DESIGNER DREAM HOMES™

VACATION

& GETAWAY HOME PLANS

OVER 200

BEST-SELLING PLANS

PRESIDENT Angela Santerini

PUBLISHER Dominic Foley

EDITOR Jennifer Emmons

CONTRIBUTING EDITORS Shannon Addis, Laura Segers

CONTRIBUTING WRITERS Jennifer Bacon, Laura Hurst Brown, Sara Hockman, Matt McGarry, Paula Powers, Clare Ulik

GRAPHIC ARTISTS Kim Campeau, Emily Sessa, Bishana Shipp, Joshua Thomas, Diane Zwack

ILLUSTRATORS Architectural Art, Allen Bennetts, Greg Havens, Holzhauer, Inc., Dave Jenkins, Kurt Kauss, Barry Nathan

PHOTOGRAPHERS Everett & Soulé, Dan Forer, Tom Harper, Walter Kirk, Joseph Lapeyra, John Riley, Kim Sargent, Matthew Scott, Laurence Taylor, Happy Terrebone, Doug Thompson, Oscar Thompson, CJ Walker, Brian Willy

A DESIGNS DIRECT PUBLISHING BOOK

Printed by: Toppan Printing Co., Hong Kong

First Printing: August 2006

10 9 8 7 6 5 4 3 2 1

ISBN softcover: (10-digit) 1-932553-19-3 (13-digit) 978-1-932553-19-2

TABLE OF

CONTENTS

FEATURE PLANS

PLAN CATALOG

GOLF'S GREATEST MOMENTS

The Hennefield

FRANK BETZ ASSOCIATES, INC.

■ VPFB01-3835
■ 1-866-525-9374

Homes can give a sense of pride, but it takes a special home to make you feel good every time you see it. With its board-and-batten siding, cedar shake and cottage stone, the *Hennefield* offers an inviting, cozy appearance, recalling times past. Decorative wood brackets accent steep gables, while copper adds natural brilliance, reflecting the day's sun, or on those rainy days, evoking the warmth of a summer rain on a tin roof.

■ KITCHEN — For those who want their kitchen to be hidden during formal occasions and open for casual ones, this kitchen does not disappoint. It includes an angled serving bar, pantry and center island.

■ FOYER/DINING — The spacious, open interior welcomes with high ceilings and tall columns in the foyer and dining room, allowing the dining room to accommodate a stunning tray ceiling and ladder transoms.

■ FAMILY ROOM — In the family room, the built-in cabinetry could flank the fireplace or be modified to allow a library wall with the fireplace framed by French doors or windows.

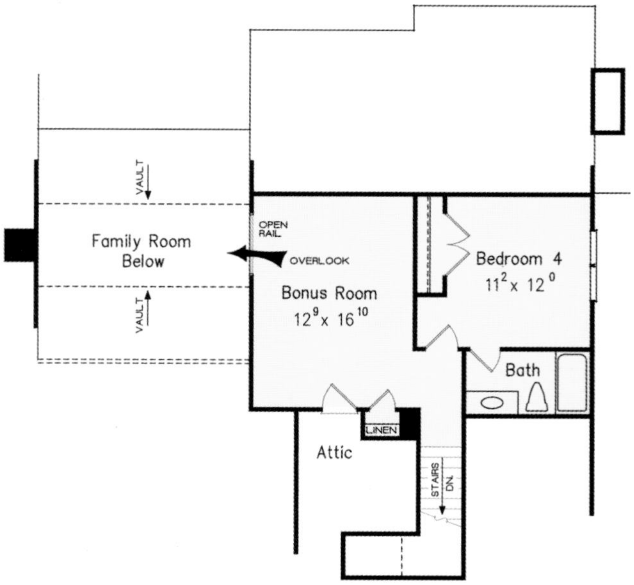

Family Room Below
VAULT
VAULT
OPEN RAIL
OVERLOOK
Bonus Room 12⁹x 16¹⁰
Bedroom 4 11²x 12⁰
Bath
LINEN
Attic
STAIRS DN.

Opt. Second Floor

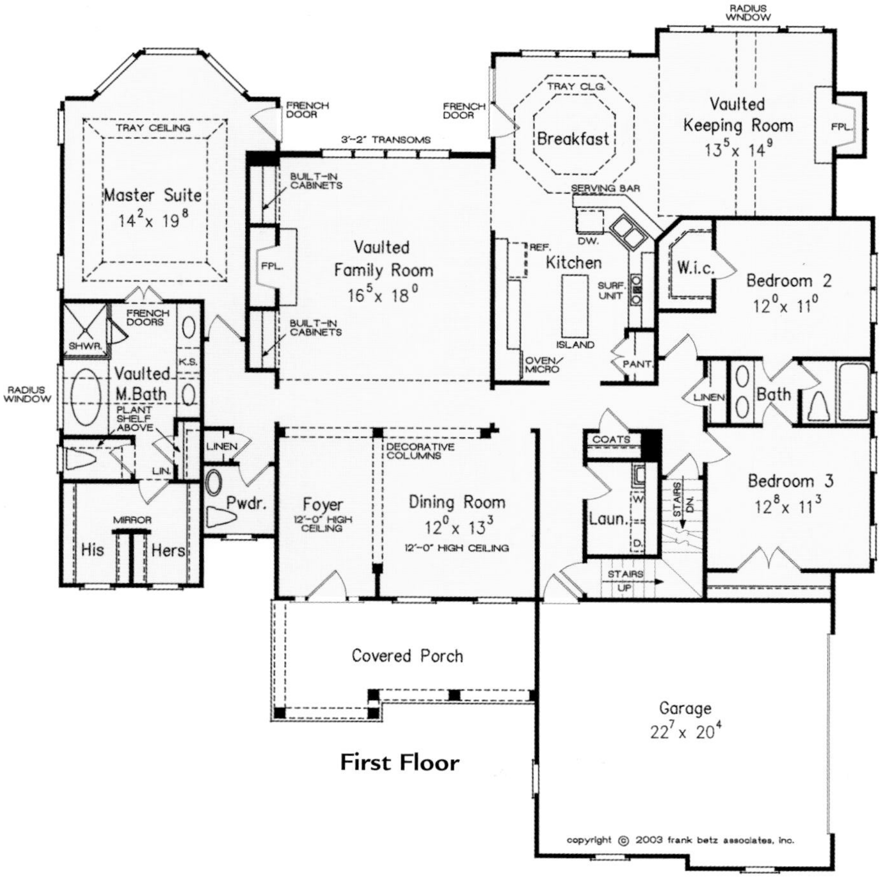

RADIUS WINDOW
TRAY CEILING
Master Suite 14²x 19⁸
FRENCH DOOR
3'-2" TRANSOMS
BUILT-IN CABINETS
FPL.
Vaulted Family Room 16⁵x 18⁰
BUILT-IN CABINETS
FRENCH DOOR
TRAY CLG.
Breakfast
SERVING BAR
Vaulted Keeping Room 13⁵x 14⁹
FPL.
RADIUS WINDOW
REF.
DW.
Kitchen
SURF. UNIT
ISLAND
OVEN/ MICRO
PANT.
W.i.c.
Bedroom 2 12⁰x 11⁰
FRENCH DOORS
SHWR.
K.S.
RADIUS WINDOW
Vaulted M.Bath
PLANT SHELF ABOVE
LIN.
LINEN
MIRROR
His
Hers
Pwdr.
Foyer 12'-0" HIGH CEILING
DECORATIVE COLUMNS
Dining Room 12⁰x 13³ 12'-0" HIGH CEILING
COATS
Laun.
W
D.
STAIRS DN.
STAIRS UP
LINEN
Bath
Bedroom 3 12⁸x 11³
Covered Porch
Garage 22⁷x 20⁴
copyright © 2003 frank betz associates, inc.

First Floor

■ KEEPING ROOM — The breakfast nook and vaulted keeping room with fireplace provide the perfect spots for morning coffee or curling up with a good book.

■ MASTER SUITE — The master suite is a sanctuary from everyday life. A tray ceiling and bay window let you know you're in an extraordinary place from the moment you enter.

■ MASTER BATH — French doors lead from the master suite into a pampering spa-styled master bath, and the large, divided walk-in closet provides plenty of room.

REAR ELEVATION

The Hennefield — VPFB01-3835 — 1-866-525-9374

Total Living	First Floor	Opt. 2nd Fl.	Bed	Bath	Width	Depth	Foundation	Price Category
2548 sq ft	2548 sq ft	490 sq ft	4	3-1/2	63' 0"	67' 6"	Basement or Crawl Space	H

Please note: Home photographed may differ from blueprint.

The Cedar Court

DONALD A. GARDNER ARCHITECTS

■ VPAL01-5004
■ 1-866-525-9374

Luxury abounds in this European-influenced home.

Stone and stucco combine with a cupola and finials to add a touch of European elegance to the *Cedar Court*.

Outdoor living is accommodated in grand style. With a decorative chimney cap, a massive fireplace highlights the screened-turret porch, extending outdoor enjoyment time. The wrapping rear porch, along with the basement-level patio, provides an abundance of recreation space.

High, decorative ceiling treatments in the great room, study and dining room increase volume and partition the common rooms without enclosing space. An art niche complements the hall leading to the master suite.

The basement level features two bedrooms and a rec room with fireplace. Each bedroom has its own walk-in closet, and the unfinished storage areas leave room for growth. Perfect for lakeside lots or those who want to capitalize on the seclusion of the mountains, the *Cedar Court* is true luxury.

■ DINING ROOM — Wooden columns punctuate the entrance to the dining room, while chocolate-colored molding frames the room.

■ GREAT ROOM — Exposed wooden beams and a serving bar connect the great room to the kitchen for a truly open feel.

■ KITCHEN — Tile and granite contrast with furniture-style cabinetry, and a large center island features a gas range and additional storage.

■ **GREAT ROOM** — Highlighting the great room, this colossal fireplace creates a grand focal point, while windows, transoms and French doors invite views inside.

■ **MASTER BEDROOM** — A tray ceiling and towering windows add to the spaciousness of the master bedroom.

■ **SITTING AREA** — The master bedroom features a bayed sitting area that is framed by a wall of windows to usher natural light throughout the room.

■ **MASTER BATH** — Intricate tile work, a double vanity and open shower create a unique master bath.

■ **REAR EXTERIOR** — Porches, patios, striking gable peaks and French doors combine to create a rear exterior that is truly stunning.

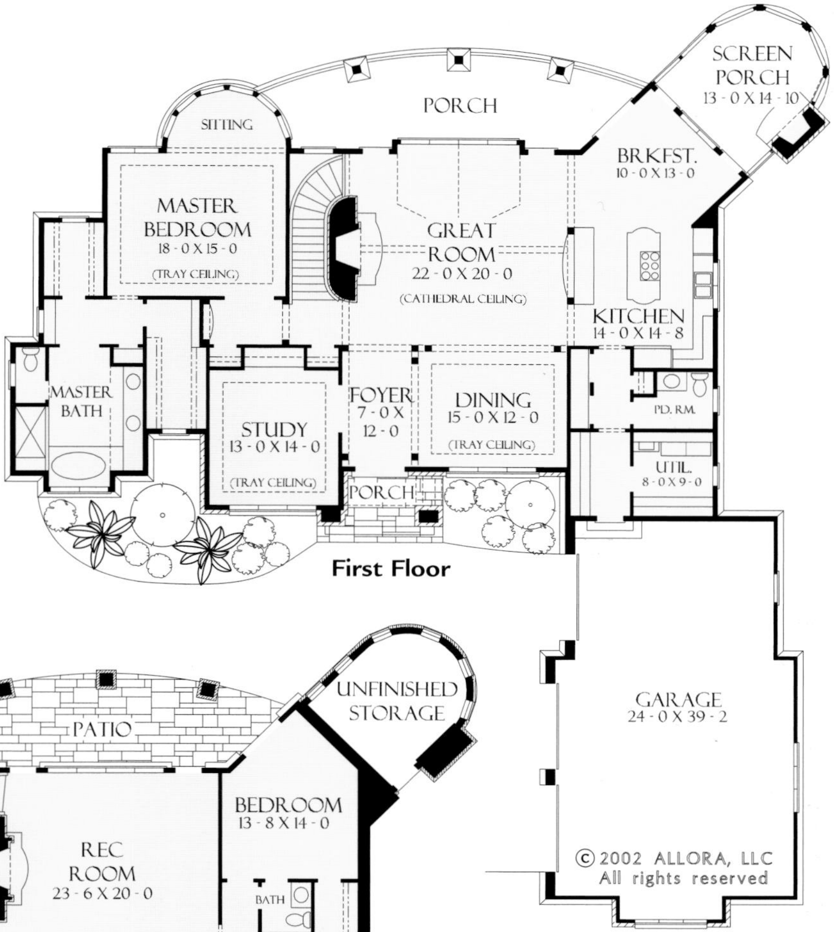

PORCH
SCREEN PORCH 13 - 0 X 14 - 10
SITTING
MASTER BEDROOM 18 - 0 X 15 - 0 (TRAY CEILING)
GREAT ROOM 22 - 0 X 20 - 0 (CATHEDRAL CEILING)
BRKFST. 10 - 0 X 13 - 0
KITCHEN 14 - 0 X 14 - 8
MASTER BATH
STUDY 13 - 0 X 14 - 0 (TRAY CEILING)
FOYER 7 - 0 X 12 - 0
DINING 15 - 0 X 12 - 0 (TRAY CEILING)
PD. RM.
UTIL. 8 - 0 X 9 - 0
PORCH
GARAGE 24 - 0 X 39 - 2
© 2002 ALLORA, LLC All rights reserved

First Floor

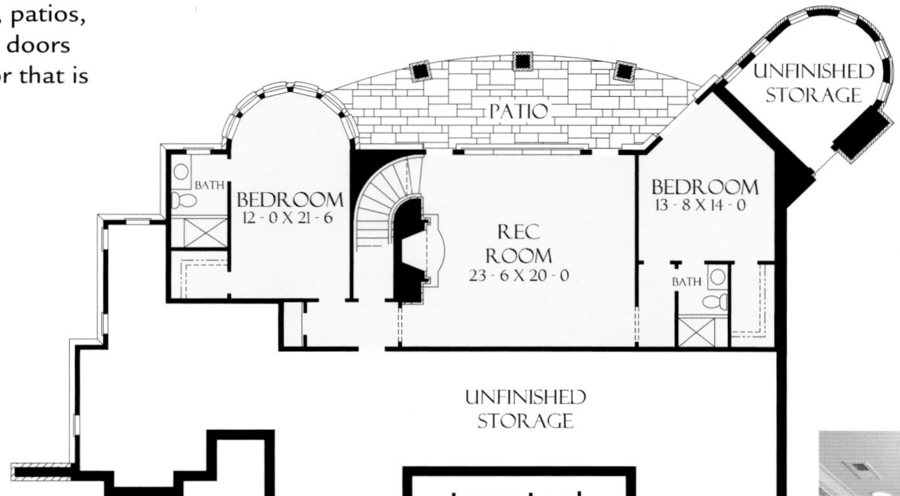

UNFINISHED STORAGE
PATIO
BATH
BEDROOM 12 - 0 X 21 - 6
REC ROOM 23 - 6 X 20 - 0
BEDROOM 13 - 8 X 14 - 0
BATH
UNFINISHED STORAGE

Lower Level

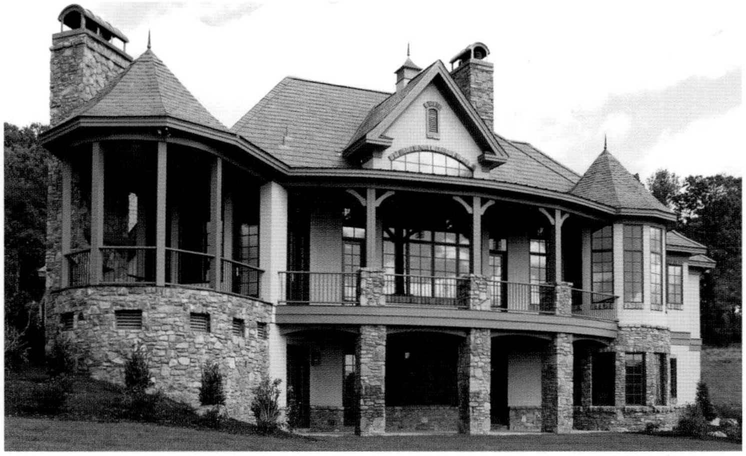

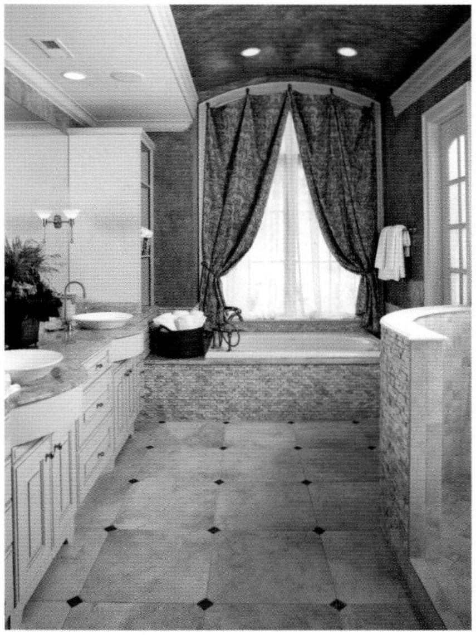

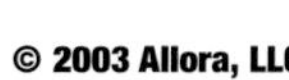

The Cedar Court — VPAL01-5004 — 1-866-525-9374

Total Living	First Floor	Lower Level	Bed	Bath	Width	Depth	Foundation	Price Category
3820 sq ft	2446 sq ft	1374	3	3-1/2	82' 4"	95' 10"	Hillside Walk-out	O

Please note: Home photographed may differ from blueprint.

Wulfert Point

SATER DESIGN COLLECTION

■ VPDS01-6688
■ 1-866-525-9374

The romantic Charleston coast is rich with timeless island communities, where relaxed attitudes and architectural styles blend — a perfect example is *Wulfert Point*. A Charleston Row courtyard — complete with a sundeck, spa and lap pool — makes this charming villa a relaxing everyday retreat. The Spanish tile roof and stucco exterior evoke memories of vacations past, and louvered shutters and circle-head windows further enhance the exterior. French doors extend the living areas and welcome sunlight and balmy breezes inside.

■ **REAR DECK** — Overlooking the pool, rows of columns and archways add symmetry and graceful elegance to the wrapping covered porch. Layering of brick and stone adds organic texture to this pampering exterior space.

■ **HALL VIEW** — A series of arches creates a shapely boundary between the dining room and kitchen.

■ **GREAT ROOM** — In the great room, lovely French doors and a row of tall windows bring the outside in. Sculpted arches add a classic formality to the relaxed spirit of the home. A sundeck and courtyard extend the living area to the outdoors, and permit scenic vistas inside.

HALLWAY — A barrel-vaulted gallery hall leads to a spacious great room through an open arrangement of the formal dining room and gourmet kitchen.

KITCHEN/DINING ROOM — Relaxed in feel and exquisite in detail, the gourmet kitchen employs columns to outline the hall and frame the view. The bar connects the two spaces allowing casual dining for two and terrific views through spans of glass facing the veranda.

DECK — The second-level master suite enjoys a covered balcony punctuated by sleek columns and custom railings — a perfect place for viewing knockout sunsets.

MASTER BEDROOM — The master retreat features a curved wall of glass and a series of French doors that grant natural light to the sitting areas.

FRONT EXTERIOR — An intricate roofline tops stucco walls with circle-head windows while louver shutters set off the cream-white exterior of this charming coastal home.

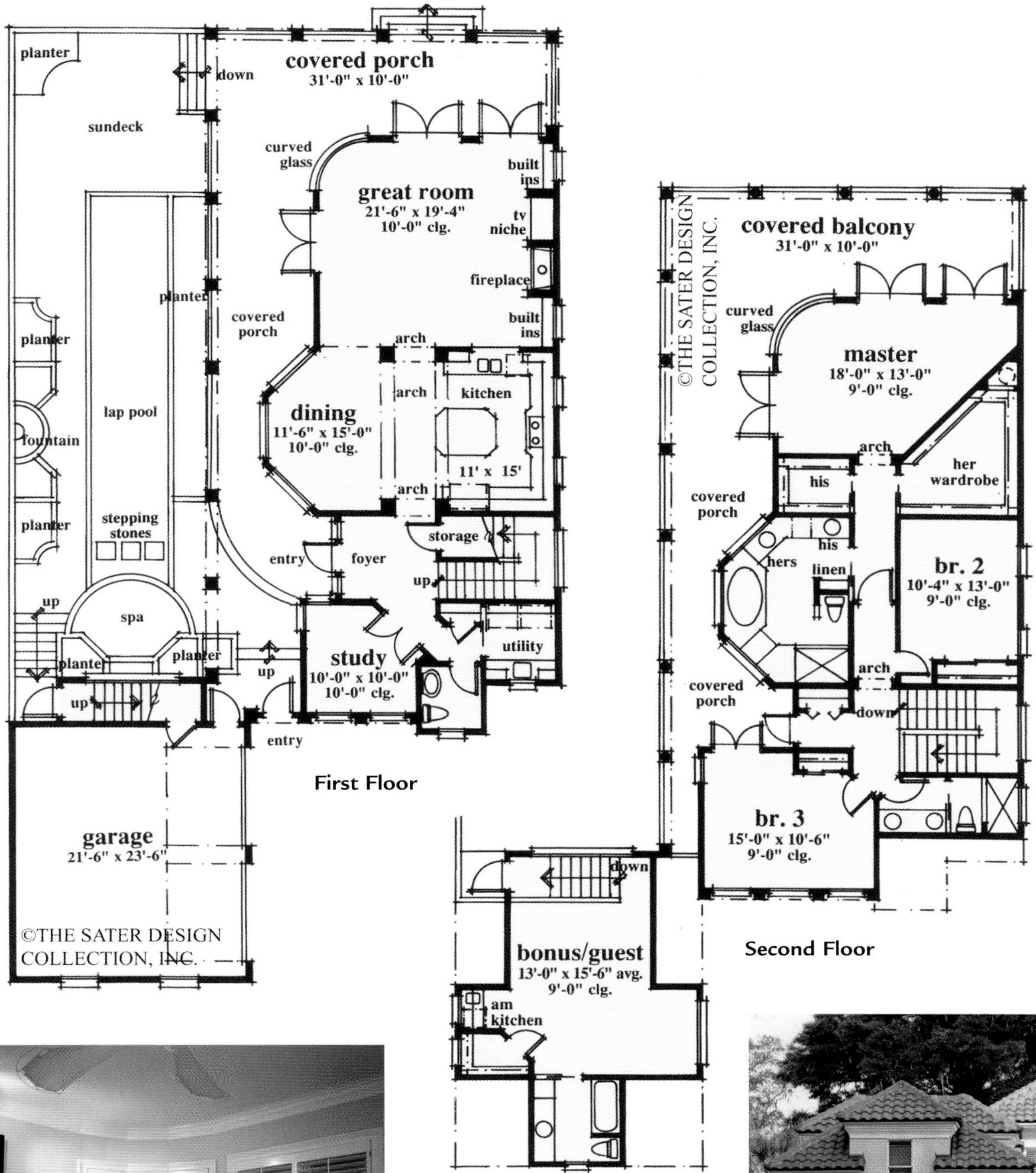

covered porch
31'-0" x 10'-0"
down
planter
sundeck
curved glass
great room
21'-6" x 19'-4"
10'-0" clg.
built ins
tv niche
fireplace
built ins
planter
covered porch
planter
lap pool
fountain
arch
dining
11'-6" x 15'-0"
10'-0" clg.
arch
kitchen
11' x 15'
arch
planter
stepping stones
entry
foyer
storage
up
up
spa
planter
planter
study
10'-0" x 10'-0"
10'-0" clg.
utility
up
up
entry
garage
21'-6" x 23'-6"

First Floor

covered balcony
31'-0" x 10'-0"
curved glass
master
18'-0" x 13'-0"
9'-0" clg.
arch
his
her wardrobe
covered porch
hers
his
linen
br. 2
10'-4" x 13'-0"
9'-0" clg.
arch
covered porch
down
br. 3
15'-0" x 10'-6"
9'-0" clg.
down
bonus/guest
13'-0" x 15'-6" avg.
9'-0" clg.
am kitchen

Second Floor

Wulfert Point — VPDS01-6688 — 1-866-525-9374

Total Living	First Floor	Second Floor	Bonus	Bed	Bath	Width	Depth	Foundation	Price Category
2873 sq ft	1293 sq ft	1154 sq ft	426 sq ft	4	3-1/2	50' 0"	90' 0"	Slab	G

Please note: Home photographed may differ from blueprint.

Adelaide

DONALD A. GARDNER ARCHITECTS

■ VPDG01-866-D
■ 1-866-525-9374

Embrace the outdoors in a comfortable environment.

Charming yet refined, the *Adelaide* is a classic combination of Craftsman home and an impressive, spacious floor plan. Twin dormers, board-and-batten siding and stone add curb appeal to this design, while the two decks, screened porch and generous patio provide space for countless hours to enjoy Mother Nature.

The large master suite features an adjacent private deck, while dual walk-in closets and the large bathroom simplify morning rituals. Located in the rear of the home, the master bedroom provides the utmost privacy. From decorative ceilings and columns, to fireplaces and a shower seat, niceties are abundant.

A bedroom/study with walk-in closet and adjacent full bath can function as a guest suite. The basement's two additional bedrooms and large rec room overlooks a covered patio. As the ideal vacation home, the *Adelaide* features your favorite amenities within a modern floor plan.

■ DINING ROOM — In the formal dining room, an elegant tray ceiling and columns that define the room's perimeter showcase architectural detail. An arched transom highlights three windows to enable a sneak peek at Mother Nature when enjoying meals.

■ GREAT ROOM — Exposed wooden beams and a cathedral ceiling enhance the lofty great room, while the stone fireplace serves as the stunning focal point.

■ GREAT ROOM — Completely open to the kitchen and breakfast room, the great room accesses a rear deck and uses windows and French doors for natural illumination.

■ KITCHEN — Wraparound countertops become instant gathering spots for snacking and chatting, while also creating an attractive partition between rooms.

■ BASEMENT REC ROOM — Built-in shelves and a wet bar bring refreshment and convenience one-step closer, while multiple sets of French doors provide stimulating scenery.

■ REAR EXTERIOR — Porches, columns and a single dormer unite for a captivating façade that easily mirrors the allure of the front exterior.

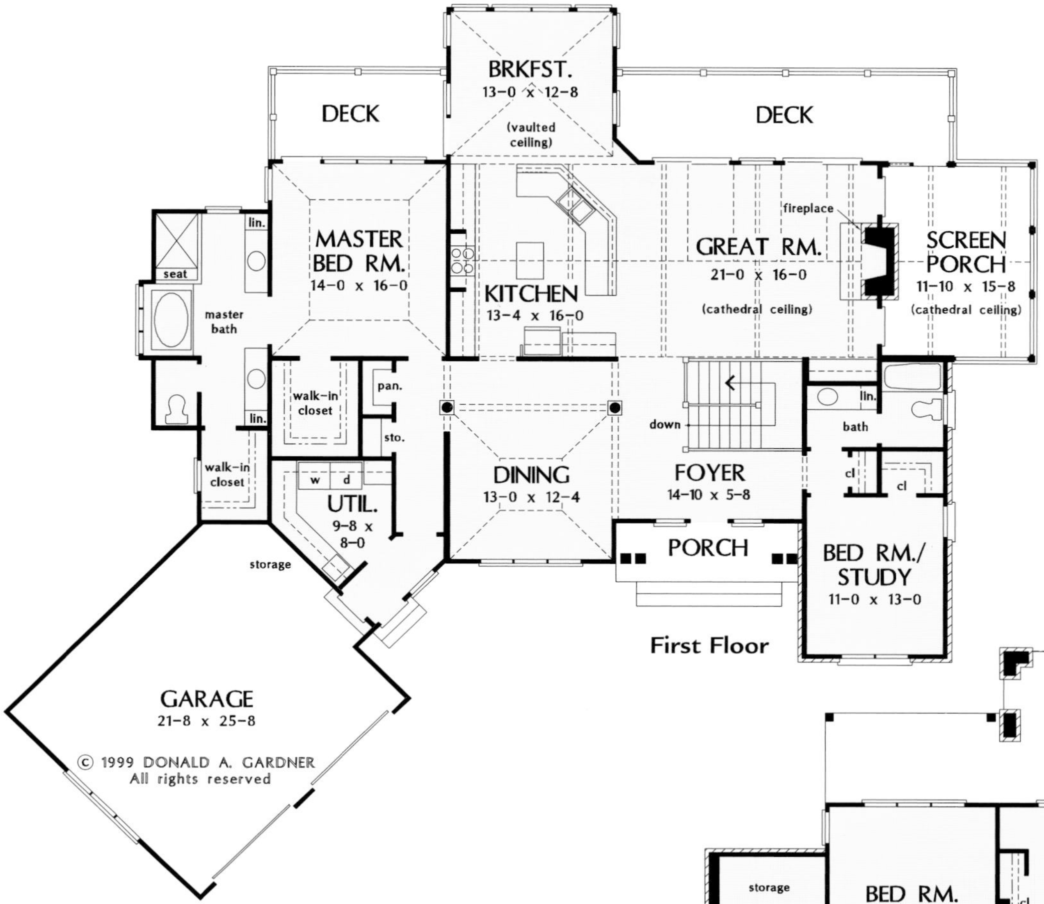
BRKFST.
13-0 x 12-8
(vaulted ceiling)
DECK
DECK
MASTER BED RM.
14-0 x 16-0
KITCHEN
13-4 x 16-0
GREAT RM.
21-0 x 16-0
(cathedral ceiling)
fireplace
SCREEN PORCH
11-10 x 15-8
(cathedral ceiling)
lin.
seat
master bath
lin.
walk-in closet
pan.
sto.
walk-in closet
w d
UTIL.
9-8 x 8-0
storage
DINING
13-0 x 12-4
down
FOYER
14-10 x 5-8
PORCH
lin.
bath
cl
cl
BED RM./ STUDY
11-0 x 13-0
GARAGE
21-8 x 25-8
© 1999 DONALD A. GARDNER
All rights reserved

First Floor

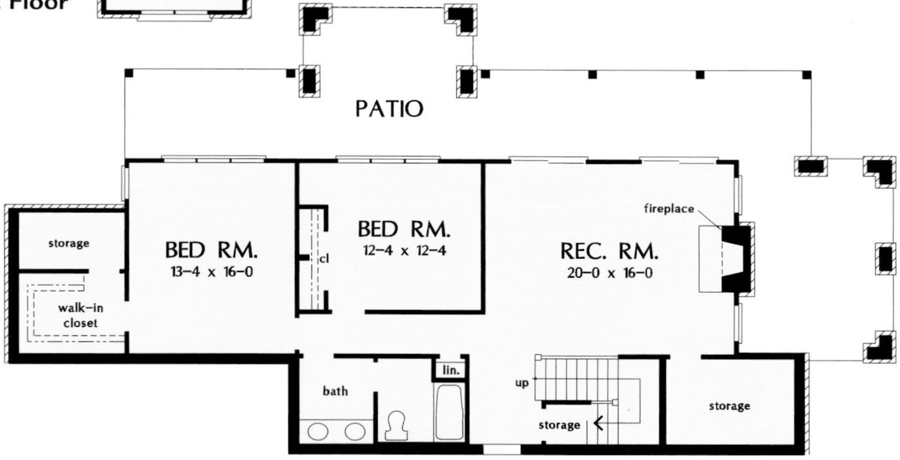
PATIO
storage
walk-in closet
BED RM.
13-4 x 16-0
cl
BED RM.
12-4 x 12-4
fireplace
REC. RM.
20-0 x 16-0
bath
lin.
up
storage
storage

Basement

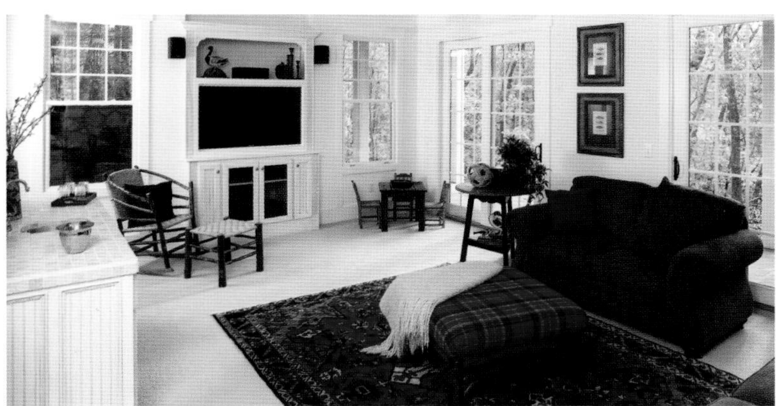

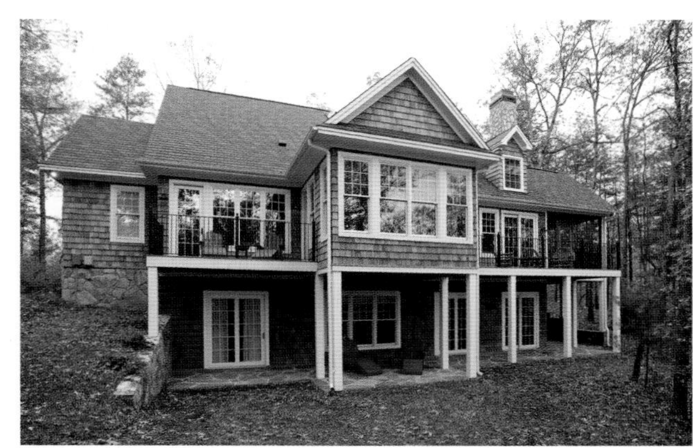

Adelaide — VPDG01-866-D — 1-866-525-9374

Total Living	First Floor	Basement	Bed	Bath	Width	Depth	Foundation	Price Category
3301 sq ft	2151 sq ft	1150	4	3	83' 0"	74' 4"	Hillside Walk-out	G

Please note: Home photographed may differ from blueprint.

Aruba Bay

SATER DESIGN COLLECTION

■ VPDS01-6840
■ 1-866-525-9374

Creative room placement in an unrestricted floor plan make the *Aruba Bay* ultra-livable as a year-round or vacation home. An elevated balcony entryway, buttery yellow siding, cloud-white trim and varied rooflines greet those who pass by. Multiple porches, a leisure room with fireplace, and upper-level bedrooms with a deck create a thoughtful, open floor plan that invites fresh breezes, wide views and good friends.

■ DINING ROOM — A large, airy dining room is just steps from the kitchen and great room. A French door to one of the main level's three porches connects the space with the outdoors and fresh spring breezes.

■ GREAT ROOM — The marble surround and classic mantle create an easy focal point for the leisure room, while arched transom windows heighten views.

■ KITCHEN — The kitchen offers lots of storage and serving space with its deep, curved counter and a long wall of cabinetry culminating in a corner pantry. Open to the dining and great rooms, it's the home's center stage.

■ MASTER SUITE — The master suite is secluded to one side of the first floor and boasts an oversized bedroom with private porch access.

■ GAME ROOM — A full wet bar, sliding doors and white-trimmed windows give the finished basement its custom feel.

■ REAR EXTERIOR — Large, layered decks make it clear that this home is made for relaxing — with good friends, good books, or a good cup of coffee.

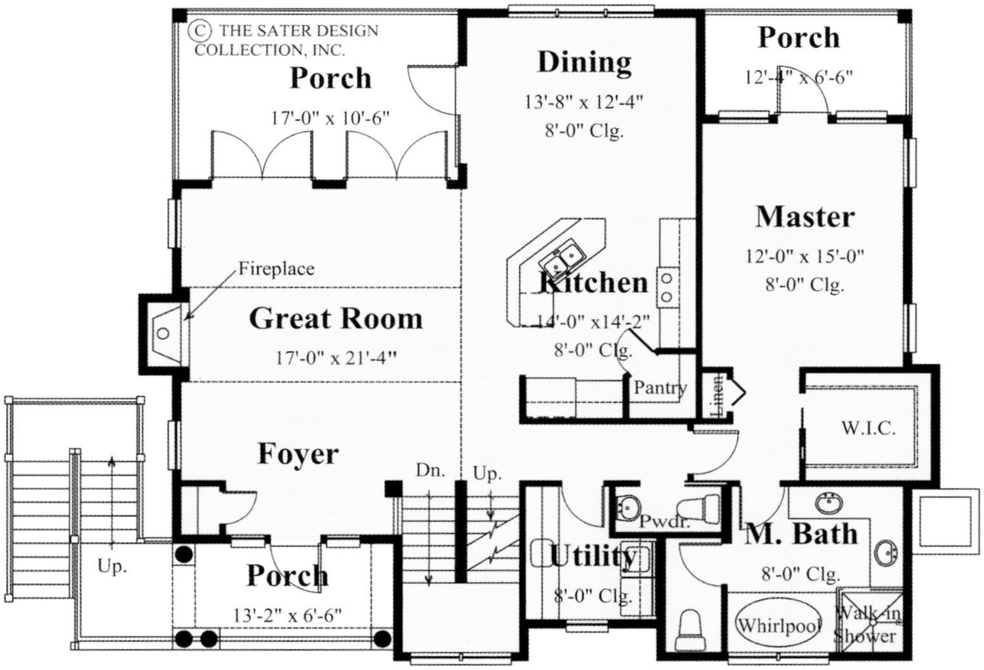

© THE SATER DESIGN COLLECTION, INC.

Porch
17'-0" x 10'-6"

Dining
13'-8" x 12'-4"
8'-0" Clg.

Porch
12'-4" x 6'-6"

Master
12'-0" x 15'-0"
8'-0" Clg.

Fireplace

Great Room
17'-0" x 21'-4"

Kitchen
14'-0" x 14'-2"
8'-0" Clg.

Pantry

Linen

W.I.C.

Foyer

Dn.

Up.

Pwdr.

M. Bath
8'-0" Clg.

Up.

Porch
13'-2" x 6'-6"

Utility
8'-0" Clg.

Whirlpool

Walk-in Shower

First Floor

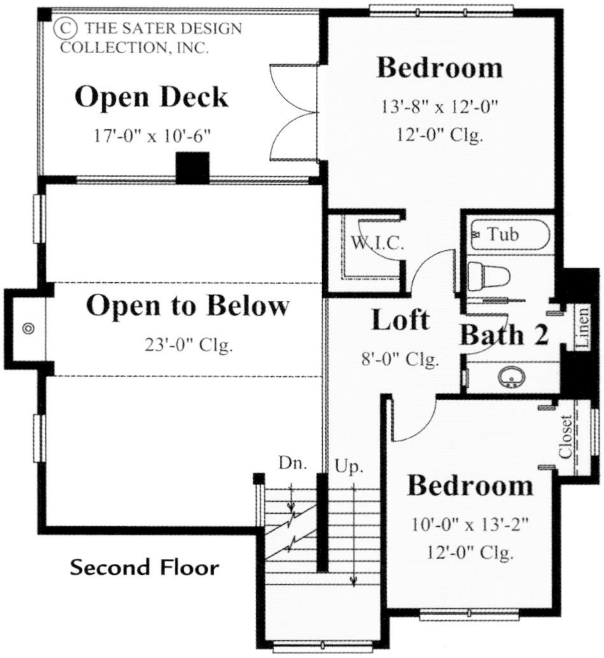

© THE SATER DESIGN COLLECTION, INC.

Open Deck
17'-0" x 10'-6"

Bedroom
13'-8" x 12'-0"
12'-0" Clg.

W.I.C.

Tub

Open to Below
23'-0" Clg.

Loft
8'-0" Clg.

Bath 2

Linen

Closet

Dn.

Up.

Bedroom
10'-0" x 13'-2"
12'-0" Clg.

Second Floor

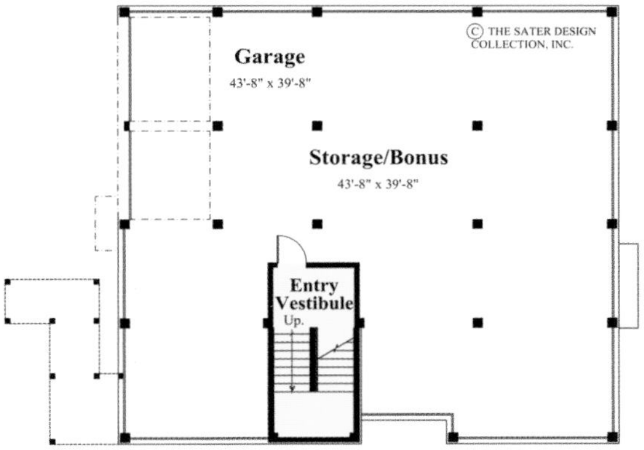

Garage
43'-8" x 39'-8"

© THE SATER DESIGN COLLECTION, INC.

Storage/Bonus
43'-8" x 39'-8"

Entry Vestibule
Up.

Lower Level

Aruba Bay — VPDS01-6840 — 1-866-525-9374

Total Living	First Floor	Second Floor	Lower Level	Bed	Bath	Width	Depth	Foundation	Price Category
1886 sq ft	1342 sq ft	511 sq ft	33 sq ft	3	2-1/2	44' 0"	40' 0"	Island Basement	G

Please note: Home photographed may differ from blueprint.

Hickory Grove

FRANK BETZ ASSOCIATES, INC.

■ VPFB01-3800
■ 1-866-525-9374

Fusing European flair and Arts-and-Crafts artistry, *Hickory Grove* is a hillside escape from the outside world.
Stone and cedar shake present architectural interest with unmistakable character, as they gracefully merge with the natural surroundings. Outdoor living areas such as the front porch, rear balcony and walkout porch bring a new level of open-air enjoyment. Beautiful windows, transoms and French doors capture breathtaking scenery and make the most of daylight hours. Box-bay windows allow room for window seats — perfect settings to welcome the morning or bid the night adieu.

■ DINING ROOM — Although defined, the dining room is open, allowing it to be enjoyed from many angles.

■ LIVING ROOM — A towering vaulted ceiling with exposed wood beams, built-in cabinetry and classic fireplace fashion an inviting family room only steps away from a cook's dream kitchen.

■ MASTER BEDROOM — The master suite enjoys privacy as the only bedroom on the main floor, and features a cozy window seat accented by decorative columns. With a tray ceiling and numerous windows, this master suite is a year round haven.

■ MASTER BATH — The master bath is a special retreat, featuring a separate tub and shower, dual sinks and a very large walk-in closet.

■ KITCHEN/NOOK — The kitchen, which includes a center range, reach-in pantry and abundant counter space, also offers a spacious breakfast nook and a much-sought-after keeping room.

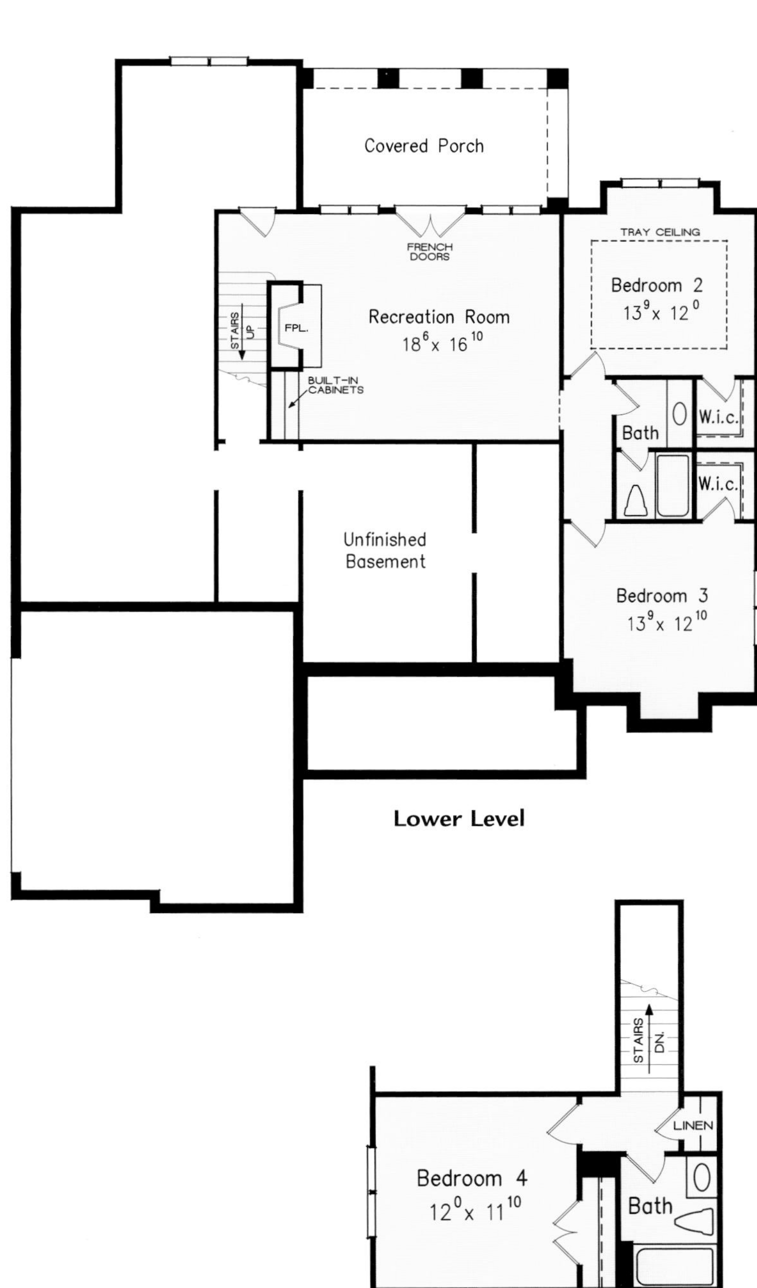

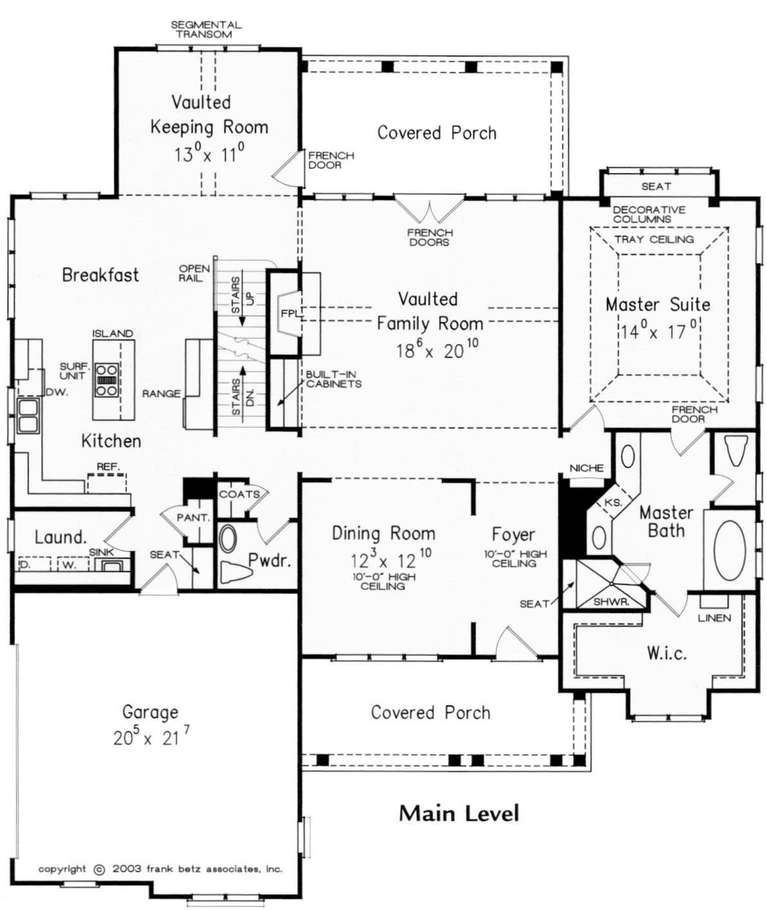

■ REAR EXTERIOR — Lazy days have found the place to be — right on this home's private rear deck.

Hickory Grove — VPFB01-3800 — 1-866-525-9374

Total Living	Main Level	Lower Level	Opt. 2nd Fl.	Bed	Bath	Width	Depth	Foundation	Price Category
2917 sq ft	1977 sq ft	940 sq ft	260 sq ft	4	3-1/2	54' 0"	63' 6"	Basement	H

Please note: Home photographed may differ from blueprint.

Riva Ridge

DONALD A. GARDNER ARCHITECTS

■ VPAL01-5013
■ 1-866-525-9374

Nature's flair embraces this rural cottage. For those whose idea of vacation is enjoying a quiet weekend in the mountains in a rustic but contemporary home, the *Riva Ridge* is for you! A stylish blend of cottage living and lavish architectural detail, the *Riva Ridge* embraces the outdoors in a comfortable and modern floor plan. An exciting ensemble of siding and stone, copper roofing and detached garage gives this Craftsman home irresistible curb appeal. For days when weather doesn't cooperate, the basement level houses the ideal media room or child's playroom. Featuring two bedrooms, the downstairs also boasts a large rec room and outdoor covered patio that perfectly melds indoor with outdoor living. For those who love all things natural, the *Riva Ridge* is a perfect fit!

■ **DINING ROOM** — Surrounded by windows and accessing the screen porch, the dining room rests in a box-bay window that provides panoramic scenery at every meal.

■ **GREAT ROOM** — The vaulted ceiling adds vertical volume, while a stone fireplace showcases elegant architectural detail.

■ **KITCHEN/DINING** — Featuring stainless steel appliances and rustic-colored cabinetry, the kitchen adds warmth to this mountain retreat. With easy access to the dining and great rooms, entertaining is a breeze.

■ GREAT ROOM — Designed for entertaining, the great room features a rear wall of windows that bathe the room with sunlight for widespread illumination. Naturally flowing into the dining room and kitchen, the great room also accesses the deck.

■ MASTER BATH — Truly luxurious, the master bathroom includes his-and-her sinks and a private toilet. The separate shower and bathtub not only promote convenience, but also add elegance to the master bath.

■ MASTER BEDROOM — Accessing a private rear deck, the master bedroom is positioned for privacy. A spacious walk-in closet grants luxury, while a cathedral ceiling increases vertical volume.

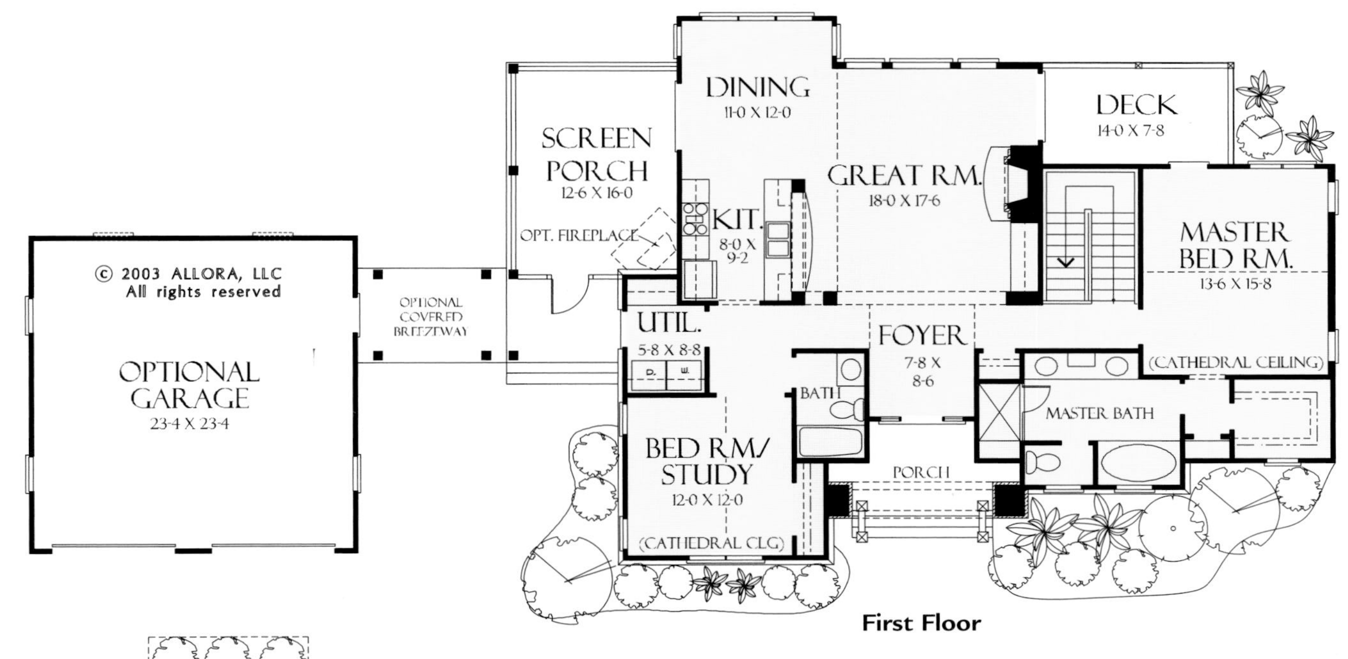

First Floor

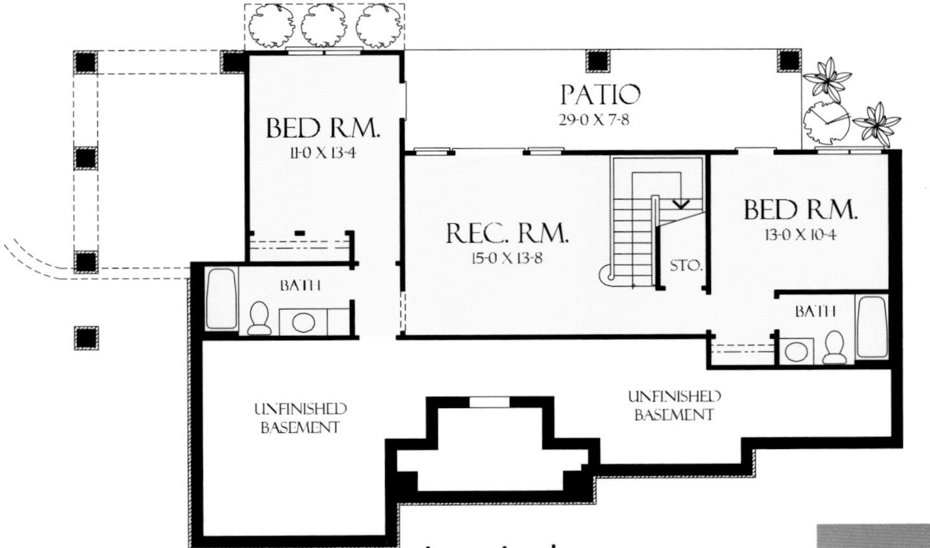

Lower Level

■ **PORCH/DECK** — When enjoying alfresco meals, the rear deck is the perfect place to entertain many or appreciate privacy. Facing the backyard, both the deck and screen porch with optional fireplace provide ample space to take in scenic views.

■ **REAR EXTERIOR** — Screen porches, decks and a box-bay window add interest and combine with stone columns and several windows for an attractive rear exterior.

Riva Ridge — VPAL01-5013 — 1-866-525-9374

Total Living	First Floor	Lower Level	Bed	Bath	Width	Depth	Foundation	Price Category
2263 sq ft	1428 sq ft	835 sq ft	4	4	60' 6"	41' 7"	Hillside Walkout	O

Please note: Home photographed may differ from blueprint.

Santa Rosa

SATER DESIGN COLLECTION

■ VPDS01-6808
■ 1-866-525-9374

A stately front porch, vista-honoring balconies and a charming cupola make a purposeful statement about the *Santa Rosa,* which is packed with warm, inviting spaces that allude to afternoons with good friends and fresh sea breezes. Typical of Southern architecture, this coastal cottage is designed for a tropical climate with its many doors and windows. Virtually every room has either outdoor views or porch access.

■ DINING ROOM — Window-laden walls with a molded tray ceiling highlight the simple elegance of the sizeable dining room, which opens invitingly to both the great room and kitchen.

■ GREAT ROOM — Soaring vaulted ceilings, generous windows and a stately fireplace elongated by geometric panels make the main-floor great room the heart of the home. Open spaces punctuated by square columns give easy entry to the adjacent kitchen and dining room.

■ KITCHEN — Flexible living space makes this home unique: Here, storage and utility rooms have been relocated downstairs to provide for a cozy breakfast nook in the cheery and functional kitchen.

■ MASTER BEDROOM — The master suite exudes charm with its exterior balcony, tray ceiling and abundant space. Just outside the entry door is an elliptical overlook to the great room below. Opposite, another door provides access to a generous walk-in-closet.

■ MEDIA ROOM — A substantial flexible living space on the ground floor has been turned into a sophisticated media room that is softly lit from a tray ceiling.

■ REAR EXTERIOR — Multiple decks and windows lend an air of subtle sophistication to the rear.

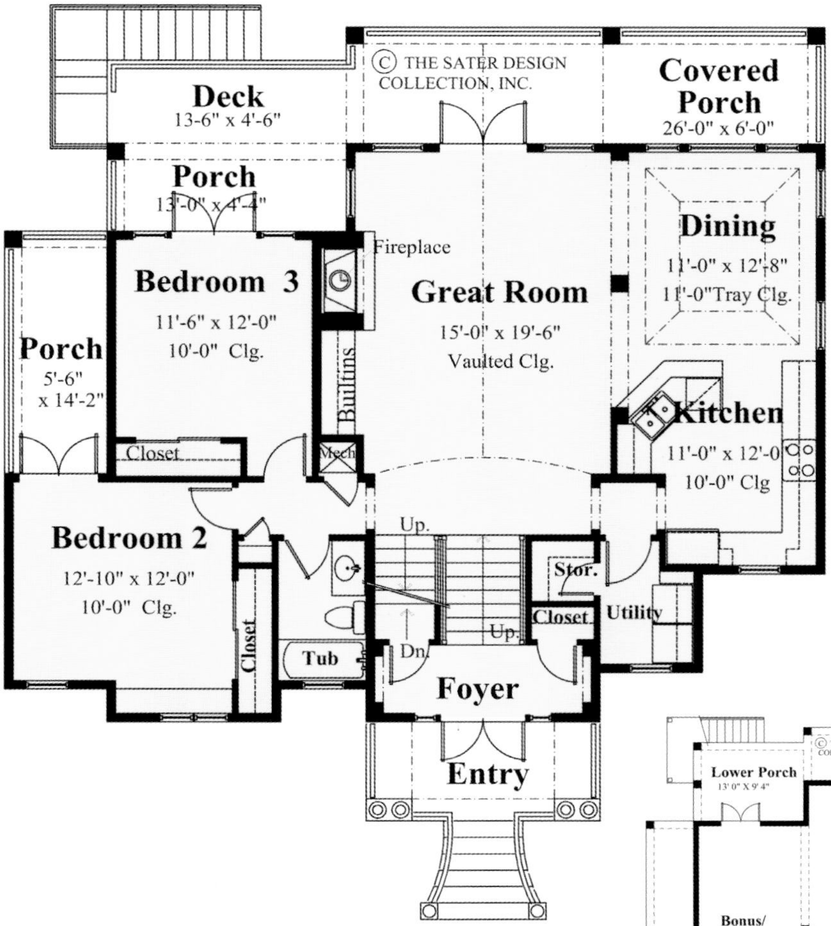

Deck
13-6" x 4'-6"

Porch
13'-0" x 4'-4"

© THE SATER DESIGN COLLECTION, INC.

Covered Porch
26'-0" x 6'-0"

Porch
5'-6" x 14'-2"

Bedroom 3
11'-6" x 12'-0"
10'-0" Clg.

Fireplace

Great Room
15'-0" x 19'-6"
Vaulted Clg.

Dining
11'-0" x 12'-8"
11'-0"Tray Clg.

Builtins

Kitchen
11'-0" x 12'-0
10'-0" Clg

Closet

Mech

Bedroom 2
12'-10" x 12'-0"
10'-0" Clg.

Closet

Tub

Up.

Dn.

Up.

Stor.

Closet

Utility

Foyer

Entry

First Floor

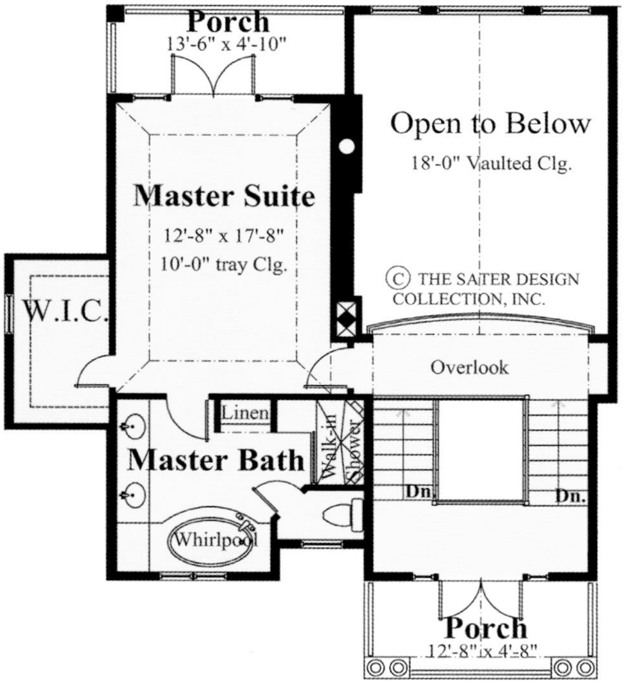

Porch
13'-6" x 4'-10"

Open to Below
18'-0" Vaulted Clg.

Master Suite
12'-8" x 17'-8"
10'-0" tray Clg.

W.I.C.

© THE SATER DESIGN COLLECTION, INC.

Overlook

Linen

Walk-in Shower

Master Bath

Whirlpool

Dn.

Dn.

Porch
12'-8" x 4'-8"

Second Floor

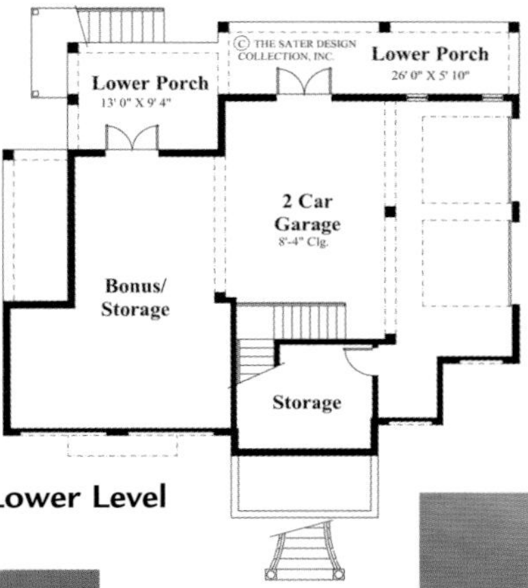

Lower Porch
13' 0" X 9' 4"

© THE SATER DESIGN COLLECTION, INC.

Lower Porch
26' 0" X 5' 10"

2 Car Garage
8'-4" Clg.

Bonus/ Storage

Storage

Lower Level

Santa Rosa — VPDS01-6808 — 1-866-525-9374

Total Living	First Floor	Second Floor	Bed	Bath	Width	Depth	Foundation	Price Category
1978 sq ft	1383 sq ft	595 sq ft	3	2	48' 0"	42' 0"	Island Basement	F

Please note: Home photographed may differ from blueprint.

Abbotts Pond

FRANK BETZ ASSOCIATES, INC.

- VPFB01-3856
- 1-866-525-9374

***Abbots Pond* exudes warmth from the moment it comes into view.**

A cozy blend of low-maintenance materials provides architectural interest, while columns invite family and friends to the charming front entrance. Both the front and rear porches offer outdoor space for morning coffee and afternoon conversations. A French door is all that separates the rear porch from the sunny breakfast nook, bringing the outdoors inside the home.

■ BREAKFAST ROOM — This arched pass-thru not only provides architectural interest, it makes the most of daylight in other areas of the home.

■ KITCHEN — With room for all of today's amenities and more than one household chef — the kitchen boasts a convenient design, with a step-saving layout, pantry and even a plant shelf for decorative plates or kitchen accessories that are meant to be used and seen.

■ LIVING ROOM — Highlighting the living room, the towering vaulted ceiling adds visual dimension and emphasizes the fireplace.

■ DINING ROOM — A vaulted ceiling and wainscoting add elegance to this formal dining room.

■ FOYER — This foyer channels the openness of the outdoors and introduces it to the interior.

■ PORCH — Accessible through a French door, the rear porch encourages outdoor recreation and relaxation.

■ MASTER BEDROOM — Modified from the original design, this master suite accommodates a cathedral ceiling just as well as a tray.

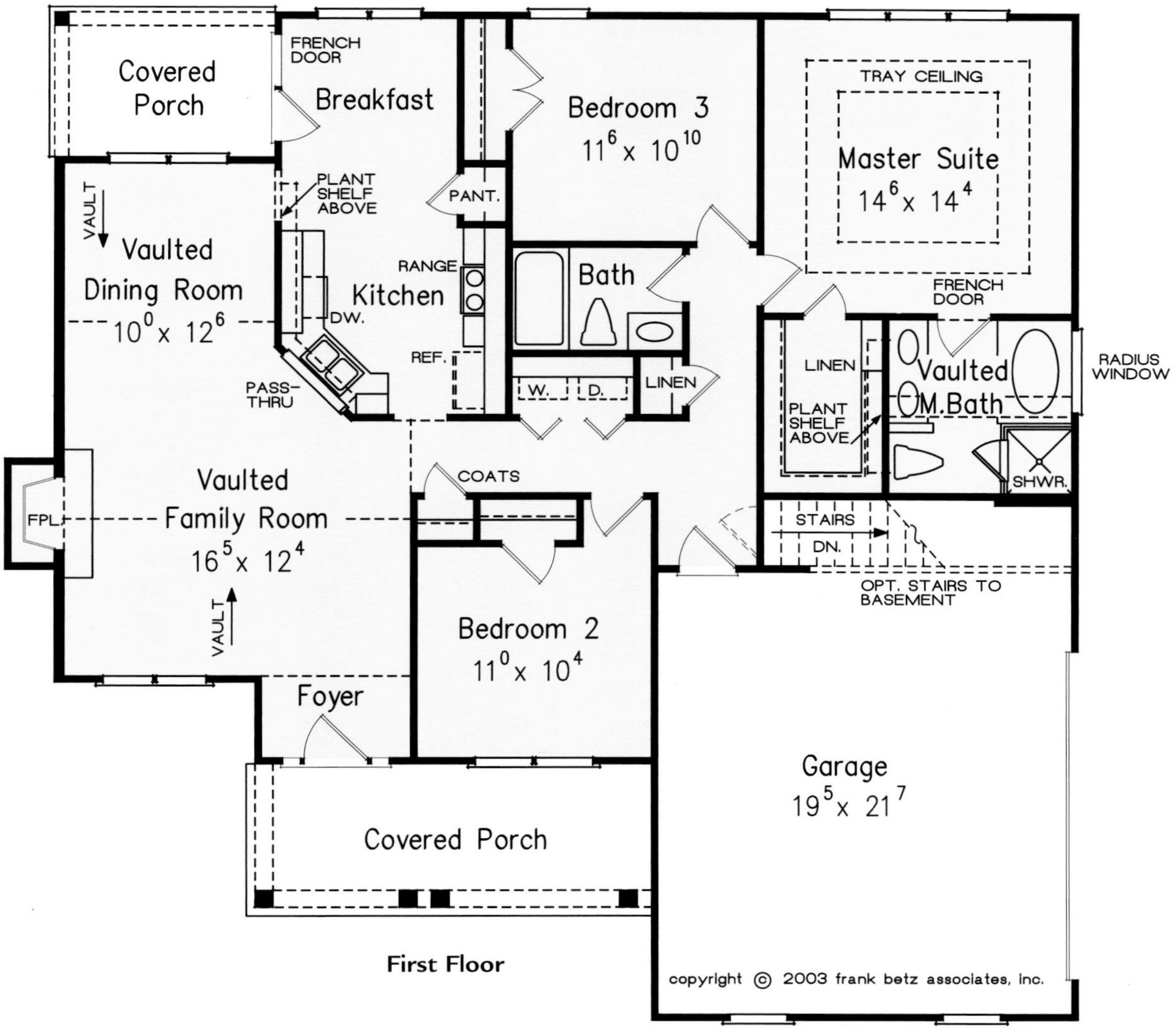
FRENCH DOOR
Covered Porch
Breakfast
Bedroom 3
11⁶ x 10¹⁰
TRAY CEILING
Master Suite
14⁶ x 14⁴
PLANT SHELF ABOVE
PANT.
VAULT
Vaulted Dining Room
10⁰ x 12⁶
RANGE
Kitchen
DW.
Bath
FRENCH DOOR
REF.
PASS-THRU
W.
D.
LINEN
LINEN
PLANT SHELF ABOVE
Vaulted M.Bath
RADIUS WINDOW
SHWR.
Vaulted Family Room
16⁵ x 12⁴
FPL.
COATS
STAIRS
DN.
OPT. STAIRS TO BASEMENT
VAULT
Bedroom 2
11⁰ x 10⁴
Foyer
Garage
19⁵ x 21⁷
Covered Porch
First Floor
copyright © 2003 frank betz associates, inc.

REAR ELEVATION

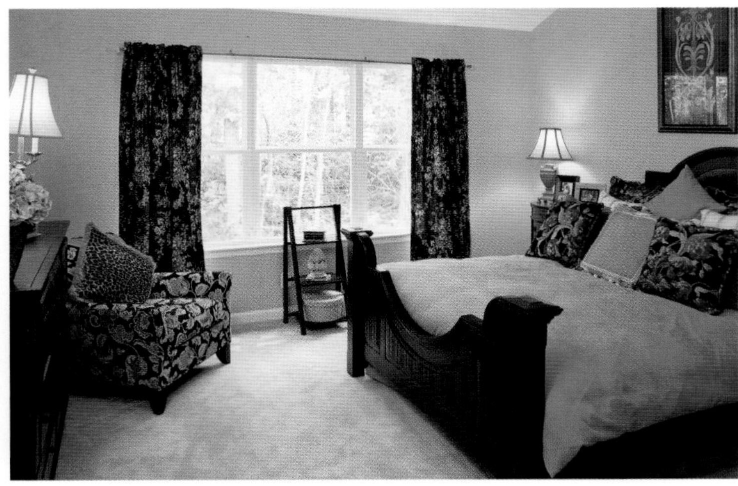

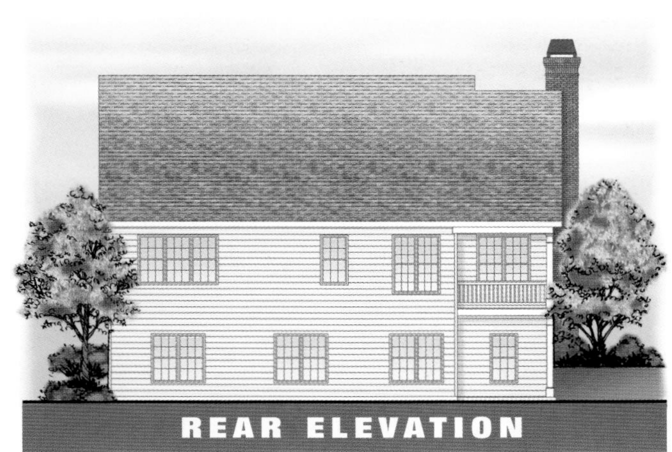

Abbotts Pond — VPFB01-3856 — 1-866-525-9374

Total Living	First Floor	Opt. Bonus	Bed	Bath	Width	Depth	Foundation	Price Category
1406 sq ft	1406 sq ft	N/A	3	2	50' 4"	49' 0"	Basement, Crawl Space, Slab	E

Please note: Home photographed may differ from blueprint.

Montego Bay

SATER DESIGN COLLECTION

- VPDS01-6800
- 1-866-525-9374

The *Montego Bay* is full of all the custom extras that add up to lavish and comfortable living, both inside and out. A corner porch provides a cozy place to visit with friends and a full-length rear veranda offers endless entertaining opportunities. Inside, multiple windows infuse almost every room with light and views. An arched foyer leads into the great room, which features a two-story coffered ceiling, triple sets of French doors opening to the backyard deck and a fireplace surrounded by built-ins. A spacious kitchen boasts a center island with cook top and a bayed dining nook. Also on the main floor, the master suite has two large walk-in closets and a luxurious bath with shower, dual sinks and a garden tub.

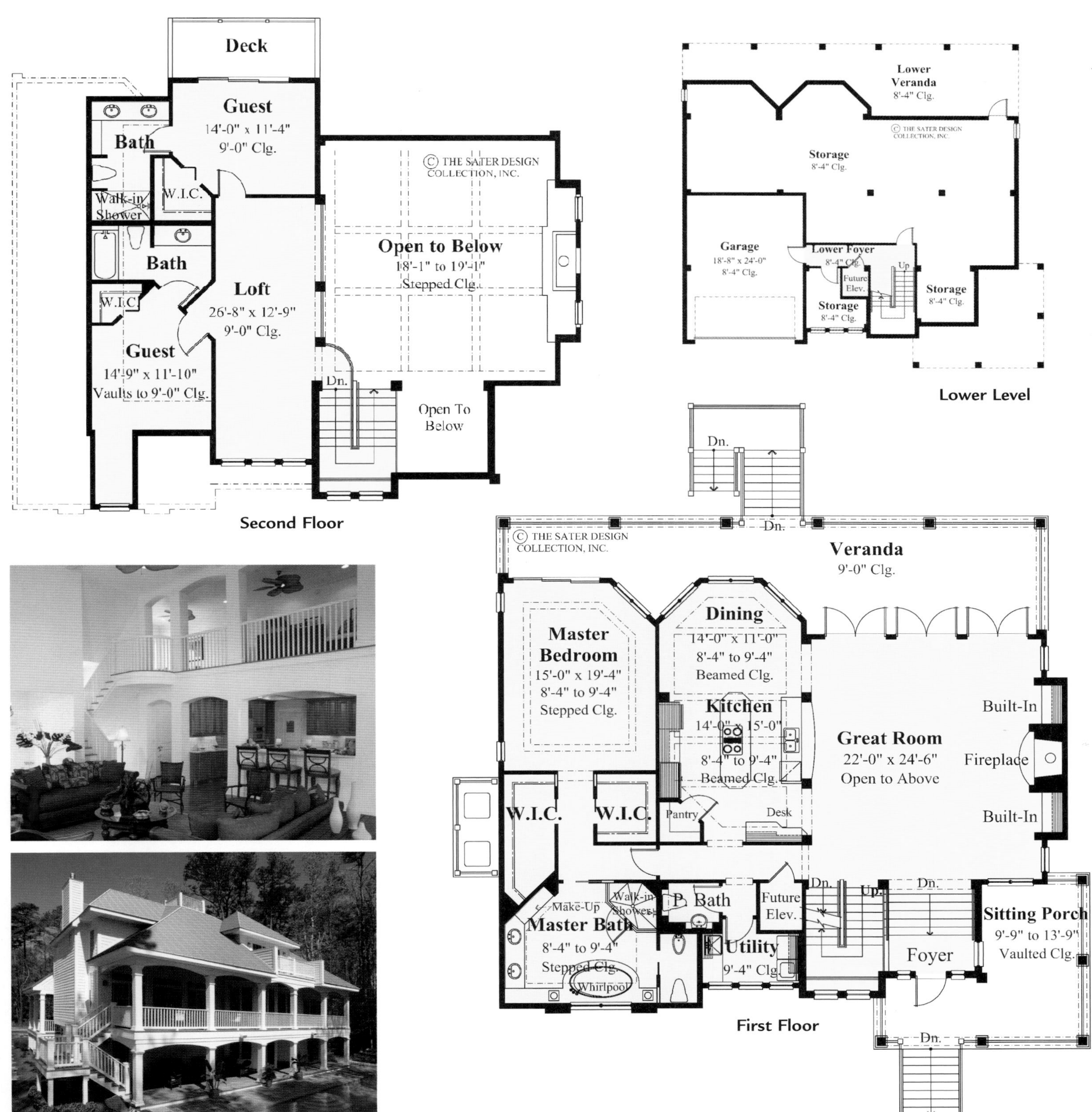

Montego Bay — VPDS01-6800 — 1-866-525-9374

Total Living	First Floor	Second Floor	Lower Foyer	Bed	Bath	Width	Depth	Foundation	Price Category
3328 sq ft	2118 sq ft	929 sq ft	281 sq ft	3	3-1/2	58' 0"	54' 0"	Island Basement	H

Please note: Home photographed may differ from blueprint.

Palm Vista

DONALD A. GARDNER ARCHITECTS

■ VPAL01-5021
■ 1-866-525-9374

Beachfront life at its finest.

Perfect for coastal living, the *Palm Vista* gives the term "vacation home" new meaning. With a captivating exterior of multiple French doors, spacious porches and an easy-to-maintain façade, the *Palm Vista* emits irresistible curb appeal.

Just off the garage, the interior produces instant convenience with a generous utility/mudroom/ bathroom combination ideal for sandy feet from the beach.

The second level consists of not one, but two, spacious master suites. Each is complete with two walk-in closets, garden tub and "his-and-her" dual sinks, ensuring even live-in relatives have the comforts of their own home. Ceiling treatments grant architectural interest, while a vaulted ceiling caps the adjacent rec room.

The third level features a private porch, wet bar and built-in seat to become an ideal relaxing space. With three luxurious floors, the *Palm Vista* captures the allure of living near the water.

■ **FRONT EXTERIOR** — Multiple sets of French doors and spacious porches give this coastal retreat a stunning exterior sure to be the envy of all the neighbors.

■ **GREAT ROOM** — The comfortable great room includes a fireplace flanked by built-in cabinetry, a wet bar, rear wall of windows and access to a screen porch and nearby patio.

■ **KITCHEN** — The rambling kitchen features expansive countertop space and a large center island that enables several chefs room to work. The kitchen, dining and great rooms combine to create a comfortable open area.

■ **REAR EXTERIOR** — This optional screen keeps nature's harsher elements out, while creating an optimal space for outdoor entertaining.

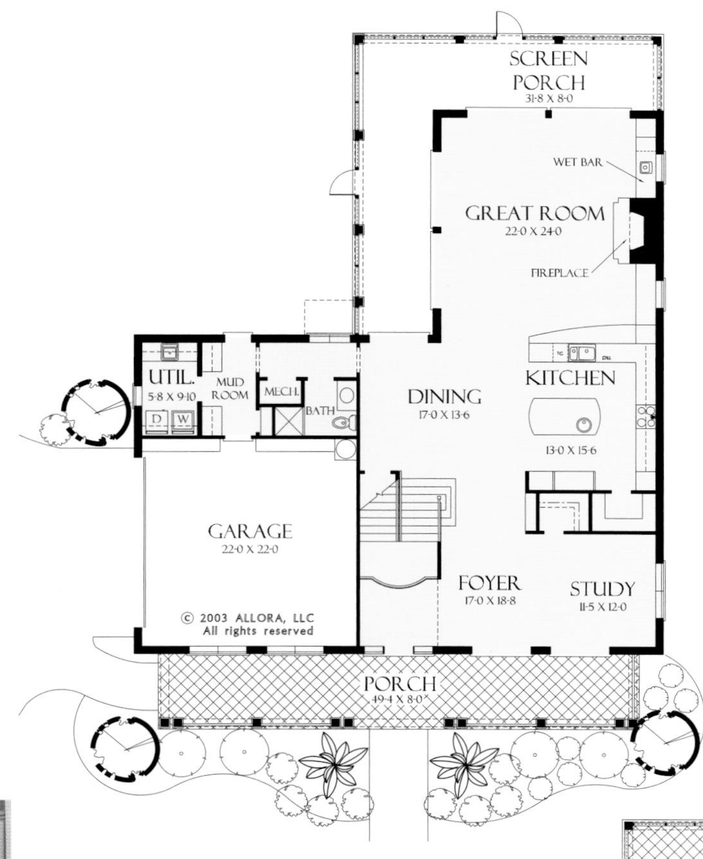

First Floor

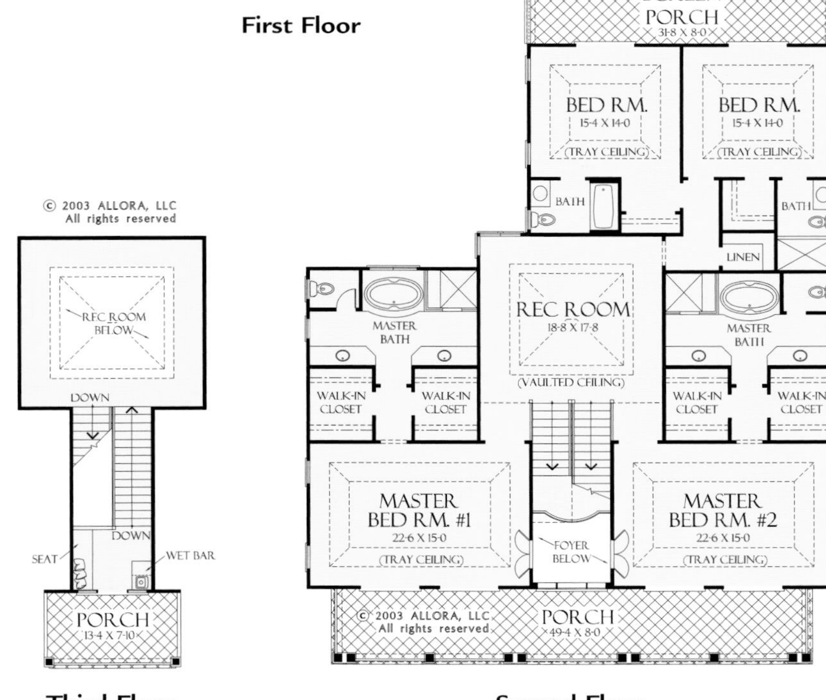

Third Floor

Second Floor

Palm Vista — VPAL01-5021 — 1-866-525-9374

Total Living	First Floor	Second Floor	Third Floor	Bed	Bath	Width	Depth	Foundation	Price Category
4441 sq ft	1885 sq ft	2495 sq ft	61 sq ft	4	5	54' 4"	73' 10"	Slab	O

Please note: Home photographed may differ from blueprint.

Stoney River

FRANK BETZ ASSOCIATES, INC.

■ VPFB01-3866
■ 1-866-525-9374

The delight of any sloping lot and adaptable to any foundation, *Stoney River* boasts an exquisite exterior of cedar shake and stone that pays tribute to its stunning surroundings. Although the front porch encourages conversation with neighbors and heart-felt waves to passers-by, the rear deck and walkout porch create private outdoor getaways for family and friends. Al fresco dining is only a few steps from the kitchen through the breakfast bay's French door.

■ KITCHEN — In this kitchen, the serving bar is a great place for quick meals, conversation and homework.

■ DINING — On two sides, columns mark entry to this gorgeous dining room, allowing its beauty to be enjoyed all day, everyday.

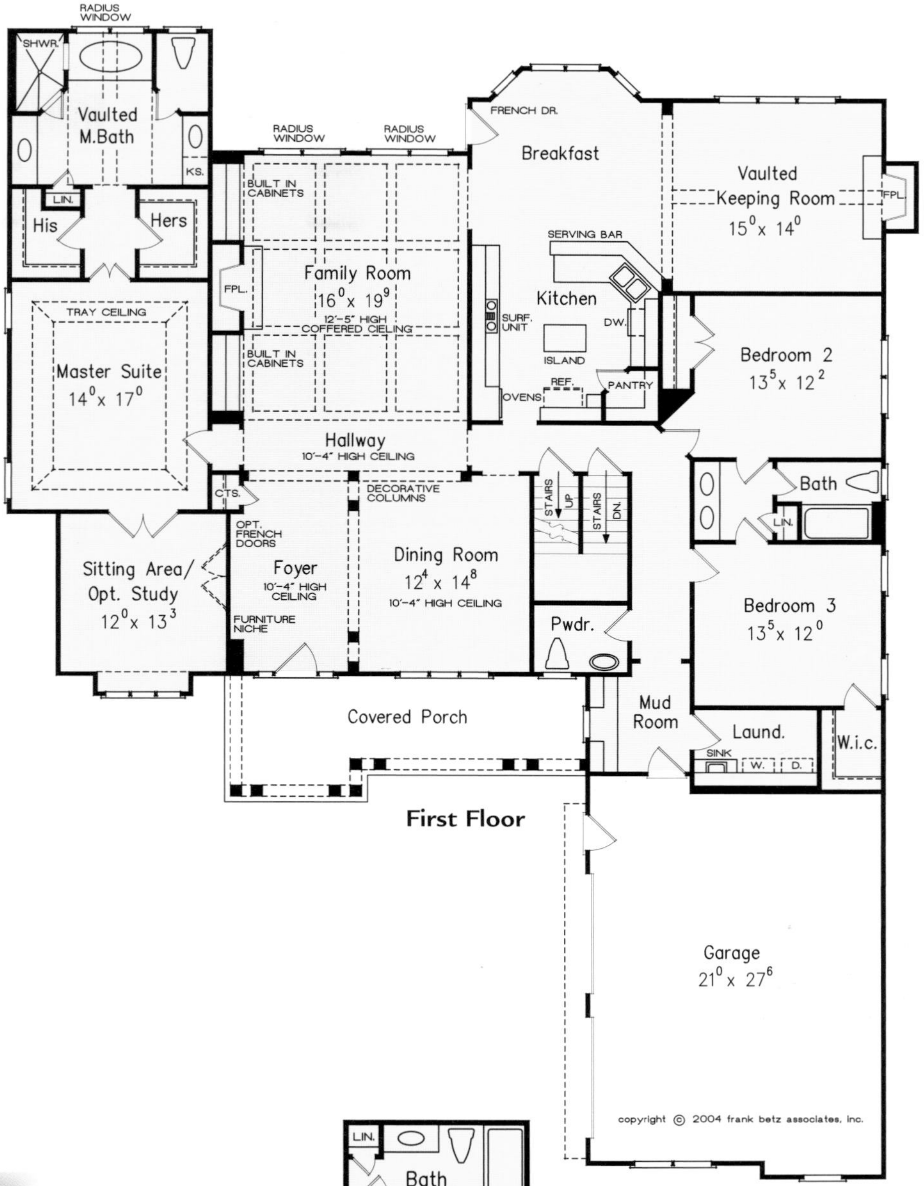

Radius Window
Shwr.
Vaulted M.Bath
KS.
Lin.
His
Hers
Tray Ceiling
Master Suite
14^0 x 17^0
Sitting Area/ Opt. Study
12^0 x 13^3
Radius Window
Radius Window
Built in Cabinets
FPL.
Family Room
16^0 x 19^9
12'-5" High Coffered Ceiling
Built in Cabinets
Hallway
10'-4" High Ceiling
CTS.
Opt. French Doors
Foyer
10'-4" High Ceiling
Furniture Niche
Decorative Columns
Dining Room
12^4 x 14^8
10'-4" High Ceiling
French Dr.
Breakfast
Serving Bar
Kitchen
Surf. Unit
DW.
Island
Ovens
Ref.
Pantry
Vaulted Keeping Room
15^0 x 14^0
FPL.
Bedroom 2
13^5 x 12^2
Bath
Lin.
Bedroom 3
13^5 x 12^0
Stairs Up
Stairs Dn.
Pwdr.
Mud Room
Laund.
Sink
W.
D.
W.i.c.
Covered Porch
Garage
21^0 x 27^6
copyright © 2004 frank betz associates, inc.

First Floor

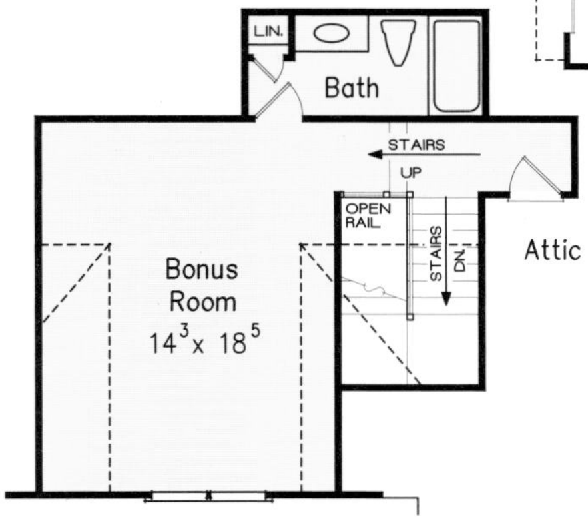

Lin.
Bath
Stairs
Up
Open Rail
Stairs Dn.
Attic
Bonus Room
14^3 x 18^5

Opt. Second Floor

Stoney River — VPFB01-3866 — 1-866-525-9374

Total Living	First Floor	Opt. 2nd Fl.	Bed	Bath	Width	Depth	Foundation	Price Category
2876 sq ft	2876 sq ft	393 sq ft	3	2-1/2	65' 4"	85' 6"	Basement or Crawl Space	H

Please note: Home photographed may differ from blueprint.

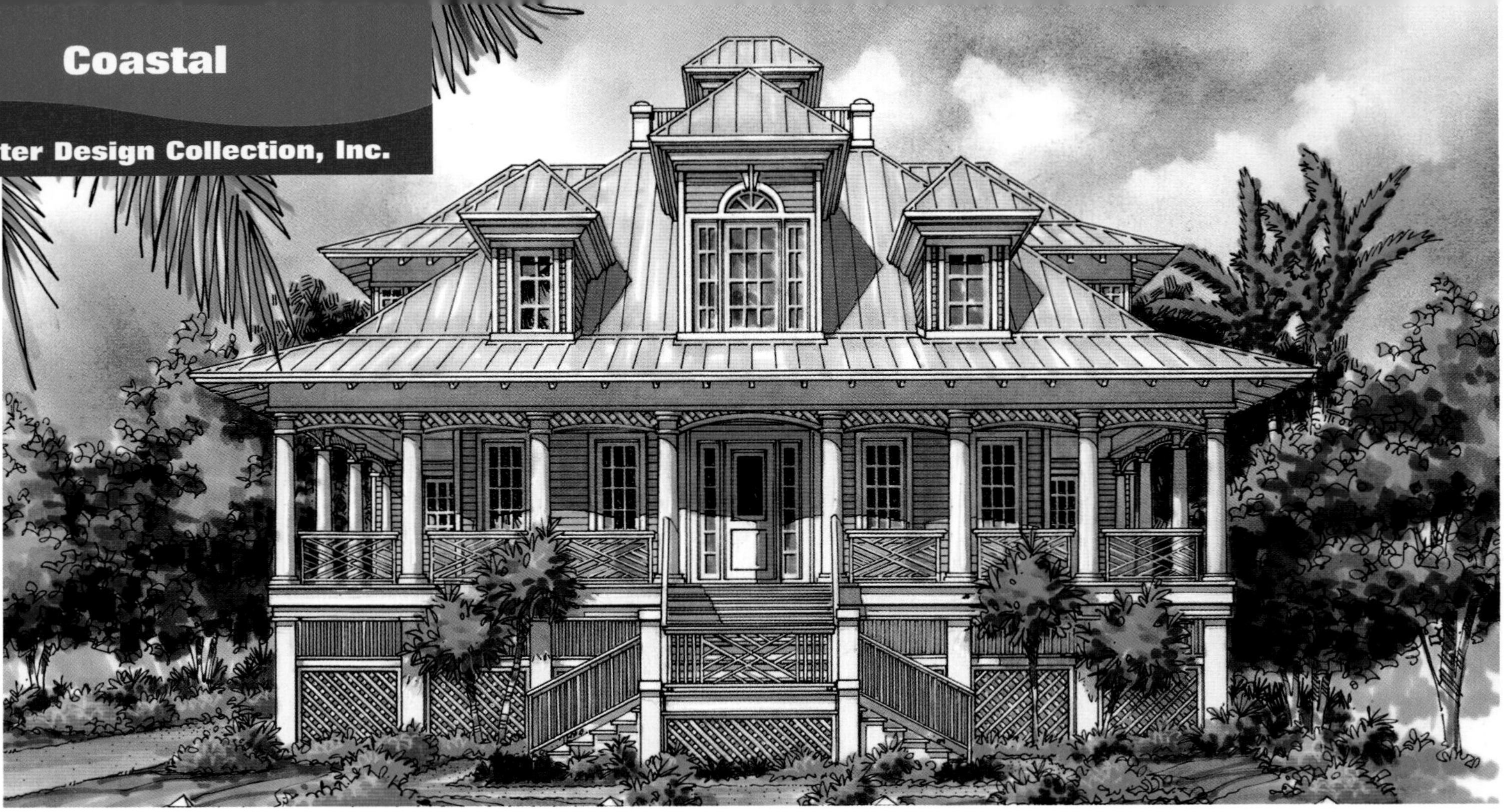

Les Anges — VPDS01-Plan 6825 — 1-866-525-9374

Total Living	First Floor	Second Floor	Lower Level	Bed	Bath	Width	Depth	Foundation	Price Category
3285 sq ft	2146 sq ft	952 sq ft	187 sq ft	3	3-1/2	56' 0"	64' 0"	Island Basement	H

Design Features

- Built-in cabinetry and a massive fireplace anchor the central living space.
- The morning nook provides a bay window and fireplace view.
- A gourmet island kitchen serves the formal dining room.
- The secluded master wing enjoys a bumped-out window and twin walk-in closets.
- The upper level boasts a catwalk that connects two secondary suites.

First Floor

Second Floor

Lower Level

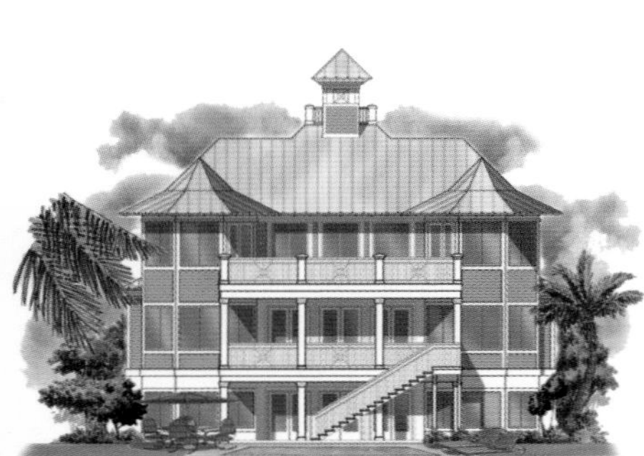

Rear Elevation

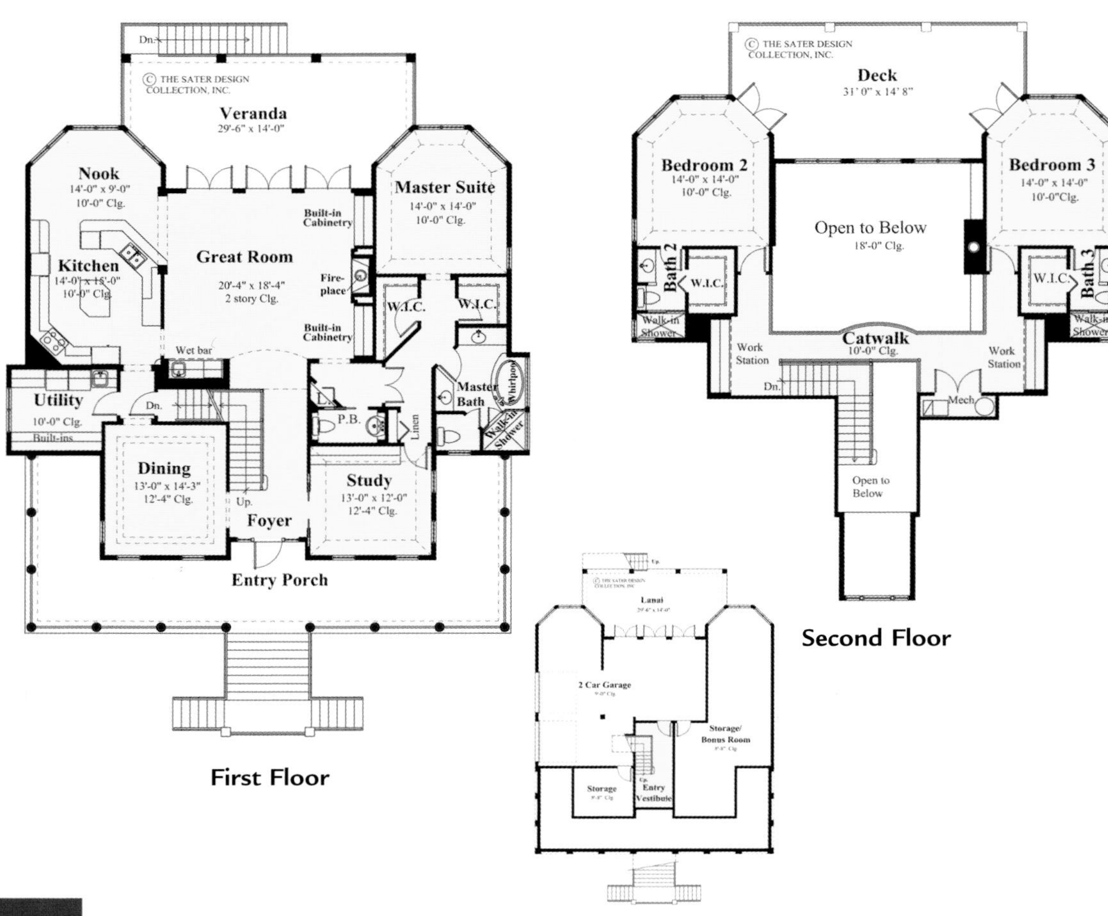

Amelia — VPFB01-3807 — 1-866-525-9374

Total Living	First Floor	Second Floor	Opt. Bonus	Bed	Bath	Width	Depth	Foundation	Price Category
2286 sq ft	1663 sq ft	623 sq ft	211 sq ft	4	3	54' 0"	48' 0"	Basement or Crawl Space	H

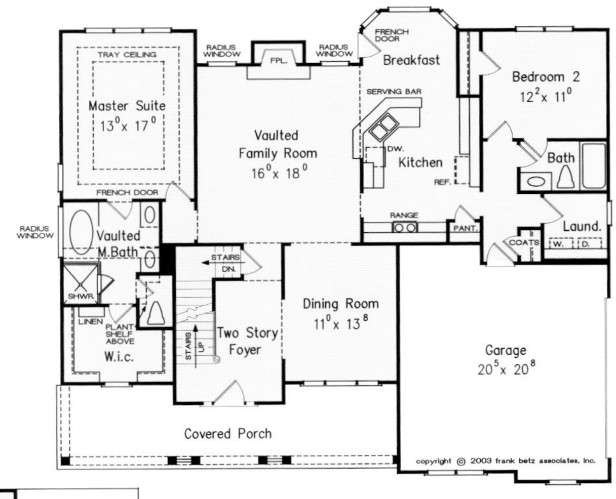

First Floor

Bedroom 3 12⁰ x 11⁰ · Family Room Below · W.i.c. · Bath · Loft 11⁰ x 10² · Bedroom 4 12⁸ x 11¹⁰ · Attic · Foyer Below · Opt. Bonus Room 12⁵ x 15⁹

Second Floor

Design Features

- The *Amelia's* façade is clean and simple, with a cozy front porch and gabled roofline.
- Louvered shutters and stone accents bring a sense of warmth that is echoed inside with a homey floor plan.
- A bedroom on the main level is also the perfect location for a home office or den.
- Upstairs, flexible areas are incorporated, giving the homeowners choices on how to use their space.
- A loft is situated among the bedrooms, making an ideal homework station or lounging area for kids.

Rear Elevation

Seabrook — VPDG01-Plan 546-C — 1-866-525-9374

Total Living	First Floor	Second Floor	Bed	Bath	Width	Depth	Foundation	Price Category
2055 sq ft	1366 sq ft	689 sq ft	3	2	49' 8"	50' 6"	Post/Pier	E

Design Features

- With an elevated pier foundation, this stunning home is perfect for waterfront properties.
- The dining room, kitchen and great room each access the wrapping rear porch.
- The great room features a ten-foot-high beamed ceiling, fireplace and built-in entertainment center.
- A grand window with arched top highlights the staircase.

Rear Elevation

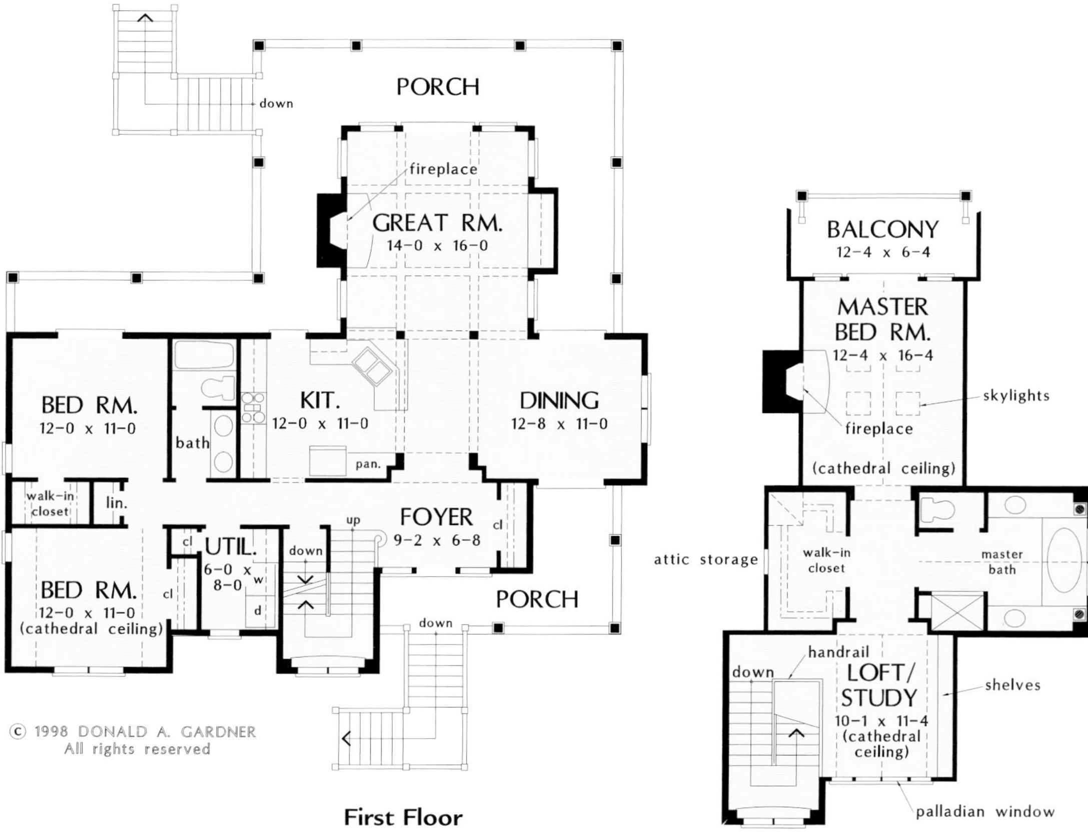

First Floor

Second Floor

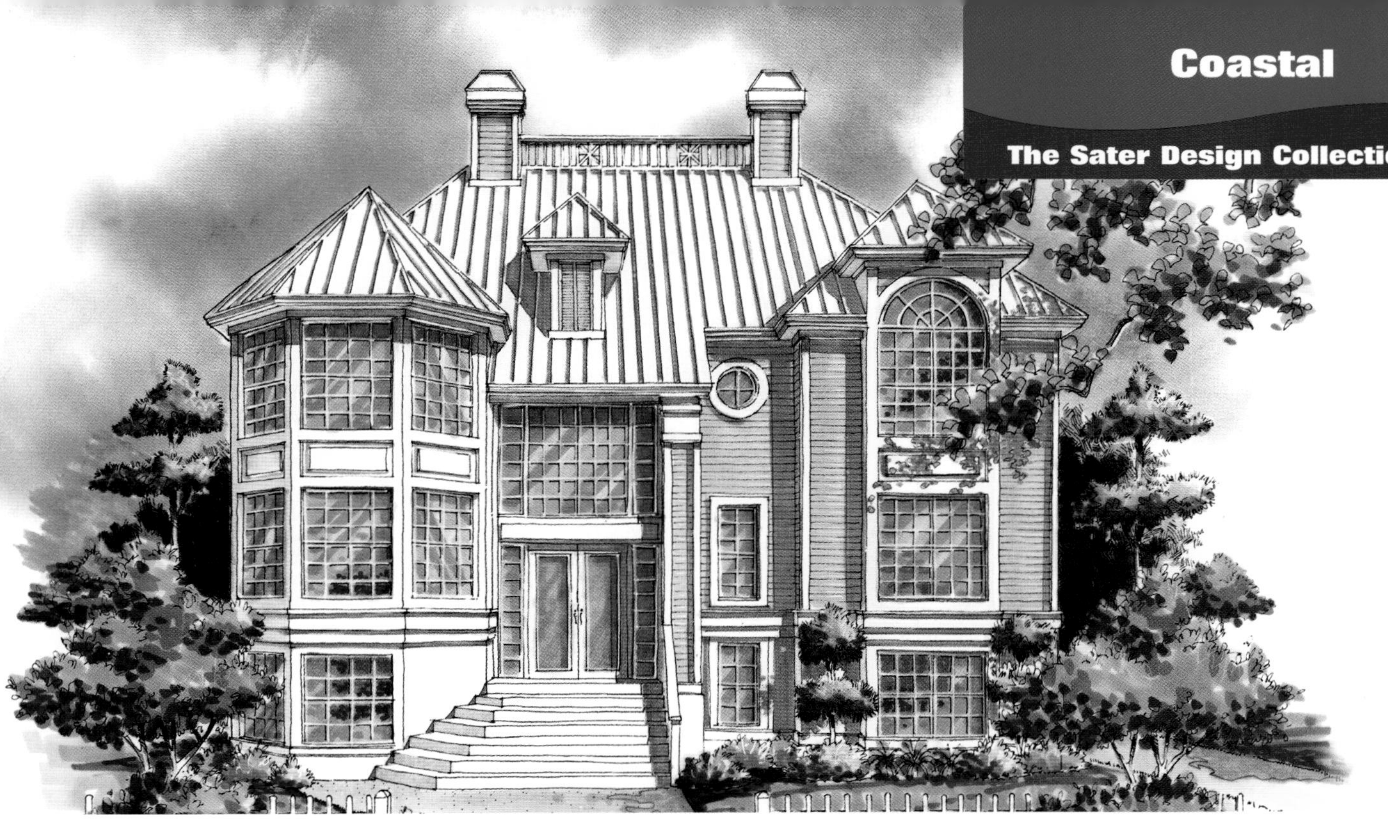

Savannah Sound — VPDS01-Plan 6698 — 1-866-525-9374

Total Living	First Floor	Second Floor	Bed	Bath	Width	Depth	Foundation	Price Category
2879 sq ft	1684 sq ft	1195 sq ft	3	3	45' 0"	52' 0"	Island Basement	G

Second Floor

First Floor

Lower Level

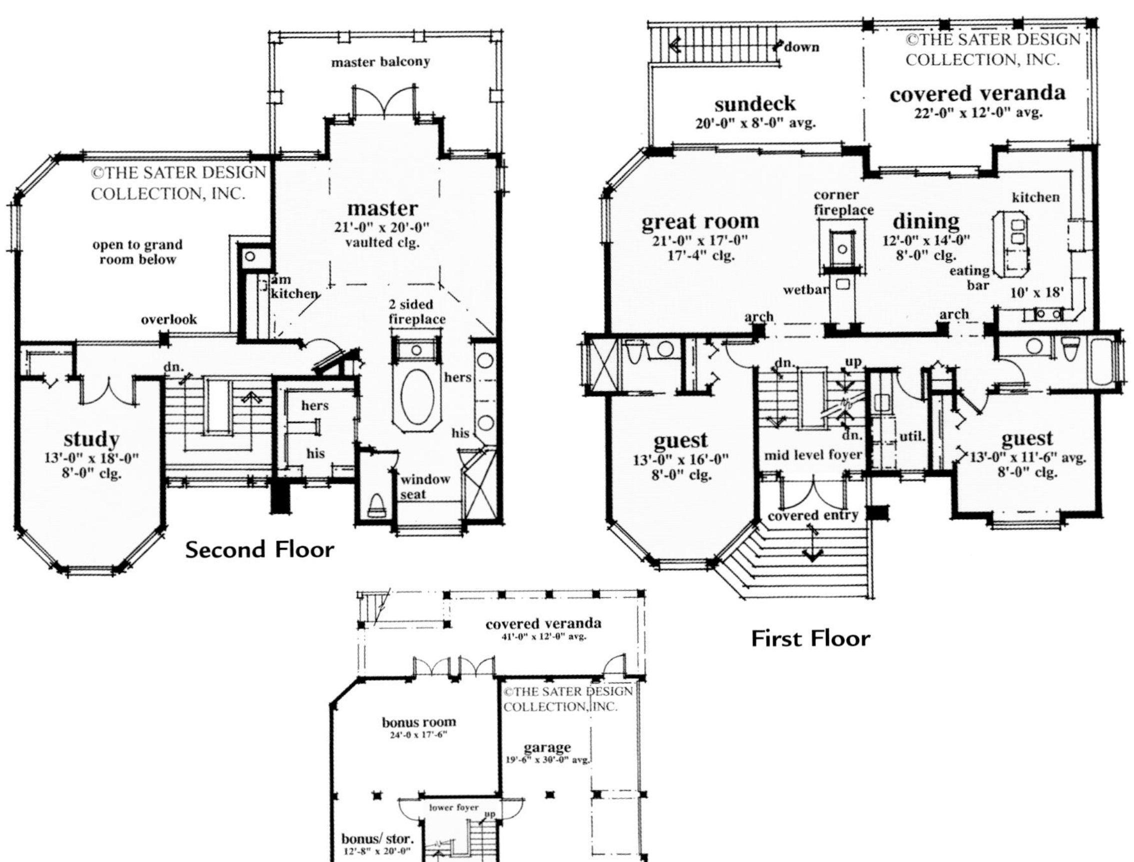

Design Features

- Two-story bay windows, dormers and a widow's peak create an impressive exterior, from all angles.
- Guests can convene around the wet bar and a corner fireplace that connect the dining and great room.
- The gourmet kitchen boasts a center island with an eating bar.
- A winding staircase leads to the upper-level master suite that features a private master balcony, morning kitchen and a two-sided fireplace that warms both the bedroom and bath.

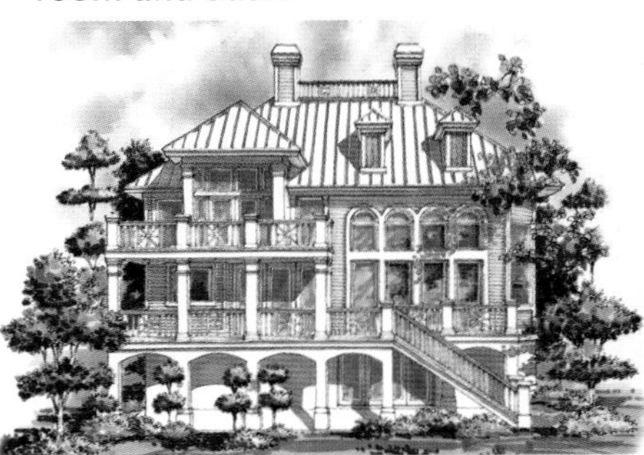

Rear Elevation

Brookhaven — VPFB01-Plan 963 — 1-866-525-9374

Total Living	First Floor	Second Floor	Opt. Bonus	Bed	Bath	Width	Depth	Foundation	Price Category
2126 sq ft	1583 sq ft	543 sq ft	251 sq ft	4	3	53' 0"	47' 0"	Basement, Crawl Space or Slab	H

Design Features

- Stone, cedar shake and siding create a Craftsman exterior on a Traditional-styled home.
- An arched walkway leads from the foyer to the family room, and an elegant tray ceiling and heavy crown moldings enhance the master bedroom.
- Rich stained cabinetry sets the tone for the stylish kitchen.
- Multiple activities take place in the bonus room. Whether bumper pool or video games, this is sure to be a family favorite.

Rear Elevation

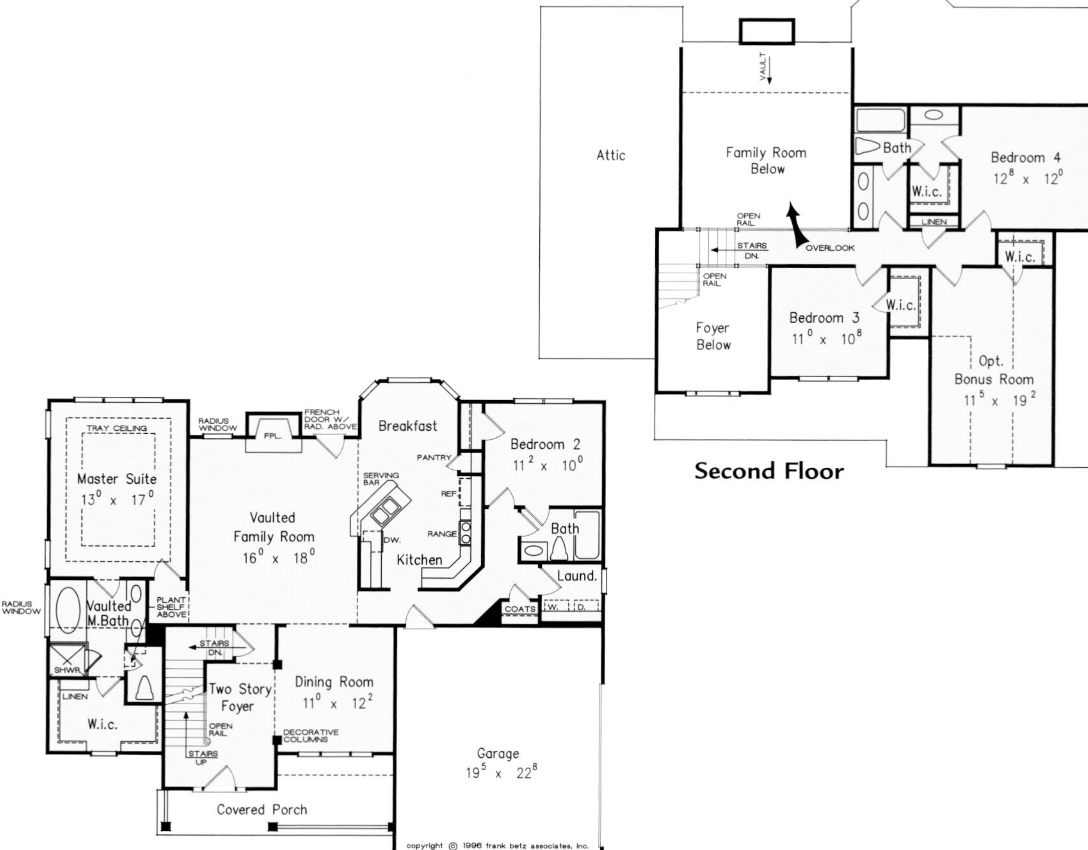

Second Floor

First Floor

Please note: Home photographed may differ from blueprint.

Palmetto — VPDG01-Plan 737-C — 1-866-525-9374

Total Living	First Floor	Second Floor	Bed	Bath	Width	Depth	Foundation	Price Category
1843 sq ft	1362 sq ft	481 sq ft	3	2-1/2	49' 4"	44' 10"	Post/Pier	D

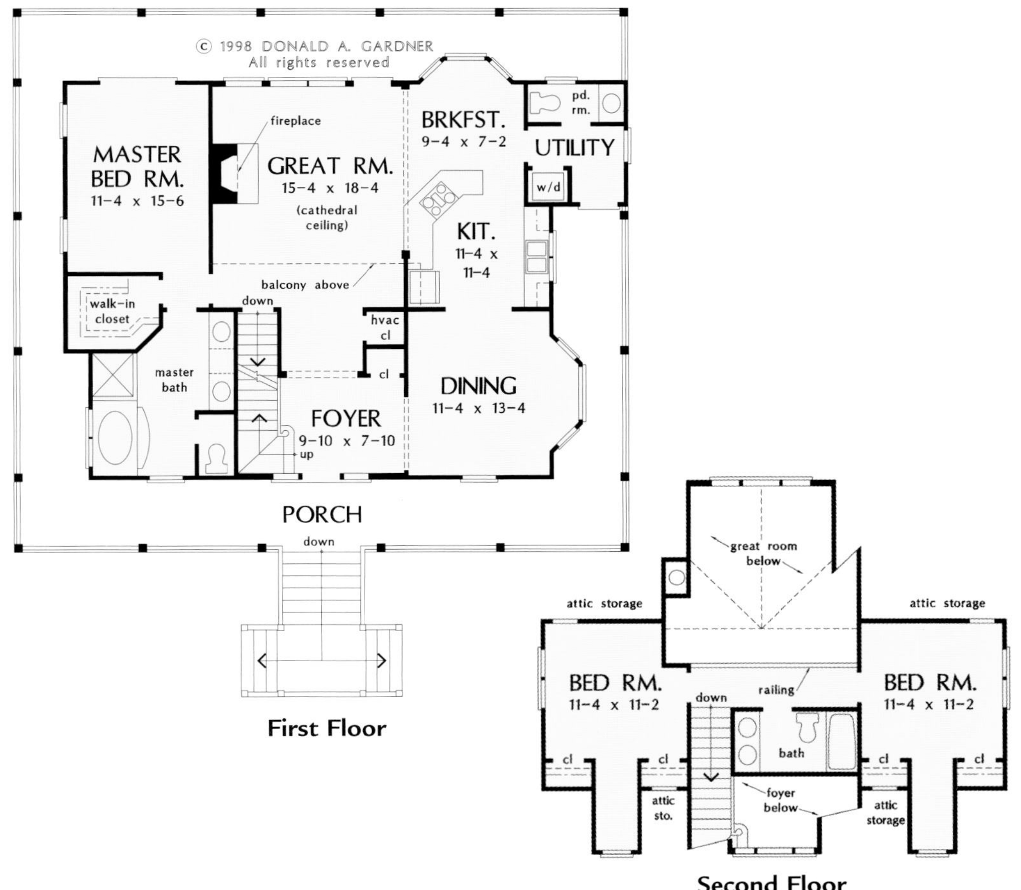

First Floor

Second Floor

Design Features

- An enchanting wraparound porch and delightful dormers create excitement for this coastal home.
- The large center dormer brightens the vaulted foyer.
- A balcony divides the second-floor bedrooms and overlooks the great room.
- The first-floor master suite features back-porch access, a walk-in closet and pampering bath.

Rear Elevation

Galleon Bay — VPDS01-Plan 6620 — 1-866-525-9374

Total Living	First Floor	Second Floor	Bed	Bath	Width	Depth	Foundation	Price Category
2875 sq ft	2066 sq ft	809 sq ft	3	3-1/2	64' 0"	45' 0"	Slab/Island Basement	H

Design Features

- The foyer embraces the living areas accented by a glass three-sided fireplace and a wet bar.
- The gourmet kitchen features ample counter and storage space, a breakfast nook and easily interacts with the verandah for outdoor cooking and eating.
- Located on the upper level, the master suite enjoys a vaulted ceiling, walk-in closet, a private sundeck and a three-sided fireplace that connects to the luxurious bathroom.

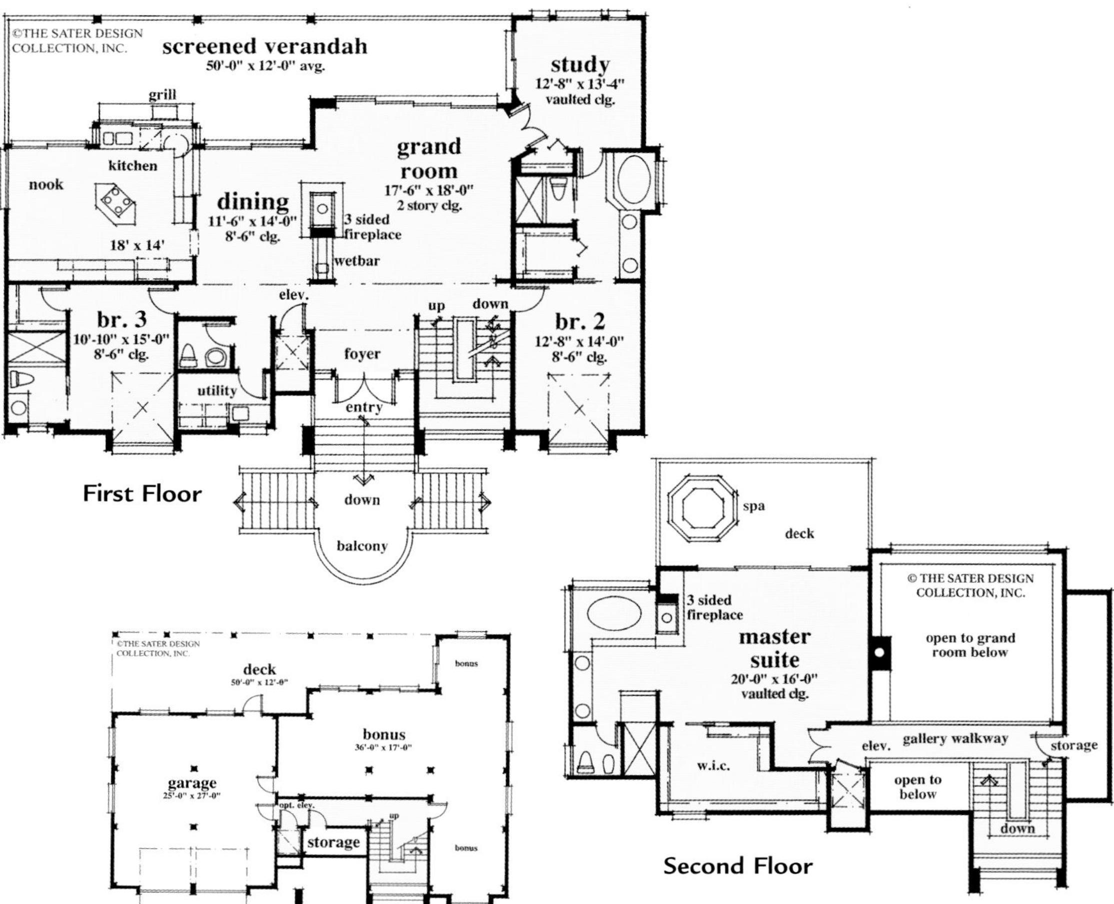

First Floor

Lower Level

Second Floor

Rear Elevation

Defoors Mill — VPFB01-Plan 3712 — 1-866-525-9374

Total Living	First Floor	Second Floor	Opt. Bonus	Bed	Bath	Width	Depth	Foundation	Price Category
2351 sq ft	1803 sq ft	548 sq ft	277 sq ft	4	3	55' 0"	48' 0"	Basement, Crawl Space or Slab	H

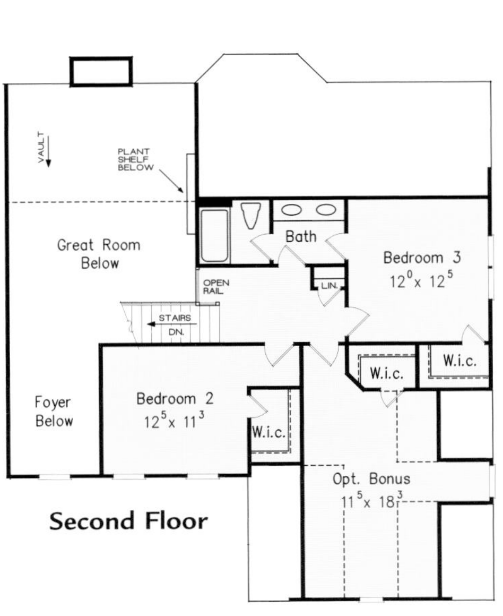

Second Floor

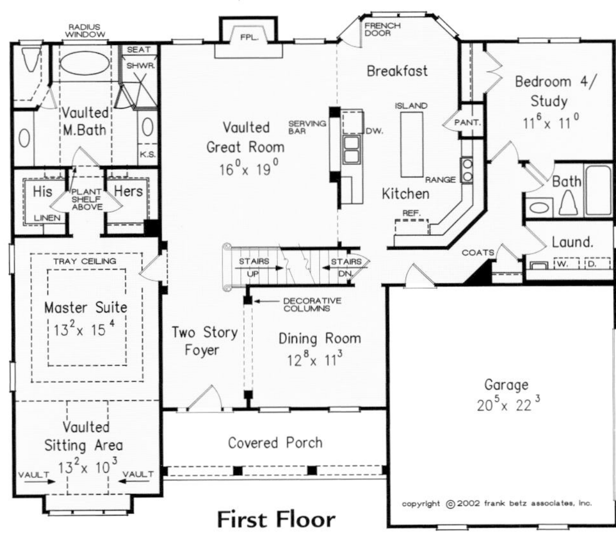

First Floor

Design Features

- A covered porch is situated on the front of the home and leads to a charming and practical floor plan.
- The master suite encompasses an entire wing of the home for comfort and privacy.
- An optional bonus room is available on the second floor.
- Special details in this home include a handy island in the kitchen, decorative columns around the dining area and a coat closet just off the garage.

Rear Elevation

Hatteras — VPDG01-Plan 739-C — 1-866-525-9374

Total Living	First Floor	Second Floor	Bed	Bath	Width	Depth	Foundation	Price Category
2362 sq ft	1650 sq ft	712 sq ft	3	2-1/2	58' 10"	47' 4"	Post/Pier	E

Design Features

- Striking gables with decorative scalloped insets adorn the exterior.
- The generous great room is expanded by a rear wall of windows.
- The kitchen features a pass-thru to the great room that doubles as a breakfast bar.
- The dining room, great room and study all access an inviting back porch.
- Two secondary bedrooms, one with its own private balcony, share a hall bath.

Rear Elevation

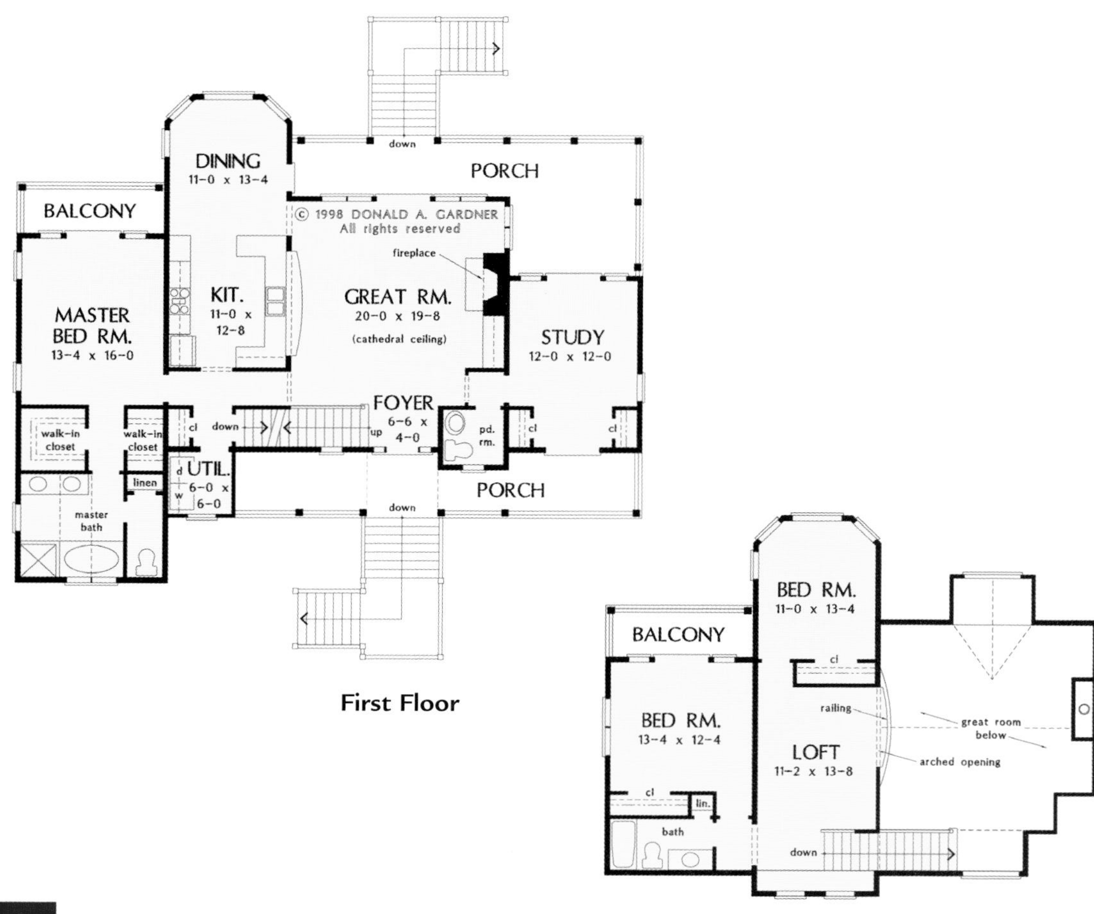

First Floor

Second Floor

Cutlass Key — VPDS01-Plan 6619 — 1-866-525-9374

Total Living	First Floor	Second Floor	Bed	Bath	Width	Depth	Foundation	Price Category
4143 sq ft	2725 sq ft	1418 sq ft	4	5-1/2	61' 4"	62' 0"	Piling with Slab	J

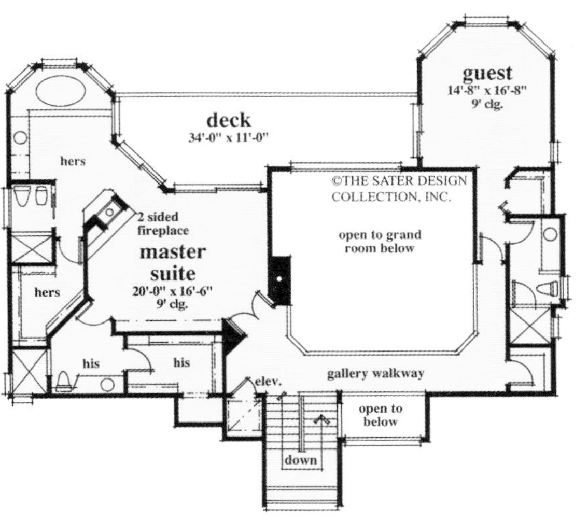

Second Floor

First Floor

Lower Level

Design Features

- The two-story grand room offers a wet bar and three-sided fireplace.
- Glass doors open to the screened veranda from the study, dining and grand room.
- The eat-in kitchen has a spacious walk-in pantry.
- The screened verandah features an outdoor grille.
- An opulent master suite gets upstairs privacy and enjoys a two-sided fireplace, along with "his-and-her" baths, walk-in closets and access to the deck.

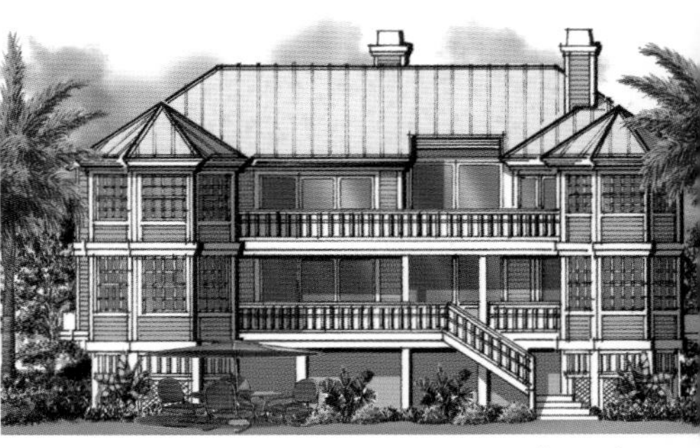

Rear Elevation

Devonhurst — VPFB01-Plan 3806 — 1-866-525-9374

Total Living	First Floor	Opt. 2nd Fl.	Bed	Bath	Width	Depth	Foundation	Price Category
2477 sq ft	2477 sq ft	555 sq ft	4	3-1/2	65' 4"	68' 0"	Basement or Crawl Space	H

Design Features

- Stepping inside you'll find a very open, unobstructed floor plan. The dining room is bordered by decorative columns, allowing effortless flow to the other living areas.
- The breakfast area and keeping room share open access to the kitchen — perfect for family gathering or parties.
- High ceilings always enhance the volume of a home, so vaults were incorporated into the keeping and family rooms.

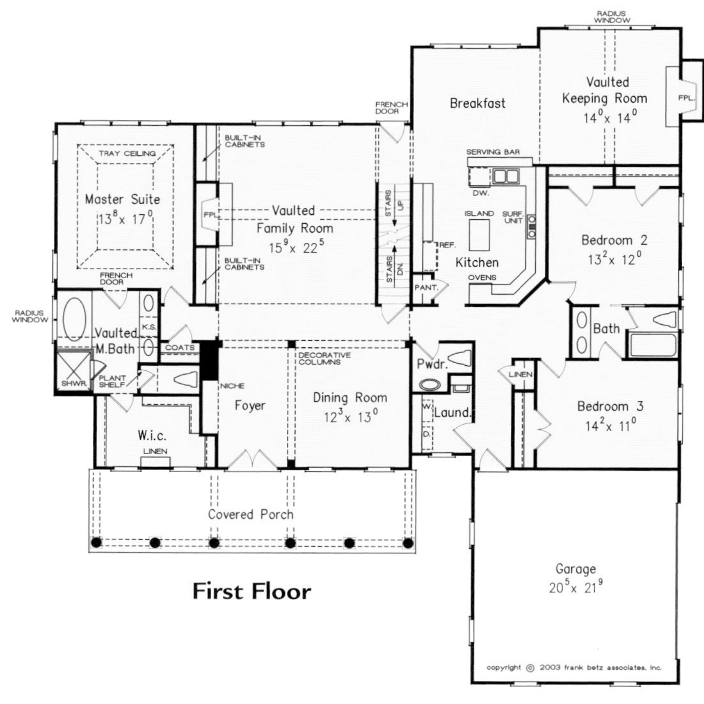

First Floor

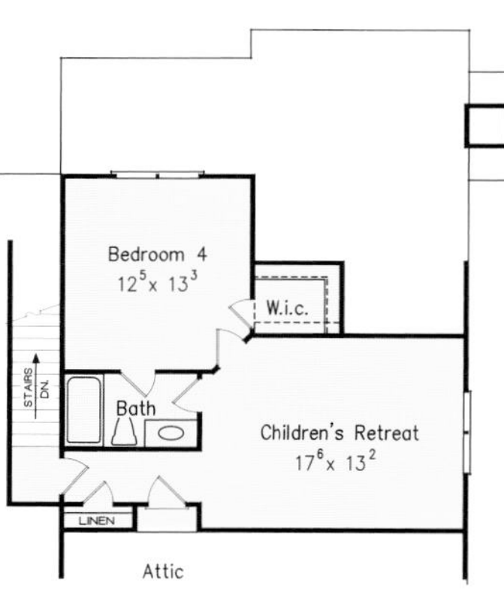

Opt. Second Floor

Rear Elevation

Sandifer — VPDG01-Plan 750-C — 1-866-525-9374

Total Living	First Floor	Second Floor	Bed	Bath	Width	Depth	Foundation	Price Category
1770 sq ft	944 sq ft	826 sq ft	3	3	30' 4"	42' 8"	Post/Pier	D

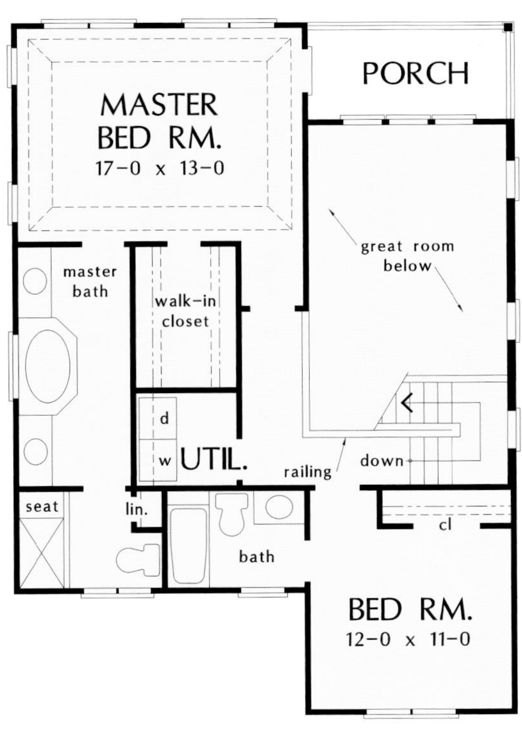

Second Floor

PORCH

DINING 11-8 x 12-10

GREAT RM. 17-2 x 15-4 (two story ceiling)

KIT. 12-2 x 12-0

up

cl

bath

cl

FOYER

STUDY/ BED RM. 12-0 x 11-0

First Floor

Design Features

- This waterfront home features a super-slim design for very narrow lots.
- A two-story ceiling amplifies the open great room with overlooking second-floor balcony.
- The back porch, dining room, kitchen and great room flow effortlessly together.
- The master suite enjoys views from its second-story porch.
- The laundry room is conveniently located on the second floor.

Rear Elevation

Admirality Pointe — VPDS01-Plan 6622 — 1-866-525-9374

Total Living	First Floor	Bonus	Bed	Bath	Width	Depth	Foundation	Price Category
2190 sq ft	2190 sq ft	N/A	3 + Study	2	58' 0"	54' 0"	Slab	F

Design Features

- An expansive great room offers a warming fireplace, sliding glass doors to the lanai, built-in shelves and a great place for an aquarium.
- A corner walk-in pantry, an eating bar open to the grand room and a windowed morning nook brighten the kitchen.
- Lower-level recreation space may be developed into a home theater, game room or hobby area.
- A secluded master wing opens to the lanai through double French doors and features dual walk-in closets and a pampering bath.

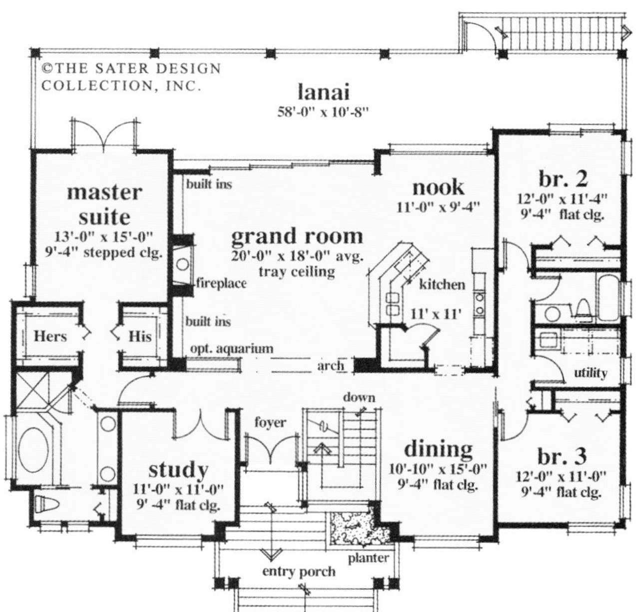

First Floor

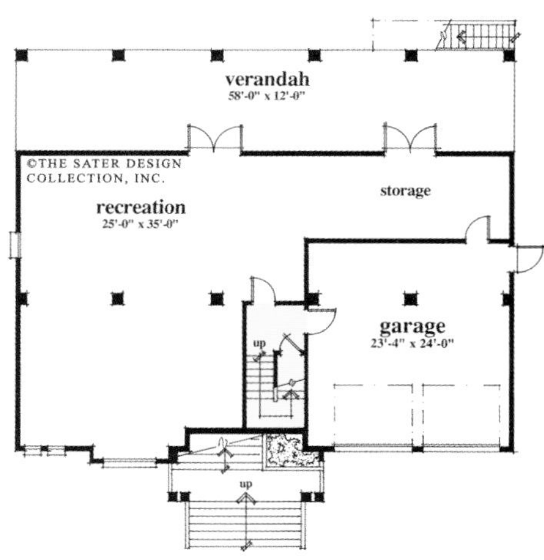

Lower Level

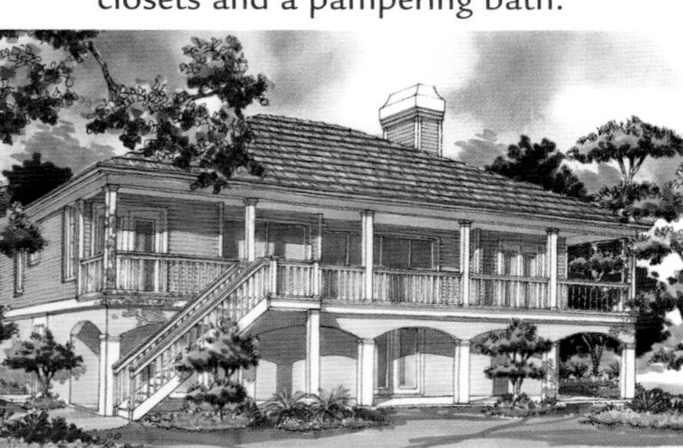

Rear Elevation

McArthur Park — VPFB01-Plan 3837 — 1-866-525-9374

Total Living	First Floor	Second Floor	Opt. Bonus	Bed	Bath	Width	Depth	Foundation	Price Category
2024 sq ft	1480 sq ft	544 sq ft	253 sq ft	3	2-1/2	52' 0"	46' 4"	Basement, Crawl Space or Slab	G

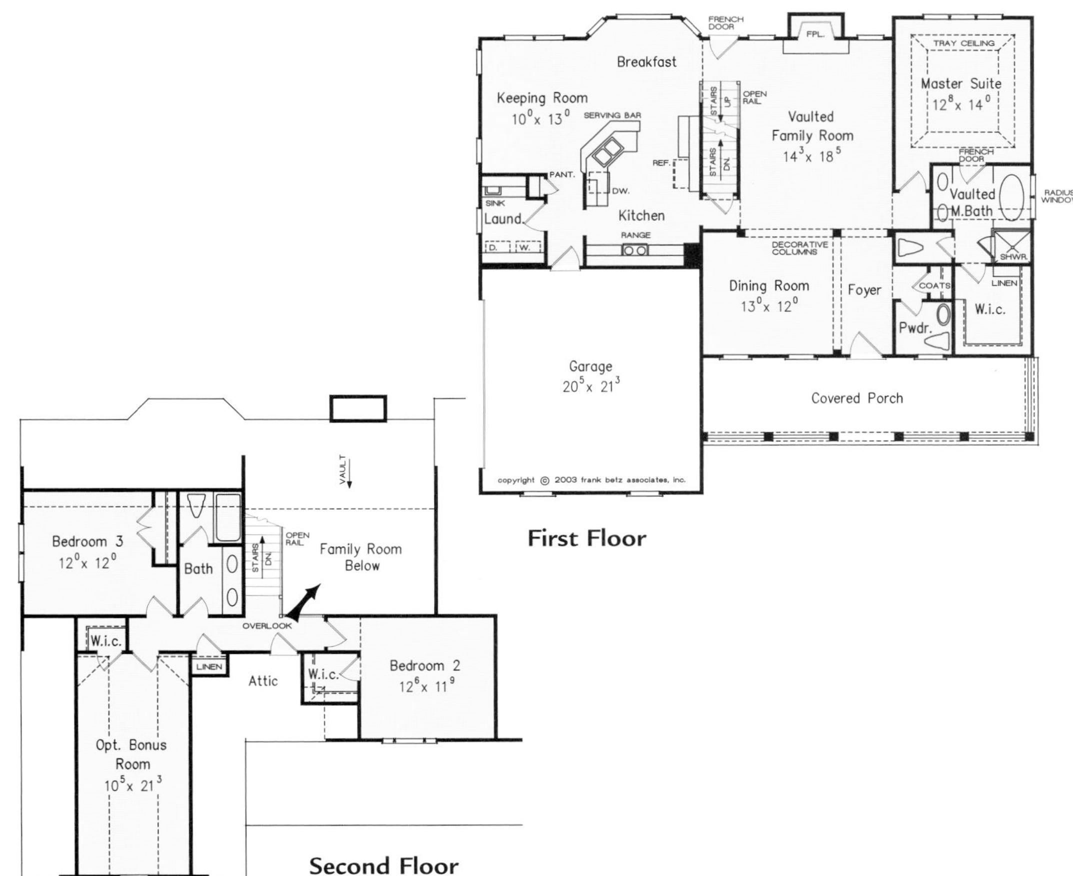

First Floor

Second Floor

Design Features

- It has been said that beauty is often found in simplicity — and the *McArthur Park* brings truth to that statement. Its understated exterior and uncomplicated roofline make this home both appealing and cost-effective to build.
- The kitchen, breakfast area and keeping room share common space, making it ideal for entertaining.
- An optional bonus room is available on the upper floor that has endless possibilities. It can be easily finished as a fourth bedroom, playroom, exercise area or craft room.

Rear Elevation

Summercrest — VPDG01-Plan 756-C — 1-866-525-9374

Total Living	First Floor	Second Floor	Bed	Bath	Width	Depth	Foundation	Price Category
2228 sq ft	1170 sq ft	1058 sq ft	4	2-1/2	30' 0"	51' 0"	Post/Pier	E

Design Features

- An elevated pier foundation, narrow width and multiple porches make this home perfect for waterfront lots.
- The great room, kitchen and breakfast area are all open for a casual and spacious feeling.
- A utility room is conveniently located on the second floor.
- Upstairs, every bedroom (plus the master bath) enjoys porch access.

Rear Elevation

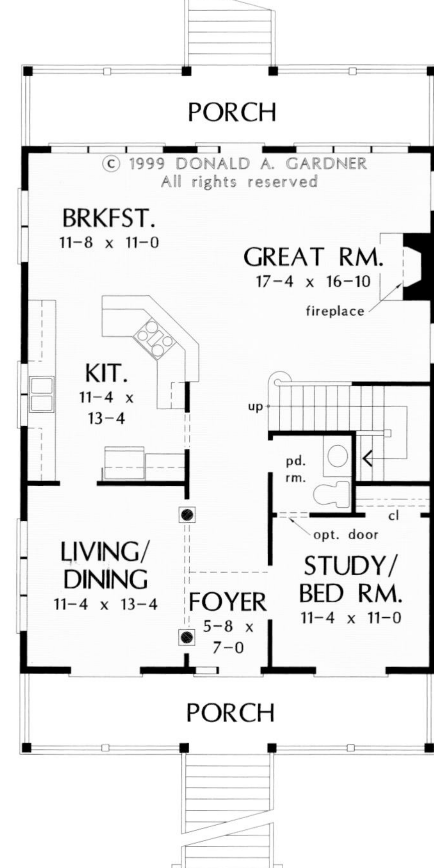

First Floor

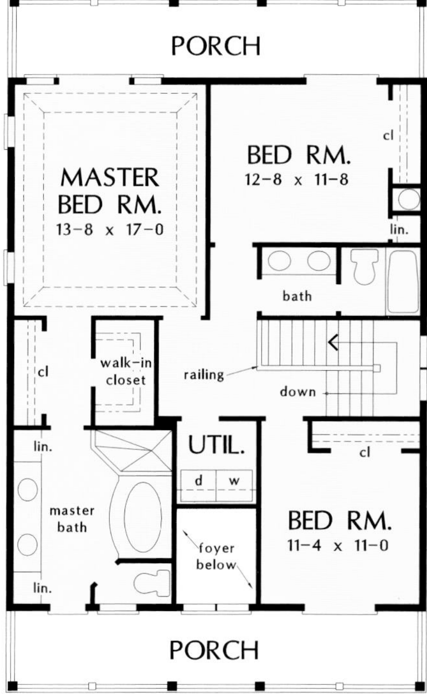

Second Floor

Gaspirilla Bay — VPDS01-Plan 6618 — 1-866-525-9374

Total Living	First Floor	Second Floor	Lower Level	Bed	Bath	Width	Depth	Foundation	Price Category
3335 sq ft	1944 sq ft	1196 sq ft	195 sq ft	4	4-1/2	68' 0"	54' 0"	Island Basement	H

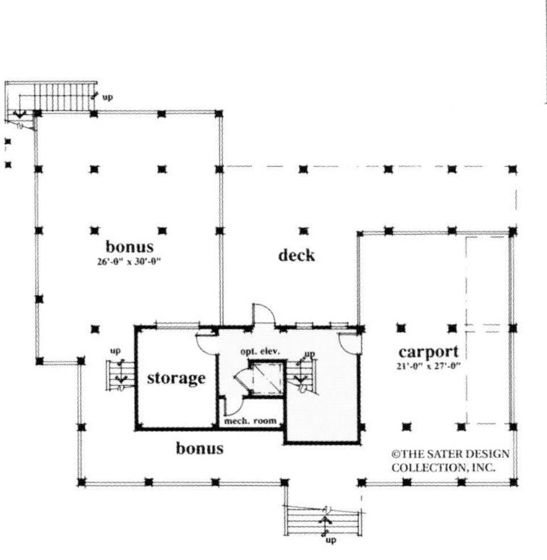

Lower Level

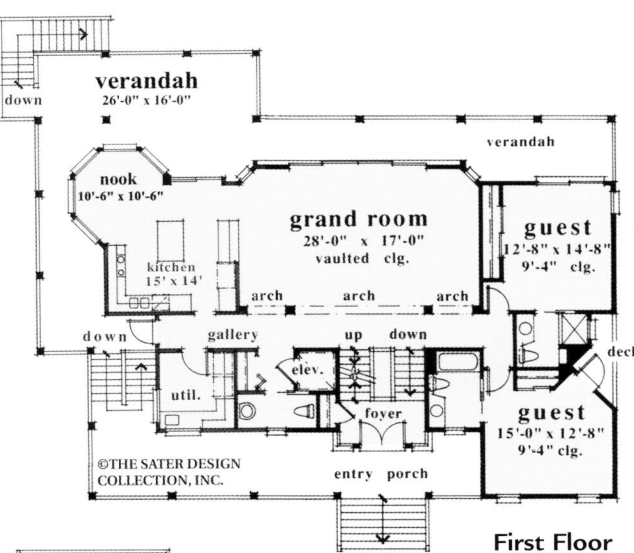

First Floor

Second Floor

Design Features

- The raised multi-level wraparound porch captures fantastic views from three sides.
- The great room sits under a vaulted ceiling and features arches, columns, a wall of glass to the veranda and easy access to the kitchen and nook.
- Planned events are a cinch in the gourmet kitchen where ample storage and counters wrap around a culinary island.
- Upstairs, a rambling master suite enjoys a private deck, a luxury bath with separate vanities and a walk-in closet with dressing area.

Rear Elevation

Roswell — VPFB01-Plan 3708 — 1-866-525-9374

Total Living	First Floor	Opt. 2nd Fl.	Bed	Bath	Width	Depth	Foundation	Price Category
1748 sq ft	1748 sq ft	303 sq ft	4	3	55' 0"	55' 0"	Basement or Crawl Space	F

Design Features

- This charming split-bedroom design has traditional elements that are comforting and familiar.
- Holiday gatherings are easily accommodated in the formal dining room that is accented with a decorative column.
- The master suite has a bright and cheery window seat that makes the perfect spot to curl up with a good book.
- The split-bedroom design allows residents the privacy they desire.

Rear Elevation

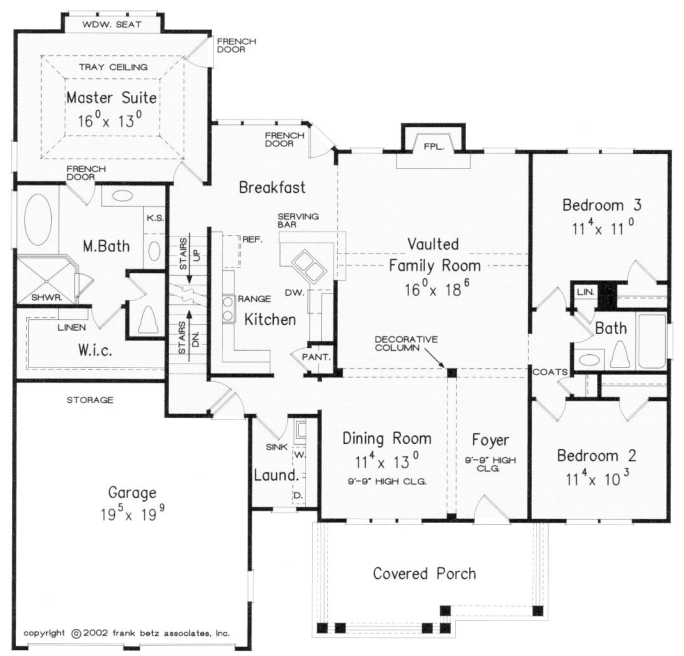

First Floor

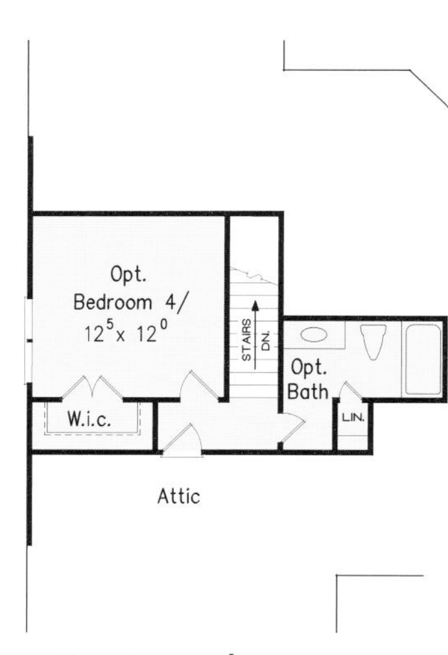

Opt. Second Foor

Mimosa — VPDS01-Plan 6861 — 1-866-525-9374

Total Living	First Floor	Bonus	Bed	Bath	Width	Depth	Foundation	Price Category
3074 sq ft	3074 sq ft	N/A	3	3-1/2	77' 0"	66' 8"	Island Basement	H

Design Features

- The enhancing portico leads to a mid-level foyer.
- A wide-open leisure room hosts a corner fireplace.
- Lower-level space offers storage and a walkout lanai.
- Glass walls and sliding doors open the leisure and living rooms to the outdoors.
- Two guest suites are secluded to one side.

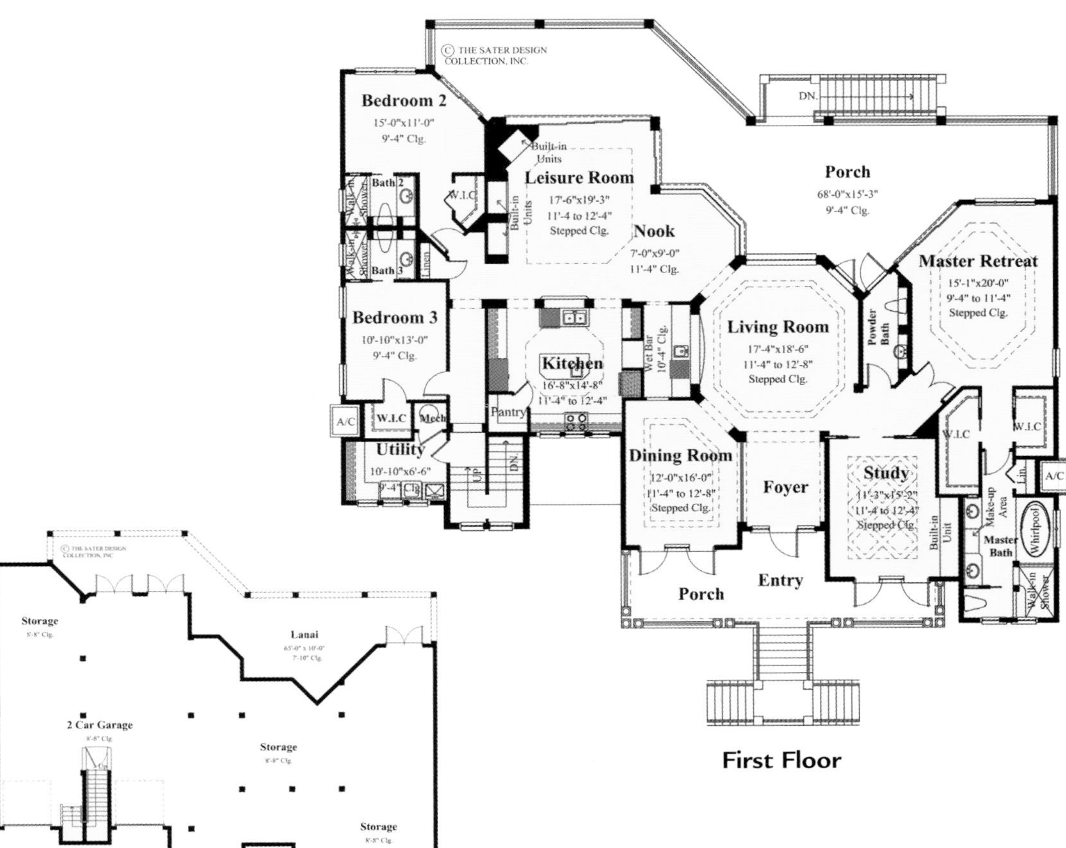

First Floor

Lower Level

Rear Elevation

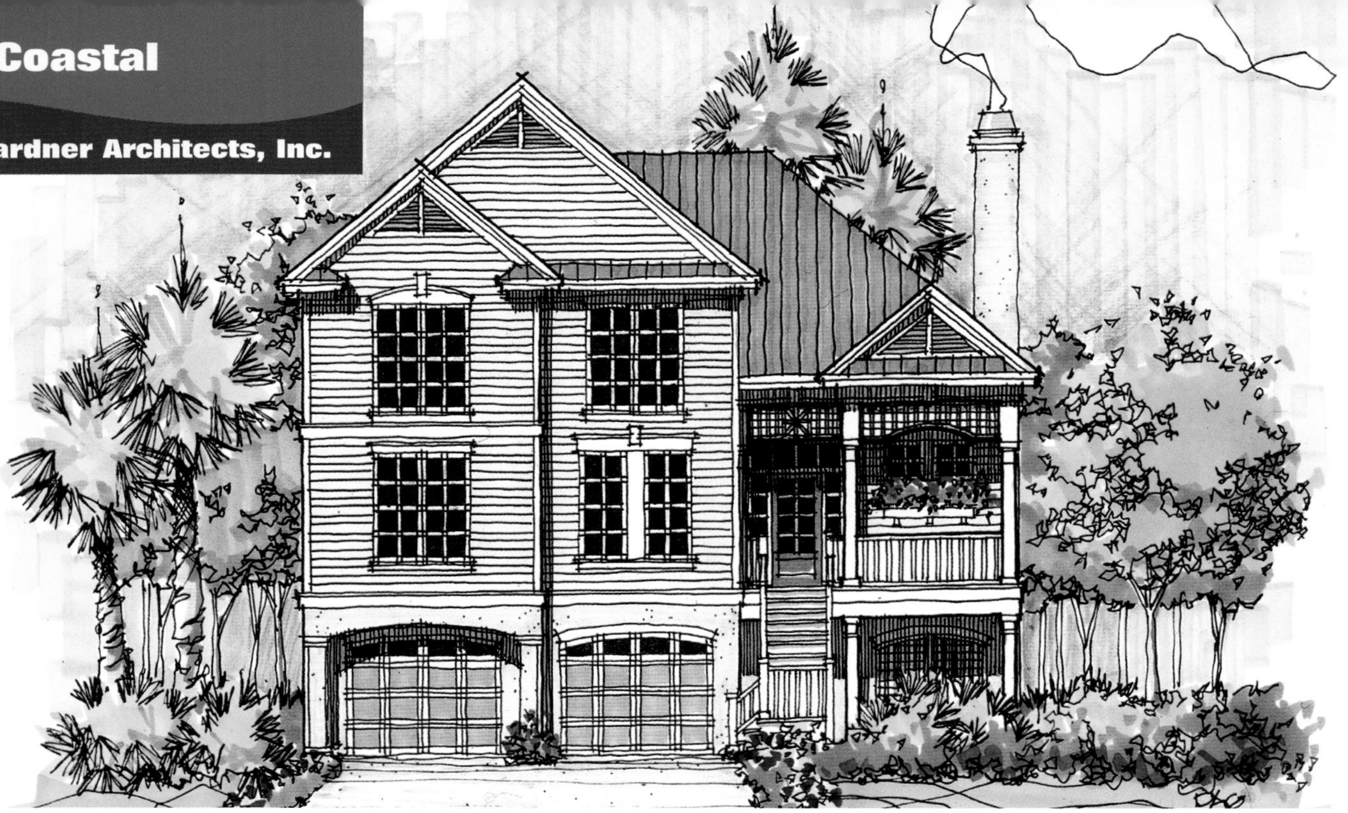

Tidewater — VPDG01-Plan 844-C — 1-866-525-9374

Total Living	First Floor	Second Floor	Bed	Bath	Width	Depth	Foundation	Price Category
2612 sq ft	1500 sq ft	1112 sq ft	4	3	42' 0"	49' 6"	Post/Pier	E

Design Features

- The main living areas are positioned at the rear of the home for the best views of the water.
- The great room features a vaulted ceiling, fireplace and back-porch access.
- The kitchen is open, sharing space with a bayed breakfast area and lovely sunroom.
- The first floor includes a bedroom/study and full bath.
- The master suite boasts a private porch and sitting room with bay window.

First Floor

Second Floor

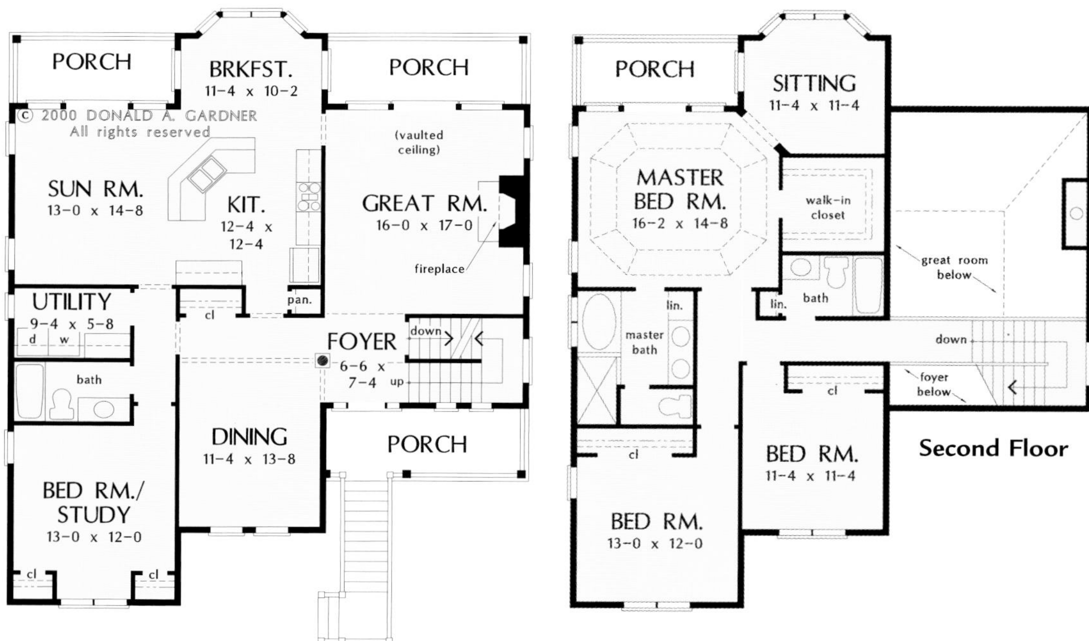

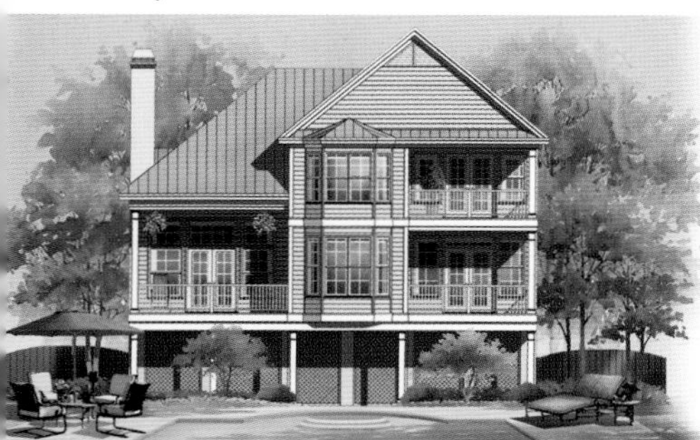

Rear Elevation

Palm Lily — VPDG01-Plan 845-C — 1-866-525-9374

Total Living	First Floor	Second Floor	Bed	Bath	Width	Depth	Foundation	Price Category
2390 sq ft	1620 sq ft	770 sq ft	3	3-1/2	49' 0"	58' 8"	Post/Pier	E

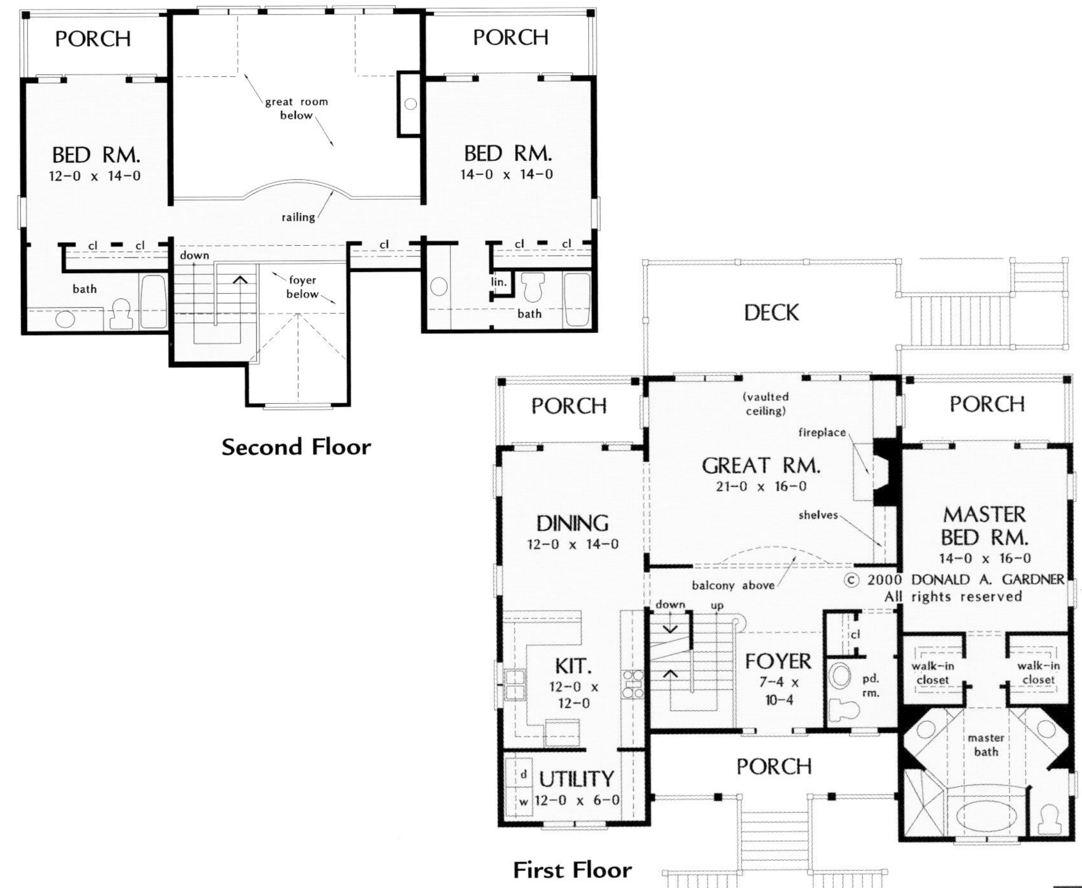

Second Floor

First Floor

Design Features

- Vaulted ceilings in the foyer and great room highlight a dramatic second-floor balcony.
- The two upstairs bedrooms each have their own bath and private porch.
- The great room is generously proportioned with built-in shelves, fireplace and rear-deck access.
- Private back porches enhance the dining room and the master suite as well.

Rear Elevation

Tullamore Square — VPFB01-Plan 3801 — 1-866-525-9374

Total Living	First Floor	Second Floor	Opt. Bonus	Bed	Bath	Width	Depth	Foundation	Price Category
2398 sq ft	1805 sq ft	593 sq ft	255 sq ft	4	3	55' 0"	48' 0"	Basement, Slab or Crawl Space	H

Design Features

- This home is every bit as quaint as its name, with a cedar-shake exterior accented with a rooftop cupola.
- A seated shower, soaking tub and "his-and-her" closets make the master bath feel like five-star luxury.
- A coat closet and a laundry room are placed just off the garage, keeping coats and shoes in their place.
- A second main-floor bedroom makes a great guest room or home office.

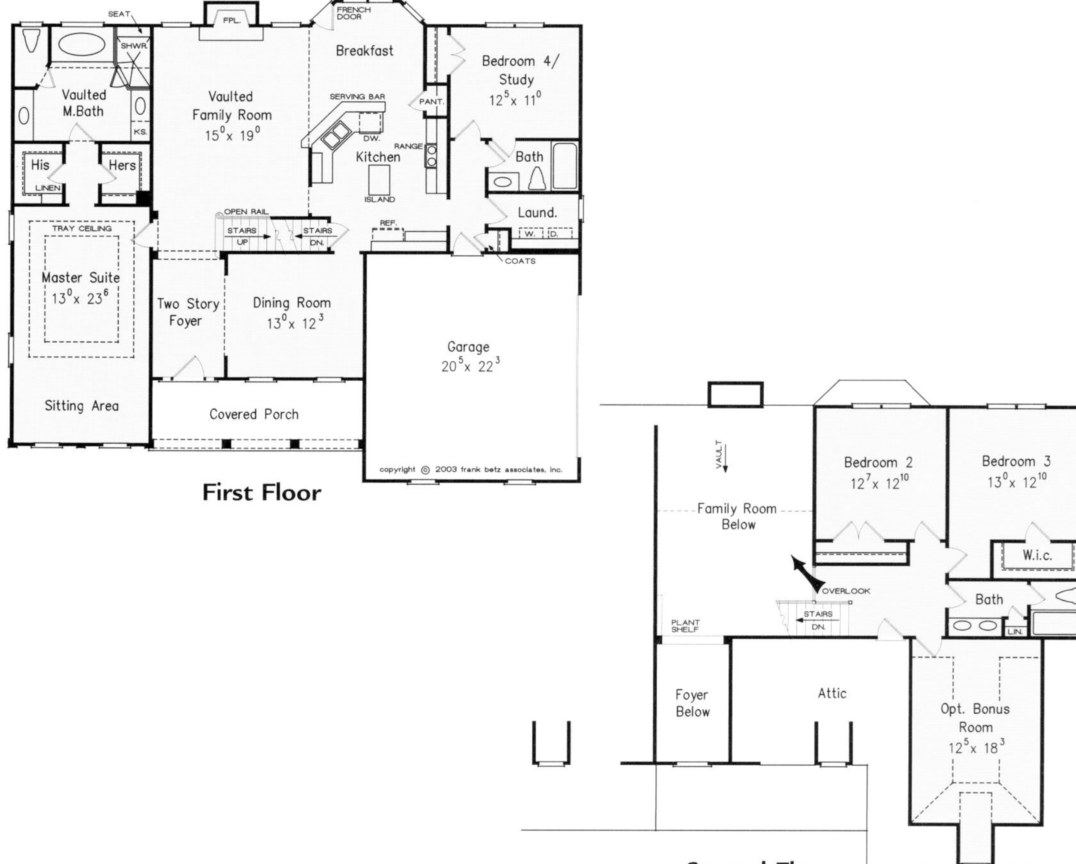

First Floor

Second Floor

Rear Elevation

Kingston Harbor — VPDS01-Plan 6621 — 1-866-525-9374

Total Living	First Floor	Second Floor	Bed	Bath	Width	Depth	Foundation	Price Category
2569 sq ft	1642 sq ft	927 sq ft	3	2-1/2	60' 0"	44' 6"	Slab	G

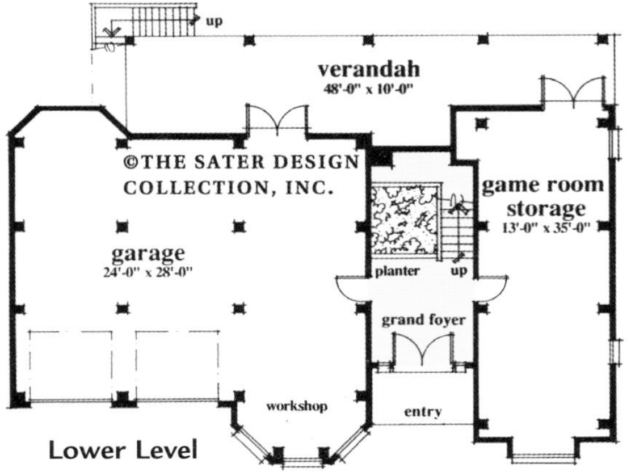

Lower Level

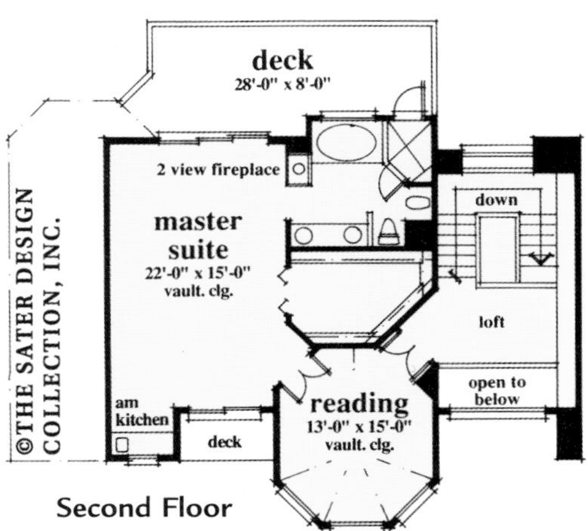

Second Floor

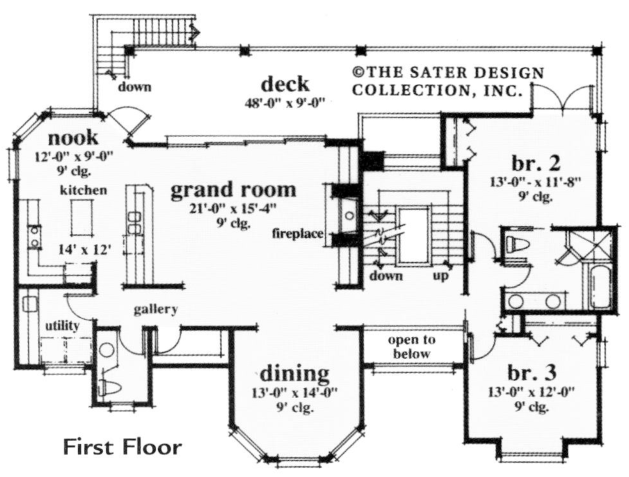

First Floor

Design Features

- The kitchen offers ample counter space, a center work island and a bay breakfast nook.
- The grand room features built-in cabinetry, a fireplace, glass doors to the deck and easy access to the nook and kitchen.
- The master retreat resides on the upper level and boasts a cozy loft area, reading room, morning kitchen, two-sided fireplace, spacious bath and French doors opening to a sun deck.

Rear Elevation

Sunburst — VPDG01-Plan 846-C — 1-866-525-9374

Total Living	First Floor	Bonus	Bed	Bath	Width	Depth	Foundation	Price Category
1970 sq ft	1970 sq ft	N/A	3	2	34' 8"	83' 0"	Post/Pier	D

Design Features

- Triple gables, front and back porches and a quartet of bay windows showcase stunning curb appeal.
- Numerous windows and volume ceilings enhance spaciousness throughout the home.
- Columns add just the right amount of definition to the open dining room.
- Two bedrooms, one with access to a private front porch, share a full bath.
- The master suite is secluded at the rear of the home with back-porch access.

Rear Elevation

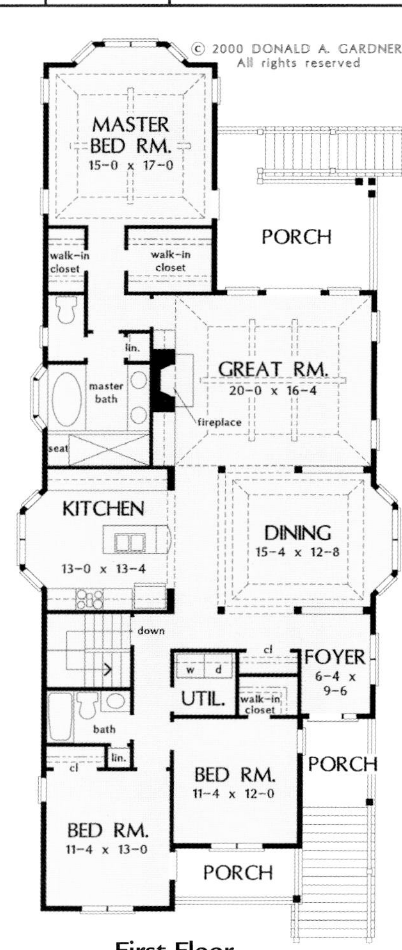

First Floor

Oleander — VPDG01-Plan 847-C — 1-866-525-9374

Total Living	First Floor	Bonus	Bed	Bath	Width	Depth	Foundation	Price Category
2413 sq ft	2413 sq ft	N/A	3	3	66' 4"	62' 10"	Post/Pier	E

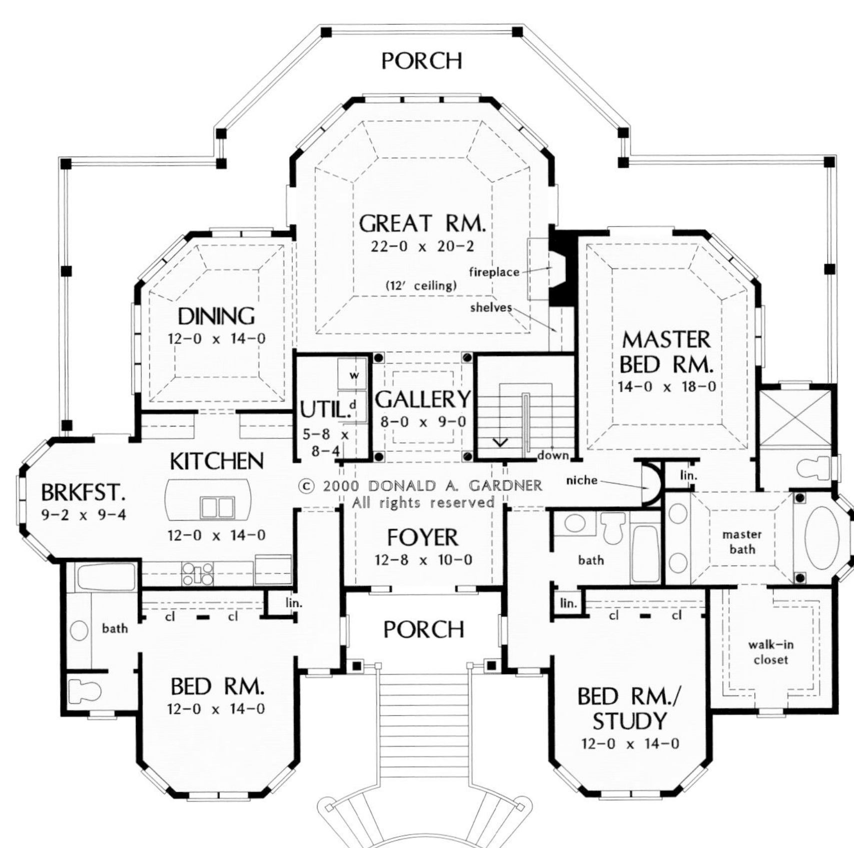

First Floor

Design Features

- Hip and turret-style roofs top the two front bedrooms of this coastal home.
- An arched window in an eyebrow dormer crowns the double-door front entrance.
- A remarkable foyer creates quite a first impression and leads into the great room.
- The great room boasts a tray ceiling, numerous windows and back-porch access.
- The kitchen is spacious with an island and delightful breakfast area with bay window.

Rear Elevation

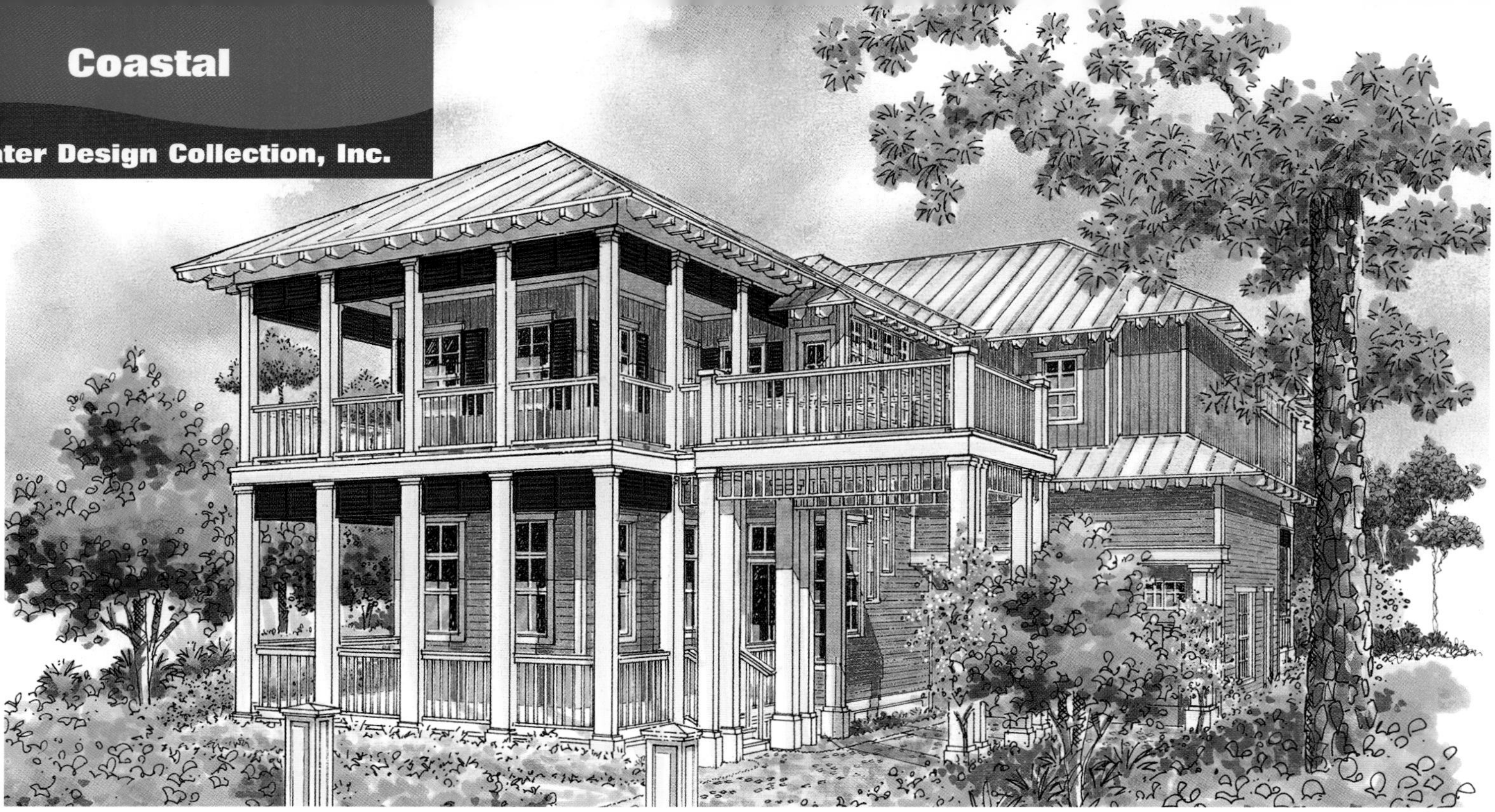

Sierra Vista — VPDS01-Plan 6757 — 1-866-525-9374

Total Living	First Floor	Second Floor	Bed	Bath	Width	Depth	Foundation	Price Category
2989 sq ft	1372 sq ft	1617 sq ft	5	5-1/2	50' 0"	83' 10"	Pier	G

Design Features

- The first floor is home to three secondary bedrooms, with each featuring a full bath, spacious closet and easy access to the media room and veranda.
- The living room sits on the upper level under a vaulted ceiling with built-in cabinetry and a fireplace, and opens into the dining room and kitchen.
- An upper veranda features an alfresco kitchen that extends the function of the dining room.

Rear Elevation

First Floor

Second Floor

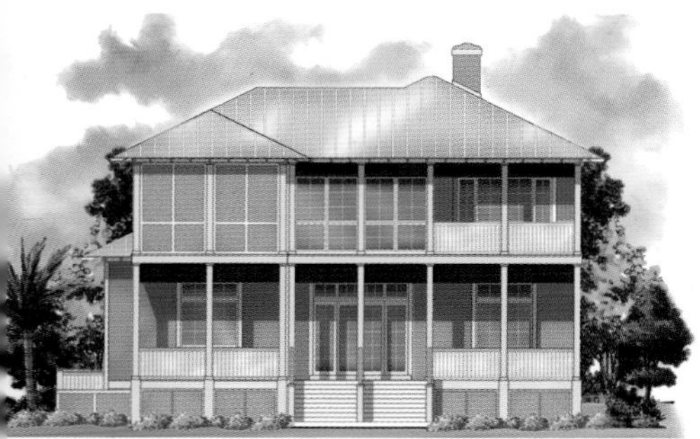

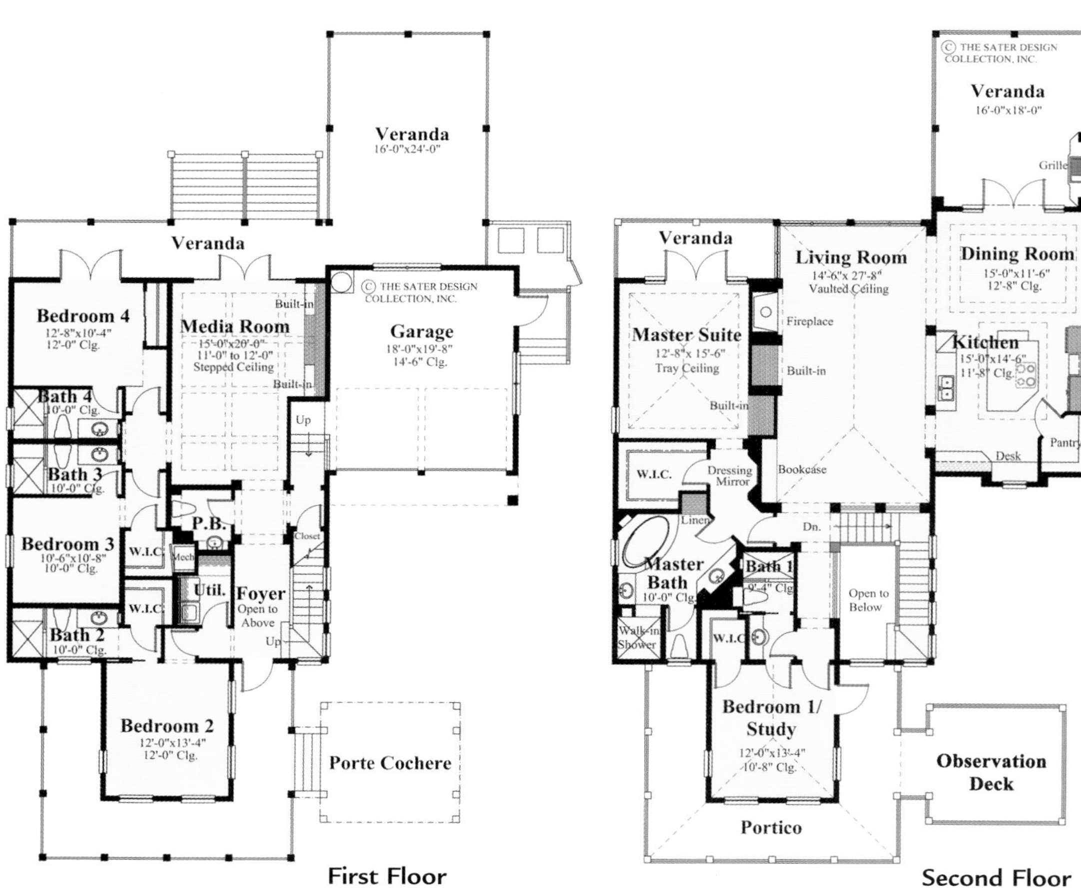

Willowbrook — VPFB01-Plan 1086 — 1-866-525-9374

Total Living	First Floor	Second Floor	Opt. Bonus	Bed	Bath	Width	Depth	Foundation	Price Category
1597 sq ft	1205 sq ft	392 sq ft	190 sq ft	3	2-1/2	50' 6"	44' 4"	Basement, Crawl Space or Slab	E

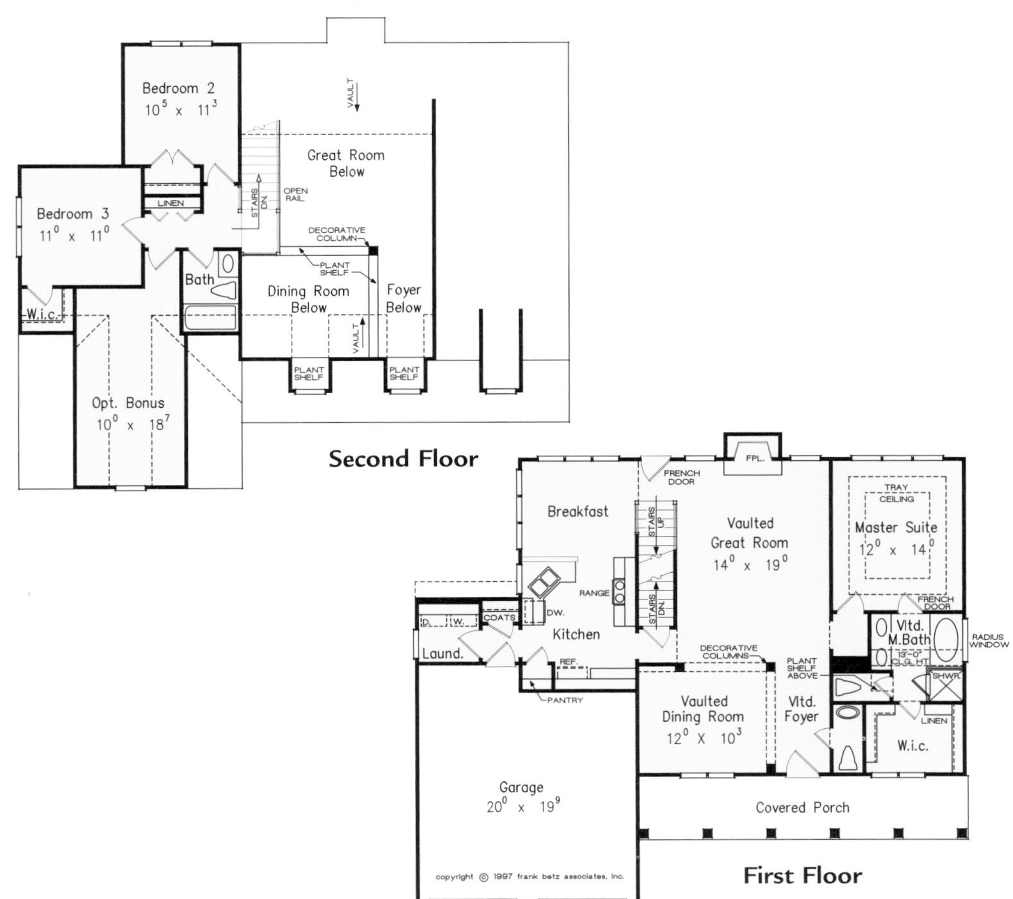

Second Floor

First Floor

Design Features

- The rocking-chair front porch gives guests a glimpse of what's inside.
- The main-level master suite offers homeowners the privacy so many desire.
- Decorative columns frame the dining room, which leads to the vaulted great room.
- Two bedrooms and an optional bonus room are located on the second floor.

Rear Elevation

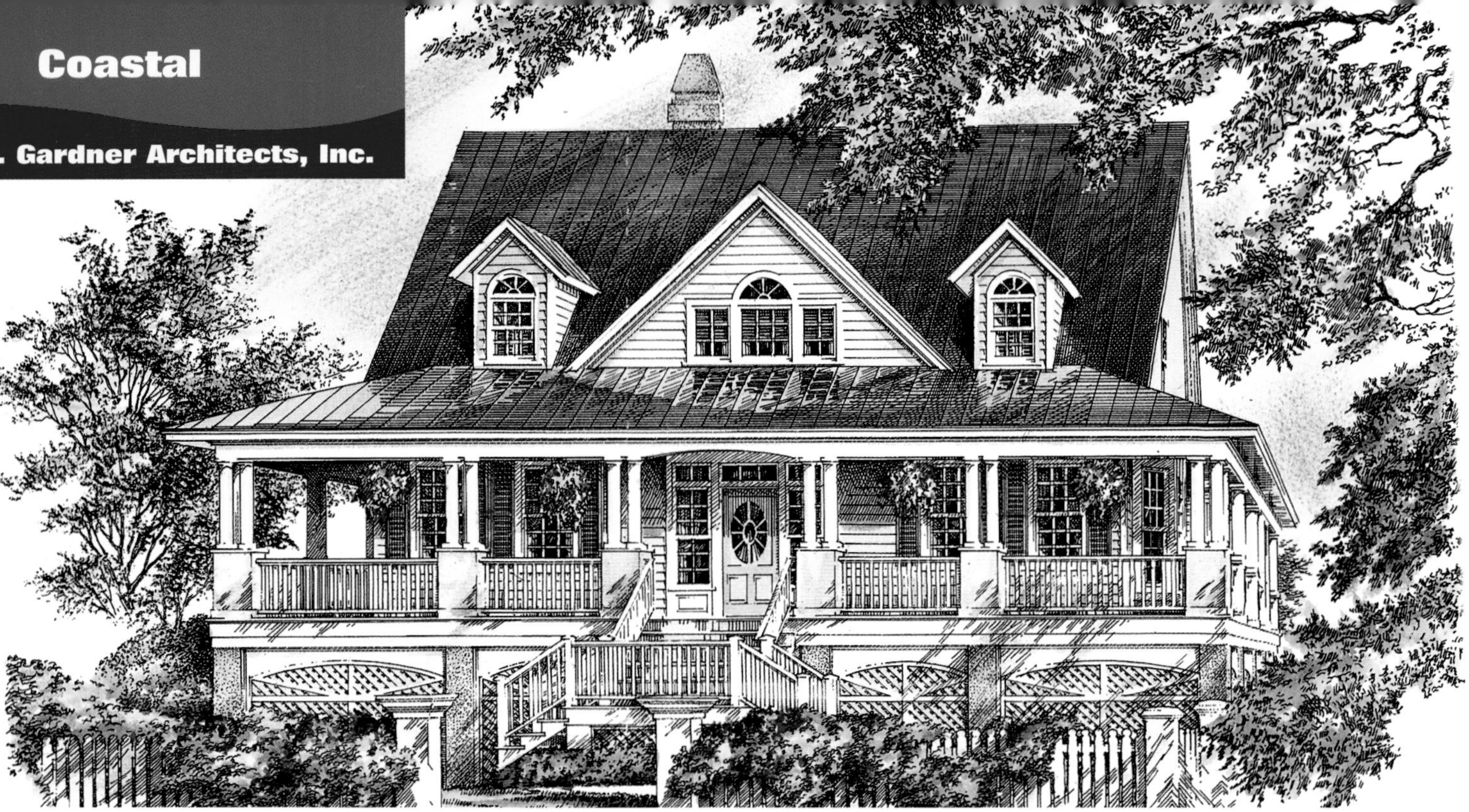

Hyacinth — VPDG01-Plan 856-C — 1-866-525-9374

Total Living	First Floor	Second Floor	Bed	Bath	Width	Depth	Foundation	Price Category
1849 sq ft	1368 sq ft	481 sq ft	3	2-1/2	49' 4"	44' 10"	Post/Pier	D

Design Features

- An irresistible wraparound porch surrounds this home with grace and comfort.
- A stunning cathedral ceiling is highlighted by a rear clerestory dormer in the great room.
- Bay windows add light, space and appeal to the dining room and breakfast area.
- The first-floor master suite enjoys French-door access to the wraparound porch.
- The second-floor hall overlooks the great room and connects two additional bedrooms and a bath.

Rear Elevation

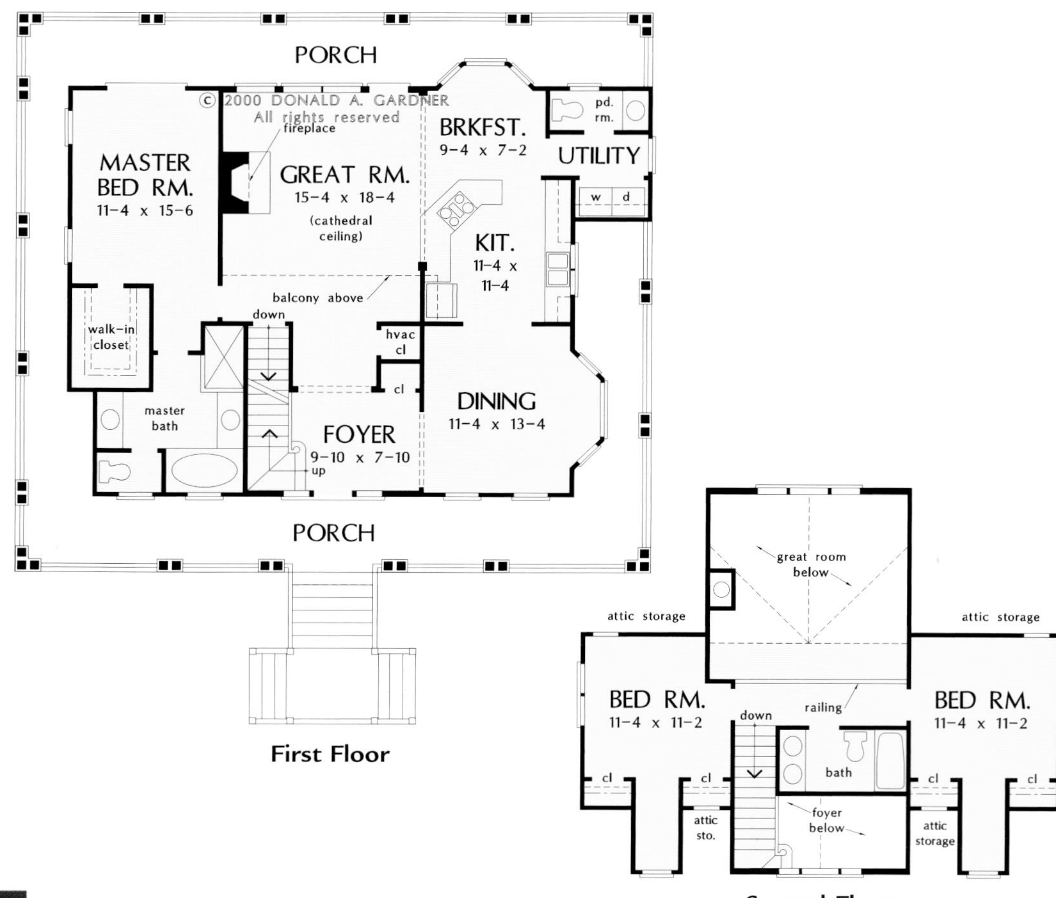

First Floor

Second Floor

Buena Vista — VPDG01-Plan 911-C — 1-866-525-9374

Total Living	First Floor	Second Floor	Bed	Bath	Width	Depth	Foundation	Price Category
2599 sq ft	1680 sq ft	919 sq ft	3	3-1/2	51' 8"	53' 6"	Post/Pier	F

Design Features

- Two porches greet from the front, while multiple French doors lead to the back porch.
- A cathedral ceiling runs from the rear clerestory window through the loft.
- Symmetrical box-bay windows grace the kitchen and master bath.
- Decorative columns mark entry into the dining room and great room.
- Enhancing the great room is a fireplace and curved second-floor balcony.

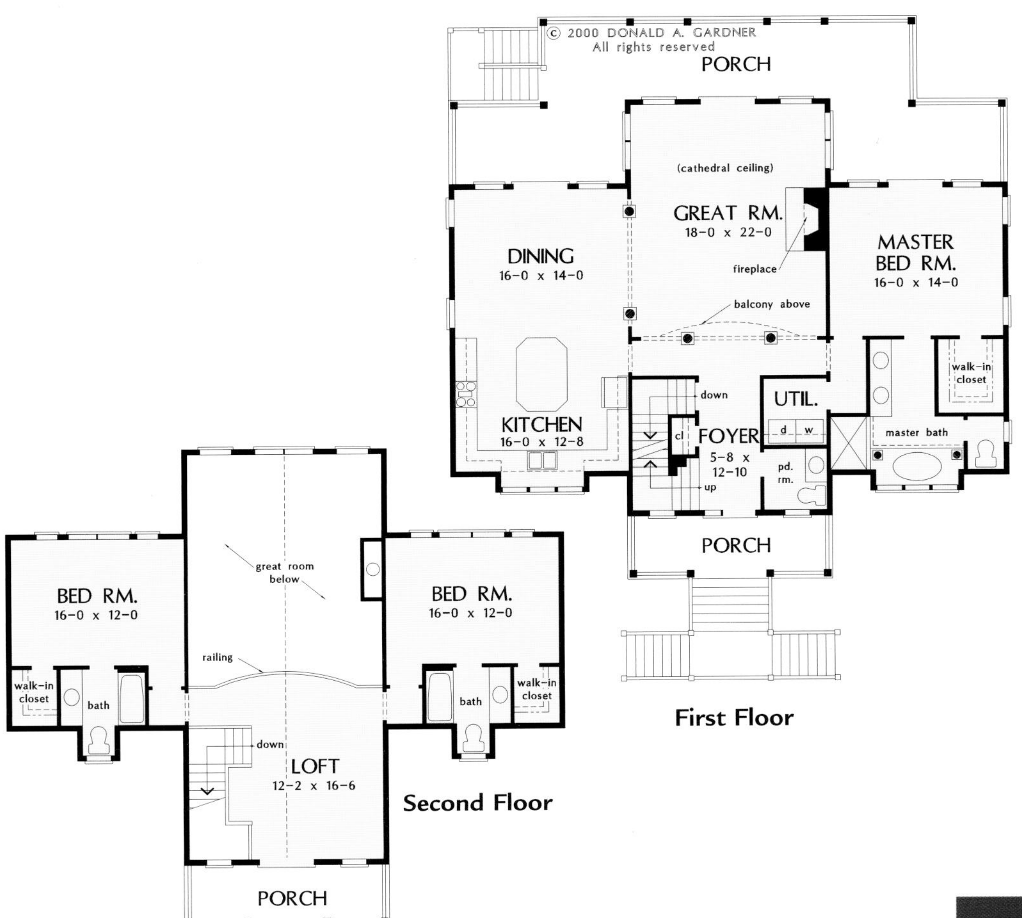

First Floor

Second Floor

Rear Elevation

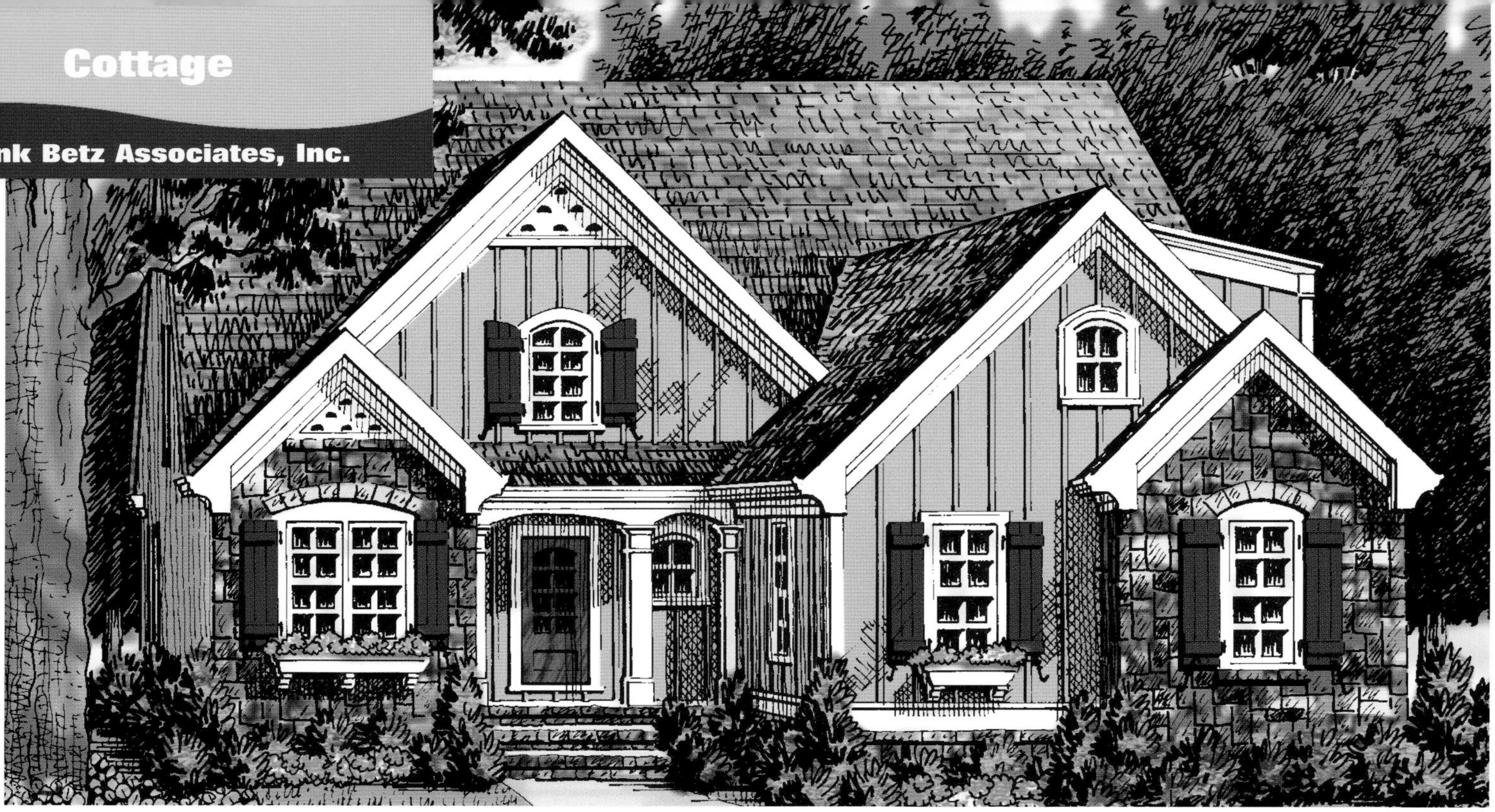

Aberdeen Place — VPFB01-3809 — 1-866-525-9374

Total Living	First Floor	Second Floor	Opt. Bonus	Bed	Bath	Width	Depth	Foundation	Price Category
1593 sq ft	1118 sq ft	475 sq ft	223 sq ft	3	2-1/2	41' 0"	45' 0"	Basement, Crawl Space or Slab	G

Design Features

- From the *Southern Living® Design Collection*
- The *Aberdeen Place* has that cozy cottage appeal with its board-and-batten exterior and stone accents. Its conservative square footage is rich in style and functional design.
- The breakfast room is bordered by windows that allow natural light to pour in.
- A generously sized master bedroom includes a tray ceiling and views to the backyard.
- An optional bonus area provides extra space that homeowners can personalize.

Rear Elevation

Second Floor

First Floor

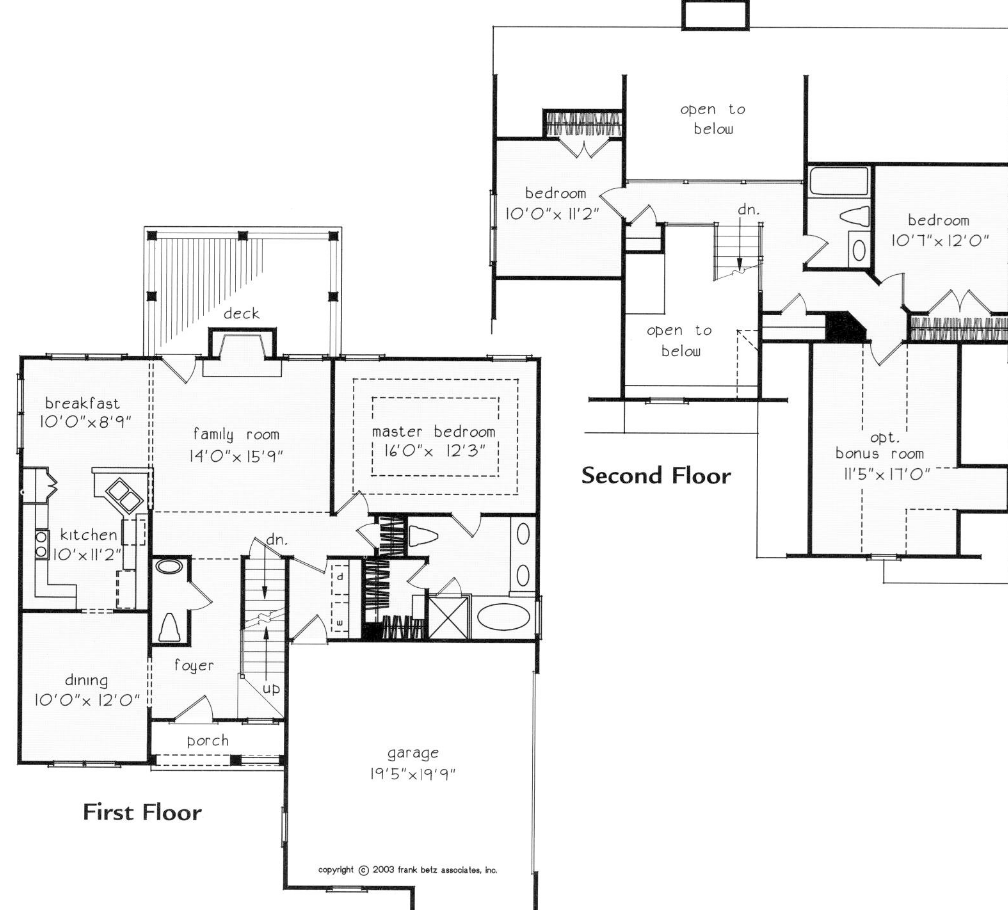

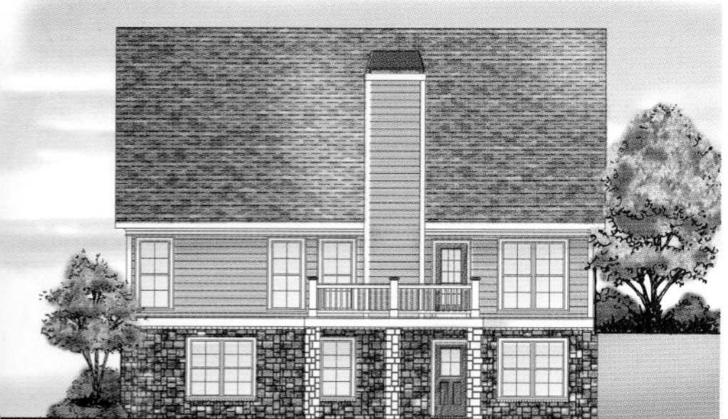

Meredith — VPDG01-355 — 1-866-525-9374

Total Living	First Floor	Second Floor	Bed	Bath	Width	Depth	Foundation	Price Category
1694 sq ft	1100 sq ft	594 sq ft	3	2	36' 8"	45' 0"	Crawl Space*	D

Second Floor

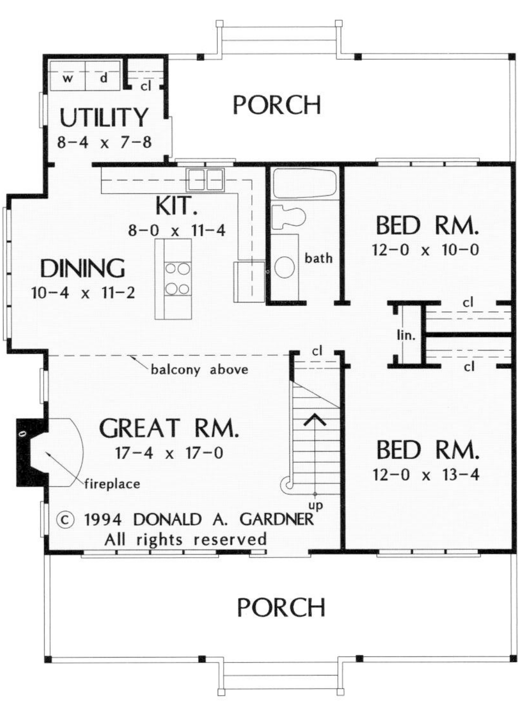

First Floor

Design Features

- This rustic home invites casual, comfortable living in impressive indoor spaces.
- The clever kitchen features an island cooktop with counter, which is ideal for entertaining.
- The second-floor master suite pampers owners with a whirlpool tub and a walk-in closet.
- Extra storage space is available in the attic.

Rear Elevation

*Other options available. See page 255.

Monserrat — VPDS01-Plan 6858 — 1-866-525-9374

Total Living	First Floor	Second Floor	Bed	Bath	Width	Depth	Foundation	Price Category
2756 sq ft	1855 sq ft	901 sq ft	3	3-1/2	66' 0"	50' 0"	Island Basement	H

Design Features

- The octagonal great room boasts a multi-faceted vaulted ceiling, a fireplace, a built-in entertainment center and three sets of French doors, which lead outside to a vaulted lanai.
- The kitchen features a pass-thru to the lanai, an island workstation and easy access to the dining and great room.
- To ensure privacy, the master suite is tucked away from the guest bedrooms and main living areas.

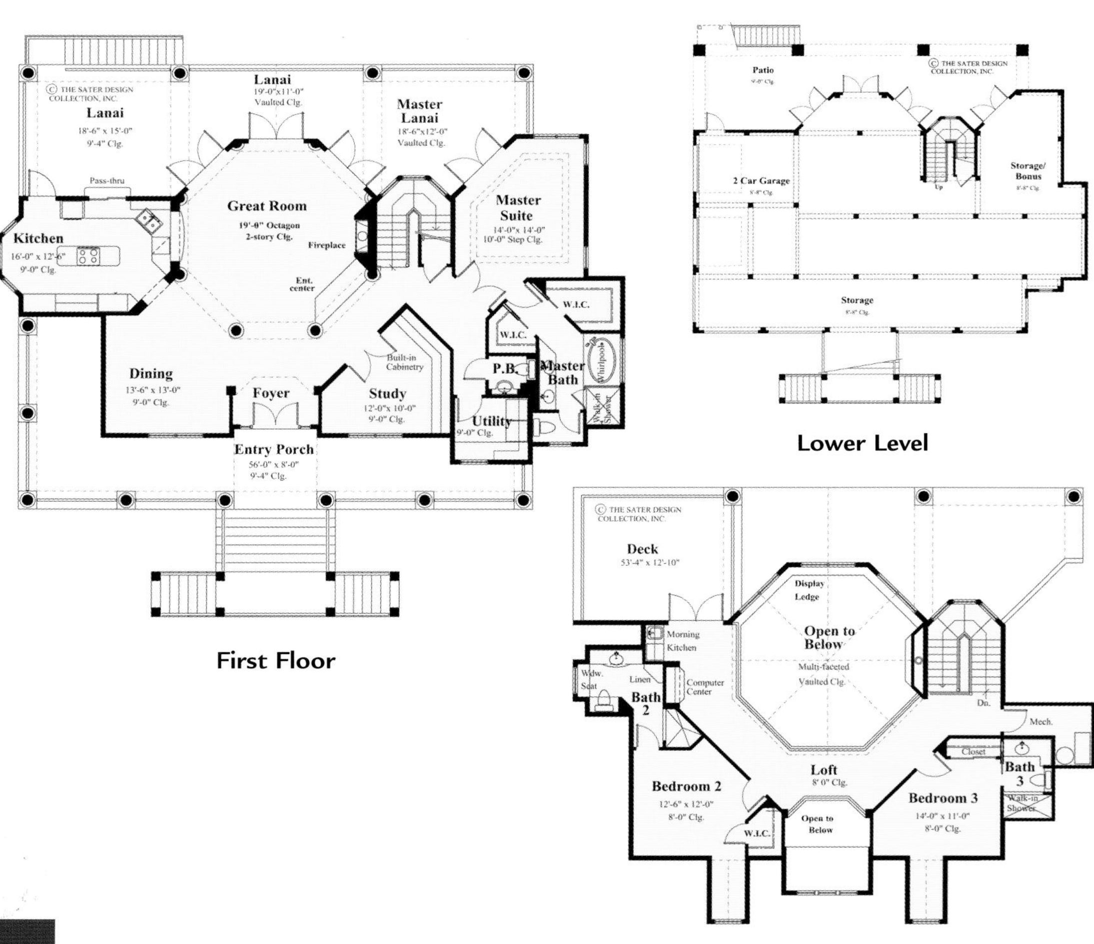

First Floor

Lower Level

Second Floor

Rear Elevation

Nassau Cove — VPDS01-6654 — 1-866-525-9374

Total Living	First Floor	Second Floor	Bed	Bath	Width	Depth	Foundation	Price Category
1853 sq ft	1342 sq ft	511 sq ft	3	2	44' 0"	40' 0"	Post/Pier	E

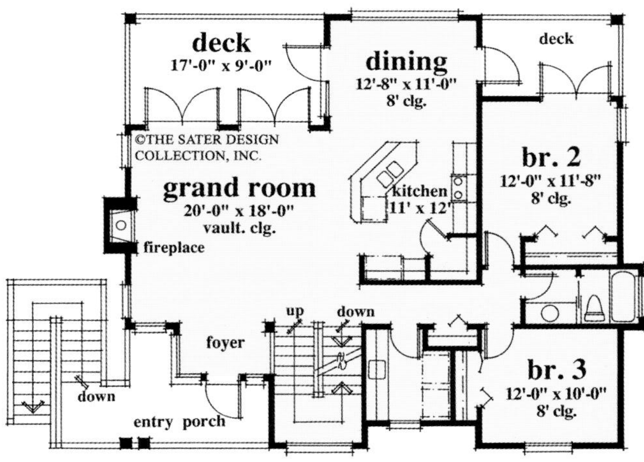

First Floor

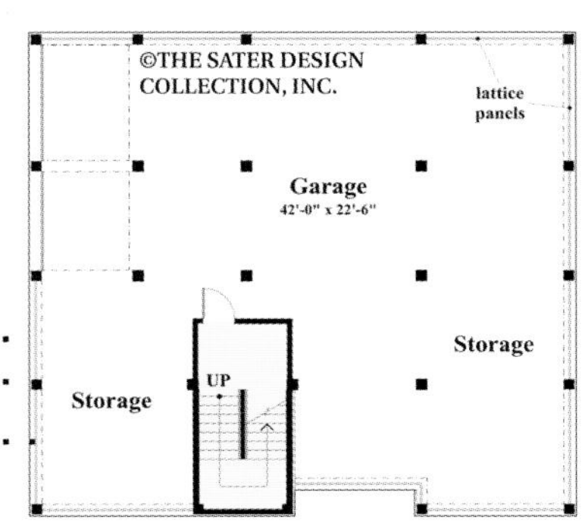

Lower Level

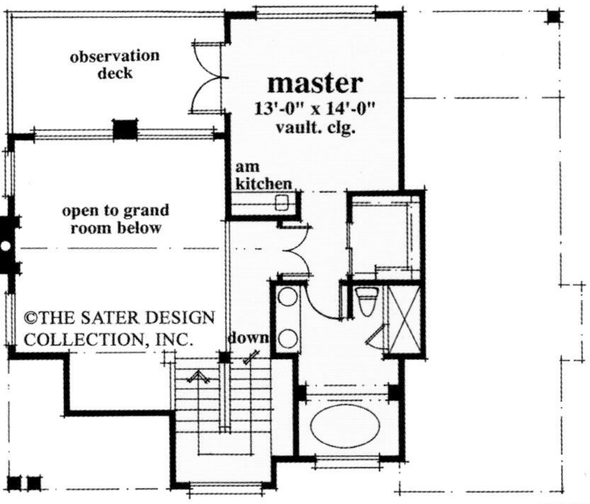

observation deck

master
13'-0" x 14'-0"
vault. clg.

am kitchen

open to grand room below

©THE SATER DESIGN
COLLECTION, INC.

down

Second Floor

Design Features

- Double French doors lead to the deck from the grand room.
- Both sides of the dining room open to decks.
- The well-appointed kitchen overlooks the living area.
- Upstairs, a hall with balcony overlook leads to the master's retreat.
- The master bath boasts a windowed whirlpool tub.

Rear Elevation

Cherbourg — VPFB01-Plan 3683 — 1-866-525-9374

Total Living	First Floor	Second Floor	Opt. Bonus	Bed	Bath	Width	Depth	Foundation	Price Category
1867 sq ft	1410 sq ft	457 sq ft	239 sq ft	4	3	40' 0"	53' 4"	Basement, Crawl Space or Slab	F

Design Features

- Vertical siding and stone make the *Cherbourg* a home that would be welcome in any neighborhood.
- The master suite is on the main level as well as an additional bedroom that can also be used as a home office.
- An optional bonus room and two bedrooms are on the second floor of this home.
- The openness of the floor plan is ideal for entertaining.

Rear Elevation

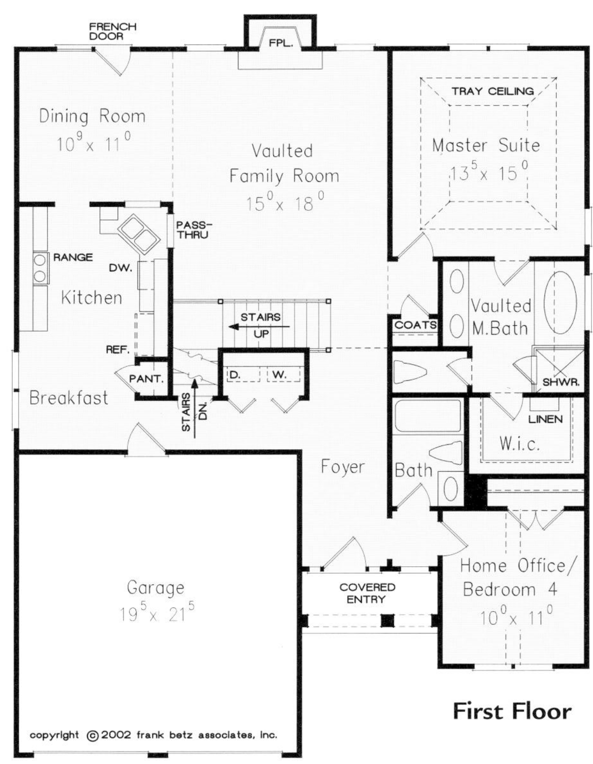

First Floor

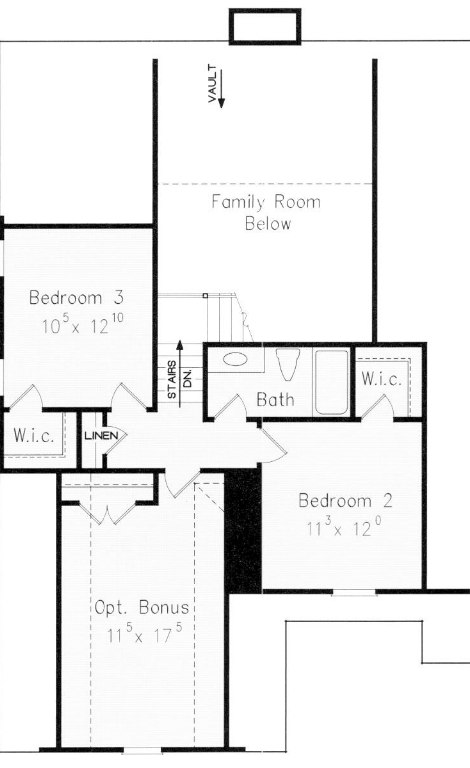

Second Floor

Hilligan — VPDG01-1015 — 1-866-525-9374

Total Living	First Floor	Bonus	Bed	Bath	Width	Depth	Foundation	Price Category
1535 sq ft	1535 sq ft	355 sq ft	3	2	59' 8"	47' 4"	Crawl Space*	D

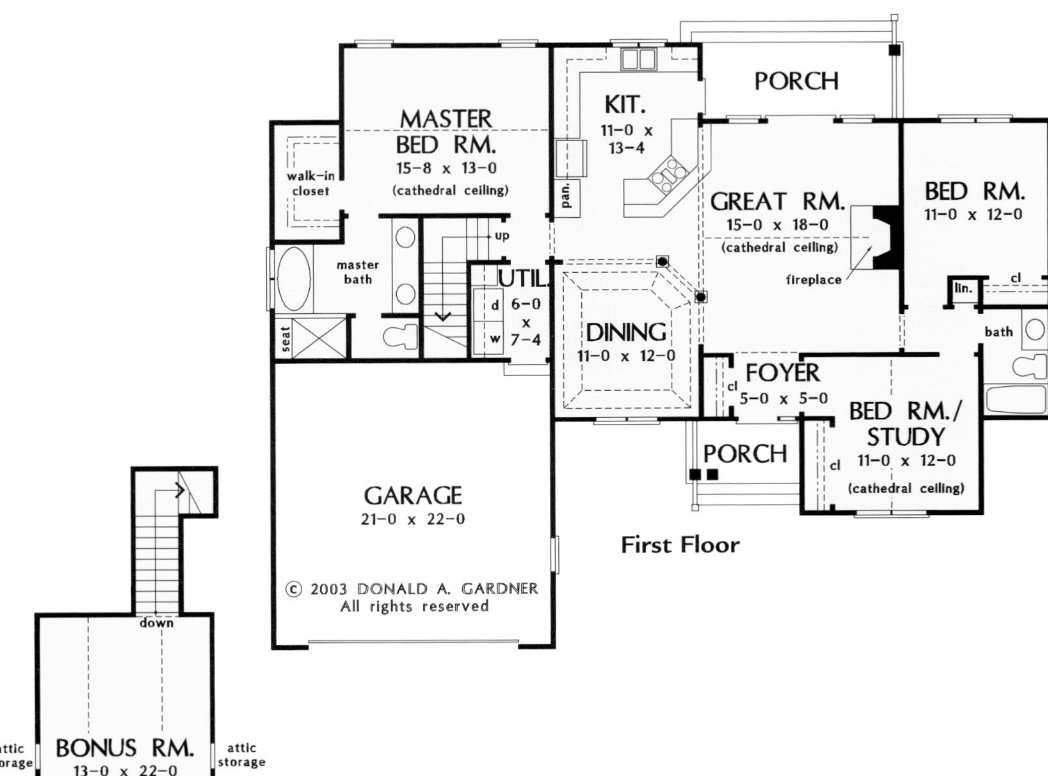

First Floor

Bonus Room

Design Features

- With a low-maintenance exterior and front-entry garage, this charmer promotes easy living.
- The family-efficient floor plan is designed as a step-saver and allows a natural traffic flow.
- A bonus room and bedroom/study provide flexibility.
- An angled cooktop counter and columns define spaces.
- The master suite is complete with a walk-in closet and master bath with a double vanity.

Rear Elevation

*Other options available. See page 255.

Bridgeport Harbor — VPDS01-Plan 6685 — 1-866-525-9374

Total Living	First Floor	Second Floor	Bed	Bath	Width	Depth	Foundation	Price Category
2520 sq ft	1305 sq ft	1215 sq ft	3	2-1/2	30' 6"	77' 6"	Slab/Island Basement	G

Design Features

- Built-ins, a fireplace, eating bar and four sets of French doors opening to the covered porch enhance the welcoming great room.
- The dining room enjoys expansive views through a bay window and easy access to the kitchen and great room.
- The upper level master suite features a spacious bath designed for two, while three sets of doors open to an observation deck with a special place for sunning and privacy.

Rear Elevation

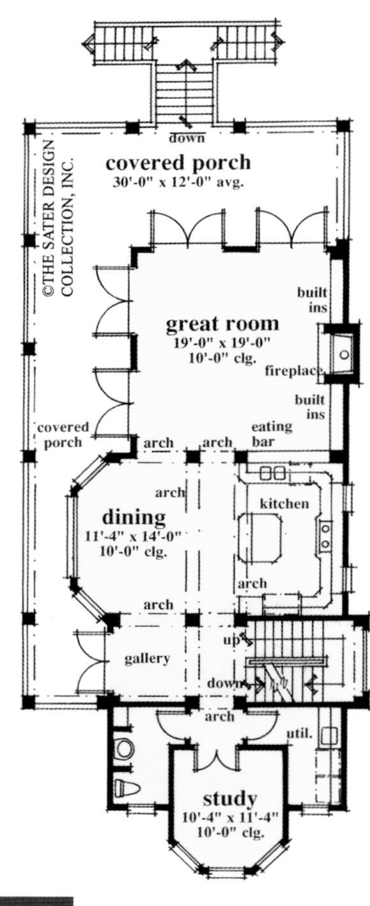

First Floor

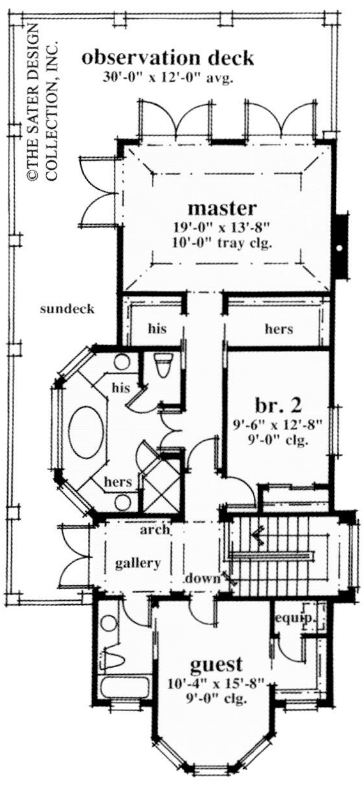

observation deck
30'-0" x 12'-0" avg.
©THE SATER DESIGN COLLECTION, INC.
master
19'-0" x 13'-8"
10'-0" tray clg.
sundeck
his
hers
his
hers
br. 2
9'-6" x 12'-8"
9'-0" clg.
arch
gallery
down
equip.
guest
10'-4" x 15'-8"
9'-0" clg.

Second Floor

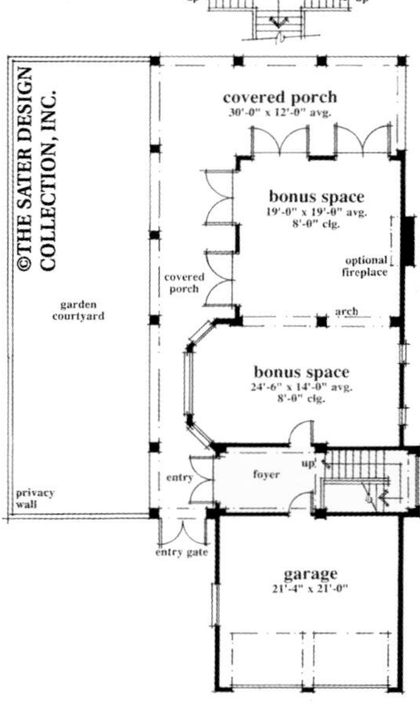

Lower Level

Lindenhurst — VPFB01-Plan 3695 — 1-866-525-9374

Total Living	First Floor	Second Floor	Opt. Bonus	Bed	Bath	Width	Depth	Foundation	Price Category
1858 sq ft	1401 sq ft	457 sq ft	305 sq ft	3	2-1/2	50' 4"	52' 0"	Basement or Crawl Space	F

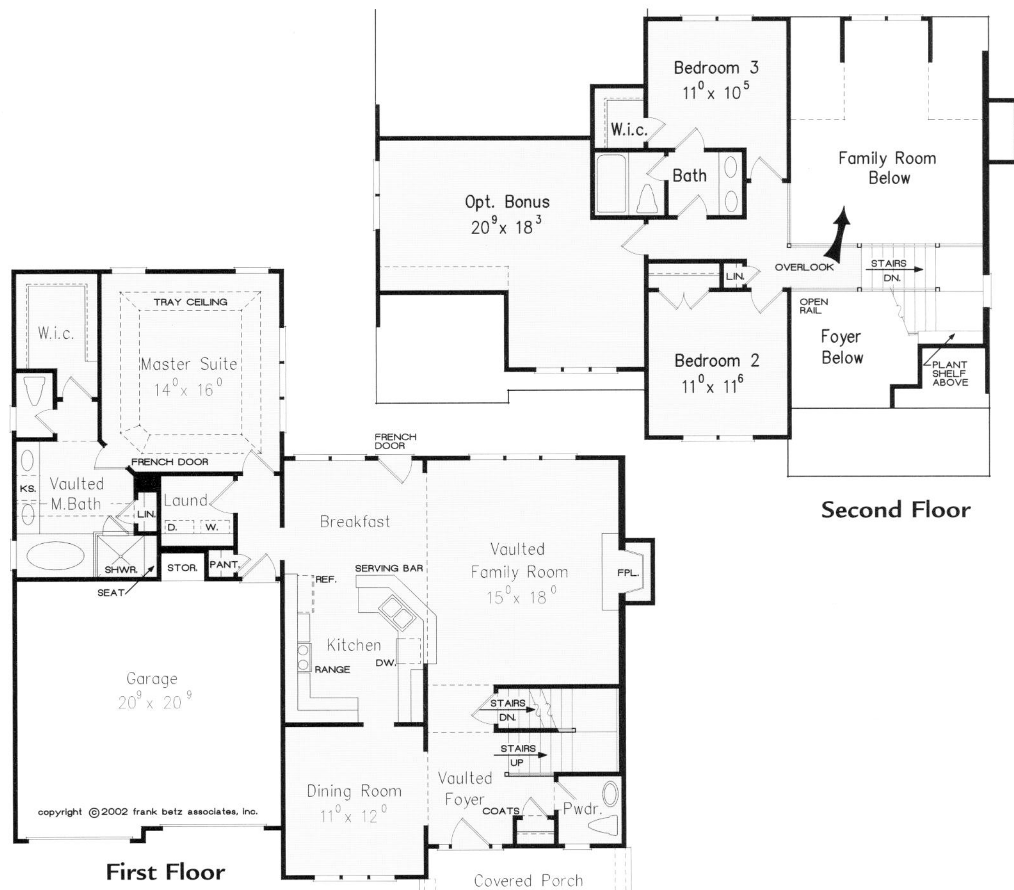

Second Floor

First Floor

Design Features

- A timeless exterior is the perfect way to describe the *Lindenhurst*.
- Inside, the master bedroom is located on the main floor, away from the other bedrooms allowing for privacy.
- A vaulted family room has rear windows that overlook the backyard and let in natural light.
- The secondary bedrooms are located upstairs are well as an optional bonus room.

Rear Elevation

Morninglory — VPDG01-236 — 1-866-525-9374

Total Living	First Floor	Second Floor	Bed	Bath	Width	Depth	Foundation	Price Category
1778 sq ft	1325 sq ft	453 sq ft	3	2-1/2	48' 4"	40' 4"	Crawl Space*	D

Design Features

- Custom-style windows dress up the exterior.
- The U-shaped kitchen has a pass-thru to the vaulted great room.
- The private, first-level master suite opens to a rear deck.
- The master bath pampers with double lavs, garden tub and shower.

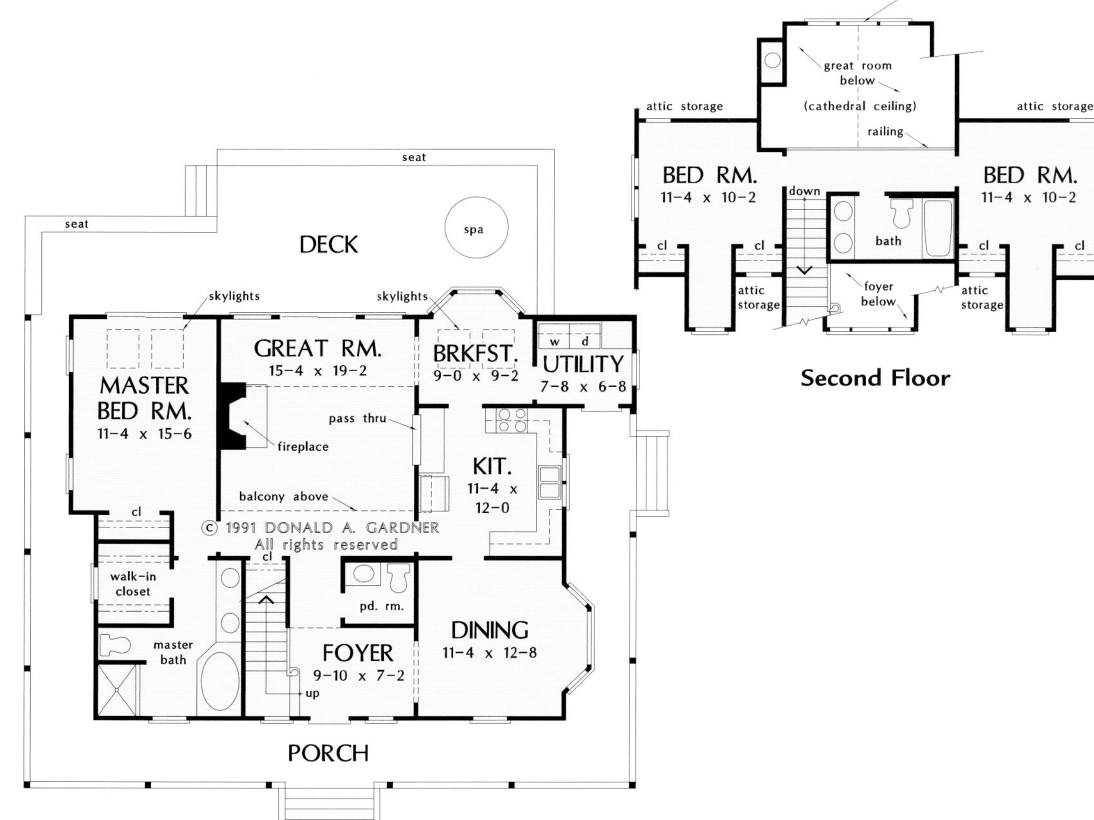

Second Floor

First Floor

Rear Elevation

*Other options available. See page 255.

Donald A. Gardner Architects, Inc.

Wicklow — VPDG01-950 — 1-866-525-9374

Total Living	First Floor	Second Floor	Bonus	Bed	Bath	Width	Depth	Foundation	Price Category
2294 sq ft	1542 sq ft	752 sq ft	370 sq ft	3	2-1/2	44' 4"	54' 0"	Crawl Space*	E

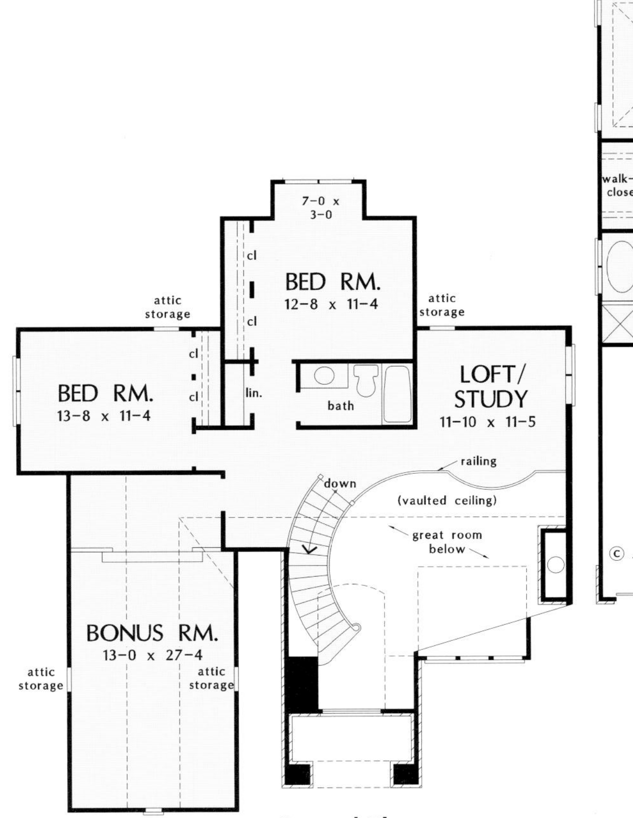

Second Floor

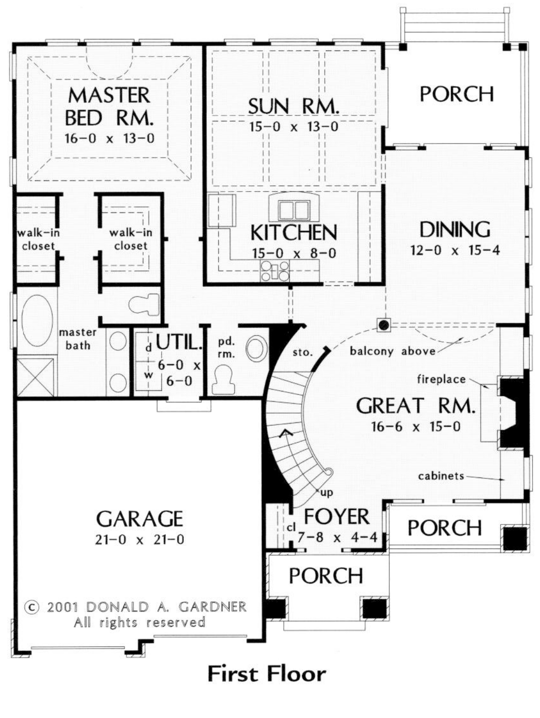

First Floor

Design Features

- Columns, decorative railing and a metal roof add architectural interest to an intimate front porch.
- A rock entryway frames a French door flanked by sidelights and crowned with a transom.
- An elegant, curved staircase highlights the grand two-story foyer and great room.
- A delightful sunroom can be accessed from the dining room and is open to the kitchen.

Rear Elevation

*Other options available. See page 255.

Newell — VPFB01-Plan 3863 — 1-866-525-9374

Total Living	First Floor	Opt. Bonus	Bed	Bath	Width	Depth	Foundation	Price Category
1847 sq ft	1847 sq ft	N/A	3	2	34' 0"	76' 0"	Slab	F

Design Features

- The *Newell* is part of the "Zero Lot Line Collection."
- This plan offers affordability, style, and spaciousness.
- The plan is a split-bedroom design allowing the homeowners privacy in the back of the home, while the two additional bedrooms are at the front.
- A patio is designed into the side of the home utilizing space within the footprint of the plan.

Side Patio Elevation

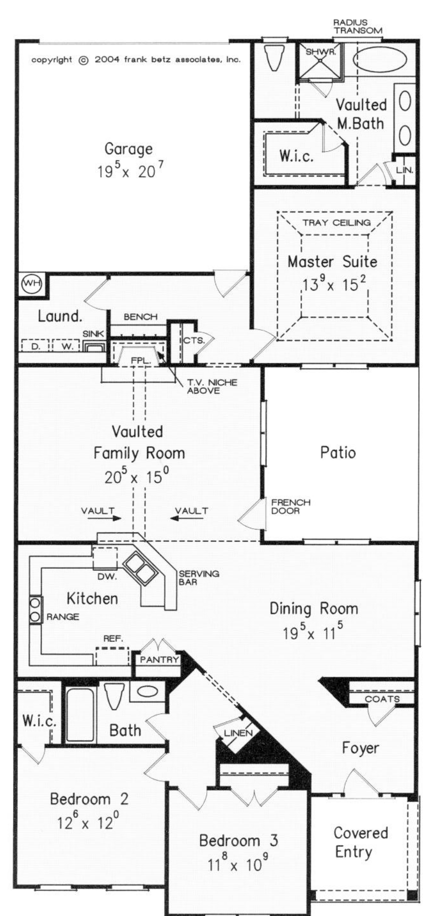

First Floor

Duvall Street — VPDS01-Plan 6701 — 1-866-525-9374

Total Living	First Floor	Second Floor	Bed	Bath	Width	Depth	Foundation	Price Category
2123 sq ft	878 sq ft	1245 sq ft	4	2-1/2	27' 6"	64' 0"	Post/Pier	F

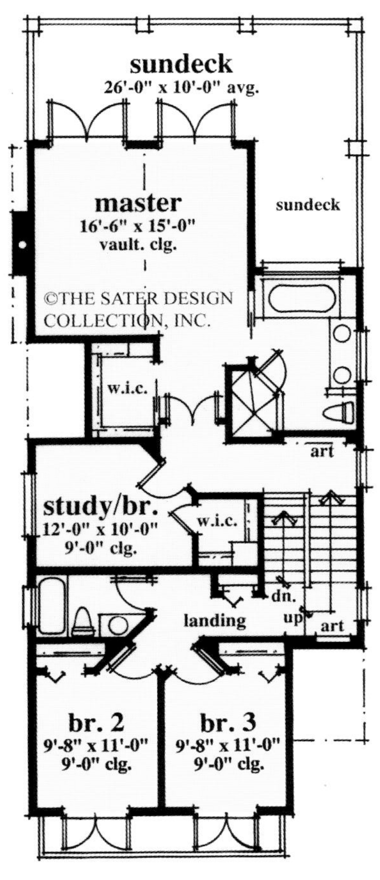

Second Floor

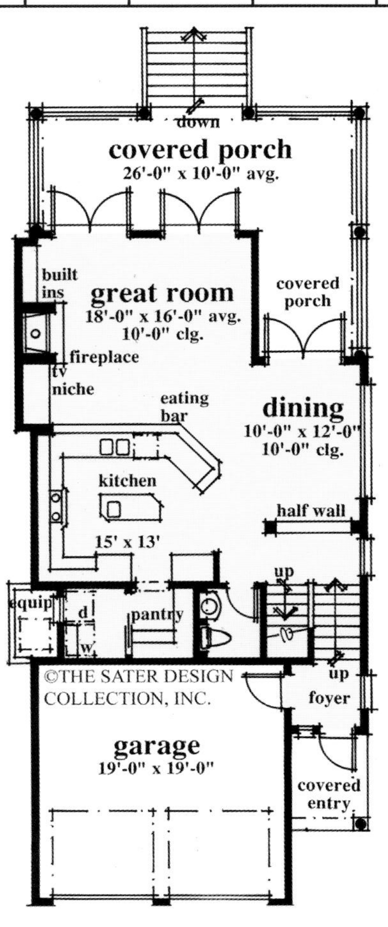

First Floor

Design Features

- Two sets of French doors open the great room to the porch.
- A gourmet kitchen boasts a prep sink and eating bar.
- The mid-level landing leads to two bedrooms and a bath.
- French doors open the master suite to a sundeck.
- The master bath has a windowed soaking tub.

Rear View

Please note: Home photographed may differ from blueprint.

Waddell — VPFB01-Plan 3886 — 1-866-525-9374

Total Living	First Floor	Opt. Bonus	Bed	Bath	Width	Depth	Foundation	Price Category
1644 sq ft	1644 sq ft	N/A	3	2	34' 0"	68' 0"	Slab	E

Design Features

- A timeless combination of clapboard siding and brick make the *Waddell* a welcome addition to any neighborhood.
- Its unique foyer — with a corner coat closet, decorative columns, and art niche — makes this design interesting from the start.
- The television niche over the fireplace creates more space for furniture arrangement in the family room.
- As part of the "Zero Lot Line Collection," this plan offers many amenities in only 1644 square feet.

Side Patio Elevation

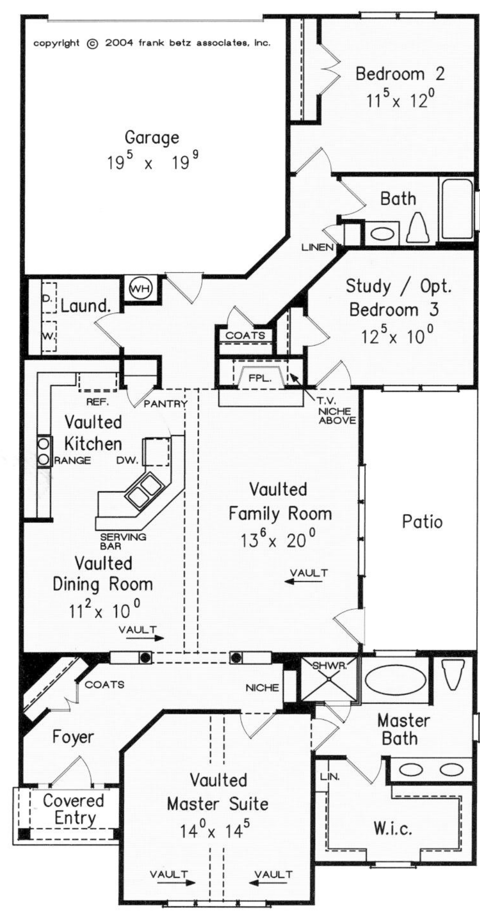

First Floor

Carmel Bay — VPDS01-Plan 6810 — 1-866-525-9374

Total Living	First Floor	Second Floor	Bed	Bath	Width	Depth	Foundation	Price Category
2513 sq ft	1542 sq ft	971 sq ft	4	3	46' 0"	51' 0"	Island Basement	G

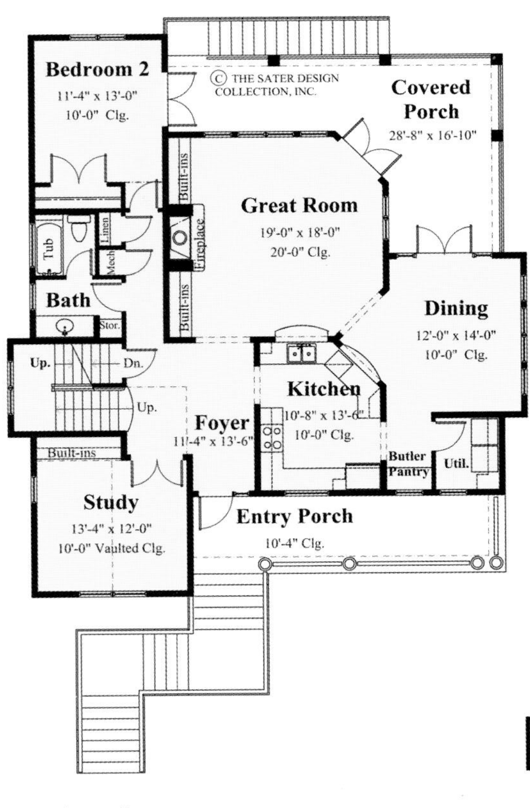

First Floor

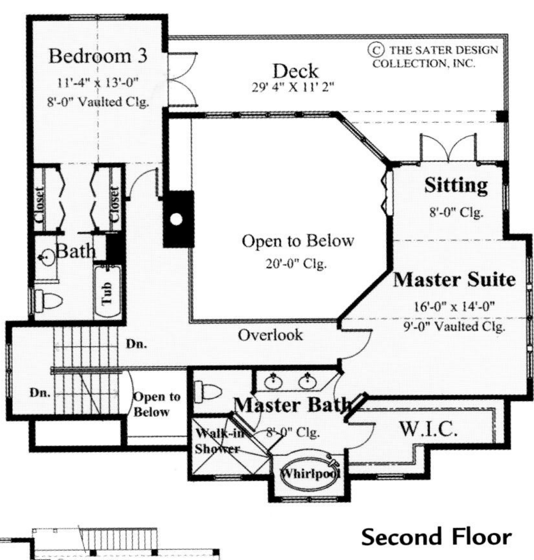

Second Floor

© THE SATER DESIGN COLLECTION, INC.

Lower Porch
28'-8" x 16'-10"

Bonus/
Storage

Up.

Up.

2 Car Garage

Storage

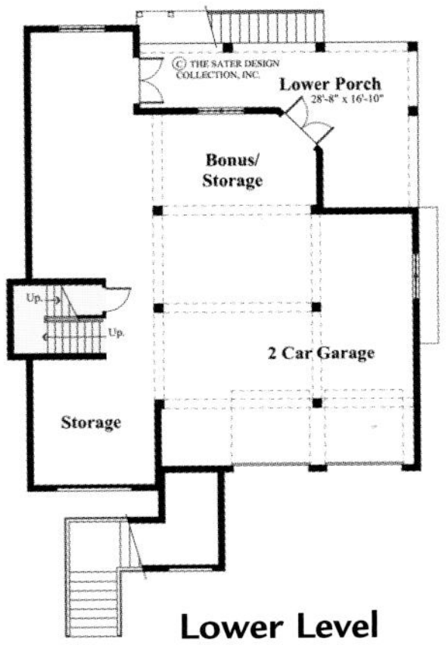

Lower Level

Design Features

- The expansive great room is accentuated with a wall of glass, built-ins and a cozy fireplace.
- An open floor plan encourages flow between the kitchen, dining and great room.
- Tucked away from the main living spaces, the master suite features a vaulted ceiling, spacious bath and private sitting room with deck access.
- Guests will enjoy spare bedrooms that access a deck and covered porch, ample closet space and private bathrooms.

Rear Elevation

Seymour — VPDG01-287 — 1-866-525-9374

Total Living	First Floor	Second Floor	Bed	Bath	Width	Depth	Foundation	Price Category
1622 sq ft	1039 sq ft	583 sq ft	3	2	37' 9"	44' 8"	Crawl Space*	D

Design Features

- This rustic three-bedroom plan takes its relaxed manner from spacious, covered front and back porches.
- The openness from the great room to the kitchen/dining area provides a spacious feeling.
- The master suite pampers with separate shower, whirlpool tub and generous walk-in closet.
- One of the two upstairs bedrooms overlooks the great room for added drama.

Rear Elevation

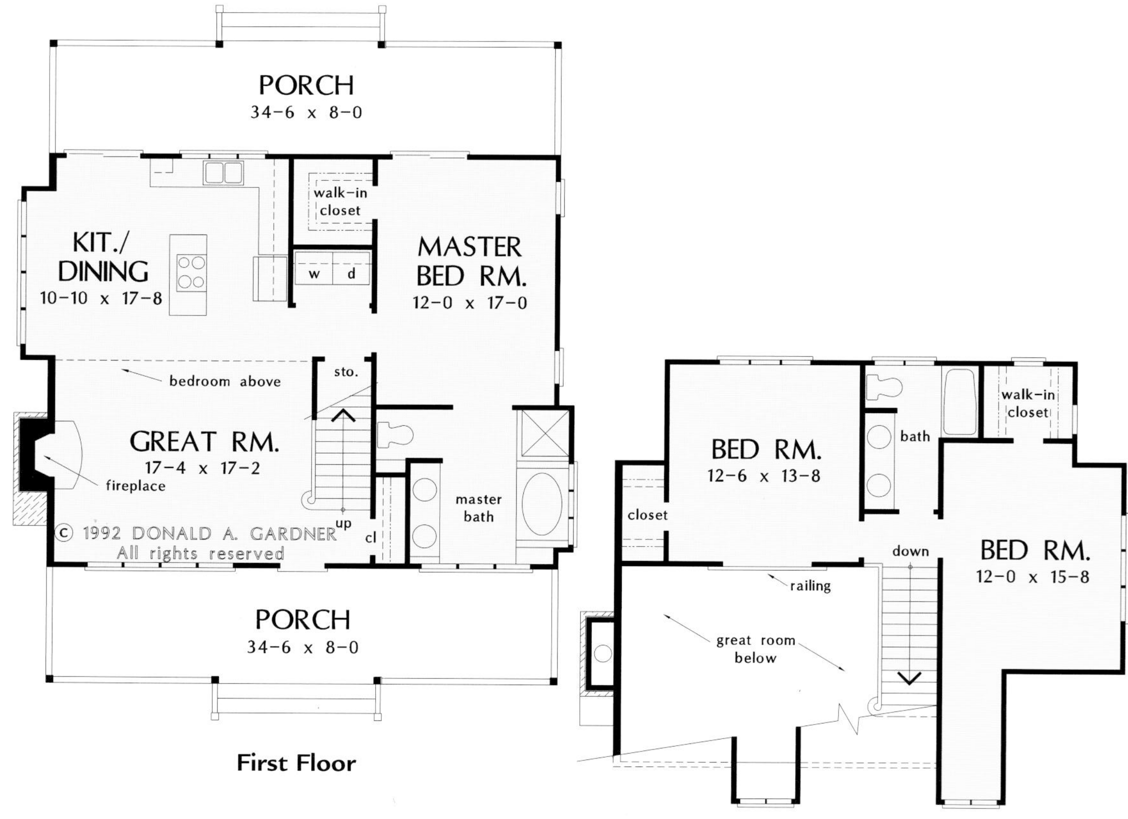

First Floor

Second Floor

*Other options available. See page 255.

Mallory Square — VPDS01-6691 — 1-866-525-9374

Total Living	First Floor	Bonus	Bed	Bath	Width	Depth	Foundation	Price Category
1288 sq ft	1288 sq ft	N/A	2	2	32' 4"	60' 0"	Crawl Space	D

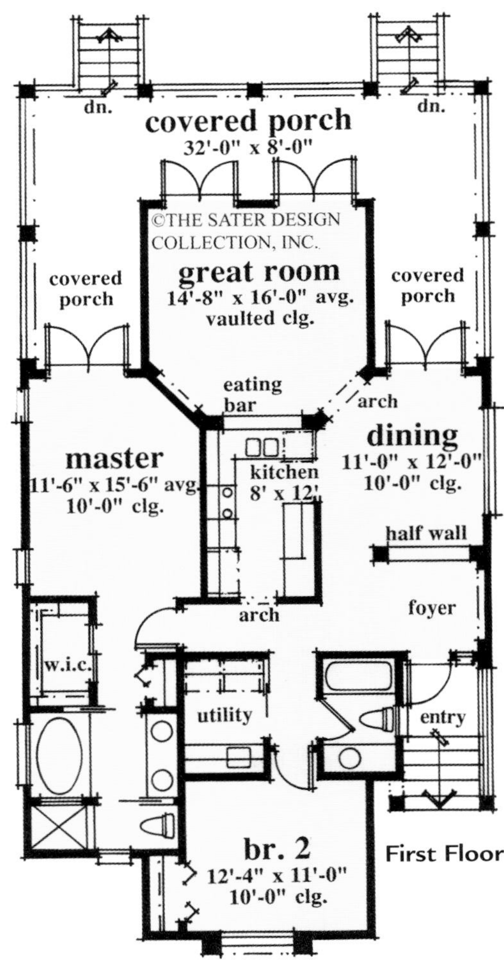

First Floor

Design Features

- An arched, covered entry greets those who stop by.
- The great room opens to backyard views.
- A galley-style kitchen has a pass-thru with views.
- French doors open the master suite, great room and dining room to the covered porch.
- Asymmetrical roof lines blend with front and rear gables.

Rear Elevation

Frank Betz Associates, Inc.

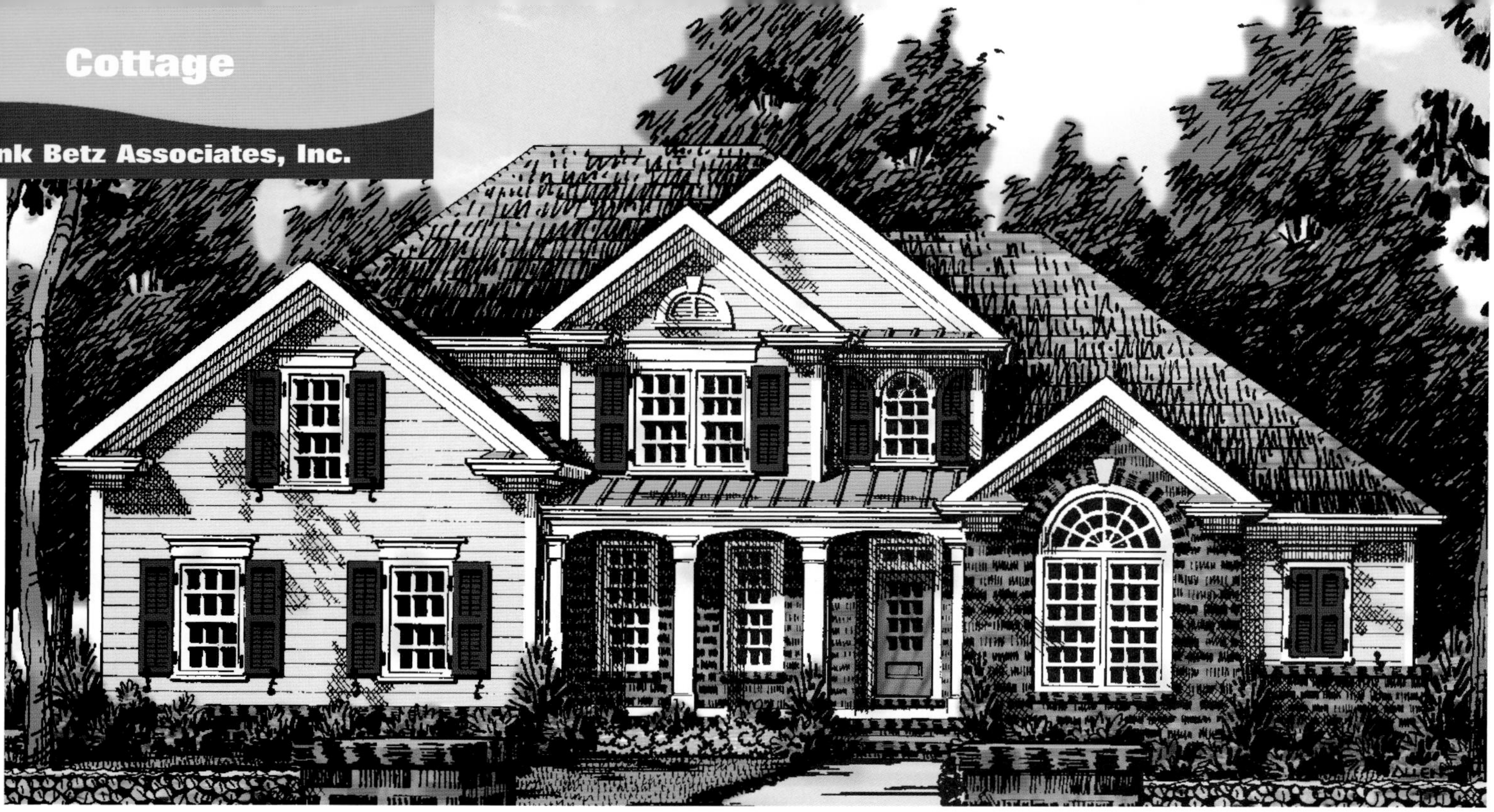

Stonington — VPFB01-Plan 3567 — 1-866-525-9374

Total Living	First Floor	Second Floor	Opt. Bonus	Bed	Bath	Width	Depth	Foundation	Price Category
2251 sq ft	1714 sq ft	537 sq ft	260 sq ft	4	3	60' 0"	42' 10"	Basement or Crawl Space	G

Design Features

- Two-story spaces in the foyer and family room make a grand impression.
- A walk-in pantry adds convenience in the kitchen.
- The secondary bedroom on the main level is just steps from the master suite and is a convenient spot for a home office or study.
- Upstairs, each secondary bedroom has a walk-in closet.

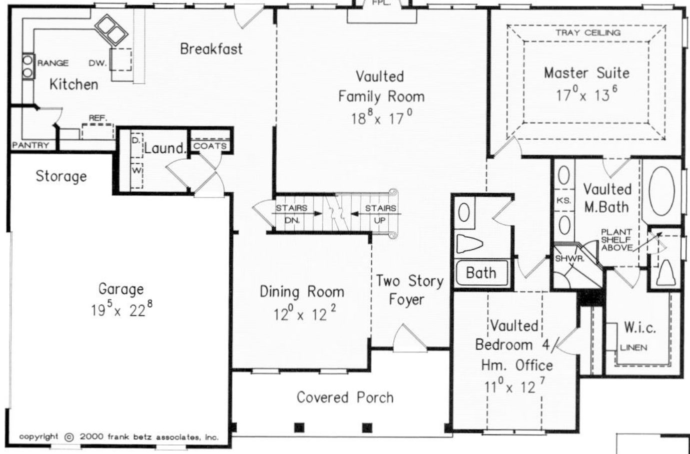

First Floor

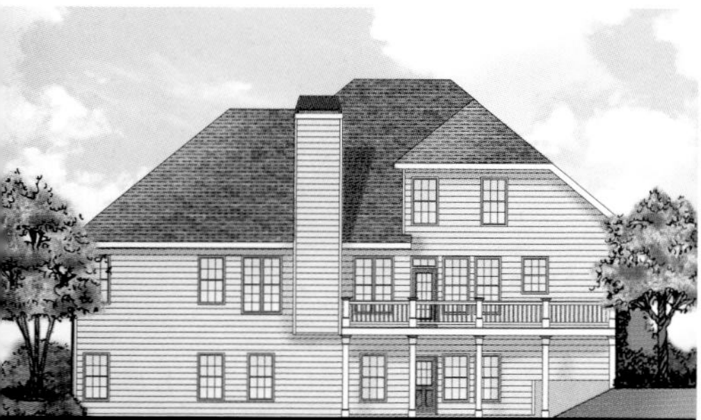

Rear Elevation

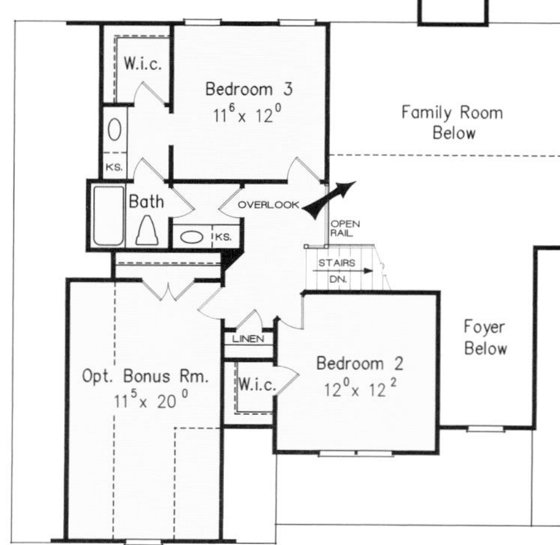

Second Floor

Nickerson — VPFB01-3839 — 1-866-525-9374

Total Living	First Floor	Opt. Bonus	Bed	Bath	Width	Depth	Foundation	Price Category
1627 sq ft	1627 sq ft	N/A	3	2	37' 0"	66' 0"	Slab	E

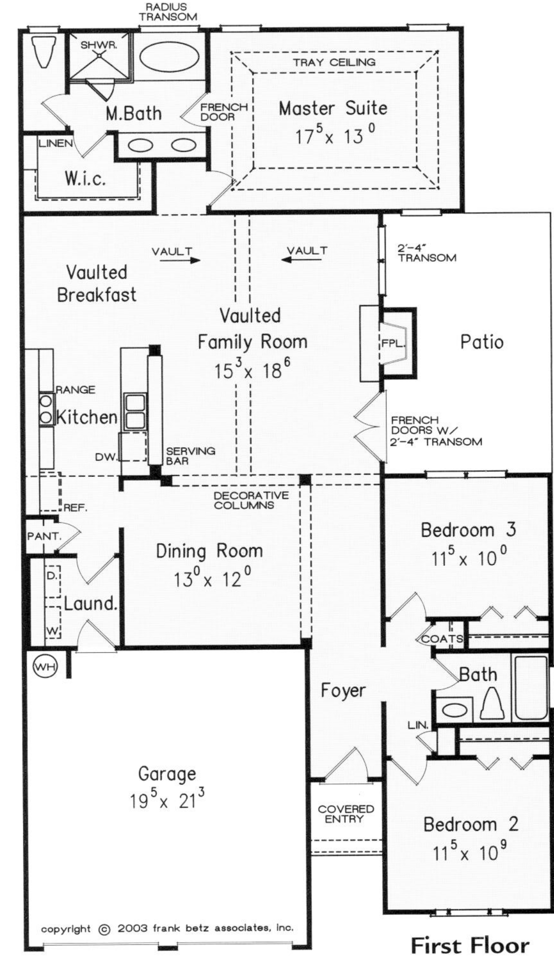

First Floor

Design Features

- This plan was designed as part of the "Zero Lot Line Collection."
- Creative design allows for excellent use of space, making this plan feel larger than its 1627 square feet.
- A private patio is enclosed within the home, giving the homeowners plenty of privacy.
- The laundry room is located off the kitchen and accessible through the garage, allowing shoes and coats a place to rest.

Side Patio Elevation

Georgetown — VPDG01-393 — 1-866-525-9374

Total Living	First Floor	Bonus	Bed	Bath	Width	Depth	Foundation	Price Category
1832 sq ft	1832 sq ft	425 sq ft	3	2	65' 4"	62' 0"	Crawl Space	D

Design Features

- Dual porches, gables and circle-top windows give this home its special country charm.
- The foyer, expanded by a vaulted ceiling, introduces a formal colonnaded dining room.
- The vaulted great room is always bright with light from the circle-top clerestory.
- A tray ceiling adds volume to the private master suite featuring a double vanity and walk-in closet.

Rear Elevation

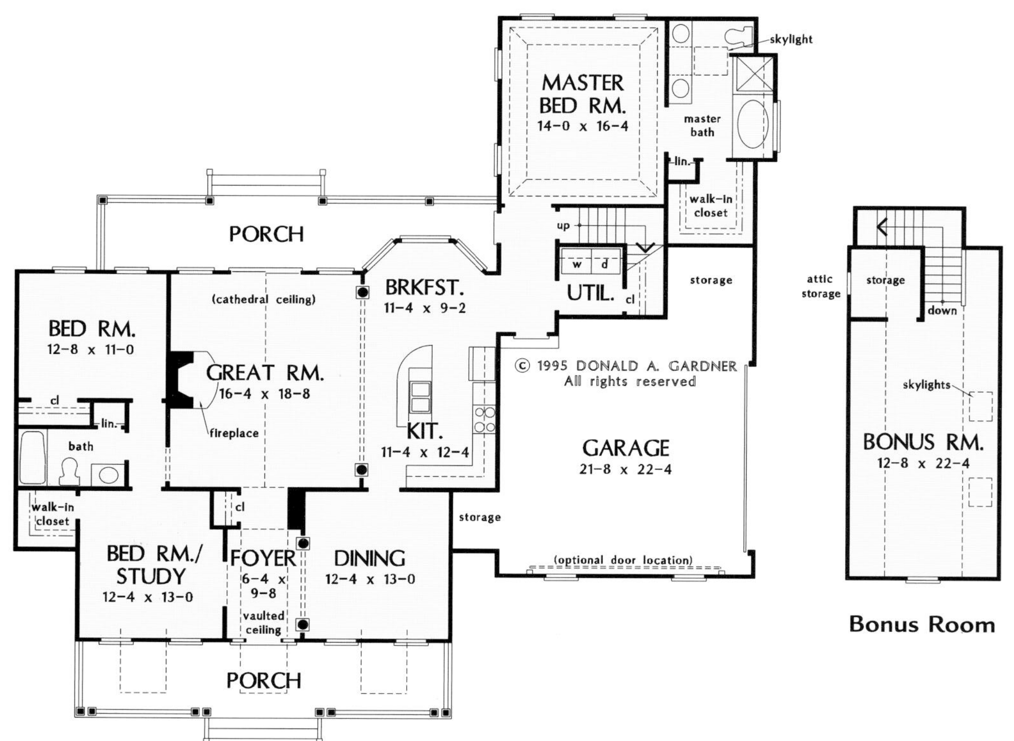

First Floor

Bonus Room

Hampton — VPDG01-390 — 1-866-525-9374

Total Living	First Floor	Bonus	Bed	Bath	Width	Depth	Foundation	Price Category
1879 sq ft	1879 sq ft	360 sq ft	3	2	66' 4"	55' 2"	Crawl Space*	D

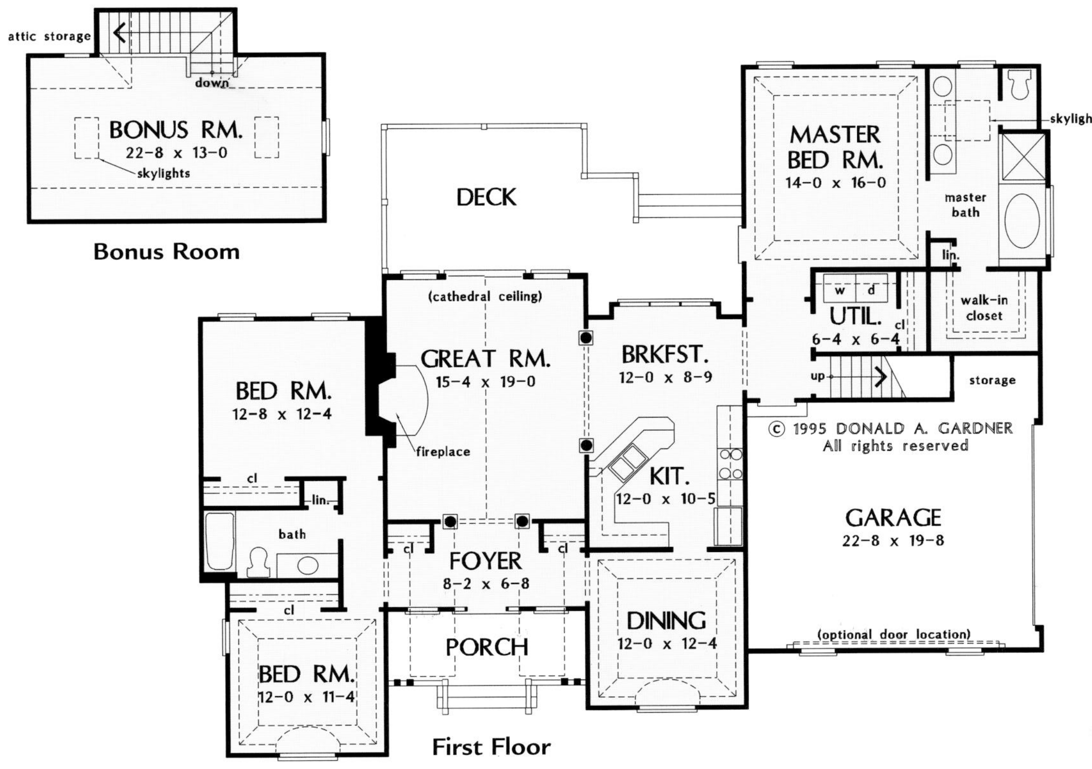

Design Features

- Dormers cast light and interest into the foyer that sets the tone in a home full of today's amenities.
- The great room, defined by columns, is conveniently located adjacent to the breakfast room and kitchen.
- Tray ceilings and picture windows with circle tops accent the front bedroom and dining room.
- A secluded master suite includes a bath with skylight, garden tub, separate shower and spacious walk-in closet.

Rear View

Please note: Home photographed may differ from blueprint.

***Other options available.** **See page 255.**

Saint Martin — VPDS01-Plan 6846 — 1-866-525-9374

Total Living	First Floor	Lower Level	Bed	Bath	Width	Depth	Foundation	Price Category
2494 sq ft	2385 sq ft	109 sq ft	3	3	60' 0"	52' 0"	Island Basement	F

Design Features

- An open floor plan allows for easy movement and communication between the kitchen, nook and great room.
- Built-ins, a vaulted ceiling and a wall of glass adorn the great room.
- A vaulted ceiling, built-ins and double doors that open onto a front balcony enhance the study.
- The master suite is secluded on the left side of the plan for privacy and features two walk-in closets and a pampering whirlpool master bath.

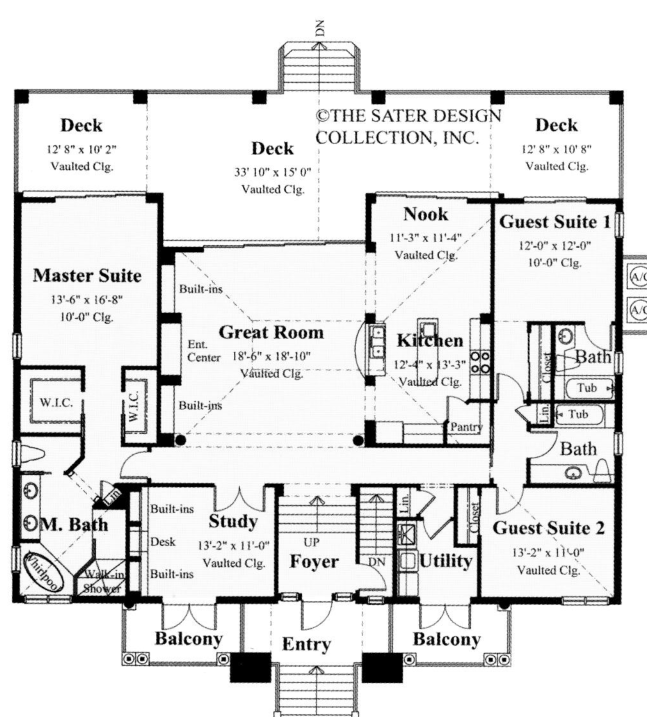

First Floor

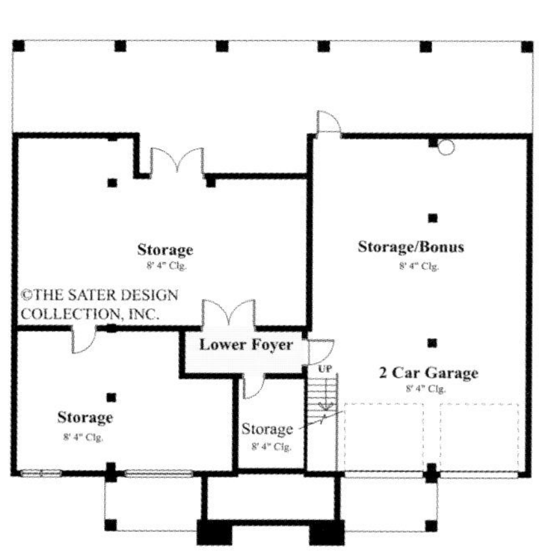

Lower Level

Rear Elevation

Tradewind Court — VPDS01-Plan 6617 — 1-866-525-9374

Total Living	First Floor	Second Floor	Bed	Bath	Width	Depth	Foundation	Price Category
1904 sq ft	1302 sq ft	602 sq ft	3	2-1/2	46' 0"	45' 0"	Piling	F

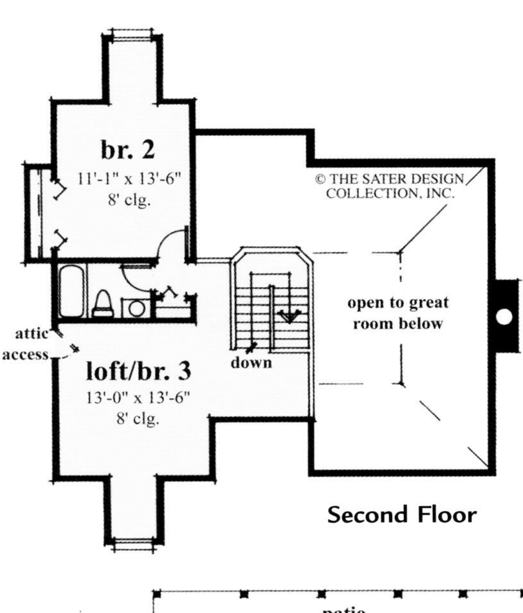

Second Floor

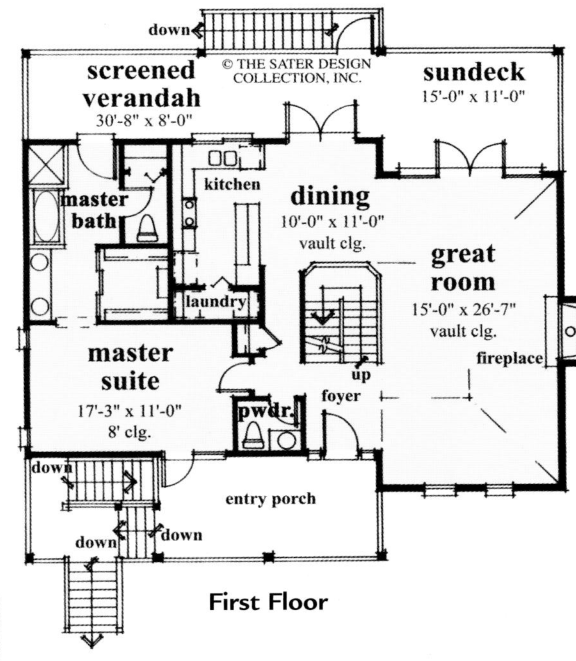

First Floor

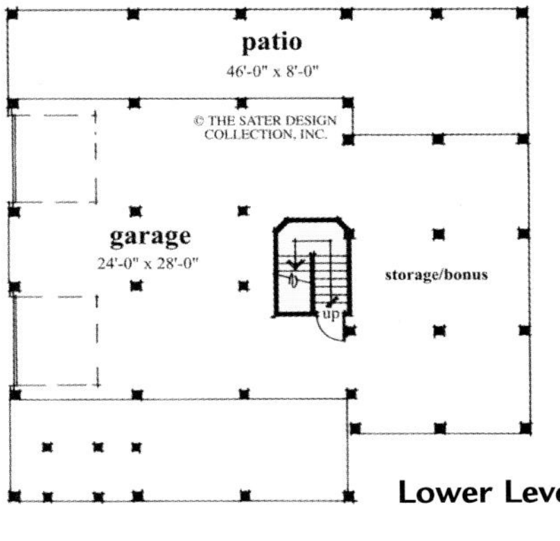

patio
46'-0" x 8'-0"
© THE SATER DESIGN COLLECTION, INC.
garage
24'-0" x 28'-0"
up
storage/bonus

Lower Level

Design Features

- The great room features a vaulted ceiling, fireplace and easy access to the dining room and kitchen.
- A windowed double sink opens the kitchen to the verandah, while a convenient laundry keeps the living area tidy.
- The master suite boasts a luxurious bath and private access to a secluded area of the verandah.
- Upstairs, a secondary bedroom shares a full bath with a cozy loft or third bedroom.

Rear Elevation

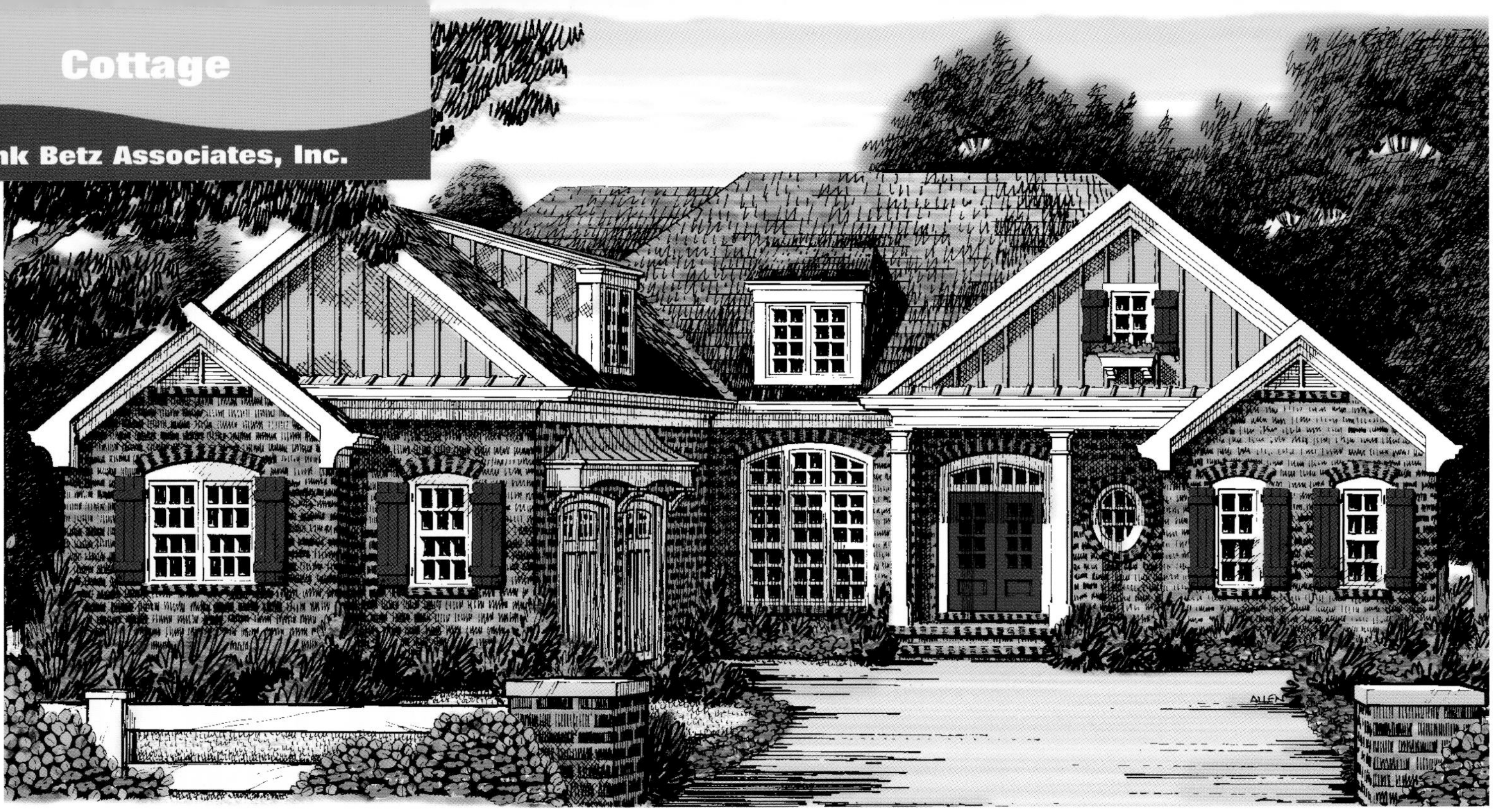

Kingsport — VPFB01-3745 — 1-866-525-9374

Total Living	First Floor	Opt. 2nd Fl.	Bed	Bath	Width	Depth	Foundation	Price Category
2282 sq ft	2282 sq ft	658 sq ft	4	3-1/2	60' 0"	74' 0"	Basement, Crawl Space or Slab	G

Design Features

- The *Kingsport* is as warm and welcoming inside as it is outside.
- The kitchen area is bright and cheery with a bay window in the breakfast area. This space caters to casual family time with a cozy keeping room connected to it.
- Transom windows brighten the breakfast and keeping rooms.
- An optional second floor provides the opportunity for a fourth bedroom, as well as additional space ideal for a customized playroom, craft room or exercise area.

Rear Elevation

First Floor

Opt. Second Floor

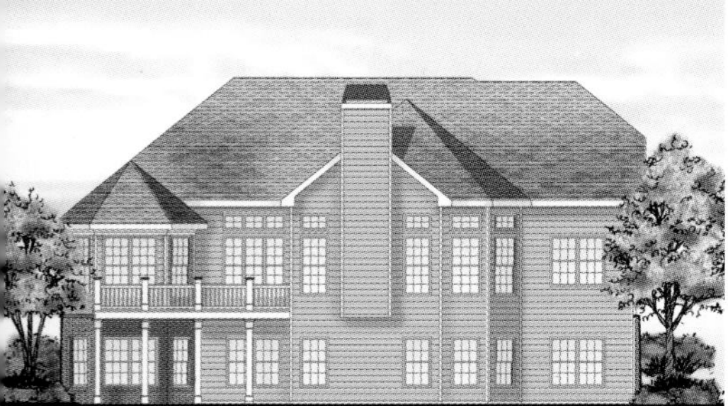

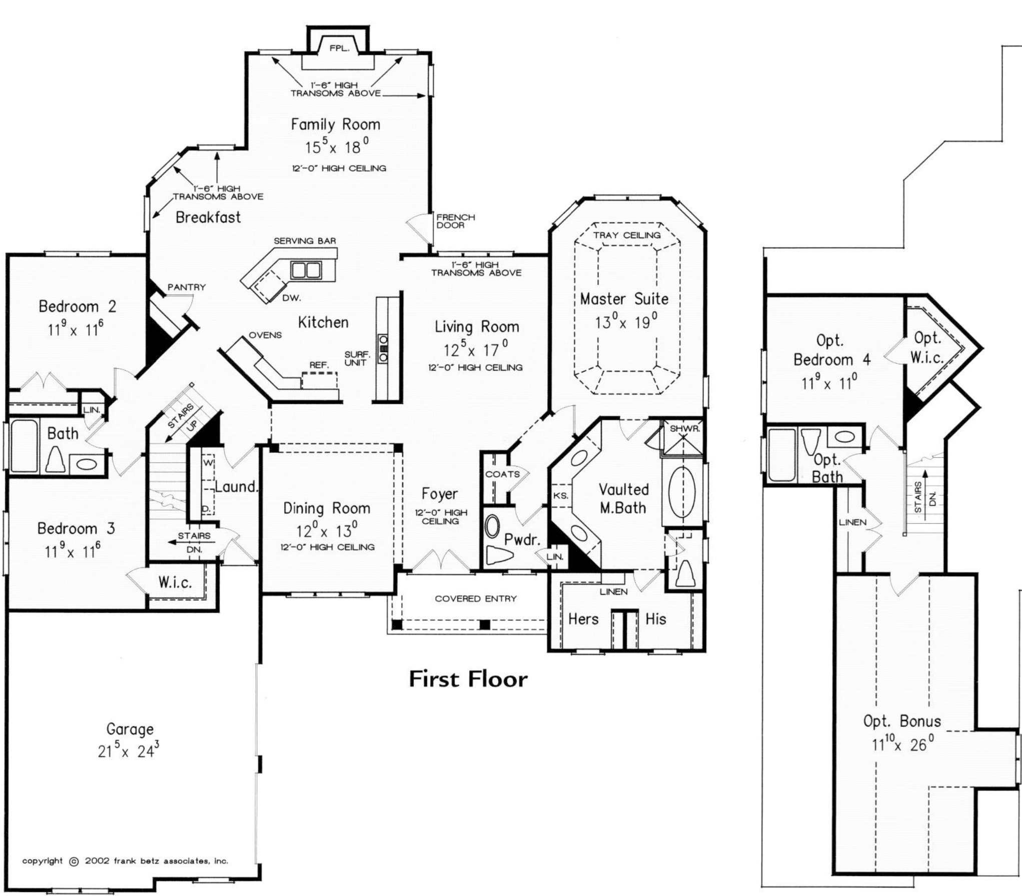

Donald A. Gardner Architects, Inc.

Newcastle — VPDG01-994 — 1-866-525-9374

Total Living	First Floor	Second Floor	Bonus	Bed	Bath	Width	Depth	Foundation	Price Category
2515 sq ft	1834 sq ft	681 sq ft	365 sq ft	3	3-1/2	50' 8"	66' 8"	Crawl Space*	F

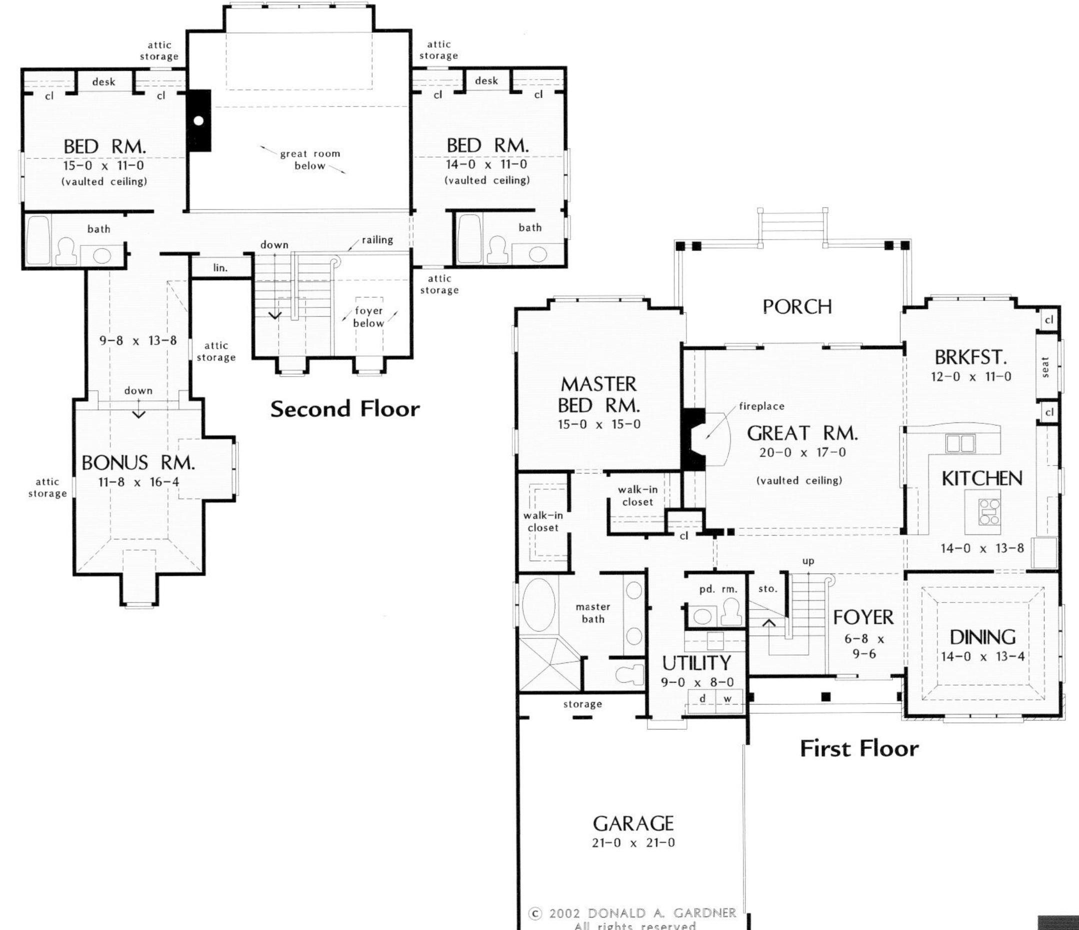

Second Floor

First Floor

Design Features

- With Old-World charm, this cottage's impressive exterior is made of stone and cedar shake.
- Inside, gathering rooms are open to each other and distinguished by columns.
- Both the foyer and great room have two-story ceilings that are brightened by dormers.
- The breakfast nook includes two pantries, while the kitchen features a cooktop island.
- Upstairs, a flexible bonus room can accommodate a growing family.

Rear Elevation

*Other options available. See page 255.

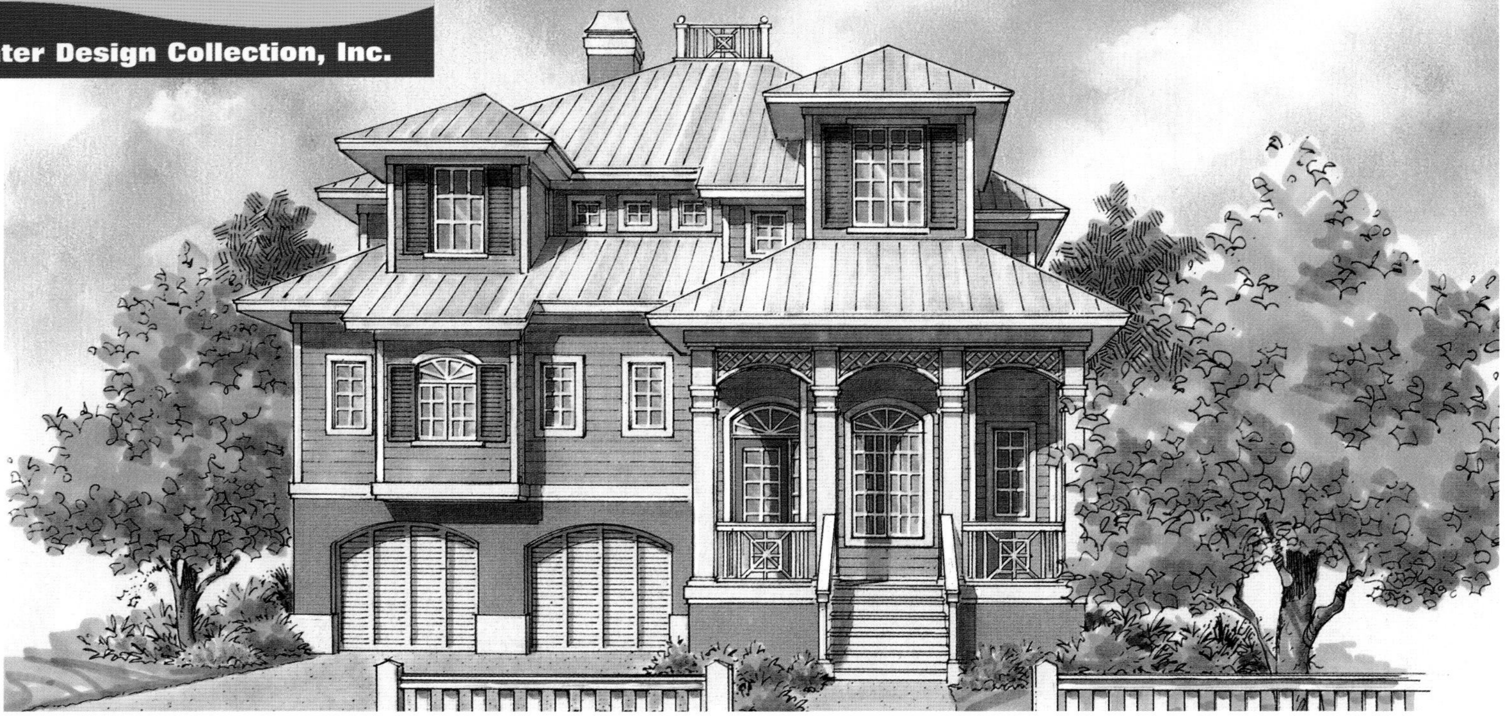

Linden Place — VPDS01-Plan 6805 — 1-866-525-9374

Total Living	First Floor	Second Floor	Bed	Bath	Width	Depth	Foundation	Price Category
2374 sq ft	1510 sq ft	864 sq ft	3	3-1/2	44' 0"	49' 0"	Island Basement	F

Design Features

- This award-winning home features a modern Mediterranean-style.
- The great room boasts a warming fireplace, built-in cabinets and two pairs of French doors that open to the rear porch.
- The master suite is enriched with a tray ceiling, tall windows and a pampering bath.
- To ensure privacy, the spare bedrooms are located on the upper level and each has its own full bath and private access to the upper deck.

Rear Elevation

Second Floor

First Floor

Lower Level

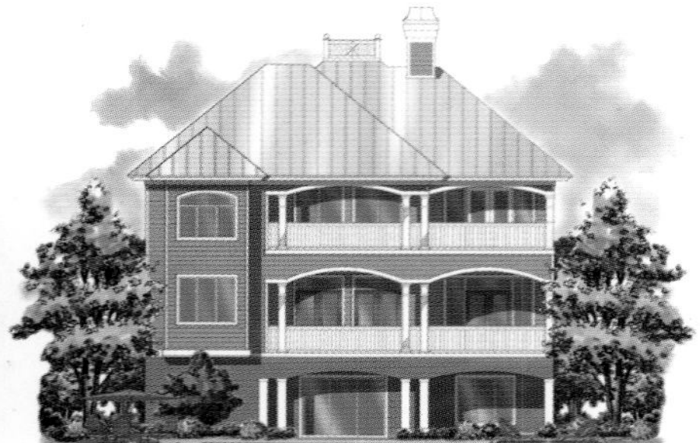

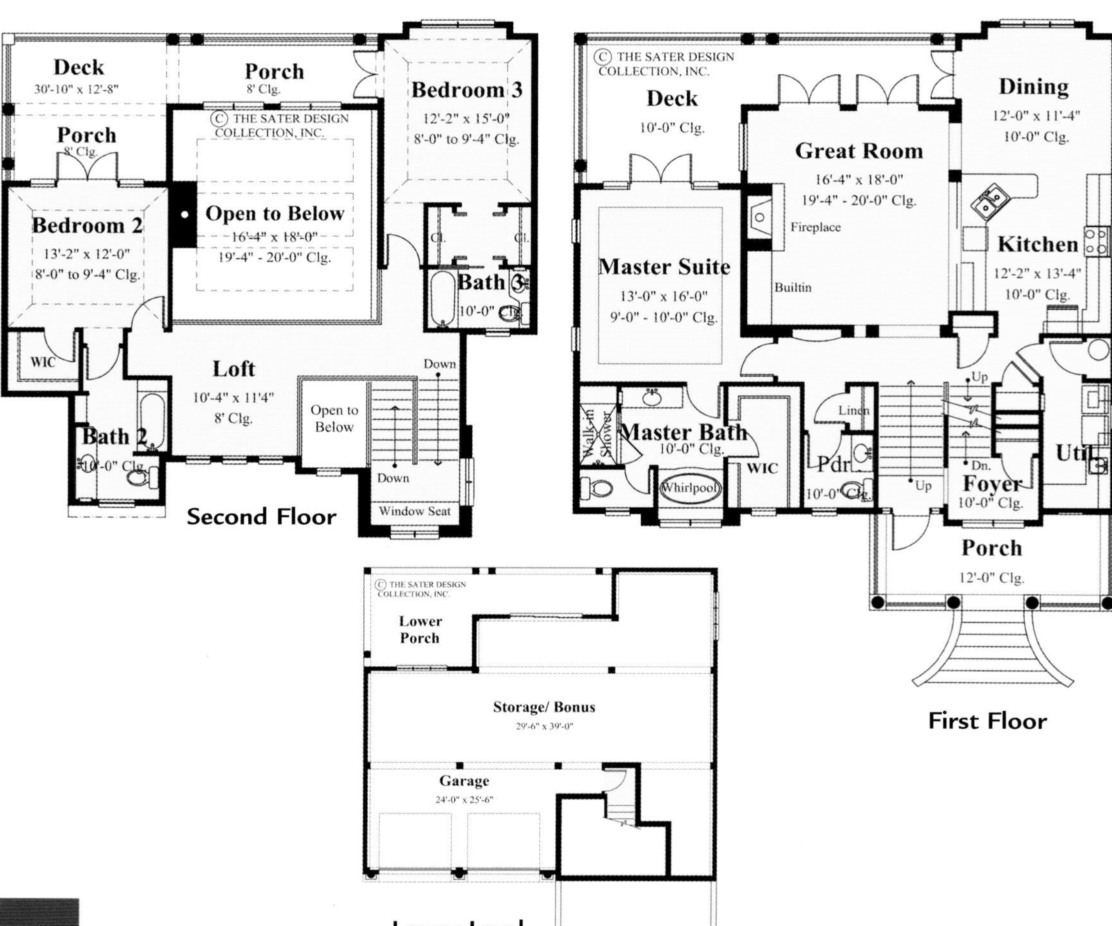

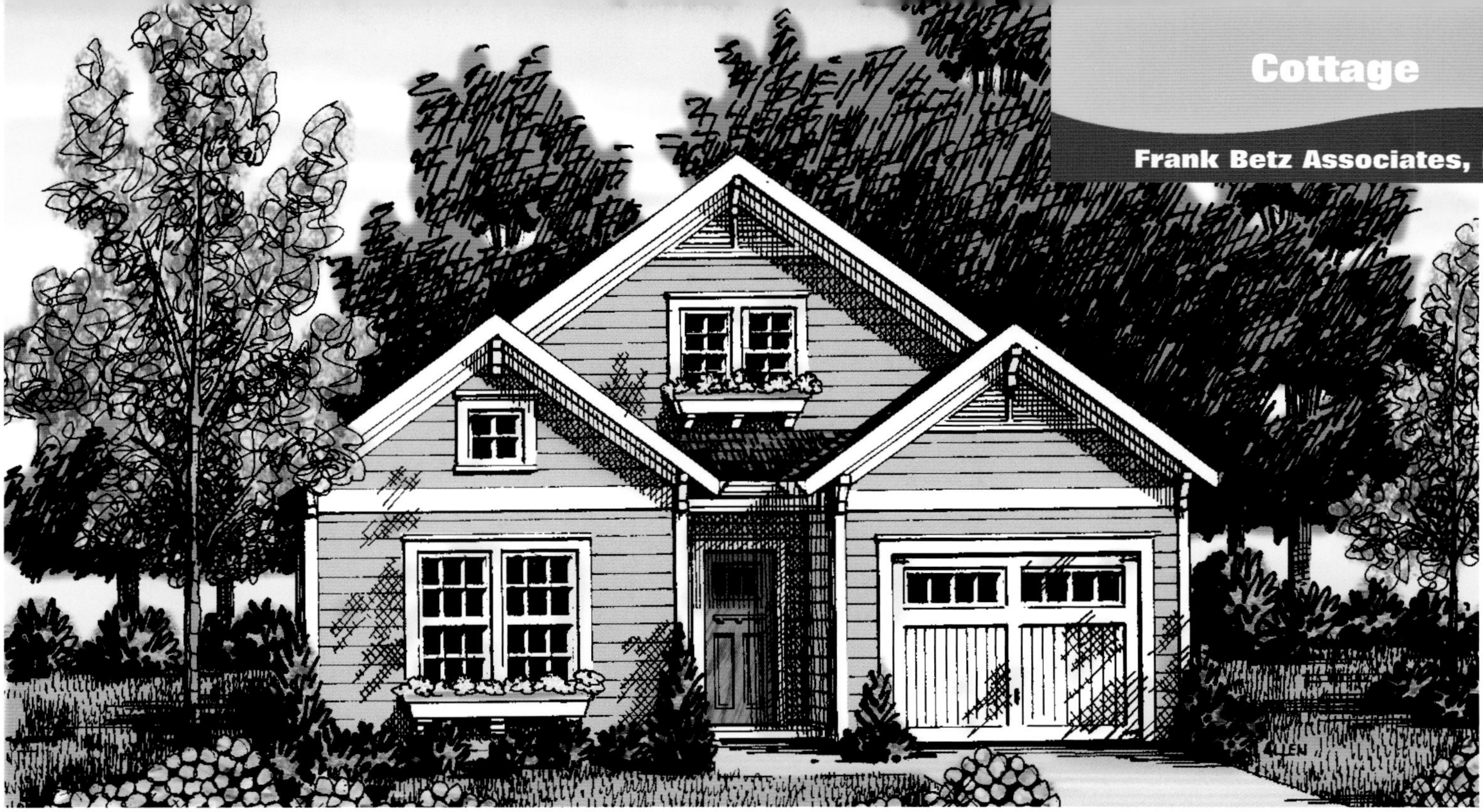

Wesley — VPFB01-Plan 3888 — 1-866-525-9374

Total Living	First Floor	Opt. Bonus	Bed	Bath	Width	Depth	Foundation	Price Category
1634 sq ft	1634 sq ft	N/A	3	2	32' 0"	68' 0"	Slab	E

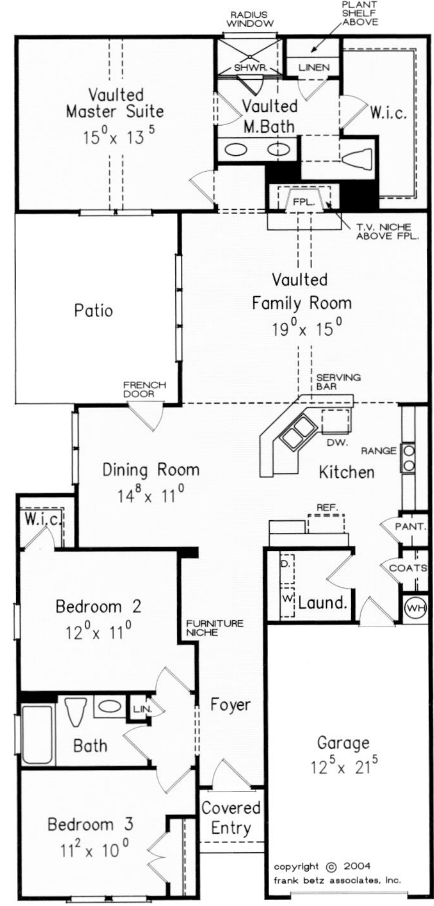

First Floor

OPT. MASTER BATH

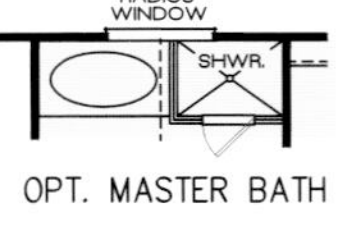

Design Features

- Three perfectly proportioned gables give the *Wesley's* façade an understated and simple elegance.
- The master suite is buffered from the other bedrooms, tucked away on the back of the home.
- The kitchen's serving bar services the family and dining rooms creating easy interaction from one space to the next.
- Designed as part of the "Zero Lot Line Collection."

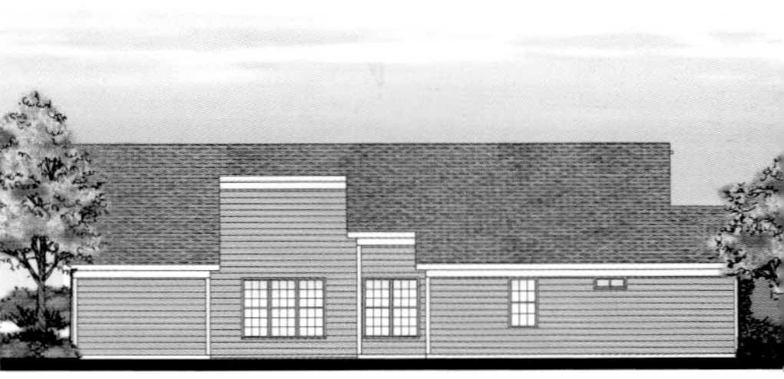

Side Patio Elevation

Satchwell — VPDG01-Plan 967 — 1-866-525-9374

Total Living	First Floor	Bonus	Bed	Bath	Width	Depth	Foundation	Price Category
2097 sq ft	2097 sq ft	352 sq ft	4	3	64' 10"	59' 6"	Crawl Space*	E

Design Features

- Welcome on any streetscape, the *Satchwell's* inviting exterior is an elegant blend of stone and siding.
- With easy access to the kitchen and great room, the dining room is an entertainer's dream.
- The kitchen overlooks the breakfast room, and its proximity to the screened porch enables family meals to easily convene outdoors.
- Positioned for privacy, the master suite accesses the screened porch and is accented by a tray ceiling.

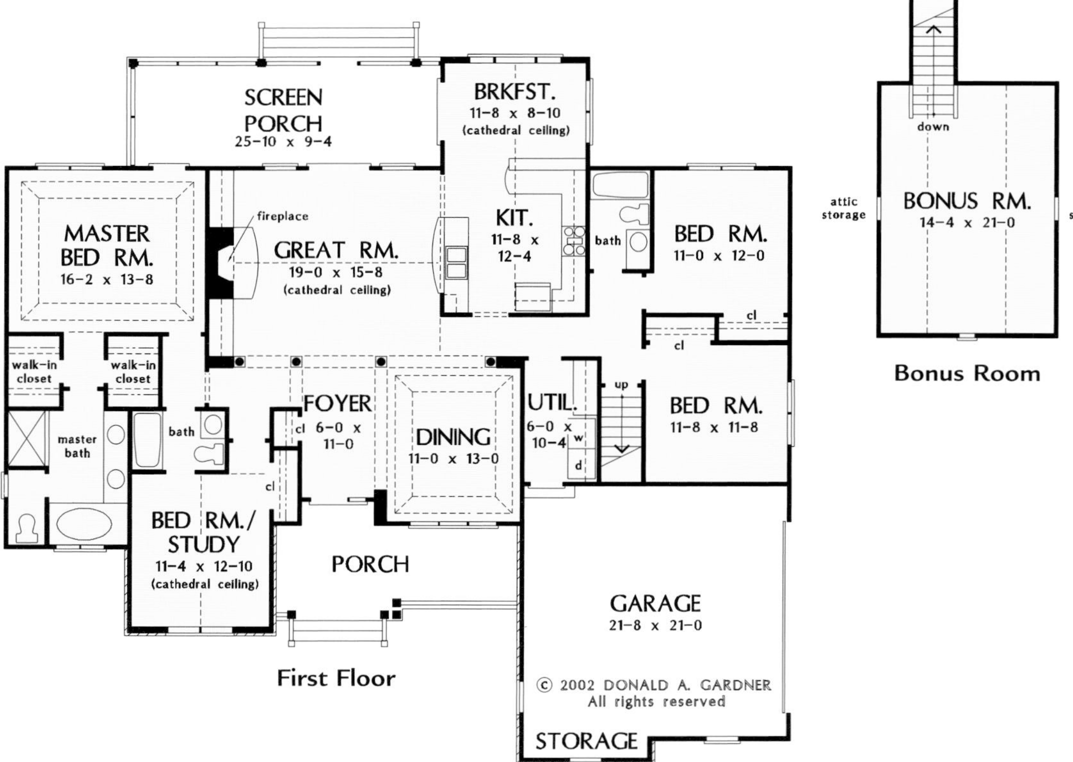

First Floor

Bonus Room

Rear View

Please note: Home photographed may differ from blueprint.

*Other options available. See page 255.

Walker Way — VPDS01-Plan 6697 — 1-866-525-9374

Total Living	First Floor	Second Floor	Bed	Bath	Width	Depth	Foundation	Price Category
2569 sq ft	1642 sq ft	927 sq ft	3	2-1/2	60' 0"	44' 6"	Slab with Pilings	G

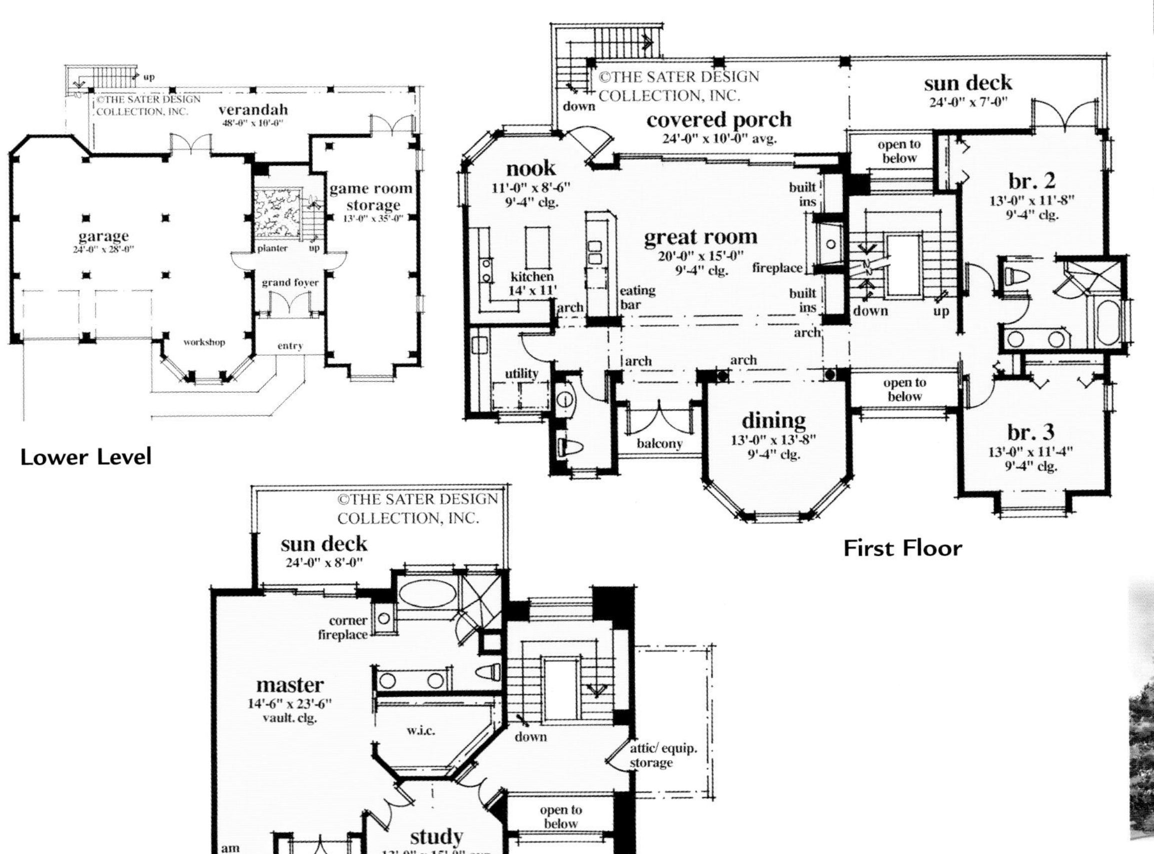

Lower Level

First Floor

Second Floor

Design Features

- The gourmet kitchen opens to the nook, which boasts its own bay windows and a single French door that leads to the verandah.
- Built-in cabinetry, a fireplace, arches, a retreating wall of glass to the covered porch and an eating bar connected to the kitchen make the great room the heart of the home.
- The upper level is dedicated to a master retreat that includes a private bayed study and a suite featuring a corner fireplace, spacious bath and a private sun deck.

Rear Elevation

Stephenson — VPFB01-3844 — 1-866-525-9374

Total Living	First Floor	Opt. Bonus	Bed	Bath	Width	Depth	Foundation	Price Category
1546 sq ft	1546 sq ft	N/A	3	2	37' 0"	65' 5"	Slab	E

Design Features

- From the street this home exudes charm with a window box, standing-seam metal trim and a covered front porch.
- The middle of the home finds the dining room overlooking the patio and kitchen with its serving bar and pantry for storage.
- The hallway access leads past the laundry room to the rear of the home where the secondary bedrooms and bath are located.
- Designed as part of the "Zero Lot Line Collection."

Side Patio Elevation

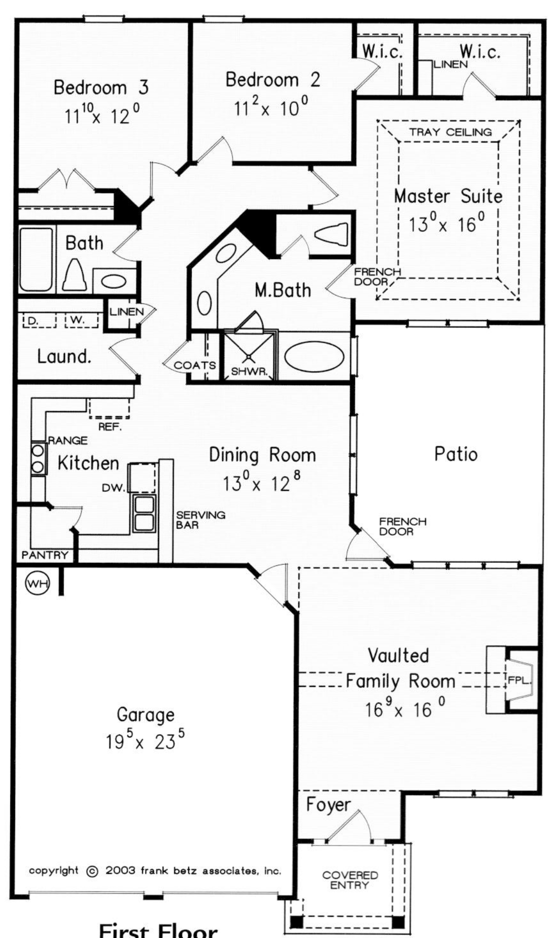

First Floor

Iverson — VPDG01-1023 — 1-866-525-9374

Total Living	First Floor	Bonus	Bed	Bath	Width	Depth	Foundation	Price Category
1547 sq ft	1547 sq ft	391 sq ft	3	2	51' 8"	59' 0"	Crawl Space*	D

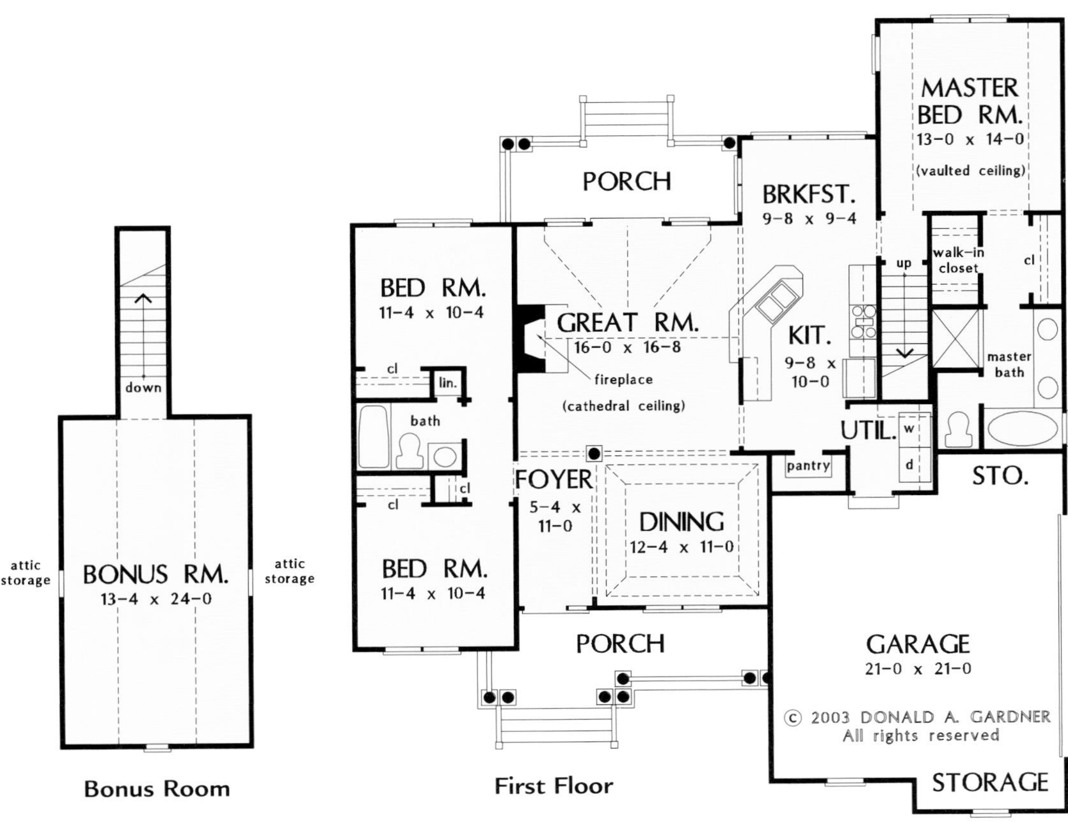

Bonus Room

First Floor

Design Features

- Custom-styled ceiling treatments crown the dining room, master bedroom and great room.
- The kitchen features an angled counter, walk-in pantry and a view of the great room's fireplace.
- Two secondary bedrooms share a full bath, and the master suite is located in the quiet zone.
- The master bath is complete with a double vanity, separate shower and garden tub.

Rear Elevation

*Other options available. See page 255.

Periwinkle Way — VPDS01-6683 — 1-866-525-9374

Total Living	First Floor	Second Floor	Bed	Bath	Width	Depth	Foundation	Price Category
1838 sq ft	1290 sq ft	548 sq ft	3	2-1/2	38' 0"	51' 0"	Basement/Crawl Space	E

Design Features

- The two-story great room features a corner fireplace.
- Columns and sweeping archways define the formal dining room.
- The main-level master suite has two lavatories.
- The second level includes a large deck.
- Two upper-level bedrooms enjoy a balcony overlook.

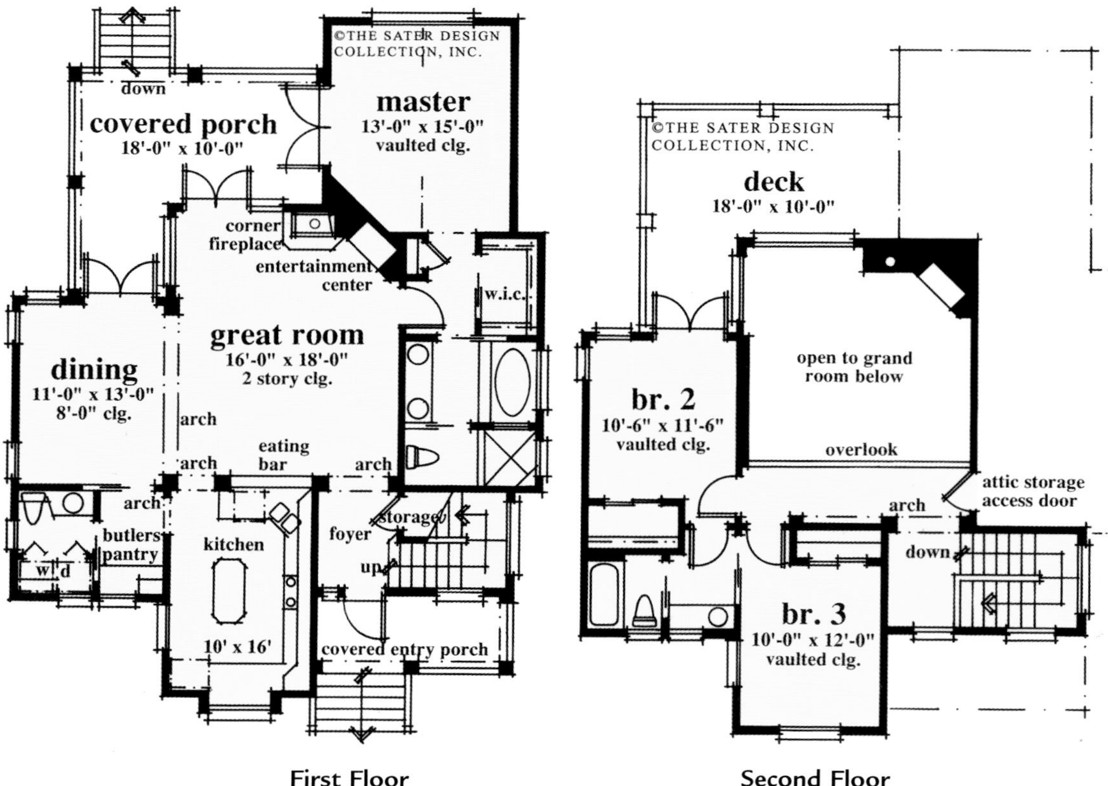

First Floor

Second Floor

Rear Elevation

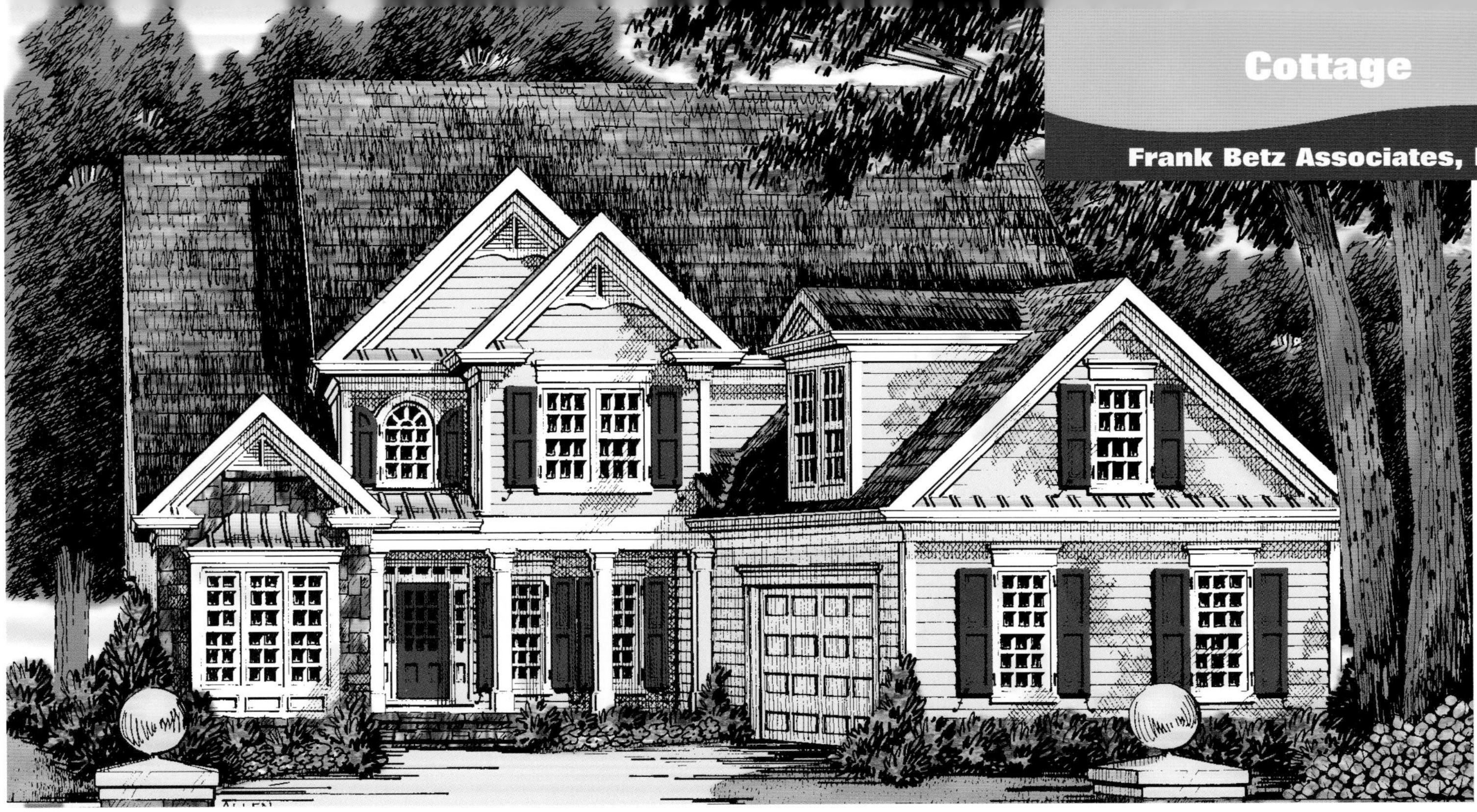

Seymour — VPFB01-Plan 1210 — 1-866-525-9374

Total Living	First Floor	Second Floor	Opt. Bonus	Bed	Bath	Width	Depth	Foundation	Price Category
2034 sq ft	1559 sq ft	475 sq ft	321 sq ft	4	3	50' 0"	56' 4"	Basement, Crawl Space or Slab	G

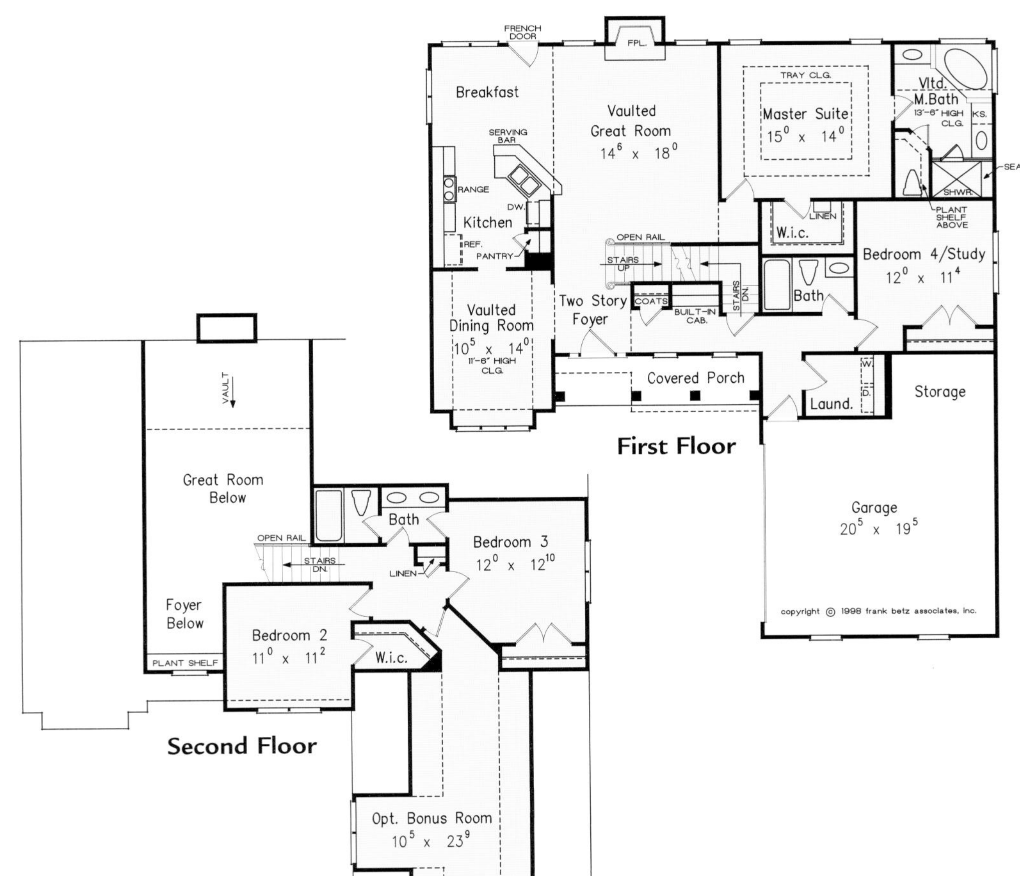

Design Features

- Style and sensibility meet to create the *Seymour*, a design that is as practical as it is beautiful.
- Fieldstone, copper accents and a courtyard entry distinguish this home from the others on the block.
- The main floor consists of the common living areas, the master bedroom and a secondary bedroom that can easily serve as the home office.
- Optional bonus space is also available on the second floor, leaving homeowners choices on how to finish it.

Rear Elevation

Wilshire — VPDG01-976 — 1-866-525-9374

Total Living	First Floor	Opt. Bonus	Bed	Bath	Width	Depth	Foundation	Price Category
1904 sq ft	1904 sq ft	366 sq ft	3	2	53' 10"	57' 8"	Crawl Space*	D

Design Features

- Blending stone with siding, this cottage has many wonderful architectural features.
- Lush amenities include built-in cabinetry, tray ceilings and a cooktop island.
- A pass-thru connects the great room and kitchen and adds convenience.
- The master suite includes dual walk-in closets, private toilet, garden tub and separate shower.

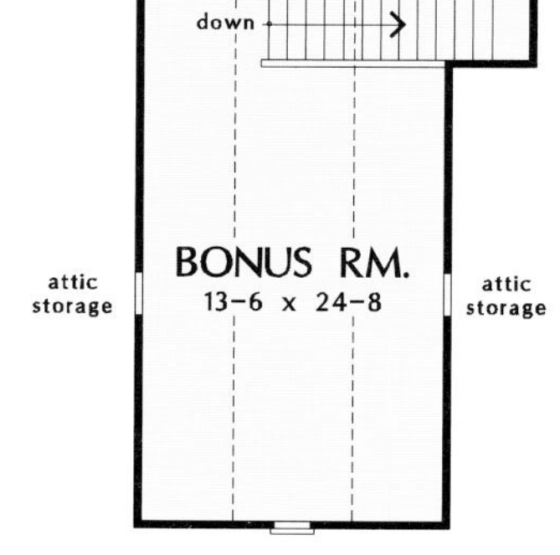

Bonus Room

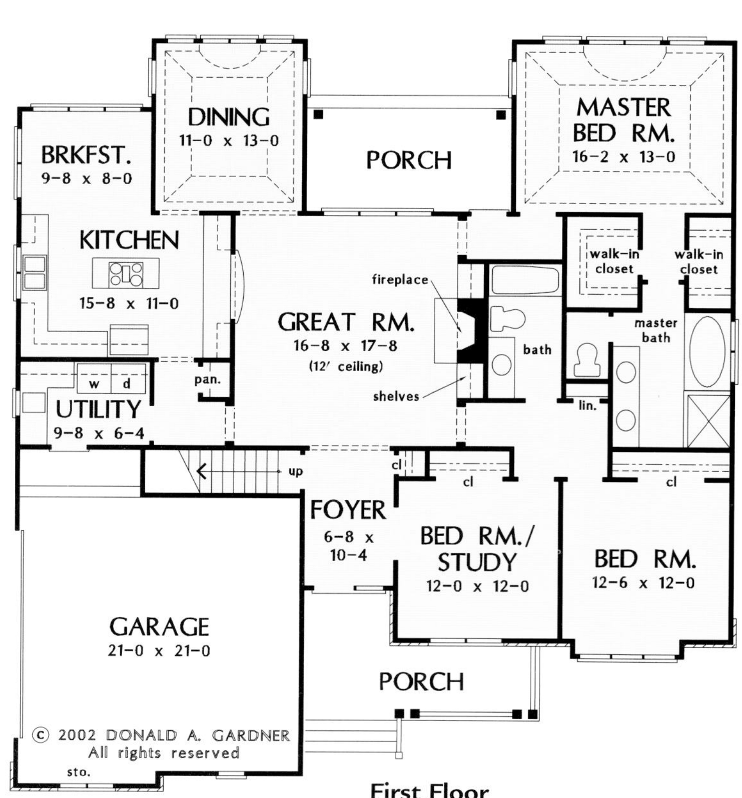

First Floor

Rear Elevation

*Other options available. See page 255.

Shadow Lane — VPDS01-6686 — 1-866-525-9374

Total Living	First Floor	Second Floor	Bed	Bath	Width	Depth	Foundation	Price Category
1684 sq ft	1046 sq ft	638 sq ft	3	3	25' 0"	72' 2"	Post/Pier	E

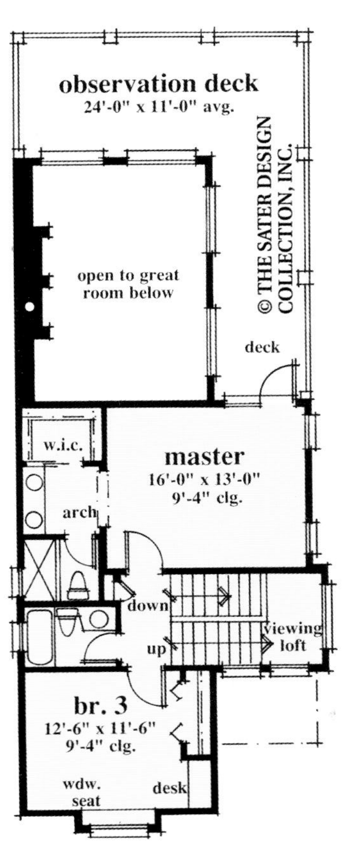

Second Floor

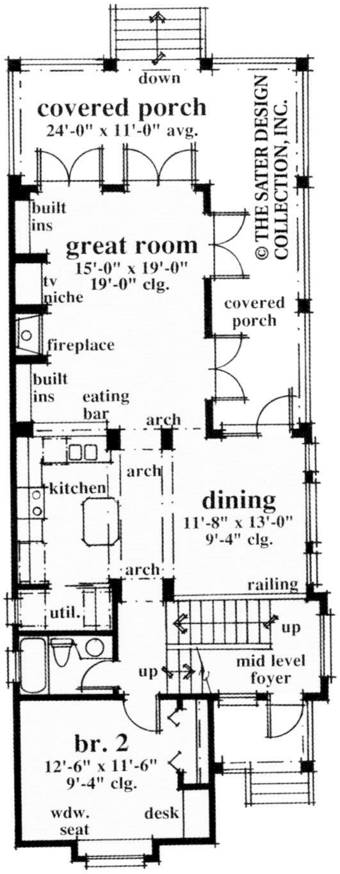

down
covered porch
24'-0" x 11'-0" avg.
© THE SATER DESIGN COLLECTION, INC.
built ins
great room
15'-0" x 19'-0"
19'-0" clg.
tv niche
covered porch
fireplace
built ins
eating bar
arch
kitchen
arch
dining
11'-8" x 13'-0"
9'-4" clg.
arch
railing
util.
up
up
mid level foyer
br. 2
12'-6" x 11'-6"
9'-4" clg.
wdw. seat
desk

First Floor

Design Features

- Built-ins and a media niche frame the fireplace in the great room.
- The formal dining room opens to the wraparound covered porch.
- The gourmet kitchen shares an eating bar with the great room.
- The second-level master suite includes a private observation deck.
- A vestibule leads to a viewing-loft stair, where a built-in window seat offers quiet relaxation.

Rear Elevation

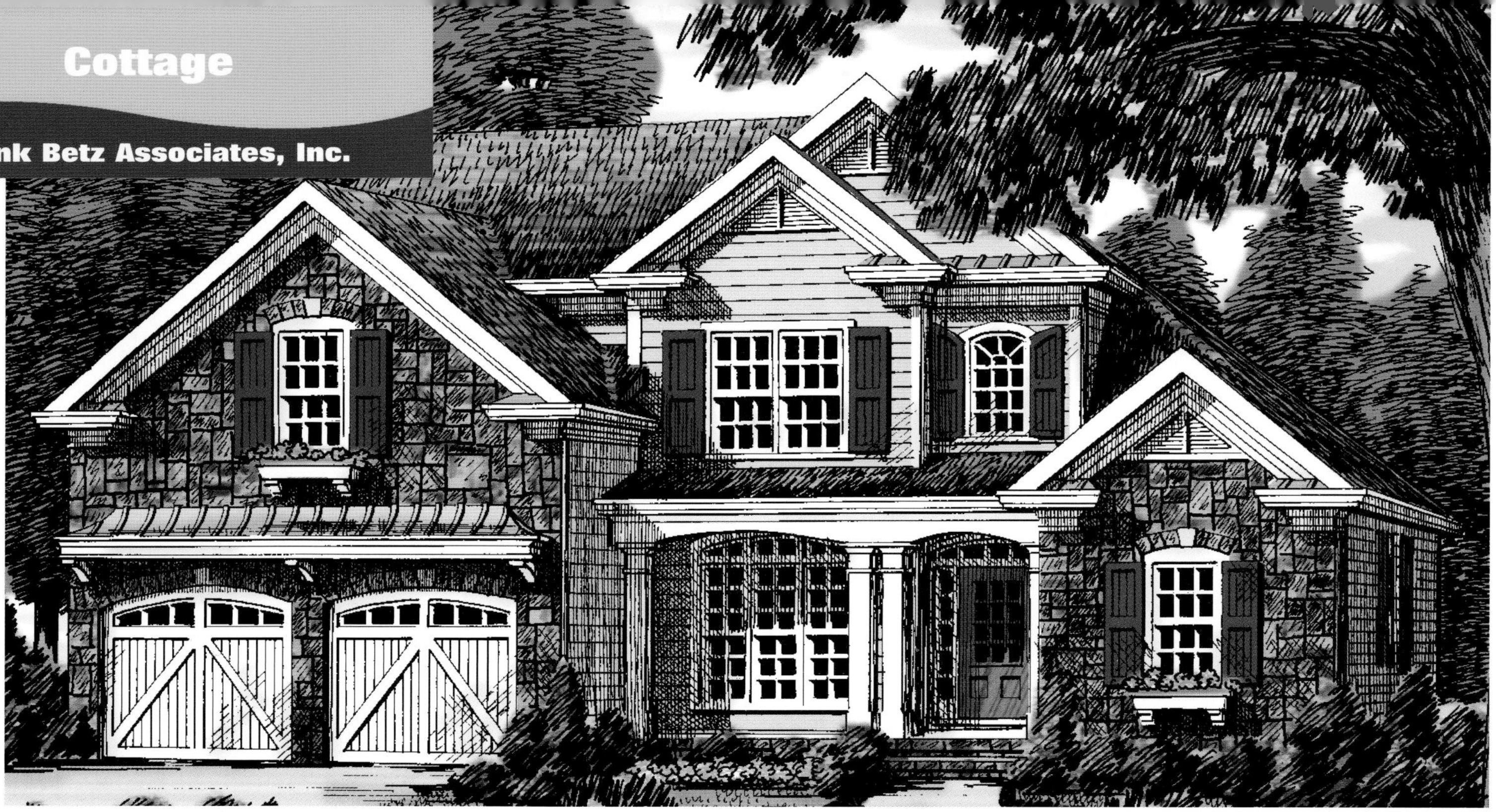

Stonechase — VPFB01-3662 — 1-866-525-9374

Total Living	First Floor	Second Floor	Opt. Bonus	Bed	Bath	Width	Depth	Foundation	Price Category
1974 sq ft	1458 sq ft	516 sq ft	168 sq ft	3	2-1/2	50' 0"	46' 0"	Basement or Crawl Space	G

Design Features

- Stone accents, carriage doors and board-and-batten shutters come together to create the cottage-like appeal that is so desirable today.
- The master suite is secluded from secondary bedrooms, encompassing an entire wing of the main level.
- A powder room and coat closet are strategically placed near the garage entrance, keeping shoes and coats in their place.
- The secondary bedrooms have an overlook to the vaulted family room.

Rear Elevation

First Floor

Second Floor

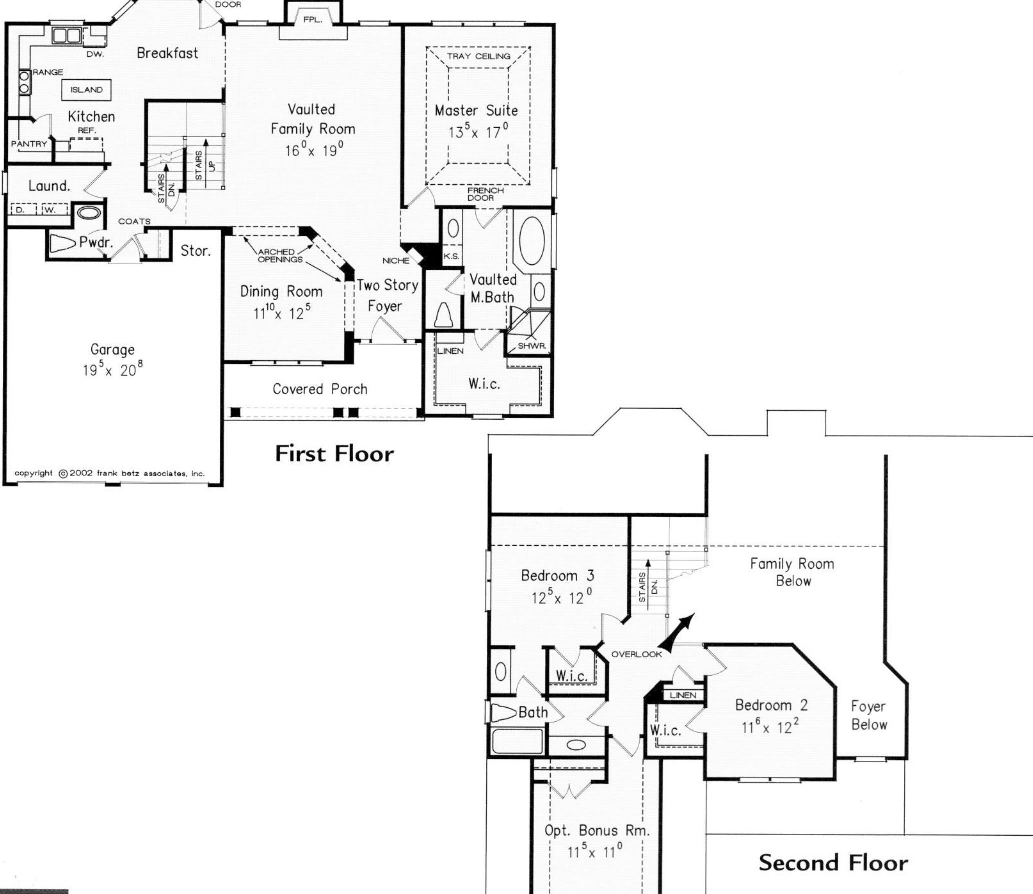

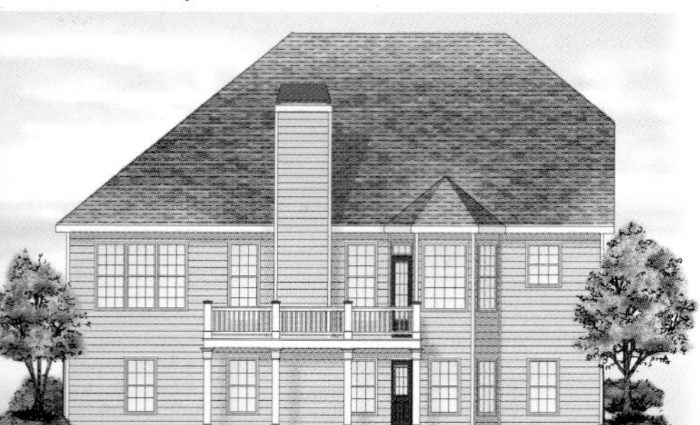

Urbandale — VPDG01-1088 — 1-866-525-9374

Total Living	First Floor	Bonus	Bed	Bath	Width	Depth	Foundation	Price Category
1685 sq ft	1685 sq ft	N/A	3	2	36' 4"	88' 8"	Crawl Space*	D

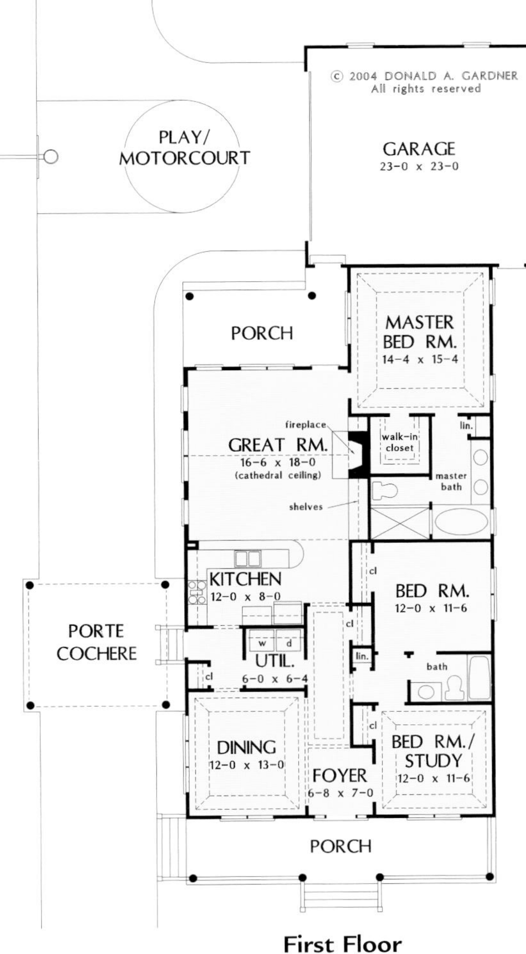

First Floor

Design Features

- Perfect for long, narrow lots, this plan combines everyday needs with exciting extras.
- The porte-cochere, defined by decorative columns, becomes quick, covered parking for vehicles.
- Wraparound countertops expand area for meal preparation in the kitchen.
- The master bedroom features "his-and-her" sinks, a garden tub and a generous walk-in closet.

Rear Elevation

*Other options available. See page 255.

Georgetown Cove — VPDS01-6690 — 1-866-525-9374

Total Living	First Floor	Second Floor	Bed	Bath	Width	Depth	Foundation	Price Category
1910 sq ft	873 sq ft	1037 sq ft	3	2-1/2	27' 6"	64' 0"	Piling/Garage on Slab	E

Design Features

- The quaint front balcony has a glass-paneled entry to the foyer.
- The great room has French doors to the outside and a fireplace framed by built-in cabinetry.
- The formal dining room opens to a private area of the covered porch.
- Double French doors fill the upper-level master suite with sunlight and open to a sundeck.
- The study has a walk-in closet and views to the side property.

Rear Elevation

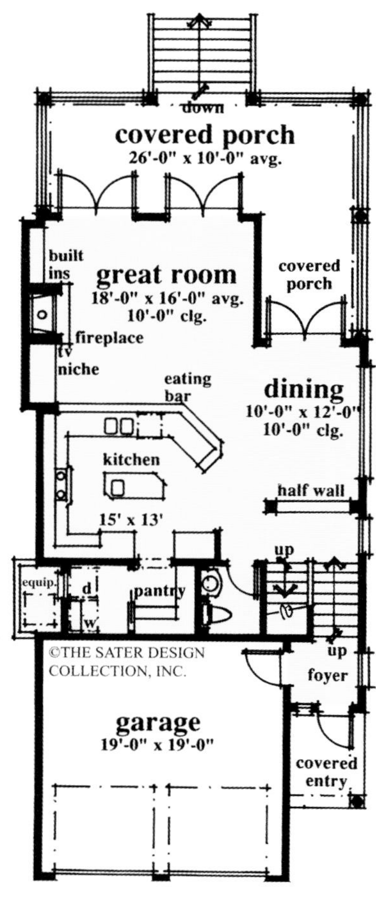

First Floor

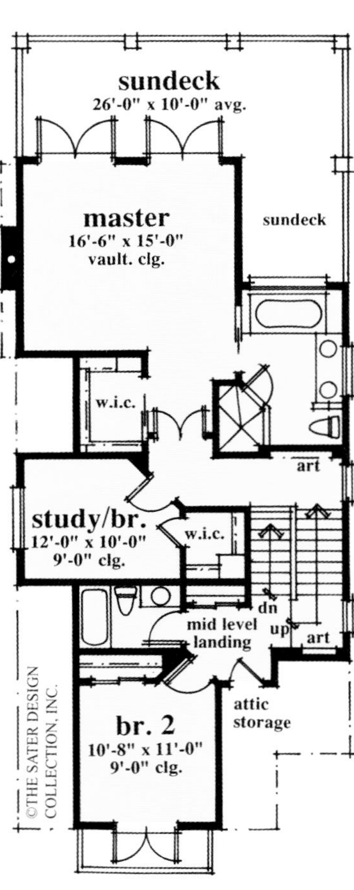

Second Floor

Summerhill — VPDG01-1090 — 1-866-525-9374

Total Living	First Floor	Bonus	Bed	Bath	Width	Depth	Foundation	Price Category
2193 sq ft	2193 sq ft	387 sq ft	3	2	56' 4"	73' 0"	Crawl Space*	E

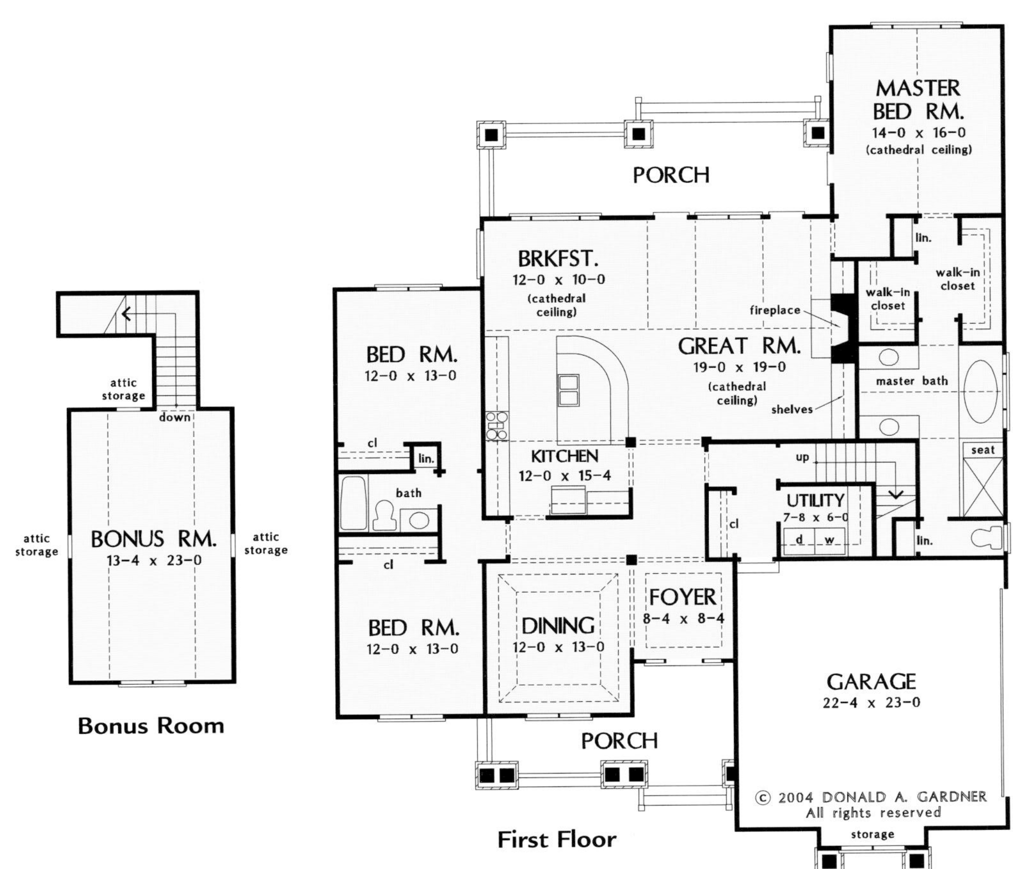

Bonus Room

First Floor

Design Features

- An Arts-n-Crafts façade boasts elegant curb appeal as double dormers echo the dual-arched portico.
- Twin sets of tapered columns provide architectural detail to this lavish exterior.
- Vaulted ceilings in the great room offer generous vertical volume throughout the open living spaces.
- A vaulted ceiling, dual sinks and walk-in closets give the master suite additional flair.

Rear Elevation

*Other options available. See page 255.

Nantucket Sound — VPDS01-Plan 6693 — 1-866-525-9374

Total Living	First Floor	Second Floor	Lower Level	Bed	Bath	Width	Depth	Foundation	Price Category
2957 sq ft	1642 sq ft	1165 sq ft	150 sq ft	3	3-1/2	44' 6"	58' 0"	Post/Pier/Slab	G

Design Features

- A cozy fireplace framed by built-ins invites gatherings, while two pairs of French doors, which frame a two-story wall of glass topped off by a graceful arch, define the open living and dining room area.
- The gourmet kitchen features an island prep area, walk-in pantry, a pass-thru counter and access to the covered porch.
- Upstairs, a gallery loft leads to a balcony overlook and two secondary bedrooms that feature private baths.

Rear Elevation

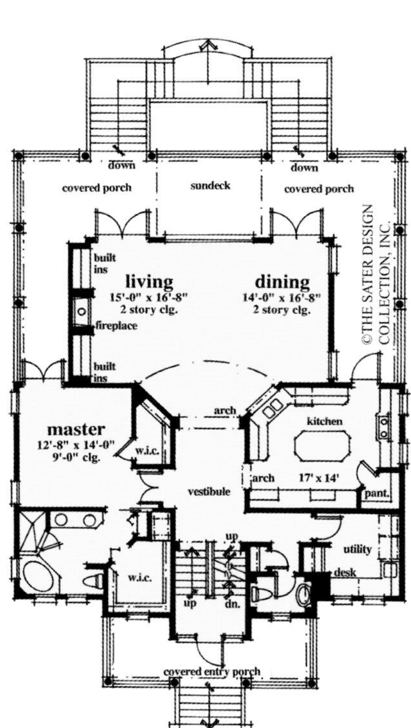

First Floor

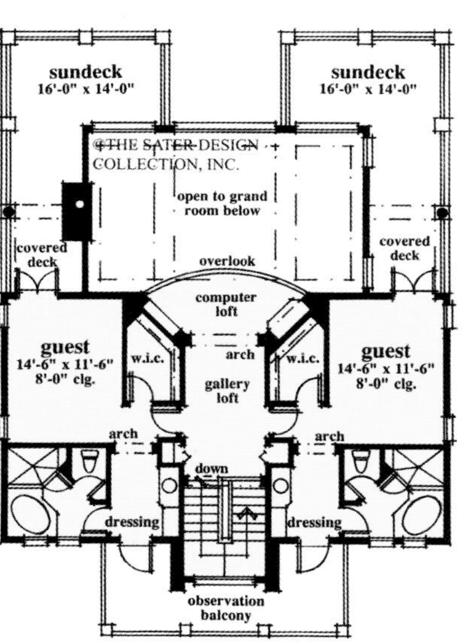

Second Floor

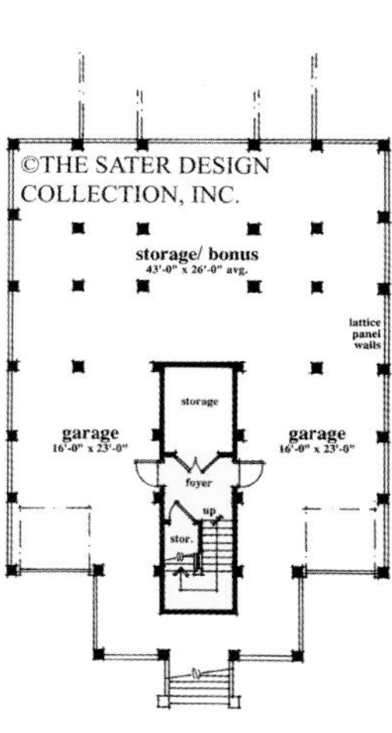

Lower Level

Donald A. Gardner Architects, Inc.

Kilpatrick — VPDG01-833 — 1-866-525-9374

Total Living	First Floor	Bonus	Bed	Bath	Width	Depth	Foundation	Price Category
1608 sq ft	1608 sq ft	437 sq ft	3	2	40' 8"	62' 8"	Crawl Space*	D

Design Features

- This three-bedroom Craftsman home packs a lot of style into its slim façade.
- A tray ceiling tops the formal dining room, while the kitchen features an efficient design.
- The master suite enjoys a space-enhancing cathedral ceiling, back-porch access and dual walk-in closets.
- The utility room is conveniently located in close proximity to the home's three bedrooms.

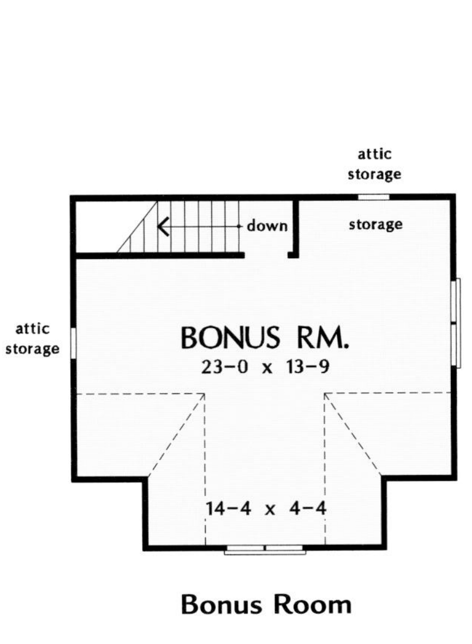

Bonus Room

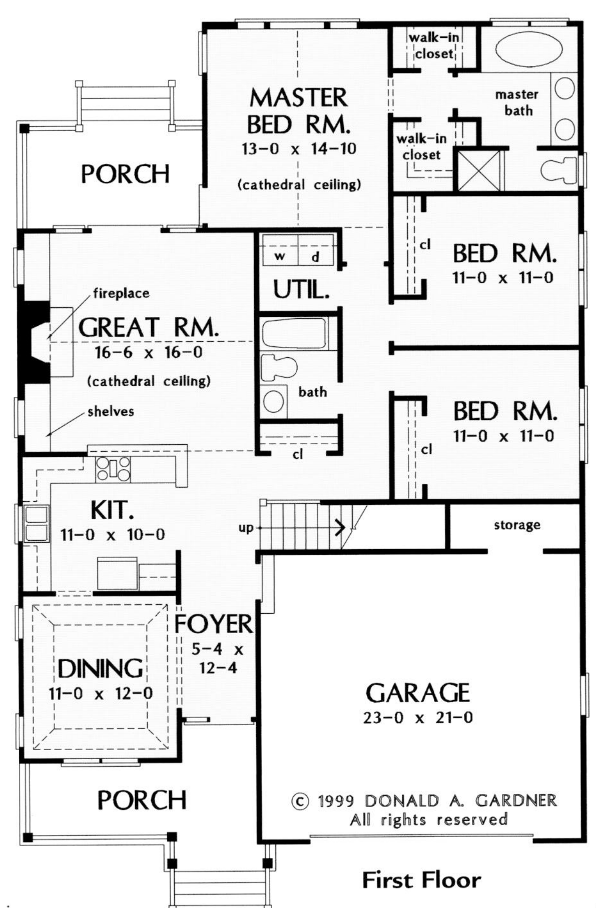

First Floor

Rear Elevation

Please note: Home photographed may differ from blueprint.

*Other options available. See page 255.

Donald A. Gardner Architects, Inc.

Gresham — VPDG01-1084 — 1-866-525-9374

Total Living	First Floor	Bonus	Bed	Bath	Width	Depth	Foundation	Price Category
1830 sq ft	1830 sq ft	354 sq ft	3	2	54' 4"	61' 4"	Crawl Space*	D

Design Features

- Gables and decorative dormers accentuate the hipped roof, while a box-bay window de-emphasizes the garage.
- The screened porch can be accessed from the versatile bed-room/study and great room.
- Other special features include a bonus room, reach-in pantry and built-in cabinetry.
- An art niche and spacious closet enhance the foyer, and the master bath is quite the retreat.

Rear Elevation

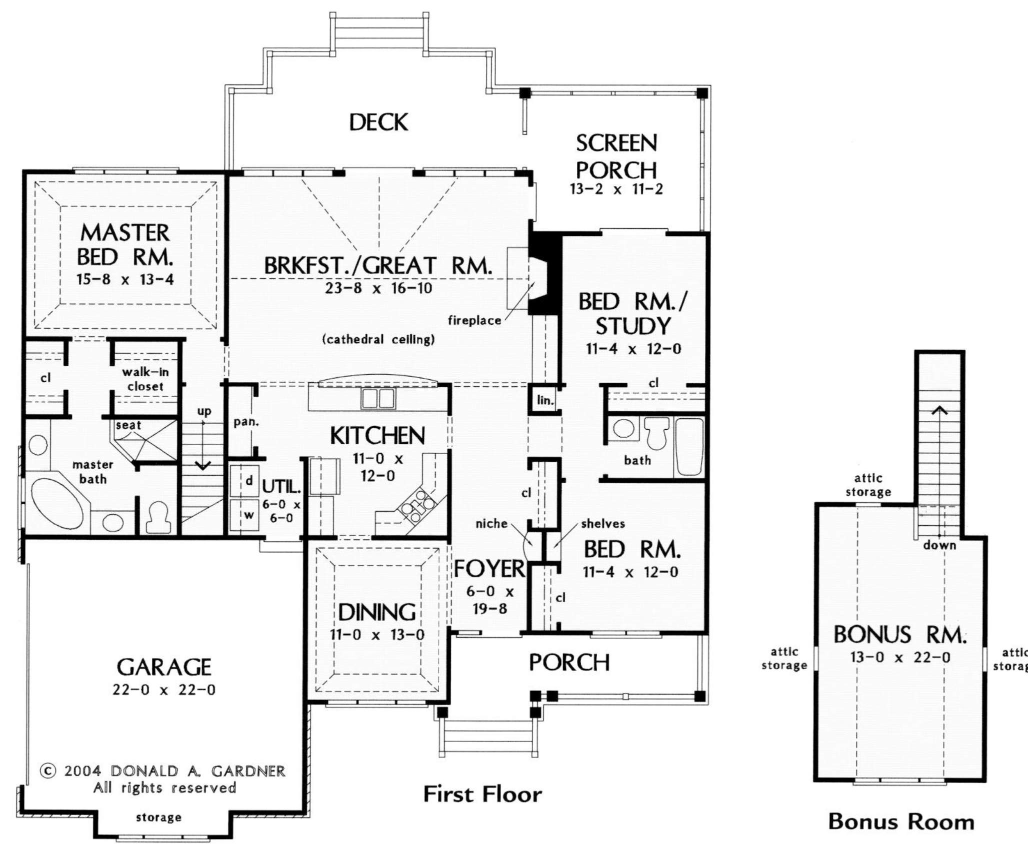

First Floor

Bonus Room

*Other options available. See page 255.

Hemingway Lane — VPDS01-Plan 6689 — 1-866-525-9374

Total Living	First Floor	Second Floor	Lower Level	Bed	Bath	Width	Depth	Foundation	Price Category
2957 sq ft	1642 sq ft	1165 sq ft	150 sq ft	5	3-1/2	44' 6"	58' 0"	Slab/Piling	G

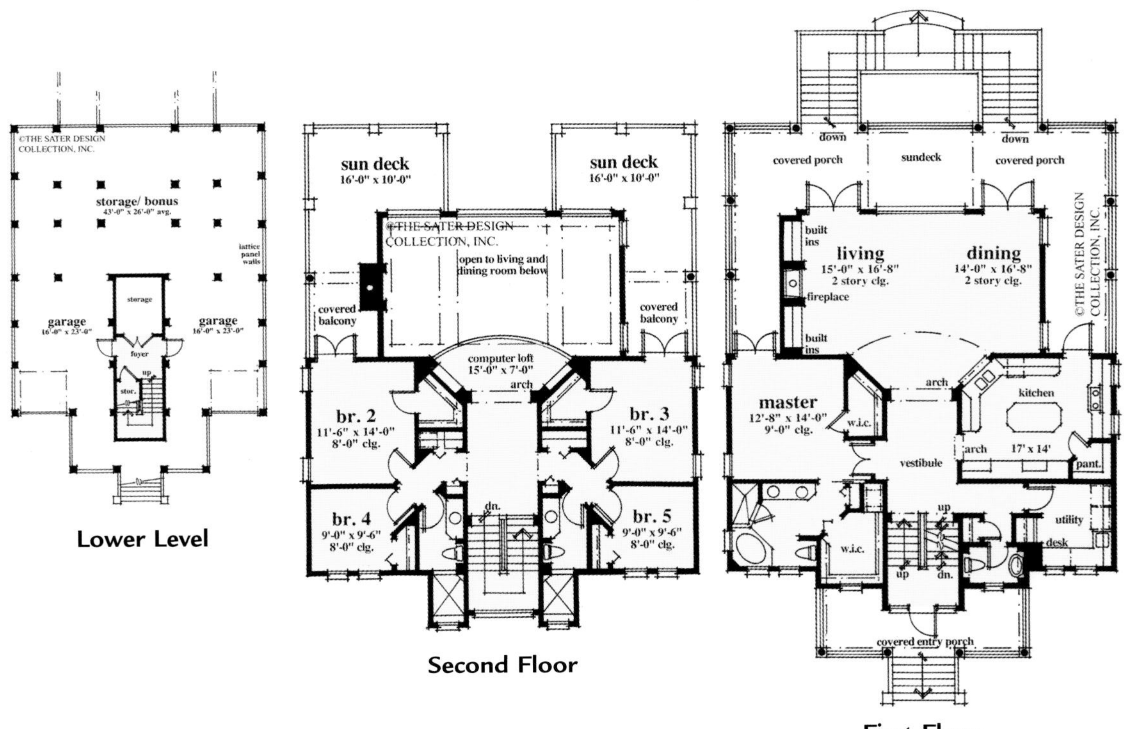

Lower Level

Second Floor

First Floor

Design Features

- A widow's peak, mirroring dormers, shutters, Doric columns and a glass-paneled arched entry adorn the exterior.
- The living/dining room area enjoys a fireplace, built-in cabinetry, two sets of French doors leading out to the sundeck and a two-story picture window that invites views in.
- The upper level features four secondary bedrooms and a central computer loft that offers built-in desk space and a balcony overlook.

Rear Elevation

Donald A. Gardner Architects, Inc.

Oakway — VPDG01-968 — 1-866-525-9374

Total Living	First Floor	Bonus	Bed	Bath	Width	Depth	Foundation	Price Category
1457 sq ft	1457 sq ft	341 sq ft	3	2	50' 4"	46' 4"	Crawl Space*	C

Design Features

- Poised and cozy, this home features a split-bedroom plan.
- The convenient front-entry garage has a versatile bonus room above for expansion purposes.
- Economical and builder-friendly, the floor plan is family-efficient and has a variety of custom-styled touches.
- The master suite is complete with a walk-in closet and master bath.
- Additional bedrooms are located on the opposite side of the house and are separated by a full bath.

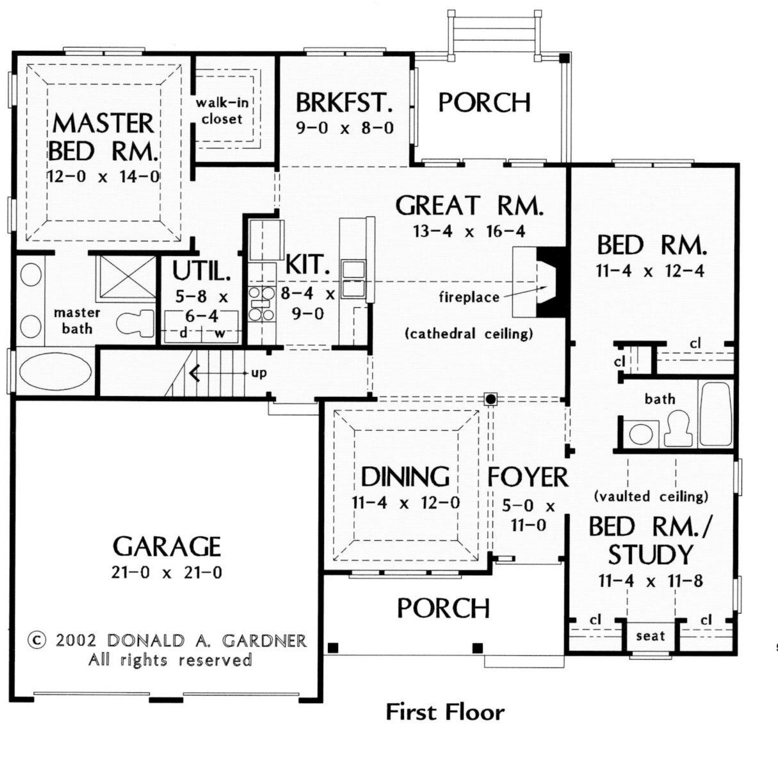

First Floor

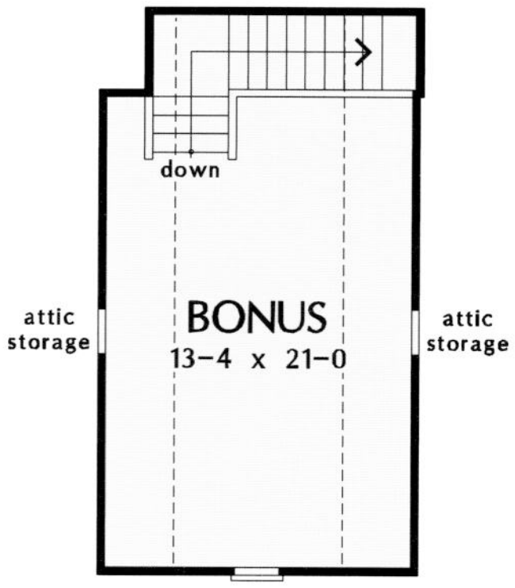

down
attic storage
BONUS
13-4 x 21-0
attic storage

Bonus Room

Rear Elevation

*Other options available. See page 255.

Key Largo — VPDS01-Plan 6828 — 1-866-525-9374

Total Living	First Floor	Second Floor	Bed	Bath	Width	Depth	Foundation	Price Category
2691 sq ft	1313 sq ft	1378 sq ft	3	2-1/2	34' 4"	63' 6"	Crawl Space	G

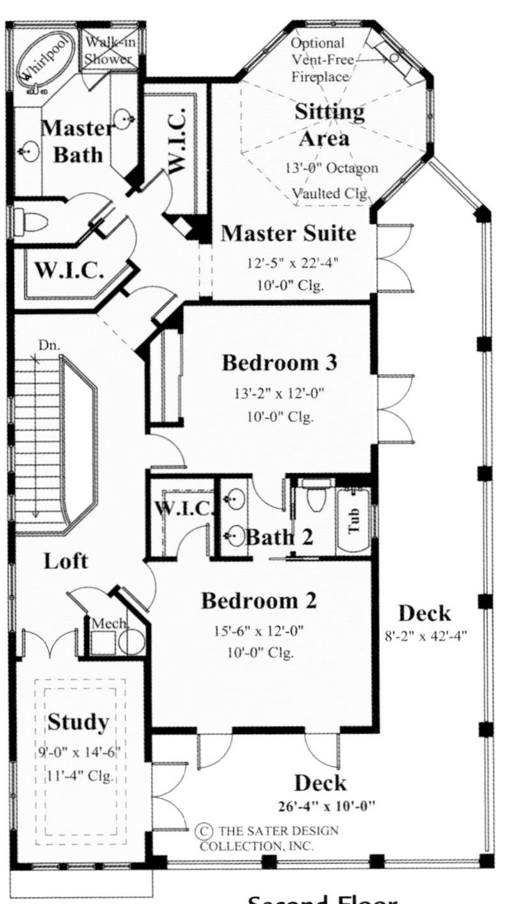

Second Floor

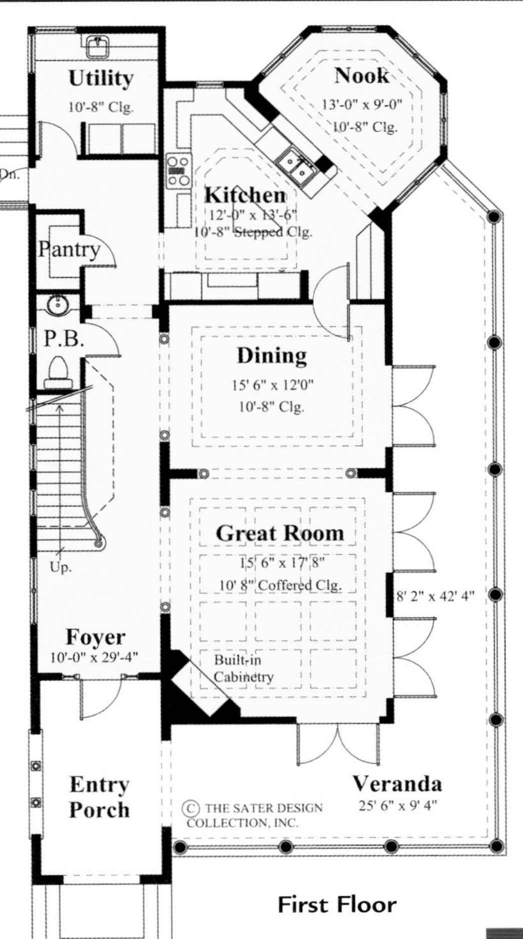

First Floor

Design Features

- Three sets of French doors to the veranda, built-in cabinetry and a coffered ceiling enhance the great room.
- On the upper level, the luxurious master suite boasts a sitting area encircled with a wall of windows, a vaulted ceiling and features a cozy two-sided fireplace.
- Two secondary bedrooms share a "Jack-and-Jill" bathroom that boasts a double-sink vanity and each room opens to the upper deck.

Rear View

Please note: Home photographed may differ from blueprint.

Shady Grove — VPDG01-Plan 262 — 1-866-525-9374

Total Living	First Floor	Second Floor	Bed	Bath	Width	Depth	Foundation	Price Code
1338 sq ft	1002 sq ft	336 sq ft	3	2	36' 9"	44' 8"	Crawl Space*	C

Design Features

- As a rural retreat, this home is a great get-a-way to the outdoors.
- Multiple porches, a stone fireplace and a box-bay window lend character to this cottage.
- The open floor plan receives volume from a cathedral ceiling over the kitchen and great room.
- The master suite features a large walk-in closet, double vanity and garden tub.
- The second-floor hall ends with a balcony that overlooks the two-story common rooms.

Rear Elevation

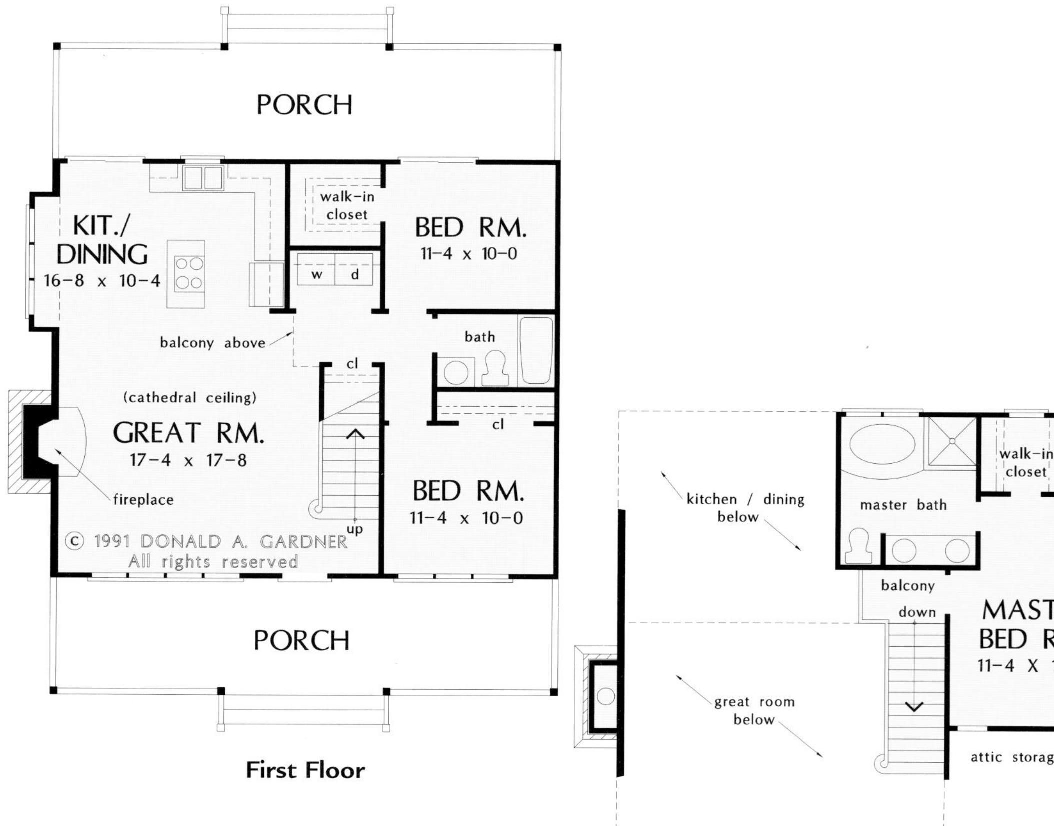

First Floor

Second Floor

*Other options available. See page 255.

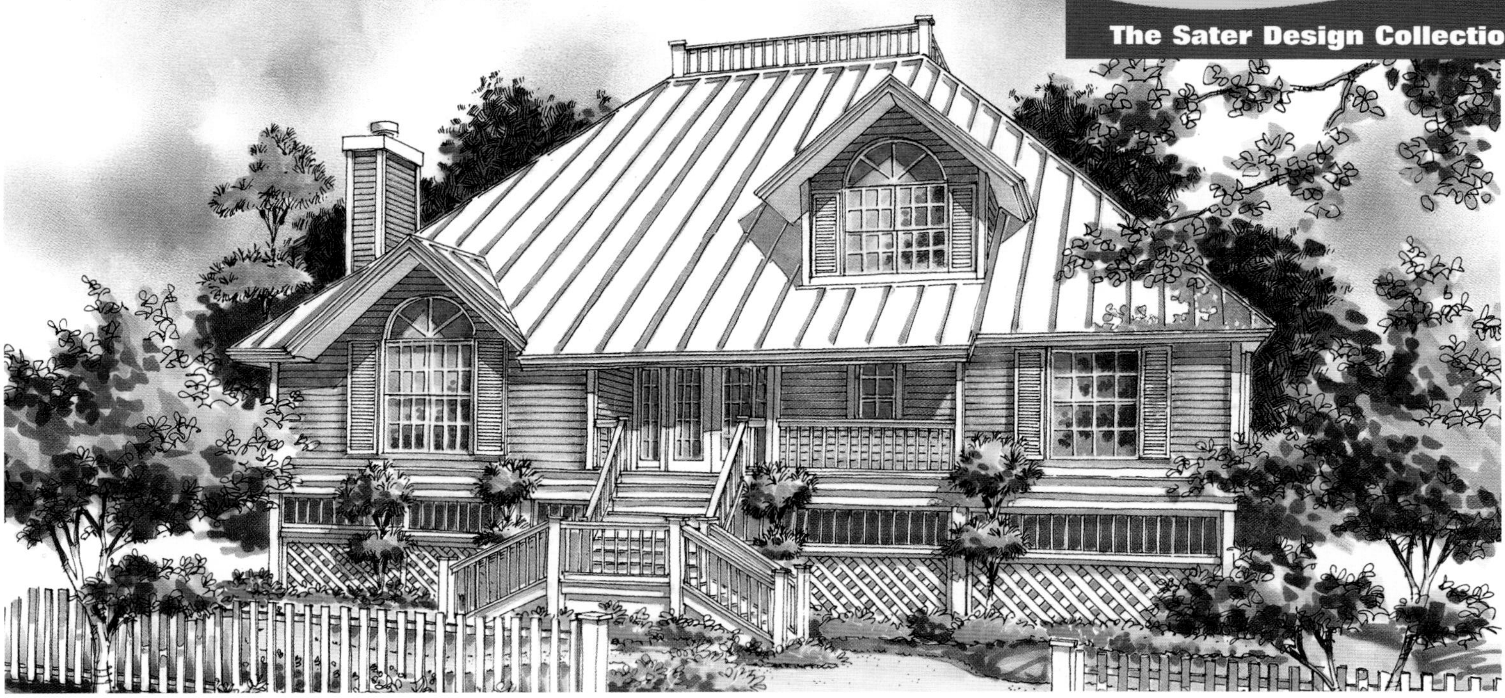

Abaco Bay — VPDS01-Plan 6655 — 1-866-525-9374

Total Living	First Floor	Second Floor	Lower Level	Bed	Bath	Width	Depth	Foundation	Price Code
2257 sq ft	1537 sq ft	575 sq ft	145 sq ft	3	2	50' 0"	44' 0"	Post/Pier	F

Second Floor

First Floor

Lower Level

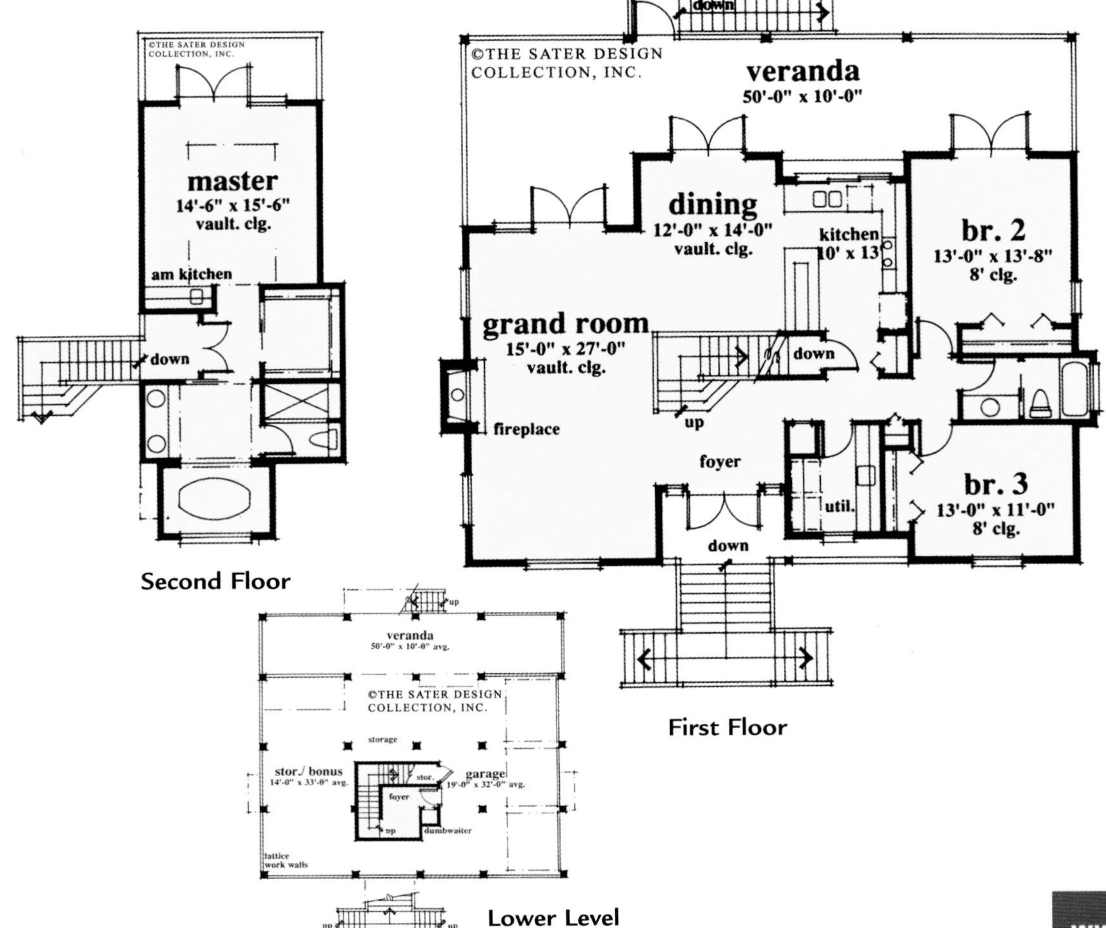

Design Features

- An open foyer leads into the expansive great room, made cozy by a warming hearth.
- The rear veranda is accessible from the grand room, dining room and a secondary bedroom.
- The upper level is dedicated to the master suite, which features a morning kitchen, access to a private deck and a vanity with an arched soffit ceiling.
- Enclosed storage plus bonus space is tucked away on the lower level.

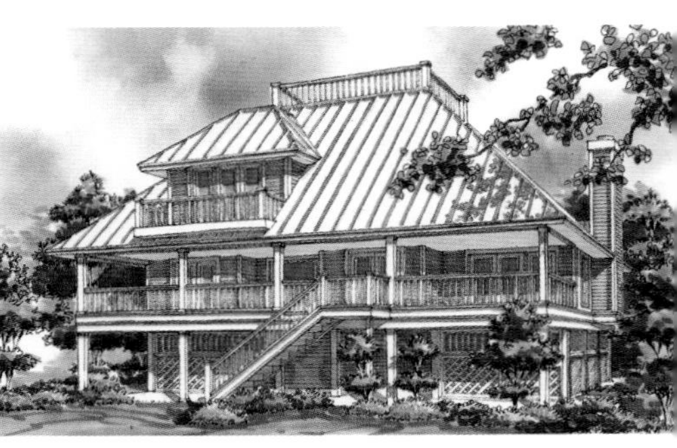

Rear Elevation

Seagrove Beach — VPDS01-Plan 6682 — 1-866-525-9374

Total Living	First Floor	Second Floor	Bed	Bath	Width	Depth	Foundation	Price Category
2659 sq ft	1637 sq ft	1022 sq ft	3	3-1/2	50' 0"	54' 0"	Piling	G

Design Features

- The great room boasts a corner fireplace and island entertainment center, and brings in spectacular views through the walls of glass.
- The gourmet kitchen includes an island eating bar, a serving bar to the veranda, ample counter space and easy access to the dining and great room.
- A vaulted ceiling soars over the master suite, which features a private balcony, "his-and-her" walk-in closets and a spacious bath.

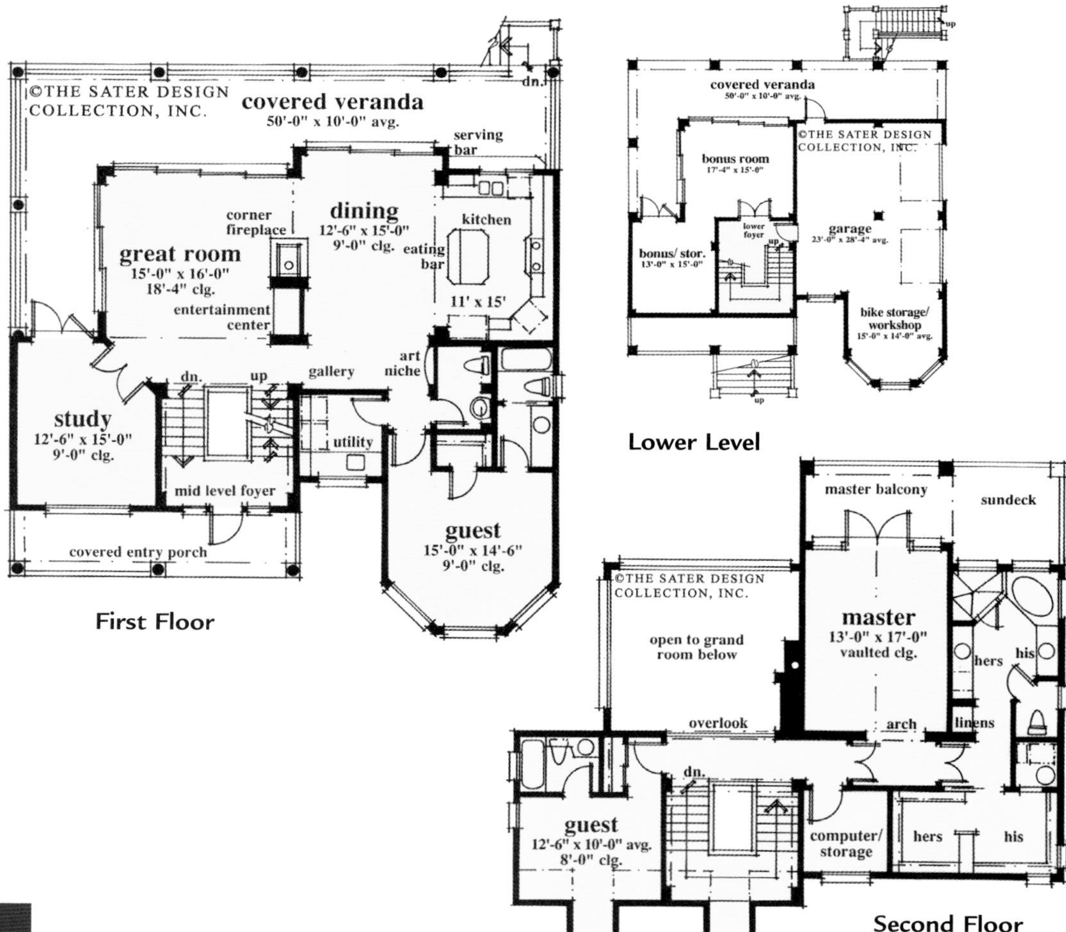

First Floor

Lower Level

Second Floor

Rear Elevation

Tucker Town Way — VPDS01-6692 — 1-866-525-9374

Total Living	First Floor	Lower Level	Bed	Bath	Width	Depth	Foundation	Price Category
2190 sq ft	2190 sq ft	N/A	3	2	59' 8"	54' 0"	Slab	F

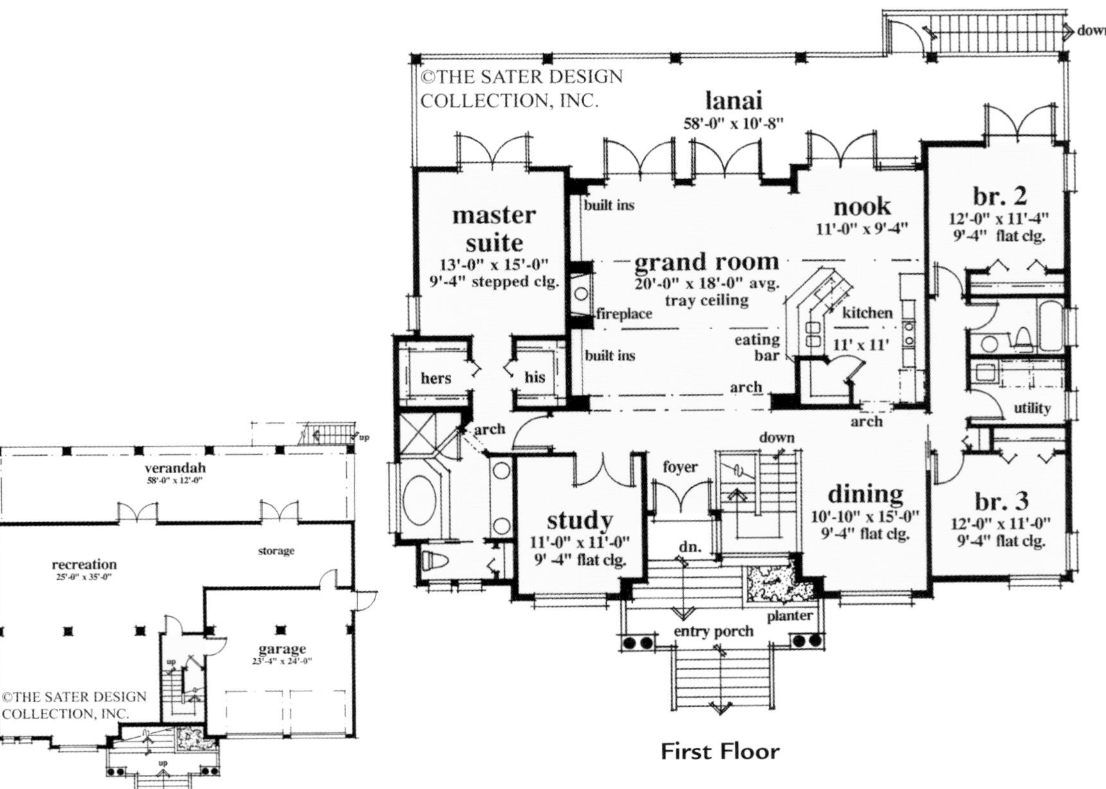

Lower Level

First Floor

Design Features

- The foyer opens to the grand room with fireplace.
- A well-crafted kitchen has wrapping counter space.
- A secluded master suite offers lanai access.
- The opulent master bath has twin lavatories.
- Two secondary bedrooms share a full bath.

Rear Elevation

Palma Rios — VPDS01-Plan 6863 — 1-866-525-9374

Total Living	First Floor	Second Floor	Bed	Bath	Width	Depth	Foundation	Price Code
2843 sq ft	1562 sq ft	1281 sq ft	4	2-1/2	40' 0"	67' 0"	Slab	G

Design Features

- A central turret anchors a series of varied gables and rooflines, square columns and a spare balustrade define the entry porch, all of which enhance the exterior.
- The gourmet kitchen offers a center work island, walk-in pantry, a built-in desk and an eating bar that connects to the dining and leisure room.
- The master retreat sits under a tray ceiling and boasts a private master porch, spacious bath and large walk-in closet.

Rear Elevation

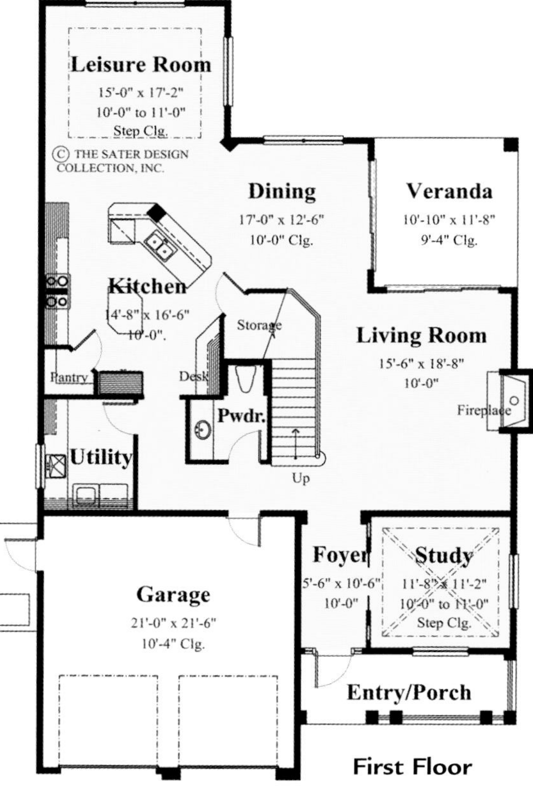

First Floor

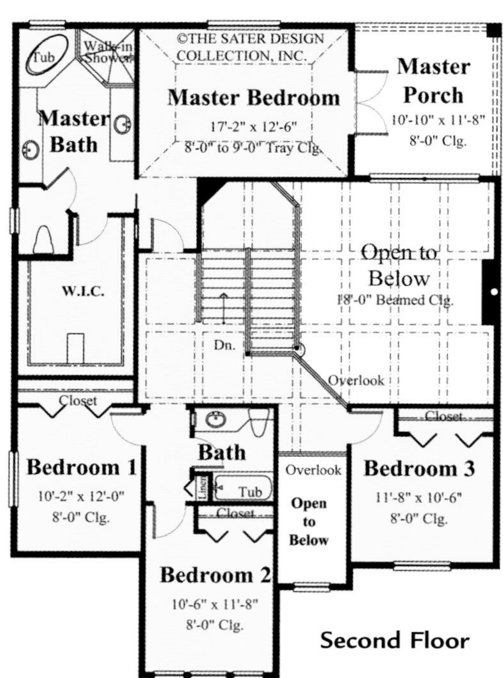

Second Floor

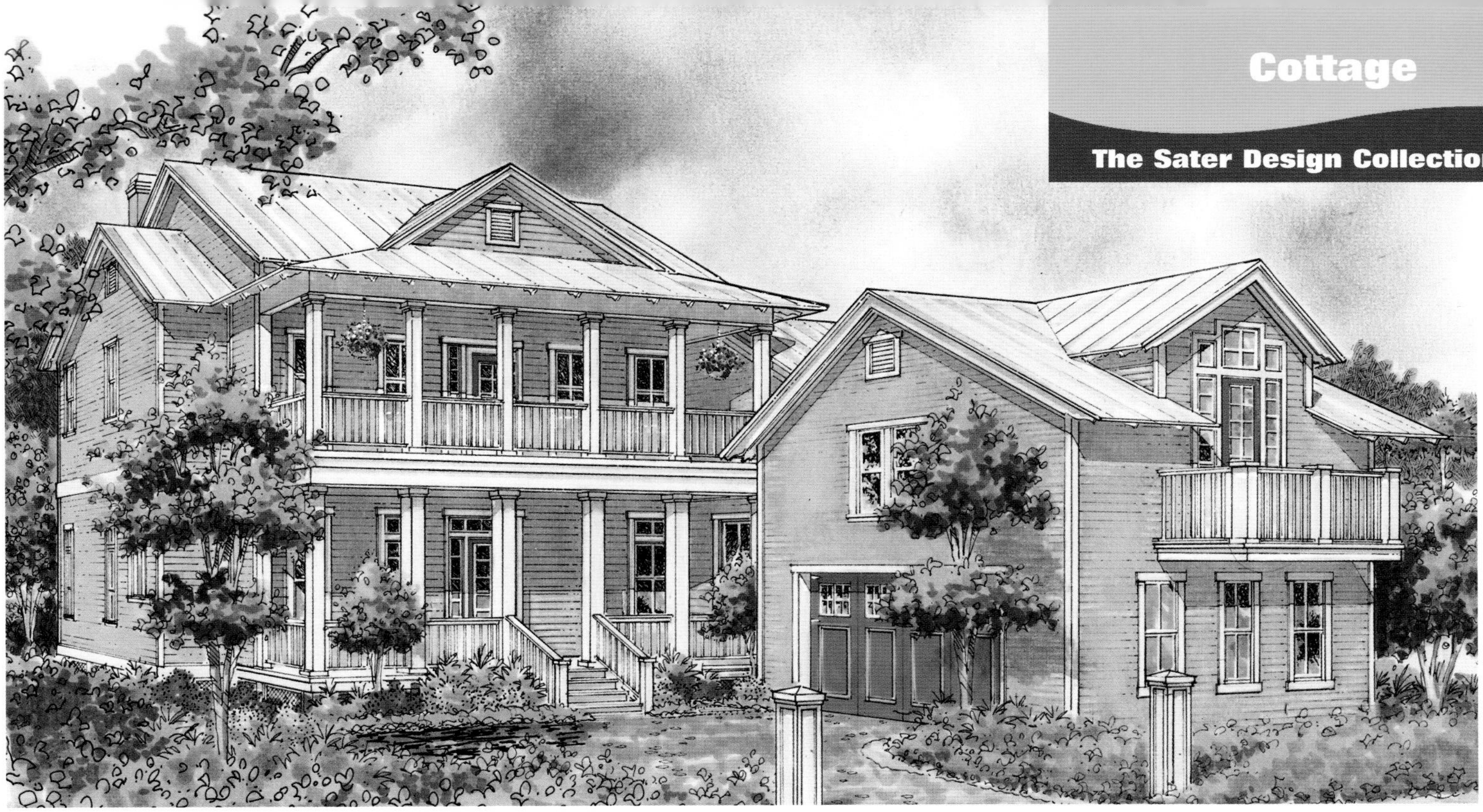

Carlile Bay — VPDS01-Plan 6755 — 1-866-525-9374

Total Living	First Floor	Second Floor	Bonus	Bed	Bath	Width	Depth	Foundation	Price Code
3348 sq ft	1766 sq ft	1582 sq ft	434 sq ft	5	5-1/2	56' 0"	80' 0"	Pier	H

First Floor

Second Floor

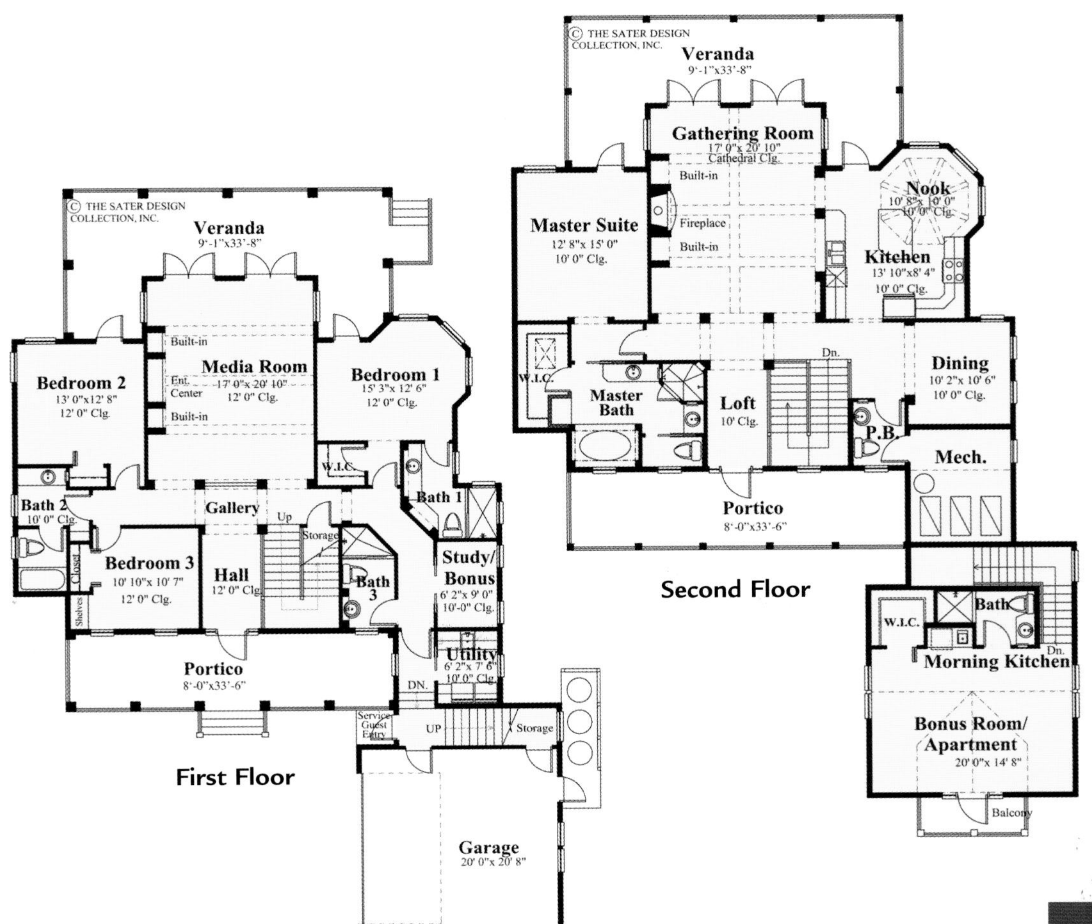

Design Features

- Wide verandas and a double portico enrich the façade of this coastal cottage.
- Both the media and gathering rooms boast dual French doors to the veranda, built-in cabinetry and a fireplace.
- The kitchen is located on the upper level and features a breakfast nook and easy access to the gathering and dining rooms.
- A bonus room/apartment is located over the garage and features a morning kitchen.

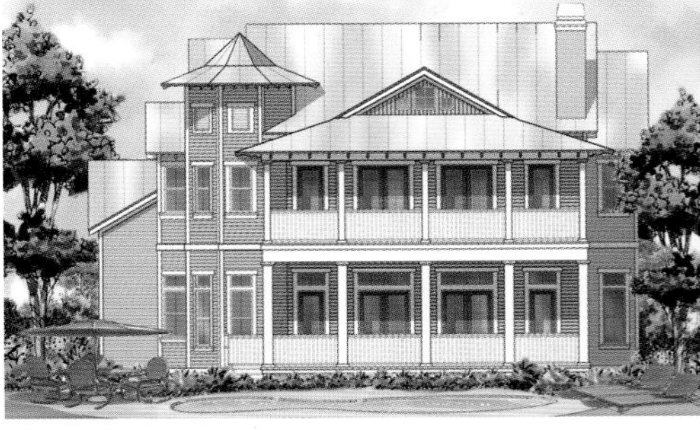

Rear Elevation

Pennyhill — VPDG01-294 — 1-866-525-9374

Total Living	First Floor	Bonus	Bed	Bath	Width	Depth	Foundation	Price Category
1867 sq ft	1867 sq ft	422 sq ft	3	2-1/2	71' 0"	56' 4"	Crawl Space*	D

Design Features

- This country home surprises with an open floor plan featuring a great room with cathedral ceiling.
- The kitchen with an angled counter opens to the breakfast area and great room for easy entertaining.
- The secluded master bedroom has a cathedral ceiling and nearby access to the deck.
- Skylights over the tub accent the luxurious master bath.
- A bonus room over the garage makes expansion easy.

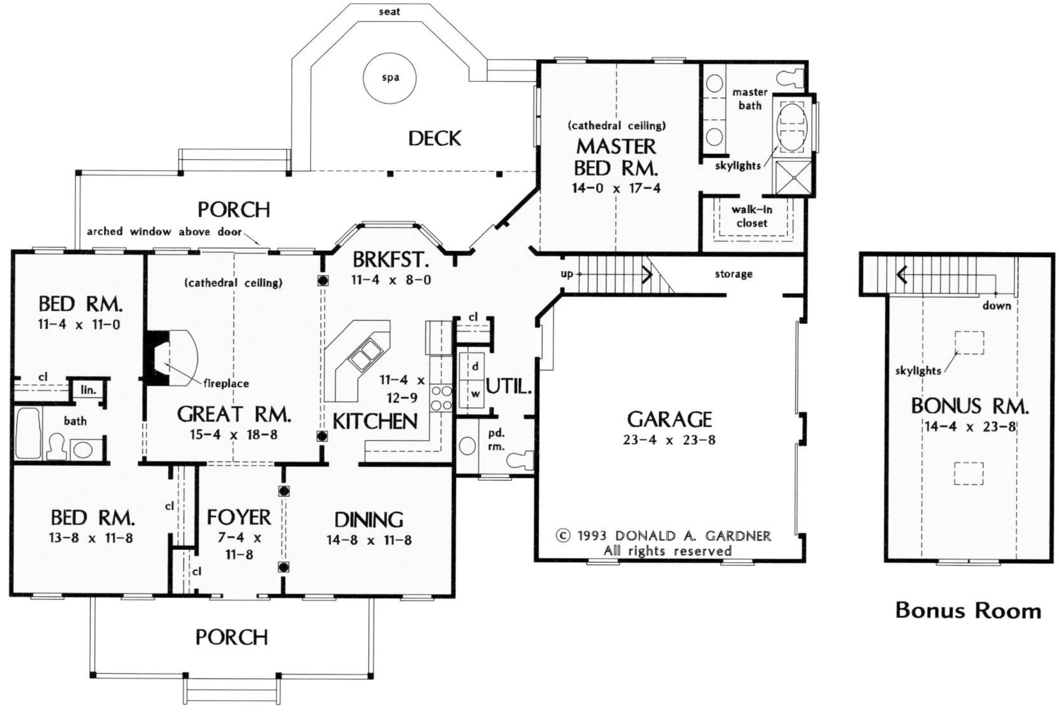

First Floor

Bonus Room

Rear View

Please note: Home photographed may differ from blueprint.

***Other options available. See page 255.**

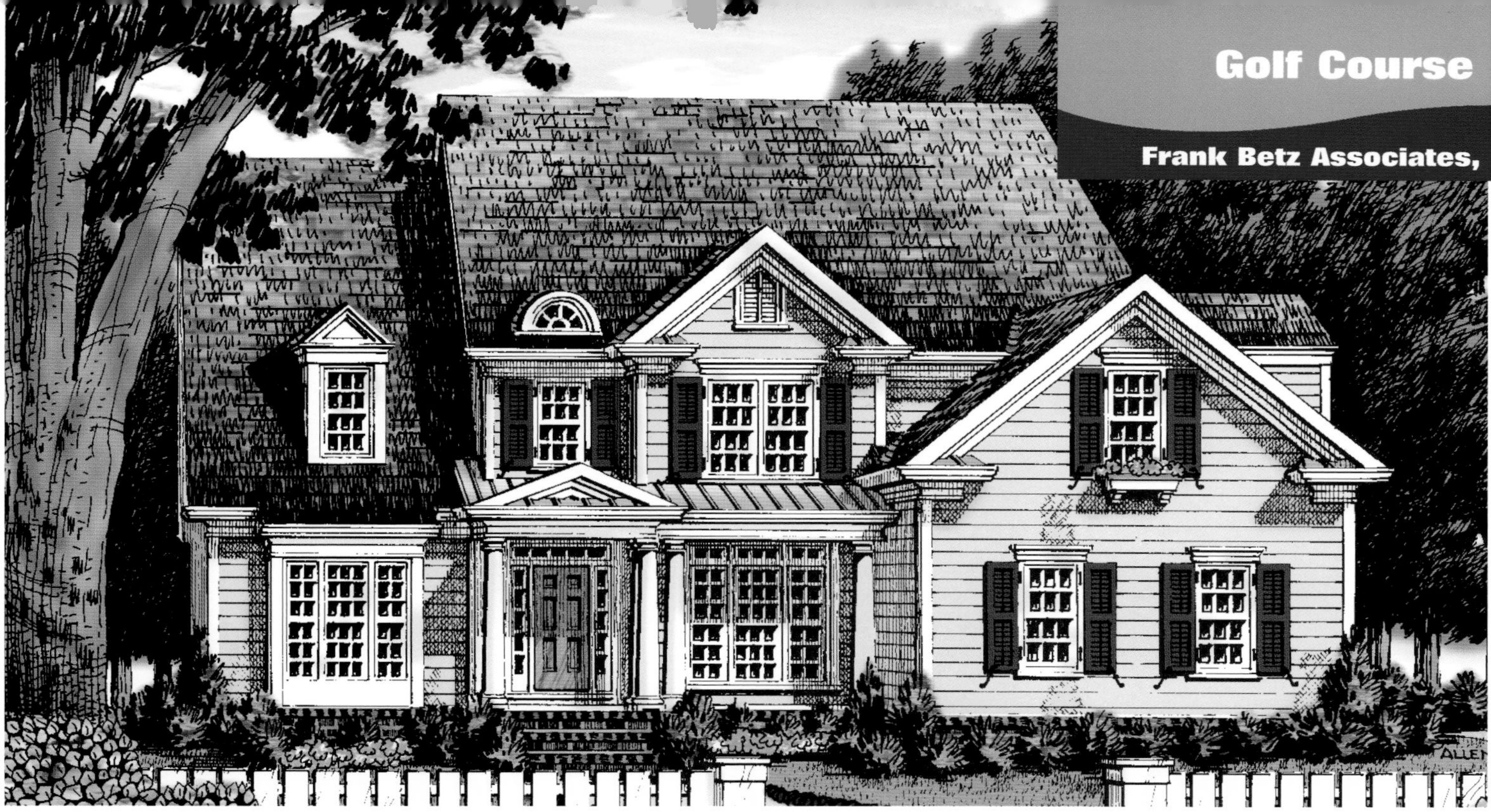

Ardsley — VPFB01-Plan 3624 — 1-866-525-9374

Total Living	First Floor	Second Floor	Opt. Bonus	Bed	Bath	Width	Depth	Foundation	Price Category
2262 sq ft	1784 sq ft	478 sq ft	336 sq ft	3	2-1/2	54' 0"	54' 6"	Basement or Crawl Space	G

First Floor

Second Floor

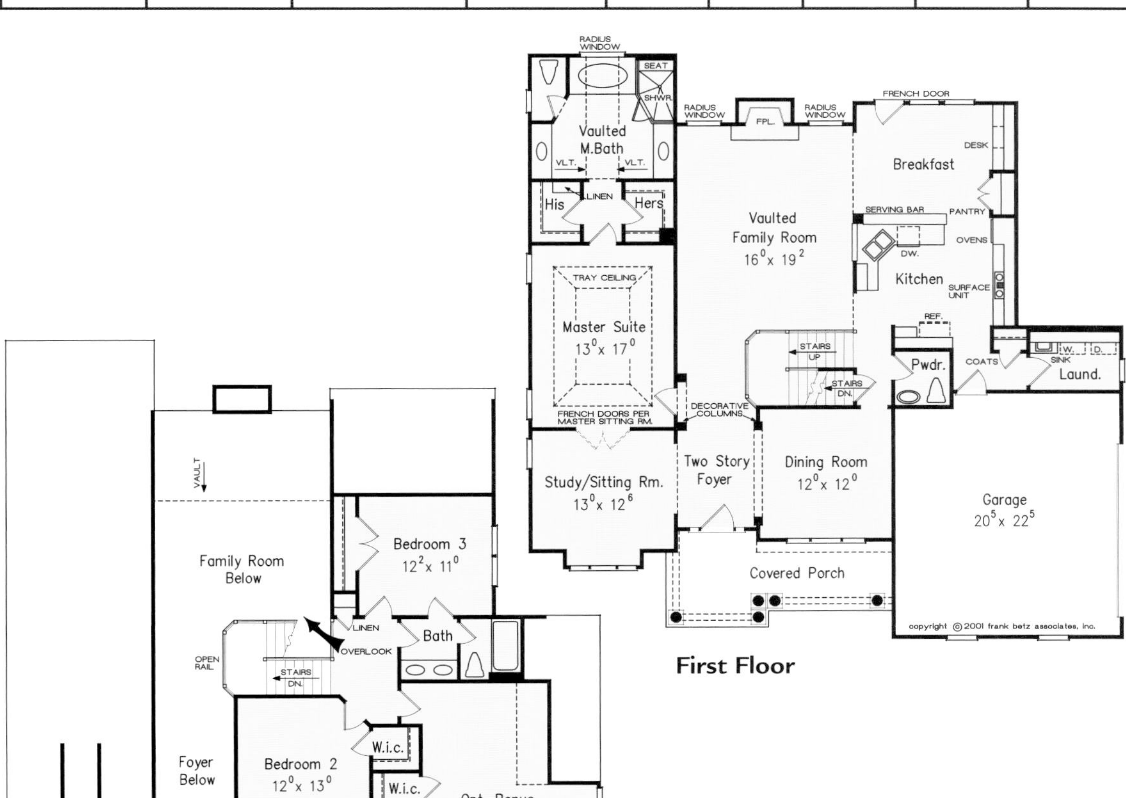

Design Features

- Nothing creates a cottage-like appeal better than a covered front porch, welcoming you in to make yourself at home.
- Just off the foyer, a study makes an ideal location for a home office which converts into a master suite sitting area if you so choose.
- Special extras, such as the built-in message center and an optional bonus room, make this design a highly functional choice for today's busy family.

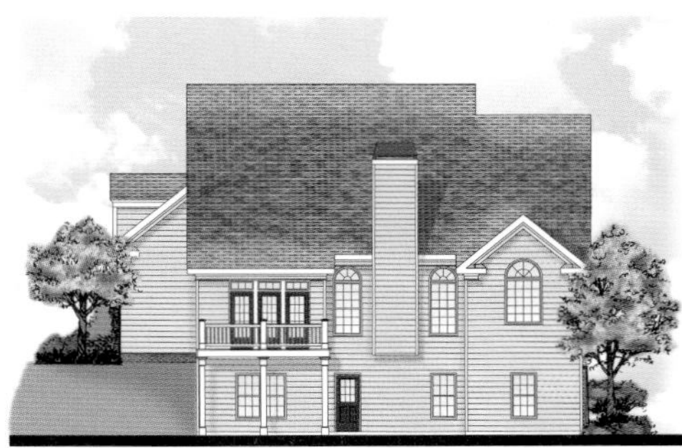

Rear Elevation

Toscana — VPDS01-6758 — 1-866-525-9374

Total Living	First Floor	Opt. Bath	Bed	Bath	Width	Depth	Foundation	Price Category
2329 sq ft	2329 sq ft	70 sq ft	3 + Study	2	65' 0"	55' 2"	Slab	F

Design Features

- Arches and columns maintain a constant theme throughout this home.
- The contemporary gourmet kitchen has ample cabinet and countertop space.
- The airy great room and leisure room have retreating doors to the loggia.
- An oversized walk-in shower spans the width of the bath behind the whirlpool tub.
- Striking tray and coffered ceilings are throughout the home.

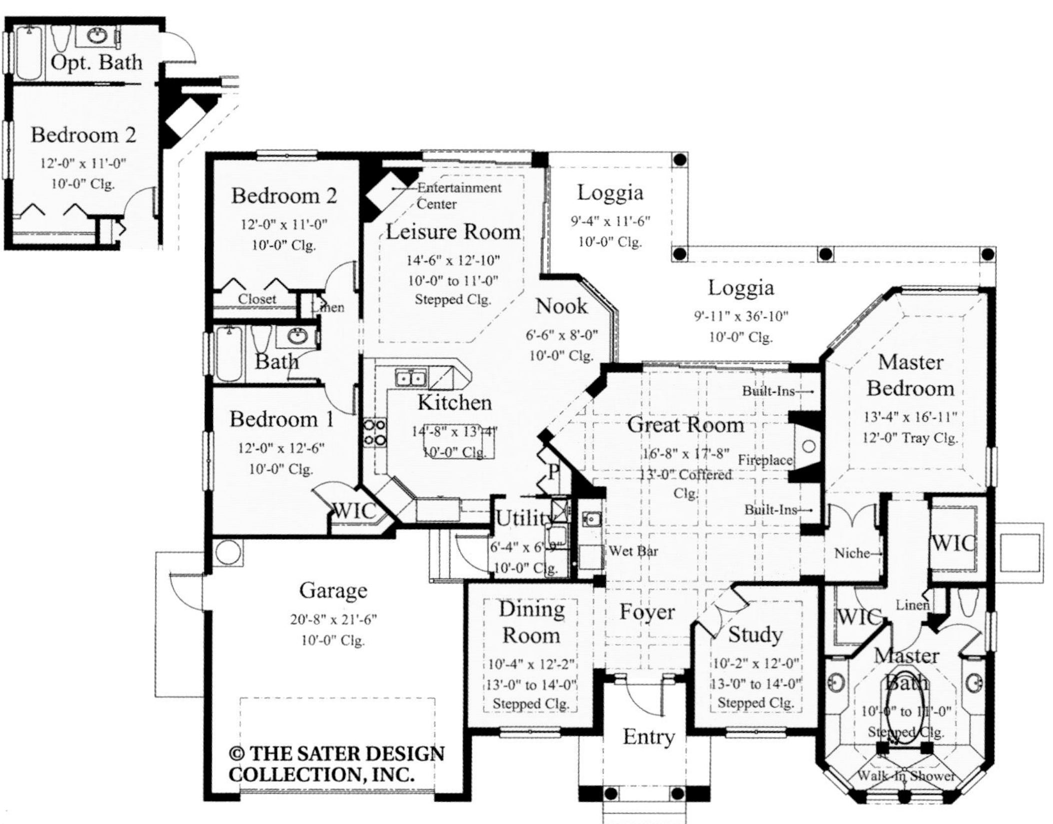

First Floor

Pool & Loggia View

Please note: Home photographed may differ from blueprint.

Not available for construction in Lee or Collier Counties, Florida.

Edgewater — VPDG01-Plan 1009 — 1-866-525-9374

Total Living	First Floor	Bonus	Bed	Bath	Width	Depth	Foundation	Price Category
2818 sq ft	2818 sq ft	N/A	4	3	70' 0"	69' 10"	Crawl Space*	F

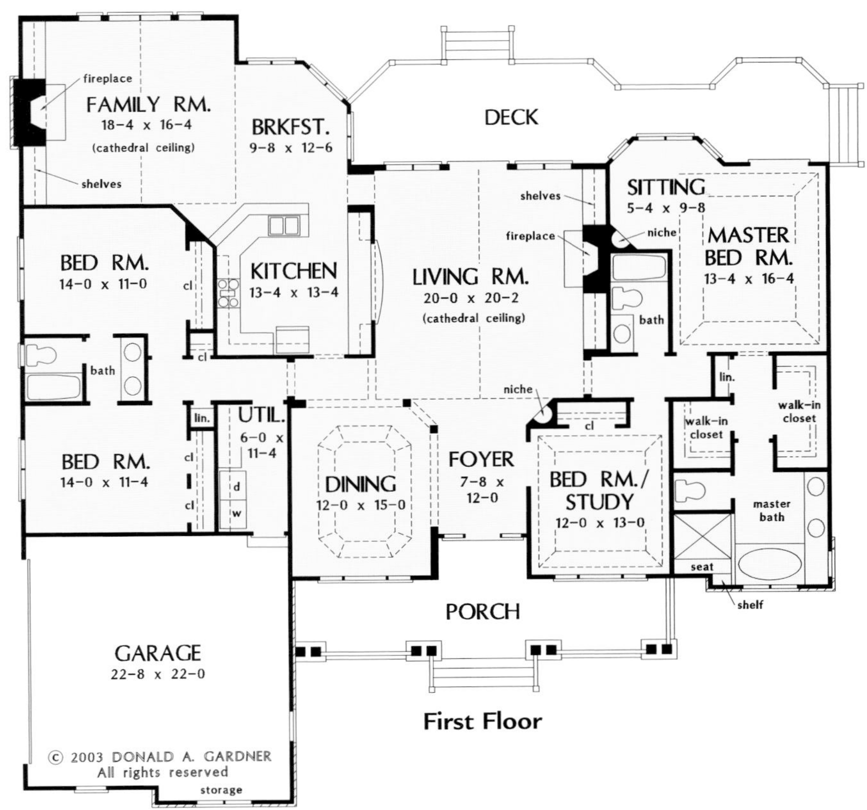

First Floor

Design Features

- For the family that needs a lot of square footage in a one-story design but doesn't want to live on two floors, the *Edgewater* is home.
- The kitchen has a handy pass-thru to the great room and features angled countertops.
- Tucked away, the family room is just off the breakfast room and is complete with fireplace.
- Columns and a tray ceiling distinguish the dining room, creating a formal room for entertaining.

Rear View

Please note: Home photographed may differ from blueprint.

*Other options available. See page 255.

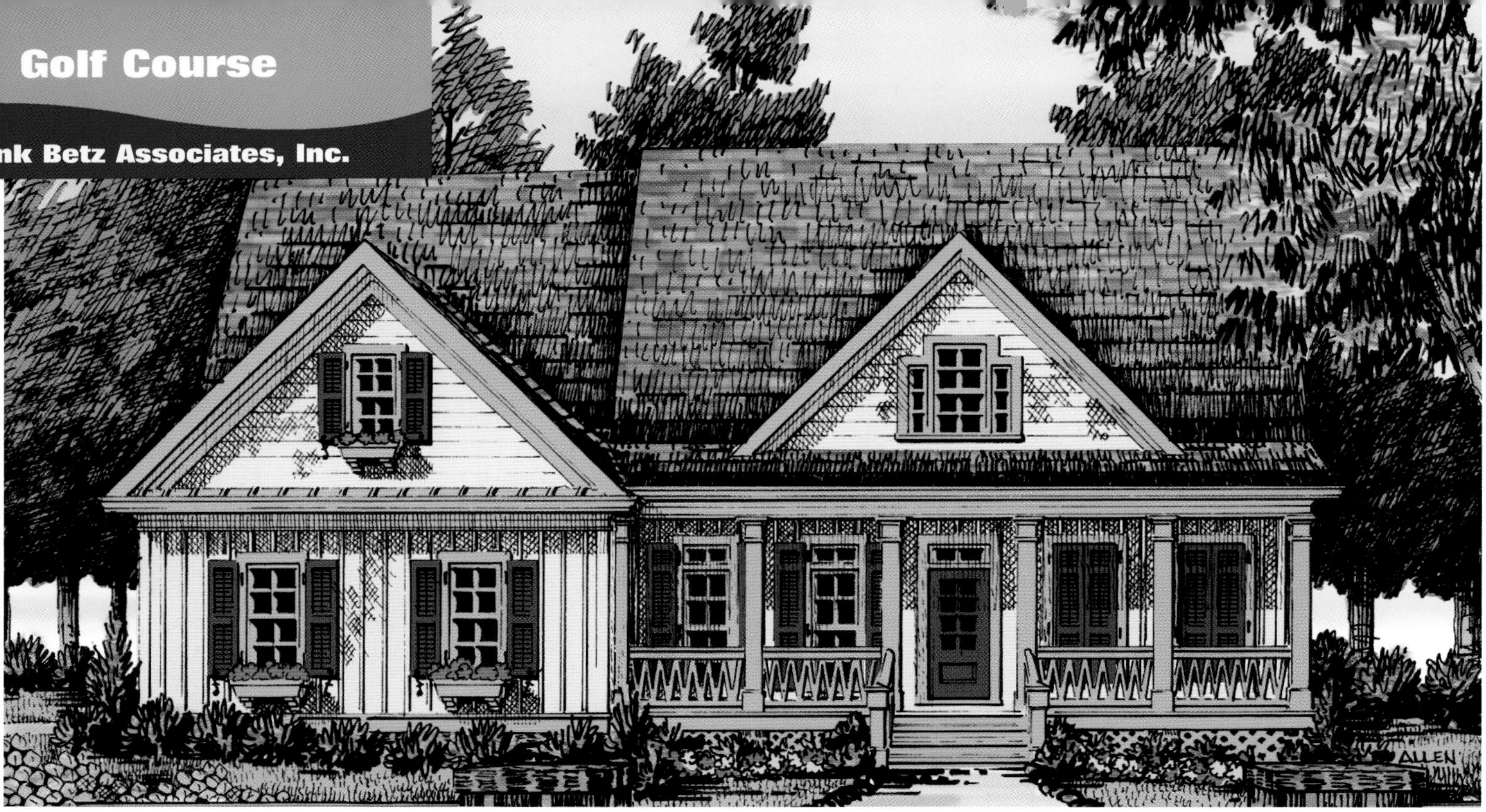

Azalea Park — VPFB01-Plan 3894 — 1-866-525-9374

Total Living	First Floor	Second Floor	Bed	Bath	Width	Depth	Foundation	Price Category
2182 sq ft	1455 sq ft	727 sq ft	3	2-1/2	53' 0"	55' 0"	Basement, Crawl Space or Slab	G

Design Features

- This cozy cottage is as functional inside as it is charming on the outside.
- The kitchen is equipped with a center island to aid in meal preparation.
- A mudroom off the garage adjoins the laundry room, keeping coats and shoes in their place.
- The screened porch makes a great spot for relaxing or outdoor entertaining.

First Floor

Second Floor

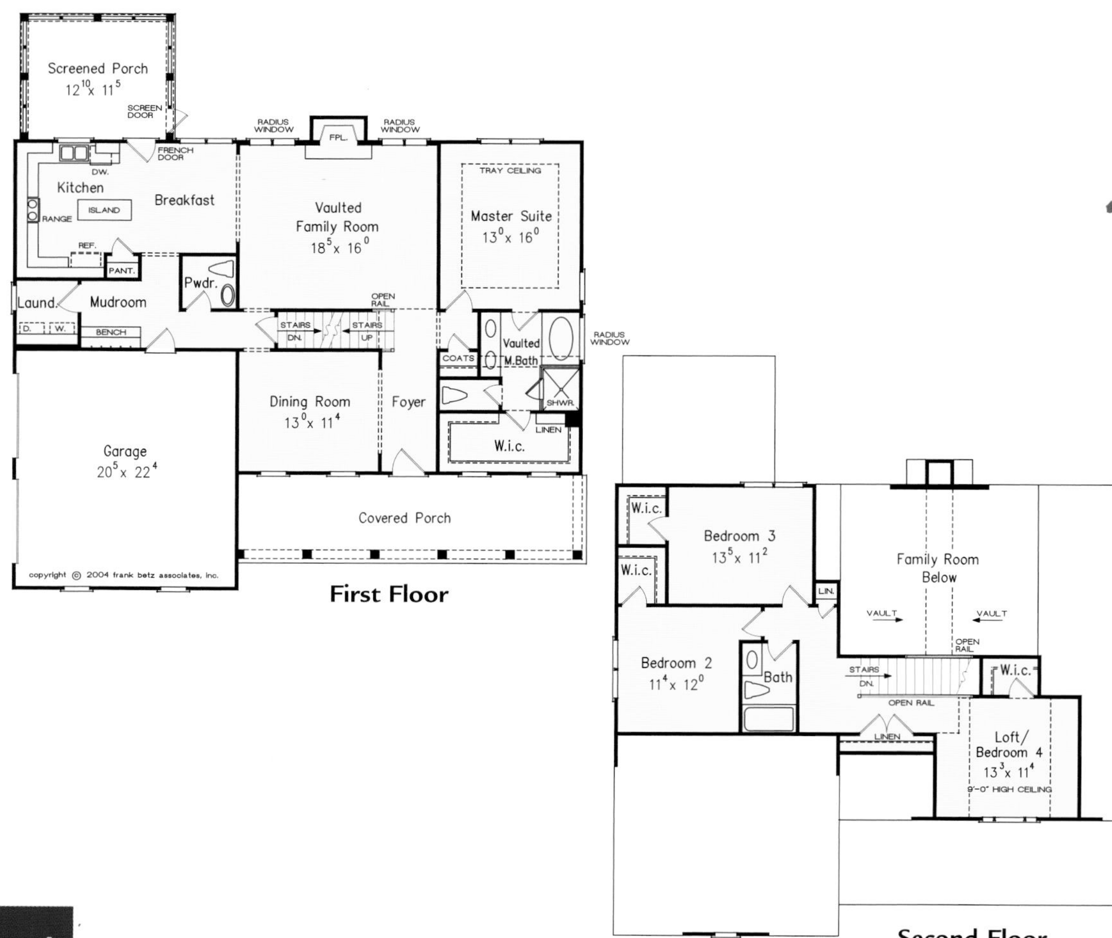

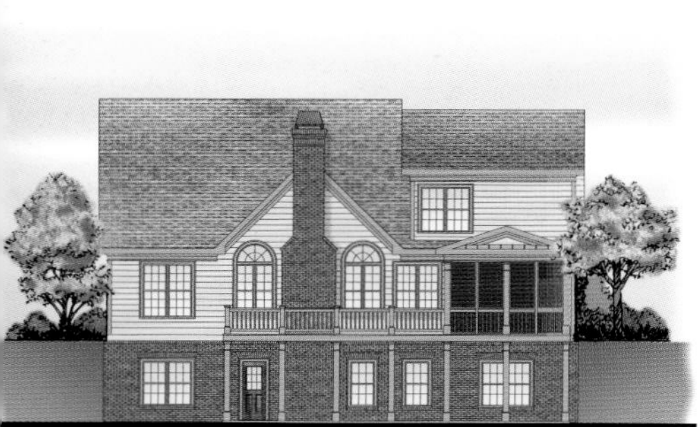

Rear Elevation

St. Thomas — VPDS01-6770 — 1-866-525-9374

Total Living	First Floor	Bonus	Bed	Bath	Width	Depth	Foundation	Price Category
1911 sq ft	1911 sq ft	N/A	3 + Study	2	64' 0"	55' 0"	Slab	E

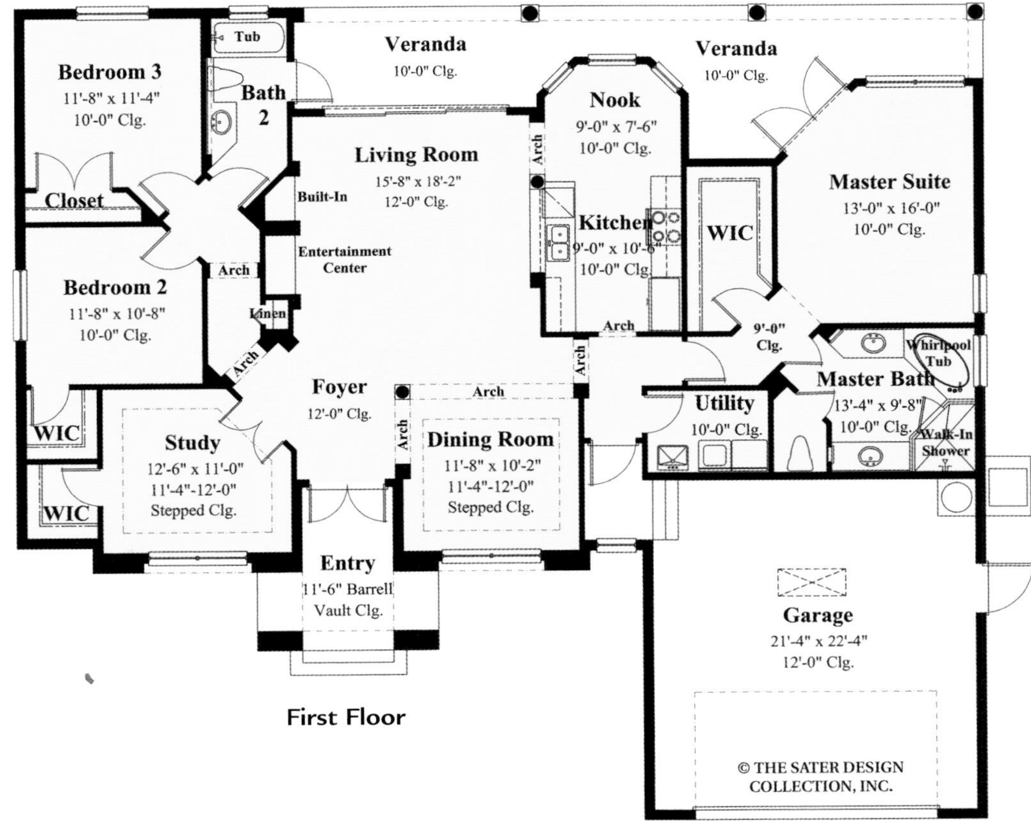

First Floor

Design Features

- Double-doors open to a foyer through an arched covered entry.
- This split-bedroom plan offers privacy from the public spaces.
- A generous living room with built-ins opens to the veranda through a wall of glass.
- Secondary bedrooms share a bath that doubles as a pool bath.
- Arched entries throughout the home add a touch of elegance.

Rear Elevation

Not available for construction in Collier County, Florida.

Crowne Canyon — VPDG01-Plan 732-D — 1-866-525-9374

Total Living	First Floor	Basement	Bed	Bath	Width	Depth	Foundation	Price Category
4776 sq ft	3040 sq ft	1736 sq ft	5	4-1/2	106' 5"	104' 2"	Hillside Walkout	J

Please note: Home photographed may differ from blueprint.

Design Features

- Exposed wood beams enhance the magnificent cathedral ceilings throughout the home.
- Fireplaces add warmth and ambience to the multiple rooms.
- The kitchen is complete with its center island, pantry and ample room for cooking.
- A three-and-a-half car garage allows space for storage or a golf cart.

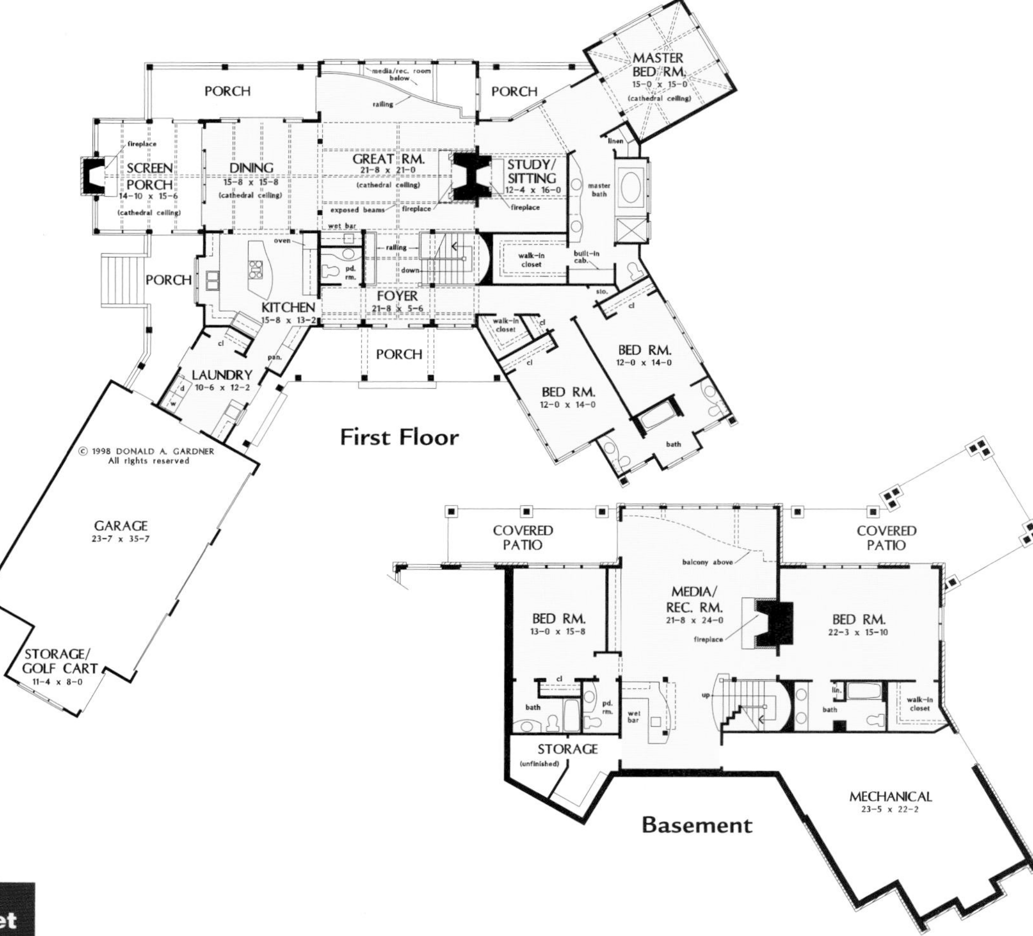

Rear Elevation

Colonnade — VPFB01-Plan 3699 — 1-866-525-9374

Total Living	First Floor	Second Floor	Opt. Bonus	Bed	Bath	Width	Depth	Foundation	Price Category
2138 sq ft	1589 sq ft	549 sq ft	248 sq ft	4	3	53' 0"	47' 6"	Basement or Crawl Space	H

First Floor

Second Floor

Design Features

- Today, function and flexibility are a must. The *Colonnade* was created to provide both.
- The family room, kitchen and breakfast area connect to create the home's center point.
- The size and location of the main-floor bedroom also make it a perfect home office or den.
- Optional bonus space on the upper level of this home gives homeowners the opportunity to add additional living space to their home.

Rear Elevation

Cerafino — VPDS01-Plan 6504 — 1-866-525-9374

Total Living	First Floor	Bonus	Bed	Bath	Width	Depth	Foundation	Price Category
1608 sq ft	1608 sq ft	N/A	2 + Study	2	44' 0"	74' 0"	Slab	F

Design Features

- The front elevation features a grand recessed arch entryway, transom windows and decorative corbels.
- The master suite, great room and dining room open to the Solana.
- The kitchen offers a center work island, plenty of counter space and easy access to the dining and great room.
- To ensure privacy, the master bedroom is tucked away from the guest room and primary living space.
- The rear Solana is complete with corner fireplace and outdoor grille.

Rear Elevation

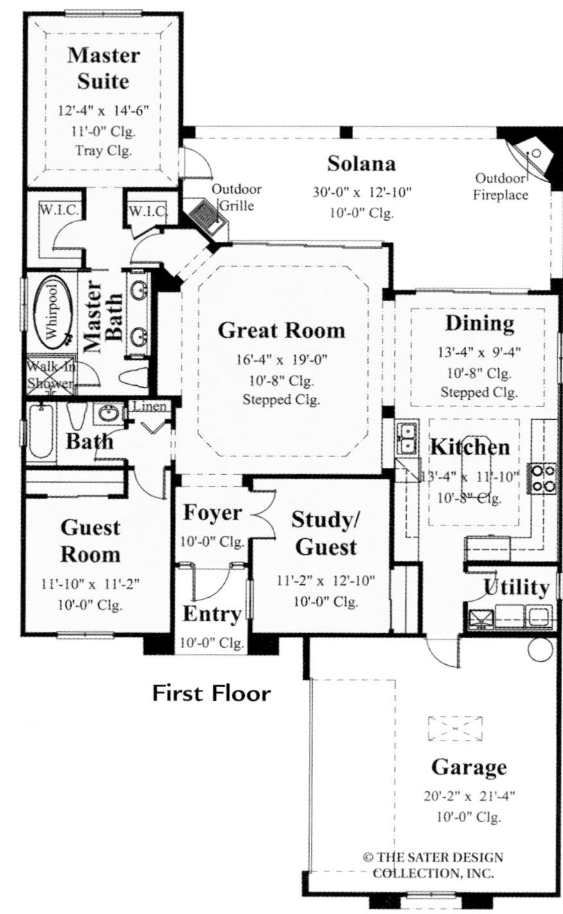

First Floor

Not available for construction in Myrtle Beach, South Carolina

Ryecroft — VPDG01-824-D — 1-866-525-9374

Total Living	First Floor	Basement	Bed	Bath	Width	Depth	Foundation	Price Category
2815 sq ft	1725 sq ft	1090 sq ft	3	3-1/2	59' 0"	59' 4"	Hillside Walkout	F

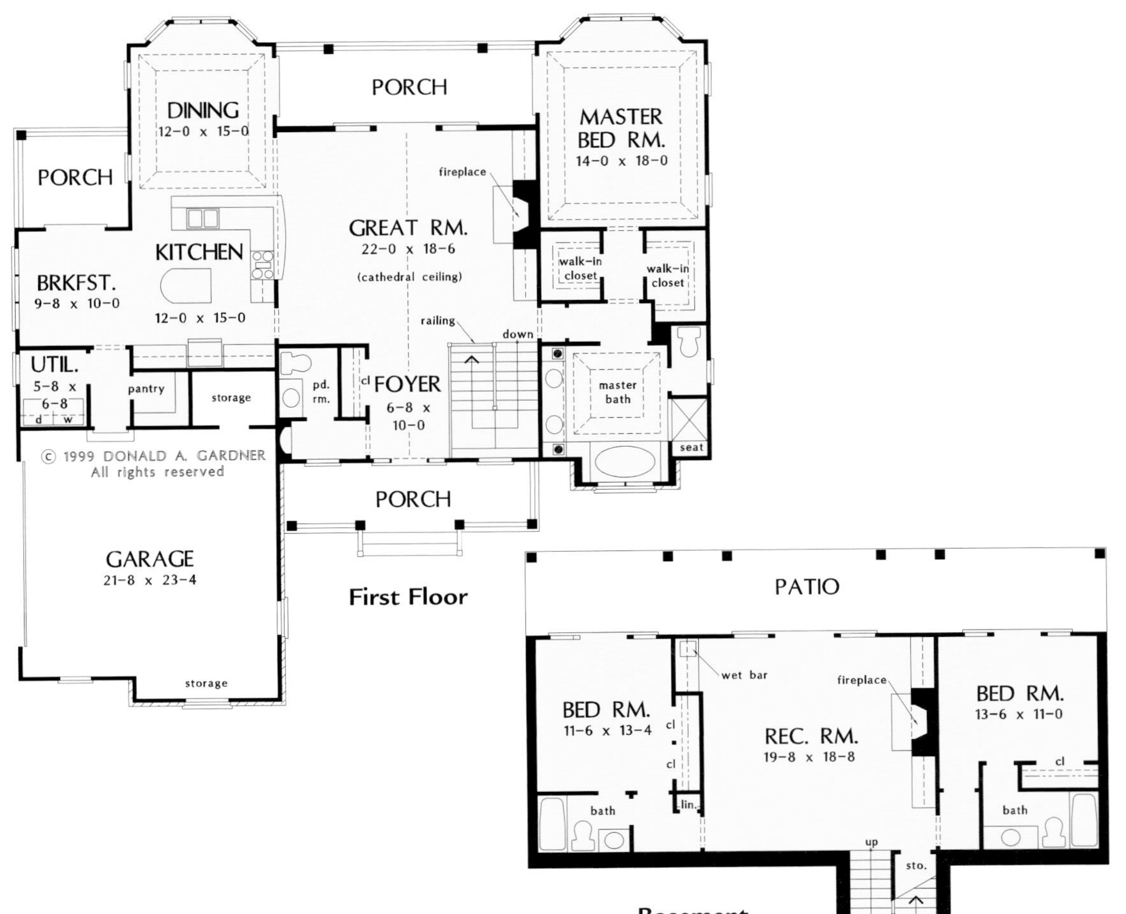

First Floor

Basement

Design Features

- Designed for sloping lots, this home positions its common living areas and master suite on the first floor.
- A generous rec room and two family bedrooms reside on the lower level.
- With a bay window and back-porch access, the master suite boasts dual walk-ins and a luxurious bath.
- Downstairs, two bedrooms and baths flank the rec room with fireplace and wet bar.

Rear View

Please note: Home photographed may differ from blueprint.

Gramercy — VPFB01-Plan 3902 — 1-866-525-9374

Total Living	First Floor	Opt. 2nd Fl.	Bed	Bath	Width	Depth	Foundation	Price Category
2050 sq ft	2050 sq ft	418 sq ft	4	3	60' 0"	56' 0"	Basement, Crawl Space or Slab	F

Design Features

- This quaint one-story home is the perfect starter, empty nester or vacation home.
- With views to the back of the home this house would be ideal in a golf course or mountain community.
- Four bedrooms and an optional second floor ensure there is room for everyone.
- The split-bedroom design gives each resident their privacy.

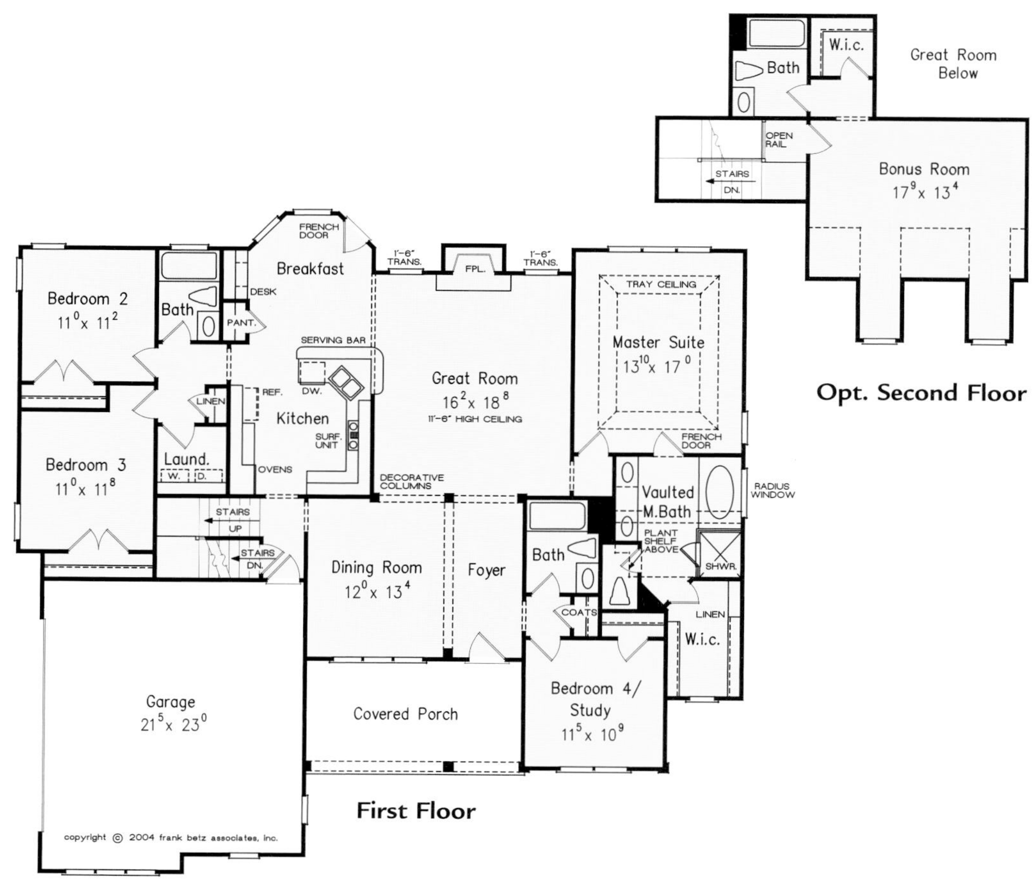

Opt. Second Floor

First Floor

Rear Elevation

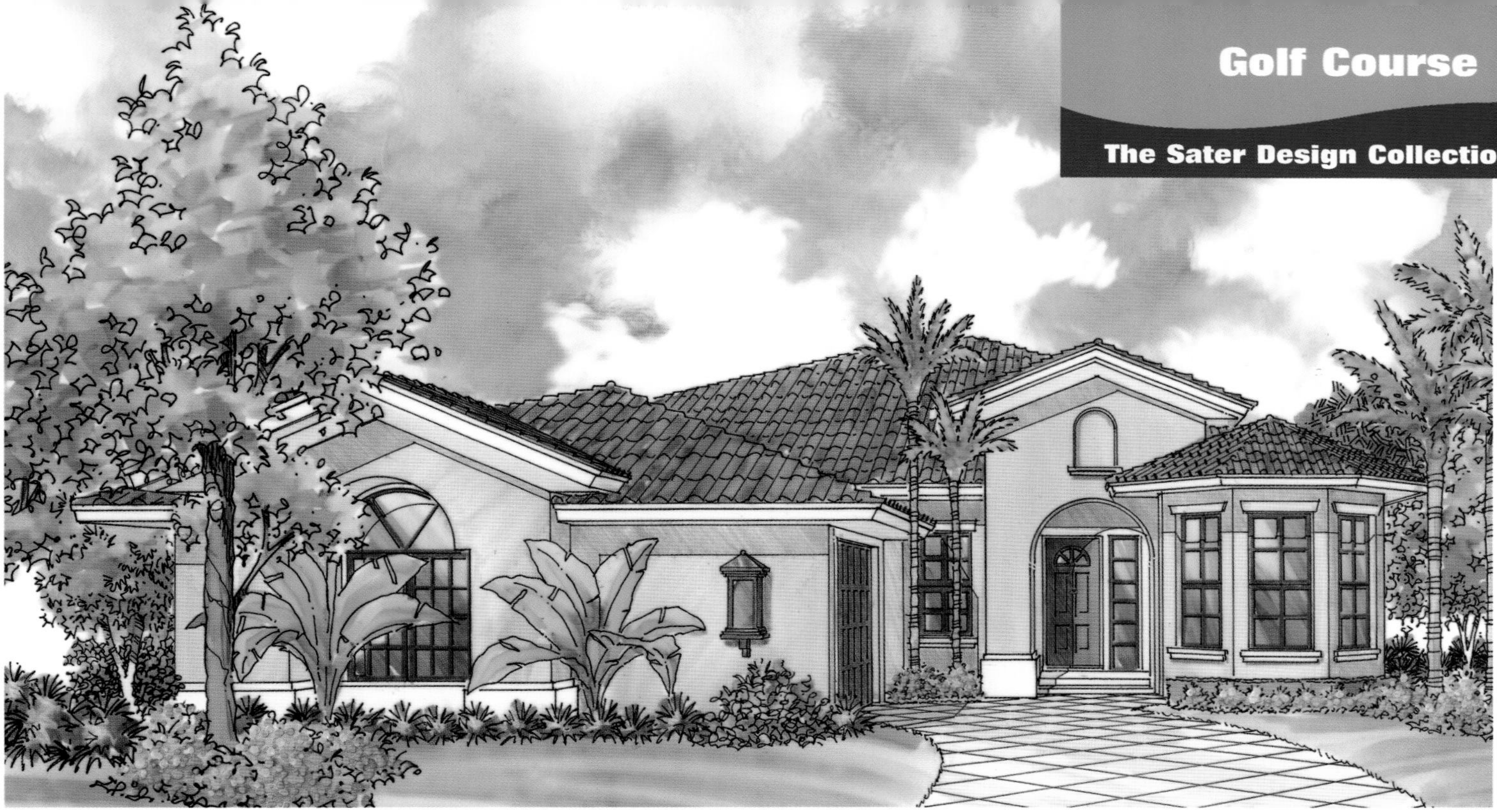

Bianca — VPDS01-Plan 6506 — 1-866-525-9374

Total Living	First Floor	Bonus	Bed	Bath	Width	Depth	Foundation	Price Category
1404 sq ft	1404 sq ft	N/A	2 + Study	2	42' 8"	63' 4"	Slab	E

First Floor

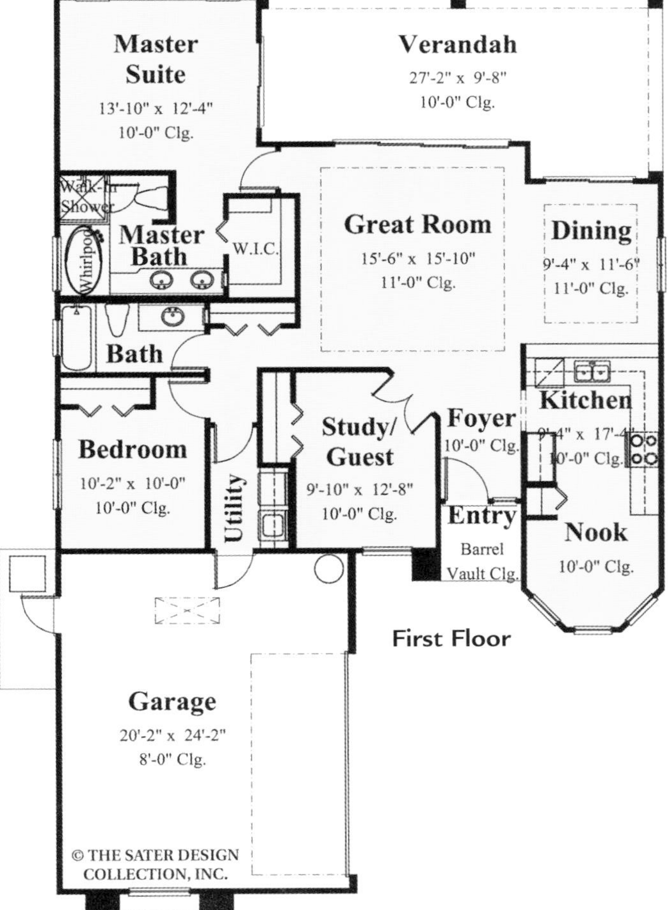

Design Features

- A turreted breakfast nook greets visitors aside the entryway, which features a striking barrel vault ceiling.
- The foyer looks ahead through a disappearing wall of glass that opens the great room to the verandah.
- A pass-thru bar opens the kitchen to the spacious great room and dining room.
- The master suite is tucked away from the common living area and features a luxurious bath and access to the verandah.

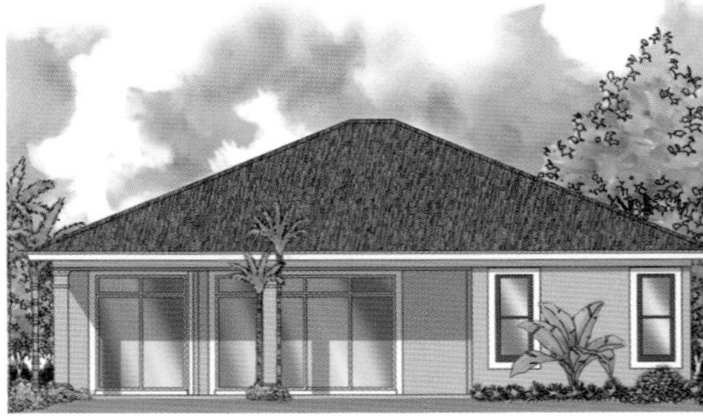

Rear Elevation

Not available for construction in Myrtle Beach, South Carolina

Berkshire — VPDG01-748-D — 1-866-525-9374

Total Living	First Floor	Basement	Bed	Bath	Width	Depth	Foundation	Price Category
3281 sq ft	2065 sq ft	1216 sq ft	4	3-1/2	82' 2"	43' 6"	Hillside Walkout	G

Design Features

- Stone, siding and multiple gables combine beautifully on this walkout basement home.
- Capped by a cathedral ceiling, the great room features a fireplace and built-in shelves.
- Twin walk-in closets and a private bath create a luxury master suite.
- The nearby powder room offers an optional full bath, allowing the study to double as a bedroom.
- Downstairs, a large media/recreation room with wet bar and fireplace separates two bedrooms.

Rear Elevation

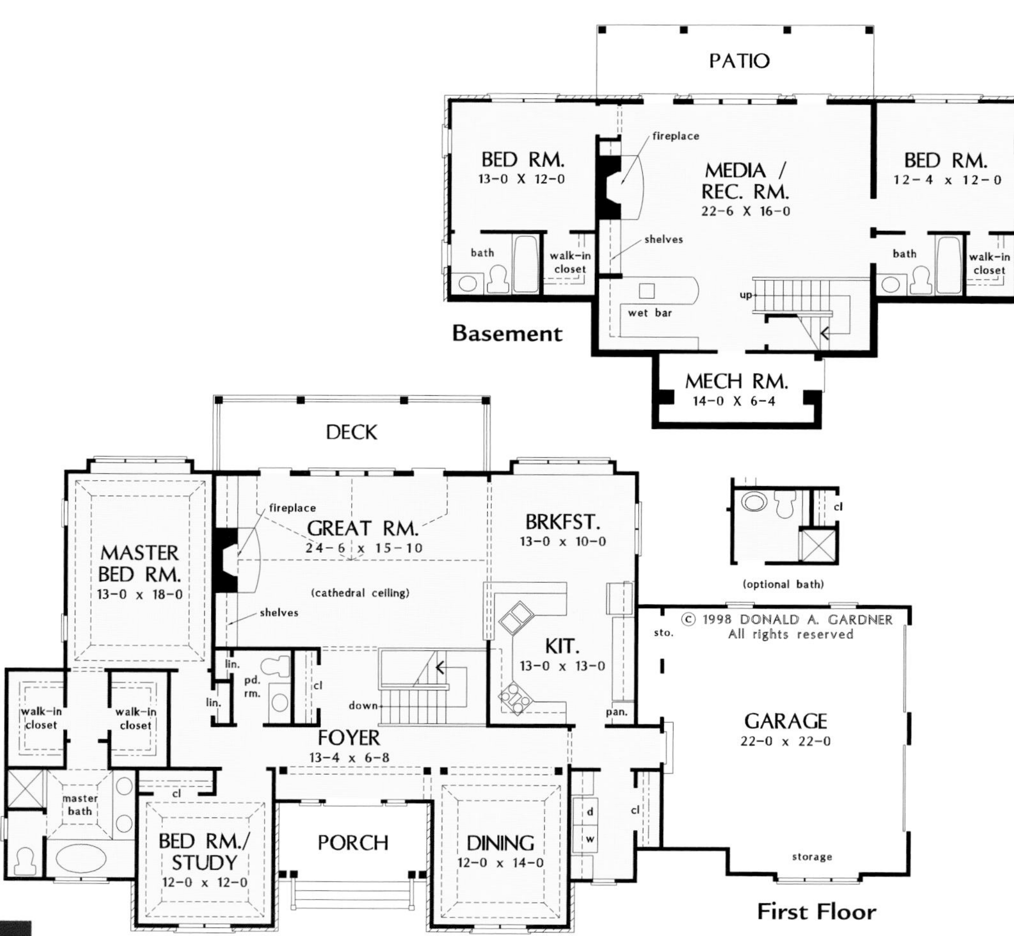

Basement

First Floor

Musgrave — VPFB01-Plan 3526 — 1-866-525-9374

Total Living	First Floor	Second Floor	Opt. Bonus	Bed	Bath	Width	Depth	Foundation	Price Category
2444 sq ft	1720 sq ft	724 sq ft	212 sq ft	4	3	58' 0"	47' 0"	Basement, Crawl Space or Slab	H

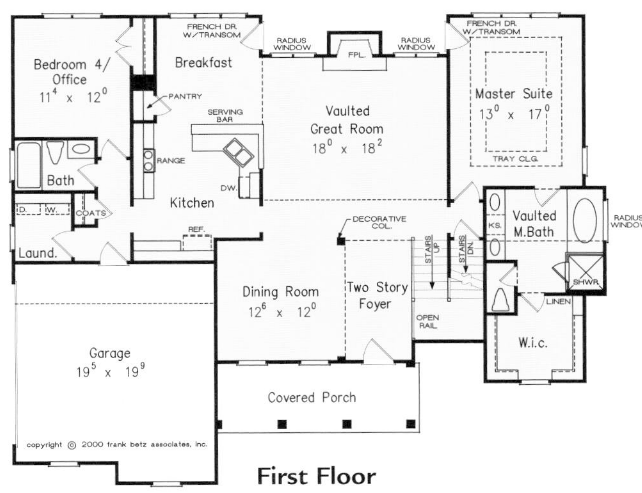

First Floor

Design Features

- A main-floor bedroom is the ideal location for a guest suite with direct access to a full bath.
- Telecommuters may opt to use this space as a home office.
- The second-floor bedrooms have walk-in closets and share a divided bath.
- A computer nook has been thoughtfully incorporated into the upper level, giving children a private and convenient homework station.

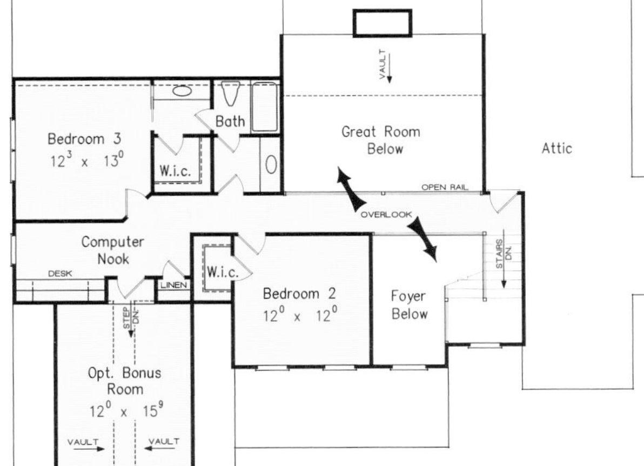

Second Floor

Rear Elevation

Del Rosa — VPDS01-Plan 6510 — 1-866-525-9374

Total Living	First Floor	Bonus	Bed	Bath	Width	Depth	Foundation	Price Category
1919 sq ft	1919 sq ft	N/A	3 + Study	2	47' 2"	78' 0"	Slab	F

Design Features

- The turreted, recessed entry garners attention and gives a sophisticated elegance to the façade of this Mediterranean home.
- The spacious kitchen opens into the dining and great rooms, which feature stepped ceilings and access to the Solana.
- With privacy in mind, the master suite and two secondary bedrooms are located on one side of the home, the dining room and kitchen on the other.

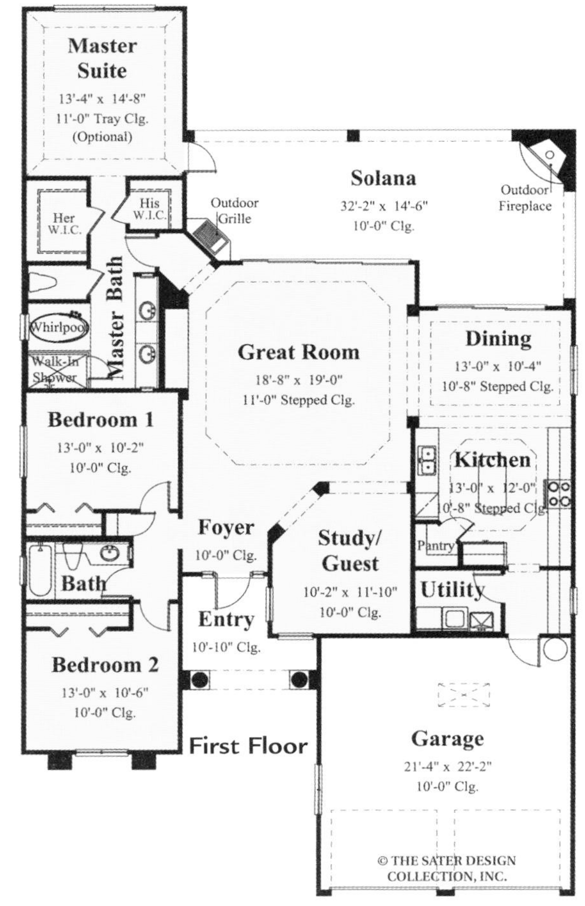

Rear Elevation

Not available for construction in Myrtle Beach, South Carolina

Questling — VPDG01-1004-D — 1-866-525-9374

Total Living	First Floor	Basement	Bed	Bath	Width	Depth	Foundation	Price Category
2971 sq ft	1938 sq ft	1033 sq ft	4	4	77' 6"	42' 7"	Hillside Walkout	F

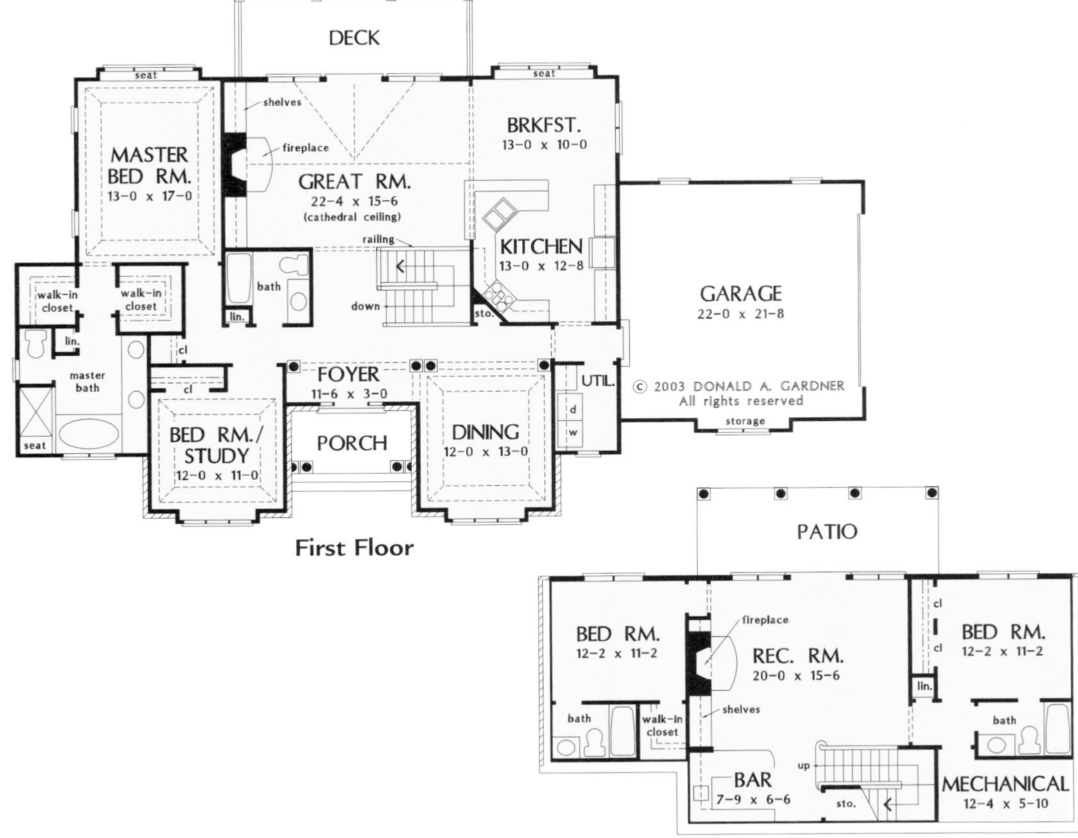

First Floor

Basement

Design Features

- This hillside walkout features traditional style and a more defined floor plan.
- Box-bay windows with metal roofs, decorative windows and transoms create curb appeal.
- A U-shaped stair leads to the lower level with rec room, bar and secondary bedrooms with baths.
- Decorative ceilings, window seats and built-in cabinetry add custom features.

Rear Elevation

Stoneleigh Cottage — VPFB01-Plan 3919 — 1-866-525-9374

Total Living	First Floor	Second Floor	Opt. Bonus	Bed	Bath	Width	Depth	Foundation	Price Category
1975 sq ft	1448 sq ft	527 sq ft	368 sq ft	3	2-1/2	46' 0"	62' 0"	Basement or Crawl Space	G

Design Features

- Especially designed for small and corner lots, the *Stoneleigh Cottage* offers amenities usually reserved for much larger homes.
- Inside, the open floor plan allows for easy flow between rooms, making entertaining a breeze.
- Upstairs, there are two additional bedrooms, both with walk-in closets and an optional bonus room.
- The master suite encompasses one wing of the home. This suite has a back wall of windows allowing in both natural light and rear views.

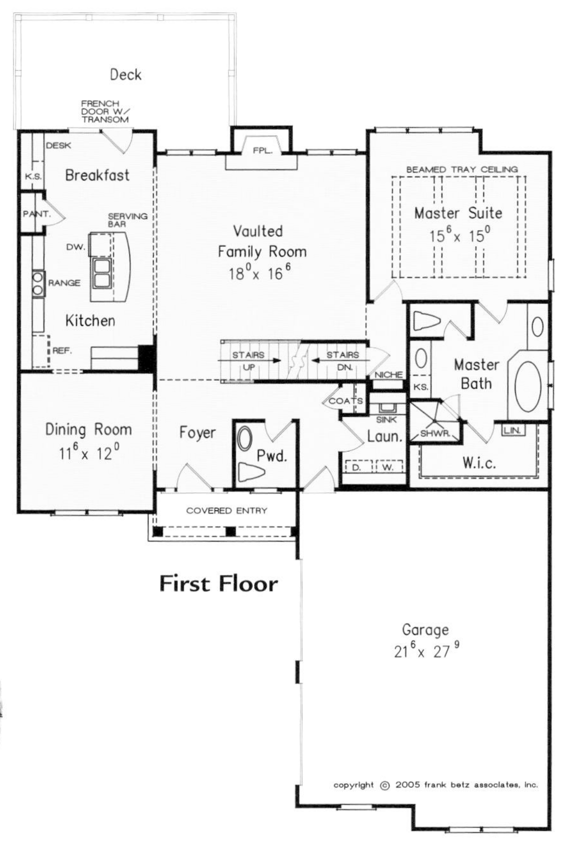

First Floor

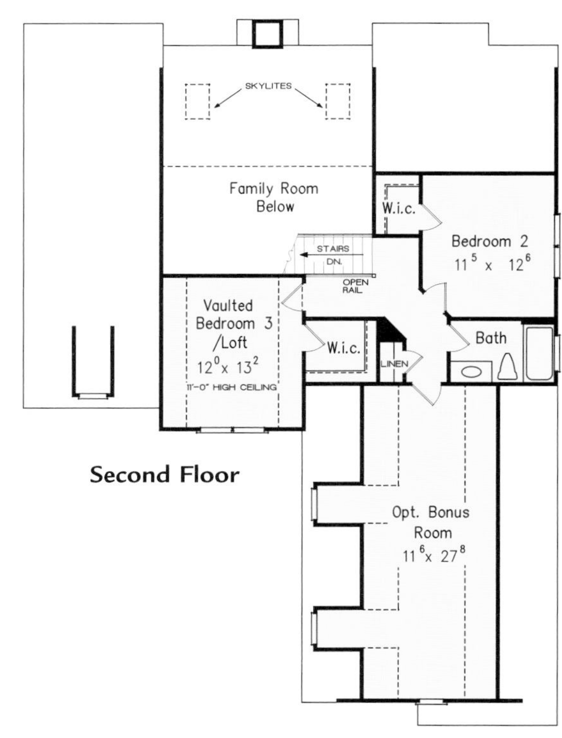

Second Floor

Rear Elevation

Aldwin — VPDS01-6771 — 1-866-525-9374

Total Living	First Floor	Bonus	Bed	Bath	Width	Depth	Foundation	Price Category
2028 sq ft	2028 sq ft	N/A	3	2	60' 8"	59' 10"	Slab	F

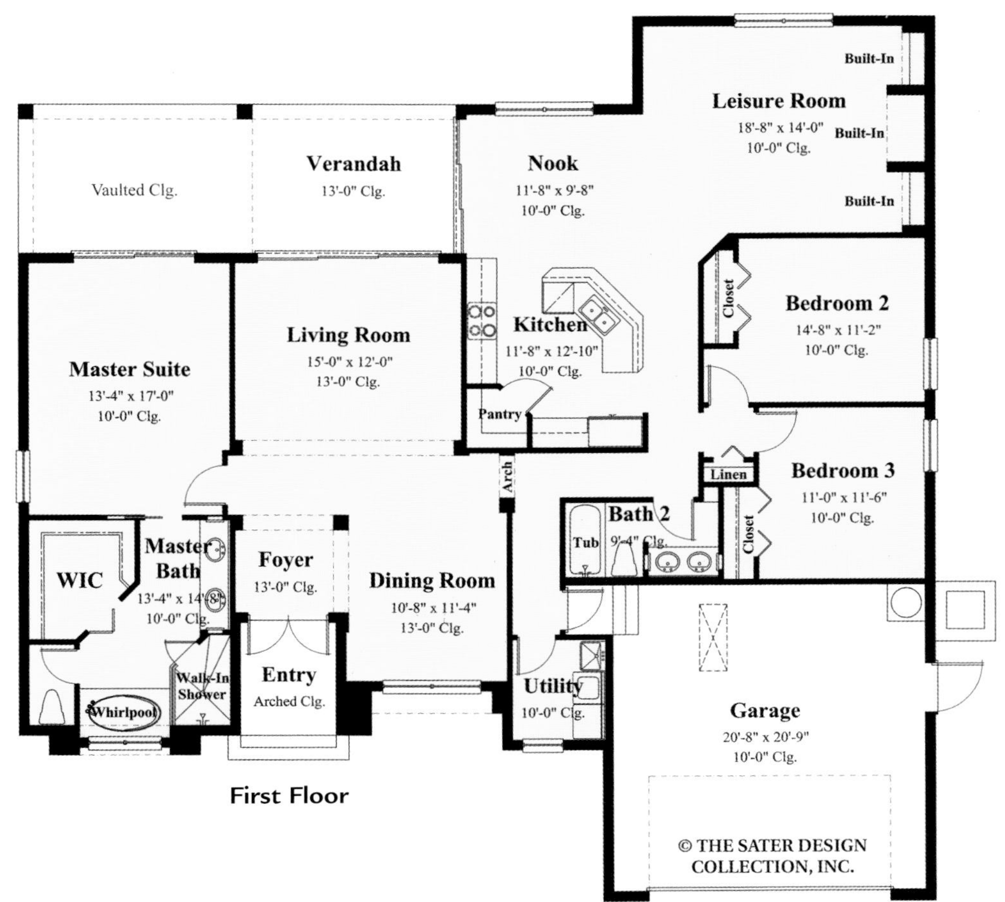

First Floor

Design Features

- Circular vents accent a hip and gabled roofline.
- An arched entry ceiling preceeds an elegant double-door with overhead transom.
- The large leisure room has a wall of built-ins.
- A gourmet kitchen offers a breakfast bar and pantry.
- An elegant dining room sits just off the foyer.
- An airy living room offers glass-door access to the verandah.
- The master suite boasts a free-standing whirlpool tub.

Rear Elevation

Not available for construction in Collier County, Florida.

Ingraham — VPDG01-332 — 1-866-525-9374

Total Living	First Floor	Bonus	Bed	Bath	Width	Depth	Foundation	Price Category
1977 sq ft	1977 sq ft	430 sq ft	3	2	69' 8"	59' 6"	Crawl Space*	D

Design Features

- With an elegant exterior, this executive home makes both every-day life and entertaining a breeze.
- A Palladian window floods the foyer with light for a dramatic entrance.
- The screened porch, breakfast area and master suite access the deck with optional spa.
- The large master suite, located in the rear for privacy, features a luxurious skylit bath with separate shower.

Rear View

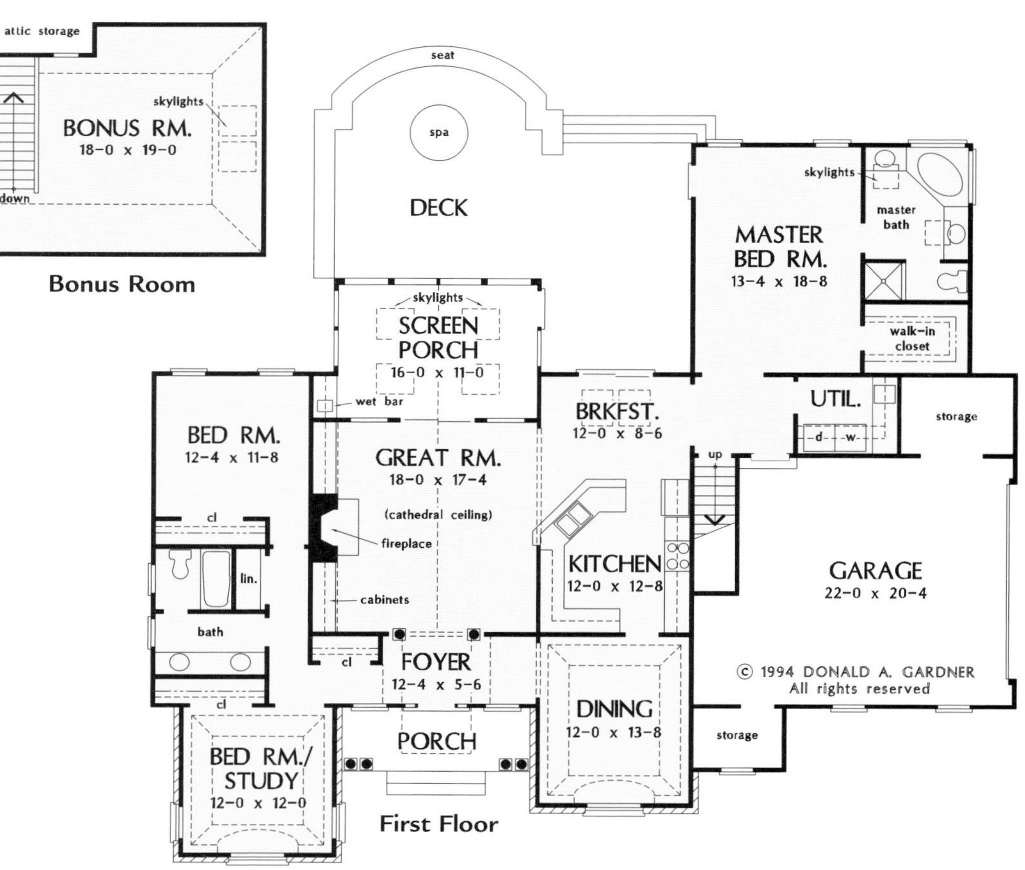

First Floor

Please note: Home photographed may differ from blueprint.

*Other options available. See page 255.

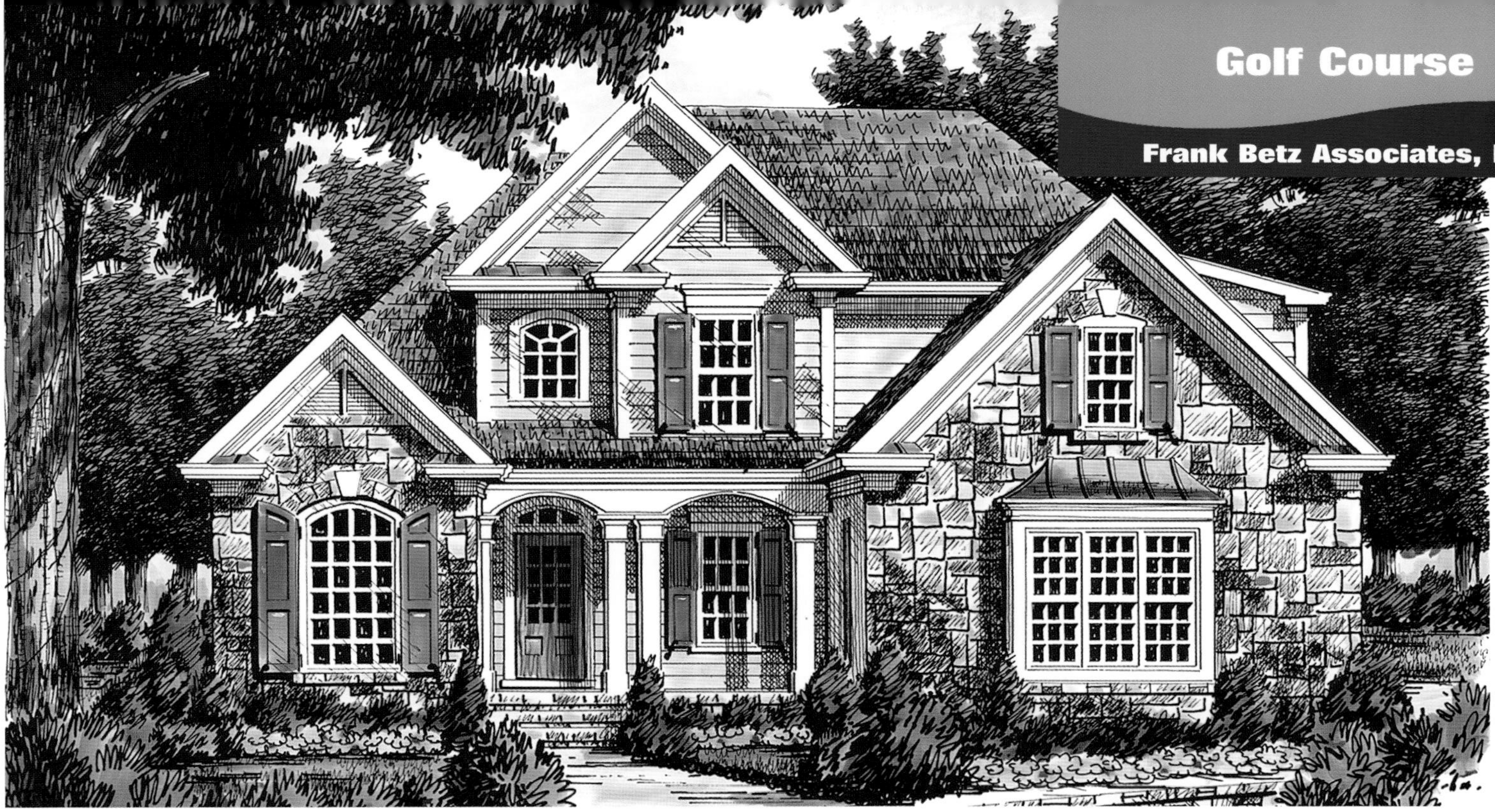

Bouldercrest — VPFB01-3674 — 1-866-525-9374

Total Living	First Floor	Second Floor	Opt. Bonus	Bed	Bath	Width	Depth	Foundation	Price Category
1879 sq ft	1407 sq ft	472 sq ft	321 sq ft	3	2-1/2	48' 0"	53' 10"	Basement or Crawl Space	F

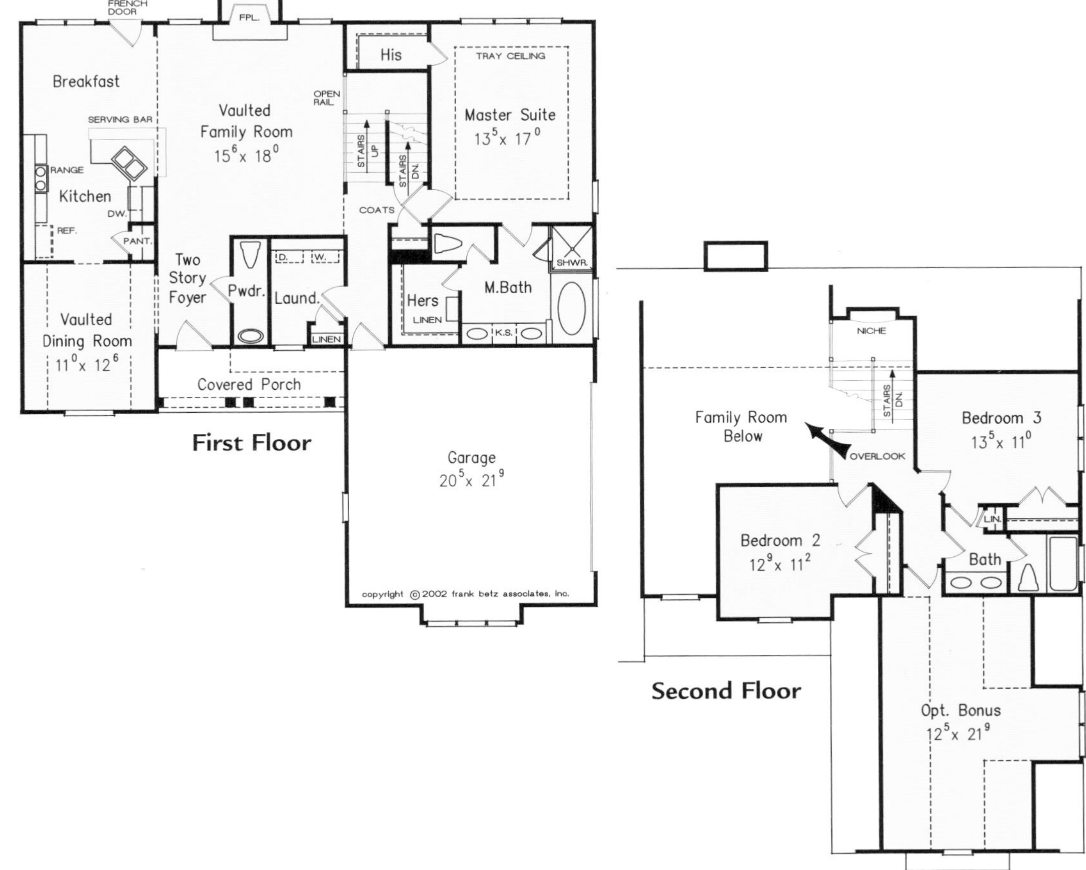

Design Features

- Stacked stone and siding give this Old-World elevation an up-to-date look.
- The spacious "his-and-her" closets are just one special feature in this main-level master home.
- The kitchen boasts a serving bar, perfect for doing homework or a quick meal on the run.
- Two bedrooms, a bath and an optional bonus room complete the second floor.

Rear Elevation

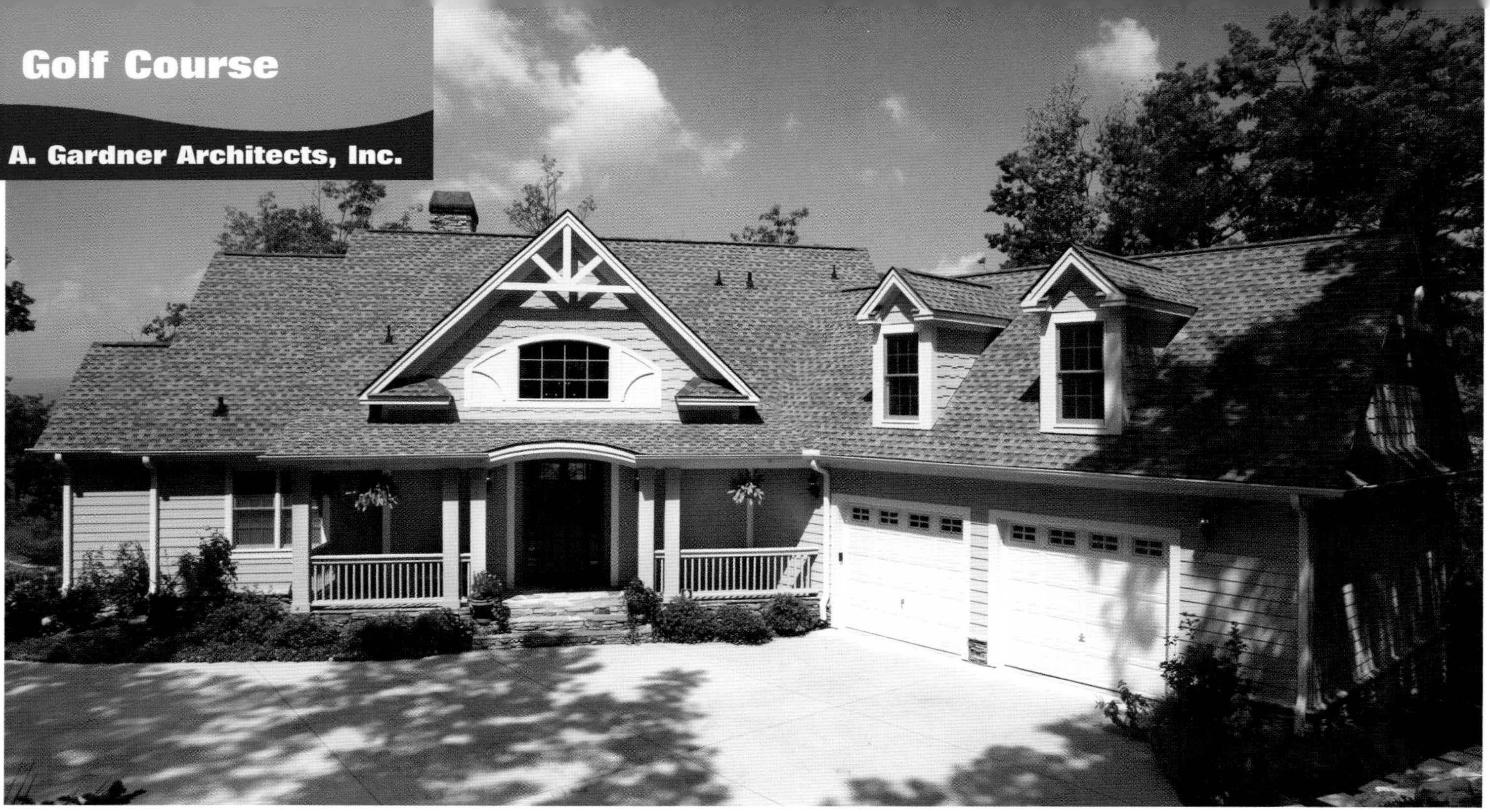

Peekskill — VPDG01-Plan 780-D — 1-866-525-9374

Total Living	First Floor	Second Floor	Basement	Bonus	Bed	Bath	Width	Depth	Foundation	Price Category
2953 sq ft	1662 sq ft	585 sq ft	706 sq ft	575 sq ft	4	3-1/2	81' 4"	68' 8"	Hillside Walkout	F

Design Features

- A stunning center dormer with arched window embellishes the exterior.
- The dormer's arched window floods light into the foyer with built-in niche.
- A generous back porch extends the great room, which features a vaulted ceiling.
- The master bedroom, which has a tray ceiling, enjoys back-porch access.
- Note the huge bonus room over the three-car garage.

Basement

Second Floor

First Floor

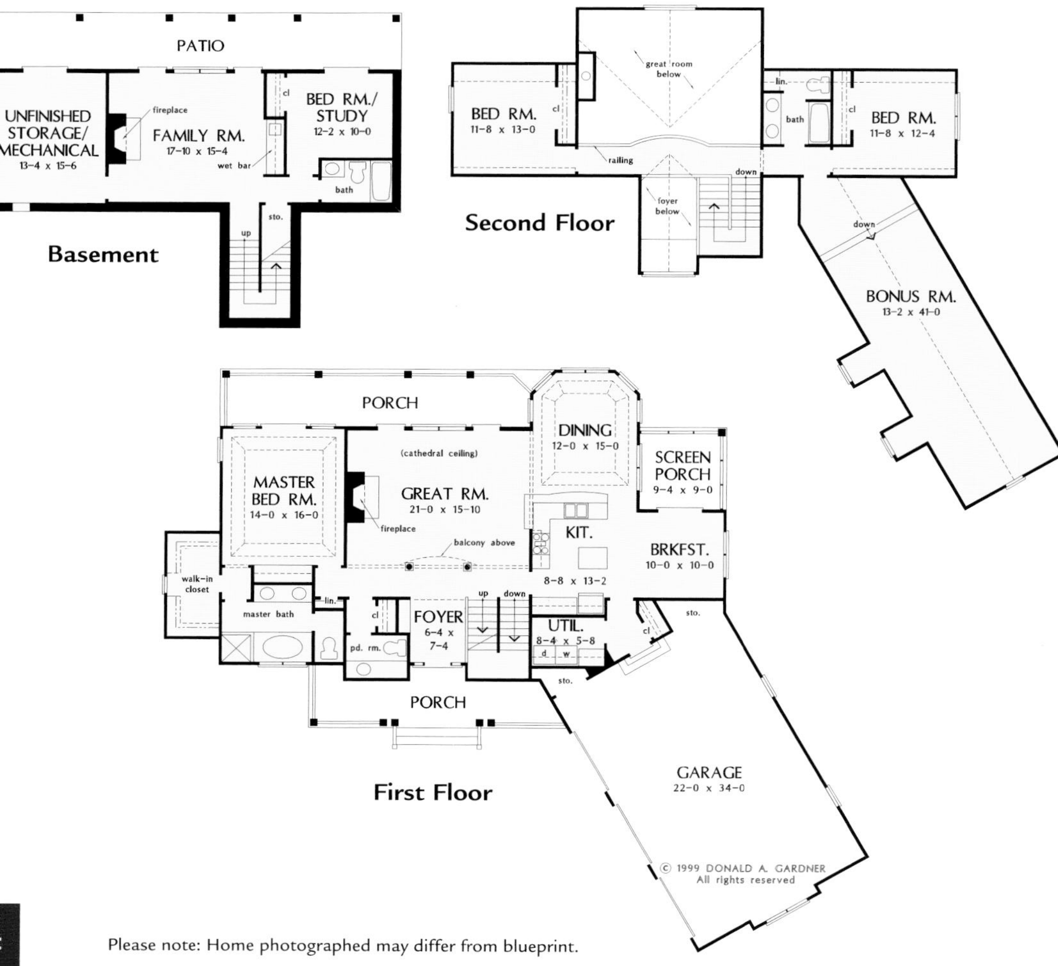

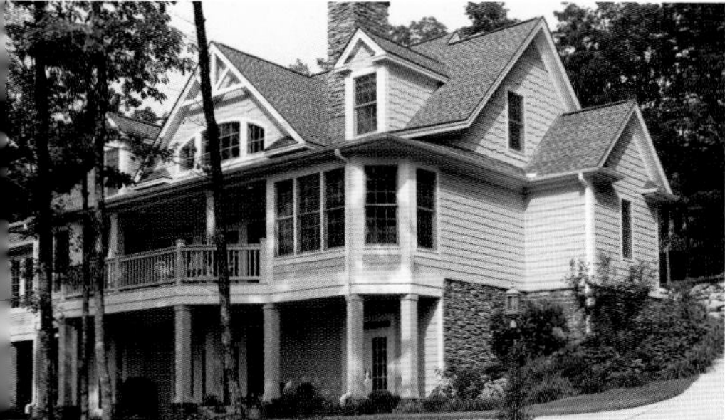

Rear View

Please note: Home photographed may differ from blueprint.

Tessier — VPFB01-Plan 3922 — 1-866-525-9374

Total Living	First Floor	Second Floor	Opt. Bonus	Bed	Bath	Width	Depth	Foundation	Price Category
2234 sq ft	1690 sq ft	544 sq ft	254 sq ft	3	2-1/2	55' 0"	48' 0"	Basement, Crawl Space or Slab	I

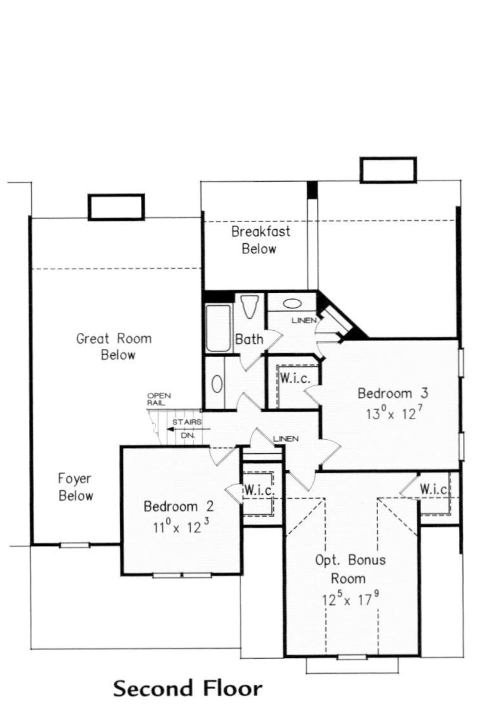

Second Floor

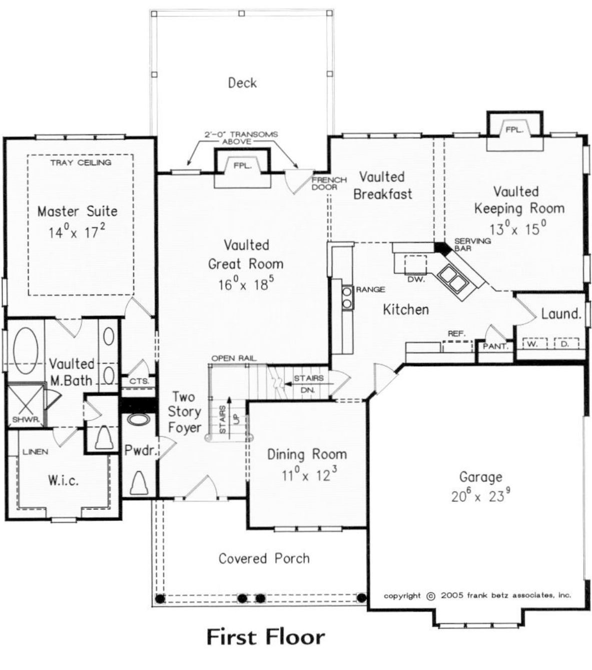

First Floor

Design Features

- The main-floor or master-suite plan possesses all the amenities of a much larger home.
- The spacious master bedroom encompasses one wing of the home.
- The keeping room with a fireplace is a special feature so many are looking for in homes today.
- The back deck is the perfect place to relax at the end of the day.

Rear Elevation

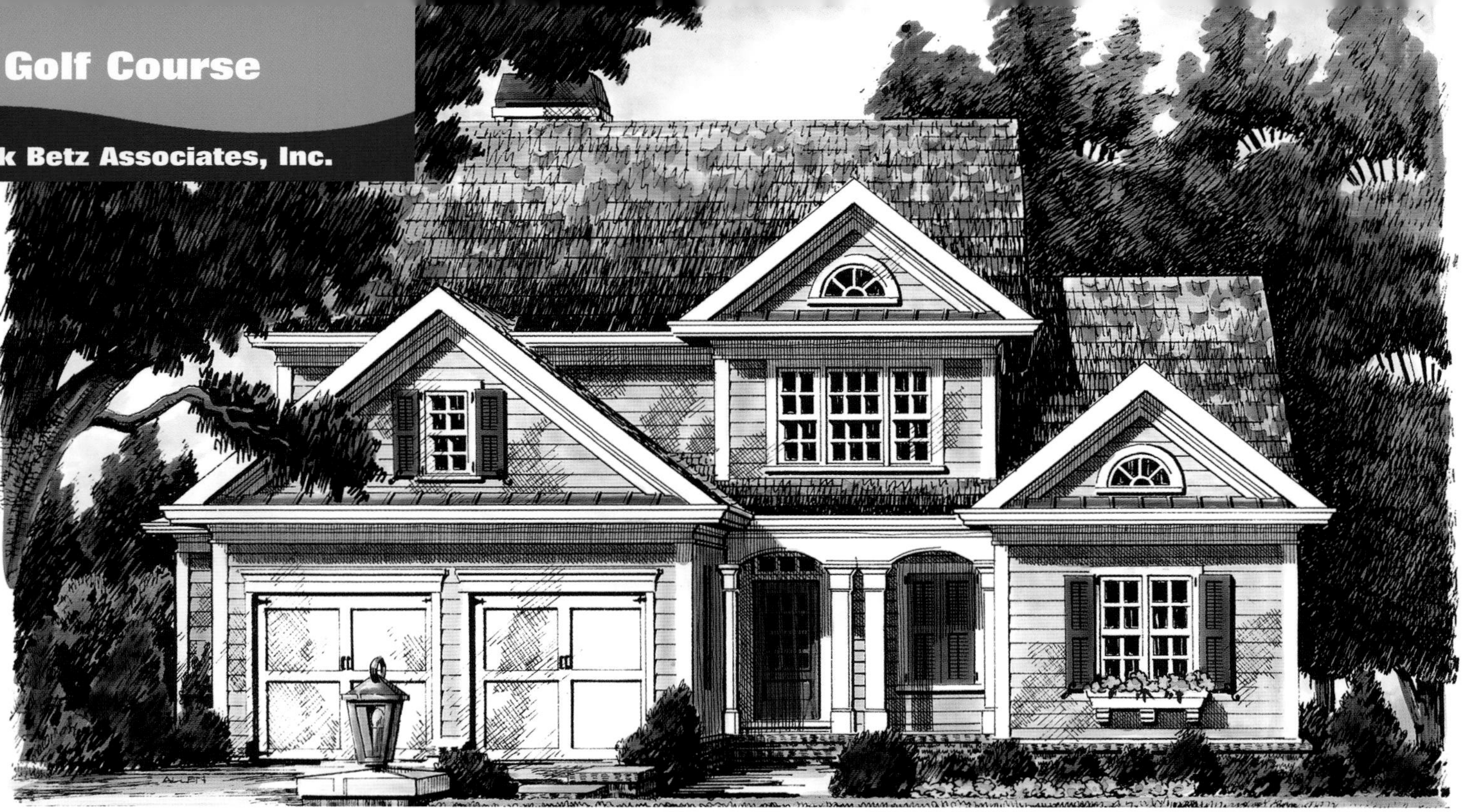

Willow Ridge — VPFB01-Plan 3692 — 1-866-525-9374

Total Living	First Floor	Second Floor	Bed	Bath	Width	Depth	Foundation	Price Category
2011 sq ft	1387 sq ft	624 sq ft	4	2-1/2	49' 0"	52' 4"	Basement or Crawl Space	F

Design Features

- The *Willow Ridge* offers the traditional floor plan many people are looking for today.
- The master suite is on the main level, allowing the homeowners the privacy many seek.
- The master bathroom offers dual sinks, a separate tub and shower and a large walk-in closet.
- Three additional bedrooms are on the second floor.

First Floor

Second Floor

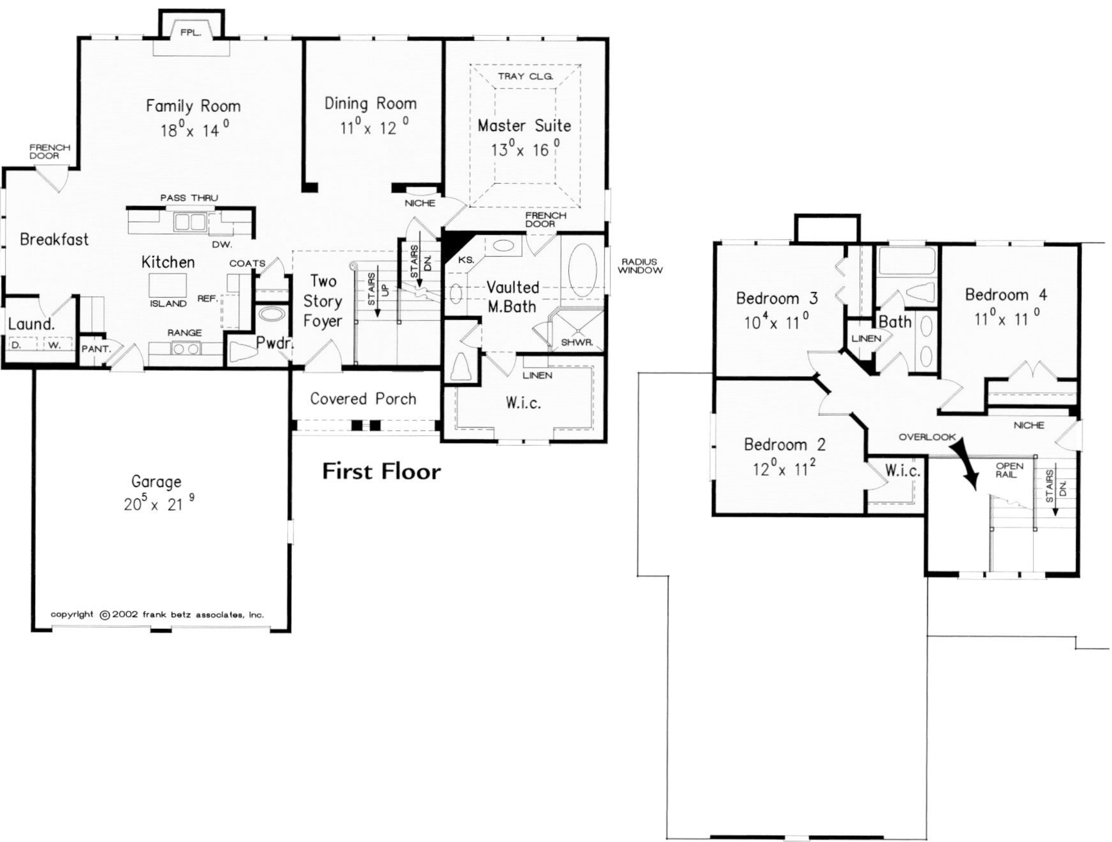

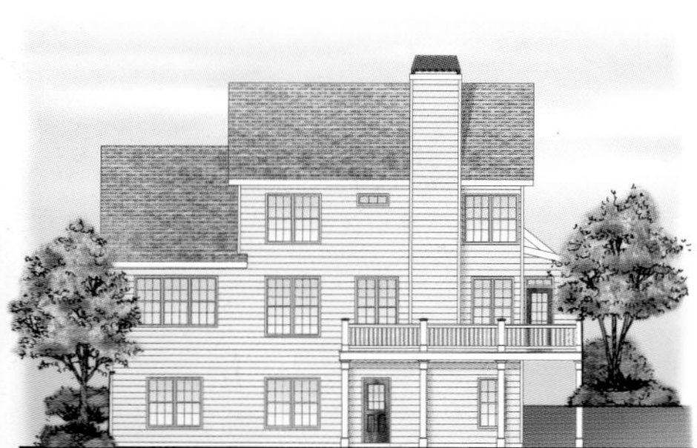

Rear Elevation

Churchdown — VPDG01-867 — 1-866-525-9374

Total Living	First Floor	Second Floor	Bonus	Bed	Bath	Width	Depth	Foundation	Price Category
3499 sq ft	2755 sq ft	744 sq ft	481 sq ft	3	3-1/2	92' 6"	69' 10"	Crawl Space*	G

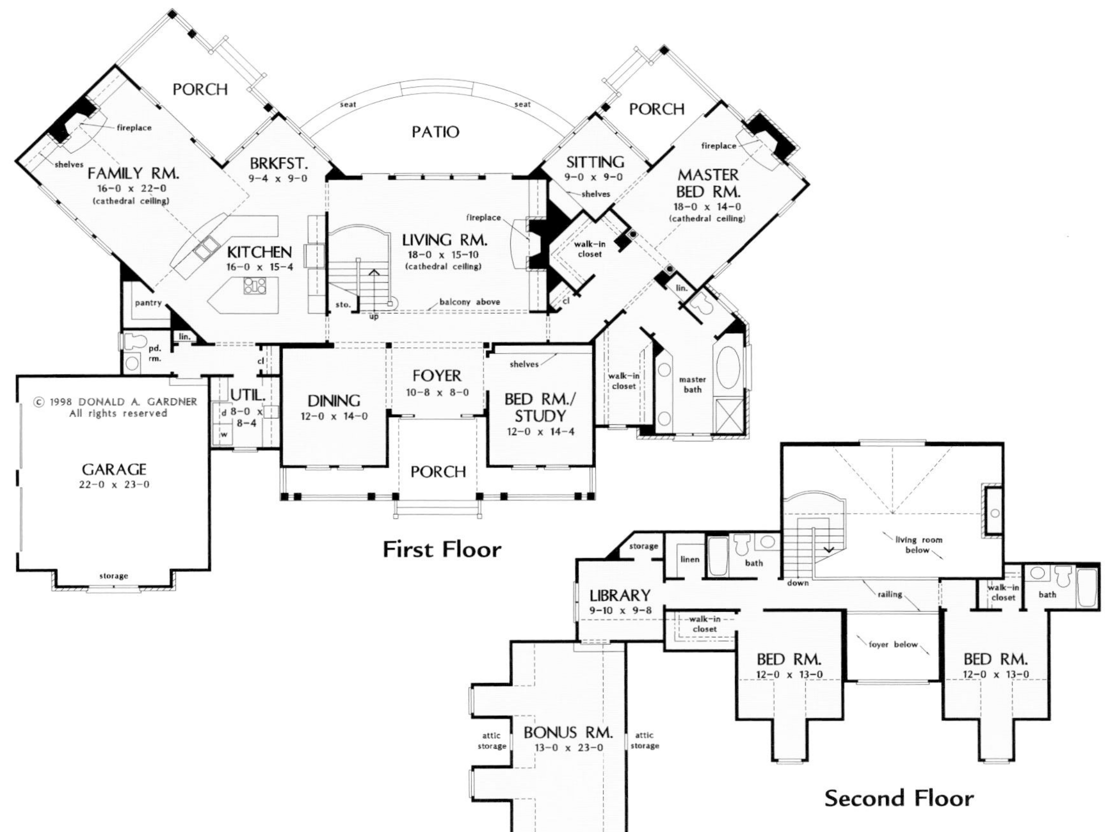

Design Features

- The master suite features two walk-in closets, sitting area and a private porch.
- In addition to the living room, this plan also has a family room with a cathedral ceiling.
- Built-in shelves enhance the private study.
- Secondary bedrooms, two full bathrooms, a library and bonus room complete the second level.

Rear Elevation

*Other options available. See page 255.

Broadmoor — VPFB01-1088 — 1-866-525-9374

Total Living	First Floor	Second Floor	Opt. Bonus	Bed	Bath	Width	Depth	Foundation	Price Category
1658 sq ft	1179 sq ft	479 sq ft	338 sq ft	3	2-1/2	41' 6"	54' 4"	Basement, Crawl Space or Slab	E

Design Features

- Quaint and charming outside and in, the *Broadmoor* combines function with beauty to make a wonderful home.
- The courtyard entry leads to a stunning two-story foyer.
- The great room, breakfast area and kitchen are all connected, making conversation and traffic flow effortless.
- The laundry room and a coat closet are thoughtfully placed just off the garage, keeping coats and shoes in their place.
- An optional bonus area upstairs has endless possibilities. This could be the ideal playroom, fitness area or home office.

Rear Elevation

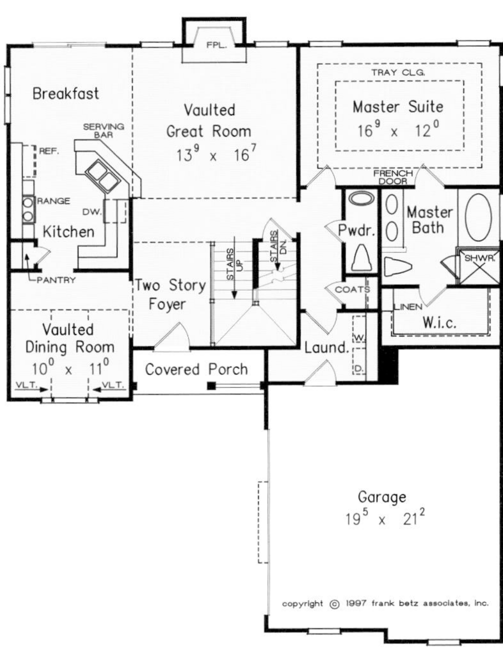

First Floor

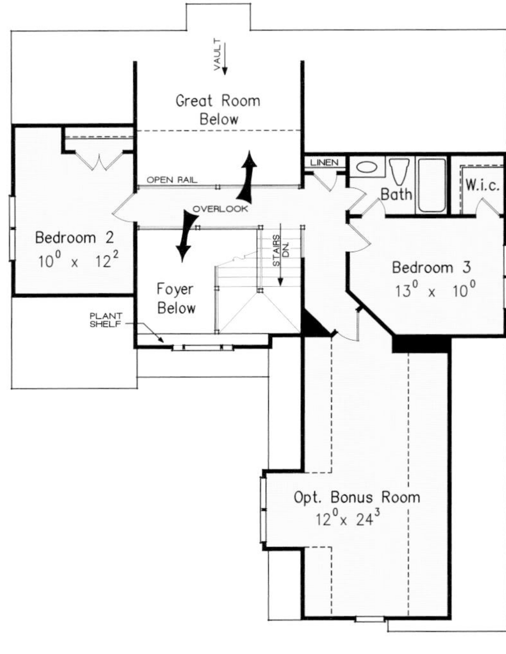

Second Floor

Edelweiss — VPDG01-1013 — 1-866-525-9374

Total Living	First Floor	Bonus	Bed	Bath	Width	Depth	Foundation	Price Category
1929 sq ft	1929 sq ft	335 sq ft	3	2	54' 8"	68' 4"	Crawl Space	D

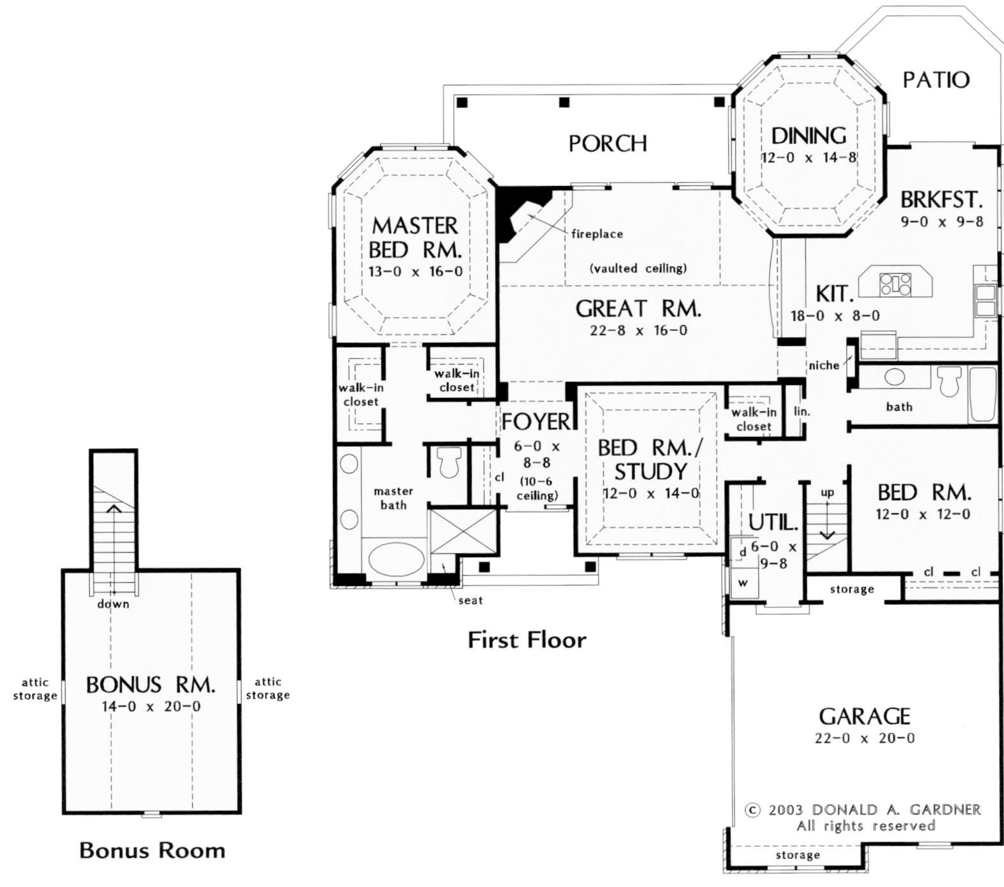

First Floor

Bonus Room

Design Features

- Stone, siding and a hipped roof create cottage charm.
- Arches contrast with gables to provide architectural interest, and custom transoms usher in natural light.
- A vaulted ceiling tops the great room, which includes French doors and a corner fireplace.
- A cooktop island keeps the kitchen open, and a private patio is adjacent to the breakfast nook.
- Expanded by a bay, the master suite is positioned for privacy.

Rear Elevation

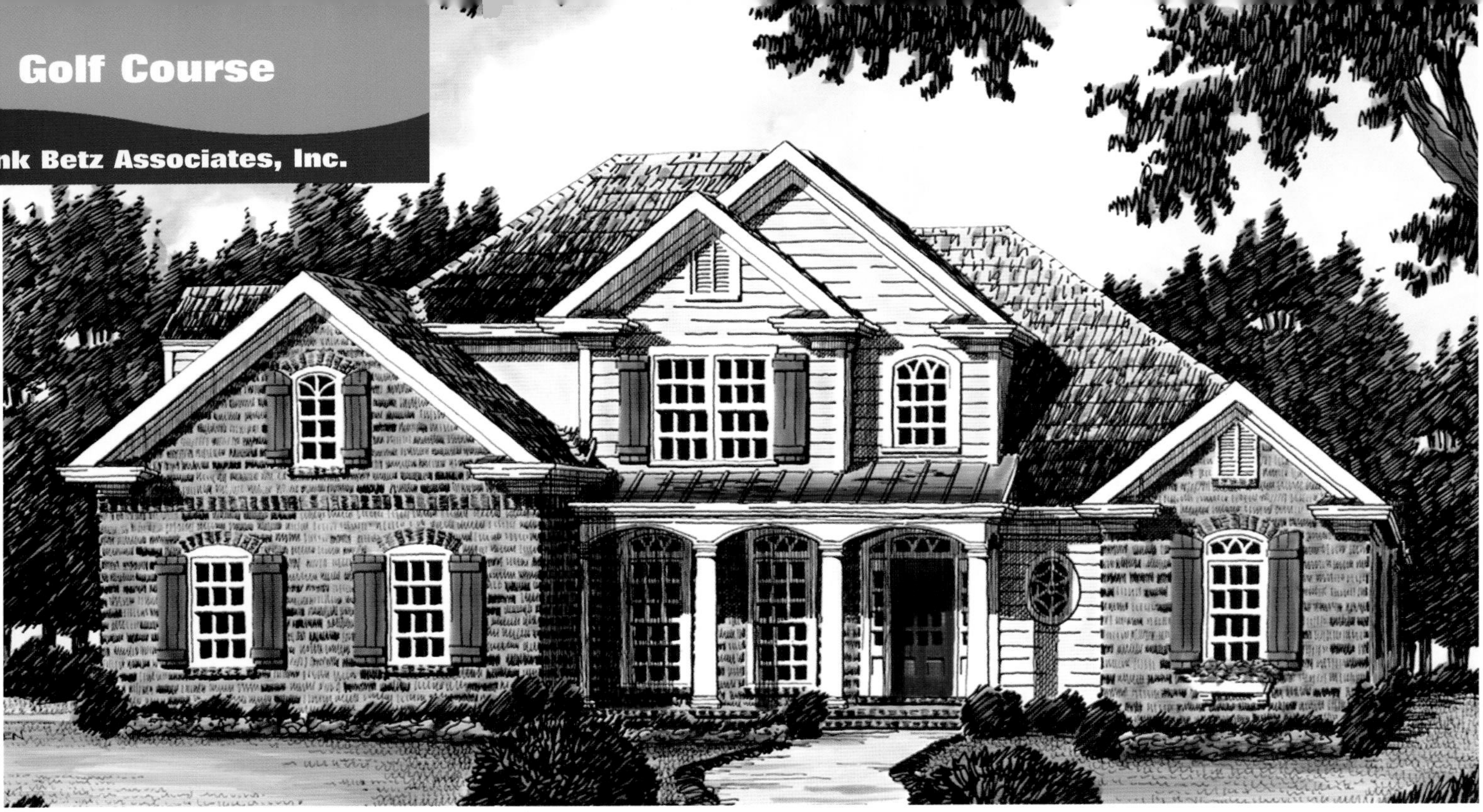

Carlton Square — VPFB01-3588 — 1-866-525-9374

Total Living	First Floor	Second Floor	Opt. Bonus	Bed	Bath	Width	Depth	Foundation	Price Category
2481 sq ft	1961 sq ft	520 sq ft	265 sq ft	4	3	60' 0"	53' 0"	Basement or Crawl Space	G

Design Features

- A clean-lined combination of brick and siding creates a façade of understated simplicity.
- The interior spaces connect with ease, generating effortless traffic flow from one room to the next.
- Also on the main level, a bedroom can be easily converted into a home office — perfect for telecommuters or retirees.
- Optional bonus space is designed into the second floor.

First Floor

Second Floor

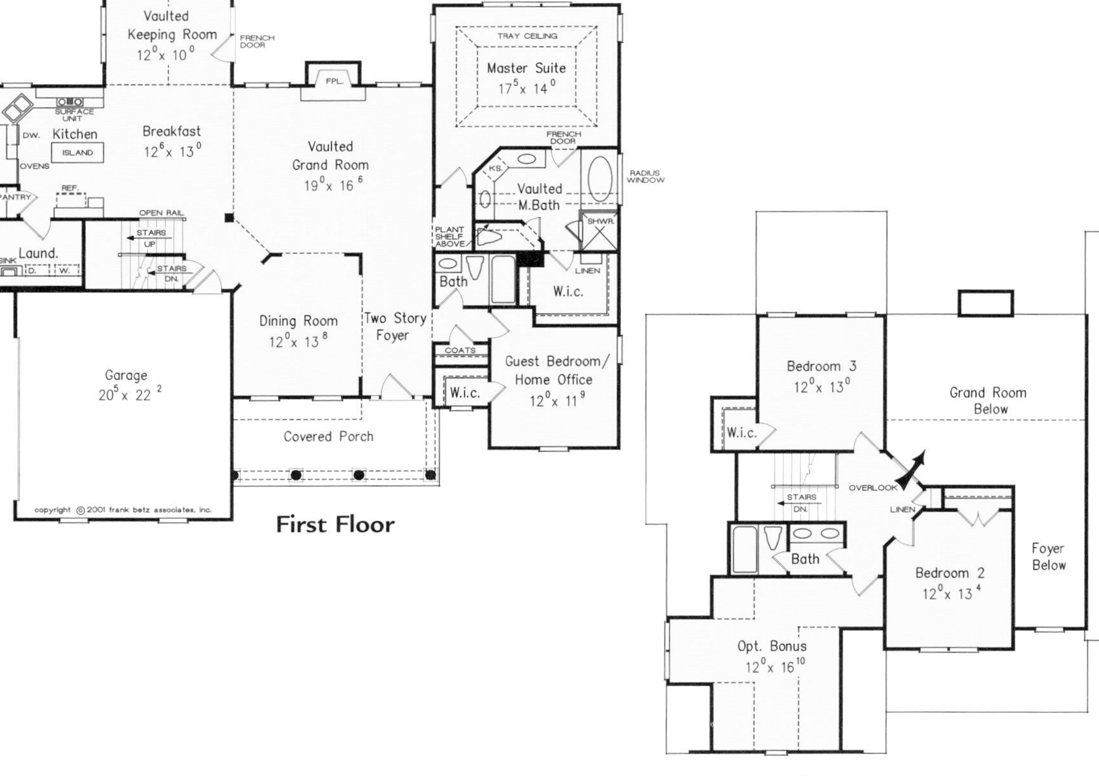

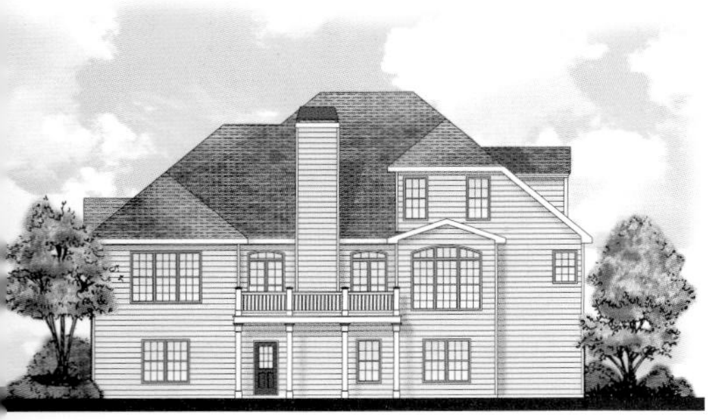

Rear Elevation

Peachtree — VPDG01-524 — 1-866-525-9374

Total Living	First Floor	Second Floor	Bonus	Bed	Bath	Width	Depth	Foundation	Price Category
2298 sq ft	1743 sq ft	555 sq ft	350 sq ft	4	3	78' 0"	53' 2"	Crawl Space*	E

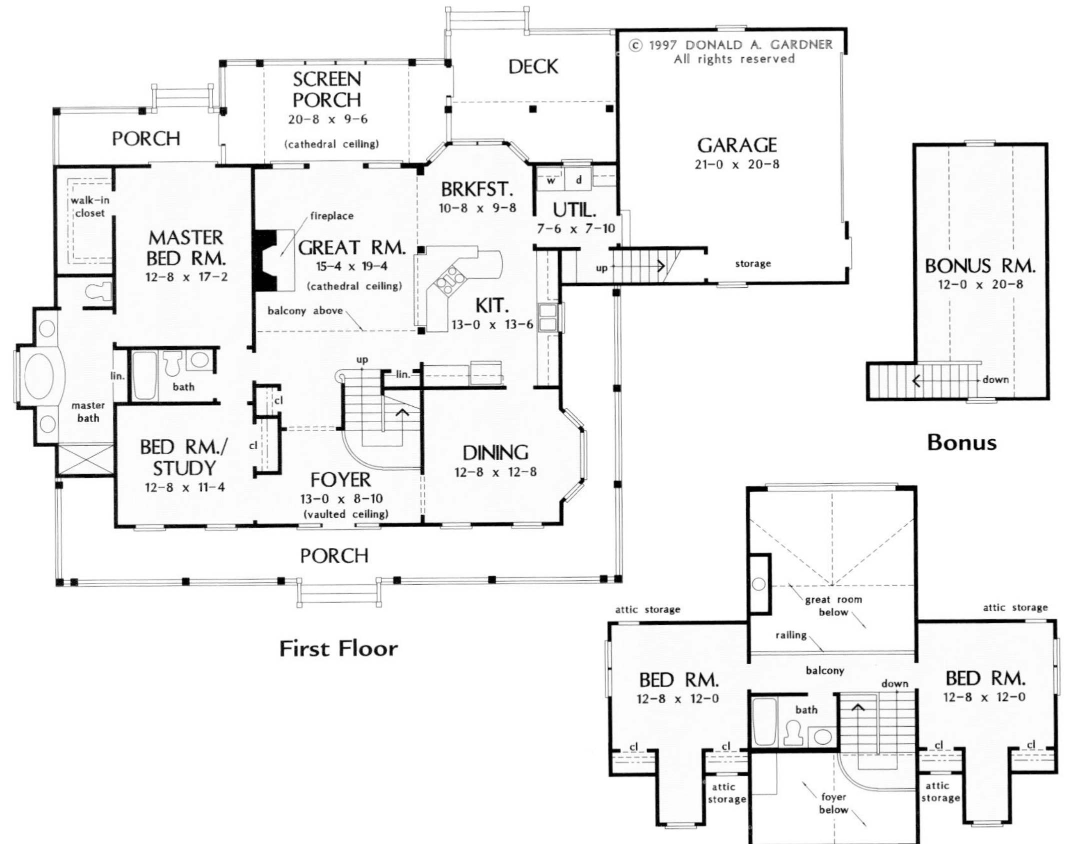

First Floor

Bonus

Second Floor

Design Features

- Nine-foot ceilings are standard throughout the first and second floors of this classic country design.
- The foyer, great room and screened porch enjoy vaulted and cathedral ceilings.
- Bay windows perk up the dining room and breakfast area.
- The master suite features back-porch access, walk-in closet and a lavish bath.

Rear Elevation

*Other options available. See page 255.

Delaney — VPFB01-3744 — 1-866-525-9374

Total Living	First Floor	Opt. 2nd Fl.	Bed	Bath	Width	Depth	Foundation	Price Category
1996 sq ft	1996 sq ft	258 sq ft	4	4	60' 0"	47' 6"	Basement or Crawl Space	G

Design Features

- The eye-catching exterior of the *Delaney* draws attention to three graceful arches across the front of the home.
- Traffic flows easily from the kitchen area into the great room, creating functional space for entertaining.
- The study easily converts into a fourth bedroom for larger families or overnight guests.
- The optional second floor gives the homeowners the ability to create a larger home by finishing the bonus room, bath and closet.

Rear Elevation

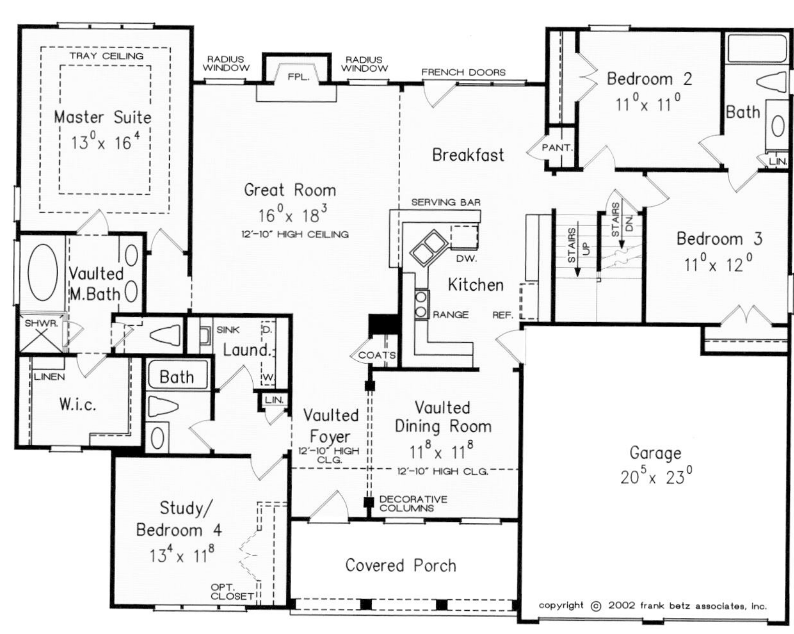

First Floor

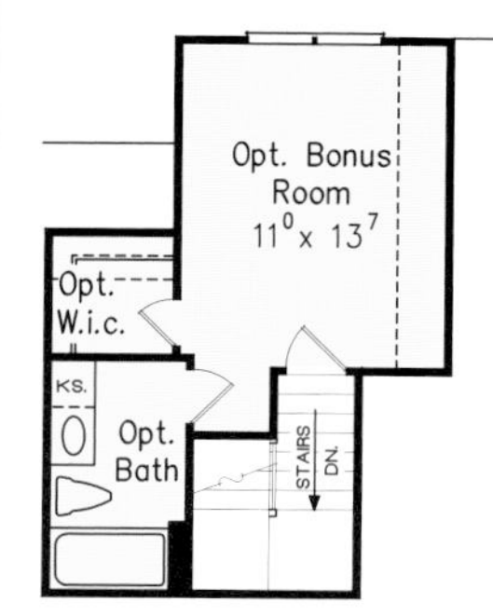

Opt. Second Floor

Holly Springs — VPFB01-3821 — 1-866-525-9374

Total Living	First Floor	Second Floor	Opt. Bonus	Bed	Bath	Width	Depth	Foundation	Price Category
2338 sq ft	1761 sq ft	577 sq ft	305 sq ft	4	3	56' 0"	48' 0"	Basement or Crawl Space	G

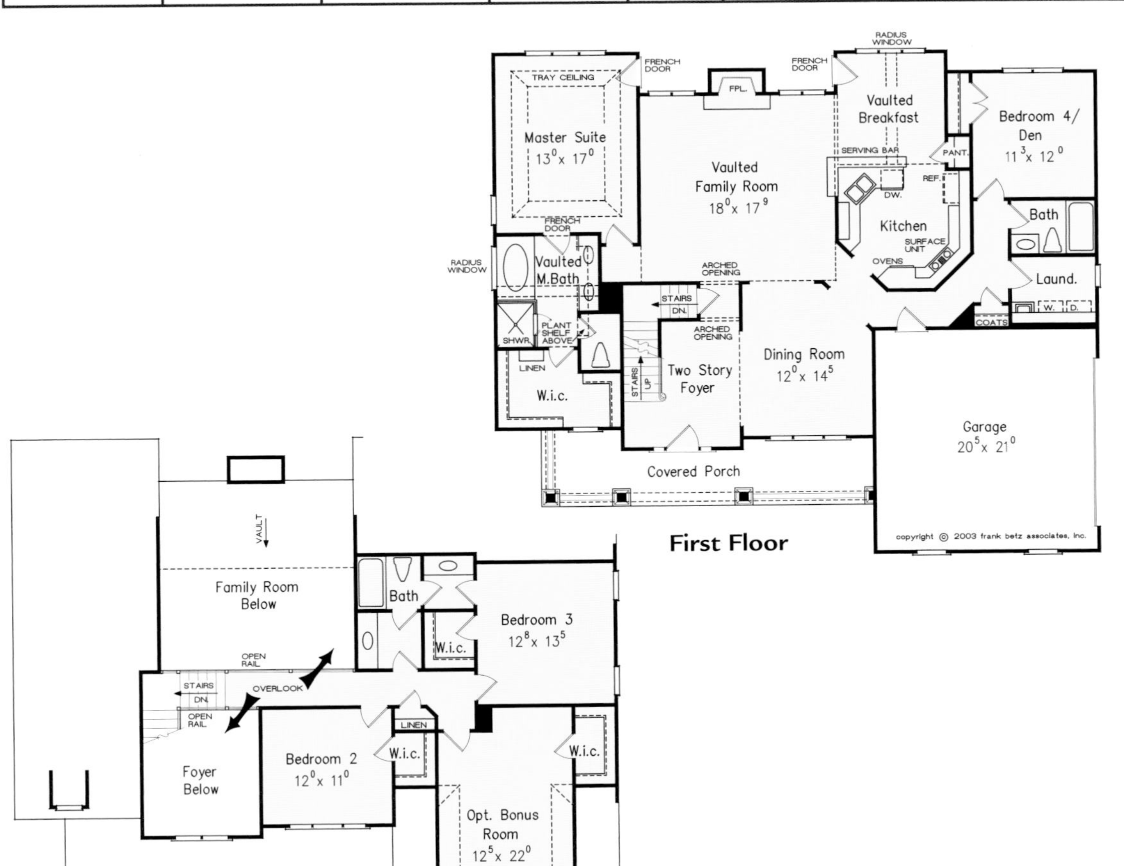

First Floor

Second Floor

Design Features

- The façade of the *Holly Springs* is eye-catching and original, with its unique windows, battered columns and varied exterior materials.
- Its main floor houses the master suite, as well as an additional bedroom that makes an ideal guest bedroom with a bath in close proximity.
- A vaulted breakfast area connects to the kitchen, complete with double ovens and a serving bar.
- Additional niceties include an arched opening leading to the family room from the foyer and a linen closet in the master suite.

Rear Elevation

Arbordale — VPDG01-452 — 1-866-525-9374

Total Living	First Floor	Second Floor	Bonus	Bed	Bath	Width	Depth	Foundation	Price Category
3163 sq ft	2086 sq ft	1077 sq ft	403 sq ft	4	3-1/2	82' 10"	51' 8"	Crawl Space*	G

Design Features

- The master suite is quietly tucked away downstairs with no bedrooms directly above.
- The cook of the family will love the spacious U-shaped kitchen.
- The bonus room is easily accessible from the back stairs or second floor.
- Storage space abounds with walk-ins, hall shelves and a linen closet upstairs.
- A curved balcony borders a versatile loft/study that overlooks the two-story great room.

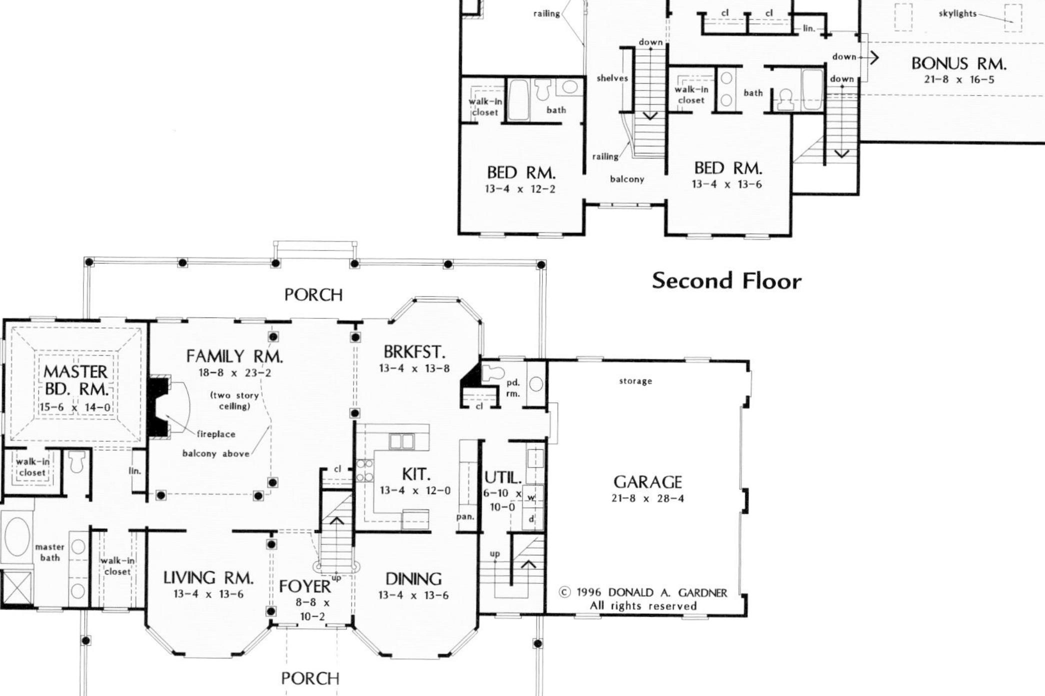

Second Floor

First Floor

Rear View

Please note: Home photographed may differ from blueprint. ***Other options available. See page 255.**

Mallory — VPFB01-992 — 1-866-525-9374

Total Living	First Floor	Second Floor	Opt. Bonus	Bed	Bath	Width	Depth	Foundation	Price Category
2155 sq ft	1628 sq ft	527 sq ft	207 sq ft	3	2-1/2	54' 0"	46' 10"	Basement, Crawl Space or Slab	I

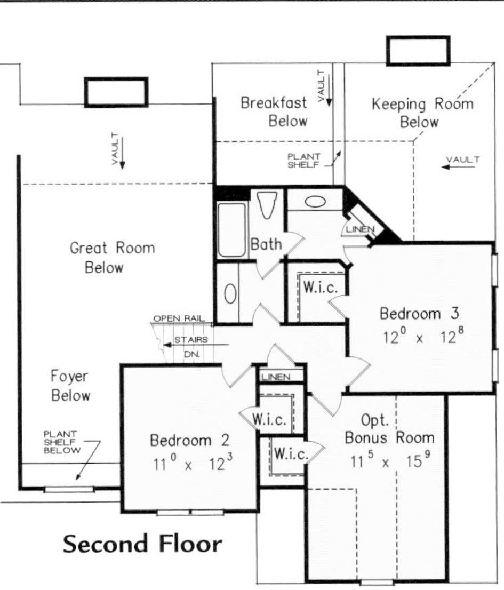

Second Floor

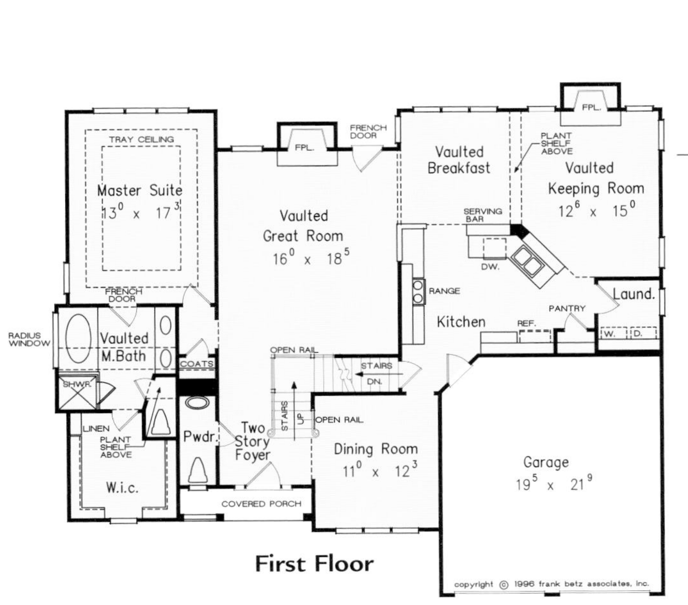

First Floor

Design Features

- Earthy fieldstone and cedar shake accents give the *Mallory* a casual elegance that Old-World style encompasses.
- A vaulted breakfast area and keeping room with fireplace adjoin the kitchen.
- Two secondary bedrooms—each with a walk-in closet—share a divided bathing area on the second floor.
- An optional bonus room is ready to finish into a fourth bedroom, playroom or exercise area.

Rear Elevation

Southerland — VPDG01-971 — 1-866-525-9374

Total Living	First Floor	Second Floor	Bonus	Bed	Bath	Width	Depth	Foundation	Price Category
2521 sq ft	1798 sq ft	723 sq ft	349 sq ft	4	3-1/2	66' 8"	49' 8"	Crawl Space*	F

Design Features

- Columns make a grand impression both inside and outside.
- Transoms above French doors brighten both the front and rear of the floor plan.
- The mud room/utility area is complete with a sink.
- An upstairs bedroom has its own bath and can be used as a guest suite.

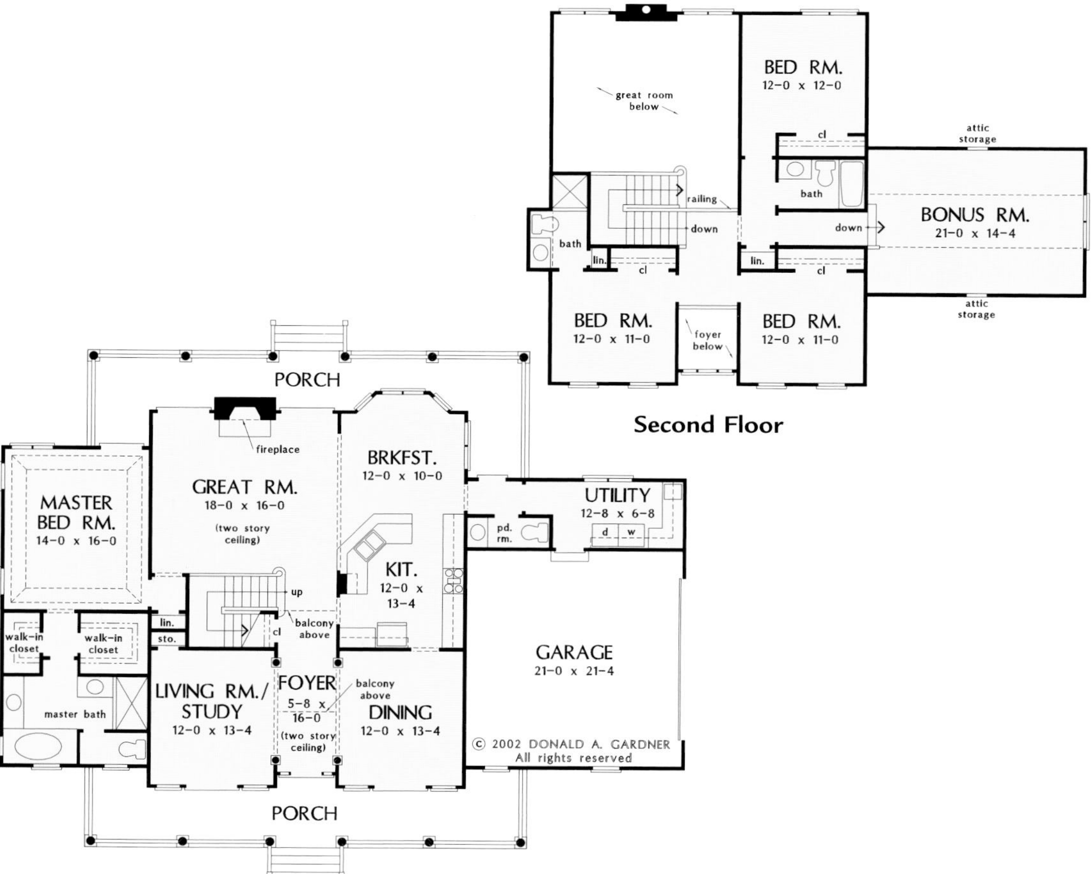

Second Floor

First Floor

Rear Elevation

*Other options available. See page 255.

Colemans Bluff — VPFB01-3896 — 1-866-525-9374

Total Living	First Floor	Opt. 2nd Fl.	Bed	Bath	Width	Depth	Foundation	Price Category
2066 sq ft	2066 sq ft	556 sq ft	4	3-1/2	63' 0"	79' 4"	Basement, Crawl Space or Slab	F

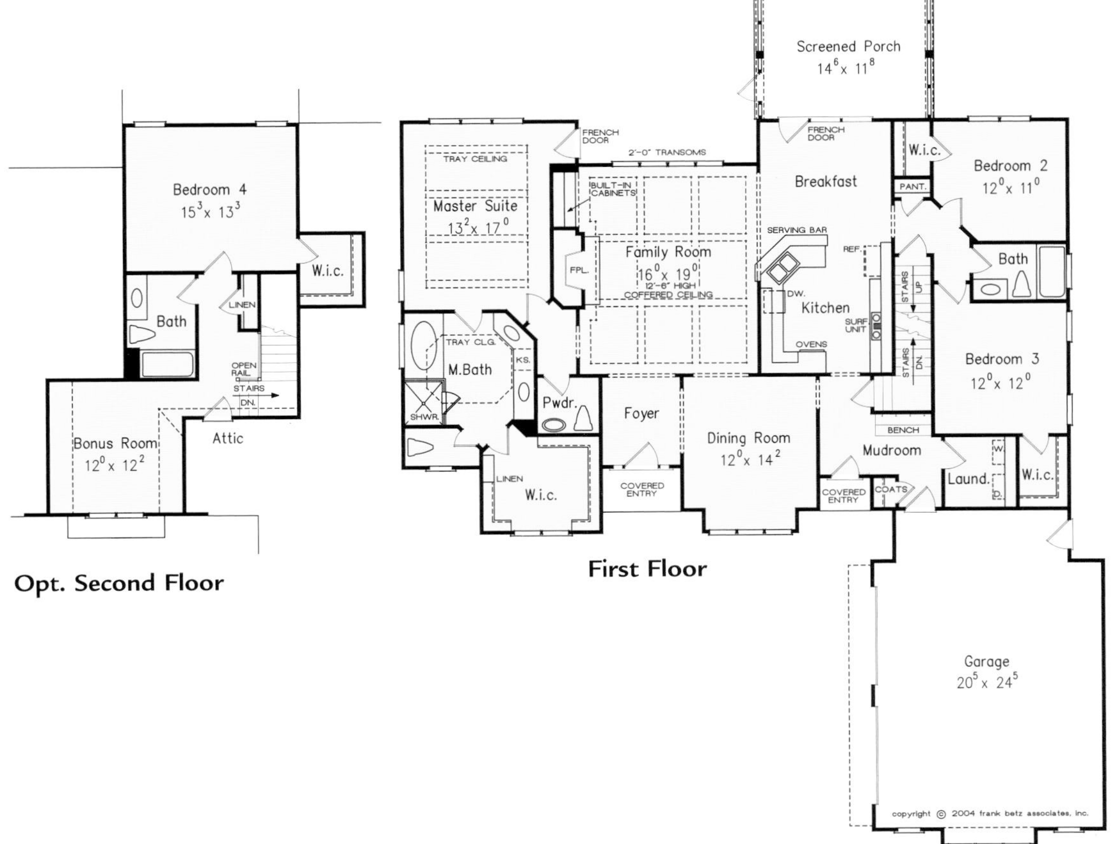

Opt. Second Floor

First Floor

Design Features

- *Colemans Bluff* floor plan is inviting, with a coffered ceiling providing a unique canopy over the family room. A large screened porch off the breakfast area provides easy outdoor living.
- The garage entry filters traffic through the mudroom, fully equipped with a coat closet, bench, wall hooks and access to the laundry room.
- Finishing the optional second floor adds a bedroom, bath and bonus room to the design.

Rear Elevation

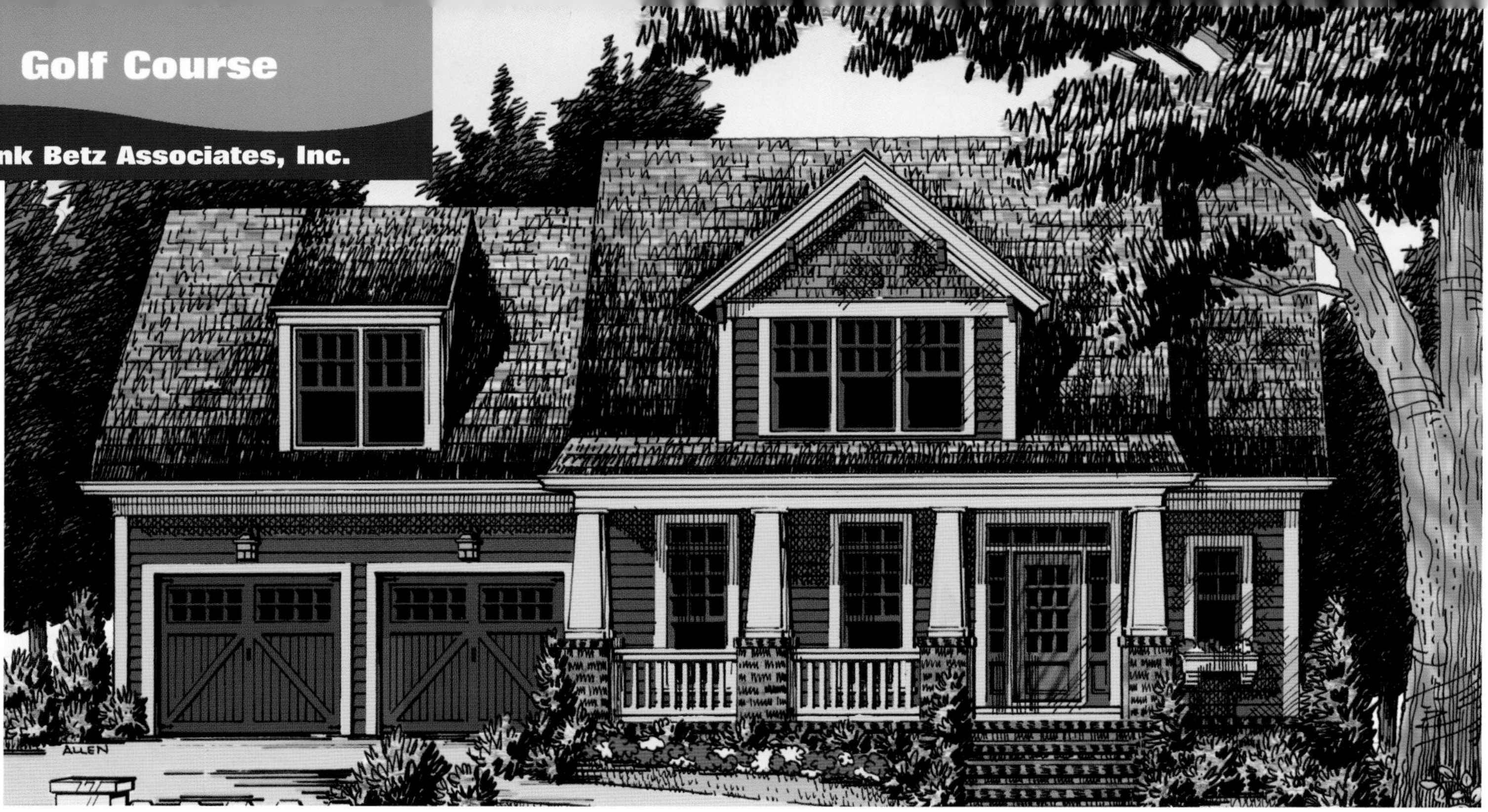

Pasadena — VPFB01-3756 — 1-866-525-9374

Total Living	First Floor	Second Floor	Opt. Bonus	Bed	Bath	Width	Depth	Foundation	Price Category
2139 sq ft	1561 sq ft	578 sq ft	274 sq ft	3	2-1/2	50' 0"	57' 0"	Basement, Crawl Space or Slab	H

Design Features

- Charm and character abound from the façade of the *Pasadena*, with its tapered architectural columns and carriage doors.
- Inside, the master suite is tucked away on the rear of the main level, giving the homeowner a peaceful place to unwind.
- An art niche is situated in the breakfast area, providing the perfect spot for a favorite art piece or floral arrangement.
- The kitchen is complete with pantry and large prep island.

Rear Elevation

First Floor

Second Floor

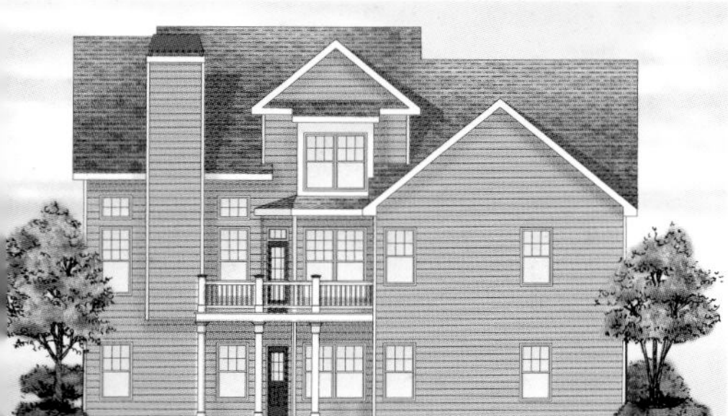

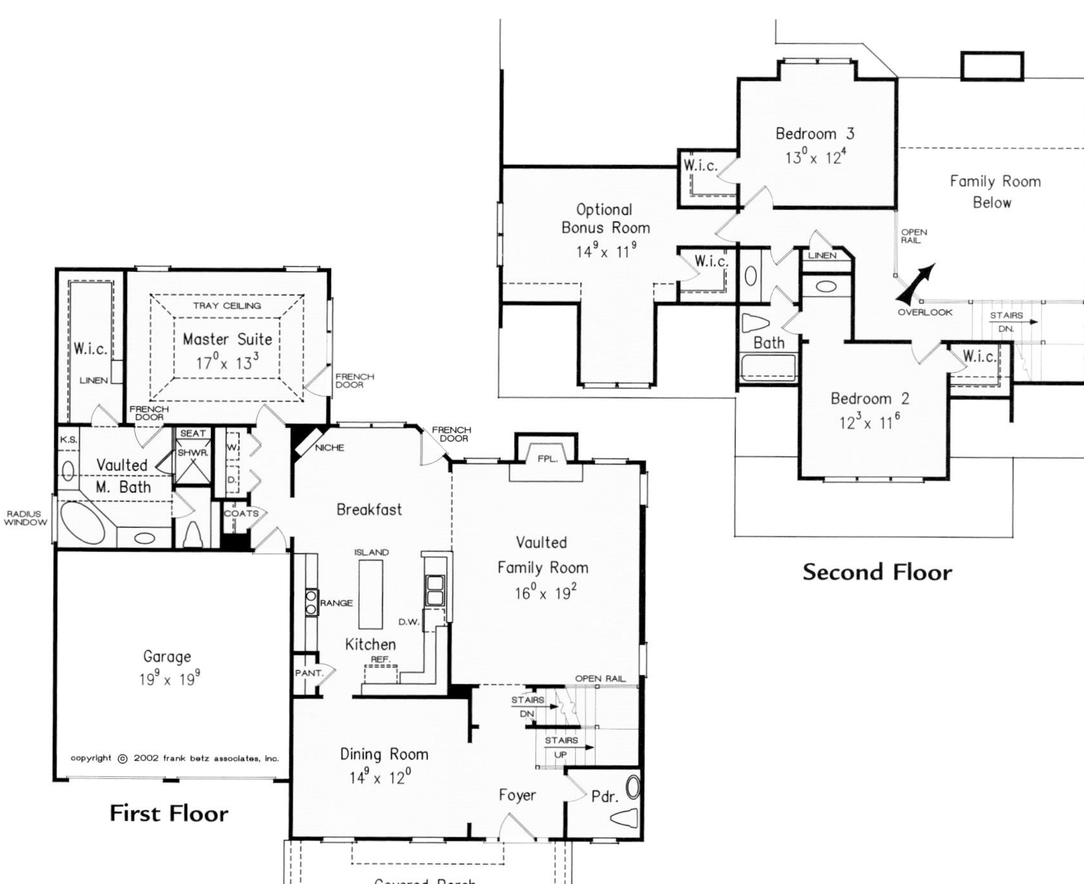

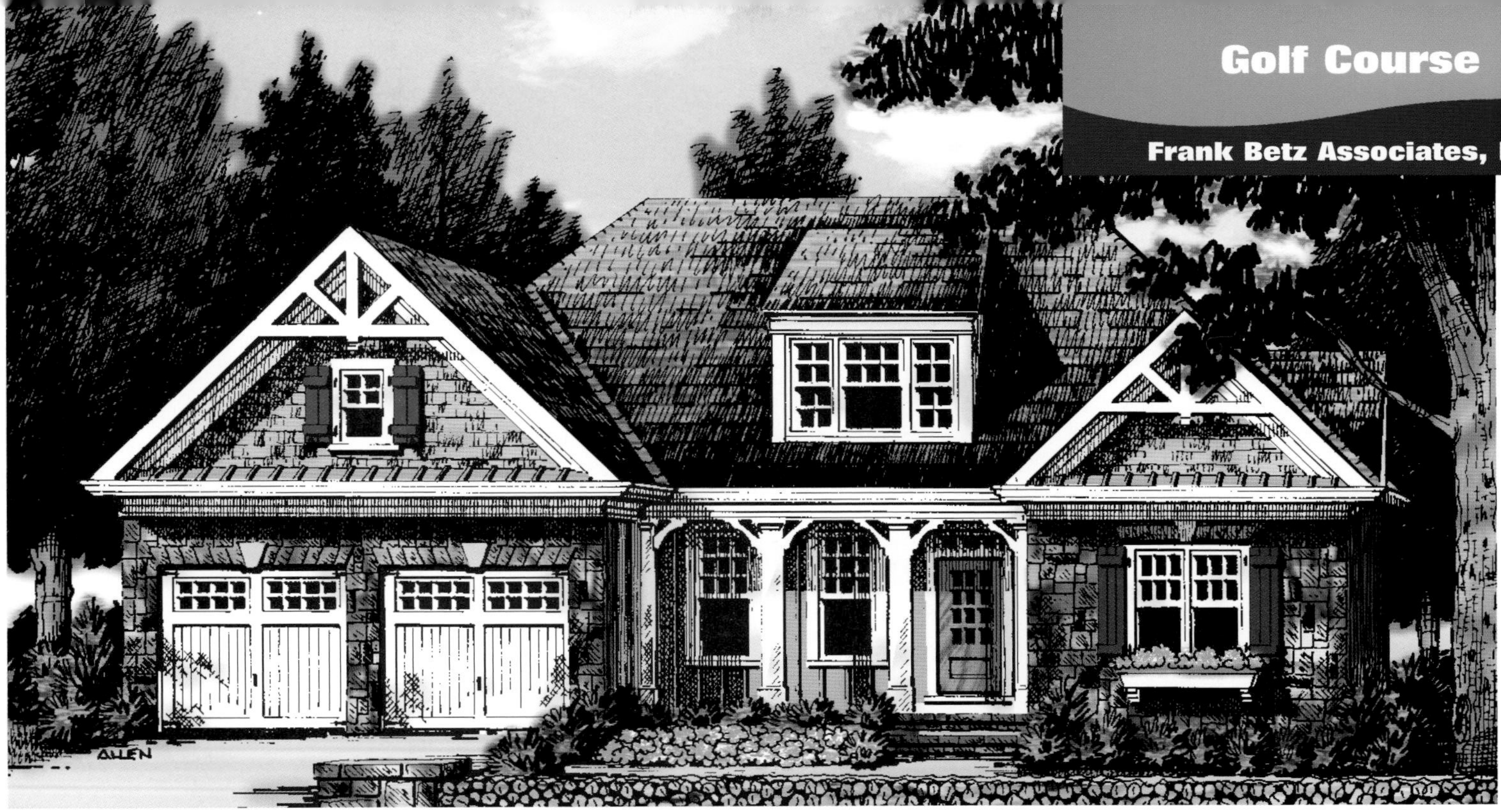

Laurel Springs — VPFB01-3854 — 1-866-525-9374

Total Living	Main Level	Lower Level	Opt. 2nd Fl.	Bed	Bath	Width	Depth	Foundation	Price Category
2201 sq ft	1381 sq ft	820 sq ft	331 sq ft	4	3-1/2	51' 0"	44' 4"	Basement	G

Main Level

Opt. Second Floor

Lower Level

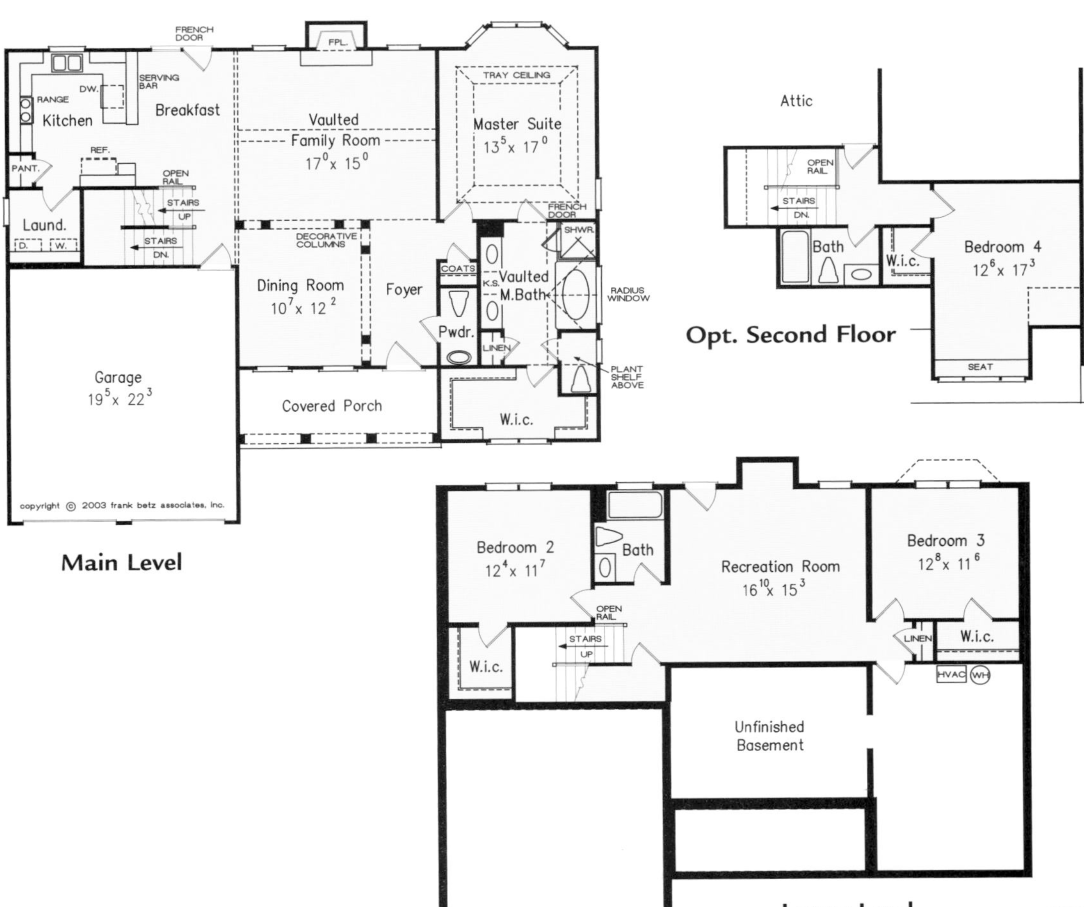

Design Features

- Decorative columns create a promenade through the foyer leading to the family room and kitchen area.
- The master suite enjoys the privacy of being the only bedroom on the main level of the home.
- The others are located in the lower level, divided by a recreation room.
- An optional second floor can be easily added, providing a fourth bedroom with generous dimensions and a window seat, as well as an additional full bath.

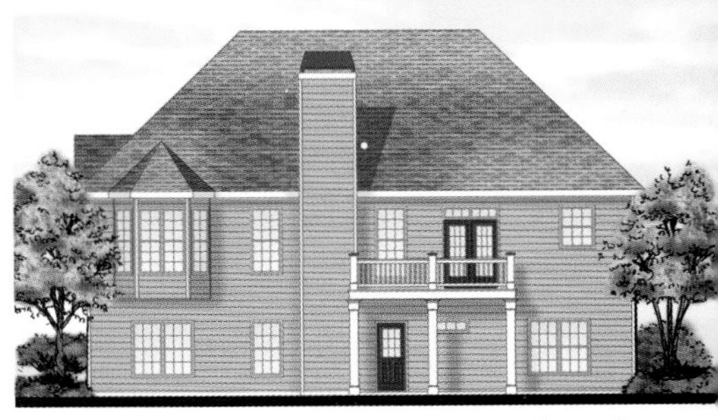

Rear Elevation

Rivermeade — VPFB01-3668 — 1-866-525-9374

Total Living	First Floor	Second Floor	Opt. Bonus	Bed	Bath	Width	Depth	Foundation	Price Category
1879 sq ft	1359 sq ft	520 sq ft	320 sq ft	3	2-1/2	45' 0"	52' 4"	Basement or Crawl Space	G

Design Features

- Volume makes this home feel larger than it is, with vaulted, tray and two-story ceilings throughout the main level.
- The laundry area can also be a mudroom with direct access off the garage.
- A handy pass-thru from the kitchen to the great room makes entertaining easier.
- A large covered porch adds interest to the front façade.

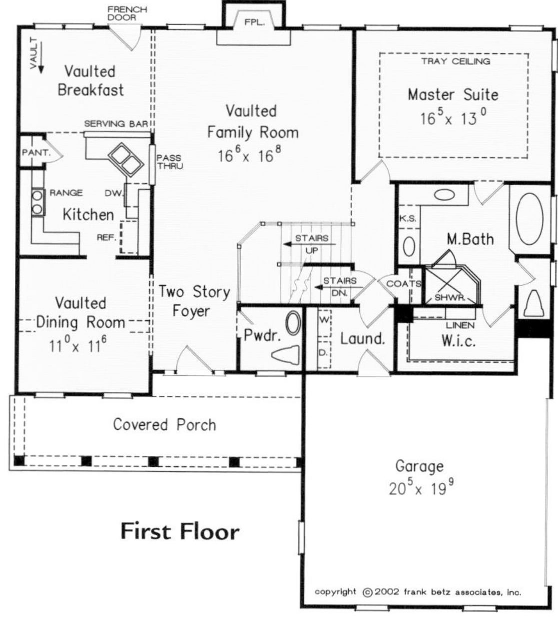

First Floor

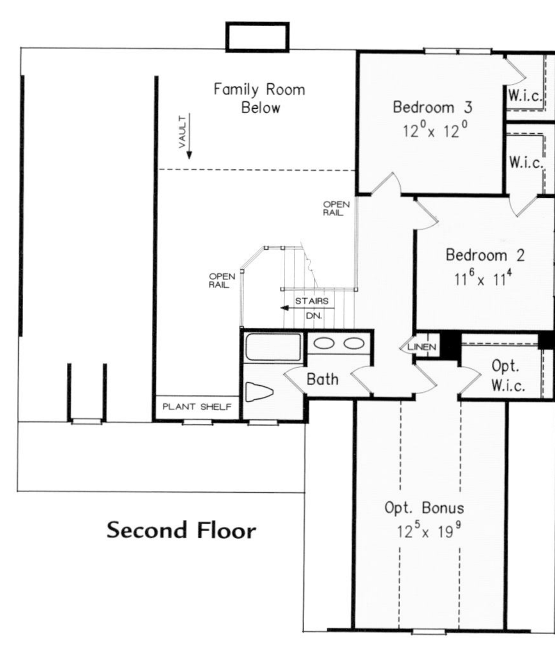

Second Floor

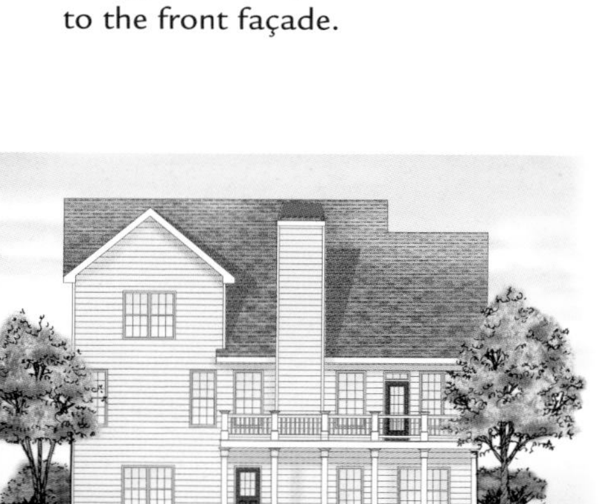

Rear Elevation

Walnut Grove — VPFB01-3865 — 1-866-525-9374

Total Living	First Floor	Opt. 2nd Fl.	Bed	Bath	Width	Depth	Foundation	Price Category
2275 sq ft	2275 sq ft	407 sq ft	3	3-1/2	59' 4"	69' 0"	Basement or Crawl Space	H

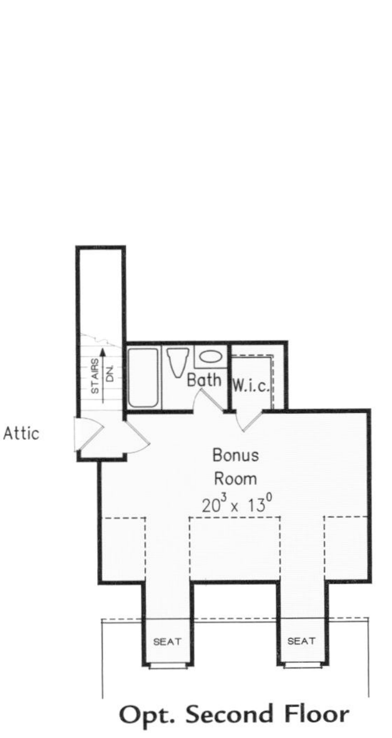

Opt. Second Floor

First Floor

Design Features

- This design was created for the homeowner who wants upscale features on one level. Its cozy fieldstone exterior sets that stage for an equally impressive design inside.
- Two separate living spaces — the keeping and family rooms — give residents and guests alike options on where to gather.
- Double ovens and a serving bar in the kitchen make meal preparation and entertaining fun and easy.
- The master suite is private from the other bedrooms, and features a tray ceiling, a corner soaking tub and serene backyard views.

Rear Elevation

Bainbridge — VPDS01-Plan 7051 — 1-866-525-9374

Total Living	First Floor	Bonus	Bed	Bath	Width	Depth	Foundation	Price Category
2555 sq ft	2555 sq ft	N/A	3	2-1/2	70' 6"	76' 6"	Crawl Space	G

Design Features

- Beamed, coffered, stepped and tray ceilings, numerous built-ins, a dynamic split floor plan and an abundance of wide, open spaces enhance the interior.
- The gourmet kitchen boasts a glass hutch, center work island, built-in desk, breakfast nook and an eating bar connecting to the great room.
- Retreat to the master suite, which offers dual walk-in closets, a luxurious bath and glass doors to the back porch.

Rear View

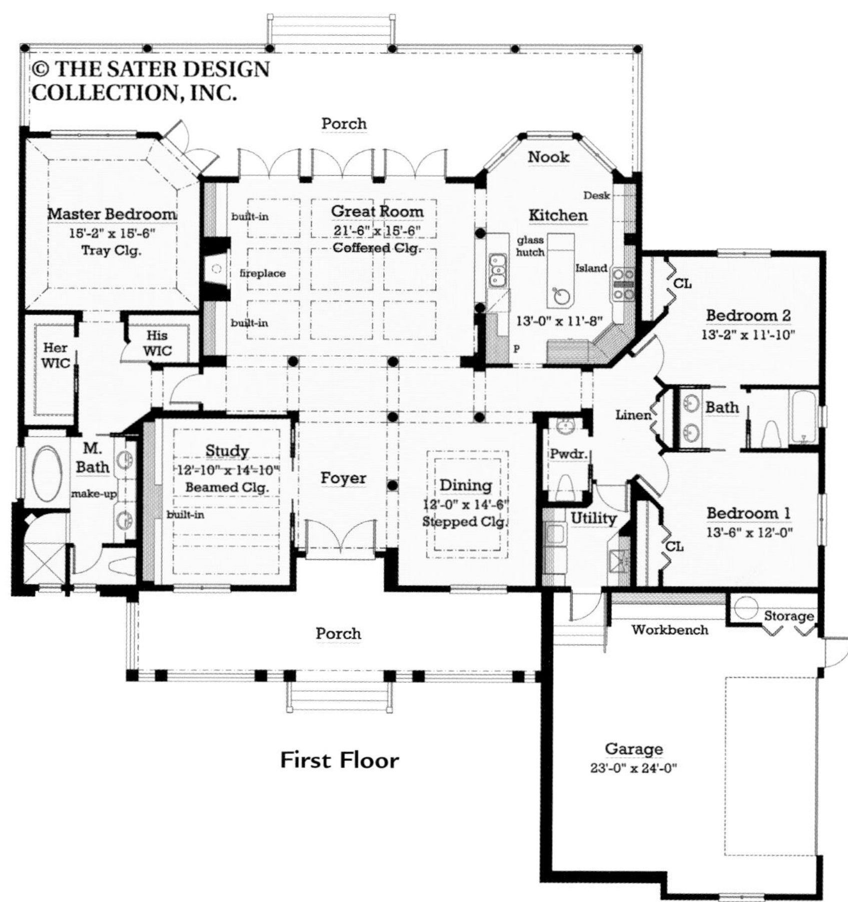

First Floor

Please note: Home photographed may differ from blueprint.

Camden Lake — VPFB01-3828 — 1-866-525-9374

Total Living	First Floor	Opt. 2nd Fl.	Bed	Bath	Width	Depth	Foundation	Price Category
2395 sq ft	2395 sq ft	660 sq ft	4	3-1/2	62' 6"	77' 4"	Basement or Crawl Space	H

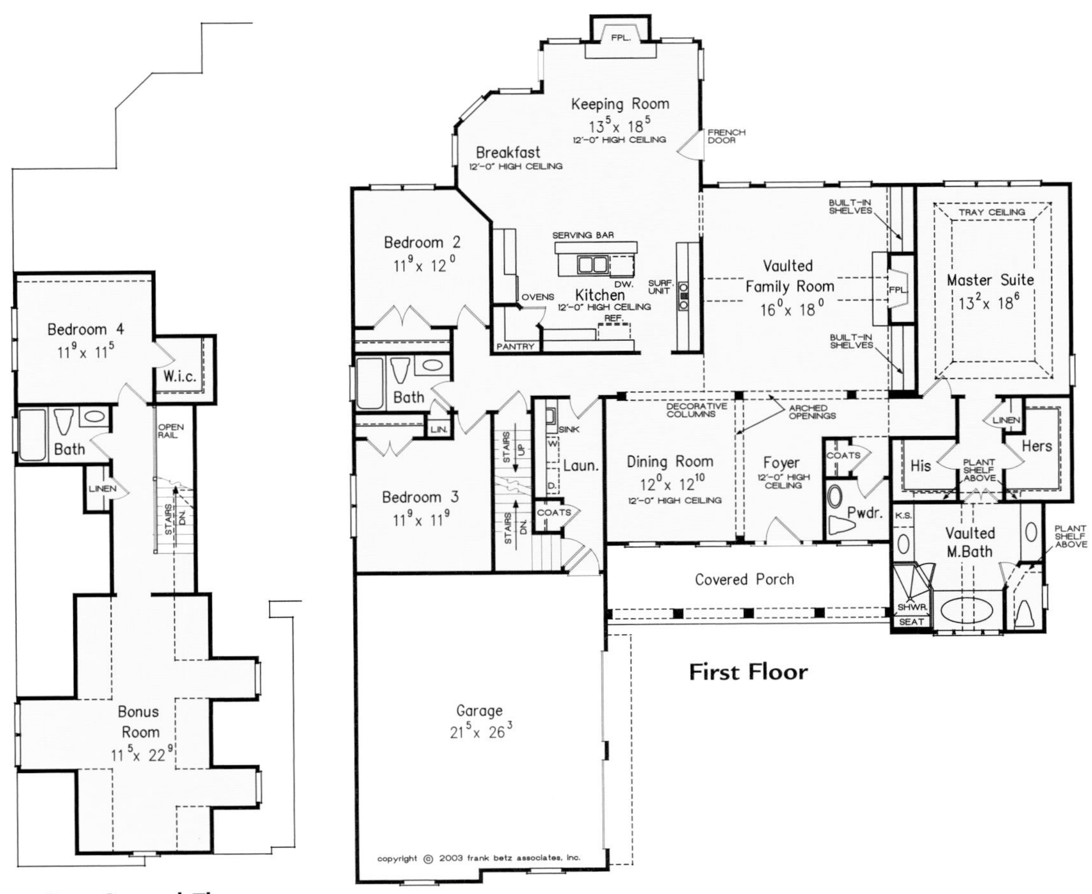

First Floor

Bedroom 4
11^9x 11^5

W.i.c.

Bath

LINEN

OPEN RAIL

Bonus Room
11^5x 22^9

Opt. Second Floor

Design Features

- One glance will tell you that this home is original and unique in its design and details. Beamed gables and cedar shake create an appealing Craftsman-style elevation.
- The pleasant surprises keep coming inside where entertainers will fall in love with this floor plan!
- The kitchen is adorned with many added extras that make it a fun place to be. Double ovens, a serving bar and a liberally sized pantry make it a user-friendly room.

Rear Elevation

Marchbanks — VPDG01-855 — 1-866-525-9374

Total Living	First Floor	Bonus	Bed	Bath	Width	Depth	Foundation	Price Category
2290 sq ft	2290 sq ft	355 sq ft	4	3	53' 0"	80' 10"	Crawl Space*	E

Design Features

- Decorative wood brackets embellish the gables of this four-bedroom home.
- Tray ceilings create formality in the foyer, dining room, bedroom/study and master bedroom.
- A cathedral ceiling expands the great room and highlights a rear clerestory dormer.
- Bay windows enhance the dining room and breakfast area.
- French doors access the back porch via the great room, kitchen and master bedroom.

Rear Elevation

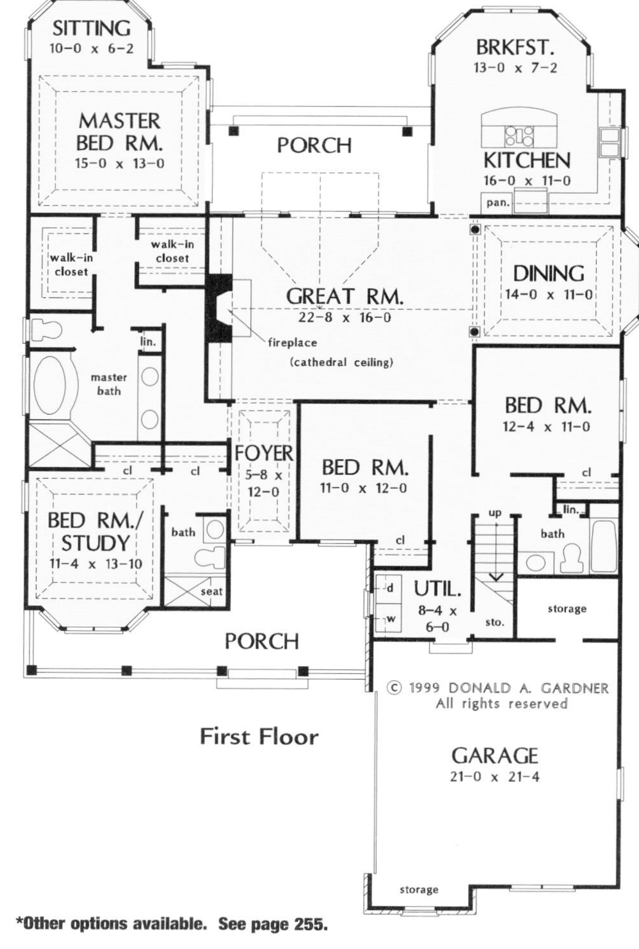

First Floor

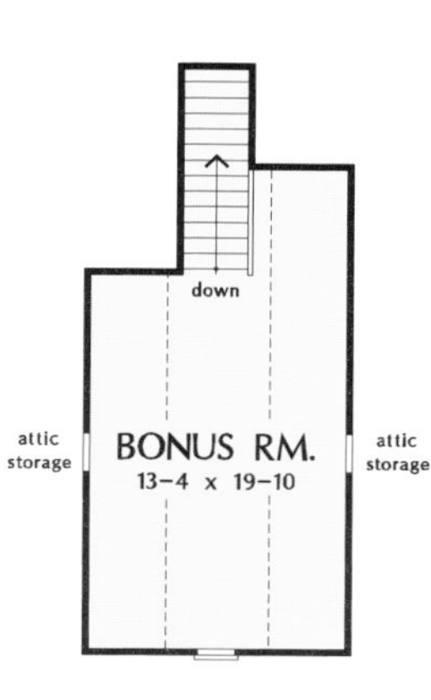

Bonus Room

*Other options available. See page 255.

Edgewood Trail — VPDS01-6667 — 1-866-525-9374

Total Living	First Floor	Second Floor	Bed	Bath	Width	Depth	Foundation	Price Category
3190 sq ft	2241 sq ft	949 sq ft	4	2-1/2	69' 8"	61' 10"	Basement/Slab	H

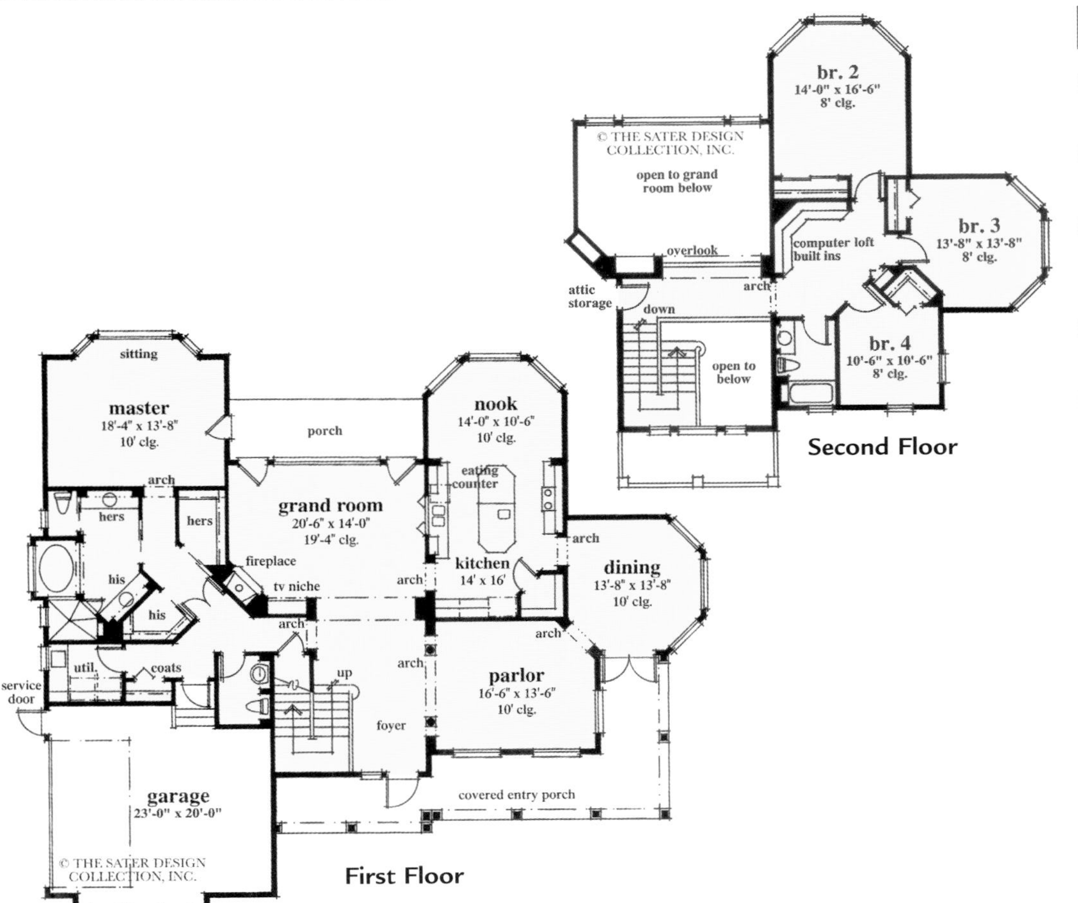

Design Features

- Formal rooms cluster near the foyer.
- A wraparound porch is perfect for stargazing.
- Dominated by a bay window, the master suite offers a spacious sitting area.
- An upper-level overlook leads to a computer loft.
- The kitchen has a food prep island and snack counter.

Rear View

Please note: Home photographed may differ from blueprint.

Sacramento — VPFB01-1047 — 1-866-525-9374

Total Living	First Floor	Opt. Bonus	Bed	Bath	Width	Depth	Foundation	Price Category
1432 sq ft	1432 sq ft	N/A	3	2	49' 0"	52' 4"	Basement, Crawl Space or Slab	E

Design Features

- This home has the charm and amenities of larger homes.
- A bay window sits at the rear of the house, letting warm sunlight flood into the breakfast room and kitchen.
- Situated near the entry is an elegant dining room with columns and an arched opening.
- Split-bedroom design allows residents their privacy.

Rear Elevation

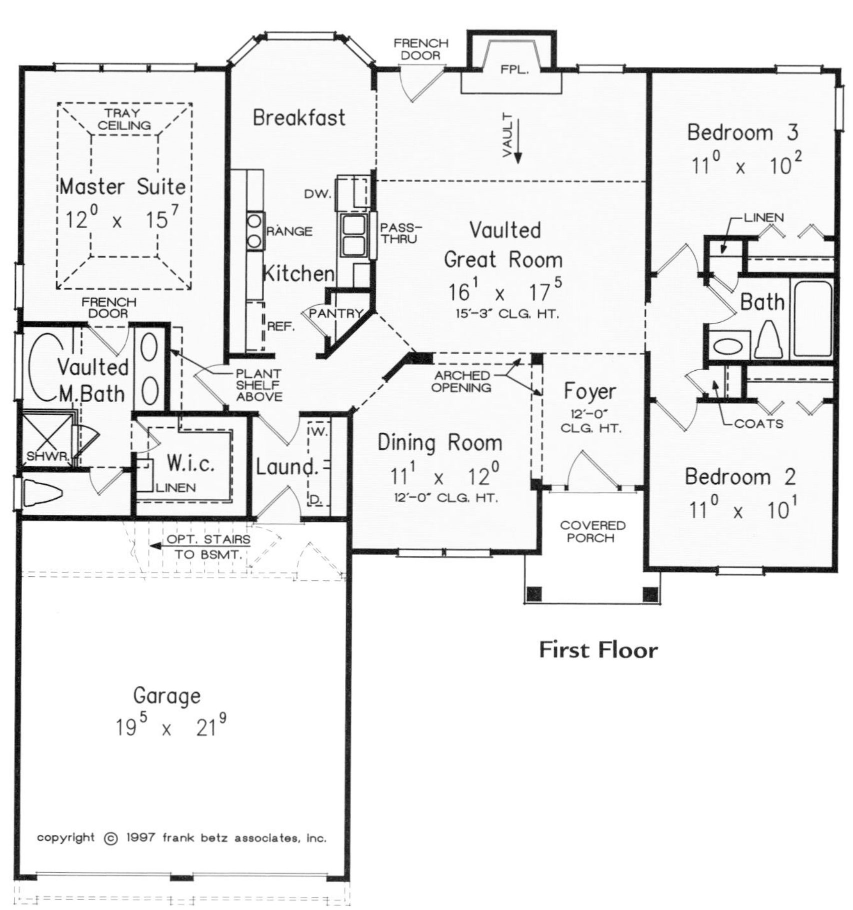

First Floor

Dewfield — VPDG01-1030 — 1-866-525-9374

Total Living	First Floor	Bonus	Bed	Bath	Width	Depth	Foundation	Price Category
1676 sq ft	1676 sq ft	376 sq ft	3	2	56' 8"	48' 4"	Crawl Space*	D

Design Features

- The curve of a Palladian window softens the strong stone wall and gable.
- The common rooms and the master bedroom are positioned to take advantage of rear views.
- A cathedral ceiling and fireplace highlight the great room.
- The bedrooms are grouped together to form a quiet zone.
- The master bedroom features a large walk-in closet and bath.

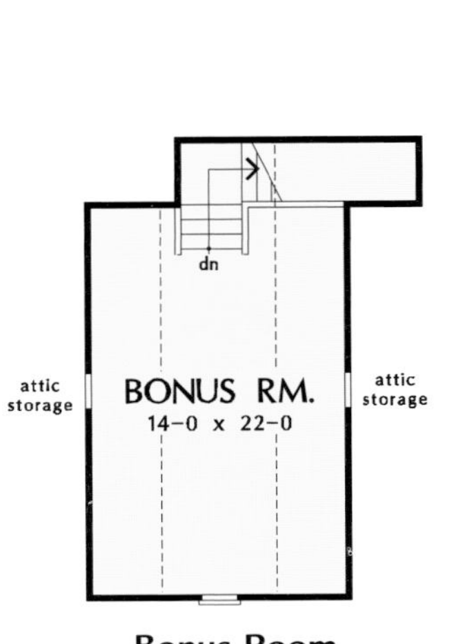

Bonus Room

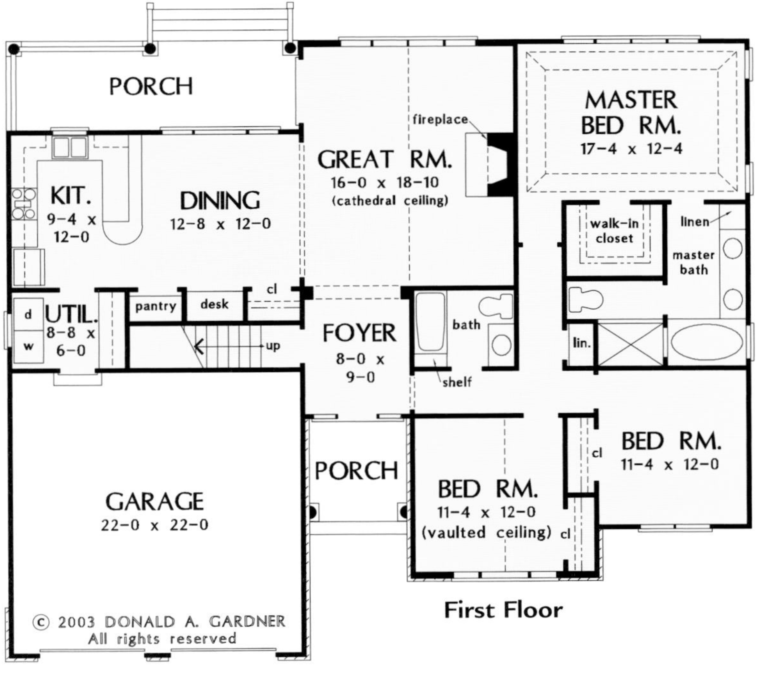

First Floor

Rear Elevation

*Other options available. See page 255.

Lexington — VPDS01-Plan 7065 — 1-866-525-9374

Total Living	First Floor	Bonus	Bed	Bath	Width	Depth	Foundation	Price Category
2454 sq ft	2454 sq ft	256 sq ft	3	2	80' 6"	66' 6"	Crawl Space	F

Design Features

- The expansive great room and study boast built-ins and specialty ceilings as well as share a double-sided fireplace.
- Six sets of French doors flood the kitchen, dining area and great room with sunlight and give access to the rear porch.
- The openness of the kitchen, dining and great room create an inviting atmosphere.
- To ensure privacy, the master suite is placed away from the guest rooms and features a bayed window, "his-and-her" walk-in closets, a luxurious bath and a private entry.

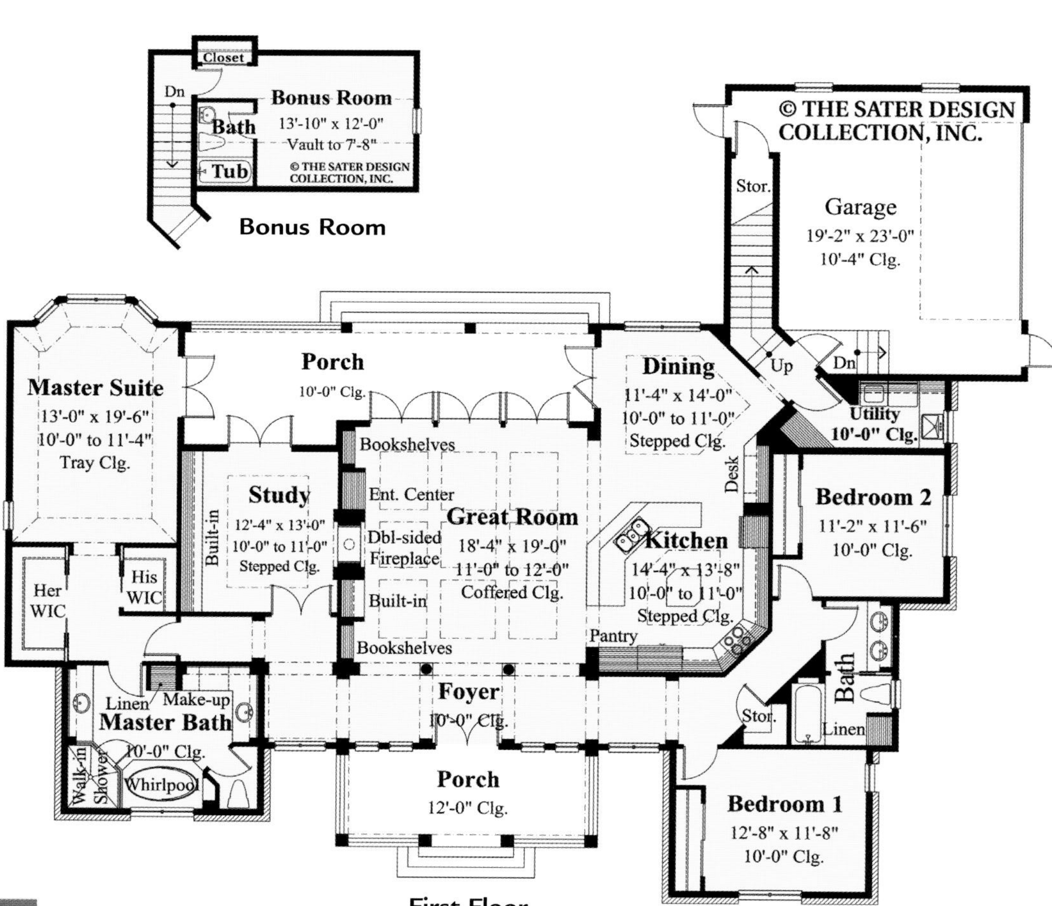

First Floor

Rear Elevation

Brentwood — VPFB01-3711 — 1-866-525-9374

Total Living	First Floor	Second Floor	Opt. Bonus	Bed	Bath	Width	Depth	Foundation	Price Category
1634 sq ft	1177 sq ft	457 sq ft	249 sq ft	3	2-1/2	41' 0"	48' 4"	Basement or Crawl Space	F

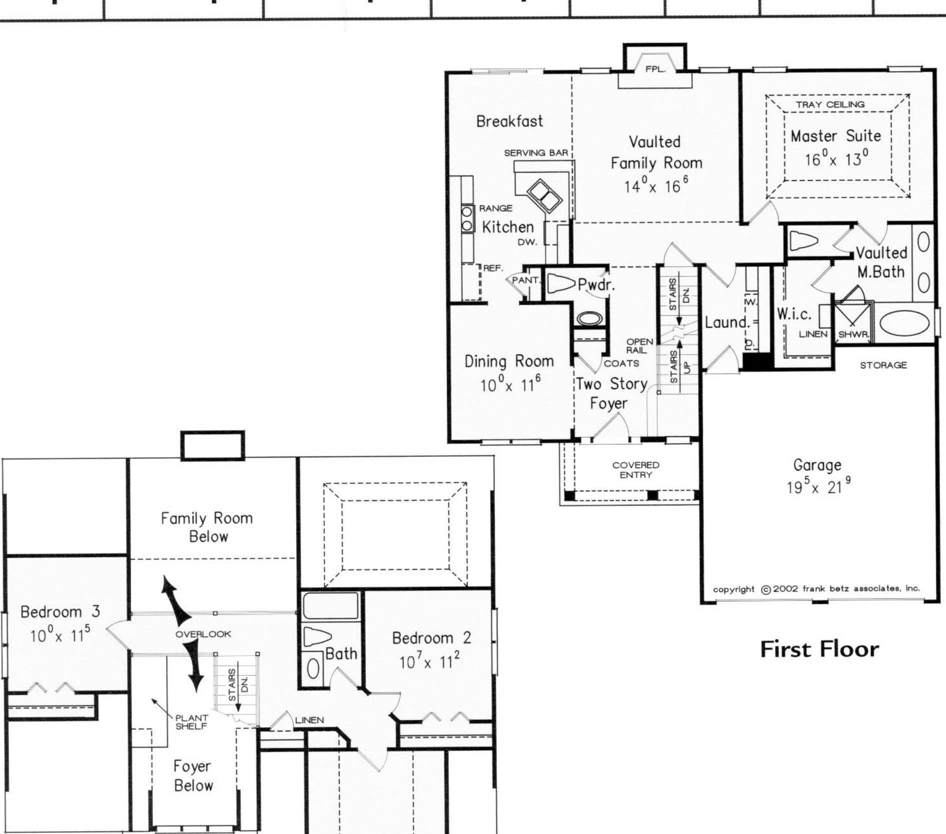

First Floor

Second Floor

Design Features

- A sheltered entry leads to a two-story foyer and wide interior vistas that extend to the back property. Rooms in the public zone are open, allowing the spaces to flex for planned events as well as family gatherings.
- At the heart of the home, the vaulted family room frames a fireplace with tall windows that bring in natural light.
- The main-level master suite boasts a tray ceiling, while two upper-level bedrooms are connected by a balcony bridge that overlooks the foyer and family room.

Rear Elevation

Donald A. Gardner Architects, Inc.

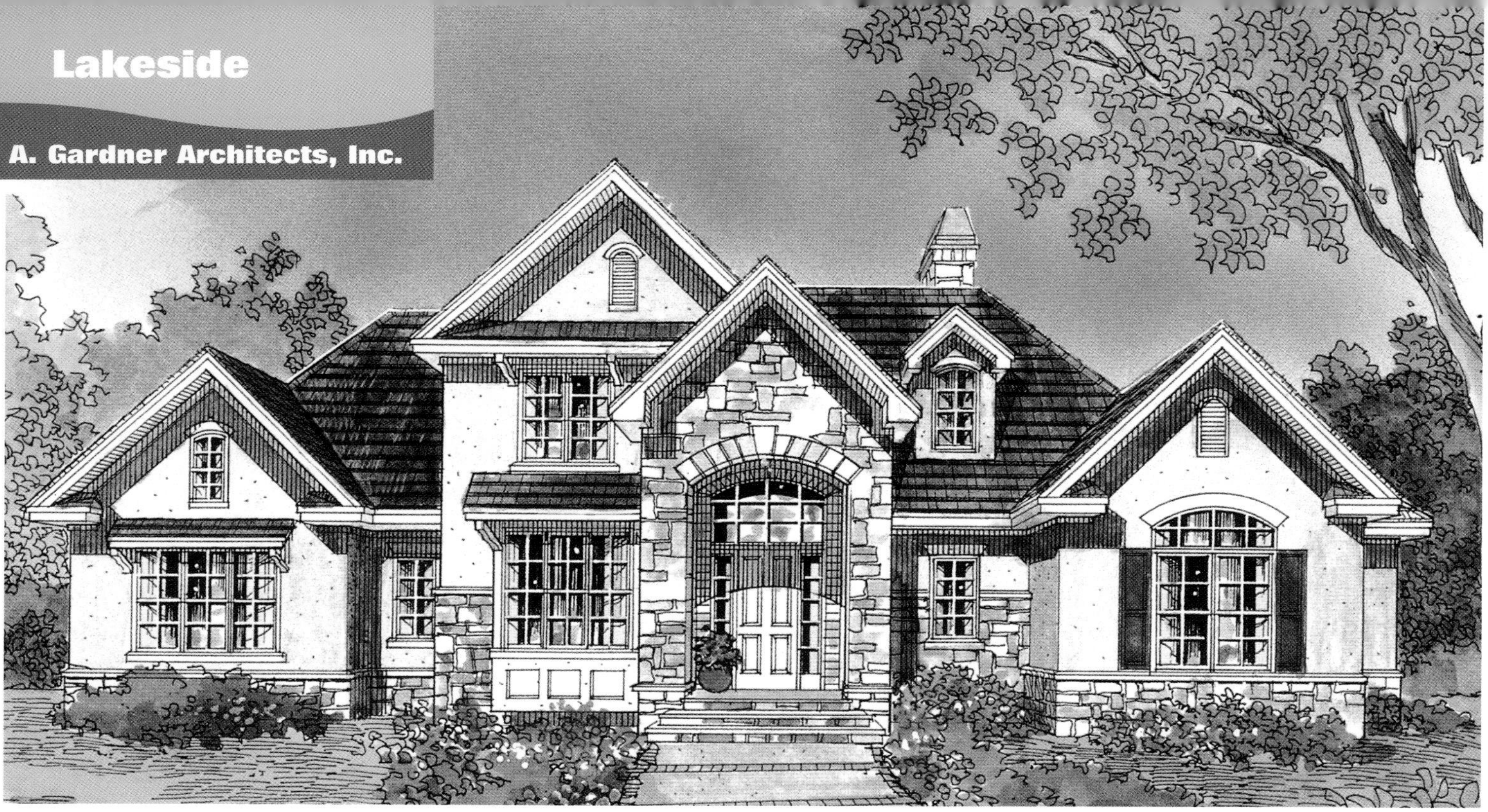

Hyde Park — VPDG01-816 — 1-866-525-9374

Total Living	First Floor	Second Floor	Bonus	Bed	Bath	Width	Depth	Foundation	Price Category
2387 sq ft	1918 sq ft	469 sq ft	374 sq ft	4	3	73' 3"	43' 6"	Crawl Space*	E

Design Features

- A two-story ceiling adds height and drama to the formal foyer.
- The adjacent dining room is enriched by a box-bay window with lovely window seat.
- The vaulted great room features a stunning rear clerestory dormer and a fireplace.
- A second-floor balcony overlooks both the great room and foyer.

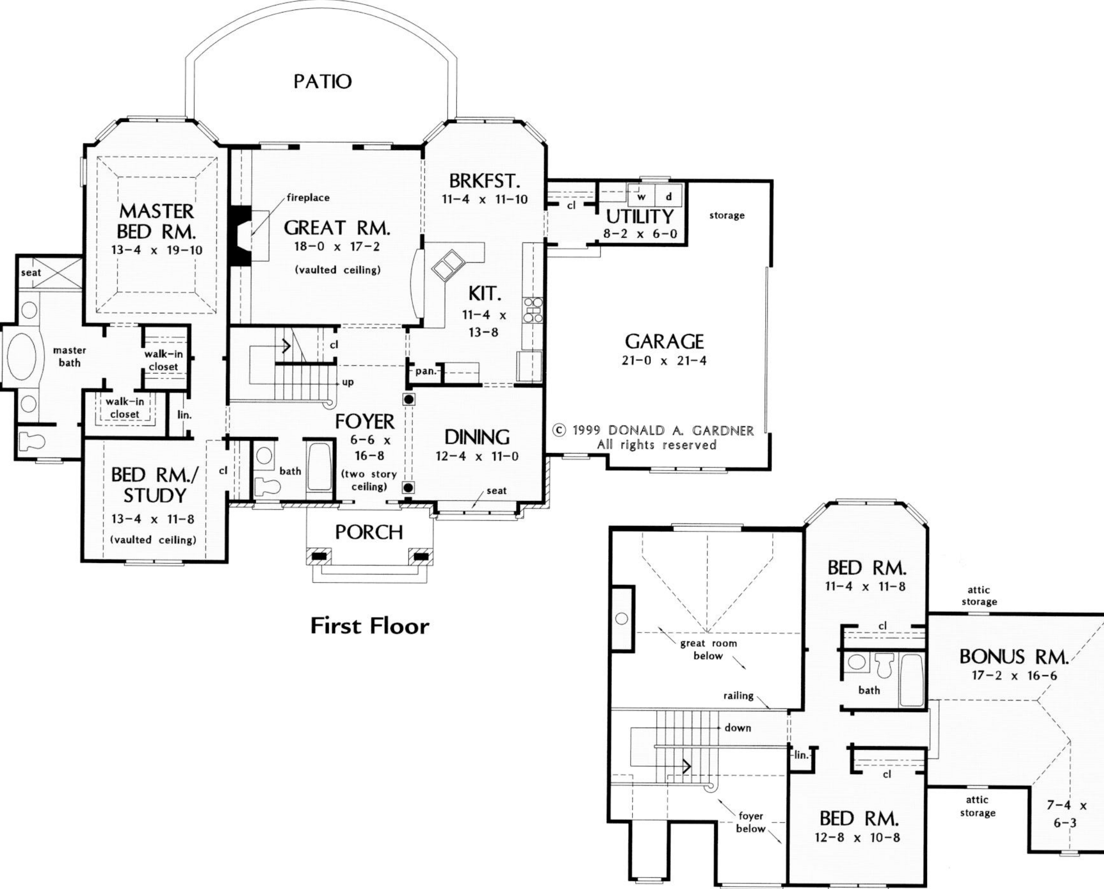

First Floor

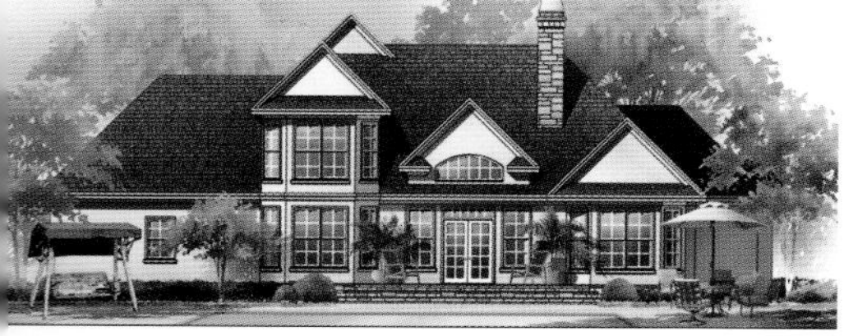

Rear Elevation

Second Floor

*Other options available. See page 255.

Sandusky — VPDS01-Plan 7062 — 1-866-525-9374

Total Living	First Floor	Second Floor	Bonus	Bed	Bath	Width	Depth	Foundation	Price Category
3082 sq ft	2138 sq ft	944 sq ft	427 sq ft	3	3-1/2	77' 8"	64' 0"	Crawl Space, Opt. Finished Basement	H

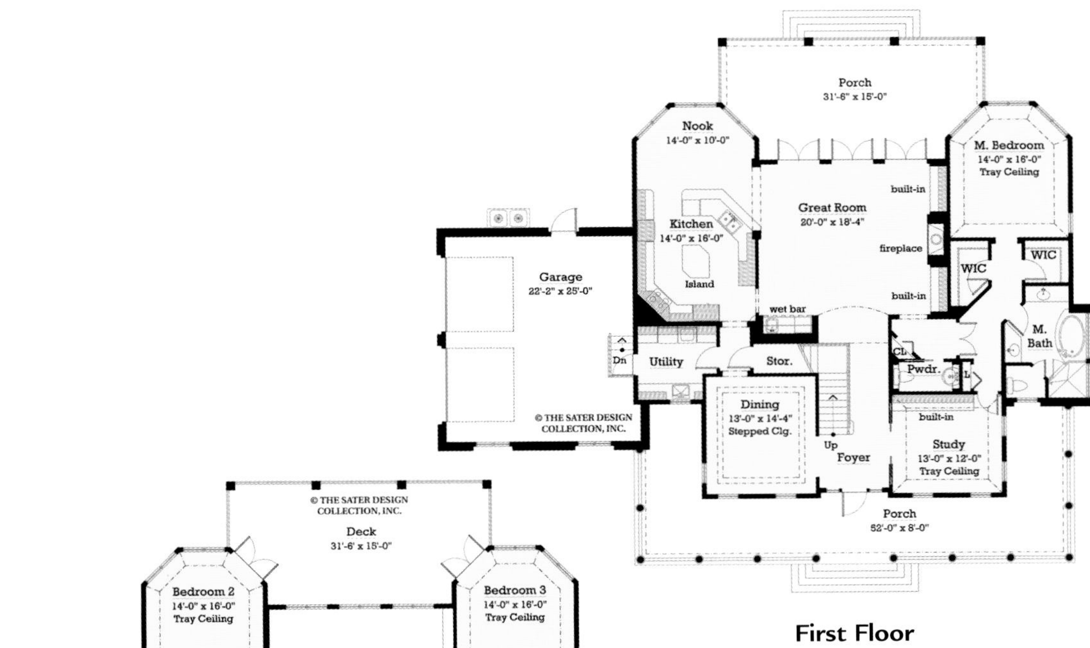

First Floor

Second Floor

Design Features

- Built-in cabinetry, a massive fire-place and a host of French doors highlight the central living space, which also features a wet bar.
- An island kitchen provides ample counter and storage space, a work island and easy access to the break-fast nook and great room.
- A quiet study features pocket doors, built-ins and a tray ceiling.
- The upper level boasts a catwalk that connects the two secondary suites featuring tray ceilings, glass corners, walk-in closets, spacious baths and individual access to the upper deck.

Rear Elevation

Guilford — VPFB01-Plan 3689 — 1-866-525-9374

Total Living	First Floor	Opt. 2nd Fl.	Bed	Bath	Width	Depth	Foundation	Price Category
1933 sq ft	1933 sq ft	519 sq ft	4	3-1/2	62' 0"	50' 0"	Basement or Crawl Space	G

Design Features

- Quaint? Timeless? Classic? All of these so accurately describe the charm that the *Guilford* exudes.
- From the cheery dormers to the board-and-batten shutters, this design stepped off the streets of yesteryear.
- Inside, the master suite features a wall of windows with views to the backyard.
- Two additional bedrooms share a divided bath.

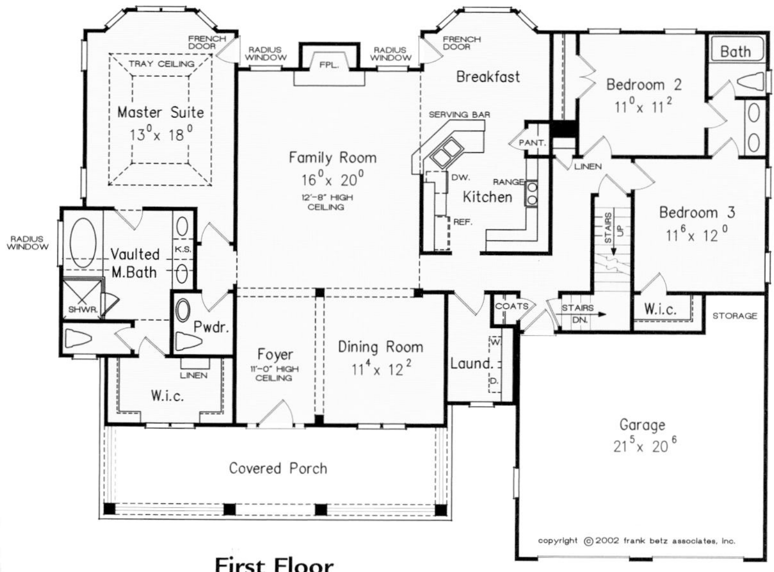

First Floor

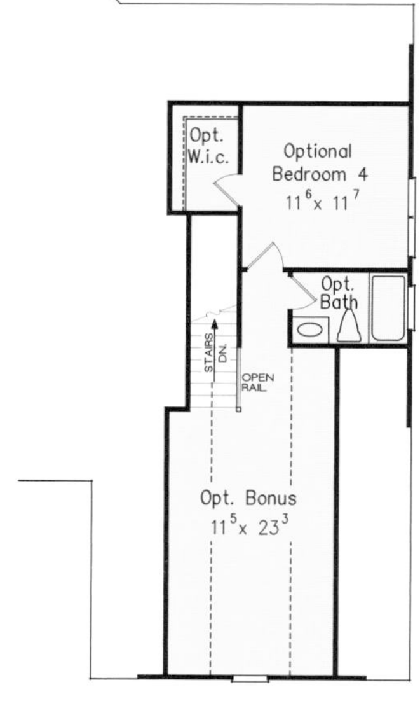

Opt. Second Floor

Rear Elevation

Nottingham — VPDG01-854 — 1-866-525-9374

Total Living	First Floor	Bonus	Bed	Bath	Width	Depth	Foundation	Price Category
2353 sq ft	2353 sq ft	353 sq ft	4	2	65' 8"	67' 10"	Crawl Space*	E

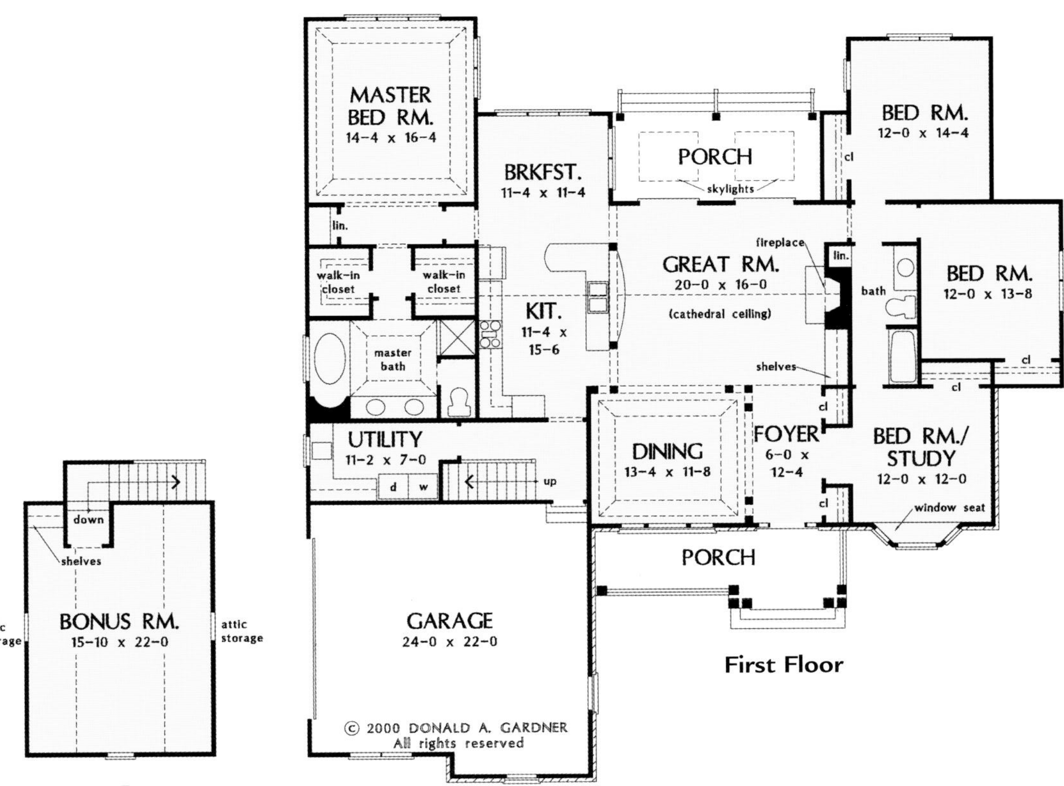

First Floor

Bonus Room

Design Features

- An exciting cathedral ceiling unifies the open great room and kitchen.
- The great room features a fireplace, built-in shelves and access to the skylit back porch.
- Note the spacious utility room with laundry sink and cabinets.
- Tray ceilings top the master bedroom and bath, which are separated by two walk-in closets.

Rear Elevation

*Other options available. See page 255.

Lunden Valley — VPDS01-7050 — 1-866-525-9374

Total Living	First Floor	Opt. 2nd Fl.	Bed	Bath	Width	Depth	Foundation	Price Category
2555 sq ft	2555 sq ft	N/A	3 + Study	2-1/2	70' 0"	76' 6"	Crawl Space	G

Design Features

- This home features a charming front porch which supports a distinctive front gable.
- A column-lined hall leads to private areas of the home.
- The master has rear-porch access.
- Natural light from the rear porch fills the great room and kitchen.
- A dining room and study border the foyer.

Rear Elevation

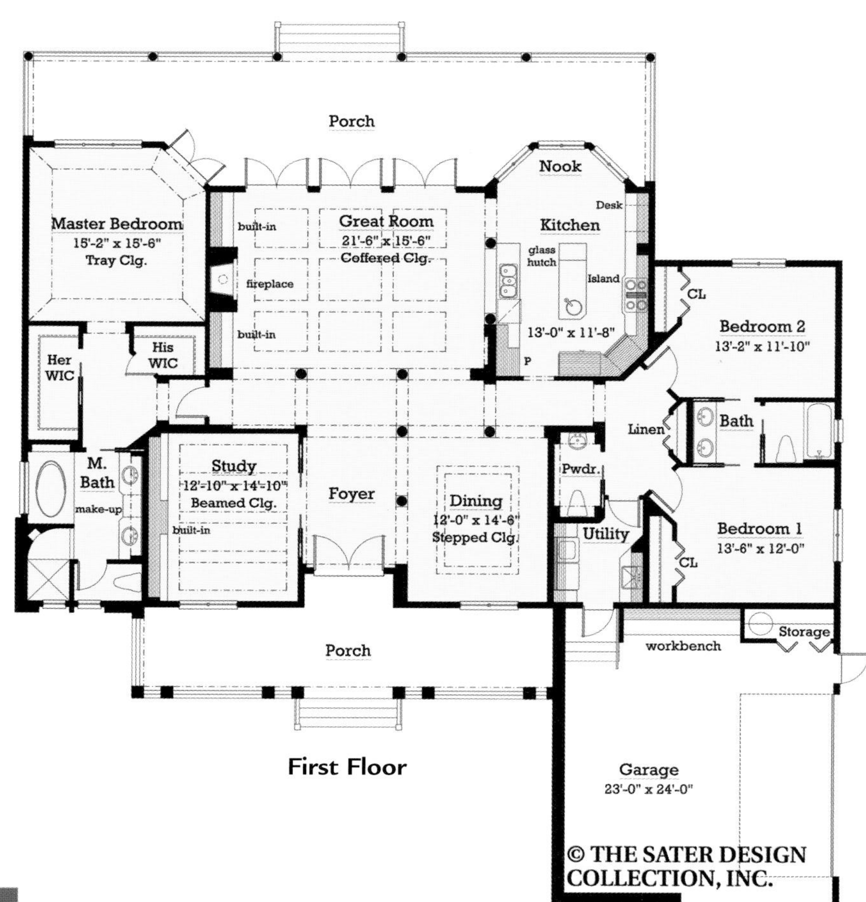

First Floor

Hedgerow — VPFB01-Plan 3945 — 1-866-525-9374

Total Living	First Floor	Second Floor	Opt. Bonus	Bed	Bath	Width	Depth	Foundation	Price Category
2324 sq ft	1769 sq ft	555 sq ft	287 sq ft	3	2-1/2	59' 0"	52' 0"	Basement, Crawl Space or Slab	H

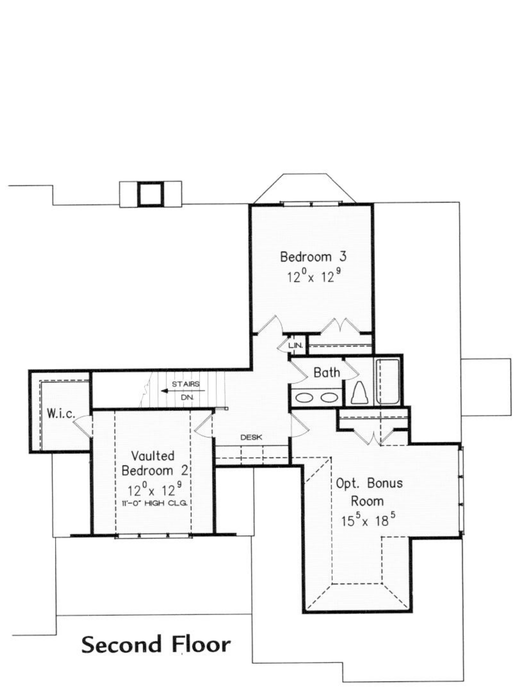

Second Floor

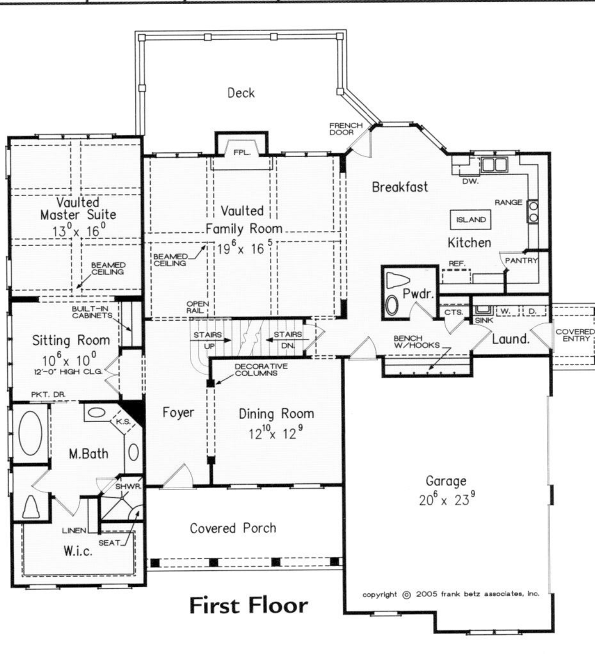

First Floor

Design Features

- From the front porch to the main-level master suite, the *Hedgerow* offers many luxuries that much larger homes provide.
- The laundry room offers a side entrance with a built-in bench and hooks, providing the ideal place for shoes, coats and book bags.
- This main-level master floor plan offers a sitting room with built-in bookshelves.
- A covered entry off of the laundry room allows children and guests to enter and leave their belongings on a built-in bench with coat hooks.

Rear Elevation

Laycrest — VPDG01-995-D — 1-866-525-9374

Total Living	First Floor	Basement	Bonus	Bed	Bath	Width	Depth	Foundation	Price Category
3320 sq ft	1720 sq ft	1600 sq ft	N/A	4	3-1/2	59' 0"	59' 4"	Hillside Walkout	G

Design Features

- With Arts-n-Crafts charm, this hillside design starts with an exterior of siding and stone.
- A rear clerestory frames the sky and places it under the great room's cathedral ceiling.
- Built-in cabinetry and fireplaces enhance the great room and rec room.
- An angled counter separates the kitchen from the dining room and great room.
- A wet bar, bay windows and tray ceilings add custom style.

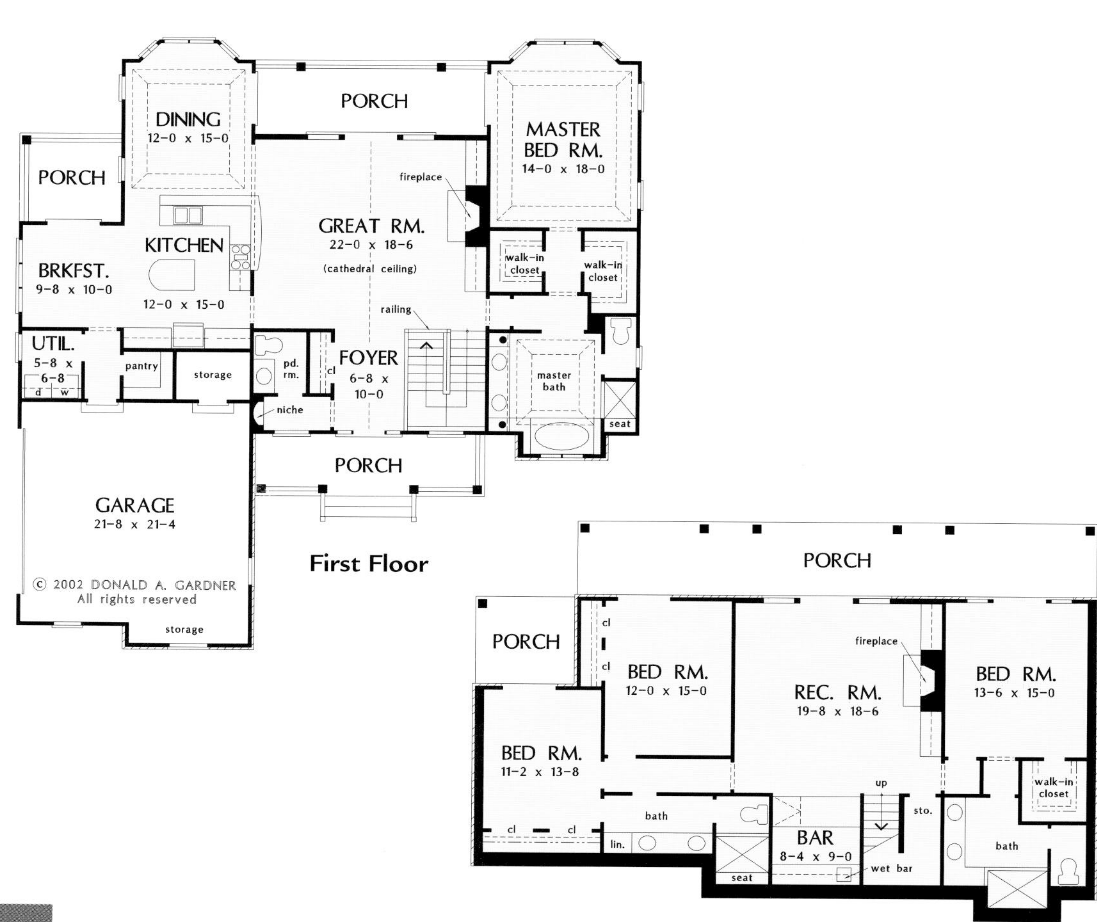

First Floor

Basement

Rear Elevation

Chantel — VPDS01-7011 — 1-866-525-9374

Total Living	First Floor	Bonus	Bed	Bath	Width	Depth	Foundation	Price Category
1822 sq ft	1822 sq ft	N/A	3 + Study	2	58' 0"	67' 2"	Basement/Opt. Fin. Basement	E

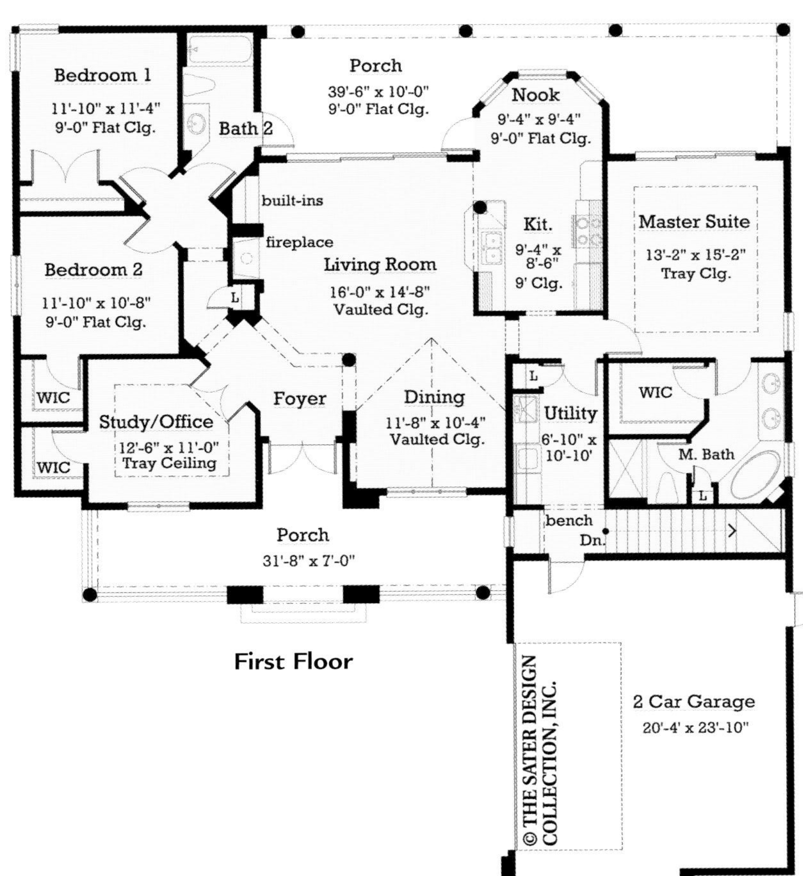

First Floor

Design Features

- A sheltering front porch is the home's main focal point.
- The living and dining rooms have vaulted ceilings.
- The living and master open to the rear porch.
- A U-shaped kitchen has a convenient pass-thru.
- Louvered shutters accentuate the office window.

Rear Elevation

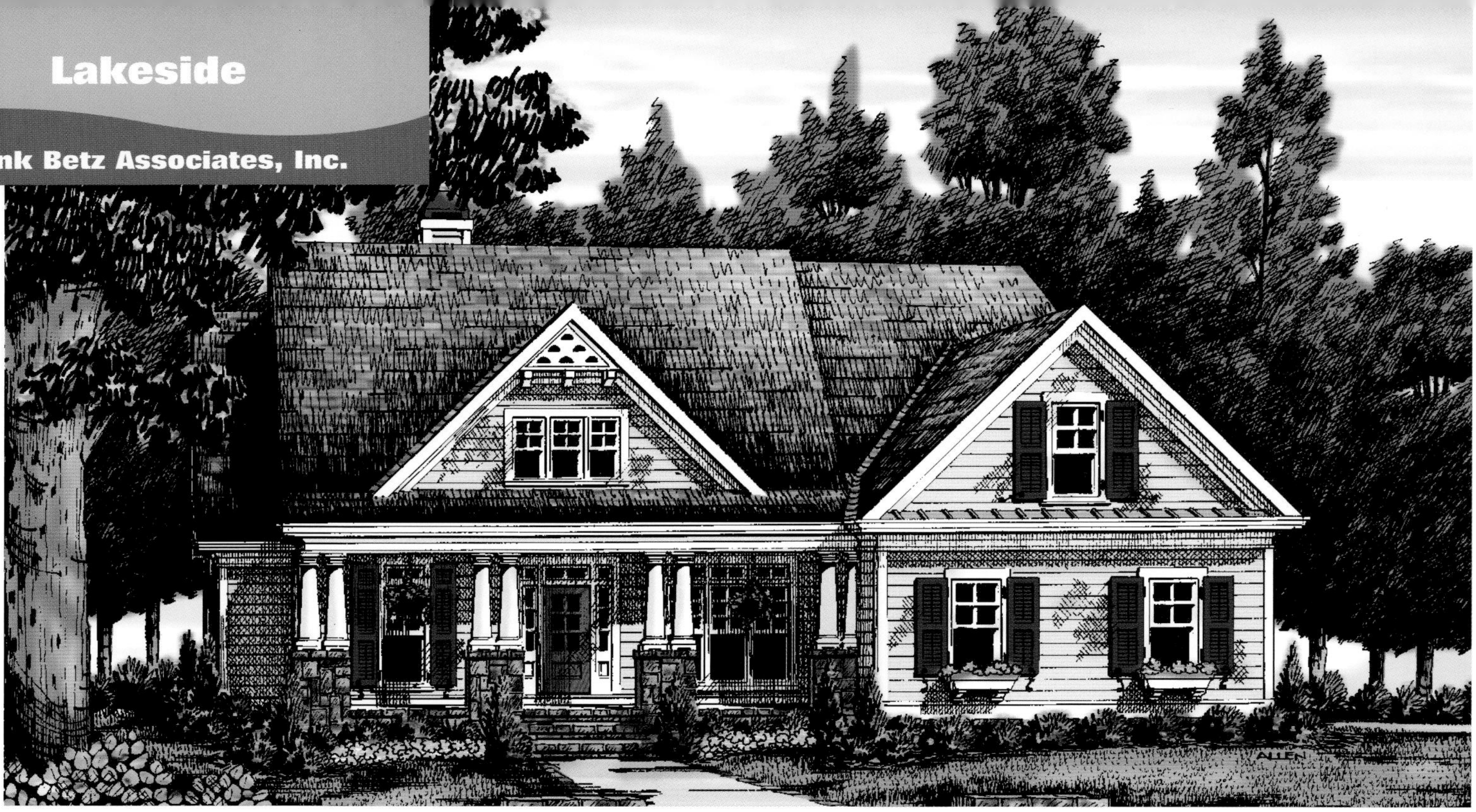

Macallen — VPFB01-Plan 3899 — 1-866-525-9374

Total Living	First Floor	Second Floor	Opt. Bonus	Bed	Bath	Width	Depth	Foundation	Price Category
2299 sq ft	1774 sq ft	525 sq ft	300 sq ft	4	3	56' 0"	63' 4"	Basement, Crawl Space or Slab	G

Design Features

- The *Macallen* has those special touches that personalize a home.
- A beamed ceiling gives the master suite a rustic and casual elegance that makes it feel like a cottage retreat.
- Radius transom windows in the great room let the natural light pour into this space.
- A screened porch is perfect for outdoor entertaining and relaxation.

First Floor

Second Floor

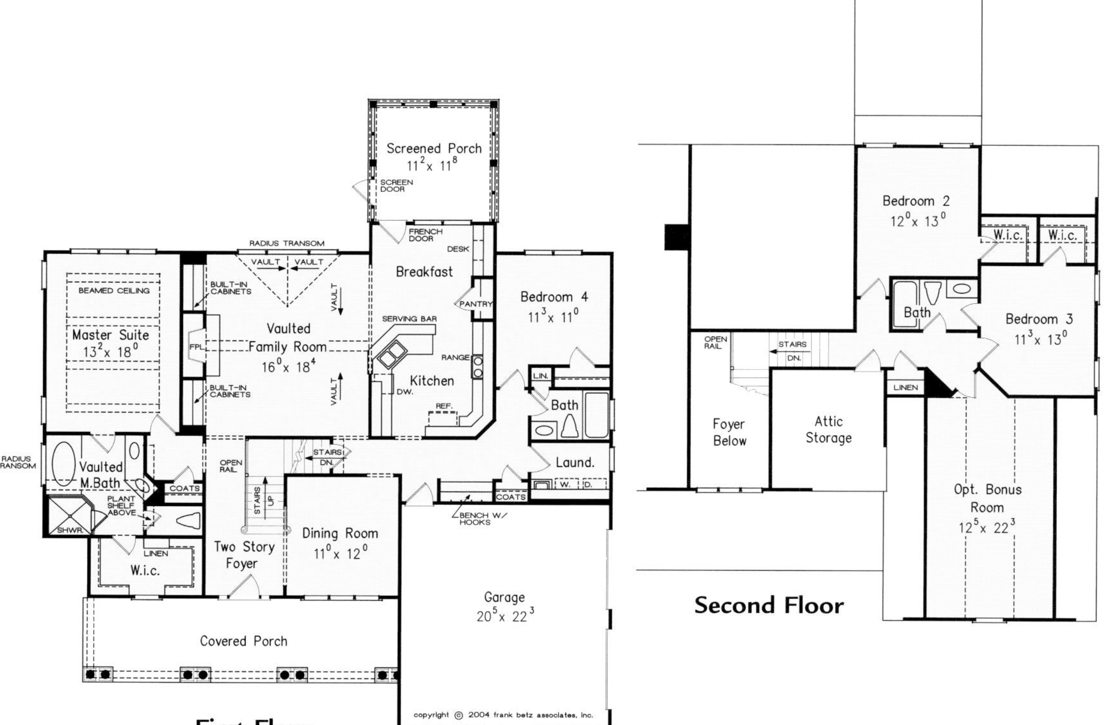

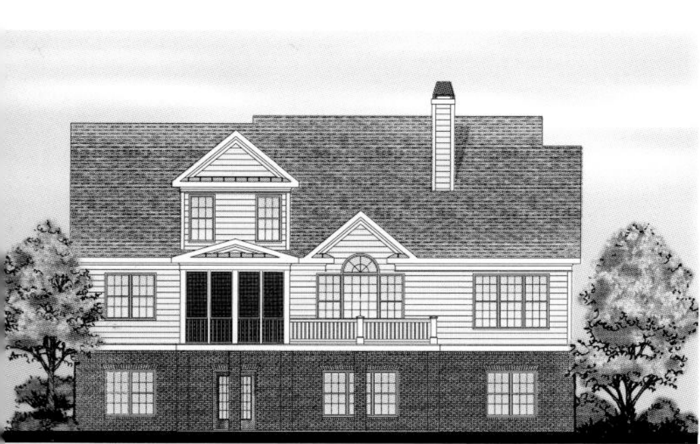

Rear Elevation

Colridge — VPDG01-1012-D — 1-866-525-9374

Total Living	First Floor	Basement	Bonus	Bed	Bath	Width	Depth	Walls/Foundation	Price Category
2652 sq ft	1732 sq ft	920 sq ft	N/A	3	3	70' 6"	59' 6"	Hillside Walkout	F

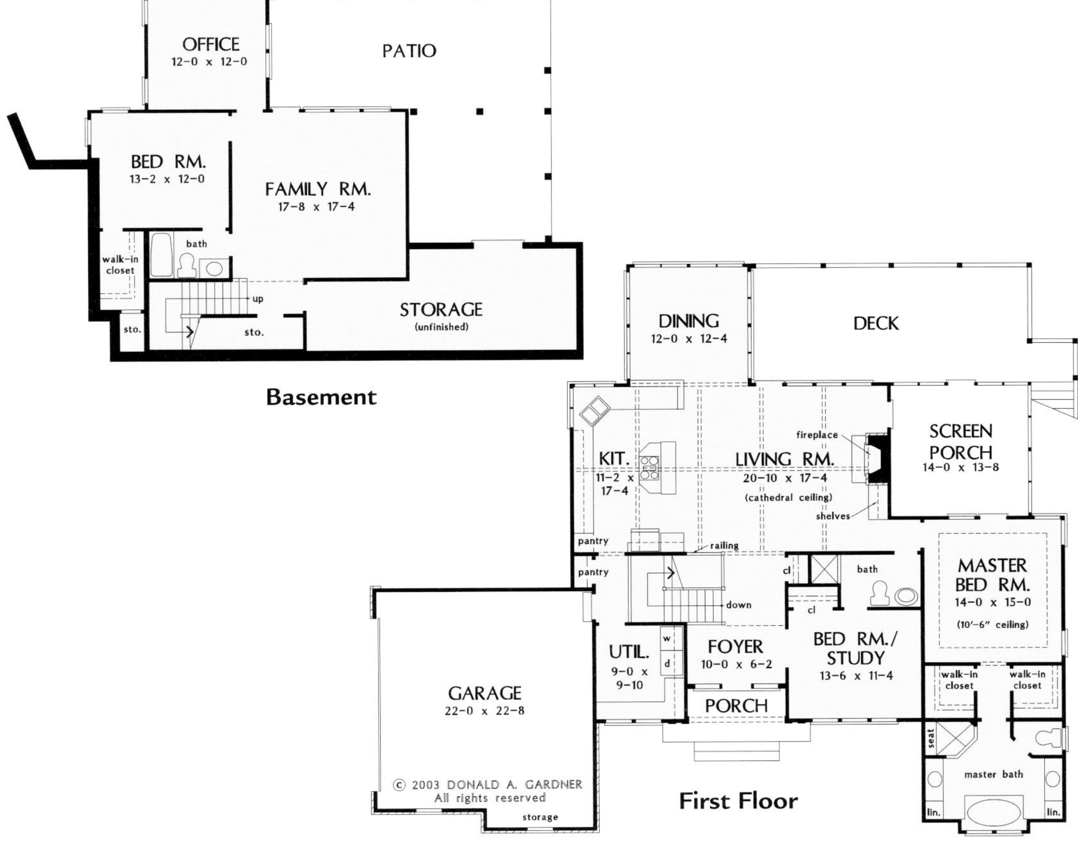

Basement

First Floor

Design Features

- A mixture of exterior materials enhances the curb appeal of this hillside walkout.
- A large deck, screened porch and patio promote outdoor living.
- A cathedral ceiling with exposed beams crowns the kitchen and great room, creating volume.
- The master suite is complete with a tray ceiling in the bedroom and screened-porch access.

Rear View

Please note: Home photographed may differ from blueprint.

Marcella — VPDS01-7005 — 1-866-525-9374

Total Living	First Floor	Bonus	Bed	Bath	Width	Depth	Foundation	Price Category
2487 sq ft	2487 sq ft	N/A	3 + Study	2	70' 0"	72' 0"	Slab/opt. Basement	F

Design Features

- A clever roofline is punctuated by shutters and a copper-topped office roof.
- Glass doors expand the dining and living rooms to the rear porch.
- The large kitchen maintains easy access to the dining room and nook.
- A study/office has built-in bookshelves and a front-yard view.
- The privacy of the master suite is protected by double entry doors.

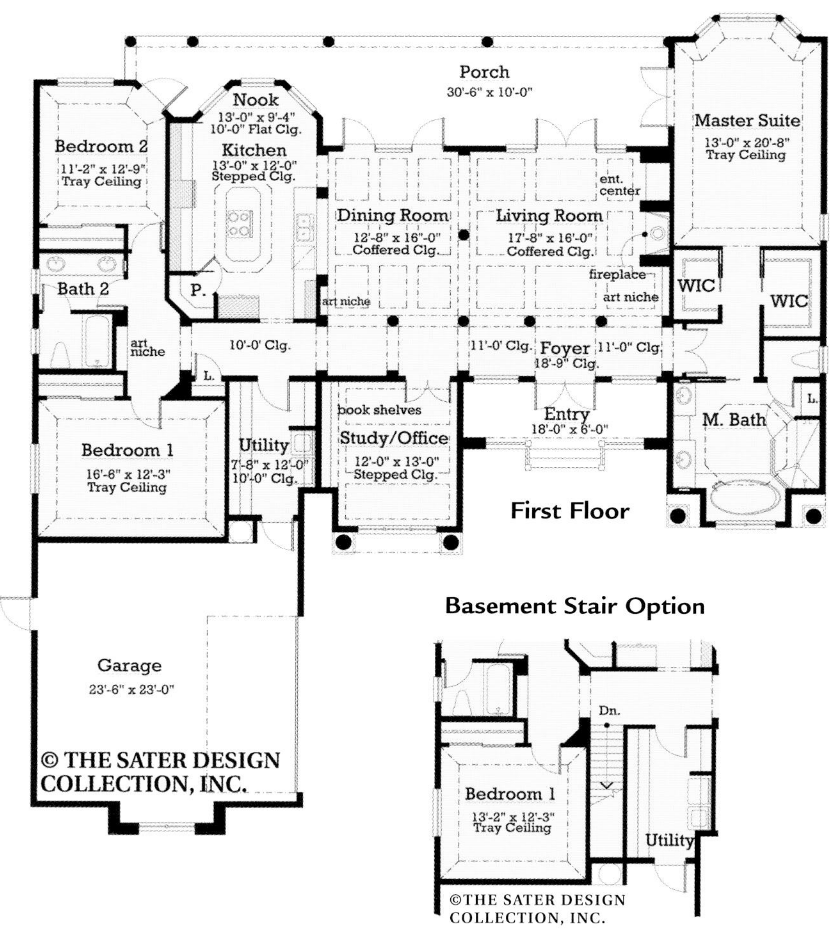

Rear Elevation

Waterston — VPFB01-Plan 3904 — 1-866-525-9374

Total Living	First Floor	Second Floor	Opt. Bonus	Bed	Bath	Width	Depth	Foundation	Price Category
2196 sq ft	1472 sq ft	724 sq ft	300 sq ft	4	2-1/2	52' 4"	52' 0"	Basement, Crawl Space or Slab	G

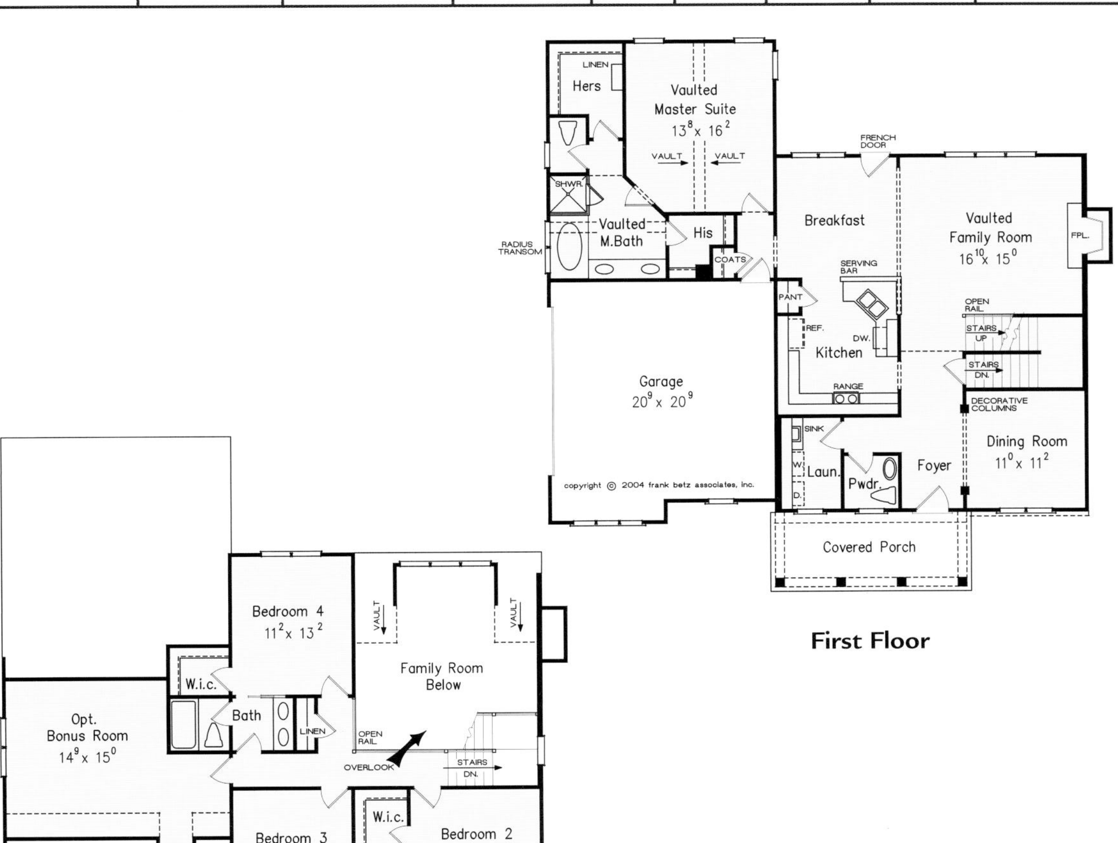

First Floor

Second Floor

Design Features

- Board-and-batten accents and stately brick were commonplace years ago and are again in high demand.
- The *Waterston*'s master suite is well appointed with vaulted ceilings and a lavish bath.
- Decorative columns enhance the dining room, making a bold architectural statement from the foyer.
- Optional bonus space upstairs can be finished into a playroom, bedroom or home office.

Rear Elevation

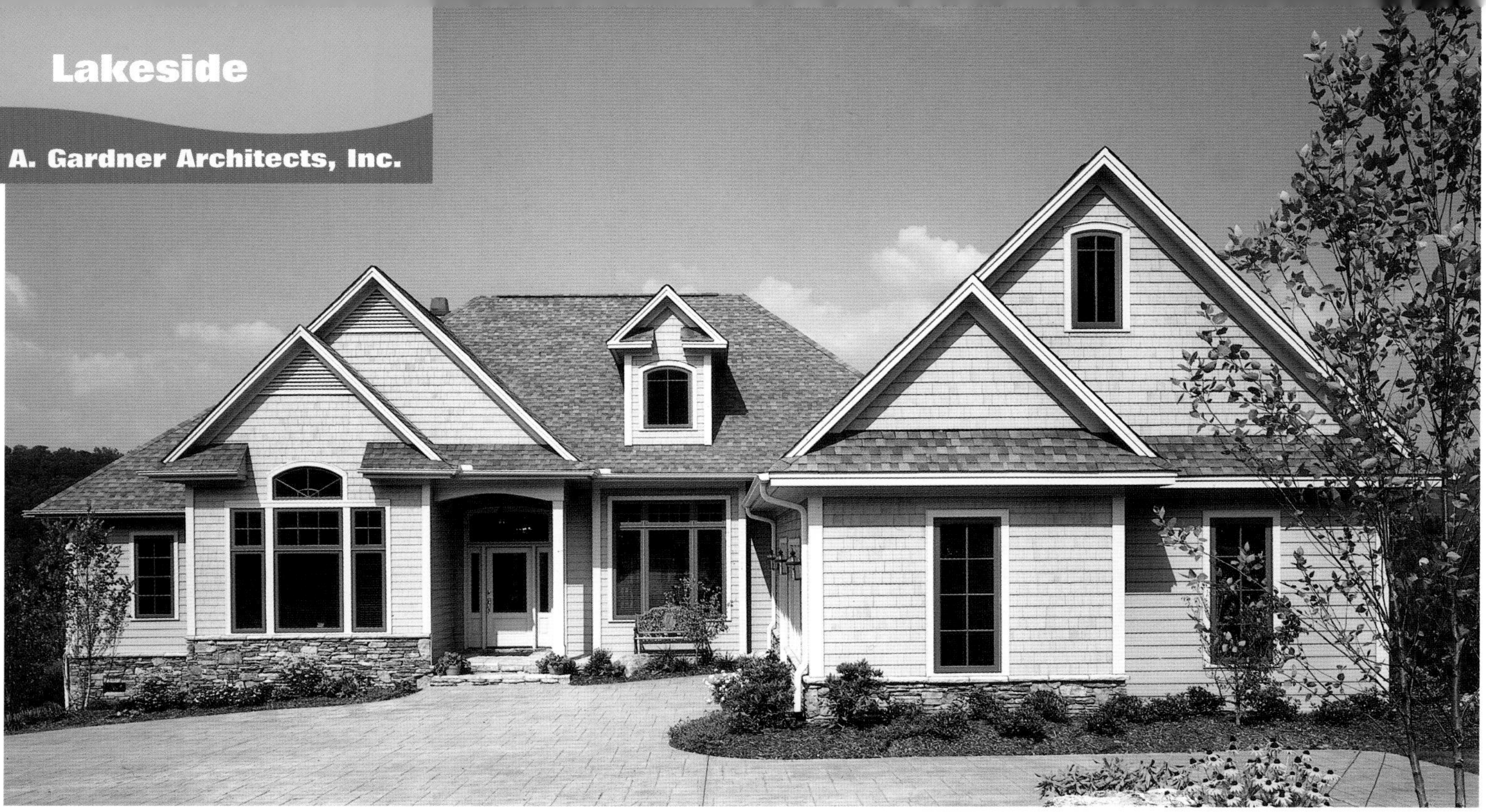

Monte Vista — VPDG01-Plan 711-D — 1-866-525-9374

Total Living	First Floor	Basement	Bed	Bath	Width	Depth	Foundation	Price Category
3509 sq ft	2297 sq ft	1212 sq ft	5	5-1/2	70' 10"	69' 0"	Hillside Walkout	H

Design Features

- Cedar shake, stone and siding embellish the exterior of this sloping-lot home.
- An expansive deck allows for spectacular rear views.
- Ceiling treatments enhance the open living and dining rooms, as well as the versatile bedroom/study.
- The kitchen features a center cook-top island and adjoining breakfast bay with rear-deck access.
- Note the convenient first-floor master suite and secondary bedrooms.

First Floor

Basement

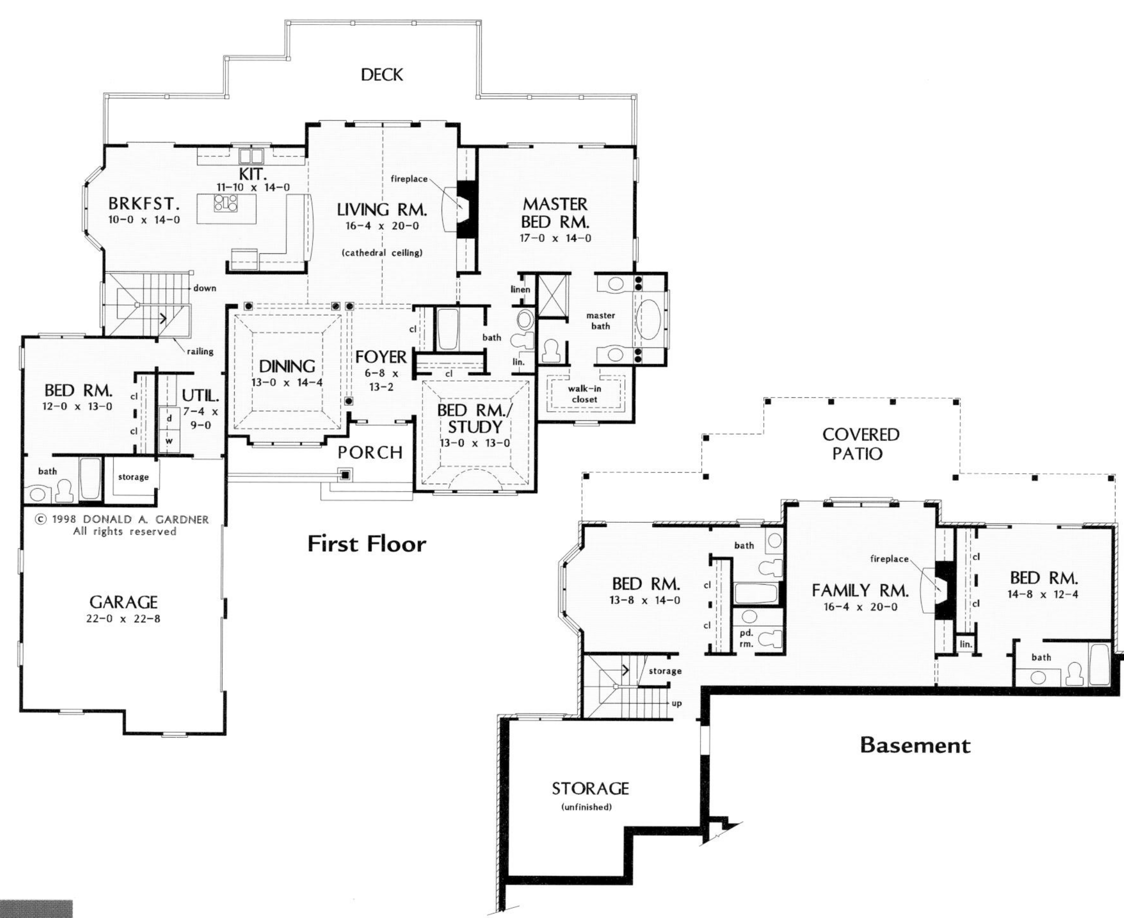

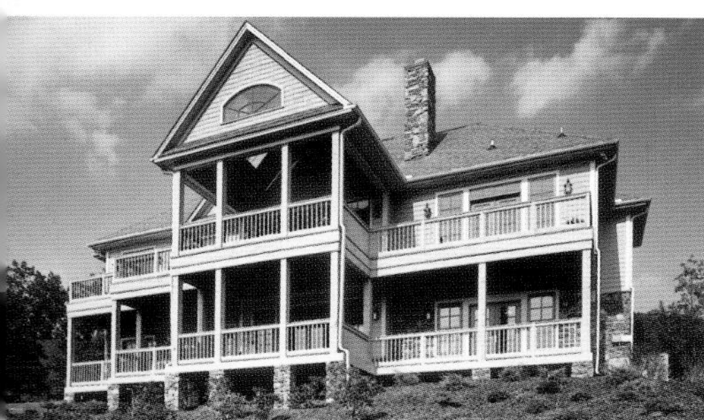

Rear View

Please note: Home photographed may differ from blueprint.

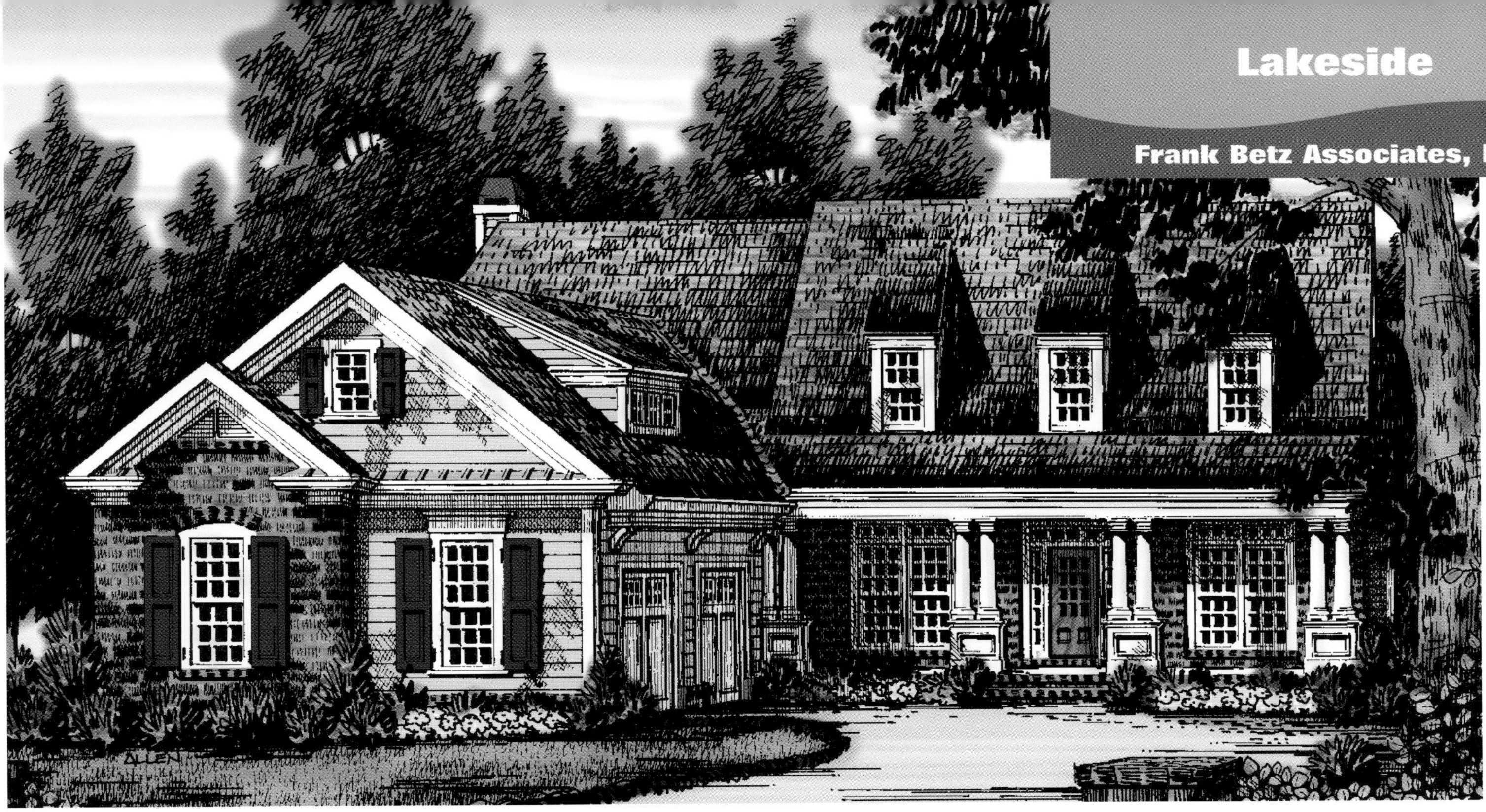

Westvale — VPFB01-Plan 3845 — 1-866-525-9374

Total Living	First Floor	Opt. 2nd Fl.	Bed	Bath	Width	Depth	Foundation	Price Category
2214 sq ft	2214 sq ft	377 sq ft	4	3-1/2	59' 4"	73' 0"	Basement or Crawl Space	G

Opt. Second Floor

First Floor

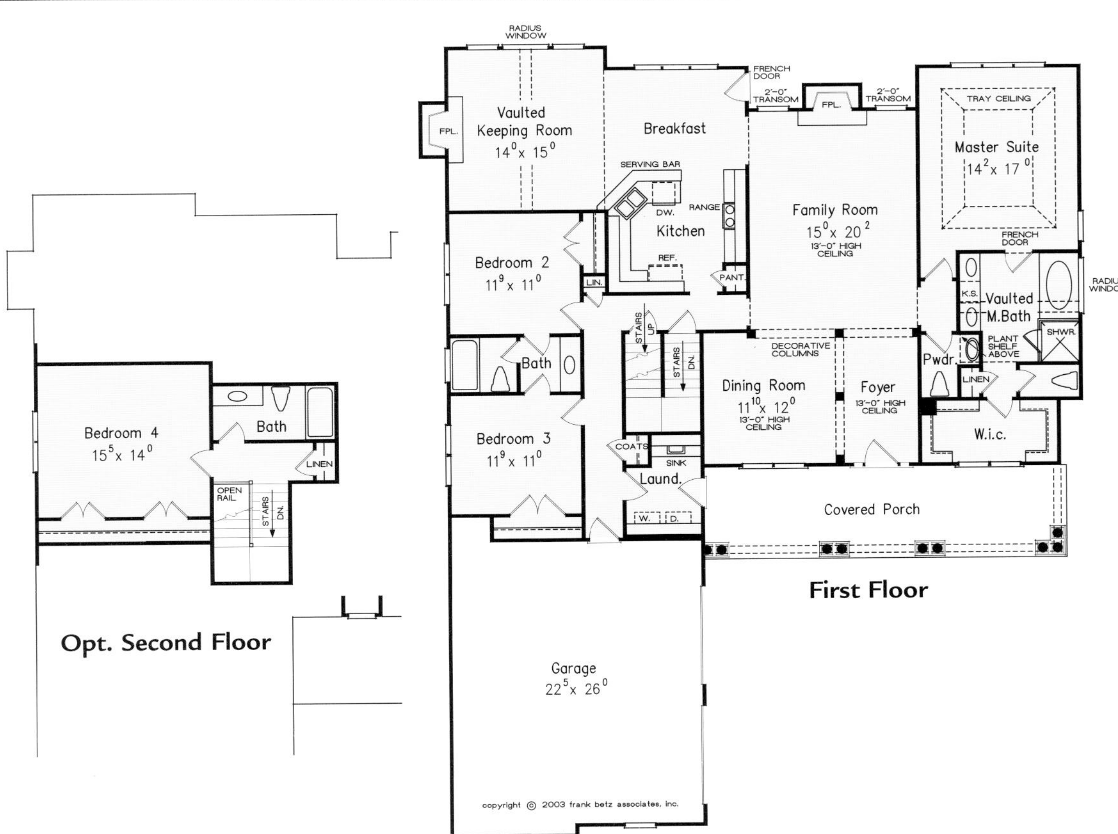

Design Features

- Friendly dormers canopy a columned front porch on the *Westvale,* extending a warm welcome to visitors and homeowners alike.
- A vaulted keeping room off the kitchen overlooks the backyard, making a cozy and casual place to unwind after meal times.
- Homeowners will love the privacy of the master suite that exclusively occupies the right side of the home.
- Decorative columns lining the dining room and foyer add a special character to this design.

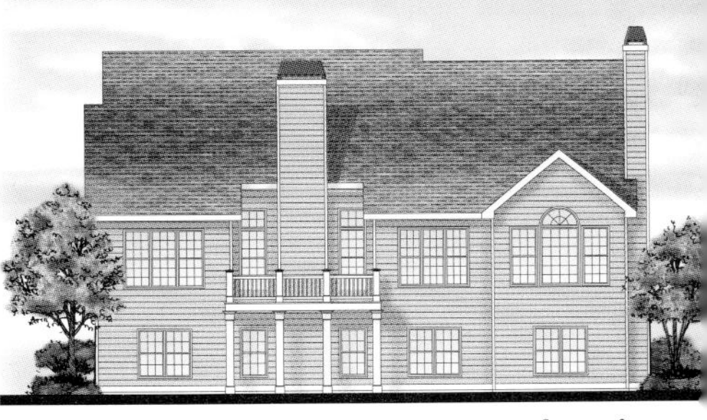

Rear Elevation

Peppermill — VPDG01-1034 — 1-866-525-9374

Total Living	First Floor	Second Floor	Bonus	Bed	Bath	Width	Depth	Foundation	Price Category
2586 sq ft	1809 sq ft	777 sq ft	264 sq ft	4	3-1/2	70' 7"	48' 4"	Crawl Space*	F

Design Features

- A traditional brick exterior with two country porches creates a modern exterior.
- Bold columns and a metal roof welcome guests inside an equally impressive interior.
- Both the foyer and great room have two-story ceilings, and a tray ceiling tops the master bedroom.
- A bay window expands the breakfast nook, while French doors lead to the rear porch.
- The living room/study and bonus room add flexibility for changing needs.

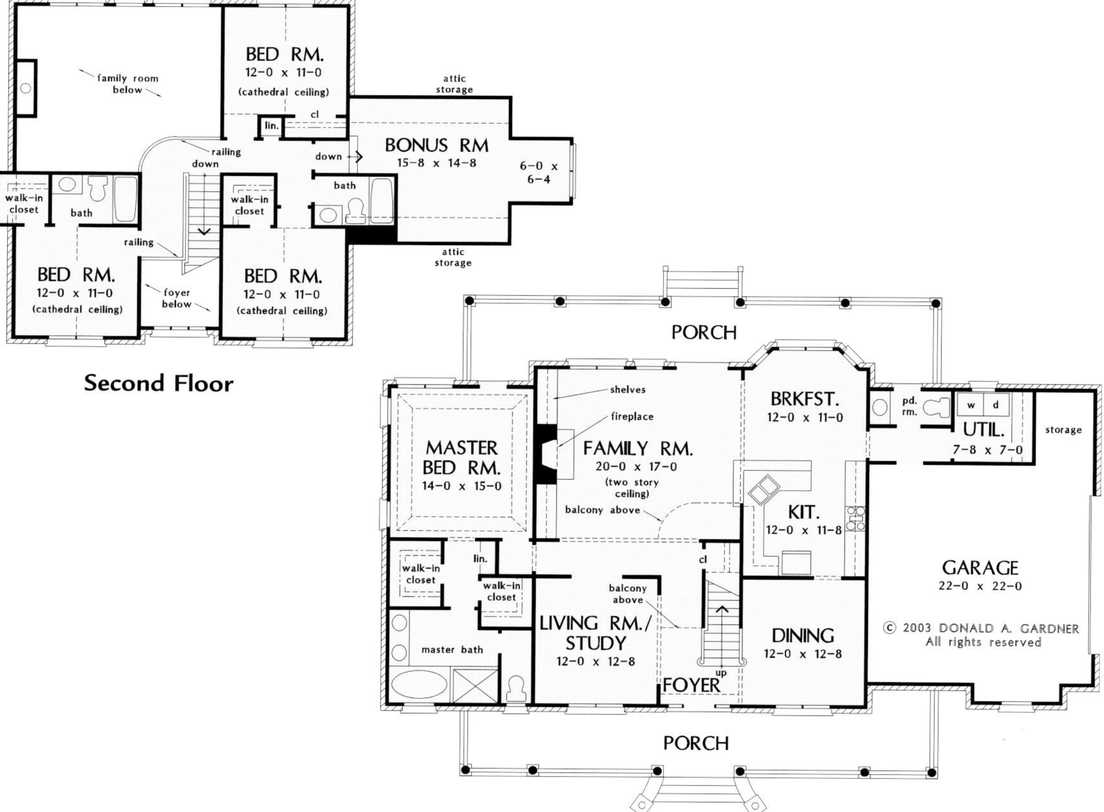

Second Floor

First Floor

Rear Elevation

*Other options available. See page 255.

Charlevoix — VPDG01-1086 — 1-866-525-9374

Total Living	First Floor	Bonus	Bed	Bath	Width	Depth	Foundation	Price Category
2607 sq ft	2607 sq ft	413 sq ft	4	3	77' 0"	58' 0"	Crawl Space*	F

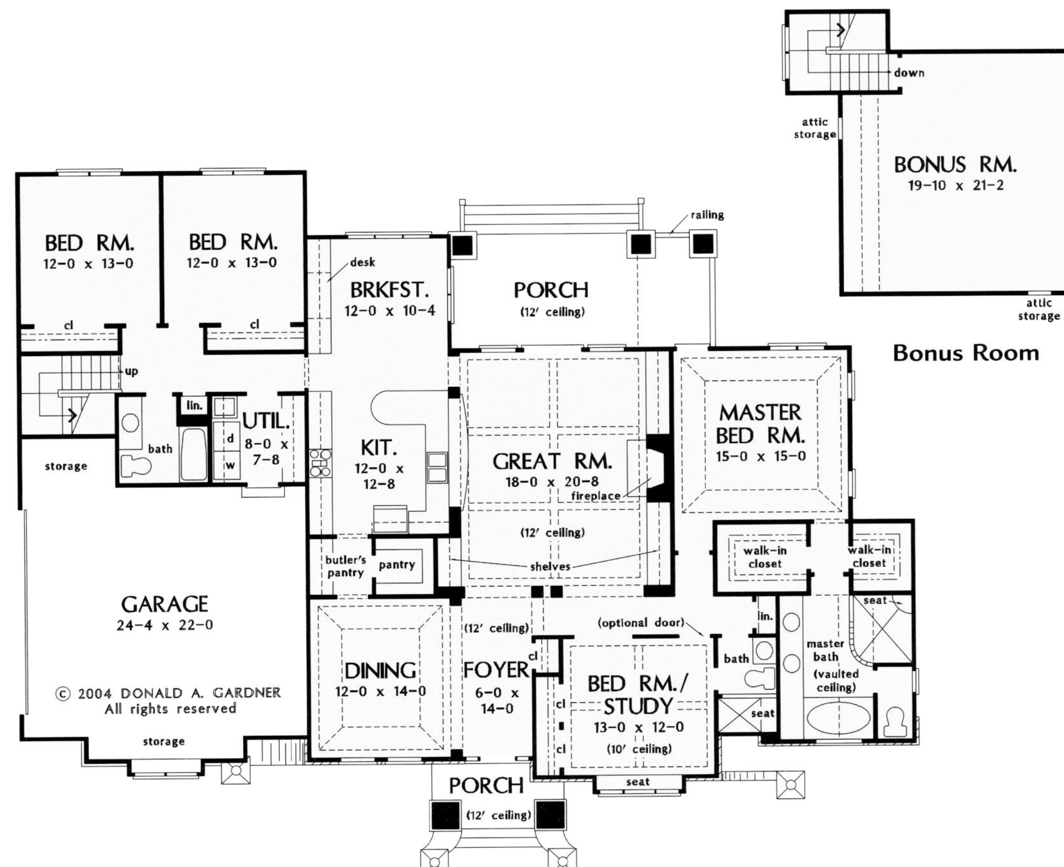

Bonus Room

First Floor

Design Features

- A stone portico makes an impressive entry to this stone-and-siding home that showcases European charm.
- A coffered ceiling, window seat and double doors enhance the bedroom/study.
- A built-in desk turns the breakfast nook into a computer hub or a place to organize the grocery list.
- The butler's pantry, large walk-in pantry and serving bar add special touches that make this home live easily.

Rear Elevation

*Other options available. See page 255.

Seabrooke — VPFB01-3842 — 1-866-525-9374

Total Living	First Floor	Opt. 2nd Fl.	Bed	Bath	Width	Depth	Foundation	Price Category
2057 sq ft	2057 sq ft	327 sq ft	3	2	56' 4"	62' 0"	Basement, Crawl Space or Slab	G

Design Features

- Modern design features inside make this house as family-friendly as it is charming.
- A vaulted keeping room is situated just off the kitchen area, giving families a comfortable place to spend casual time together.
- Decorative columns surround the dining room, serving as a subtle divider from the rest of the home.
- Optional bonus space is available that gives room for expansion.

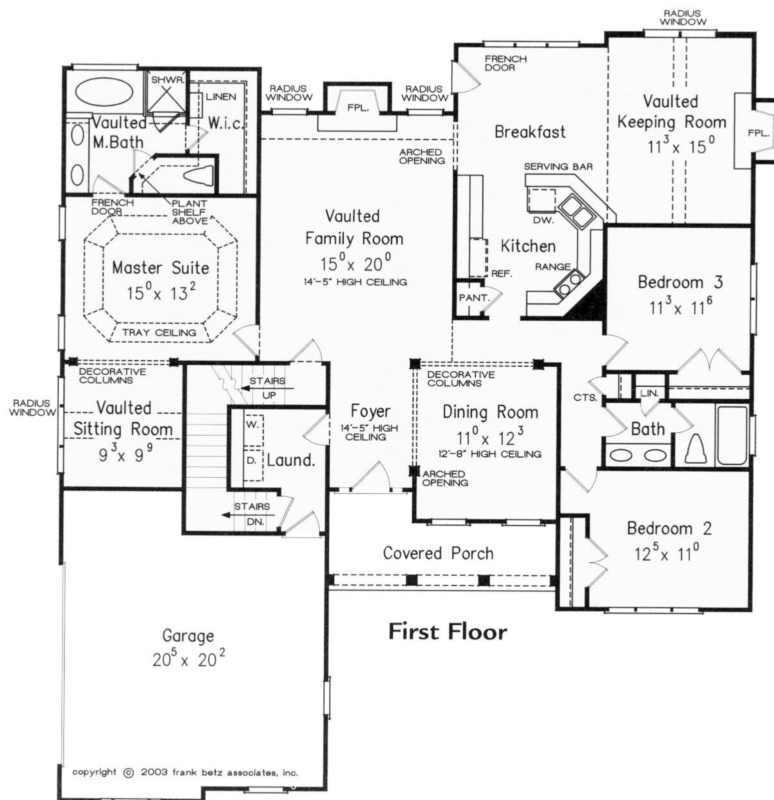

First Floor

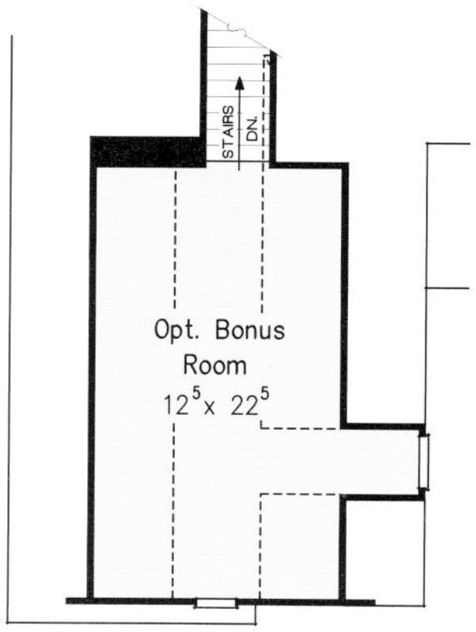

Stairs Dn.

Opt. Bonus Room
12^5x 22^5

Opt. Second Floor

Rear Elevation

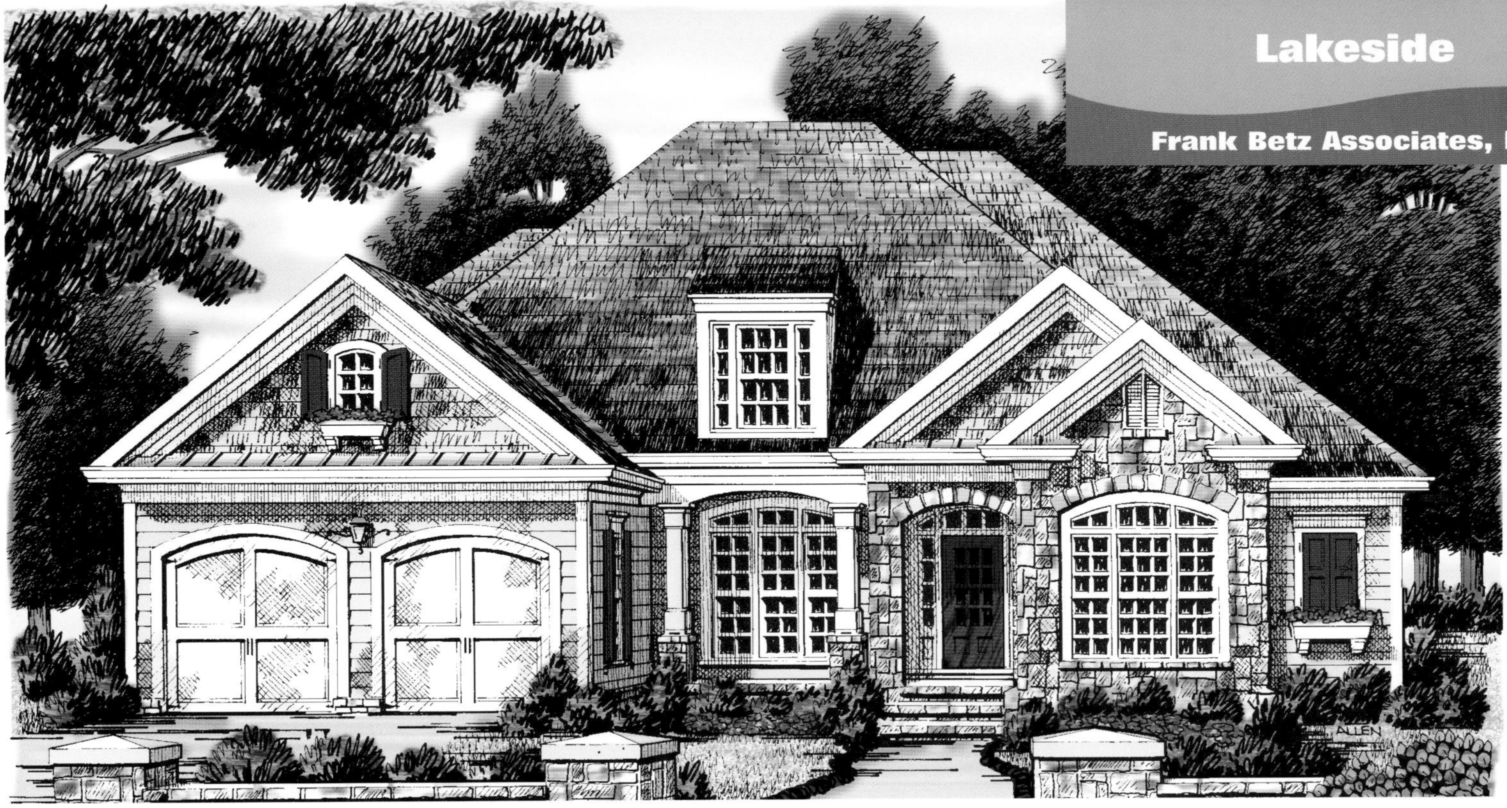

Ferdinand — VPFB01-3727 — 1-866-525-9374

Total Living	First Floor	Opt. 2nd Fl.	Bed	Bath	Width	Depth	Foundation	Price Category
2054 sq ft	2054 sq ft	304 sq ft	4	4	60' 0"	54' 6"	Basement or Crawl Space	G

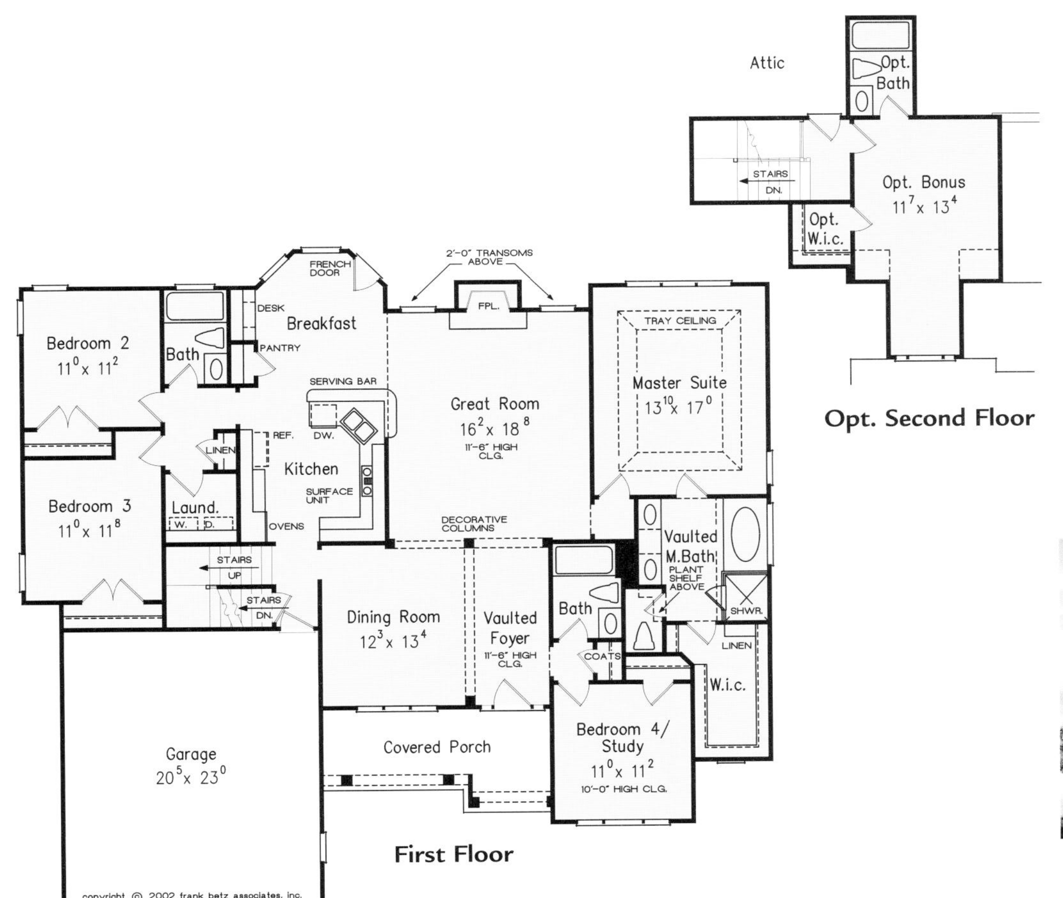

Design Features

- The extra details — like those in the *Ferdinand* — make all the difference when it comes to convenience for day-to-day living.
- A handy coat closet is tucked away just off the foyer, keeping jackets and shoes in their place.
- A desk is designed into the breakfast area so mail, calendars and schoolwork have their place.
- Transom windows in the family room allow natural light.
- The fourth bedroom can be converted into a study or home office.

Opt. Second Floor

First Floor

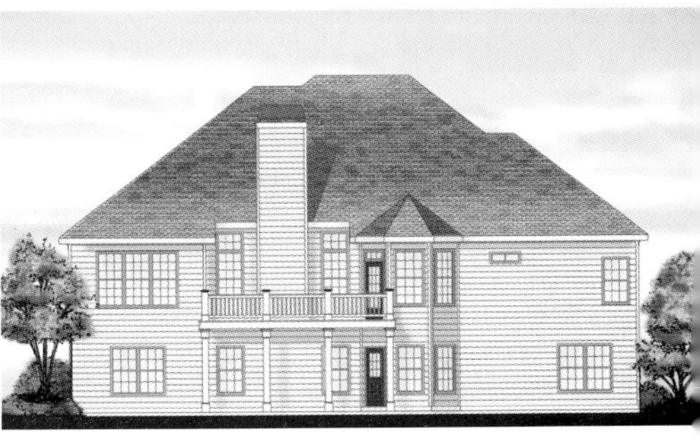

Rear Elevation

Southland Hills — VPFB01-3747 — 1-866-525-9374

Total Living	First Floor	Opt. 2nd Fl.	Bed	Bath	Width	Depth	Foundation	Price Category
1725 sq ft	1725 sq ft	256 sq ft	3	3	58' 0"	54' 6"	Basement, Crawl Space or Slab	F

Design Features

- Cheery dormers grace the exterior of the home and invite you in.
- Each bedroom is buffered from the others, providing personal space for each resident.
- The master suite is designed as its own entity, tucked away off the breakfast area, creating a private haven for the homeowner.
- Additional bedrooms are separated by a bath and a laundry room.
- A fourth bedroom or home office is readily available by finishing the optional bonus space.

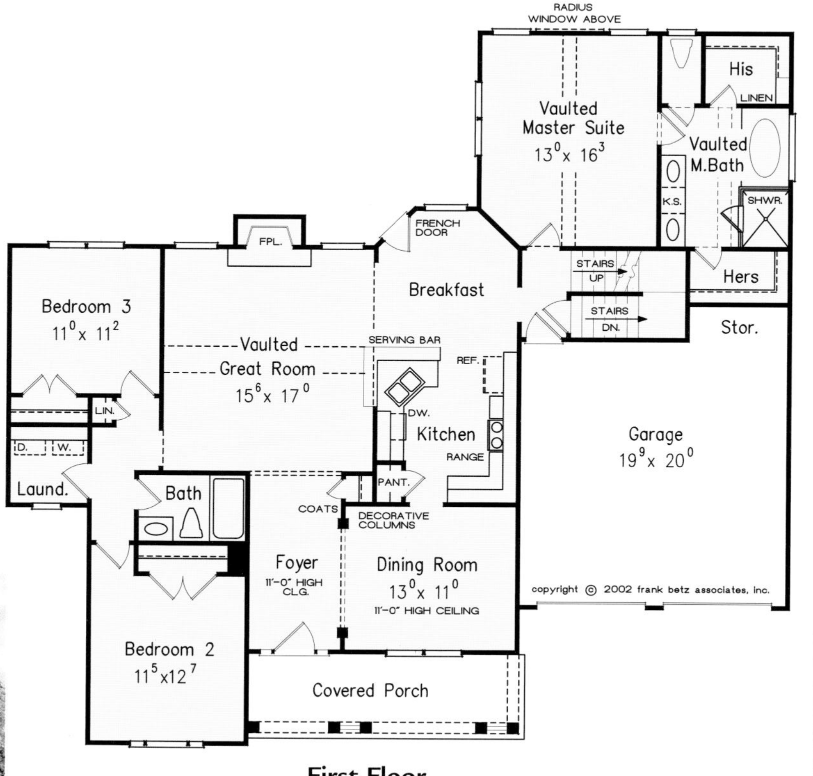

First Floor

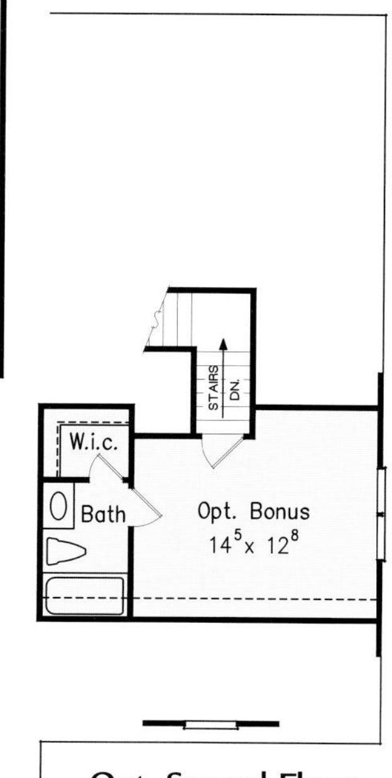

W.i.c.
STAIRS DN.
Bath
Opt. Bonus 14^5x 12^8

Opt. Second Floor

Rear Elevation

River Hill — VPFB01-3915 — 1-866-525-9374

Total Living	First Floor	Opt. 2nd Fl.	Bed	Bath	Width	Depth	Foundation	Price Category
1656 sq ft	1656 sq ft	717 sq ft	4	3	54' 0"	54' 0"	Basement, Crawl Space or Slab	F

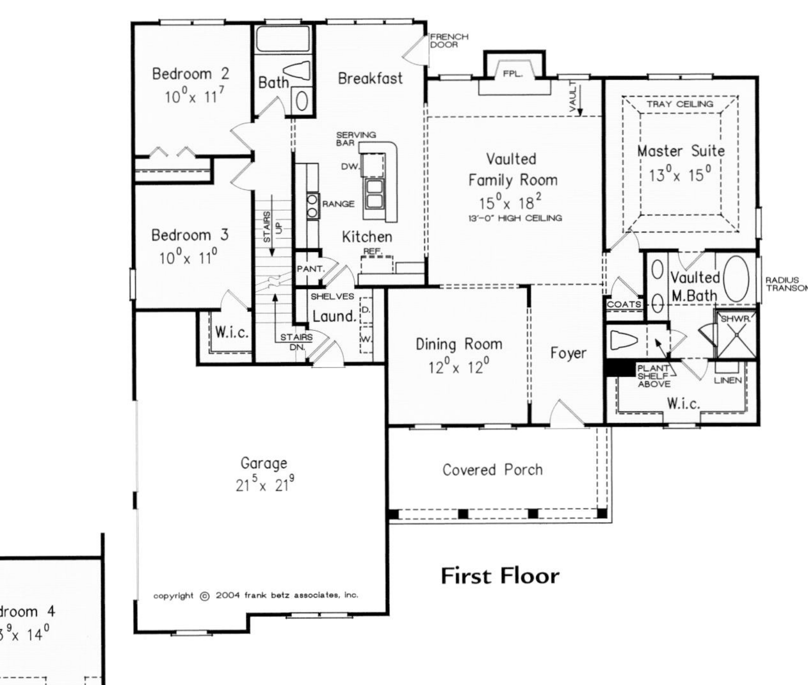

First Floor

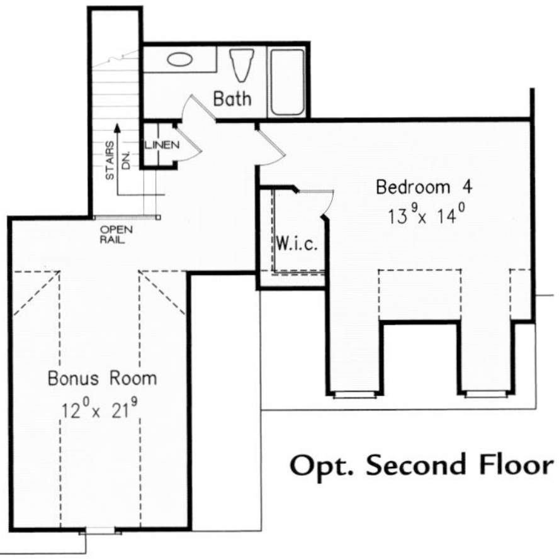

Bath
STAIRS DN.
LINEN
OPEN RAIL
Bedroom 4
13^9x 14^0
W.i.c.
Bonus Room
12^0x 21^9

Opt. Second Floor

Design Features

- A vaulted family room is the focal point from the foyer, with a cozy fireplace as its backdrop.
- The master suite is secluded from the other bedrooms giving homeowners privacy.
- A serving bar in the kitchen caters to the breakfast area and family room — convenient for entertaining.
- Optional second floor adds a bedroom and bath, as well as a bonus room that can be used as the homeowners wish.

Rear Elevation

Cranford — VPFB01-Plan 1222 — 1-866-525-9374

Total Living	First Floor	Second Floor	Opt. Bonus	Bed	Bath	Width	Depth	Foundation	Price Category
1780 sq ft	1332 sq ft	448 sq ft	212 sq ft	3	2-1/2	50' 0"	44' 4"	Basement or Crawl Space	E

Design Features

- Thoughtful design details give *Cranford* that little extra something that many homeowners are in search of.
- Decorative columns create a subtle border around the dining room.
- Transom windows in the great room allow extra natural light to flow in.
- The staircase to the upper level is creatively tucked away, not taking up any unnecessary space.
- Both secondary bedrooms feature a walk-in closet.

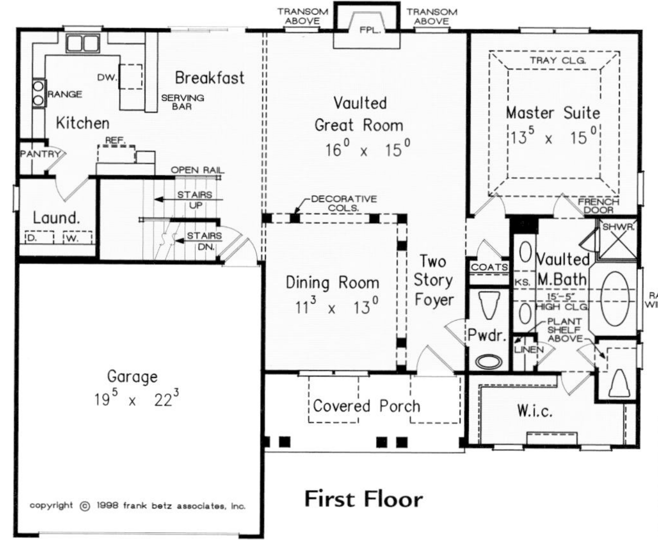

First Floor

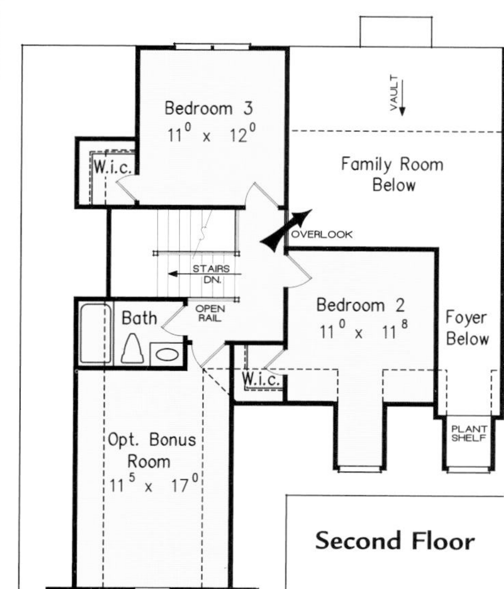

Second Floor

Rear Elevation

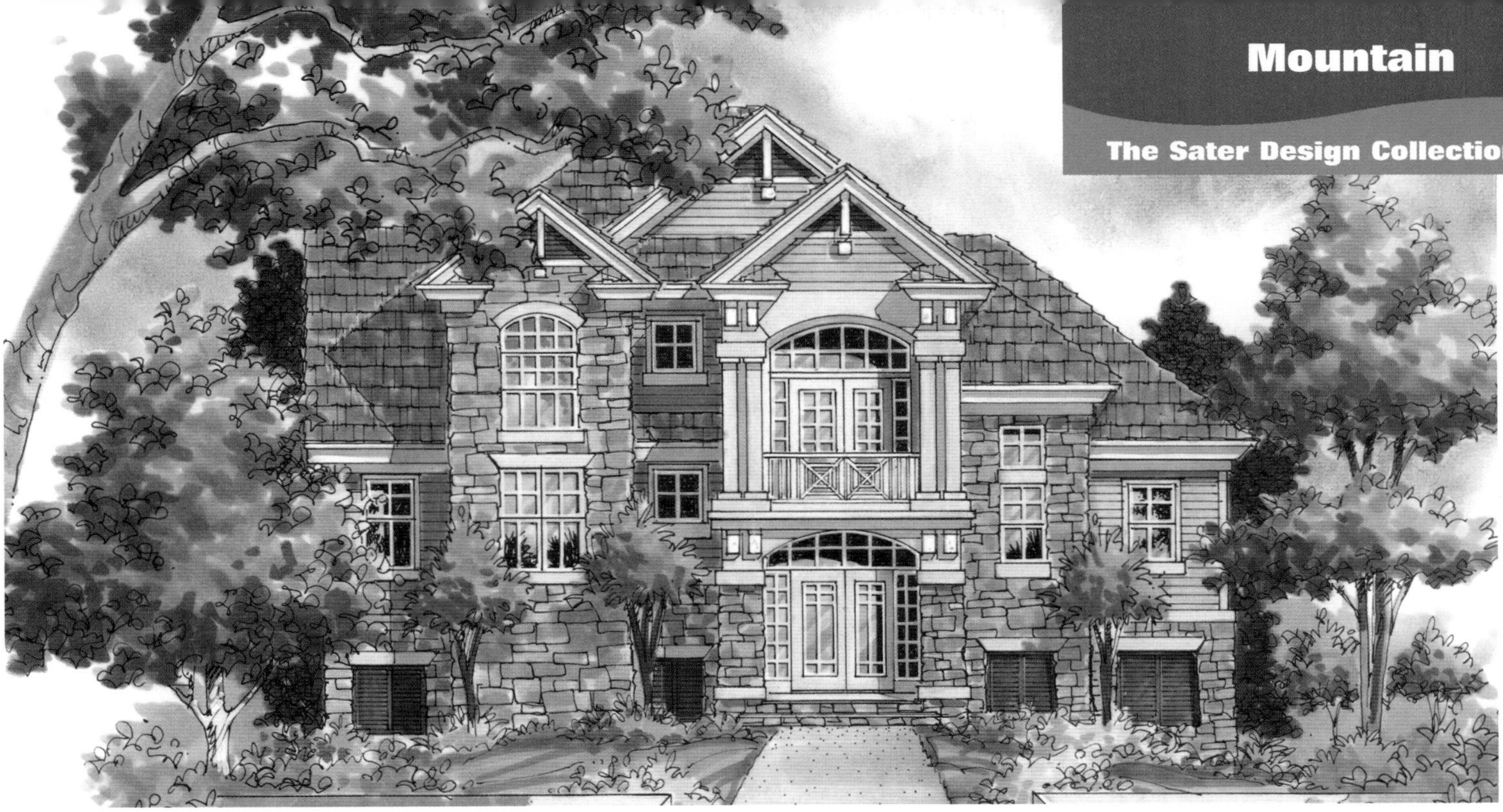

Buckhurst Lodge — VPDS01-Plan 6807 — 1-866-525-9374

Total Living	First Floor	Second Floor	Bed	Bath	Width	Depth	Foundation	Price Category
1978 sq ft	1383 sq ft	595 sq ft	3	2	48' 0"	42' 0"	Unfinished Walk-out Basement	E

First Floor

Second Floor

Lower Level

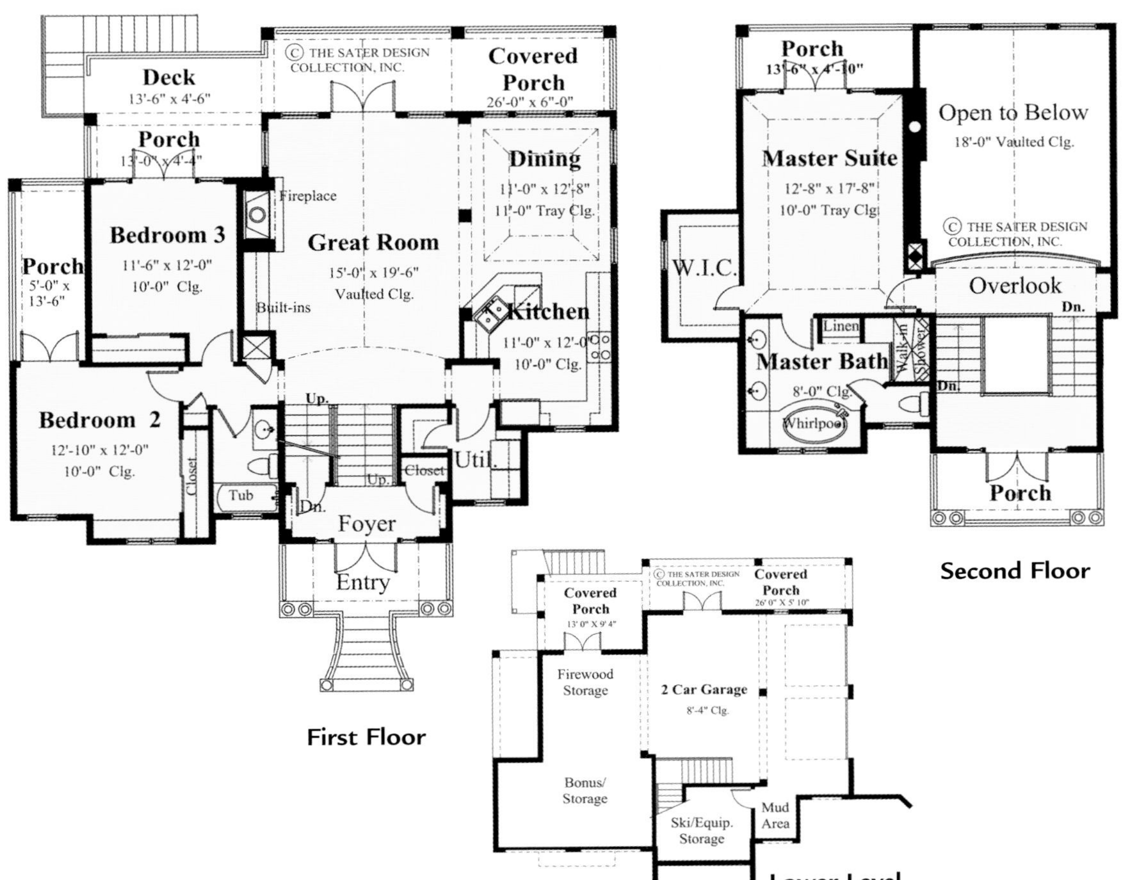

Design Features

- The open floor plan encourages flow between the great room, kitchen, dining room and covered porch.
- Built-ins, a fireplace, vaulted ceiling and extensive views through a wall of windows add to the appeal of the great room.
- Wrapping counters, an angled double sink and ample storage enhance the kitchen.
- Located on the upper level away from the main living spaces, the master suite ensures privacy.

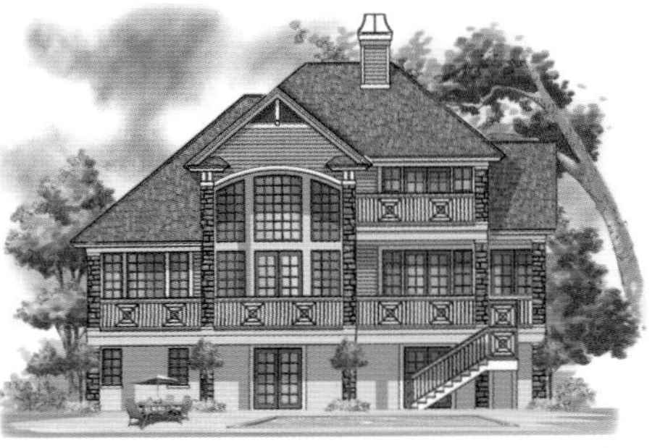

Rear Elevation

Gilchrist — VPDG01-734-D — 1-866-525-9374

Total Living	First Floor	Basement	Bonus	Bed	Bath	Width	Depth	Foundation	Price Category
3132 sq ft	2094 sq ft	1038 sq ft	494 sq ft	4	3-1/2	62' 3"	76' 7"	Hillside Walkout	G

Design Features

- A partial basement foundation makes this home perfect for hillside lots.
- The great room features a cathedral ceiling and fireplace with flanking built-in shelves.
- A convenient pass-thru in the step-saving kitchen keeps everyone connected.
- A generous recreation room and guest suite comprise the lower level.

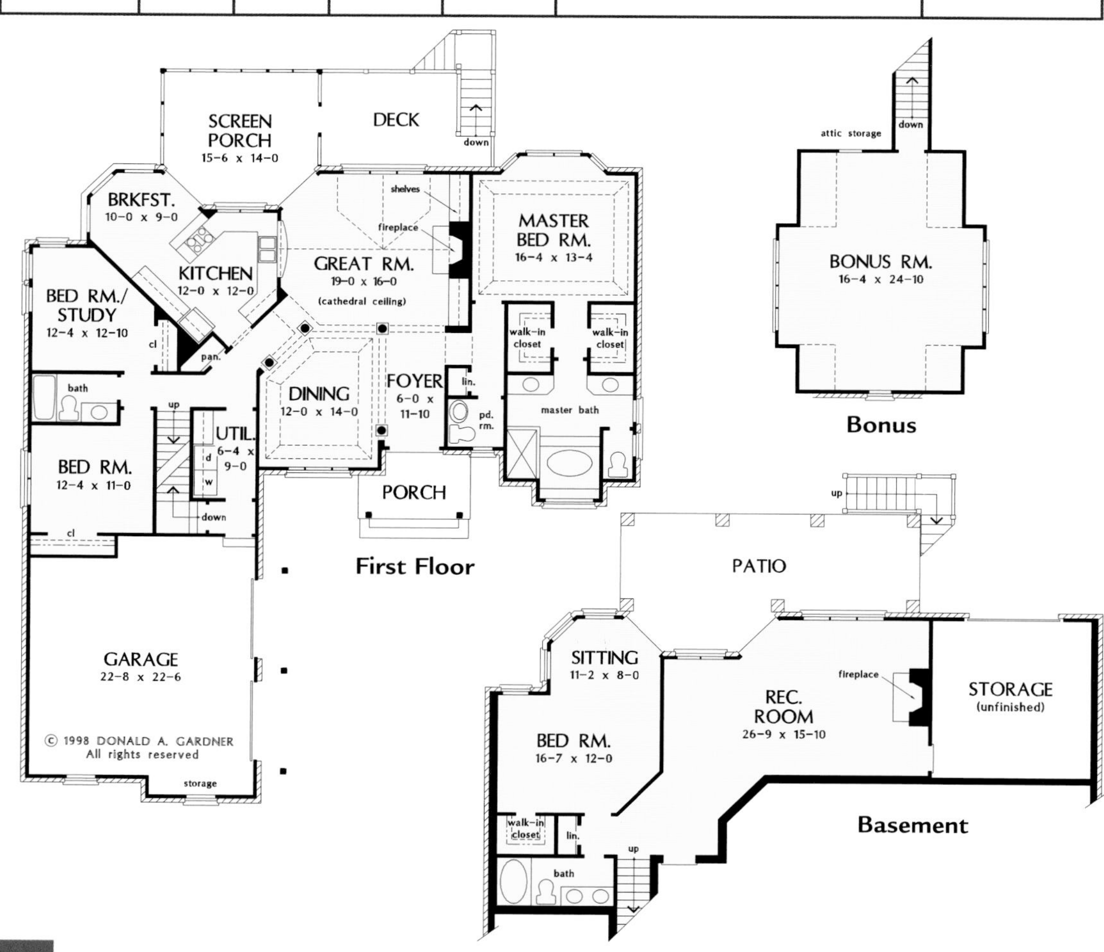

Rear View

Please note: Home photographed may differ from blueprint.

Elinor Park — VPFB01-Plan 3943 — 1-866-525-9374

Total Living	First Floor	Opt. 2nd Fl.	Bed	Bath	Width	Depth	Foundation	Price Category
2240 sq ft	2240sq ft	369 sq ft	5	4	57' 0"	68' 0"	Basement or Crawl Space	H

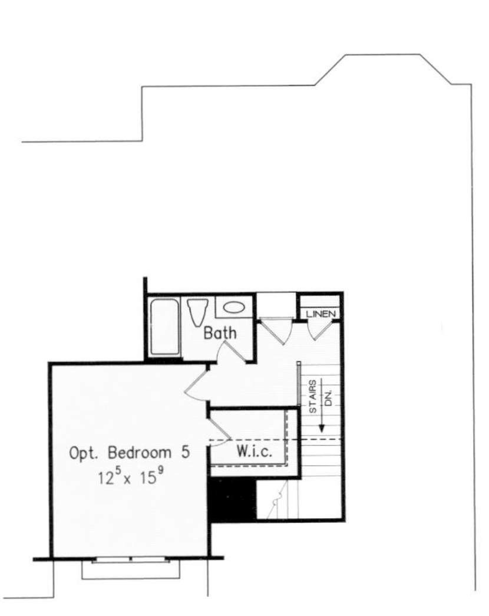

Opt. Second Floor

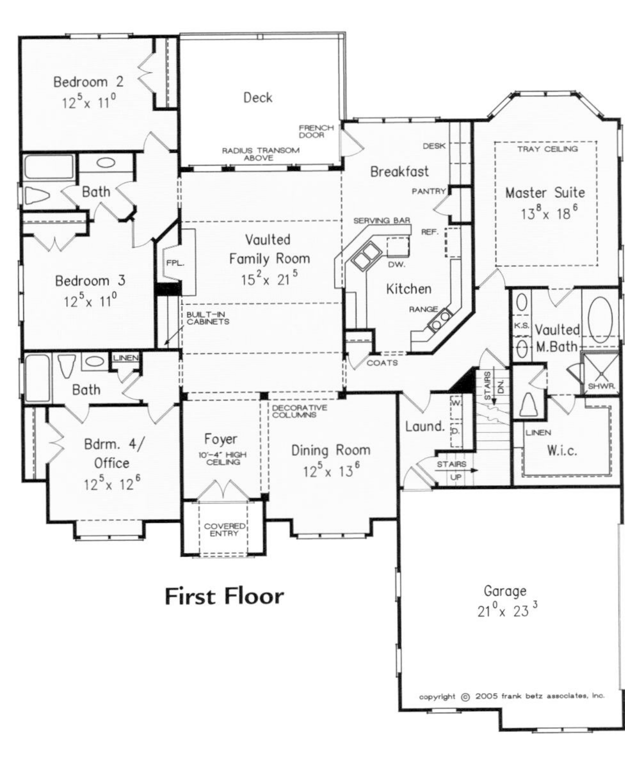

First Floor

Design Features

- The stone and brick façade of the *Elinor Park* are reminiscent of traditional homes of yesteryear.
- This one-level home offers an open and airy floor plan, allowing easy transition from one room to another.
- The optional second floor also gives homeowners choices on how to finish this space.
- The deck on the rear of the home is the perfect place for entertaining.

Rear Elevation

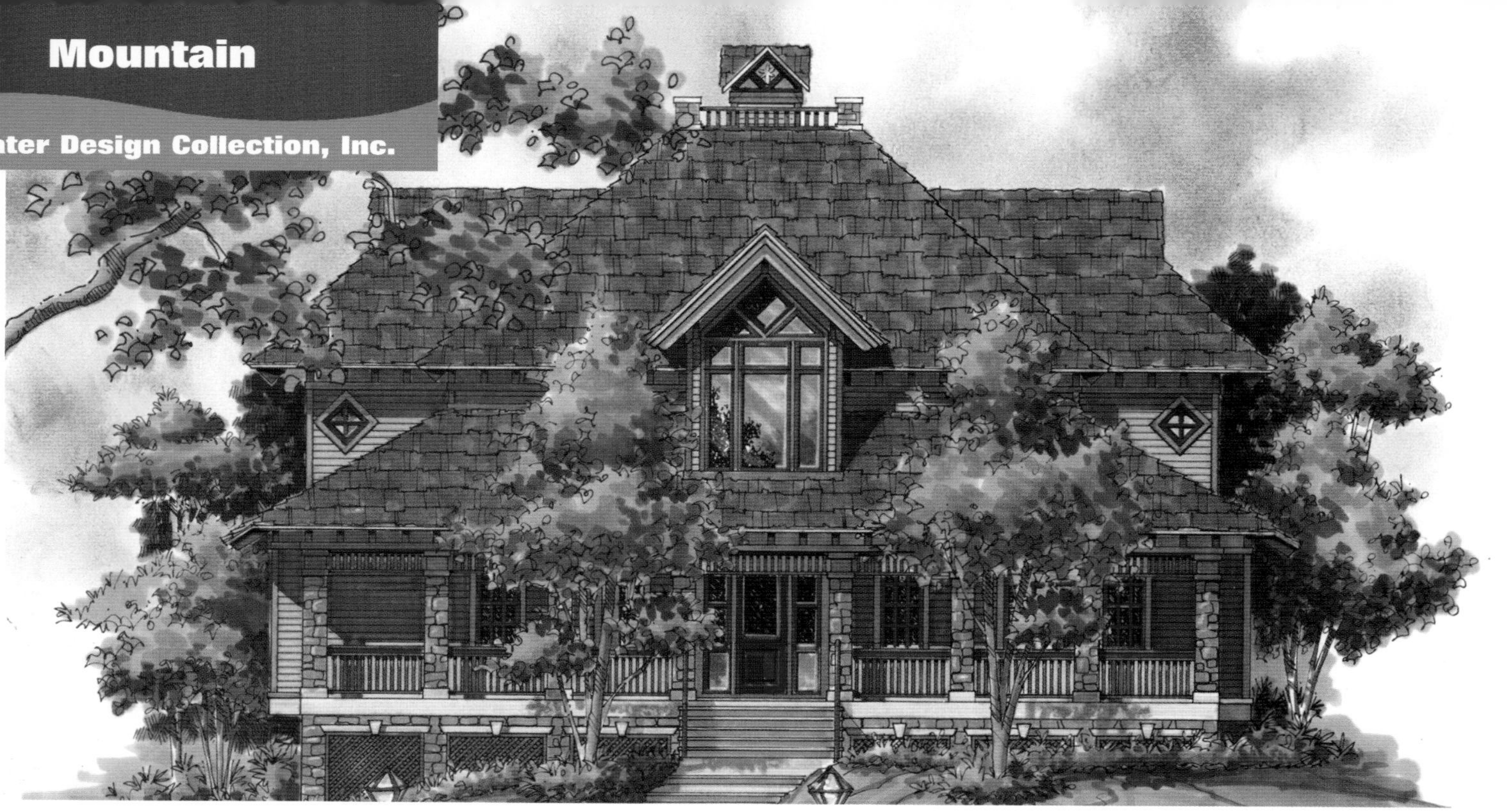

Wolf Summit — VPDS01-Plan 6826 — 1-866-525-9374

Total Living	First Floor	Second Floor	Bed	Bath	Width	Depth	Foundation	Price Category
3285 sq ft	2146 sq ft	952 sq ft	3	3-1/2	52' 0"	65' 4"	Unfinished Walkout Basement	H

Design Features

- A wraparound porch, striking gable, widow's peak and a cupola all combine to create an impressive façade.
- The great room features a wet bar, built-in cabinetry, a fireplace and three sets of French doors to the back porch.
- The kitchen boasts ample storage space, an eating bar and easy access to the nook and great room.
- Secondary bedrooms are placed on the upper level and offer walk-in closets, full baths, workstations and access to the upper deck.

First Floor

Second Floor

Lower Level

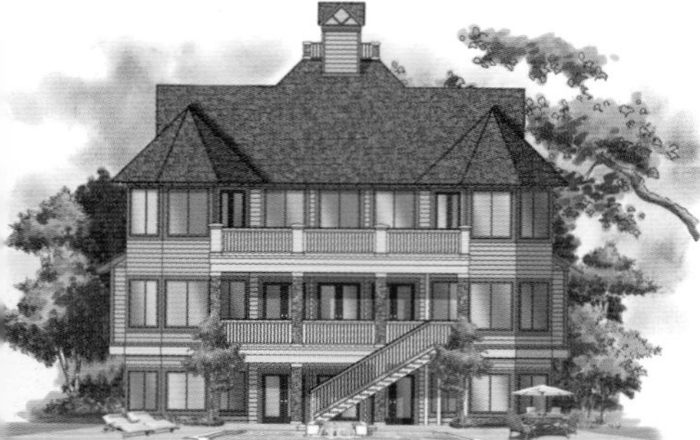

Rear Elevation

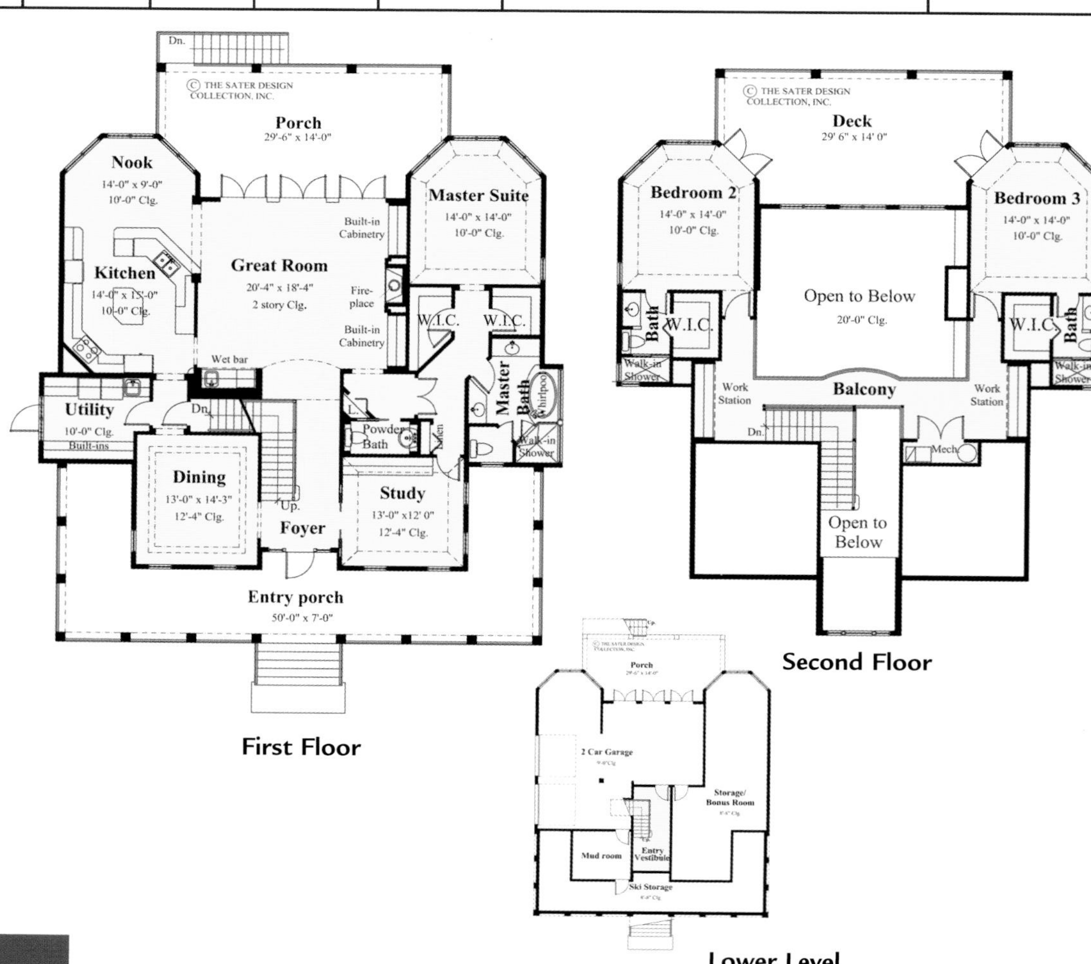

Jerivale — VPDG01-Plan 1033 — 1-866-525-9374

Total Living	First Floor	Second Floor	Bonus	Bed	Bath	Width	Depth	Foundation	Price Category
3647 sq ft	2766 sq ft	881 sq ft	407 sq ft	3	3-1/2	92' 5"	71' 10"	Crawl Space*	H

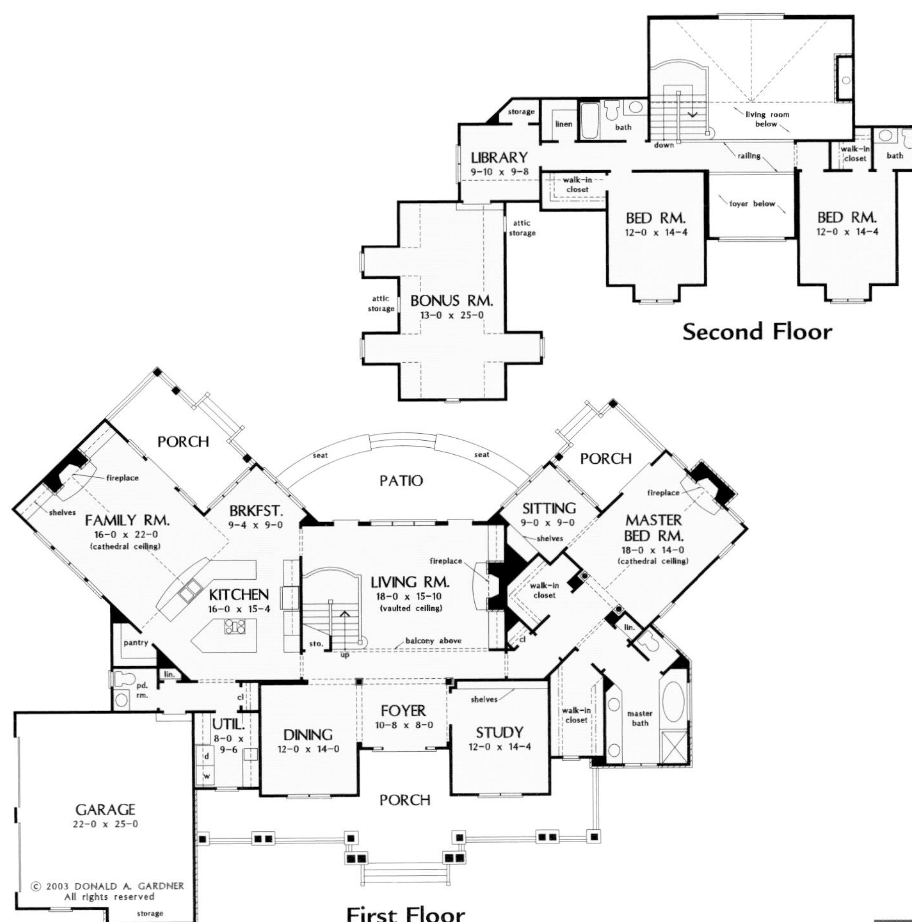

Second Floor

First Floor

Design Features

- Cedar shake, stone and siding complement a metal roof over the front porch.
- The two-story foyer has impressive views of the study, dining room, living room and balcony.
- Built-ins, three fireplaces and a walk-in pantry add special touches.
- Every bedroom has walk-in closets.
- The master bedroom's sitting area, upstairs library and versatile bonus room produce additional luxury.

Rear Elevation

*Other options available. See page 255.

Hilliard — VPFB01-Plan 3729 — 1-866-525-9374

Total Living	First Floor	Second Floor	Bonus	Bed	Bath	Width	Depth	Foundation	Price Category
2097 sq ft	1579 sq ft	518 sq ft	360 sq ft	3	2-1/2	53' 0"	47' 6"	Basement or Crawl Space	F

Design Features

- The *Hilliard's* easy-going exterior appeal continues inside with a casual and cozy keeping room, an extension of the kitchen area.
- The keeping room, combined with a vaulted family room, gives families plenty of gathering places to spend their time.
- Optional bonus space upstairs can be personalized into a playroom, home office or gym.
- The master suite on the main level is a feature many people are seeking in their homes today.

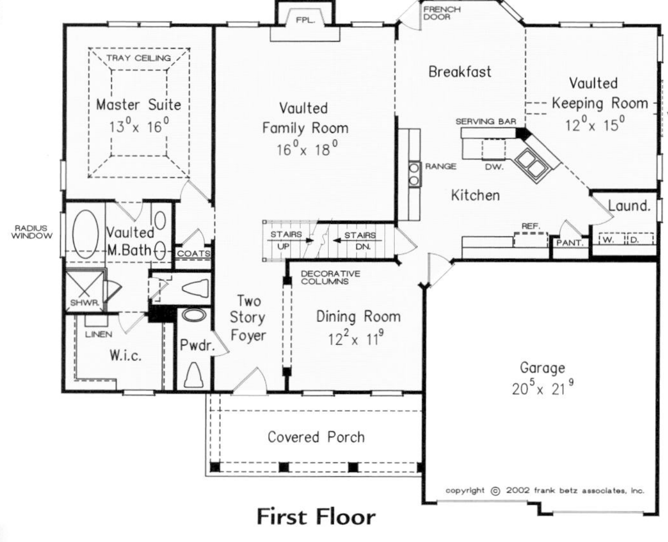

First Floor

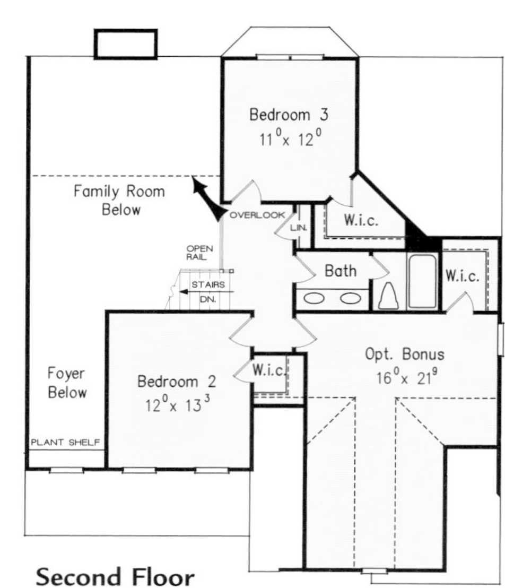

Second Floor

Rear Elevation

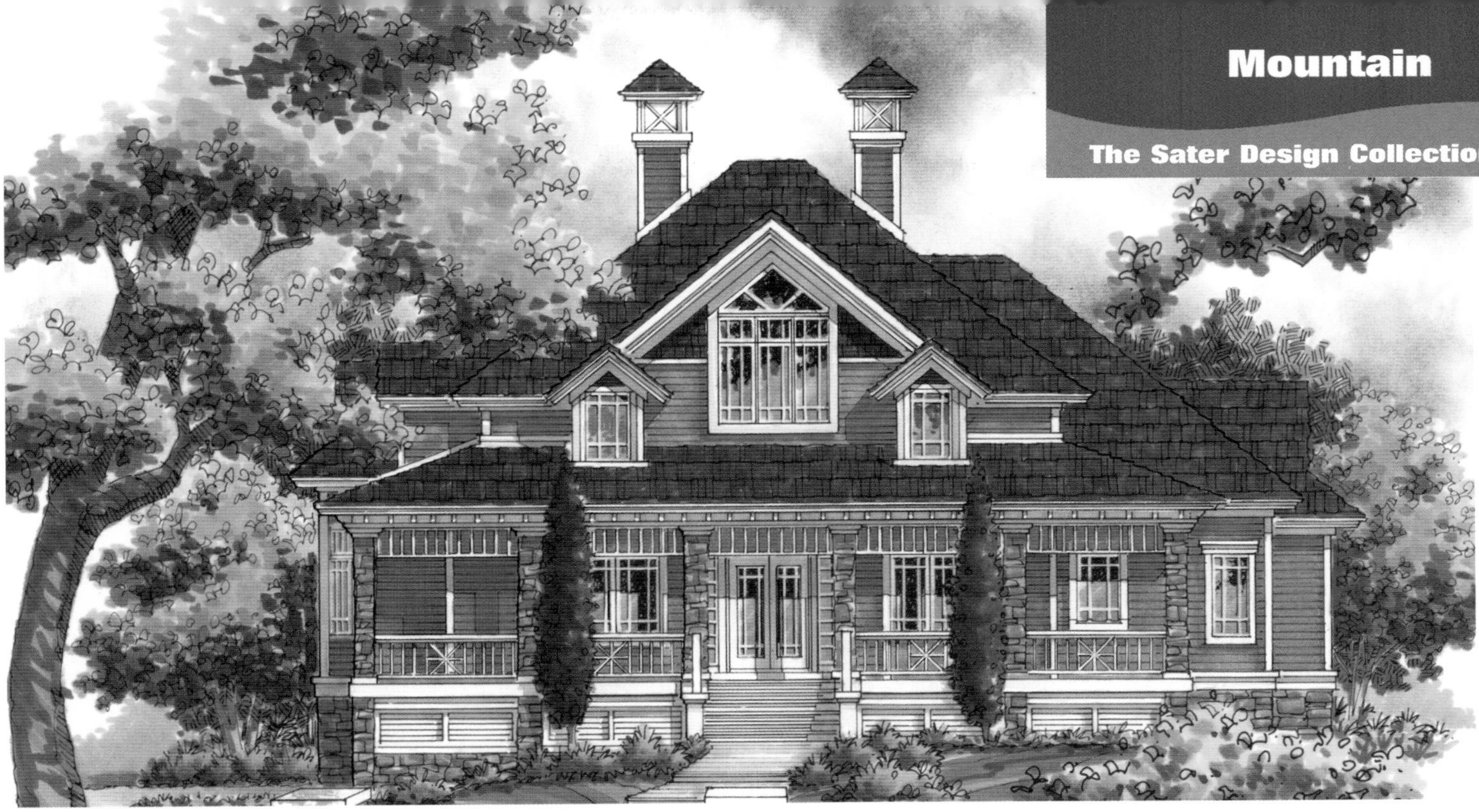

Bradley House — VPDS01-Plan 6859 — 1-866-525-9374

Total Living	First Floor	Second Floor	Bed	Bath	Width	Depth	Foundation	Price Category
2819 sq ft	1855 sq ft	964 sq ft	3	3-1/2	66' 0"	50' 0"	Unfinished Walkout Basement	G

Lower Level

First Floor

Second Floor

Design Features

- The octagonal great room features a multi-faceted vaulted ceiling, fireplace, built-in entertainment center and three sets of French doors, which lead to a vaulted porch.
- The gourmet kitchen boasts a pass-thru to the porch, ample counter and storage space, a center island and easy access to the dining and great room.
- Guests will enjoy the privacy of two secondary bedrooms placed on the upper level that feature full baths, spacious closets, a morning kitchen and a private deck.

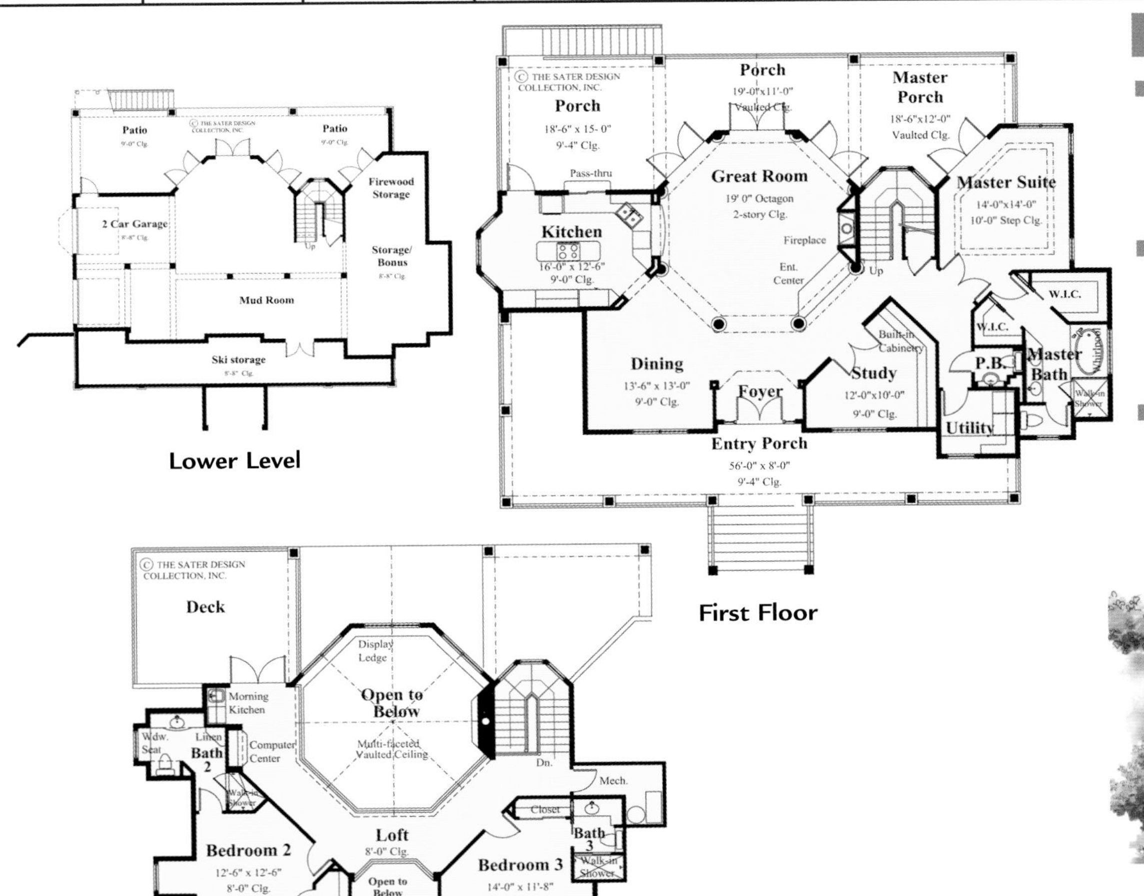

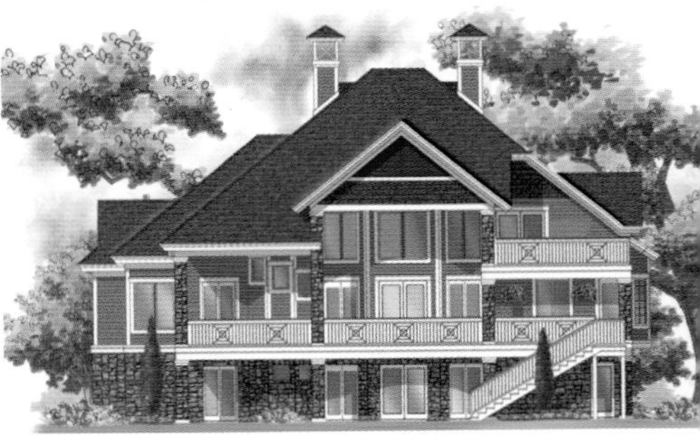

Rear Elevation

Oak Abbey — VPAL01-Plan 5003 — 1-866-525-9374

Total Living	First Floor	Basement	Bonus	Bed	Bath	Width	Depth	Foundation	Price Category
4547 sq ft	3006 sq ft	1541 sq ft	480 sq ft	4	4-1/2	93' 11"	80' 9"	Hillside Walkout	O

Design Features

- This hillside walkout features an open floor plan and plenty of outdoor living areas.
- Cathedral ceilings top the great room, master bedroom and screened porch.
- Three fireplaces, built-in cabinetry and an art niche add custom touches.
- Downstairs, each bedroom has its own walk-in closet and bath.
- Note the service entry for convenience.

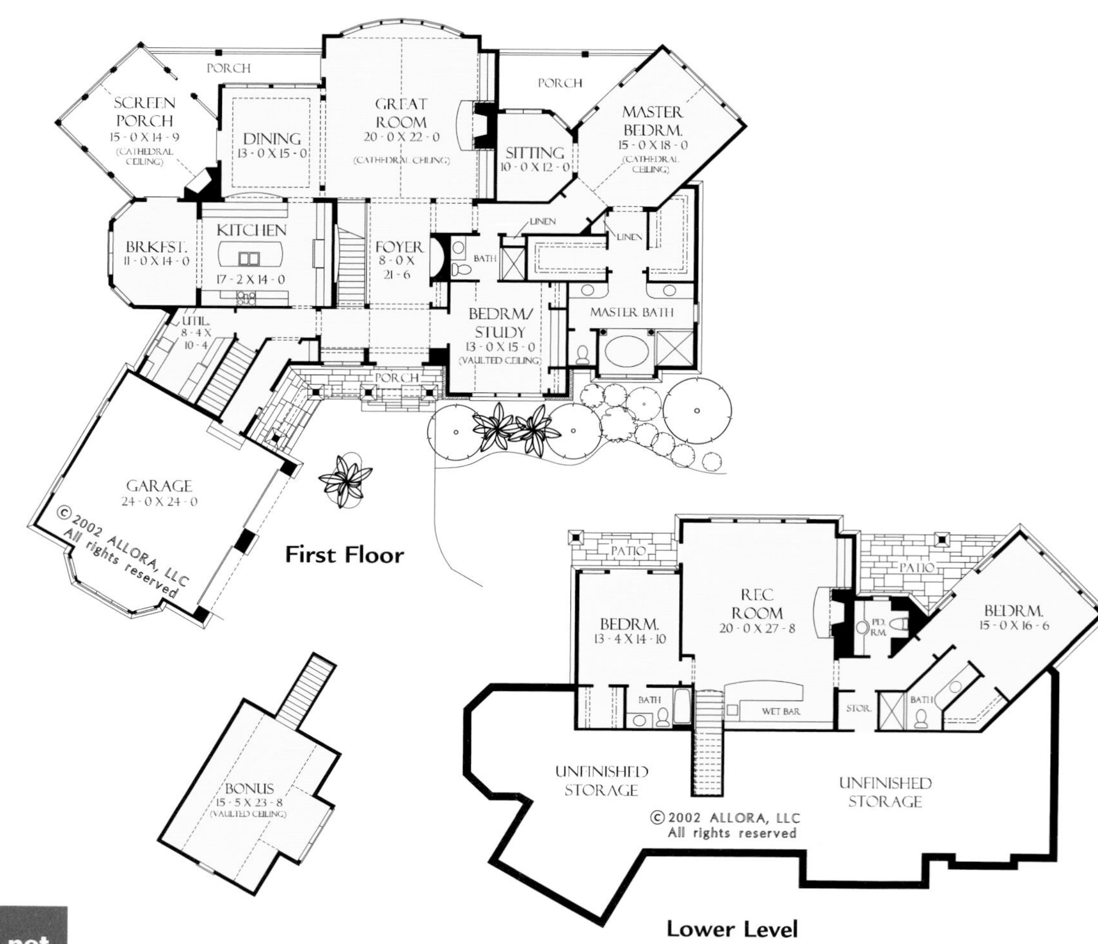

First Floor

Lower Level

Rear Elevation

Maplewood — VPFB01-Plan 3878 — 1-866-525-9374

Total Living	First Floor	Opt. 2nd Fl.	Bed	Bath	Width	Depth	Foundation	Price Category
2400 sq ft	2400 sq ft	845 sq ft	4	2-1/2	61' 0"	70' 6"	Basement or Crawl Space	G

Design Features

- The *Maplewood's* inviting exterior is just a taste of what's waiting inside.
- Transom windows along the back of the home welcome in plenty of sunshine, brightening each room.
- A coffered ceiling, fireplace and built-in cabinetry in the family room make for an attractive center point of the home.
- The master suite is a delight. The bath offers dual sinks and a separate tub and shower. A huge walk-in closet is also a special feature.

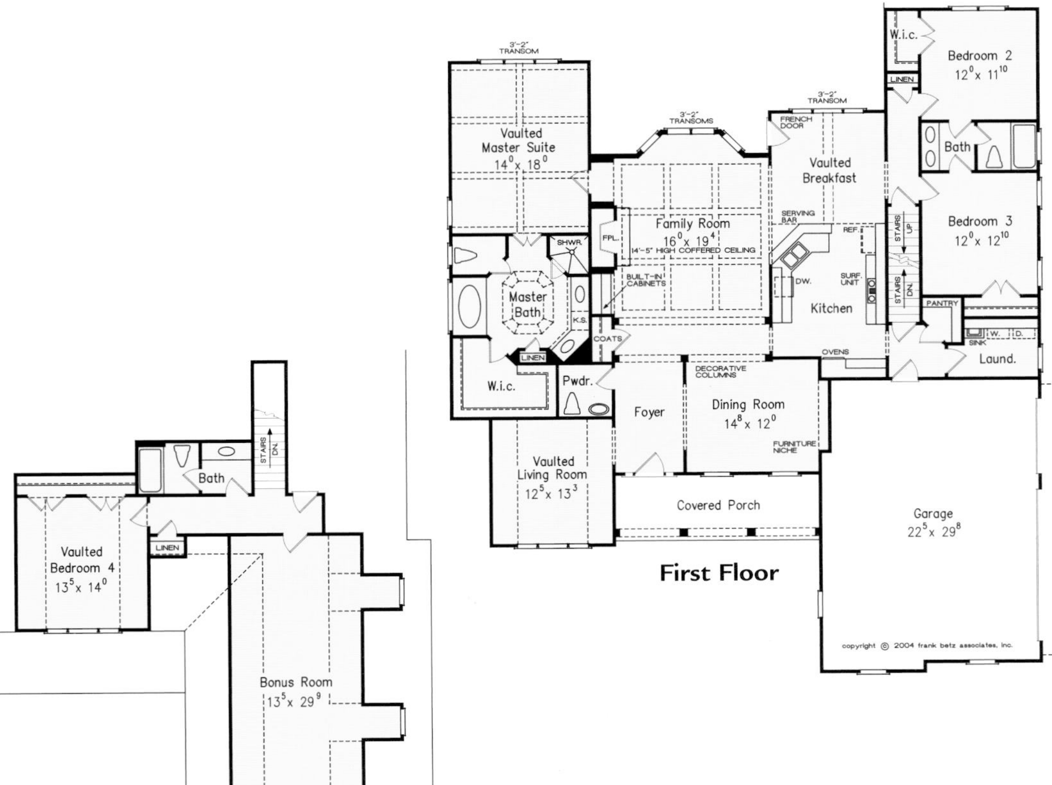

First Floor

Opt. Second Floor

Rear Elevation

Stonebridge — VPDS01-Plan 6832 — 1-866-525-9374

Total Living	First Floor	Second Floor	Bed	Bath	Width	Depth	Foundation	Price Category
2698 sq ft	1798 sq ft	900 sq ft	3	3-1/2	54' 0"	57' 0"	Crawl Space	G

Design Features

- A coffered two-story sloped ceiling soars over the great room that features built-in cabinetry, French doors to the rear porch and easy access to the kitchen, and is connected to the dining room by a two-sided fireplace.
- To ensure privacy, secondary bedrooms are placed on the upper floor away from the master suite and feature walk-in closets and private baths.

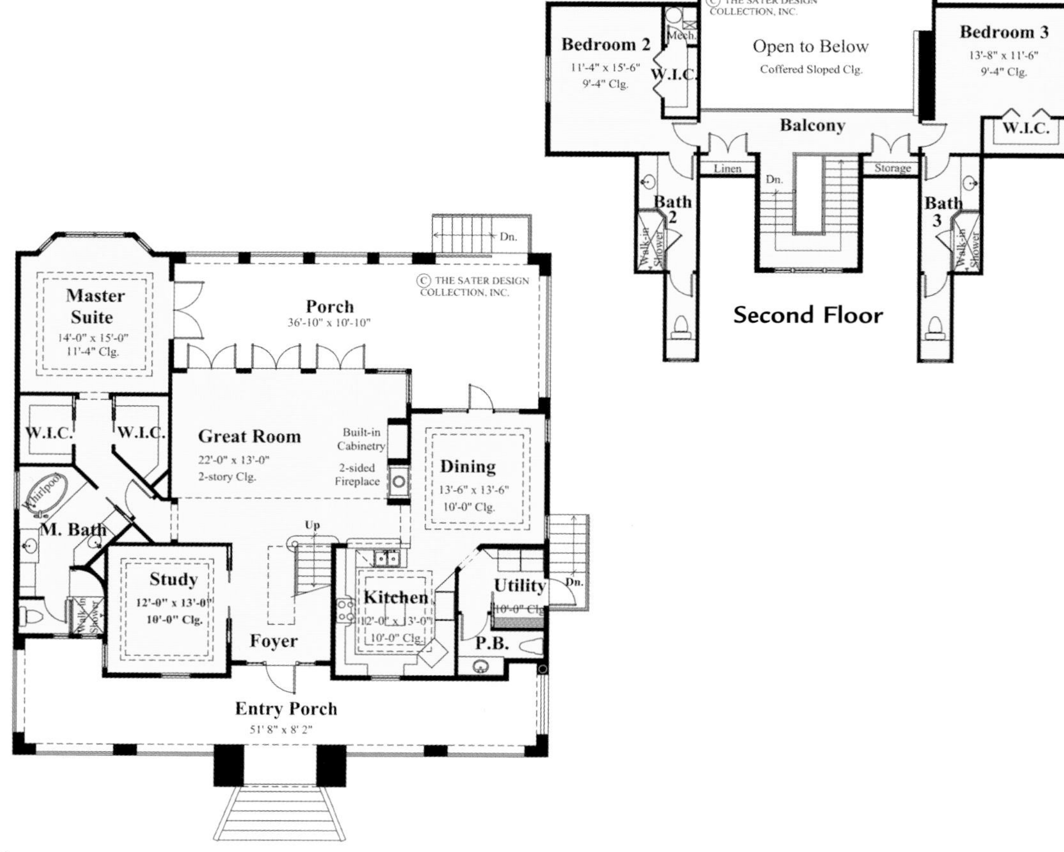

Second Floor

First Floor

Rear Elevation

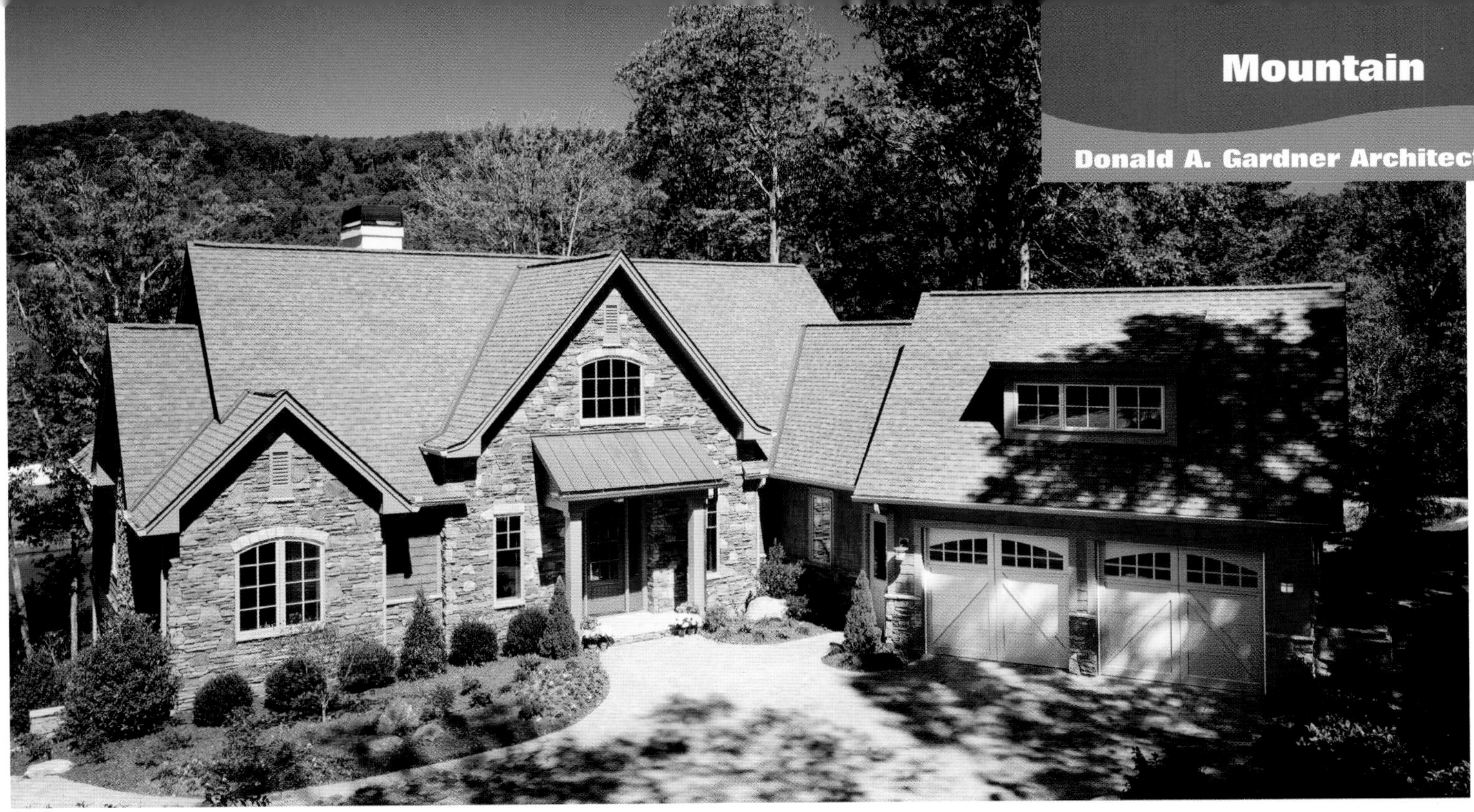

Dogwood Ridge — VPAL01-Plan 5005 — 1-866-525-9374

Total Living	First Floor	Basement	Bed	Bath	Width	Depth	Foundation	Price Category
3201 sq ft	2090 sq ft	1111 sq ft	3	3-1/2	71' 1"	78' 6"	Hillside Walkout	O

Please note: Home photographed may differ from blueprint.

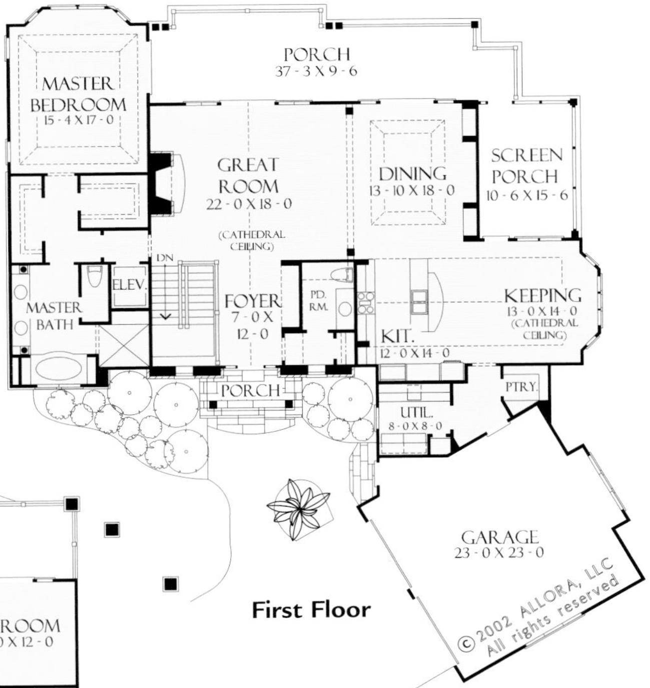

MASTER BEDROOM 15 - 4 X 17 - 0

PORCH 37 - 3 X 9 - 6

GREAT ROOM 22 - 0 X 18 - 0 (CATHEDRAL CEILING)

DINING 13 - 10 X 18 - 0

SCREEN PORCH 10 - 6 X 15 - 6

MASTER BATH

ELEV.

DN

FOYER 7 - 0 X 12 - 0

PD. RM.

KEEPING 13 - 0 X 14 - 0 (CATHEDRAL CEILING)

KIT. 12 - 0 X 14 - 0

PORCH

PTRY

UTIL. 8 - 0 X 8 - 0

GARAGE 23 - 0 X 23 - 0

First Floor

COVERED PATIO 52 - 0 X 9 - 0

BEDROOM 15 - 4 X 12 - 0

REC ROOM 16 - 10 X 18 - 0

BEDROOM 14 - 0 X 12 - 0

BATH

BATH

ELEV.

STORAGE

MECH/ STORAGE

OPT. GUEST 12 - 0 X 13 - 8

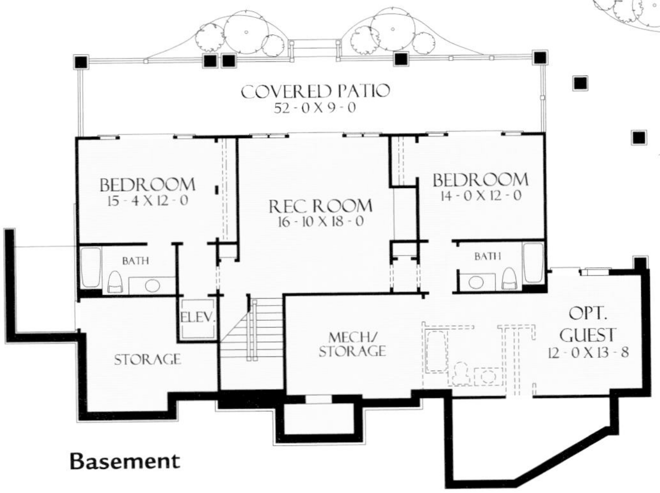

Basement

Design Features

- Stone and cedar shake combine with triumphant gables and graceful arches to create a Craftsman exterior.
- Influenced by the cottages of old, this hillside walkout boasts a rear wall of glasswork on both floors.
- The open floor plan distinguishes rooms by ceiling treatments and columns.
- Custom features include a walk-in pantry, storage space and utility room with sink.
- Along with the master suite, the secondary bedrooms take advantage of the natural scenery.

Rear View

Blackstone — VPFB01-3871 — 1-866-525-9374

Total Living	First Floor	Opt. 2nd Fl.	Bed	Bath	Width	Depth	Foundation	Price Category
2434 sq ft	2434 sq ft	307 sq ft	5	4	63' 0"	64' 6"	Basement or Crawl Space	I

Design Features

- From the *Southern Living® Design Collection*
- A vaulted master suite is divided from the other bedrooms making a private haven for homeowners to enjoy.
- The breakfast area leads to a screened porch and oversized deck on the back of the home — perfect for outdoor entertaining.
- A mudroom buffers the living area from the garage, ensuring that coats and shoes stay in their place.

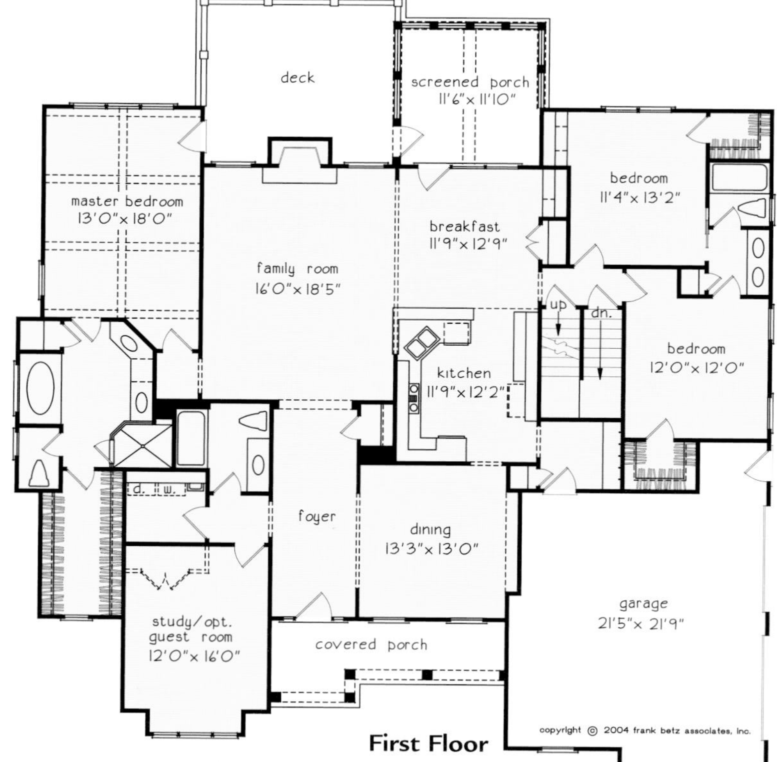

First Floor

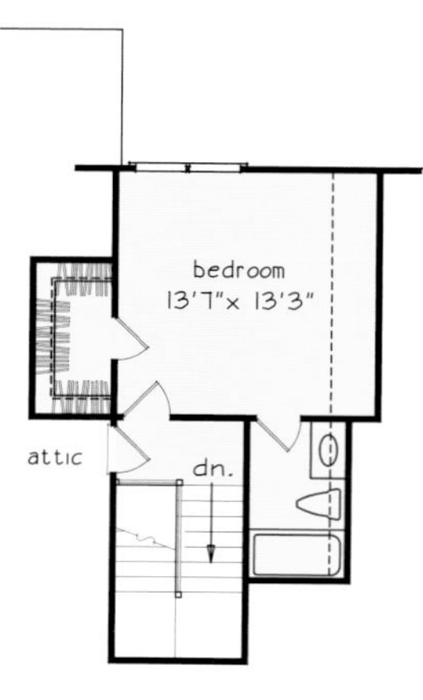

Opt. Second Floor

Rear Elevation

Wedgewood — VPDS01-Plan 6841 — 1-866-525-9374

Total Living	First Floor	Second Floor	Bed	Bath	Width	Depth	Foundation	Price Category
1853 sq ft	1342 sq ft	511 sq ft	3	2-1/2	44' 0"	40' 0"	Island Basement	E

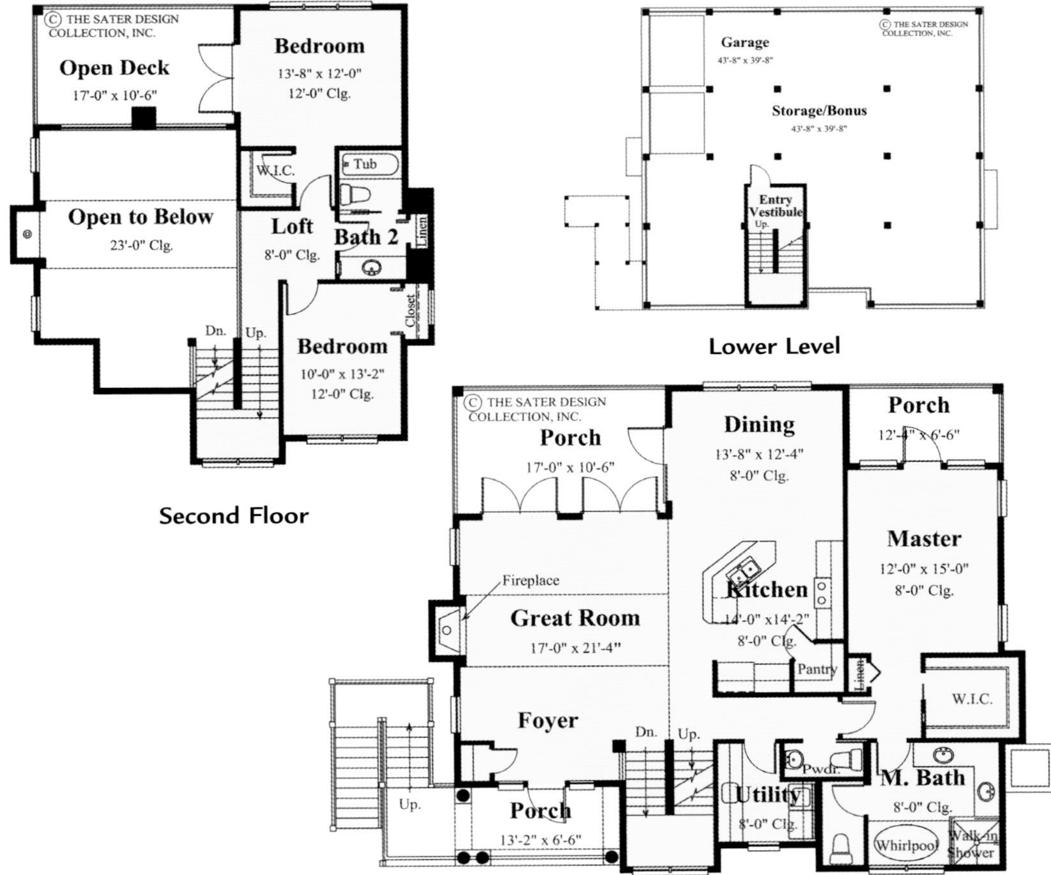

Second Floor

Lower Level

First Floor

Design Features

- The foyer opens into the kitchen, great room and dining room, encouraging movement and conversation throughout the main living area.
- The great room is made cozy by a warming fireplace and opens to the rear porch through two French doors.
- The master suite features a private porch, spacious bath and walk-in closet.
- Guests will enjoy privacy on the upper level in two secondary bedrooms, which share a bath, and one room accesses a sun deck.

Rear Elevation

Granville — VPAL01-Plan 5012 — 1-866-525-9374

Total Living	First Floor	Second Floor	Bed	Bath	Width	Depth	Foundation	Price Category
1925 sq ft	1500 sq ft	425 sq ft	3	3	60' 6"	41' 2"	Crawl Space*	O

Design Features

- This home instantly welcomes guests through its elegant foyer and great room.
- The spacious master suite includes rear-porch access and a pampering master bath.
- With a large walk-in closet and twin sinks, the master suite promotes convenience.
- Completing the first level is the versatile bedroom/study with an adjacent full bath.
- The upstairs features an additional bedroom and full bath, as well as a loft.

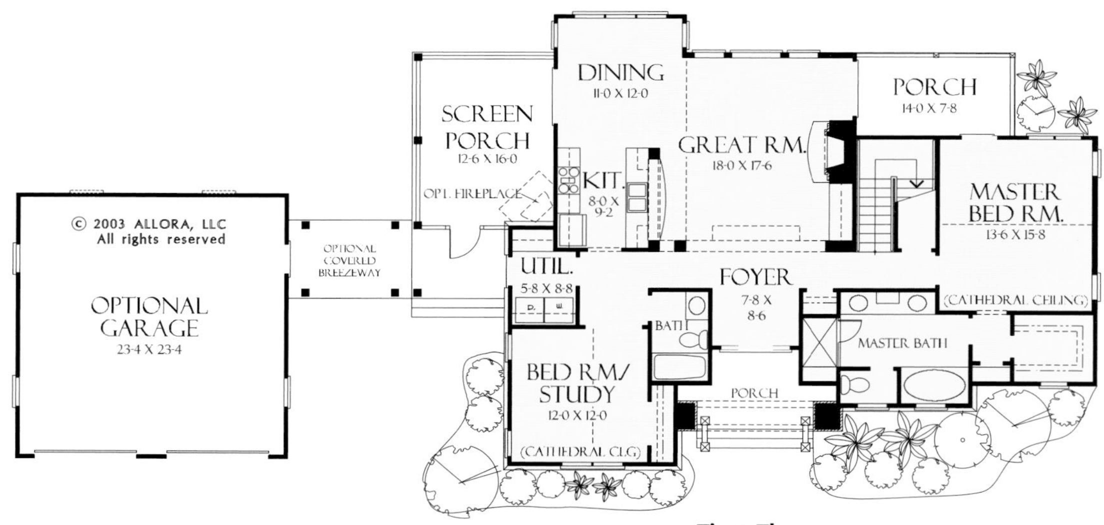

First Floor

Rear Elevation

Second Floor

*Other options available. See page 255.

Catawba Ridge — VPFB01-3823 — 1-866-525-9374

Total Living	First Floor	Second Floor	Opt. Bonus	Bed	Bath	Width	Depth	Foundation	Price Category
2389 sq ft	1593 sq ft	796 sq ft	238 sq ft	3	3-1/2	59' 8"	50' 6"	Basement, Crawl Space or Slab	I

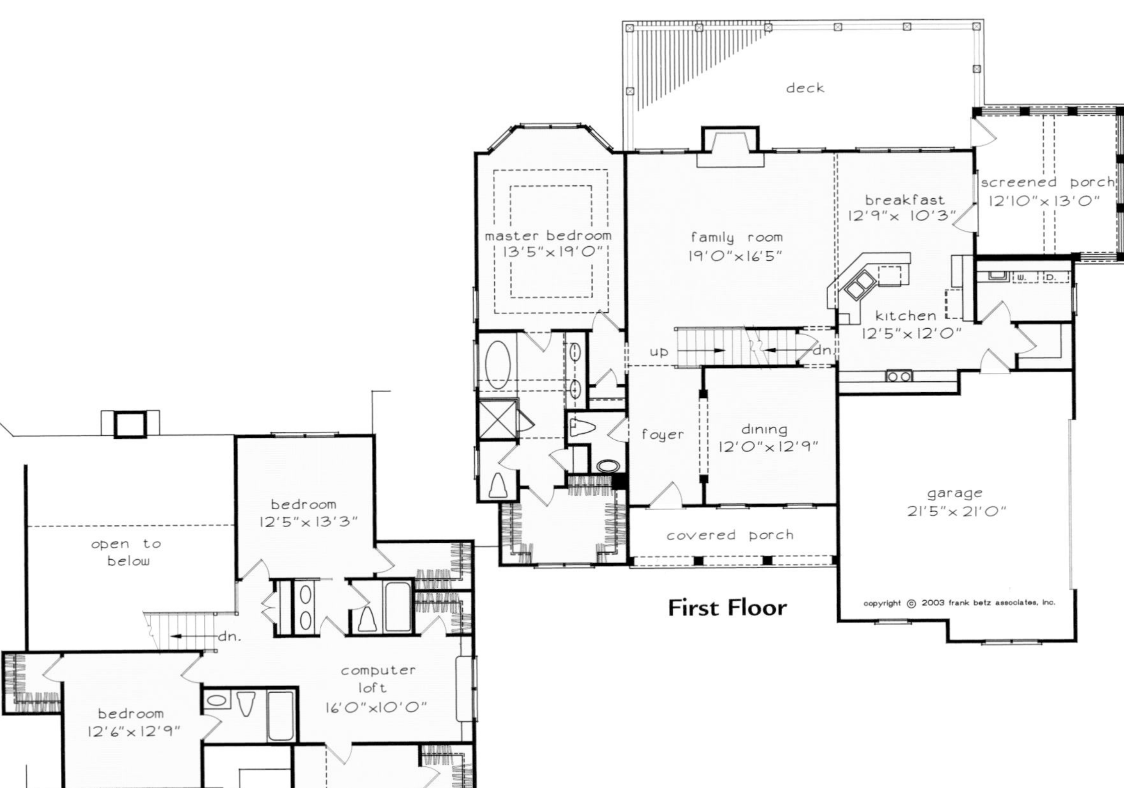

Design Features

- From the *Southern Living® Design Collection*
- A cozy front porch graces the front of the home.
- The kitchen, breakfast area and family room are conveniently grouped together for easy family interaction.
- The master suite encompasses an entire wing of the home, giving the homeowner added privacy.

Rear Elevation

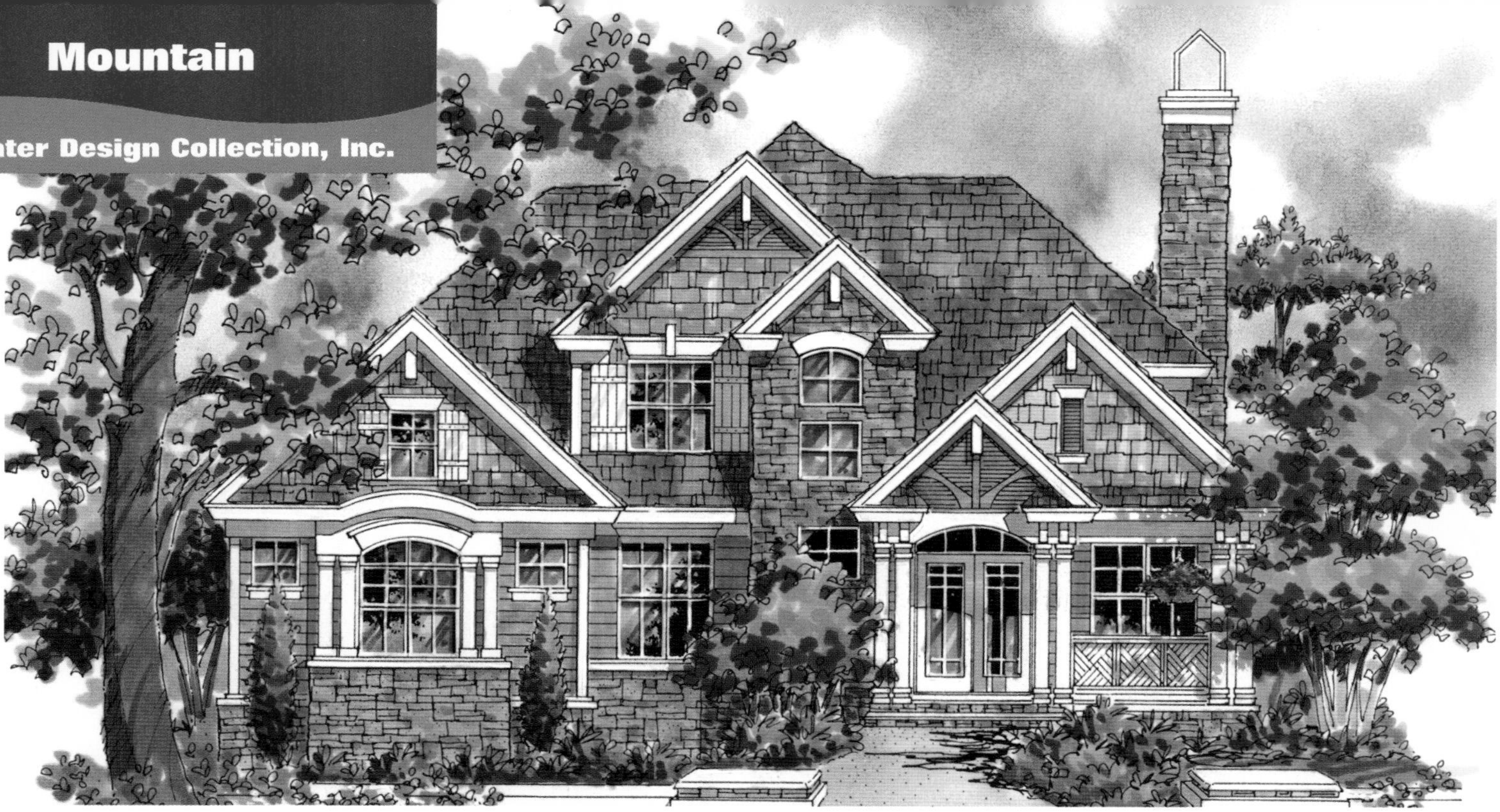

Cascade Ridge — VPDS01-Plan 6802 — 1-866-525-9374

Total Living	First Floor	Second Floor	Bed	Bath	Width	Depth	Foundation	Price Category
2988 sq ft	2096 sq ft	892 sq ft	3	3-1/2	56' 0"	54' 0"	Unfinished Walkout Basement	G

Design Features

- Steps lead down to the great room, which boasts a two-story ceiling, three sets of French doors opening to the covered veranda and a massive fireplace, flanked by built-in shelves.
- The gourmet kitchen features a centered cooktop island, walk-in pantry, easy access to the dining room and a pass-thru shared with the great room.
- On the upper level, guests will enjoy two secondary bedrooms that feature full baths and walk-in closets and one bedroom has sun deck access.

Lower Level

First Floor

Second Floor

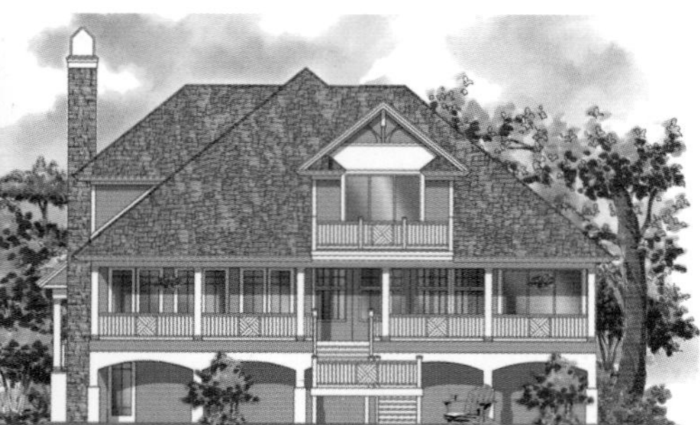

Rear Elevation

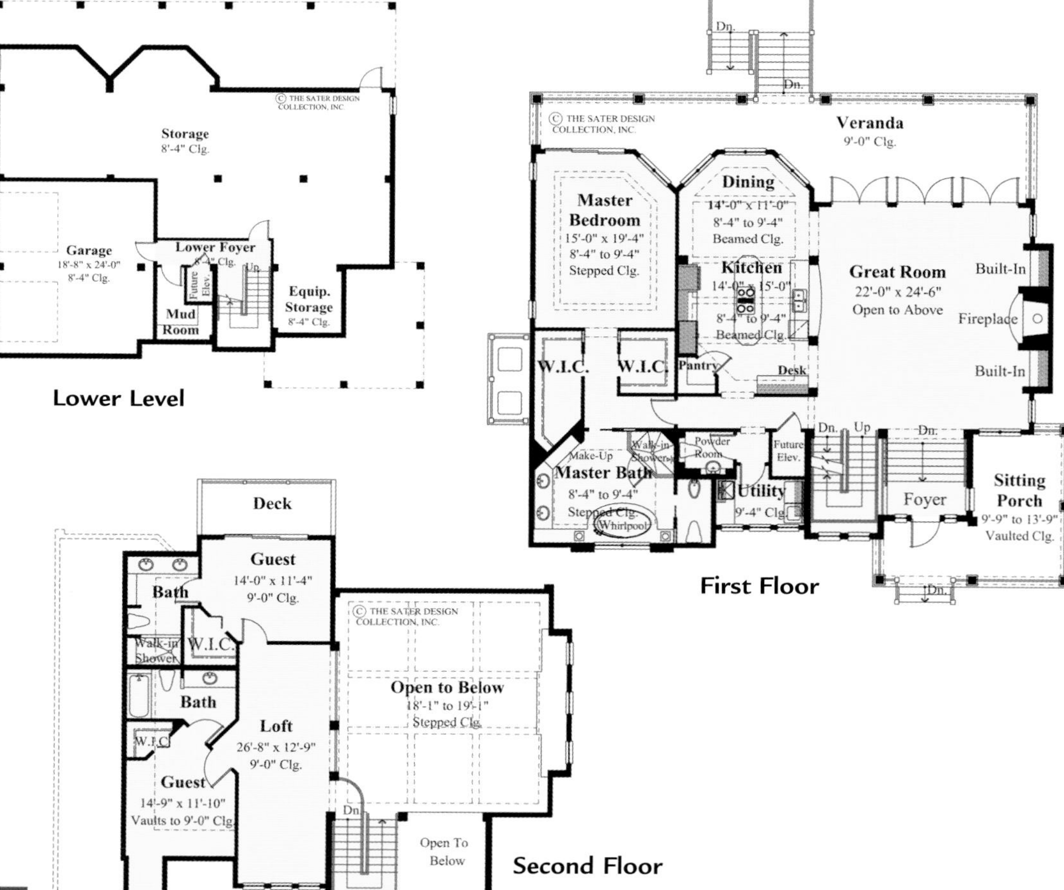

Glen Haven — VPDG01-Plan 843-D — 1-866-525-9374

Total Living	First Floor	Basement	Bed	Bath	Width	Depth	Foundation	Price Category
3104 sq ft	2000 sq ft	1104 sq ft	4	3	59' 4"	73' 2"	Hillside Walkout Foundation	G

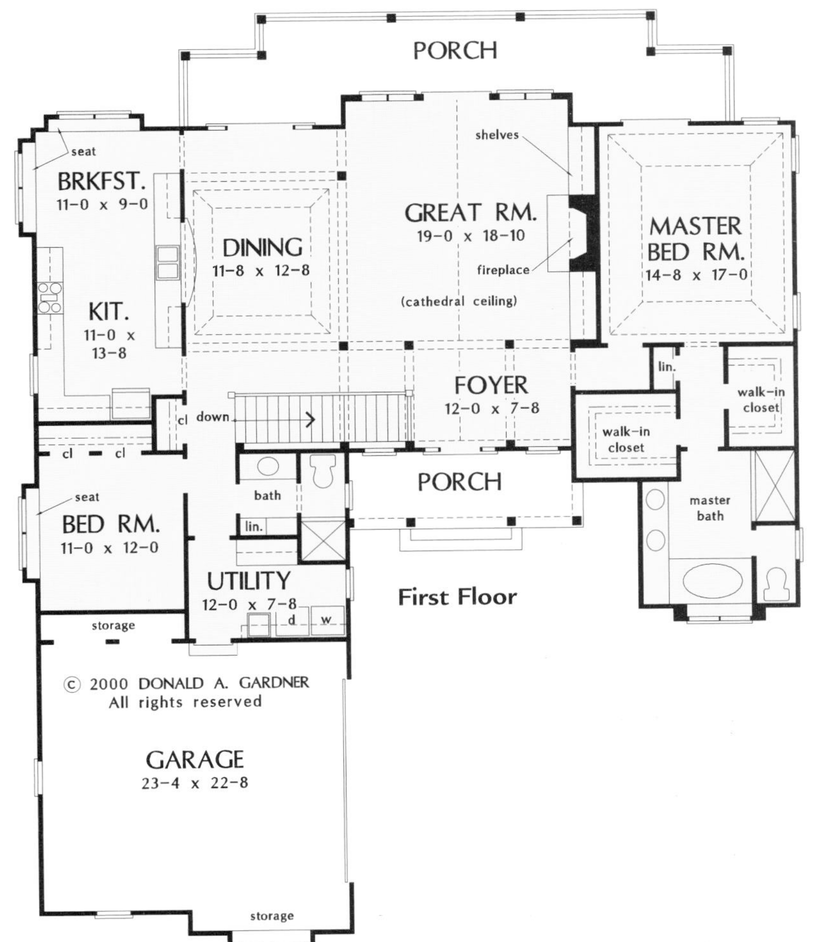

First Floor

Design Features

- In the great room, built-in shelves flank the fireplace and French doors access the back porch.
- Tray ceilings enhance the dining room and master bedroom.
- Box-bay windows with built-in window seats brighten the breakfast area.
- The master suite features two walk-in closets, a linen closet and luxurious bath.
- Bedrooms, a large family room and an unfinished storage room occupy the basement level.

Rear Elevation

Foxcrofte — VPFB01-3735 — 1-866-525-9374

Total Living	First Floor	Second Floor	Opt. Bonus	Bed	Bath	Width	Depth	Foundation	Price Category
1698 sq ft	1245 sq ft	453 sq ft	246 sq ft	3	2-1/2	50' 6"	44' 4"	Basement or Crawl Space	F

Design Features

- The *Foxcrofte* is quaint and charming with its gabled roofline and covered front porch.
- Vaulted ceilings give a roomy feeling inside the foyer and great room. The staircase to the upper floor is tucked away near the back of the home, adding to this design's spaciousness.
- The dining room is bordered by decorative columns, leaving this space open and accessible.
- Optional bonus space has been incorporated upstairs and presents the opportunity for adding a playroom, home office of craft room.

Rear Elevation

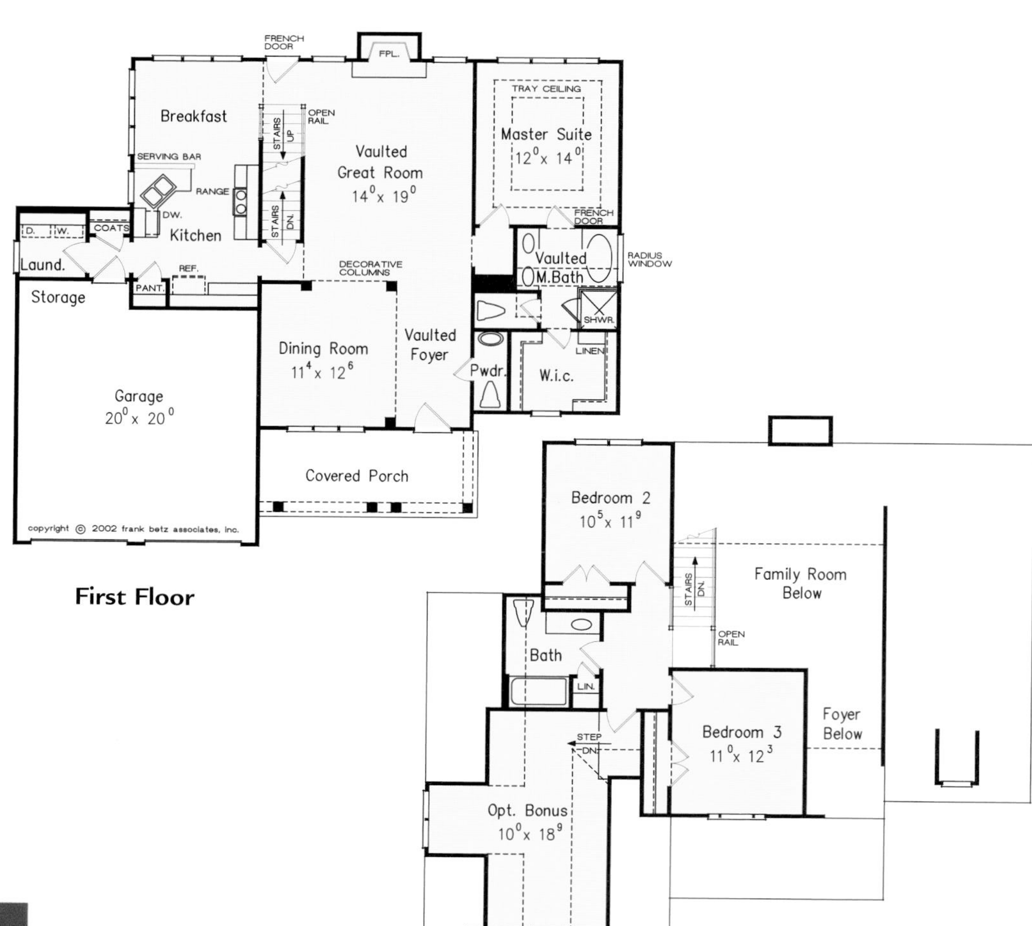

First Floor

Second Floor

Whisperwood — VPDS01-Plan 6844 — 1-866-525-9374

Total Living	First Floor	Bonus	Bed	Bath	Width	Depth	Foundation	Price Category
2137 sq ft	2137 sq ft	N/A	3	2	44' 0"	63' 0"	Unfinished Walkout Basement	F

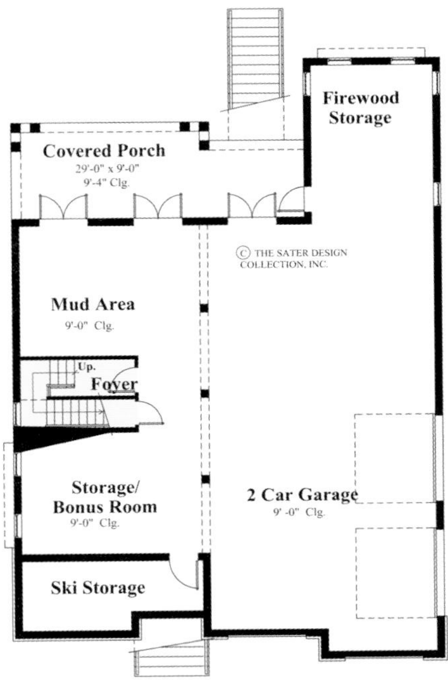

Lower Level

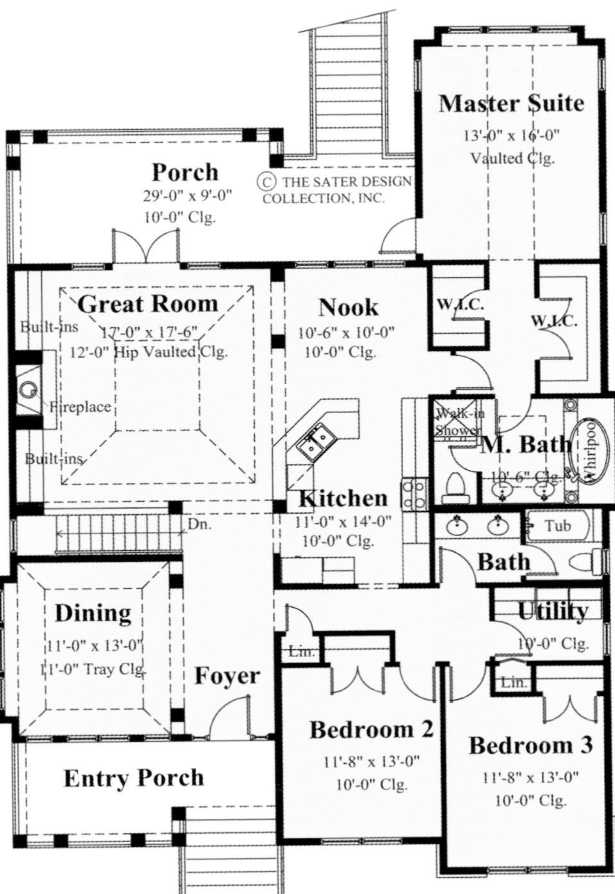

First Floor

Design Features

- A hip vaulted ceiling soars over the great room, which boasts a fireplace, built-in cabinetry, French doors to the back porch and easy access to the kitchen and dining room.
- The island kitchen shares an eating bar with the great room and offers ample counter and storage space.
- The master suite indulges with a luxiourious bath, dual walk-in closets, a vaulted ceiling and access to the back porch.

Rear Elevation

Rockledge — VPDG01-Plan 875-D — 1-866-525-9374

Total Living	First Floor	Second Floor	Basement	Bonus	Bed	Bath	Width	Depth	Foundation	Price Category
2949 sq ft	1682 sq ft	577 sq ft	690 sq ft	459 sq ft	4	3-1/2	79' 0"	68' 2"	Hillside Walkout Basement	F

Design Features

- Stone and siding combine to give this Craftsman design striking curb appeal.
- A portico sets the tone with a gentle arch and four stately columns.
- A clerestory above the front entrance floods the two-story foyer with natural light.
- Inside, Old-World charm gives way to an open, family-efficient floor plan.
- The great room features a two-story fireplace and French doors that lead to the rear porch.

Rear View

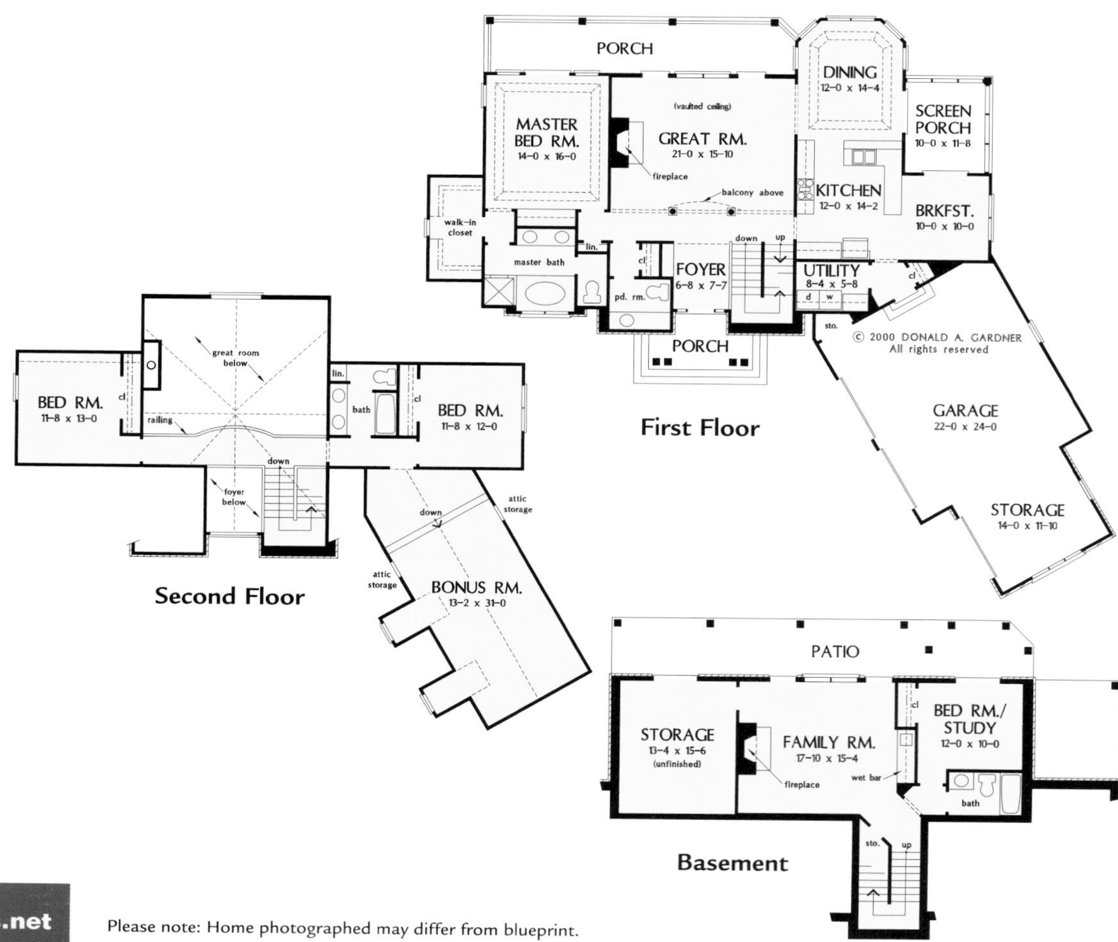

Please note: Home photographed may differ from blueprint.

Willow Creek — VPFB01-3539 — 1-866-525-9374

Total Living	First Floor	Second Floor	Opt. Bonus	Bed	Bath	Width	Depth	Foundation	Price Category
1975 sq ft	1399 sq ft	576 sq ft	221 sq ft	3	2-1/2	52' 4"	46' 10"	Basement, Crawl Space or Slab	H

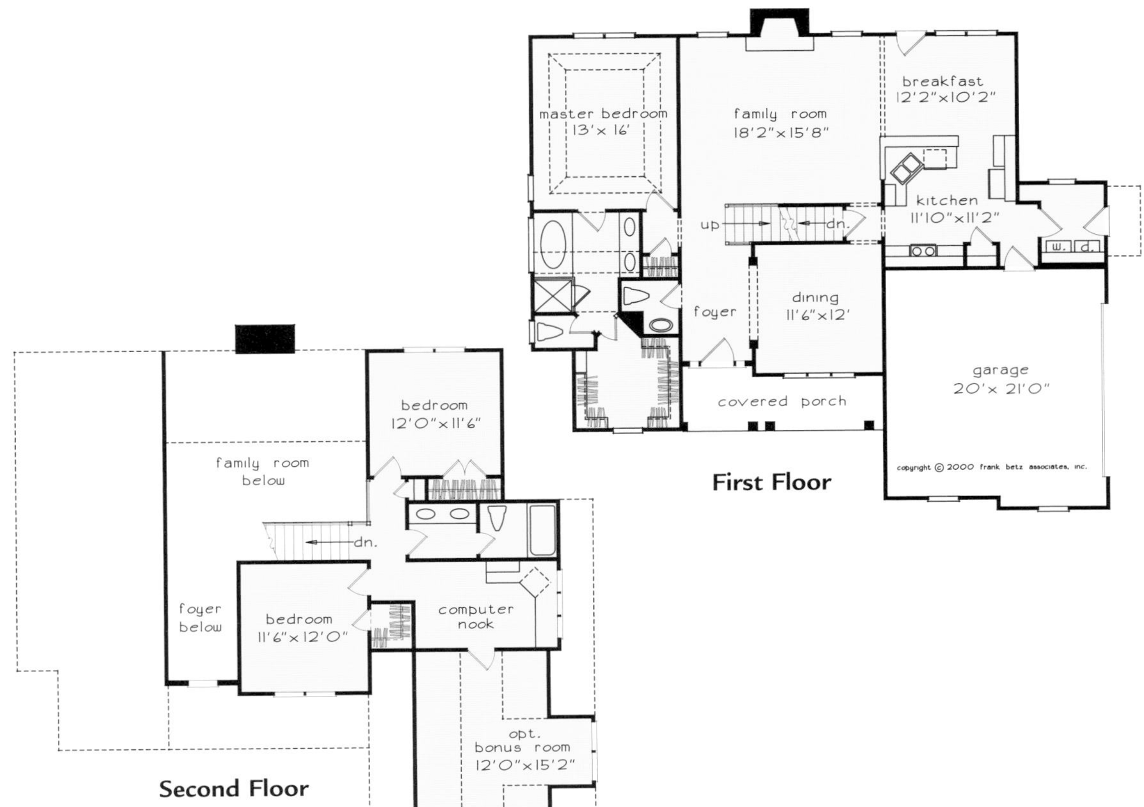

First Floor

Second Floor

Design Features

- From the *Southern Living*® *Design Collection*
- The *Willow Creek's* inviting exterior combines an attractive combination of stone and siding, graced by a columned front porch.
- The kitchen is conveniently linked to a large laundry room, which is a must-have for growing families.
- The master bath contains all the luxuries including double vanities, a garden tub, separate shower and walk-in closet.

Rear Elevation

Walden Hill — VPDS01-Plan 6803 — 1-866-525-9374

Total Living	First Floor	Second Floor	Bonus	Bed	Bath	Width	Depth	Foundation	Price Category
2374 sq ft	1510 sq ft	864 sq ft	810 sq ft	3	3-1/2	44' 0"	49' 0"	Unfinished Walkout Basement	F

Design Features

- A fireplace warms the great room, which features two sets of French doors to the rear porch and easy access to the dining room and kitchen.
- The island kitchen shares an eating bar with the great room and dining room and offers plenty of counter and storage space.
- The master retreat sits under a tray ceiling and boasts a spacious bath, walk-in closet and access to a private area of the back porch.

Rear Elevation

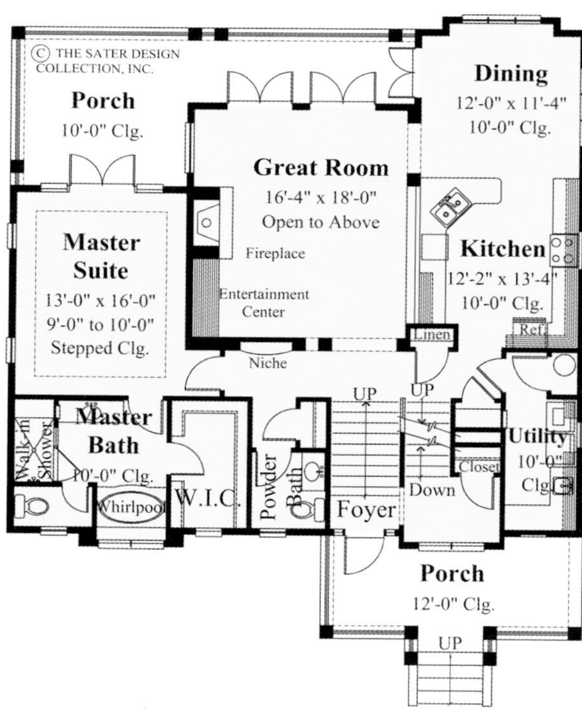

First Floor

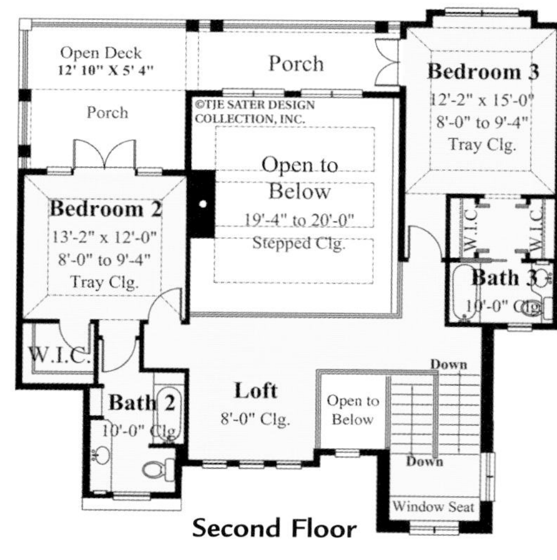

Second Floor

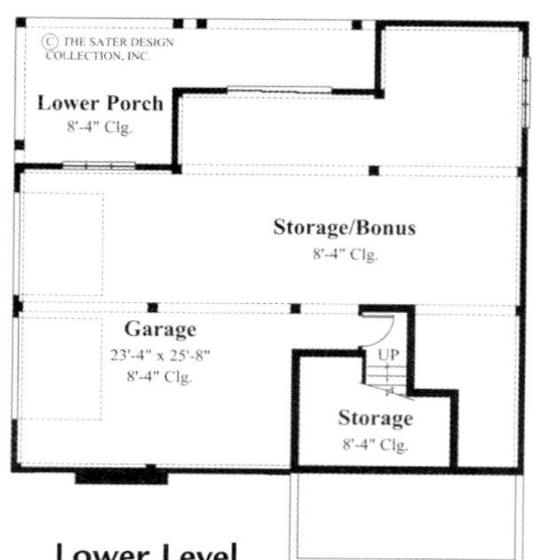

Lower Level

Evergreen — VPDG01-Plan 479 — 1-866-525-9374

Total Living	First Floor	Bonus	Bed	Bath	Width	Depth	Foundation	Price Category
1680 sq ft	1680 sq ft	N/A	3	2	62' 8"	59' 10"	Hillside Walkout Basement	D

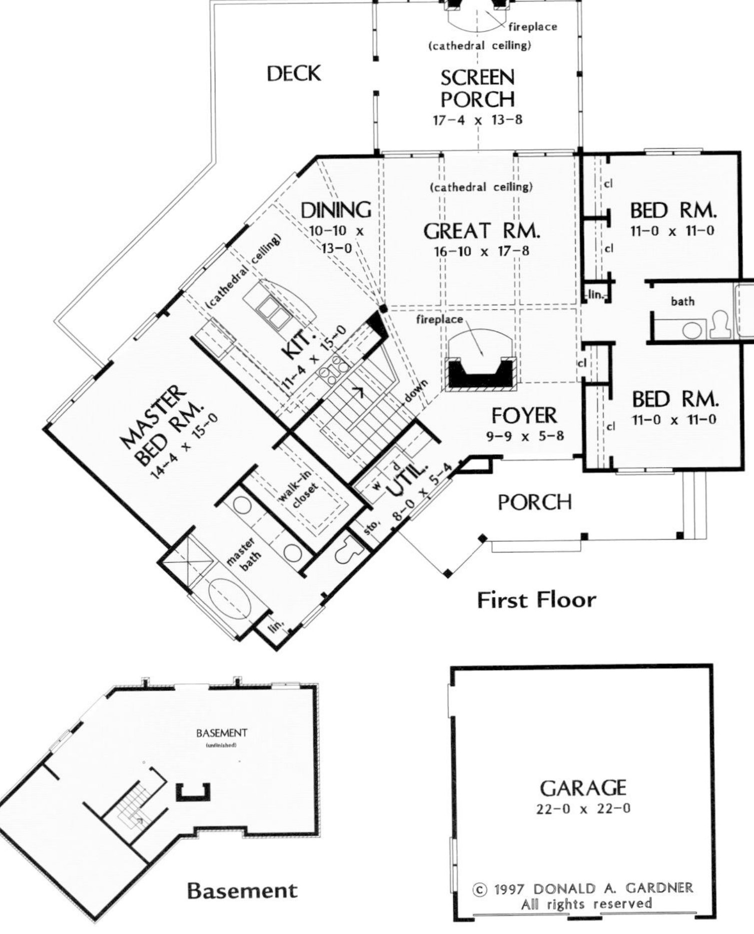

First Floor

Basement

Design Features

- Cathedral ceilings grace the great room, dining room, kitchen and screened porch.
- Outdoor living is easy with a front porch, expansive deck and screened-in porch with fireplace.
- Two bedrooms share a bath on one side of the house.
- The master suite boasts rear deck access, a walk-in closet and pampering bath.

Rear Elevation

Brewster — VPFB01-1175 — 1-866-525-9374

Total Living	First Floor	Second Floor	Opt. Bonus	Bed	Bath	Width	Depth	Foundation	Price Category
1467 sq ft	1001 sq ft	466 sq ft	292 sq ft	4	2-1/2	42' 0"	42' 0"	Basement, Crawl Space or Slab	F

Design Features

- An optional bonus room upstairs makes the perfect playroom or exercise area.
- The impressive dining room has a rare two-story ceiling; however, an optional loft or fourth bedroom can be easily incorporated.
- Vaulted ceilings and a decorative plant shelf make the main floor of this design interesting and dimensional.
- The laundry room and a handy coat closet are strategically placed just off the garage.

Rear Elevation

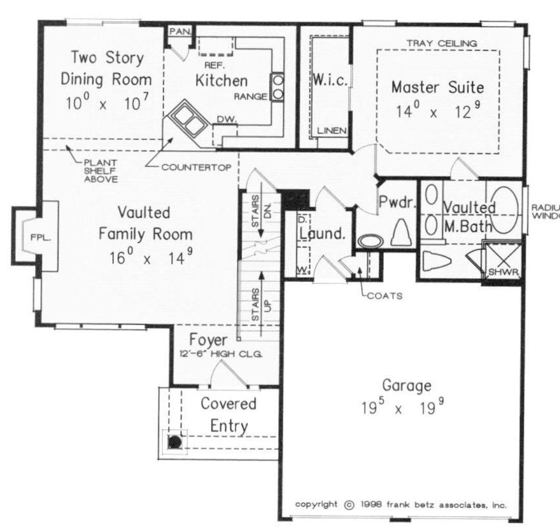

First Floor

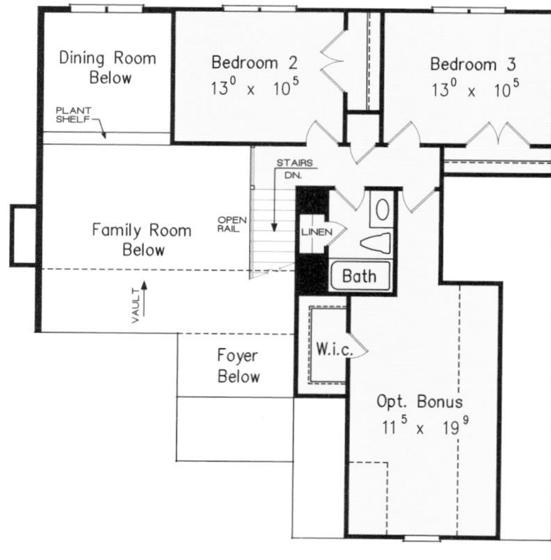

Second Floor

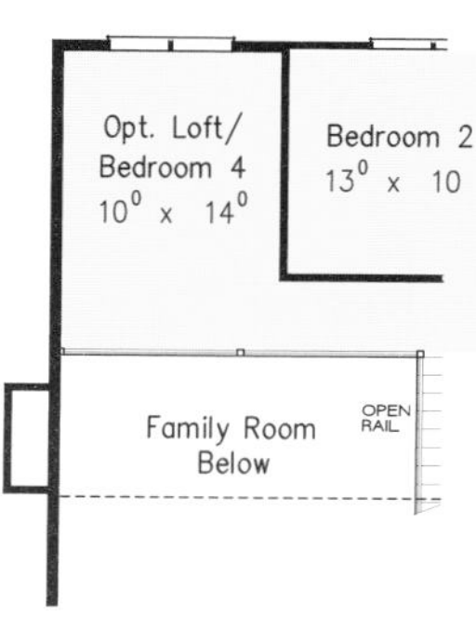

Opt. Loft or Bedroom

Heathridge — VPDG01-763-D — 1-866-525-9374

Total Living	First Floor	Basement	Bonus	Bed	Bath	Width	Depth	Foundation	Price Category
2998 sq ft	2068 sq ft	930 sq ft	N/A	3	3-1/2	72' 4"	66' 0"	Hillside Walkout	F

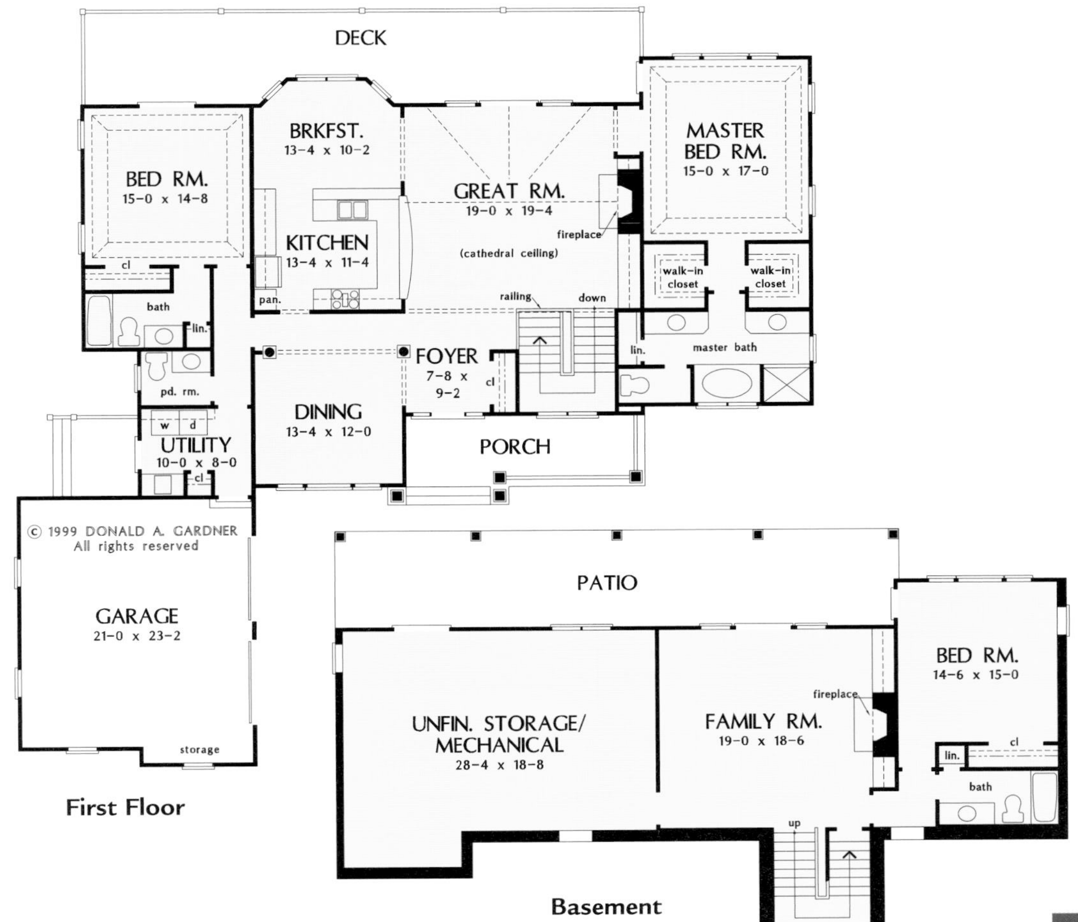

Design Features

- This Craftsman-style home takes advantage of views with its deck, patio and rear windows.
- The great room features a cathedral ceiling and a fireplace with built-in cabinets and shelves.
- The efficient kitchen serves the great and dining rooms and breakfast area with ease.
- Downstairs is a spacious family room with fireplace, a third bedroom and full bath.

Rear Elevation

Please note: Home photographed may differ from blueprint.

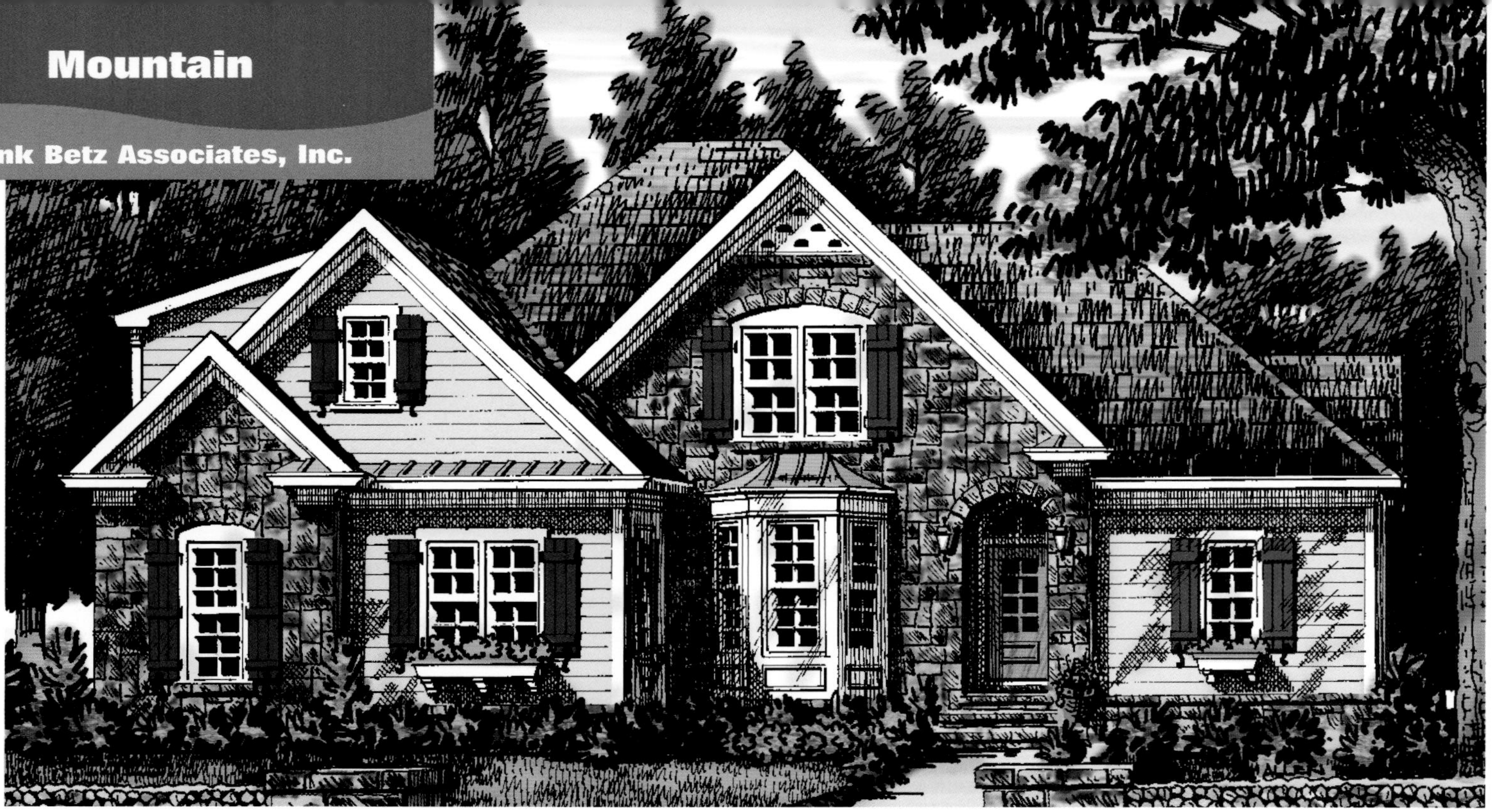

Greystone — VPFB01-3875 — 1-866-525-9374

Total Living	First Floor	Opt. 2nd Fl.	Bed	Bath	Width	Depth	Foundation	Price Category
1694 sq ft	1694 sq ft	588 sq ft	4	3	54' 0"	52' 0"	Basement or Crawl Space	F

Design Features

- A decorative column creates an unobtrusive border that defines the dining room, making the entrance of the home feel open and spacious.
- Transom windows in the family room invite plenty of sunshine into the room, keeping this space bright and cheery.
- An optional second floor has been made available for those who may need room to grow. It includes a fourth bedroom, third bath, and a bonus room.

First Floor

Opt. Second Floor

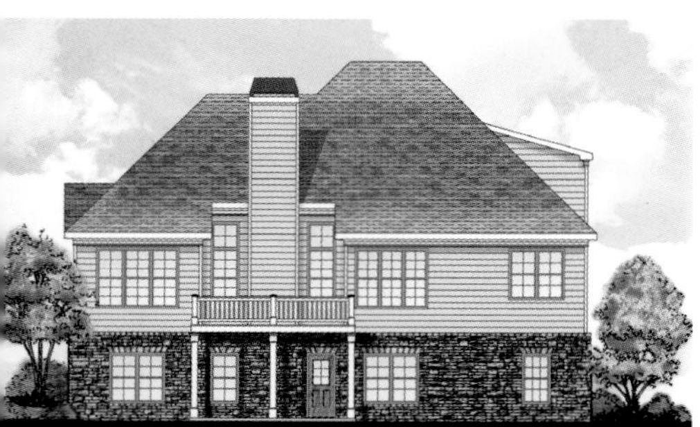

Rear Elevation

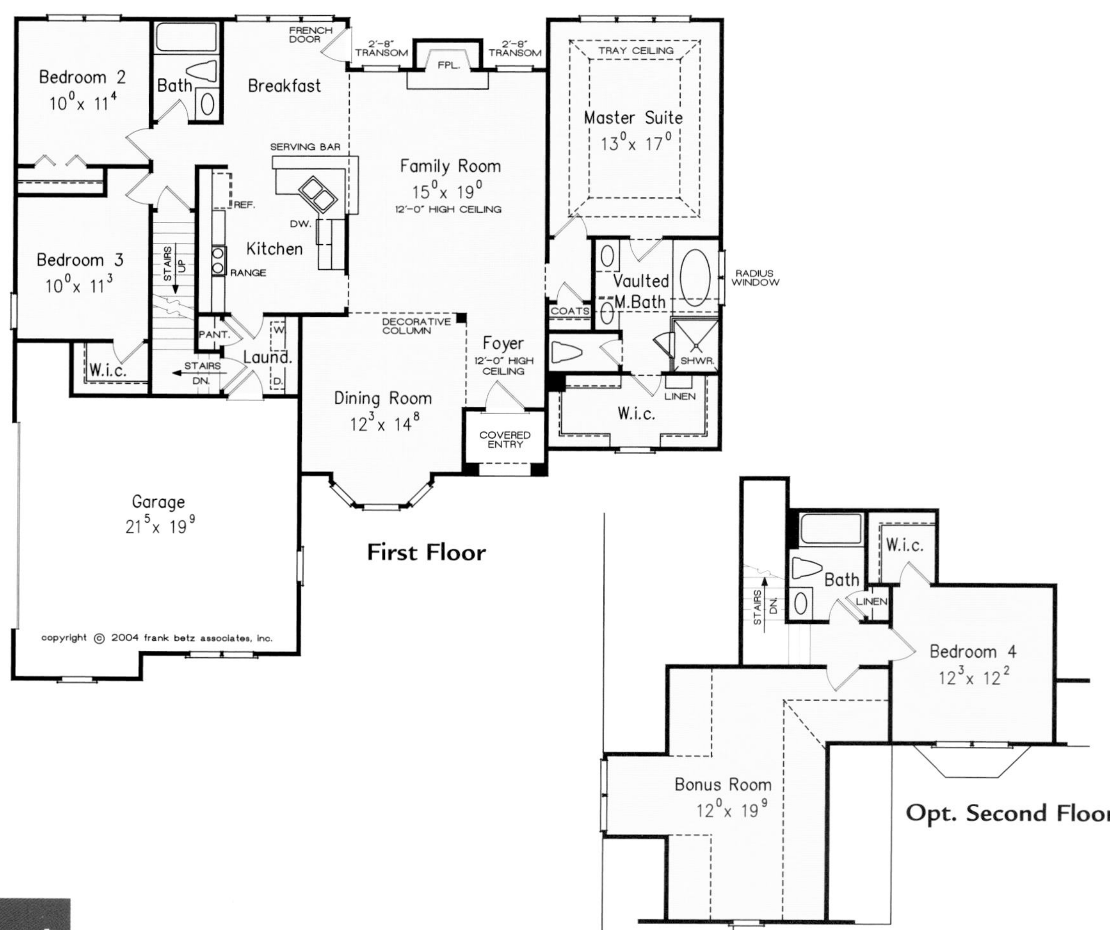

Highlands — VPDG01-852-D — 1-866-525-9374

Total Living	First Floor	Basement	Bonus	Bed	Bath	Width	Depth	Walls/Foundation	Price Category
2665 sq ft	1694 sq ft	971 sq ft	N/A	3	2-1/2	60' 6"	61' 2"	Hillside Walkout	F

Design Features

- An arched and gabled entry, Craftsman details and a mixture of stone and stucco create an appealing façade.
- Flanked by front and back porches, the great room's cathedral ceiling adds flair.
- Two back porches border the dining room with tray ceiling and arch-topped picture window.
- Downstairs, the walkout basement includes two bedrooms, storage and a recreation room.

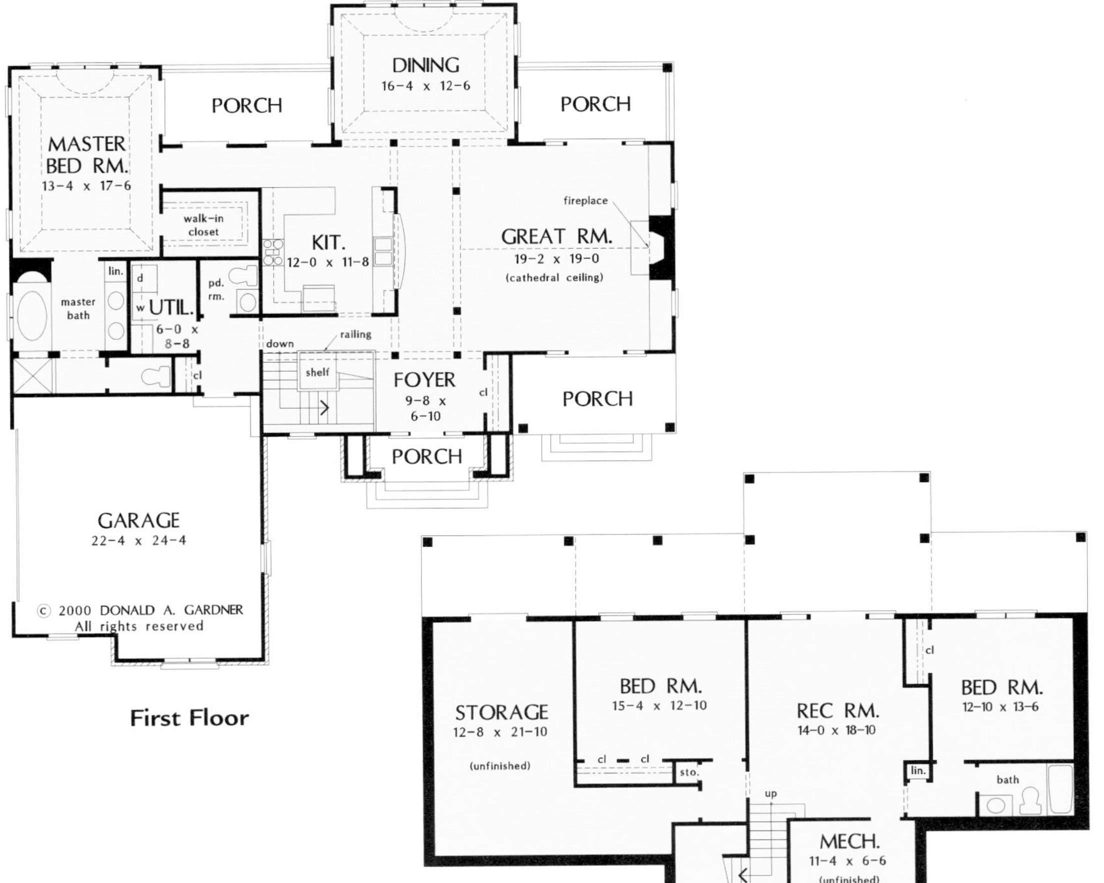

First Floor

Basement

Rear Elevation

Riverglen — VPFB01-3840 — 1-866-525-9374

Total Living	First Floor	Opt. Bonus	Bed	Bath	Width	Depth	Foundation	Price Category
1540 sq ft	1540 sq ft	N/A	3	2	52' 0"	51' 0"	Basement, Crawl Space or Slab	E

Design Features

- Fieldstone accents and dormers in the roofline give the *Riverglen* a feeling of home right from the start.
- The master suite has a private sitting area that offers a tranquil spot to start and end the day.
- Decorative columns surround the dining room giving it distinction and elegance.
- High ceilings in the foyer, family room and dining room give this design a roomy feel from the minute you walk in.

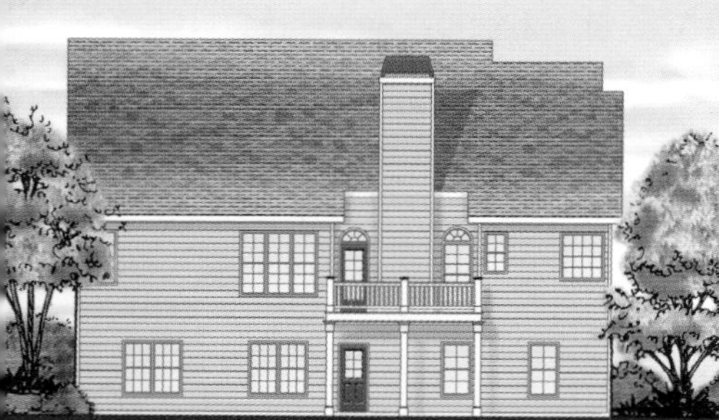

Rear Elevation

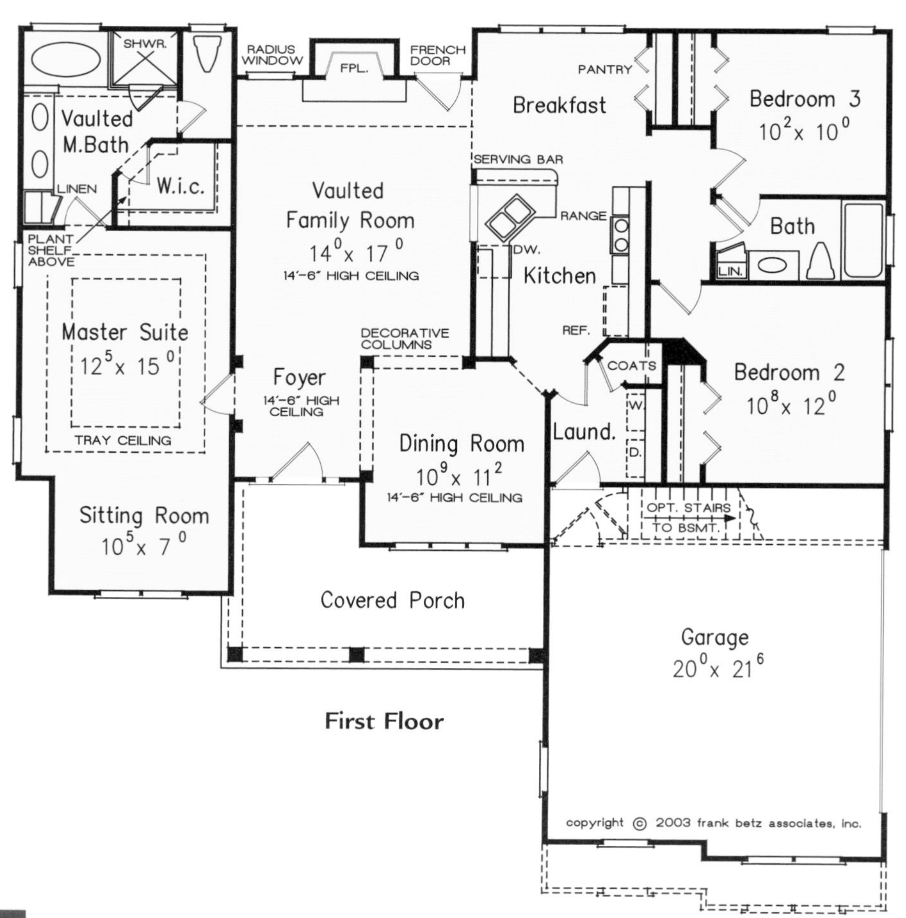

First Floor

Clairemont — VPDG01-791-D — 1-866-525-9374

Total Living	First Floor	Basement	Bonus	Bed	Bath	Width	Depth	Foundation	Price Category
3272 sq ft	2122 sq ft	1150 sq ft	N/A	4	3	83' 0"	74' 4"	Hillside Walkout	G

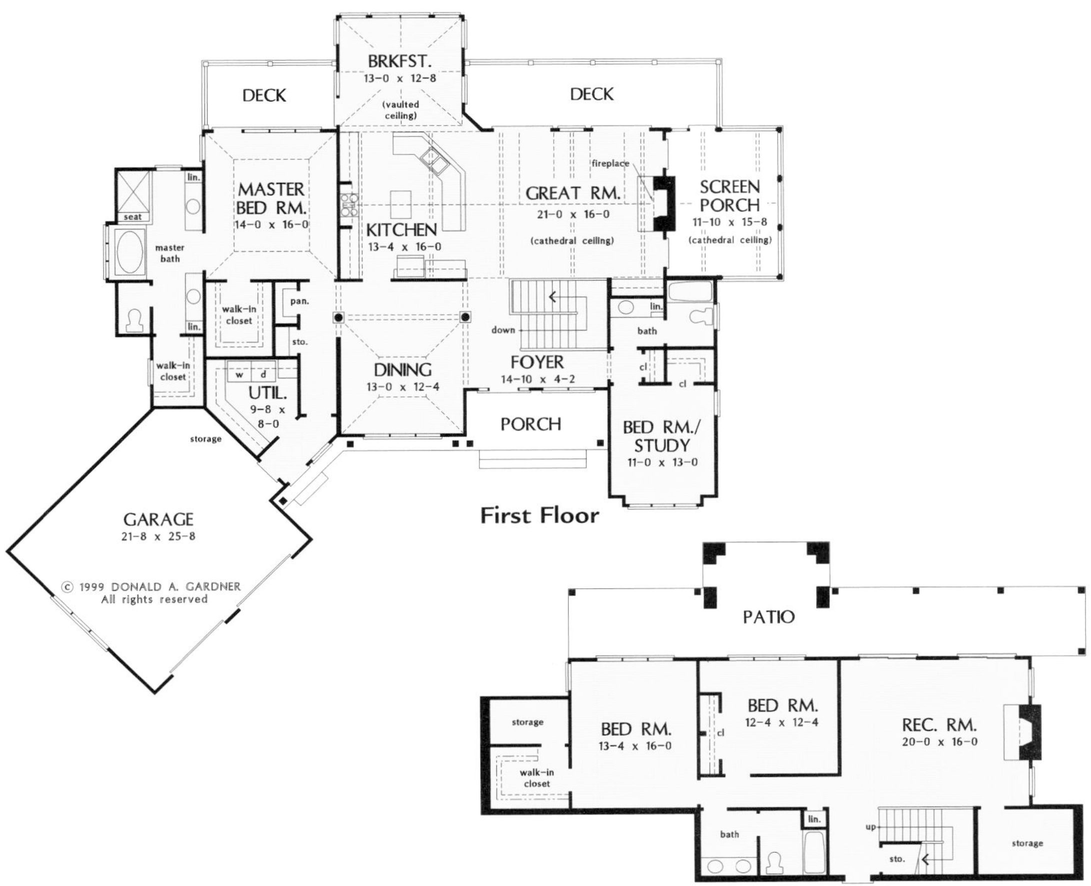

First Floor

Basement

Design Features

- A Craftsman combination of cedar shake and wood siding lends warmth to this custom home.
- A stunning cathedral ceiling spans the open great room and spacious, island kitchen.
- Two rear decks and a screened porch augment the home's ample living space.
- Note the large utility room, basement-floor recreation room and plentiful storage.

Rear Elevation

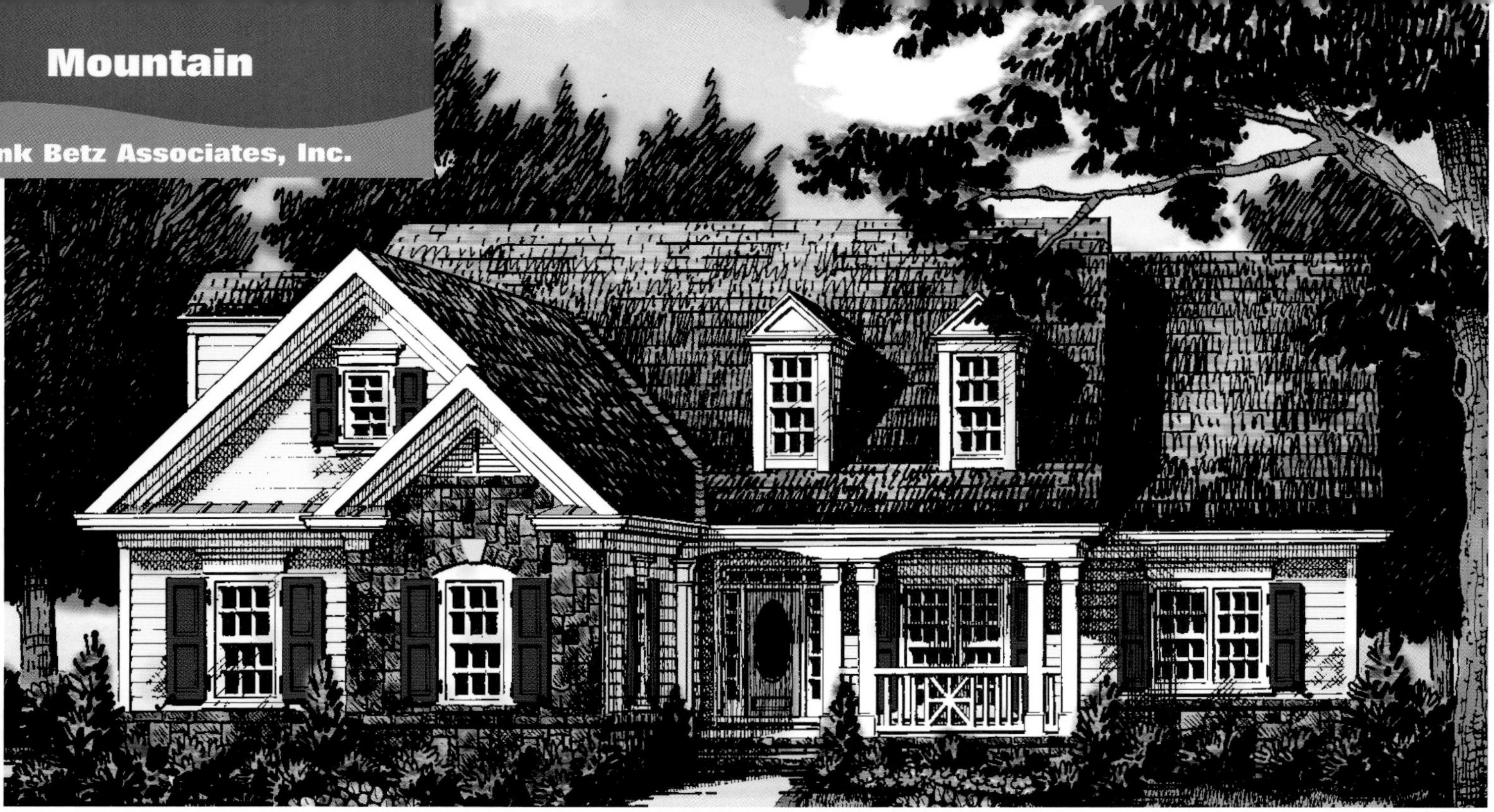

Jasmine — VPFB01-1036 — 1-866-525-9374

Total Living	First Floor	Opt. 2nd Fl.	Bed	Bath	Width	Depth	Foundation	Price Category
1604 sq ft	1604 sq ft	288 sq ft	3	2	53' 6"	55' 10"	Basement, Crawl Space or Slab	F

Design Features

- The *Jasmine* has a friendly, cottage-like appeal with its calm combination of natural stone and siding.
- Dormers accent the covered front porch that invites you in to see more.
- The dining room and kitchen have direct access to each other, making entertaining a breeze.
- Careful placement of the guest bath between the secondary bedrooms creates a comfortable separation for added privacy.

First Floor

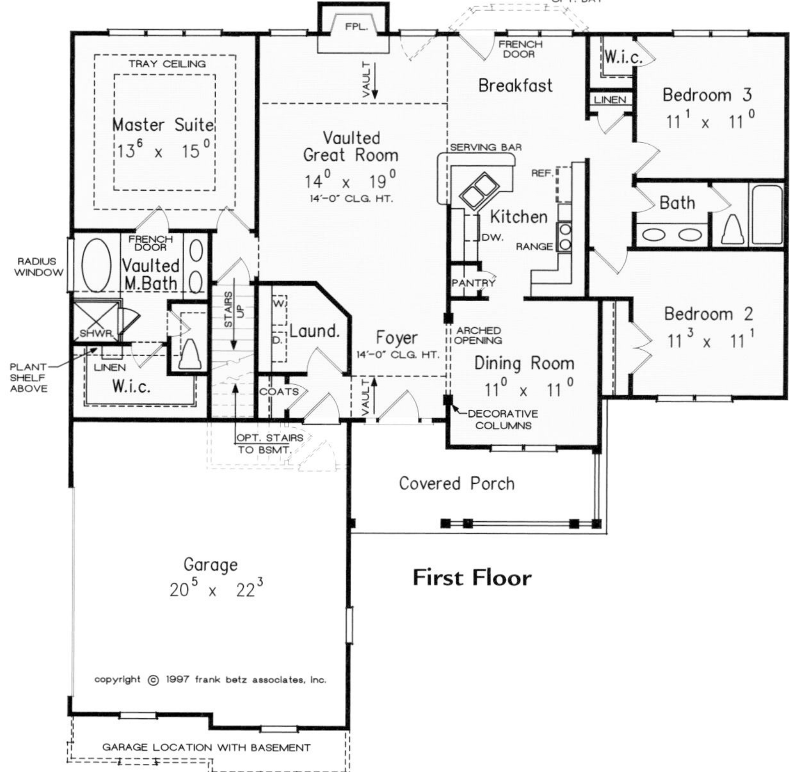

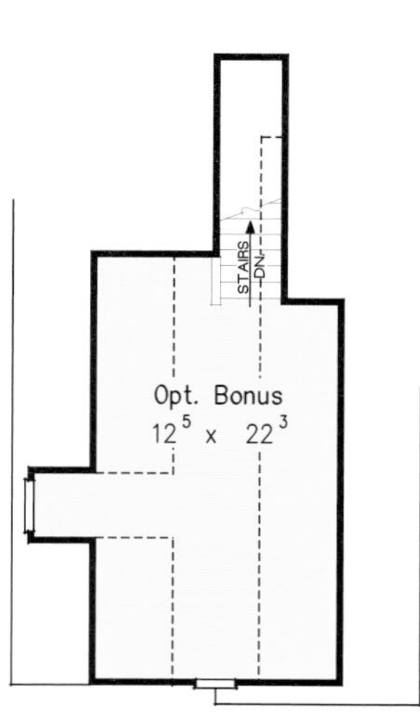

Opt. Second Floor

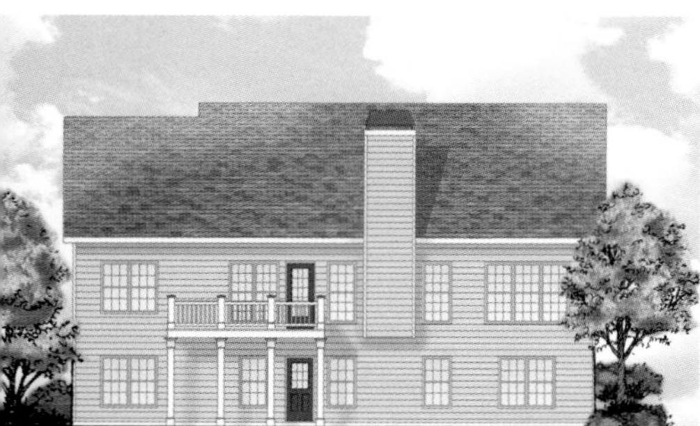

Rear Elevation

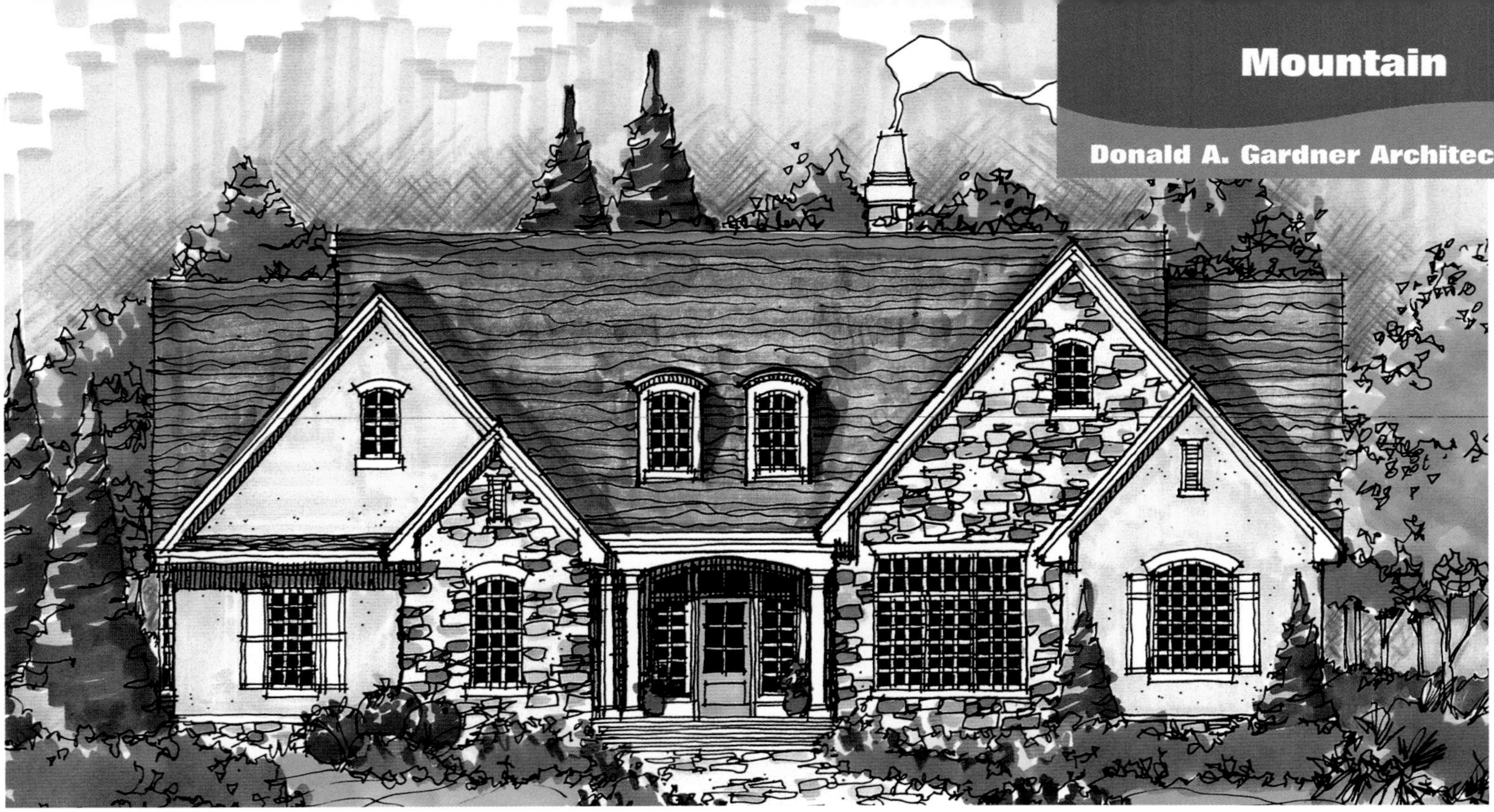

MacLachlan — VPDG01-825-D — 1-866-525-9374

Total Living	First Floor	Basement	Bonus	Bed	Bath	Width	Depth	Foundation	Price Category
2976 sq ft	1901 sq ft	1075 sq ft	N/A	4	3	64' 0"	62' 4"	Hillside Walkout	F

First Floor

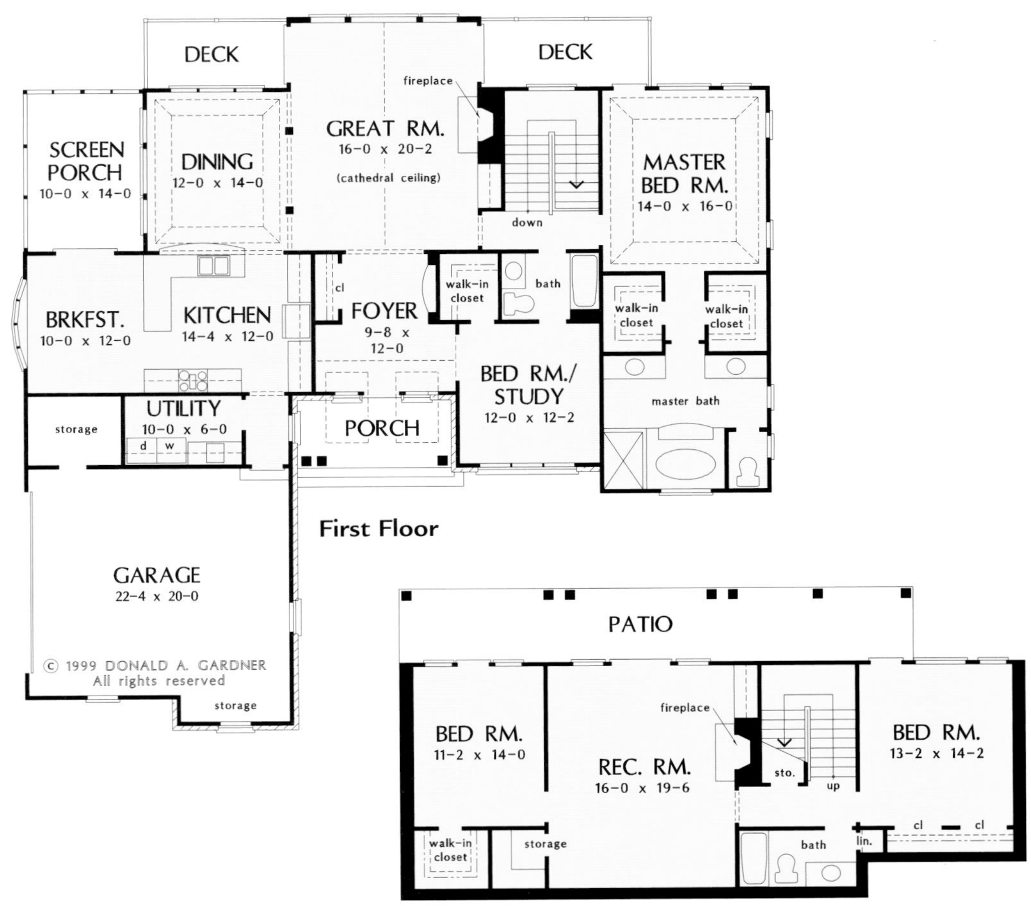

Basement

Design Features

- This stylish stone and stucco home features a partially finished walkout basement for sloping lots.
- The foyer is vaulted, receiving light from two clerestory dormer windows, and includes a niche.
- A recreation room is located on the basement level.
- Two bedrooms can be found on the first floor, while two more flank the downstairs recreation room.

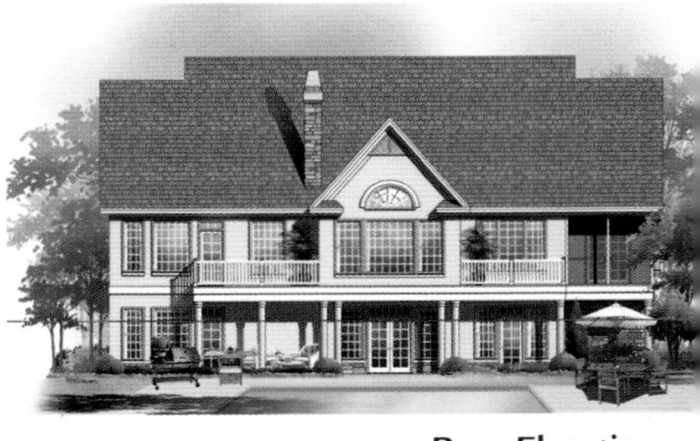

Rear Elevation

Timberlake — VPFB01-3679 — 1-866-525-9374

Total Living	First Floor	Opt. 2nd Fl.	Bed	Bath	Width	Depth	Foundation	Price Category
1814 sq ft	1814 sq ft	310 sq ft	4	3	48' 0"	56' 6"	Basement, Crawl Space or Slab	F

Design Features

- Brick, siding and board-and-batten shutters make the curb appeal of this home truly inviting.
- The vaulted family room offers a fireplace on the rear wall which is flanked by windows that allow natural light to filter in.
- The open flow of the kitchen, breakfast room and family room make entertaining a breeze.
- The master bedroom and bath offer amenities usually found in much larger homes.

Rear Elevation

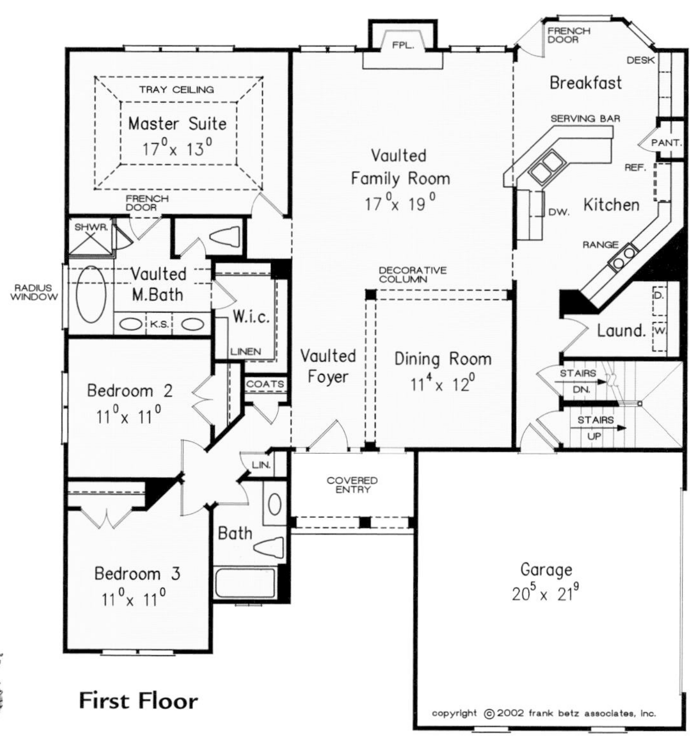

First Floor

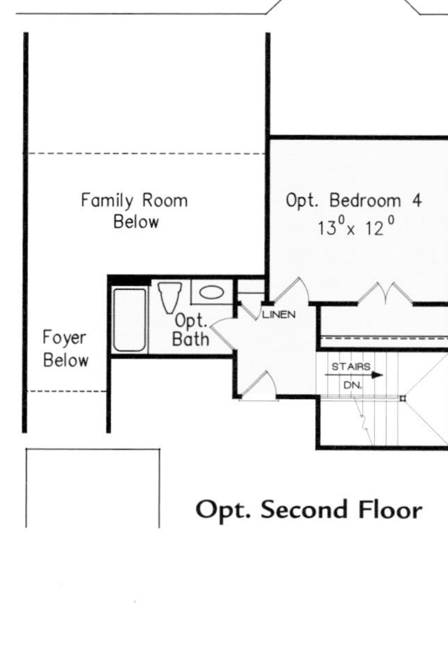

Opt. Second Floor

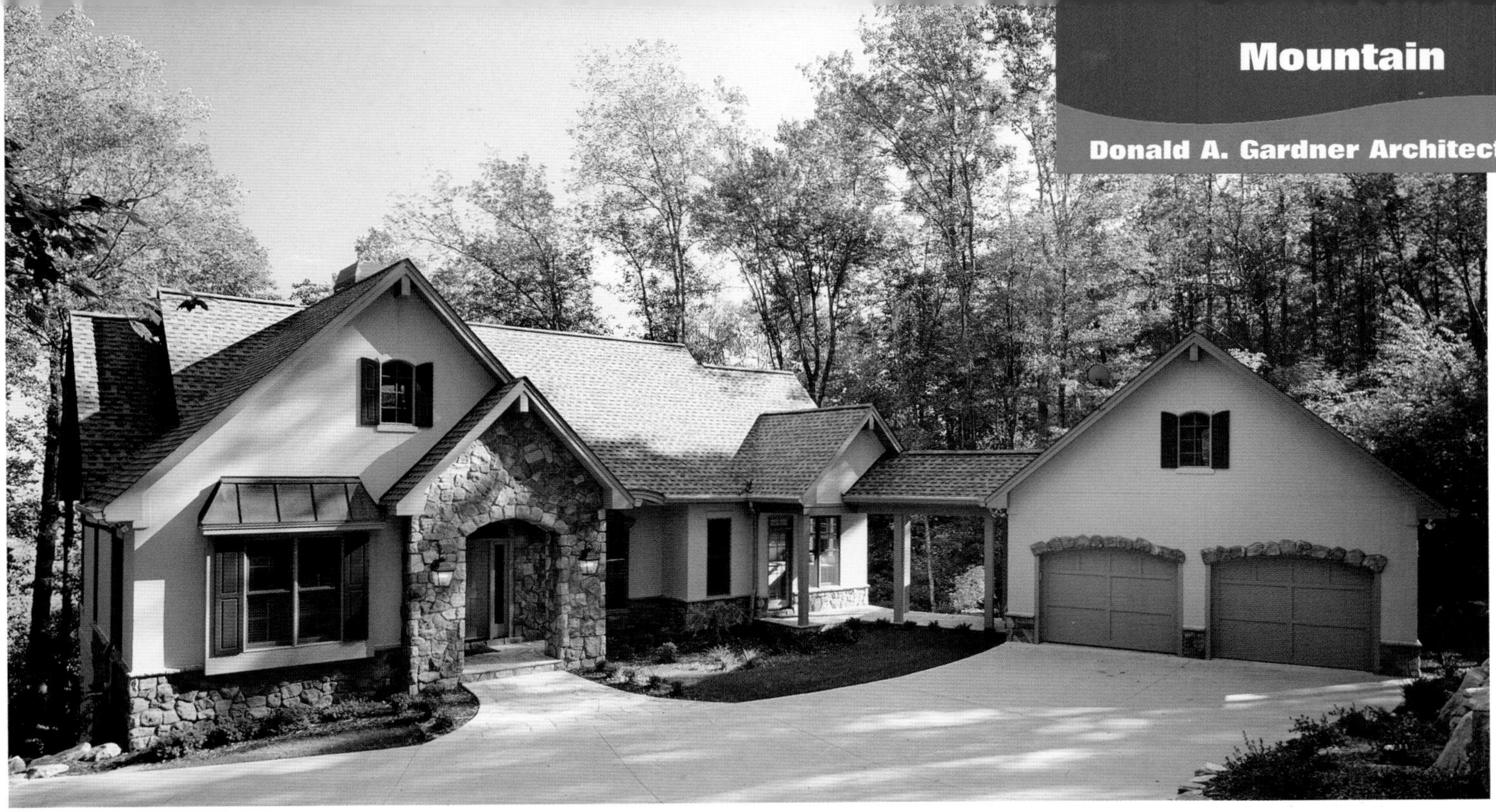

Sable Ridge — VPDG01-710-D — 1-866-525-9374

Total Living	First Floor	Basement	Bonus	Bed	Bath	Width	Depth	Foundation	Price Category
2683 sq ft	1472 sq ft	1211 sq ft	N/A	3	2-1/2	53' 8"	40' 4"	Hillside Walkout	F

First Floor

Basement

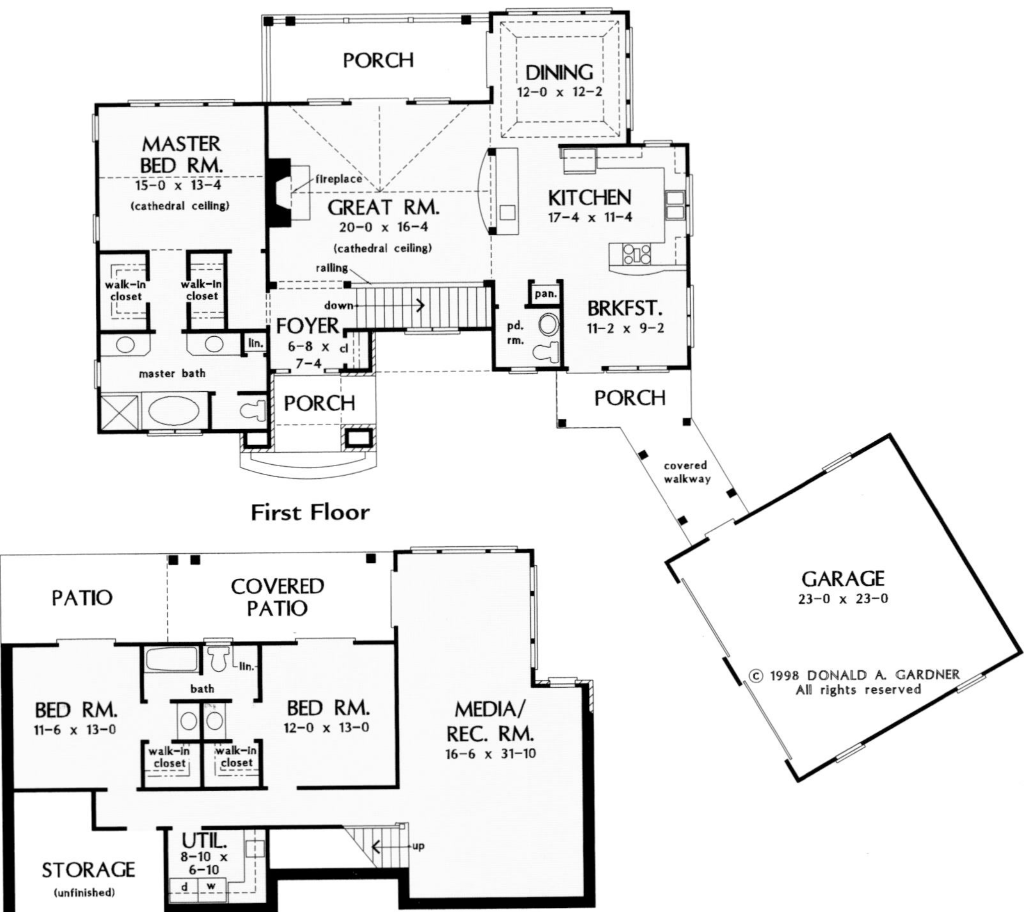

Design Features

- Designed for sloping lots, this stone and stucco home takes advantage of rear views.
- The floor plan features an open design, with cathedral ceilings in the great room and master bedroom.
- A wet bar is conveniently situated between the kitchen and great room.
- Downstairs, two bedrooms share an adjoining bath, and the enormous rec room offers flexibility.

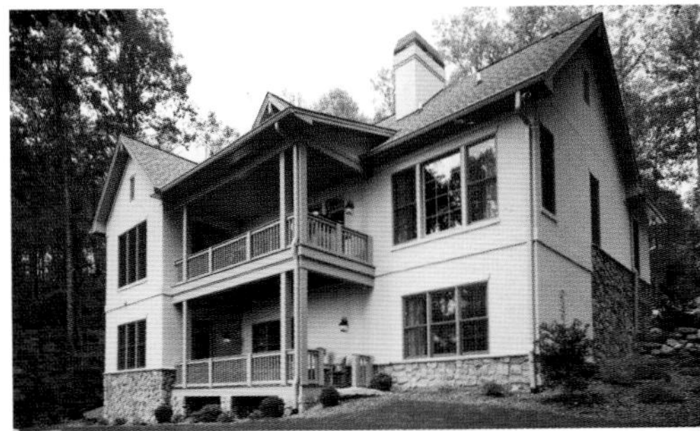

Rear View

Please note: Home photographed may differ from blueprint.

Palmdale — VPFB01-3776 — 1-866-525-9374

Total Living	First Floor	Opt. 2nd Fl.	Bed	Bath	Width	Depth	Foundation	Price Category
2073 sq ft	2073 sq ft	350 sq ft	4	3-1/2	59' 0"	57' 0"	Basement or Crawl Space	G

Design Features

- Special details and added extras give the *Palmdale* an edge over its one-level competitors.
- Step inside to find exceptional floor planning and details. A unique niche is incorporated into the foyer, providing the ideal location for that special furniture piece or artwork.
- Transom windows allow extra light to pour into the family room.
- A generously sized optional bonus area provides an additional bedroom, a home office or exercise room.

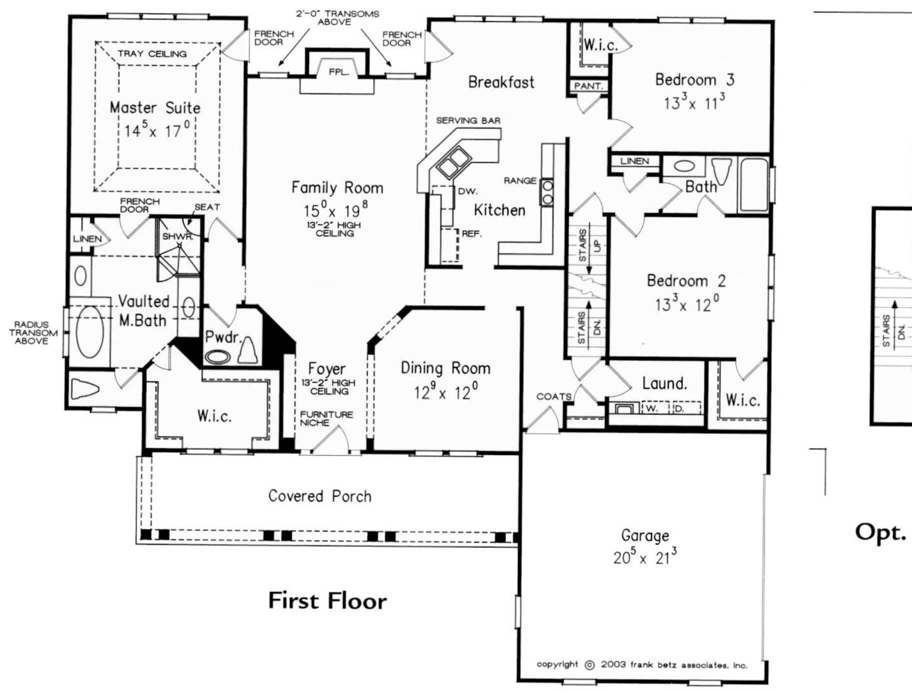

First Floor

Opt. Second Floor

Rear Elevation

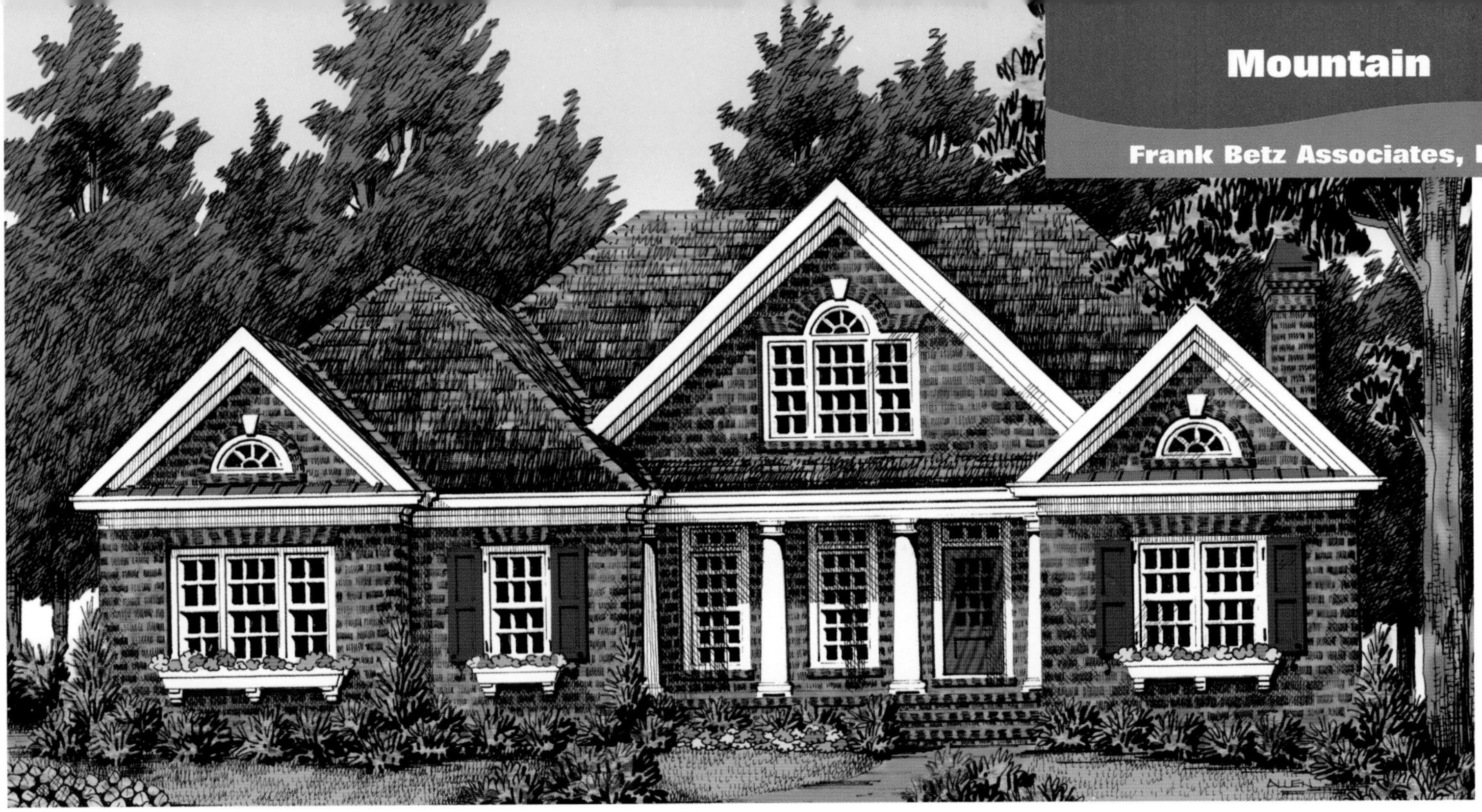

Kingsbridge — VPFB01-3936 — 1-866-525-9374

Total Living	First Floor	Opt. 2nd Fl.	Bed	Bath	Width	Depth	Foundation	Price Category
2289 sq ft	2289 sq ft	311 sq ft	3	3-1/2	57' 0"	70' 0"	Basement, Crawl Space or Slab	H

Design Features

- A brick elevation with columns makes this an inviting home.
- A keeping room is located just off the kitchen and breakfast room, and boasts a fireplace. This is a great place for families to end their day.
- The spacious family room has direct access to the covered porch and deck.
- The master suite and bath are spacious and open. A very large walk-in closet allows personal items to have their place.

Rear Elevation

Avalon — VPDG01-726 — 1-866-525-9374

Total Living	First Floor	Second Floor	Bed	Bath	Width	Depth	Foundation	Price Category
2588 sq ft	1896 sq ft	692 sq ft	3	2-1/2	84' 10"	60' 0"	Crawl Space*	F

Design Features

- Visually, the great room, dining room, kitchen, breakfast area and loft flow effortlessly together.
- A curved staircase, as well as cathedral ceilings in the great and dining rooms, enhances volume.
- "His-and-her" vanities make mornings easy.
- An abundance of storage space is accessible upstairs as well as in the garage.

Rear Elevation

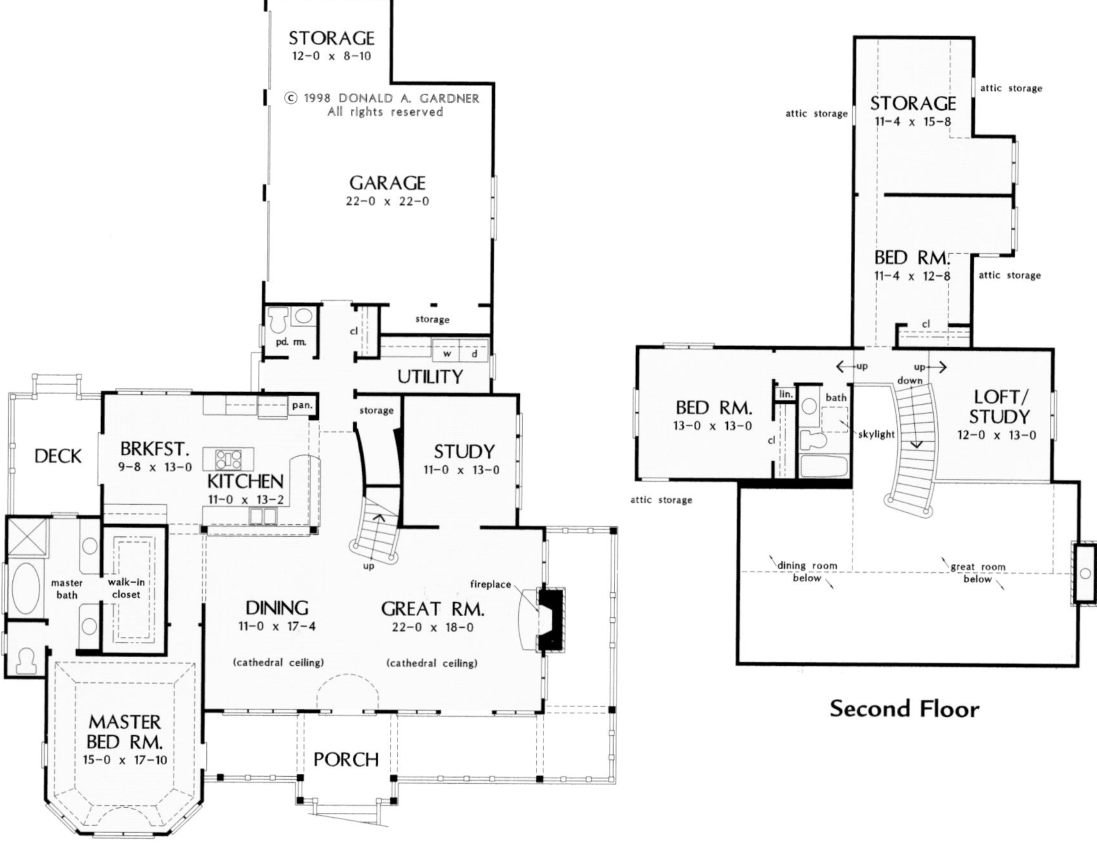

First Floor

Second Floor

Please note: Home photographed may differ from blueprint.

*Other options available. See page 255.

Rankins — VPFB01-3829 — 1-866-525-9374

Total Living	First Floor	Opt. 2nd Fl.	Bed	Bath	Width	Depth	Foundation	Price Category
2487 sq ft	2487 sq ft	306 sq ft	4	3-1/2	61' 6"	67' 6"	Basement, Crawl Space or Slab	G

Opt. Second Floor

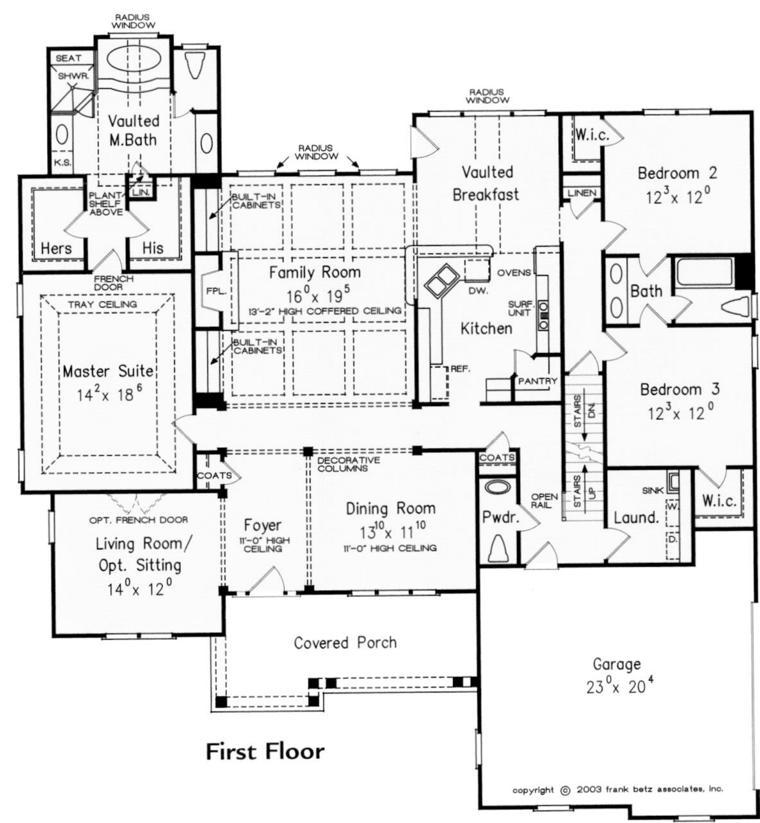

First Floor

Design Features

- Home is where the heart is — and this design has a lot of heart! It was created for that homeowner who is looking for a functional, well-planned design with upscale amenities that make a house a home.
- The core of the home is the family room that is made special with coffered ceilings and built-in cabinetry.
- The master suite is adorned with all the creature comforts imaginable, such as a seated shower, a step-up soaking tub and an optional private sitting area.

Rear Elevation

Valencia — VPDG01-Plan 907 — 1-866-525-9374

Total Living	First Floor	Second Floor	Bed	Bath	Width	Depth	Foundation	Price Category
2600 sq ft	1679 sq ft	921 sq ft	4	2-1/2	58' 0"	58' 10"	Crawl Space*	F

Design Features

- A balcony is all that separates the open foyer from the two-story great room.
- A second-floor shelf can be utilized for decorative accessories.
- A tray ceiling tops the bedroom in the master suite.
- The flexible loft/bedroom allows for expansion.
- Note the one-and two-car garages, and the box-bay window that provides extra space.

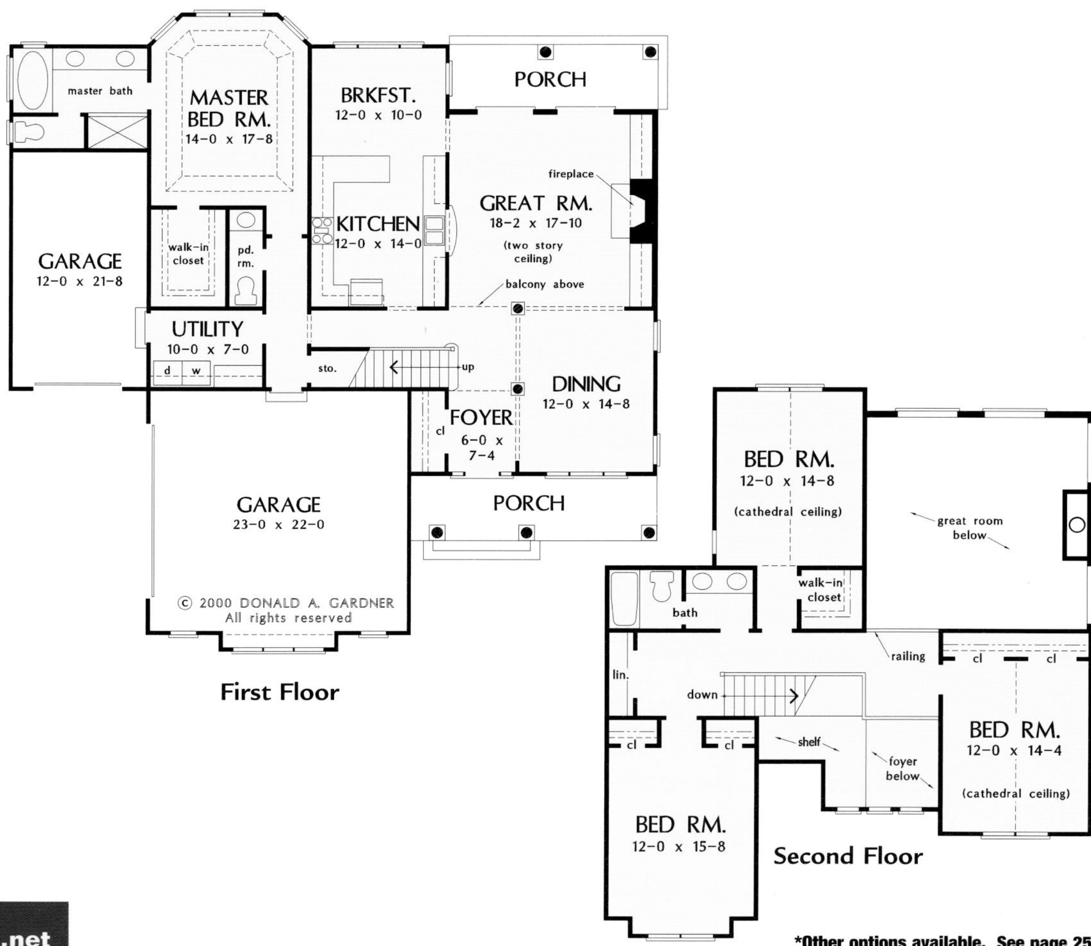

First Floor

Second Floor

Rear Elevation

*Other options available. See page 255.

Bellavita — VPDG01-Plan 1104 — 1-866-525-9374

Total Living	First Floor	Bonus	Bed	Bath	Width	Depth	Foundation	Price Category
2369 sq ft	2369 sq ft	N/A	3	2-1/2	56' 0"	70' 4"	Crawl Space*	E

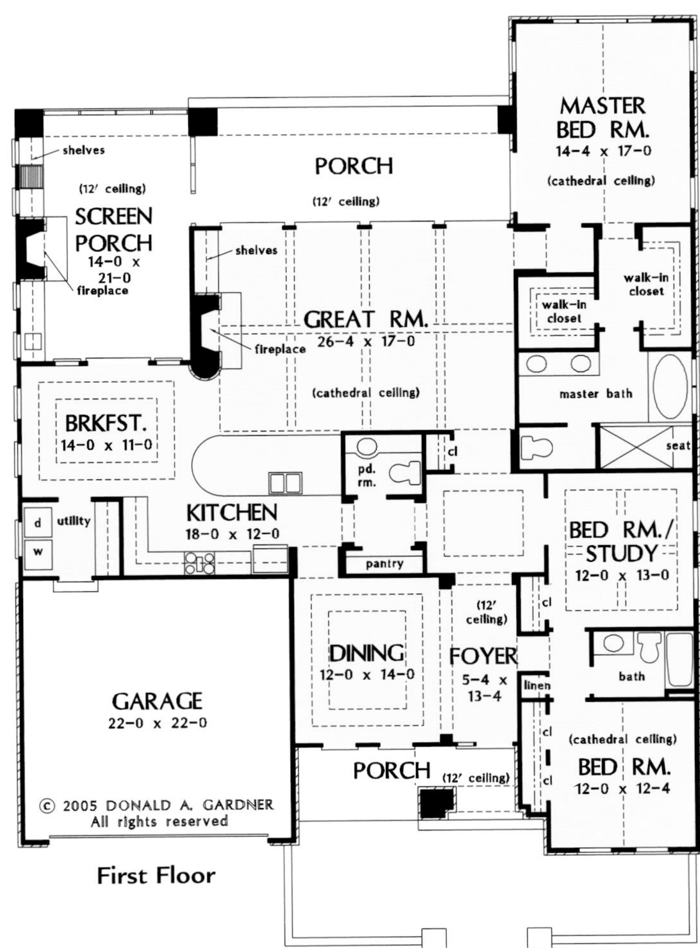

First Floor

Design Features

- This extraordinary exterior unites pizzazz with refinement.
- Ceiling treatments in multiple rooms grant striking altitude throughout the home.
- Multiple sets of French doors and a fireplace accent the oversized great room.
- A large master bedroom exits onto the covered patio in the rear of the home.
- The remainder of the suite features dual walk-in closets and sinks in the bath.

Rear Elevation

*Other options available. See page 255.

Villa

The Sater Design Collection, Inc.

Mission Hills — VPDS01-6845 — 1-866-525-9374

Total Living	First Floor	Lower Level	Bed	Bath	Width	Depth	Foundation	Price Category
2494 sq ft	2385 sq ft	109 sq ft	3	3	60' 0"	52' 0"	Island Basement	F

Design Features

- The study has double doors to the front balcony.
- Vaulted ceilings create openness throughout the living areas.
- Disappearing glass doors connect several rooms to a full-length veranda.
- A large utility room enjoys French doors to the balcony.
- A U-shaped kitchen has a center island and corner pantry.

Rear View

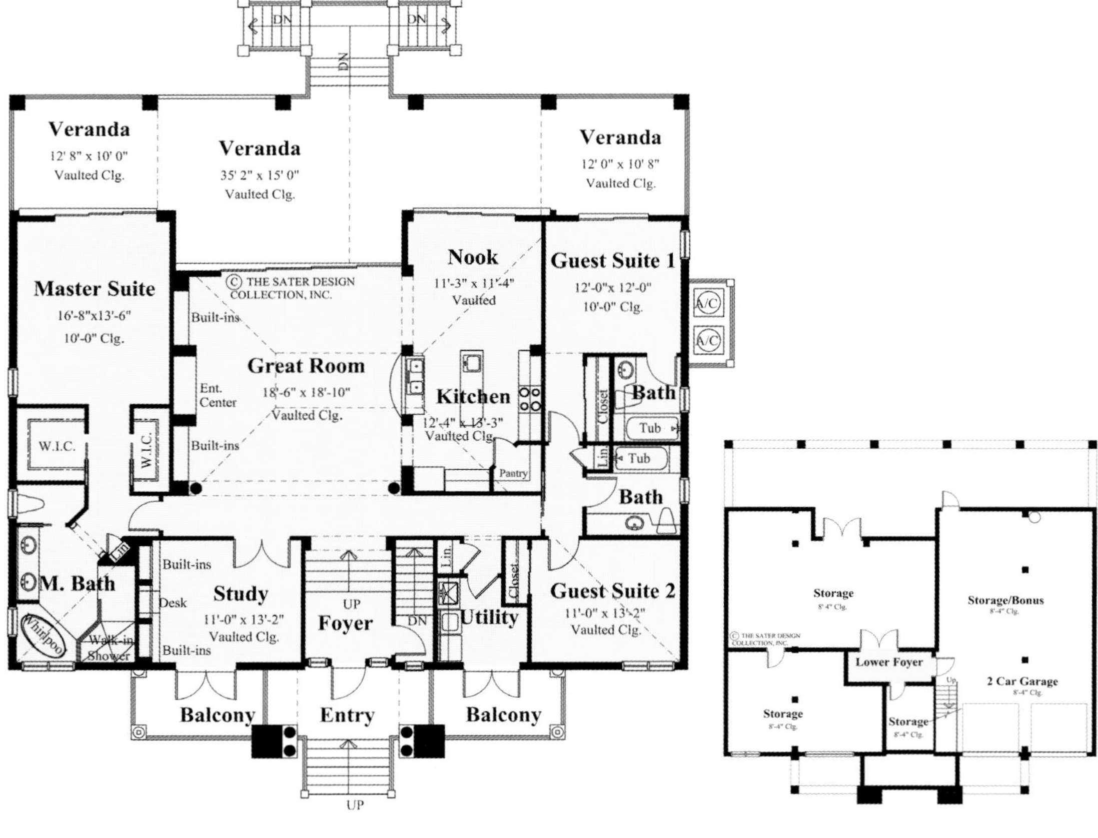

First Floor

Lower Level

Please note: Home photographed may differ from blueprint.

Southhampton Bay — VPDS01-Plan 6684 — 1-866-525-9374

Total Living	First Floor	Lower Level	Bed	Bath	Width	Depth	Foundation	Price Category
2465 sq ft	2385 sq ft	80 sq ft	3	2-1/2	60' 4"	59' 4"	Slab	F

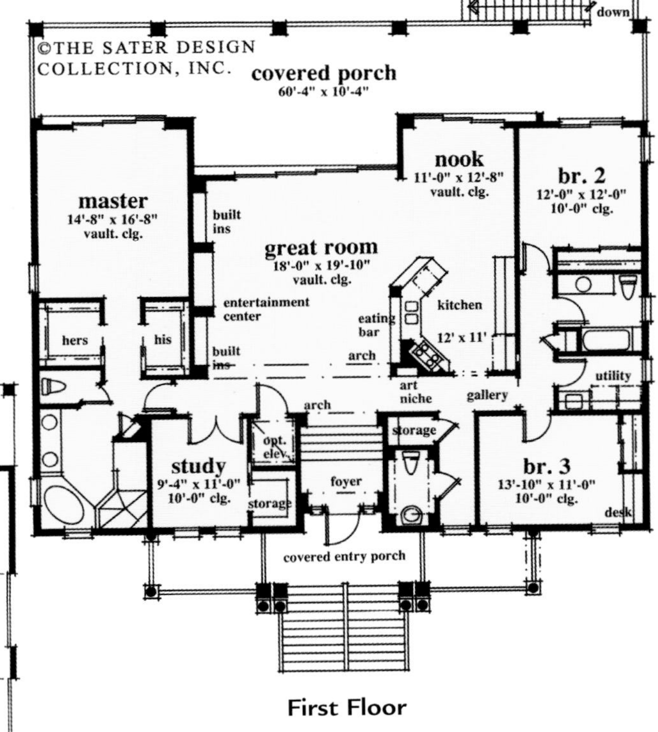

First Floor

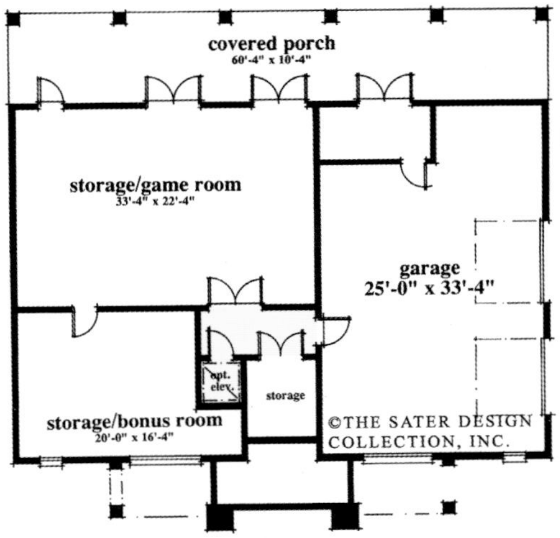

covered porch
60'-4" x 10'-4"

storage/game room
33'-4" x 22'-4"

garage
25'-0" x 33'-4"

opt. elev.

storage

storage/bonus room
20'-0" x 16'-4"

©THE SATER DESIGN COLLECTION, INC.

Lower Level

Design Features

- A cupola tops a classic pediment and low-pitched roof.
- A sunburst and sidelights set off the entry.
- The great room has a wall of built-ins for high-tech media.
- The master suite features a luxurious bath and dressing area.
- The lower level includes a game room and bonus room.

Rear Elevation

Donald A. Gardner Architects, Inc.

Firenze — VPAL01-Plan 5025 — 1-866-525-9374

Total Living	First Floor	Second Floor	Penthouse Level	Bed	Bath	Width	Depth	Foundation	Price Category
7211 sq ft	3716 sq ft	2654 sq ft	841 sq ft	5	6-1/2	60' 0"	135' 5"	Coastal Basement	O

Design Features

- The exterior features European-influenced architecture for an authentic façade.
- A wall of windows ushers natural light throughout the two-story great room.
- The penthouse level includes a rec room, wet bar, private porch and sitting area.
- Coffered ceilings crown the family room, kitchen and study.
- The spiral staircase spills into a first-level grand hall for an impressive entryway.

Rear View

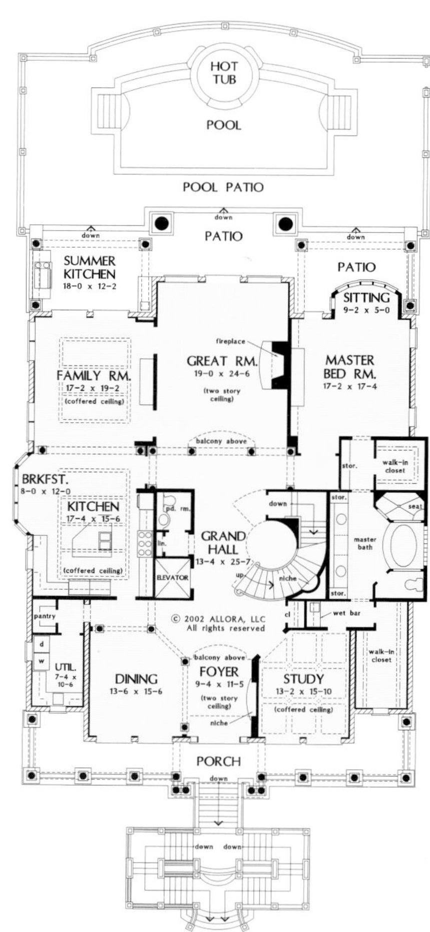

First Floor

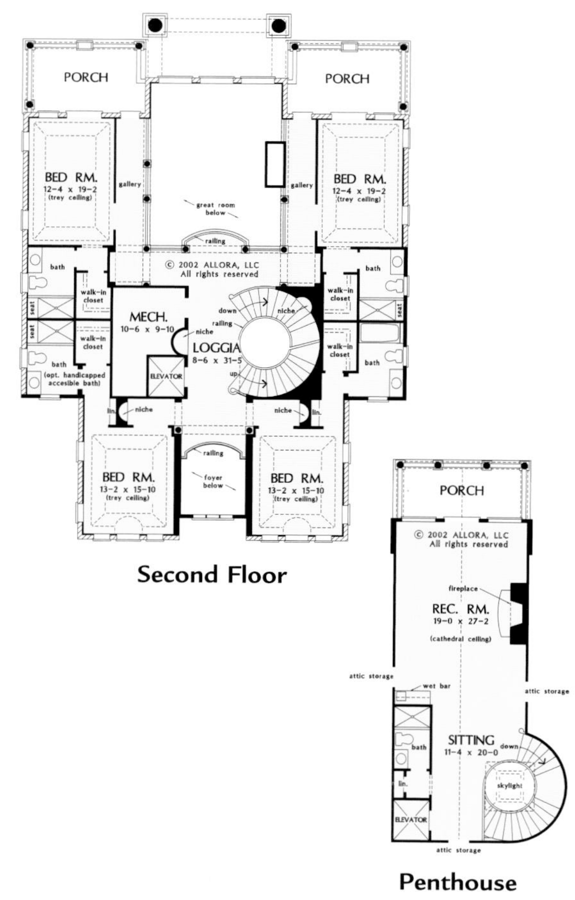

Second Floor

Penthouse

Please note: Home photographed may differ from blueprint.

Sommerset — VPDS01-Plan 6827 — 1-866-525-9374

Total Living	First Floor	Second Floor	Bed	Bath	Width	Depth	Foundation	Price Category
2650 sq ft	1296 sq ft	1354 sq ft	3	2-1/2	34' 0"	63' 2"	Slab	G

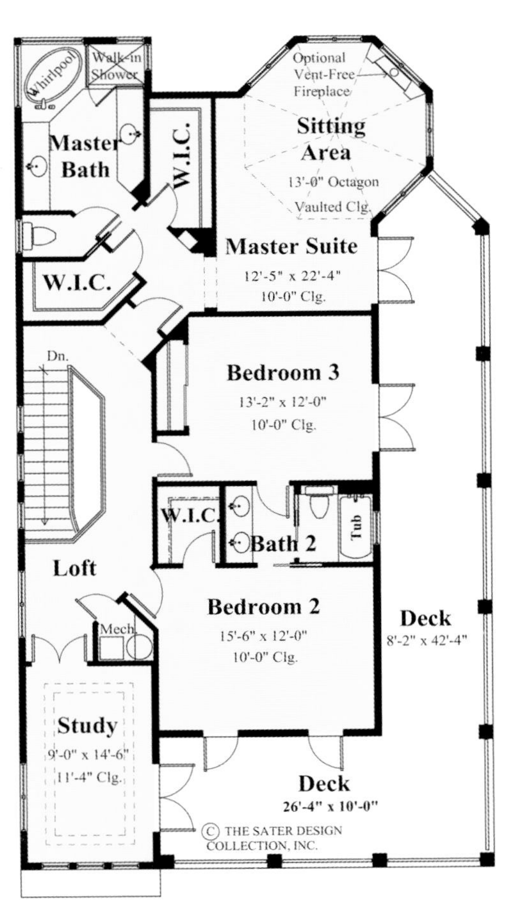

Second Floor

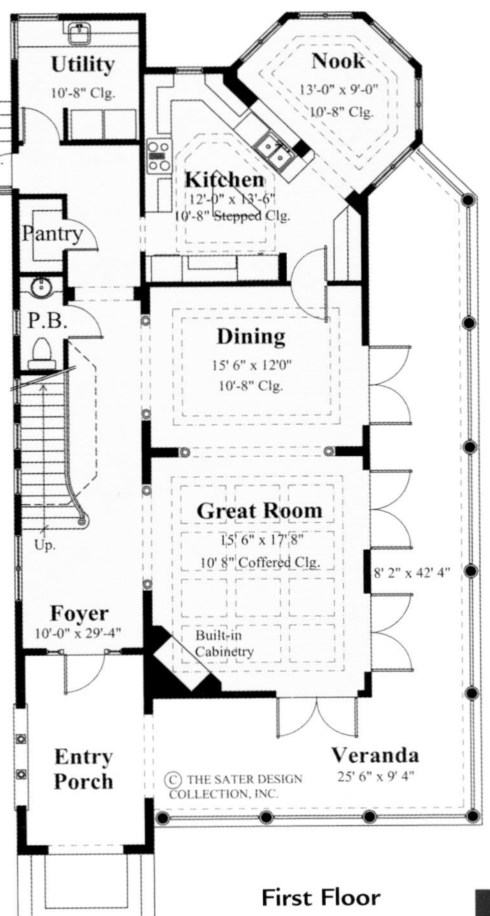

First Floor

Design Features

- A gallery-style foyer leads to a powder room and a walk-in pantry.
- Wrapping counter space provides an overlook to a breakfast nook.
- French doors bring the outdoors into the dining and great rooms.
- Upstairs, the luxurious master suite has an octagonal sitting area and deck.
- Also opening to the upper deck are two more bedrooms and a study.

Rear Elevation

Nicholas Park — VPDS01-Plan 6804 — 1-866-525-9374

Total Living	First Floor	Second Floor	Bed	Bath	Width	Depth	Foundation	Price Category
2374 sq ft	1510 sq ft	864 sq ft	3	3-1/2	44' 0"	49' 0"	Island Basement	F

Design Features

- Multiple porches, bold columns, transoms, decorative corbels and balustrades create an impressive façade.
- An open arrangement of the two-story great room, gallery kitchen and dining room enhance the welcoming atmosphere of the home.
- The great room offers warmth by the fireplace, a built-in entertainment center and double French doors that lead out to the back porch.

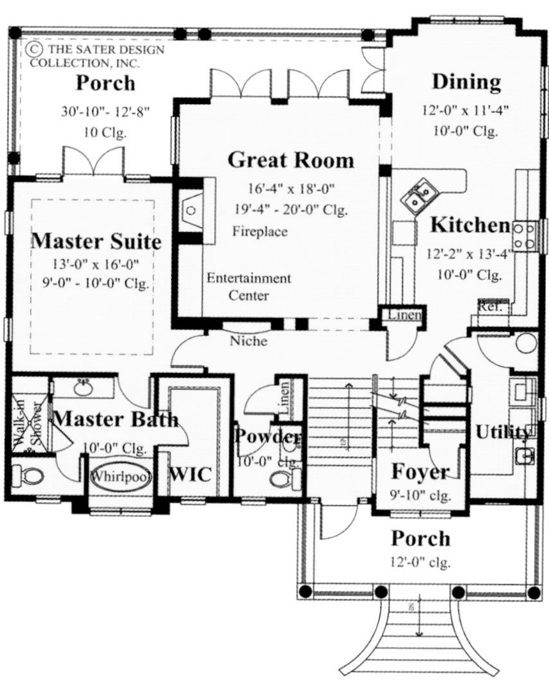

First Floor

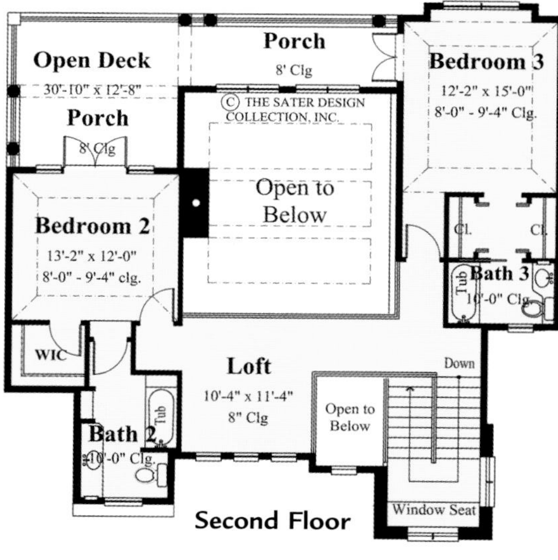

Second Floor

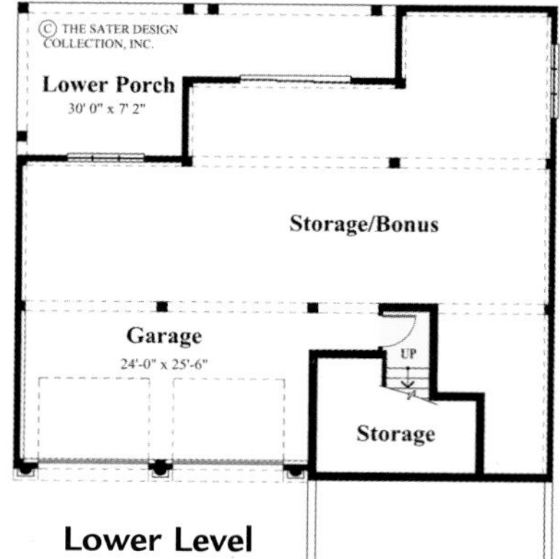

Lower Level

Rear Elevation

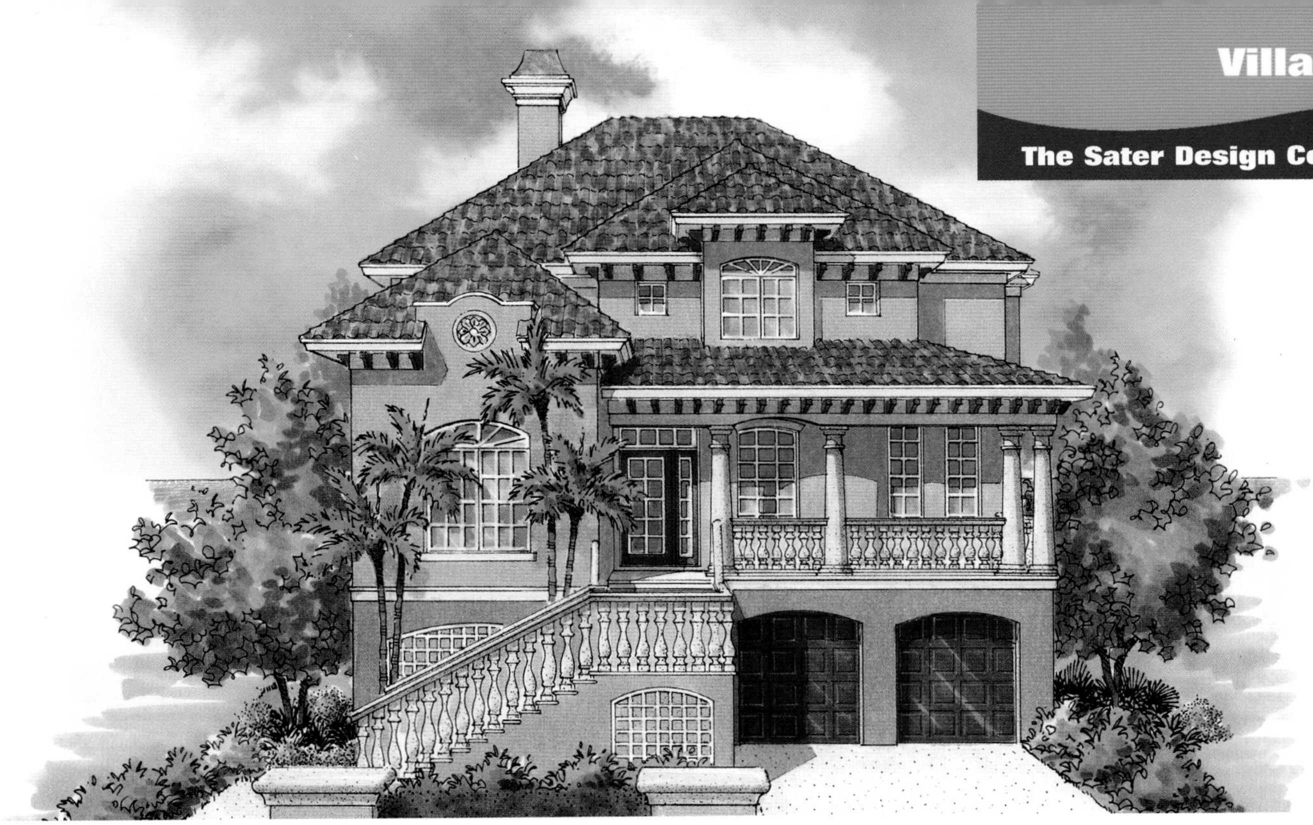

Riviera dei Fiori — VPDS01-Plan 6809 — 1-866-525-9374

Total Living	First Floor	Second Floor	Bed	Bath	Width	Depth	Foundation	Price Category
2513 sq ft	1542 sq ft	971 sq ft	4	3	46' 0"	51' 0"	Island Basement	G

Second Floor

First Floor

Lower Level

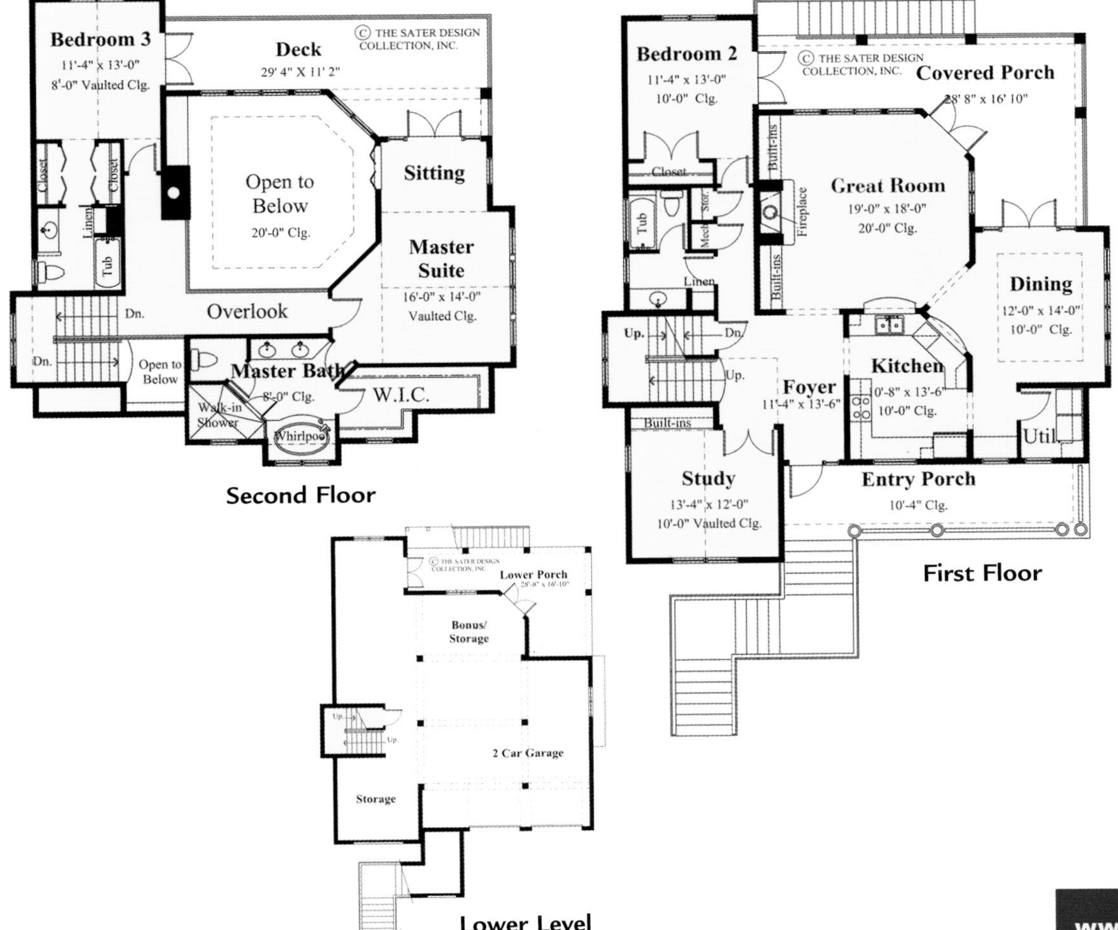

Design Features

- Elegant columns, balustrades, corbels, transoms and covered porches enhance the exterior.
- The great room features built-in cabinetry, a fireplace, glass doors that open to the rear porch and easy access to the dining room and kitchen.
- Located on the upper level away from the main living space, the master suite enjoys privacy, a vaulted ceiling, spacious bath and a private sitting area that opens to the deck.

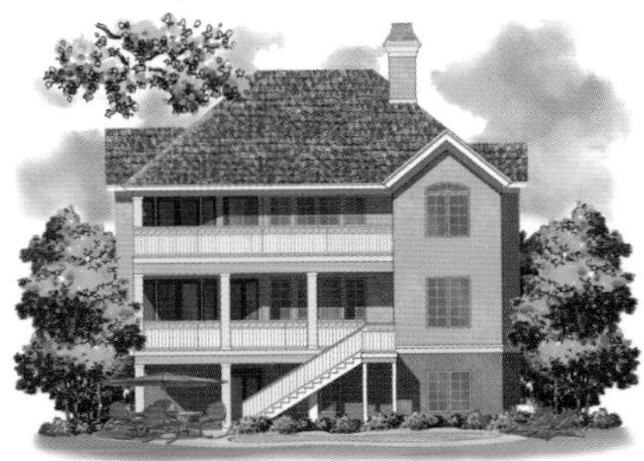

Rear Elevation

Via Pascoli — VPDS01-Plan 6842 — 1-866-525-9374

Total Living	First Floor	Bonus	Bed	Bath	Width	Depth	Foundation	Price Category
2137 sq ft	2137 sq ft	N/A	3	2	44' 0"	61' 0"	Island Basement	F

Design Features

- Lovely architecture and brilliant windows adorn this villa.
- A hip vaulted ceiling highlights the great room.
- French doors open the family space to a sheltered porch.
- Lower-level bonus spaces convert to hobby or storage rooms.
- The master suite is secluded and has many views.

Rear Elevation

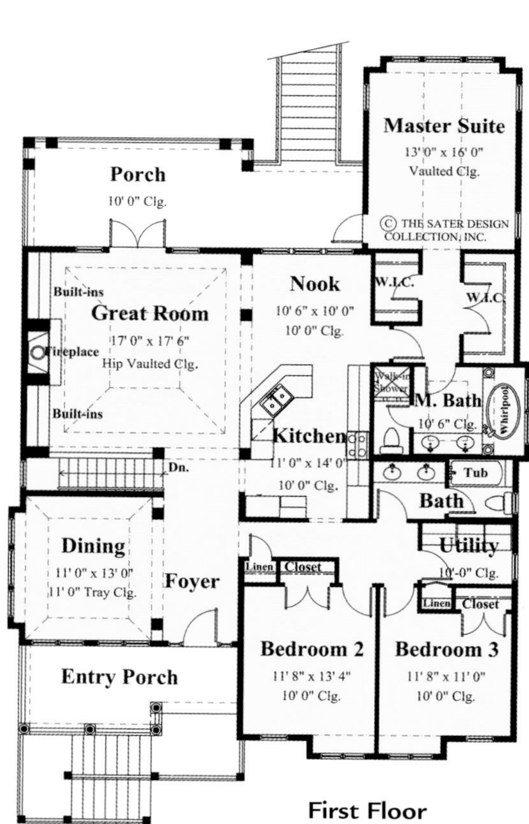

First Floor

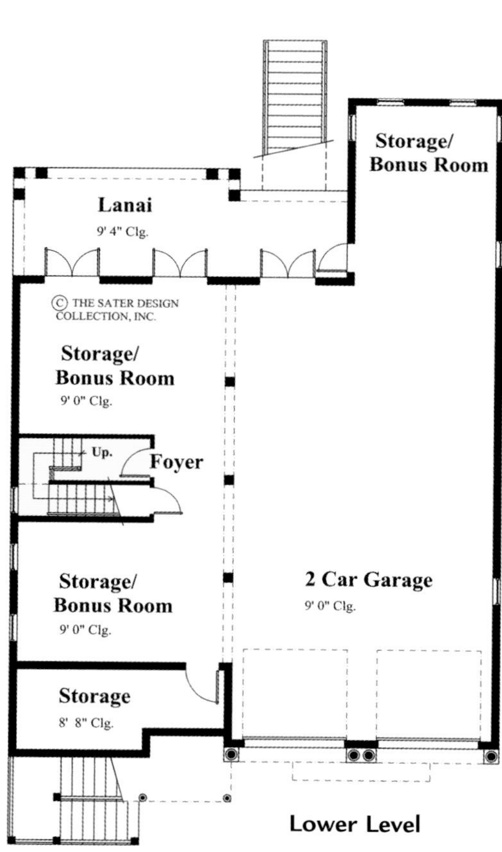

Lower Level

Vittorio Terrace — VPDS01-Plan 6866 — 1-866-525-9374

Total Living	First Floor	Second Floor	Lower Level	Bed	Bath	Width	Depth	Foundation	Price Category
1886 sq ft	1342 sq ft	511 sq ft	33 sq ft	3	2-1/2	44' 0"	40' 0"	Island Basement	E

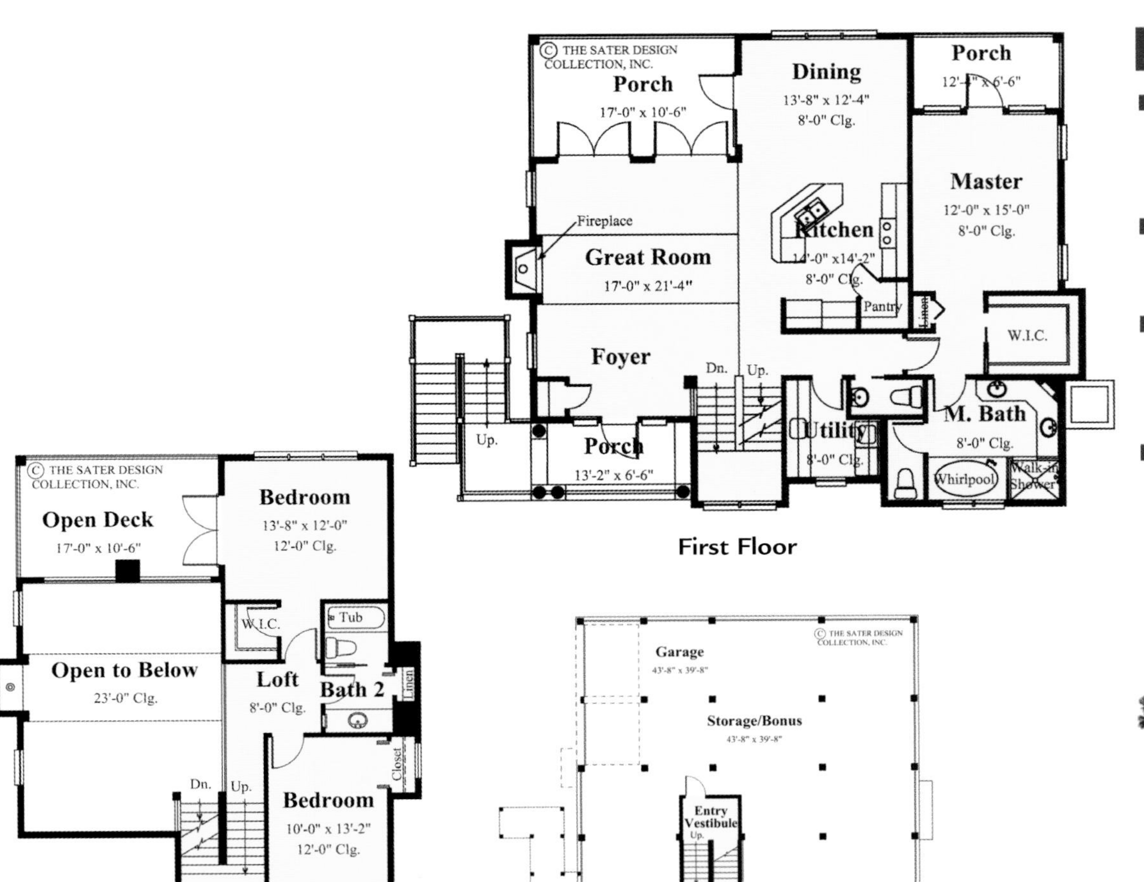

First Floor

Second Floor

Lower Level

Design Features

- The foyer provides interior vistas that extend through the great room and an open arrangement of the dining room and kitchen.
- The master suite enjoys access to a private porch, a walk-in closet and a spacious bath.
- The upper level features a computer loft with plenty of space for books, and an overlook to the great room.
- One of two secondary bedrooms opens to a sun deck with wide views of the rear property.

Rear Elevation

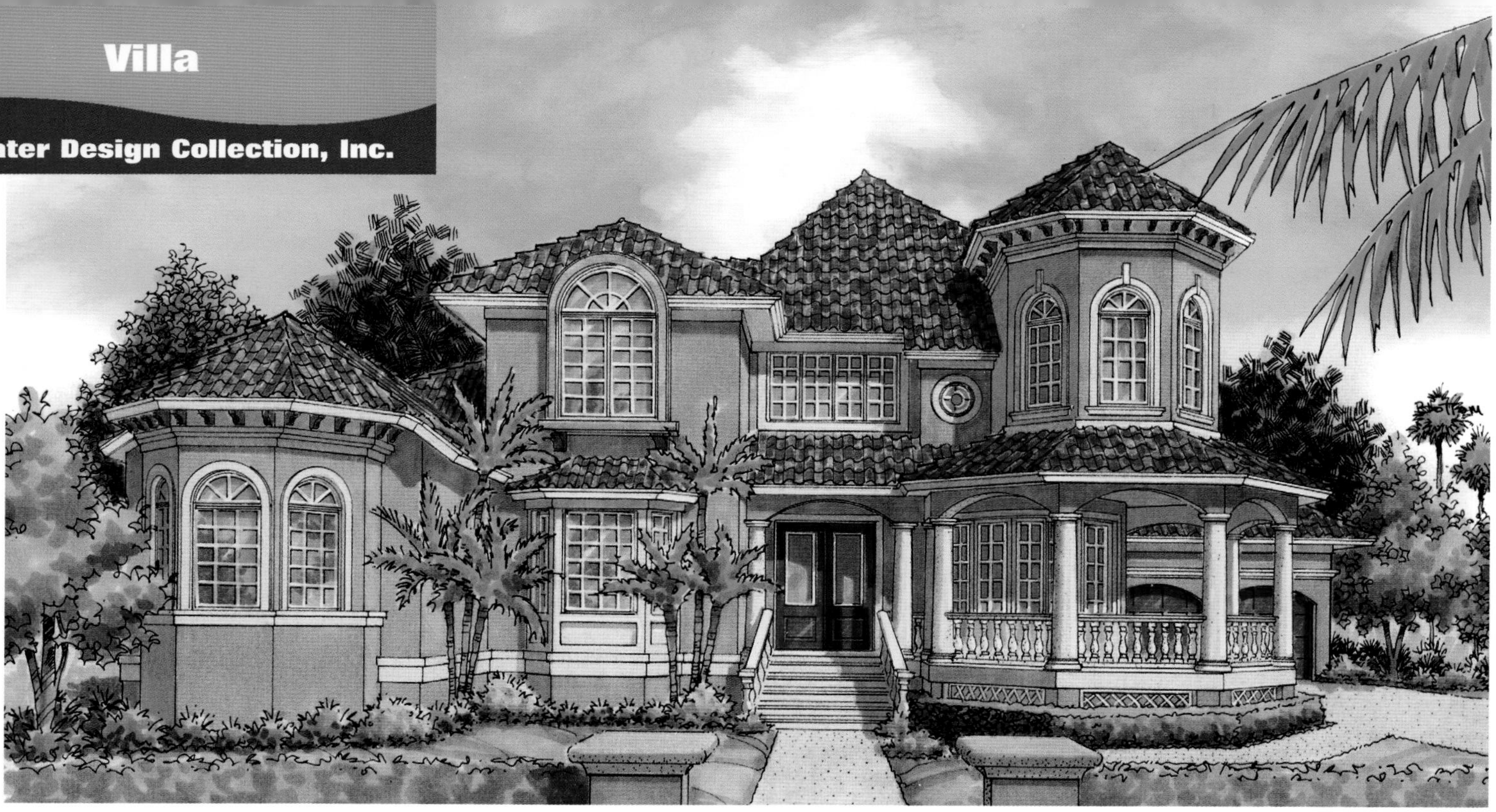

Sunset Beach — VPDS01-6848 — 1-866-525-9374

Total Living	First Floor	Second Floor	Bed	Bath	Width	Depth	Foundation	Price Category
3096 sq ft	2083 sq ft	1013 sq ft	4	3-1/2	74' 0"	88' 0"	Crawl Space	H

Design Features

- A gazebo-style front porch accents this country villa.
- The entry leads to the grand foyer and sweeping radius staircase.
- The main-level master suite boasts a private lanai.
- A study has a window seat and built-in cabinetry.
- A bayed breakfast nook and butler's pantry complete the kitchen.

Rear Elevation

First Floor

Second Floor

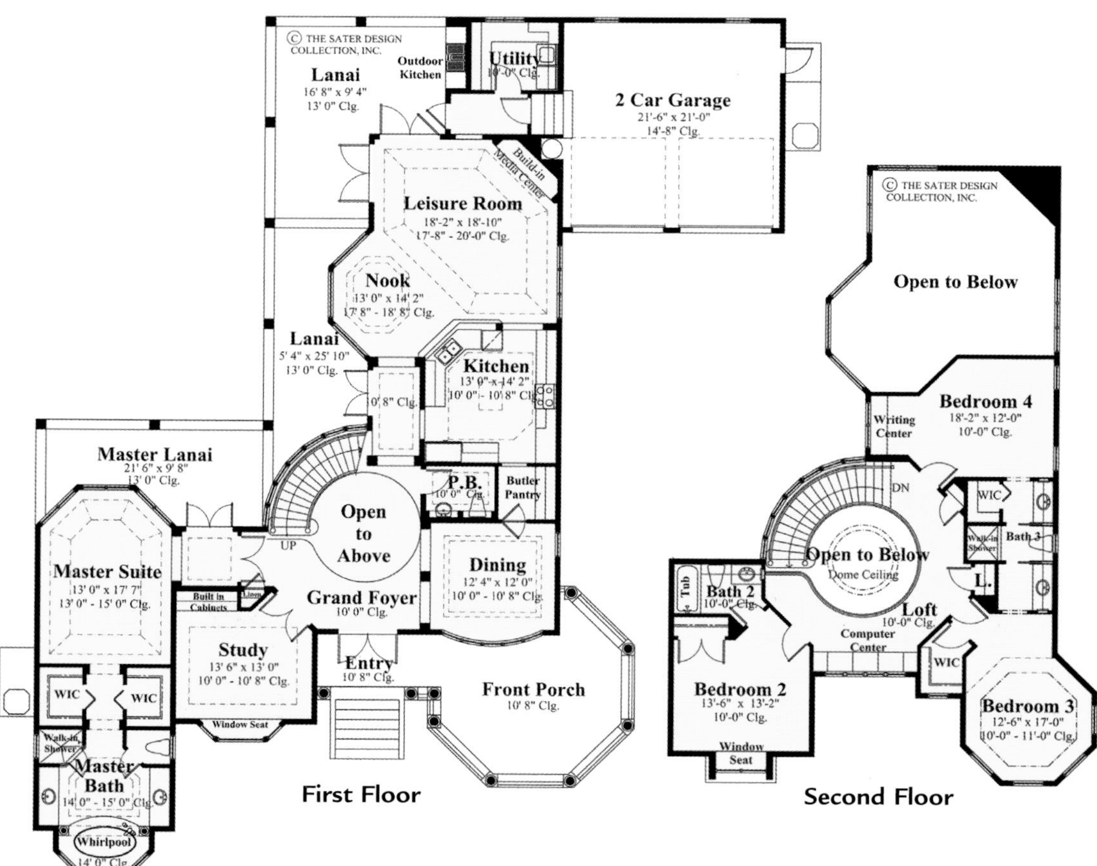

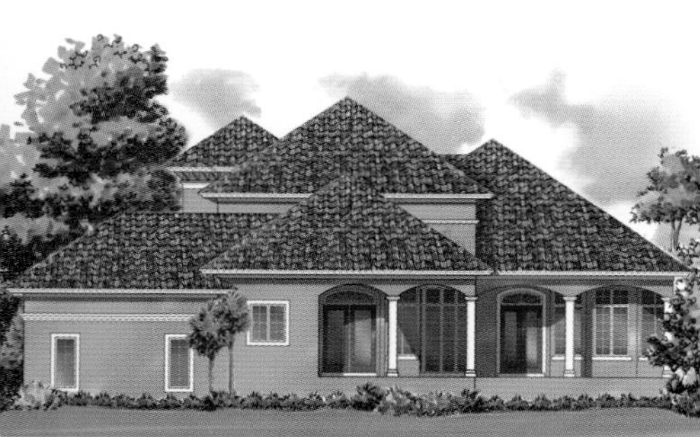

San Marino — VPDS01-Plan 6833 — 1-866-525-9374

Total Living	First Floor	Bonus	Bed	Bath	Width	Depth	Foundation	Price Category
2433 sq ft	2433 sq ft	N/A	3	3	70' 2"	53' 0"	Island Basement	F

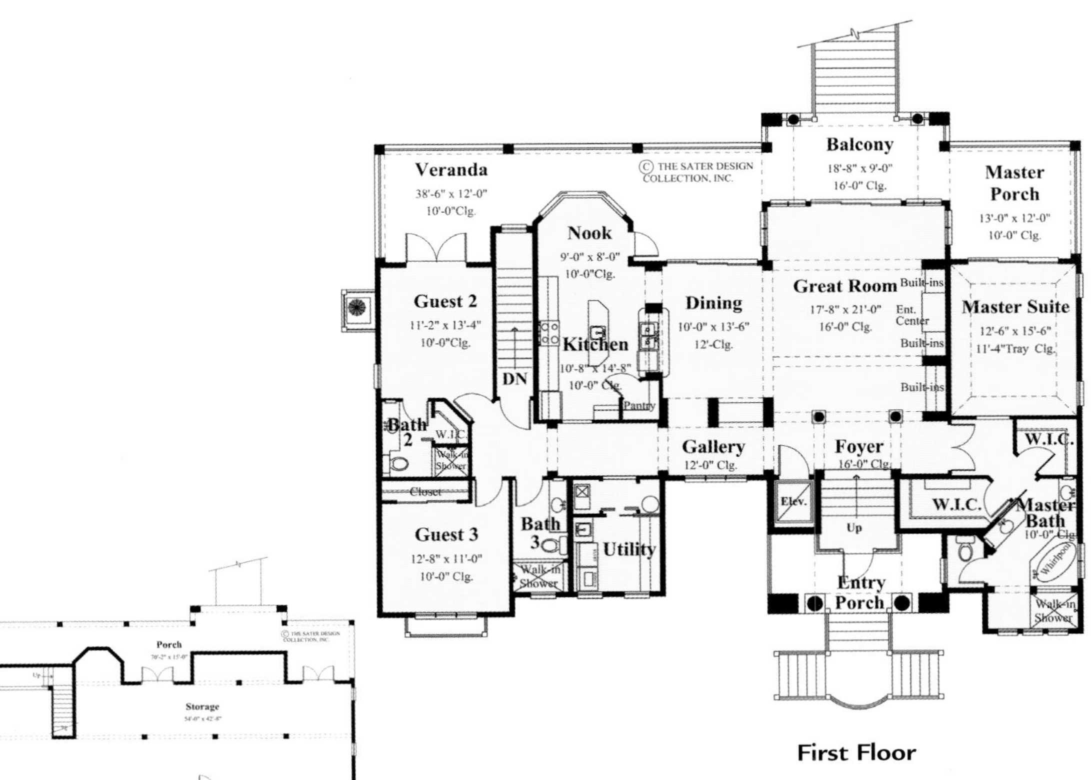

First Floor

Lower Level

Design Features

- The great room opens through columns in the central gallery hall and shares the comfort of the central fireplace and the beauty of built-in cabinetry.
- The kitchen has a food-preparation island and a service counter that opens to the dining room.
- A tray ceiling watches over the master suite that boasts two walk-in closets, a spacious master bath and a wall of glass that opens to the private porch.

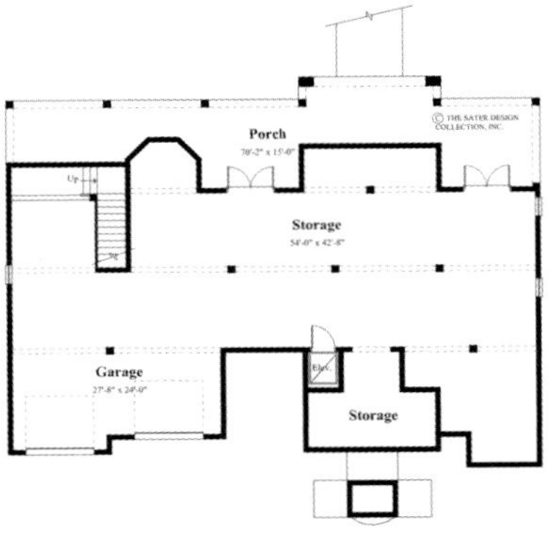

Rear Elevation

Terra di Mare — VPDS01-Plan 6806 — 1-866-525-9374

Total Living	First Floor	Second Floor	Bed	Bath	Width	Depth	Foundation	Price Category
1978 sq ft	1383 sq ft	595 sq ft	3	2	48' 0"	48' 0"	Island Basement	E

Design Features

- The foyer leads up to an open, free-flowing interior where columns separate rooms and a bounty of windows provides unrestrained views.
- The kitchen features ample counter space and an eating bar that connects to the dining and great room.
- The vaulted ceiling in the great room adds volume to the room, but the fireplace keeps it cozy.
- To ensure privacy, the master suite is located on the upper level and boasts a spacious bath, walk-in closet and French doors opening to a private porch.

Rear Elevation

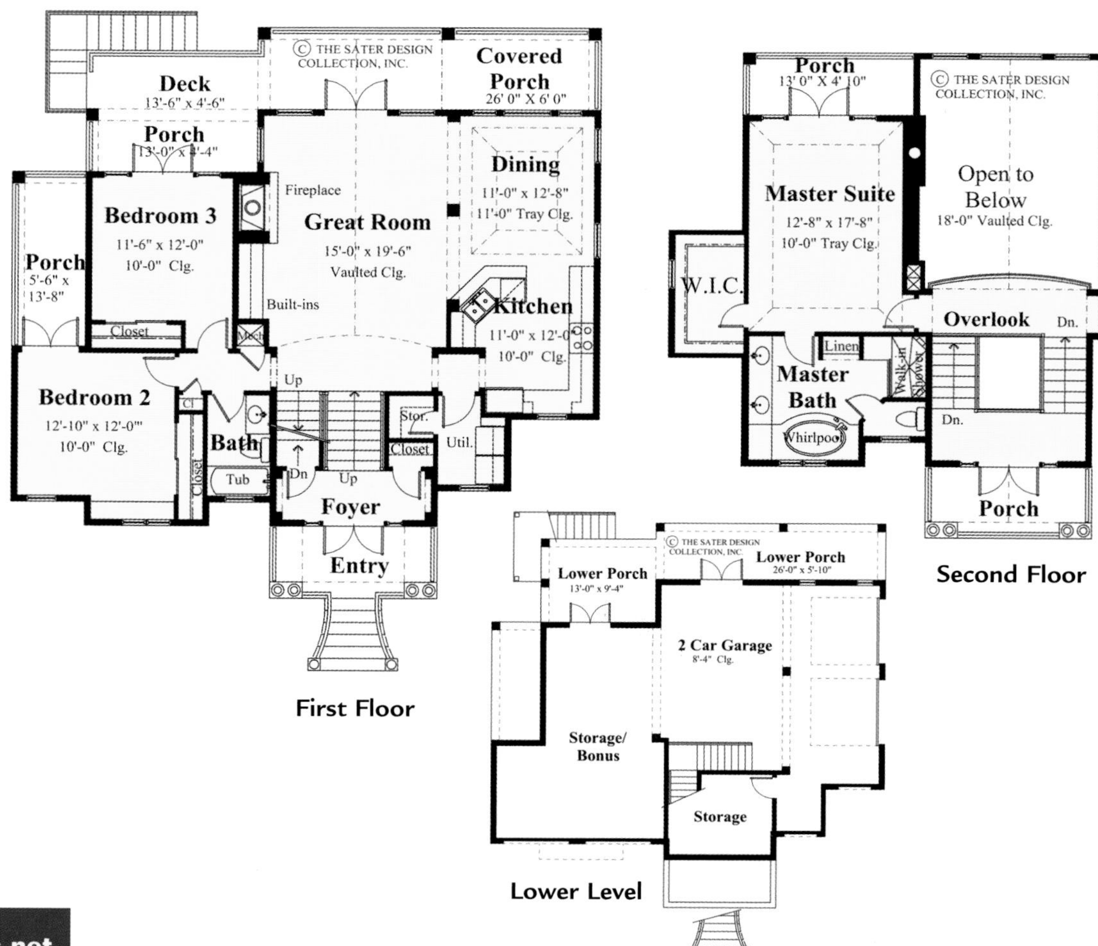

First Floor

Second Floor

Lower Level

Villa Caprini — VPDS01-Plan 6854 — 1-866-525-9374

Total Living	First Floor	Second Floor	Lower Level	Bed	Bath	Width	Depth	Foundation	Price Category
1996 sq ft	874 sq ft	880 sq ft	242 sq ft	3	2-1/2	34' 0"	40' 6"	Island Basement	E

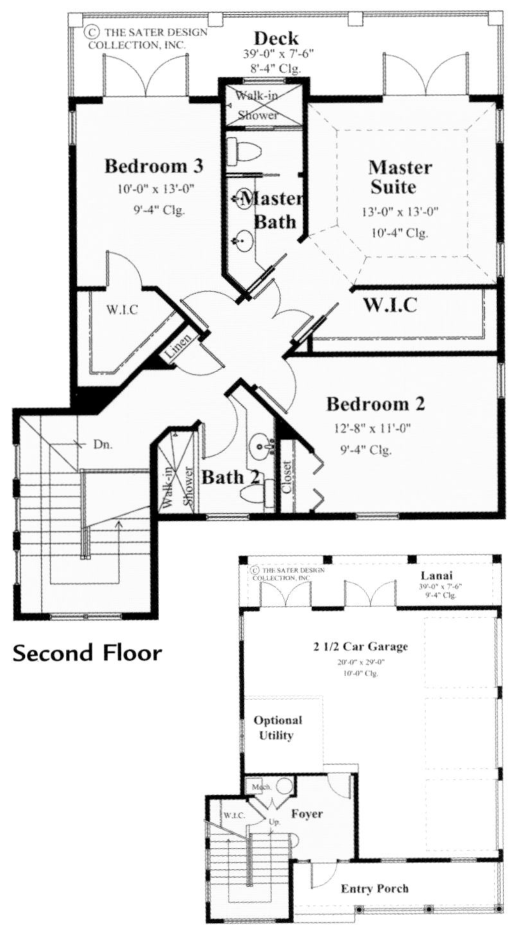

Second Floor

Lower Level

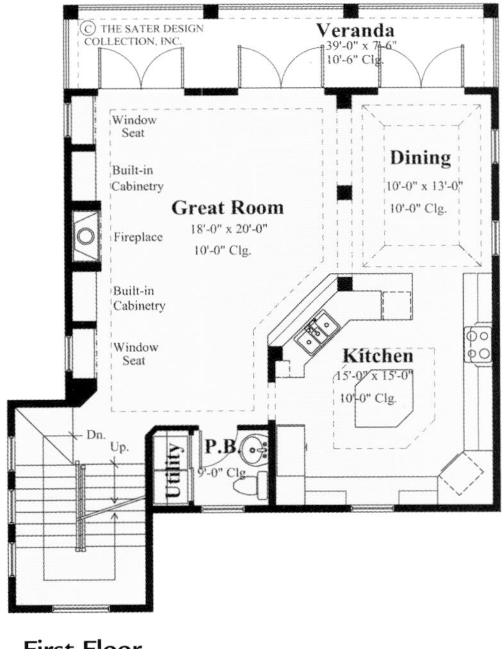

First Floor

Design Features

- Vintage details such as a high-pitched roof, faux widows walk and corner quoins enhance the façade.
- The expansive great room boasts window seats, built-in cabinetry, a fireplace and French doors that open to the veranda.
- The kitchen features a center island, ample counter and storage space and easy access to the dining and great room.
- All decked out, the back has full-length porches on every level for outdoor enjoyment.

Rear Elevation

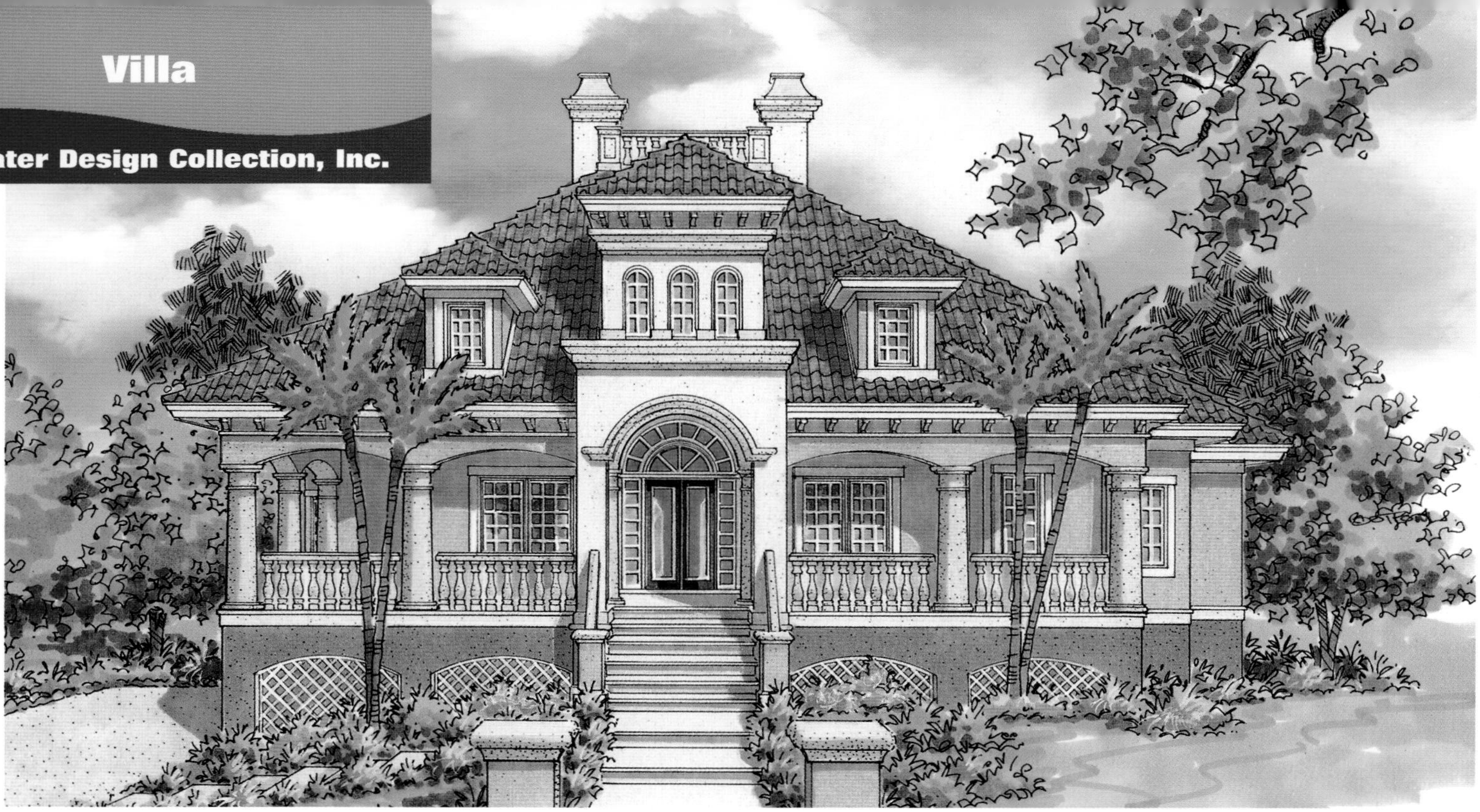

Royal Marco — VPDS01-Plan 6857 — 1-866-525-9374

Total Living	First Floor	Second Floor	Bed	Bath	Width	Depth	Foundation	Price Category
2756 sq ft	1855 sq ft	901 sq ft	3	3-1/2	66' 0"	50' 0"	Island Basement	G

Design Features

- A wraparound porch, paned windows and stately columns enhance a prominent entry.
- An octagonal great room with a multi-faceted vaulted ceiling illuminates the entire plan with a fireplace.
- The gourmet kitchen features a pass-thru to the lanai, a center island and easy access to the dining and great room.
- Tucked away from the main living spaces to ensure privacy, that master suite boasts access to the lanai.

First Floor

Lower Level

Second Floor

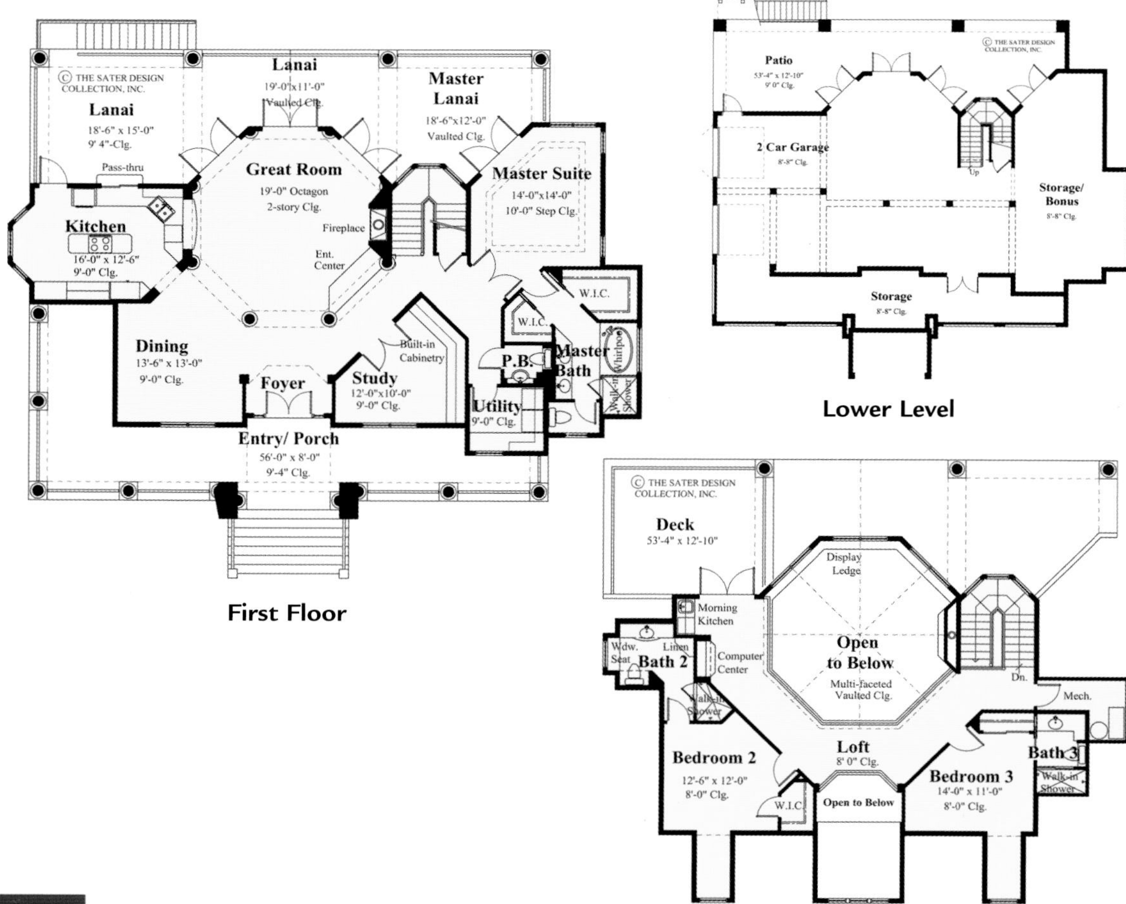

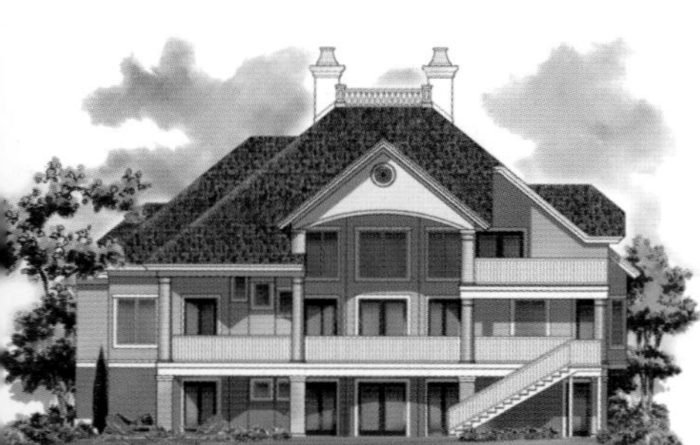

Rear Elevation

Charleston Place — VPDS01-Plan 6700 — 1-866-525-9374

Total Living	First Floor	Second Floor	Bed	Bath	Width	Depth	Foundation	Price Category
2520 sq ft	1305 sq ft	1215 sq ft	3	2-1/2	30' 6"	77' 6"	Slab or Island Basement	G

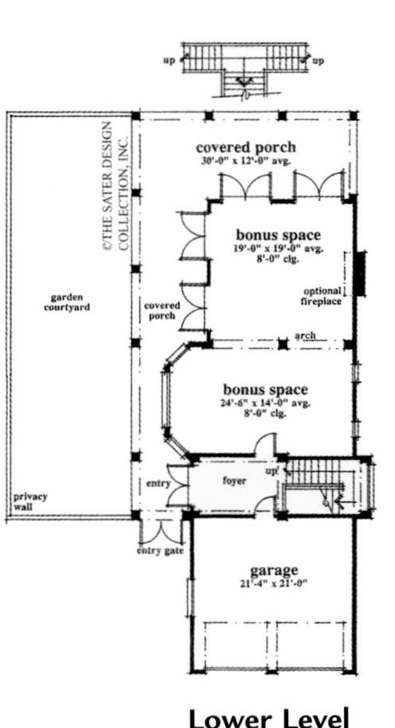

Lower Level

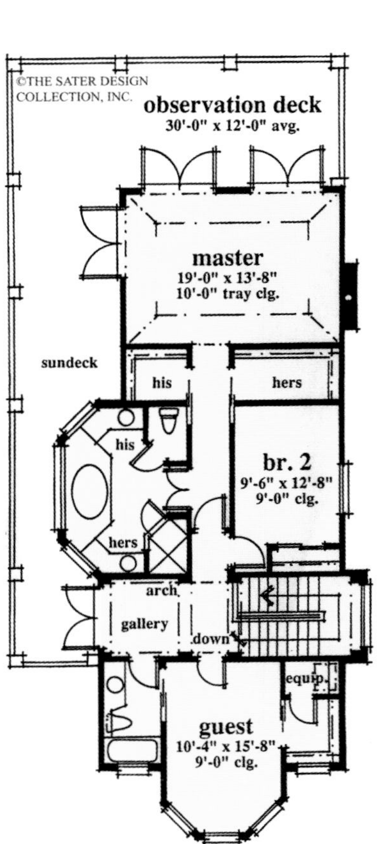

Second Floor

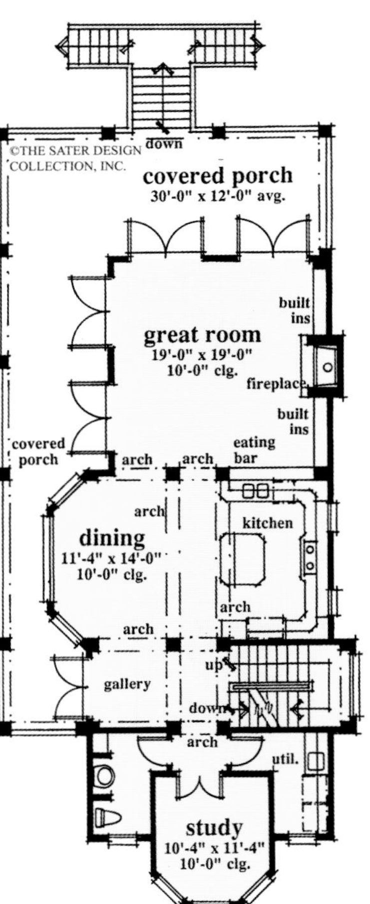

First Floor

Design Features

- Louvered shutters, balustered railings, a Spanish tile roof, stucco and quoins adorn the exterior.
- Graceful arches, a wall of built-ins, warming fireplace and four sets of French doors to the covered porch entice visitors into the great room.
- The expansive kitchen features an eating bar, a center island, plenty of counter space and easy access to the dining room.
- Three sets of French doors open the master retreat to a private observation deck.

Rear Elevation

Vasari — VPDS01-8025 — 1-866-525-9374

Total Living	First Floor	Second Floor	Bed	Bath	Width	Depth	Foundation	Price Category
4160 sq ft	1995 sq ft	2165 sq ft	5	5-1/2	58' 0"	65' 0"	Slab/Opt. Basement	J

Design Features

- A gallery foyer and loft deepen the central living/dining room.
- A two-sided fireplace warms the central area and spacious study.
- Above the entry, a sun porch with a transom brings in light.
- The loft connects the family's sleeping quarters with a guest suite.
- The main level boasts a cabana-style guest suite.

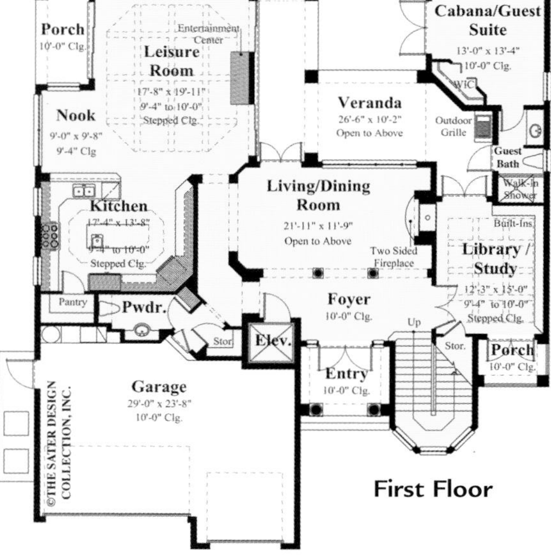

First Floor

Rear Elevation

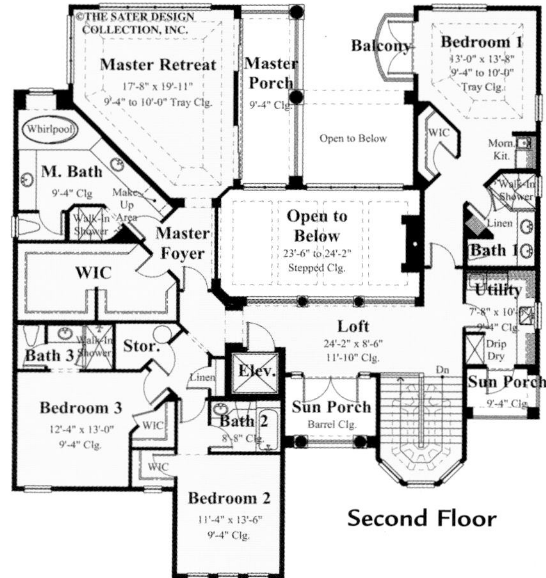

Second Floor

Bartolini — VPDS01-8022 — 1-866-525-9374

Total Living	First Floor	Second Floor	Bonus	Bed	Bath	Width	Depth	Foundation	Price Category
2736 sq ft	2084 sq ft	652 sq ft	375 sq ft	3	2-1/2	60' 6"	94' 0"	Opt. Basement/Slab	G

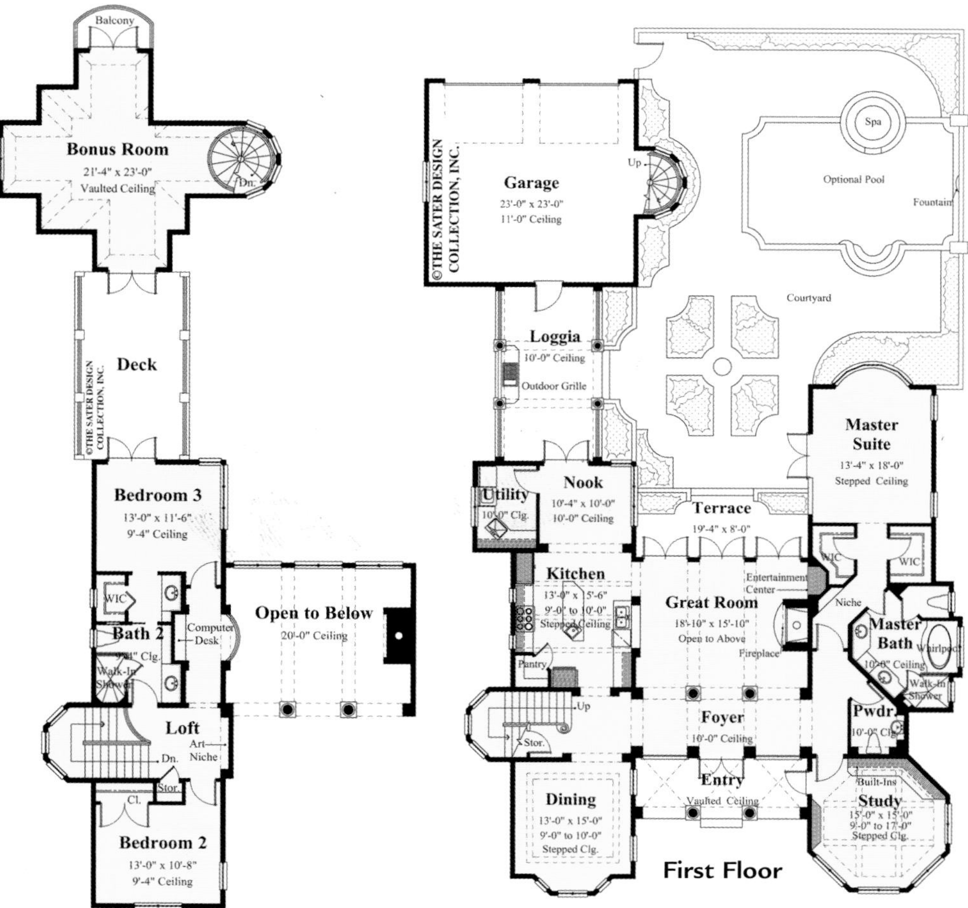

Second Floor

First Floor

Design Features

- A graceful entry arcade leads to a grand foyer.
- Three sets of French doors are all that seperate the great room from a terrace and courtyard.
- The kitchen and morning nook open to a covered loggia.
- The secluded master suite has private courtyard access.
- The upper level harbors two bedroom suites and a bonus room.

Rear Elevation

Porta Rossa — VPDS01-8058 — 1-866-525-9374

Total Living	First Floor	Bonus	Bed	Bath	Width	Depth	Foundation	Price Category
3166 sq ft	3166 sq ft	N/A	4 + Study	3-1/2	67' 0"	91' 8"	Slab	H

Design Features

- An elaborate entry turret highlights the façade and gives a Spanish Colonial feel.
- A high beamed ceiling lends character to the study.
- The master boasts a step-up spa-style tub with a private garden view.
- Two secondary bedrooms share a full bath.
- The guest suite is tucked away in the far corner of the plan and has a cabana-style bath that also serves the pool and patio.

Rear Elevation

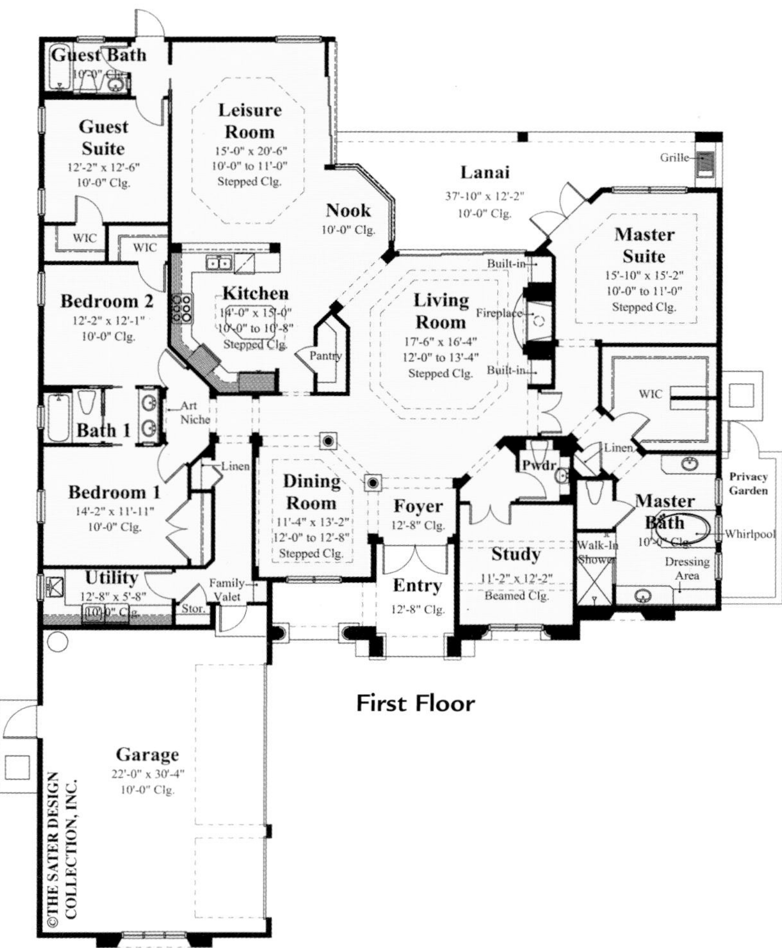

First Floor

Mercato — VPDS01-8028 — 1-866-525-9374

Total Living	First Floor	Bonus	Bed	Bath	Width	Depth	Foundation	Price Category
2191 sq ft	2191 sq ft	N/A	3 + Study	2-1/2	62' 10"	73' 6"	Slab/opt. Basement	F

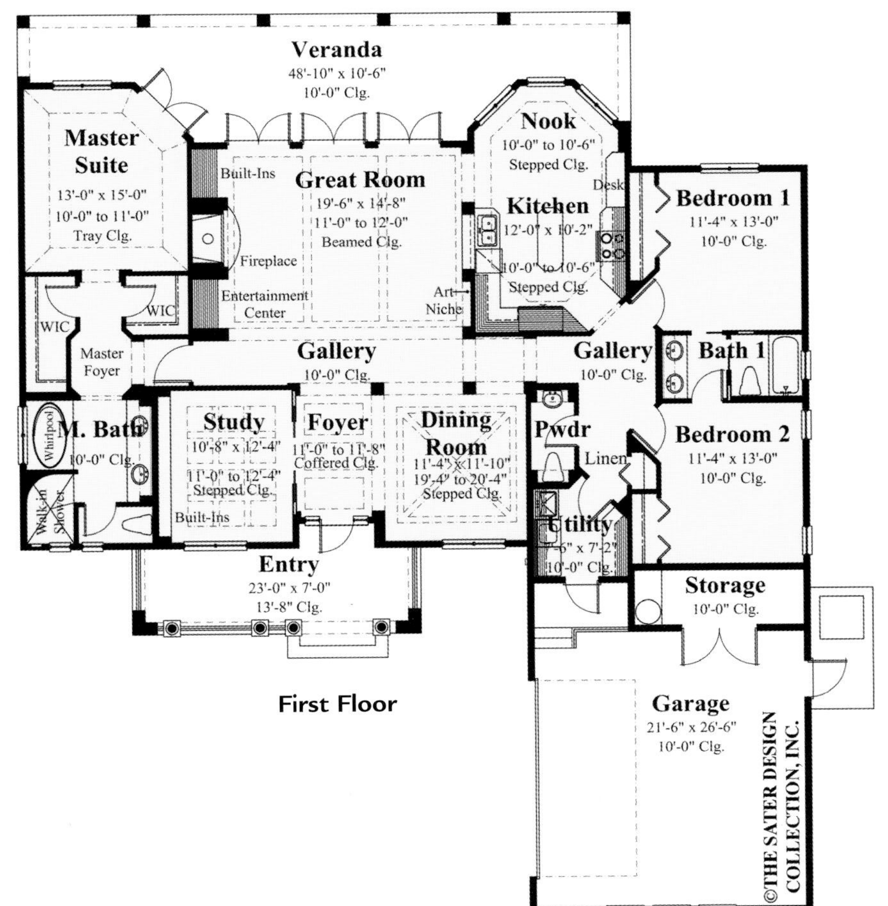

First Floor

Design Features

- An elegant covered porch is supported by tapered rope columns and a balustrade railing.
- A coffered-ceiling foyer makes a grand entry into the home.
- A gallery provides a main corridor through the home.
- A row of triple French doors open the great room to the veranda.
- The great room is anchored by a massive fireplace and built-ins on either side.
- The master wing enjoys a private foyer.

Rear Elevation

Plan Index

FRANK BETZ

*Feature Plan

Plan Index

DONALD A. GARDNER

*Feature Plan

Plan Index

DAN F. SATER, II

*Feature Plan

FOR AN EXPANDED PLAN SEARCH
OR ONLINE ORDERING
PLEASE VISIT
www.vacation-homeplans.net

BEFORE YOU ORDER

PLEASE READ THE FOLLOWING HELPFUL INFORMATION

QUICK TURNAROUND

Because you are placing your order directly, we can ship plans to you quickly. If your order is placed before noon ET, we can usually have your plans to you the next business day. Some restrictions may apply. We cannot ship to a post office box; please provide a physical street address.

OUR EXCHANGE POLICY

Since our blueprints are printed especially for you at the time you place your order, we cannot accept any returns. If, for some reason, you find that the plan that you purchased does not meet your needs, then you may exchange that plan for another plan in our collection. We allow you sixty days from the time of purchase to make an exchange. At the time of the exchange, you will be charged a processing fee of 20% of the total amount of the original order, plus the difference in price between the plans (if applicable) and the cost to ship the new plans to you. Vellums cannot be exchanged. All sets must be approved and authorization given before the exchange can take place. Please call our customer service department if you have any questions.

LOCAL BUILDING CODES AND ZONING REQUIREMENTS

Our plans are designed to meet or exceed national building standards. Because of the great differences in geography and climate, each state, county and municipality has its own building codes and zoning requirements. Your plan may need to be modified to comply with local requirements regarding snow loads, energy codes, soil and seismic conditions and a wide range of other matters. Prior to using plans ordered from us, we strongly advise that you consult a local building official.

ARCHITECTURE AND ENGINEERING SEALS

Some cities and states are now requiring that a licensed architect or engineer review and approve any set of building documents prior to construction. This is due to concerns over energy costs, safety, structural integrity and other factors. Prior to applying for a building permit or the start of actual construction, we strongly advise that you consult your local building official who can tell you if such a review is required.

DISCLAIMER

We have put substantial care and effort into the creation of our blueprints. We authorize the use of our blueprints on the express condition that you strictly comply with all local building codes, zoning requirements and other applicable laws, regulations and ordinances. However, because we cannot provide on-site consultation, supervision or control over actual construction, and because of the great variance in local building requirements, building practices and soil, seismic, weather and other conditions, WE CANNOT MAKE ANY WARRANTY, EXPRESS OR IMPLIED, WITH RESPECT TO THE CONTENT OR USE OF OUR BLUEPRINTS OR VELLUMS, INCLUDING BUT NOT LIMITED TO ANY WARRANTY OF MERCHANTABILITY OR OF FITNESS FOR A PARTICULAR PURPOSE. Please Note: Floor plans in this book are not construction documents and are subject to change. Renderings are artist's concept only.

HOW MANY SETS OF PRINTS WILL YOU NEED?

We offer a single set of prints so that you can study and plan your dream home in detail. However, you cannot build from this package. One set of blueprints is marked "NOT FOR CONSTRUCTION." If you are planning to obtain estimates from a contractor or subcontractor, or if you are planning to build immediately, you will need more sets. Because additional sets are less expensive, make sure you order enough to satisfy all your requirements. Sometimes changes are needed to a plan; in that case, we offer vellums that are reproducible and erasable so changes can be made directly to the plans. Vellums are the only set that can be reproduced; it is illegal to copy blueprints. The checklist below will help you determine how many sets are needed.

PLAN CHECKLIST

_____ **Owner** (one for notes, one for file)

_____ **Builder** (generally requires at least three sets; one as a legal document, one for inspections and at least one to give subcontractors)

_____ **Local Building Department** (often requires two sets)

_____ **Mortgage Lender** (usually one set for a conventional loan; three sets for FHA or VA loans)

_____ **Total Number of Sets**

IGNORING COPYRIGHT LAWS CAN BE A

$1,000,000 mistake!

Recent changes in the US copyright laws allow for statutory penalties of up to $150,000 per incident for copyright infringement involving any of the copyrighted plans found in this publication. The law can be confusing. So, for your own protection, take the time to understand what you cannot do when it comes to home plans.

WHAT YOU CAN'T DO!

YOU CANNOT DUPLICATE HOME PLANS

YOU CANNOT COPY ANY PART OF A HOME PLAN TO CREATE ANOTHER

YOU CANNOT BUILD A HOME WITHOUT BUYING A BLUEPRINT OR LICENSE

HOW TO ORDER BY PHONE, MAIL OR ONLINE

1-866-525-9374

Select the option that corresponds to the designer of your home plan:

Frank Betz and Associates, dial 01
Donald A. Gardner Architects, dial 02
Dan Sater - Sater Design Collection, dial 03

This puts you in DIRECT contact with the designer's office!

ADDITIONAL ITEMS**

Additional Blueprints (per set) $60.00
Full Reverse Set* $145.00

MATERIALS LIST*

Plan Categories A — E $75.00
Plan Categories F — O $80.00

FOUNDATION OPTIONS*
(basement, crawl space or slab, if different from base plan)
(no charge for Frank Betz plans, call designer for details)

Plan Categories A — C $225.00
Plan Categories D — E $250.00
Plan Categories F — M $275.00
Specification Outline* $15.00

*Call for availability. Special orders may require additional fees.

SHIPPING AND HANDLING

Overnight . . . . $45.00 Ground $22.00
2nd Day . . . . $35.00 Saturday $55.00

For shipping international, please call for a quote.

****Products and prices vary for each designer. Call for specific availability and pricing.**

BLUEPRINT PRICE SCHEDULE*

	1 STUDY SET	4 SETS	8 SETS	VELLUM
A	$465	$515	$565	$710
B	$510	$560	$610	$775
C	$555	$605	$655	$840
D	$600	$650	$700	$905
E	$645	$695	$745	$970
F	$690	$740	$790	$1035
G	$760	$810	$860	$1115
H	$835	$885	$935	$1195
I	$935	$985	$1035	$1295
J	$1035	$1085	$1135	$1395
K	$1135	$1185	$1235	$1495
L	$1235	$1285	$1335	$1595
M	$1335	$1385	$1435	$1695
N	$1435	$1485	$1535	$1795
O	Call for pricing			

* Prices subject to change without notice

Order Form

PLAN NUMBER ____________________

☐ 1-set [study only] . . . . $______
☐ 4-set building package . . . . $______
☐ 8-set building package . . . . $______
☐ 1-set of reproducible vellums . . . . $______

____ Additional Identical Blueprints @ $60 each $______
____ Full Reverse Set @ $145 fee $______

Foundation Options:
____ Crawl Space ____ Slab ____ Basement $______
(no charge for Frank Betz plans)

Sub-Total $______
Shipping and Handling $______
Sales Tax *(will be determined upon placing order)* $______

TOTAL $______

Check one: ☐ Visa ☐ MasterCard

Credit Card Number ____________________

Expiration Date ____________________

Signature ____________________

Name ____________________

Company ____________________

Street ____________________

City ____________________ State____ Zip________

Daytime Telephone Number (______)____________

Check one:

☐ Consumer ☐ Builder ☐ Developer

More Plan Books

AVAILABLE AT YOUR FAVORITE BOOK RETAILERS

DESIGNER DREAM HOMES™

ONE-STORY HOME PLANS

Over 320 best-designed home plans
from the top three residential designers

These stylish and comfortable plans all feature easy, one-level living and many have been "zoned" for comfort and privacy. Thousands of families have chosen these designs for their unique style, affordability and expanded amenities. Choose from enchanting farmhouses, traditional American bungalows, charming European cottages ranging from 1,200 to over 4,000 square feet.

$12.95 352 full-color pages

DESIGNER DREAM HOMES™

TWO-STORY HOME PLANS

Over 320 best-designed home plans
from the top three residential designers

With designs that emphasize and complement the lifestyles of today's families, this anthology showcases the most sought-after features in modern residential design, including main-floor master suites, guest bedrooms with complete baths, well-appointed open floor plans and versatile spaces with sizes ranging from 1,400 to over 8,000 square feet.

$12.95 352 full-color pages

DESIGNER DREAM HOMES™

THE ULTIMATE BOOK OF DESIGNER DREAM HOMES

Over 475 ultimate designer home plans
from the top three residential designers

An outstanding collection of designer dream homes covering the full range of sizes, styles and amenities, this collection is sure to contain the perfect home for you. Whether you're looking for a main-floor master suite in a two-story home, zoned living in a rambling one-story home or a home featuring full guest quarters, you'll find it here. Featuring full-color photography, full-color front and rear renderings, landscaping and interior design ideas and 475 best-selling home plans, this book sets a new standard in home-plan publishing.

$14.95 520 full-color pages

DAN SATER'S

COTTAGES AND VILLAS

80 Elegant cottage and waterfront home plans
from Sater Design Collection

A photo tour of 8 stunning coastal homes previews a portfolio of eighty beautifully rendered and charming clapboard cottages and grand Mediterranean villas. These highly versatile designs are big on open porches and courtyards, while balancing function with style. They bring to mind a relaxed attitude that can only come with view-oriented living.

$14.95 224 full-color pages

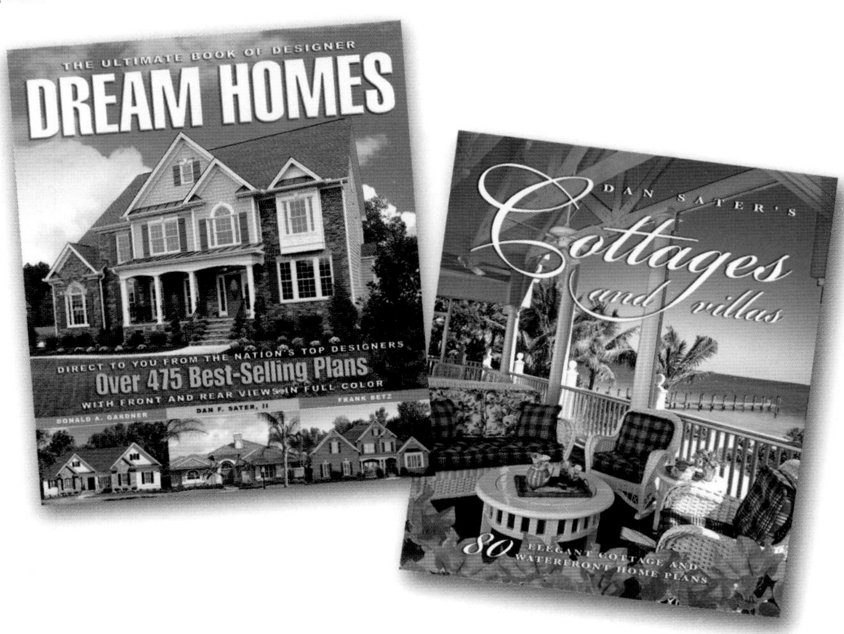